CATALOGUE
OF BENGALI PRINTED BOOKS IN THE LIBRARY OF THE BRITISH MUSEUM

CATALOGUE OF BENGALI PRINTED BOOKS IN THE LIBRARY OF THE BRITISH MUSEUM

J .F. BLUMHARDT

Published by

FacsiMile Publisher
12 Pragati Market
Ashok Vihar, Ph-2
Delhi - 110052, India
Phone: 011-47034999
Email: www.facsimilepublishers.com
info@facsimilepublishers.com

Distribution Network
gyanbooks.com
India, USA, Canada, UK, Australia

ISBN: 978-93-6896-051-5 (PB)
First Published, 1886

2nd Impression 2026

Printed at: Gyan Press, Delhi.

CATALOGUE OF BENGALI PRINTED BOOKS IN THE LIBRARY OF THE BRITISH MUSEUM
Author: J .F. BLUMHARDT

A SUPPLEMENTARY CATALOGUE

OF

BENGALI BOOKS

IN THE

LIBRARY

OF THE

BRITISH MUSEUM

ACQUIRED DURING THE YEARS 1886-1910.

COMPILED BY

J. F. BLUMHARDT, M.A.

PROFESSOR OF HINDUSTANI, AND LECTURER ON HINDI AND BENGALI AT UNIVERSITY COLLEGE, LONDON; AND TEACHER OF BENGALI AT THE UNIVERSITY OF OXFORD.

PRINTED BY ORDER OF THE TRUSTEES

London:

SOLD AT THE BRITISH MUSEUM;

AND BY

LONGMANS & CO., 39, PATERNOSTER ROW; BERNARD QUARITCH, 11, GRAFTON STREET, NEW BOND STREET, W.; ASHER & CO., 14, BEDFORD STREET, COVENT GARDEN; AND HENRY FROWDE, OXFORD UNIVERSITY PRESS WAREHOUSE, AMEN CORNER.

1910

PREFACE.

THIS Catalogue of the Bengali Printed Books acquired by the Library of the British Museum during the years 1886--1910 has been prepared by Mr. Blumhardt as a supplement to the volume compiled by him and published by order of the Trustees in 1886. In the present catalogue a classified index of titles has been added; in other respects the methods employed in the earlier volume have been closely followed in this work.

L. D. BARNETT,

Keeper of Oriental Printed Books and MSS.

BRITISH MUSEUM,

August 8, 1910.

AUTHOR'S PREFACE.

THIS Catalogue of Bengali books acquired during the last 24 years forms a supplement to the Bengali Catalogue published in 1886. It has been prepared on the same principles, and with the same system of transliteration.

The editions of the Bible, and portions of the Bible, which are entered in the Catalogue of 1886 have been embodied in the present volume, in order to make this article quite complete. All the entries under this heading have been carefully revised with the help of the "Historical Catalogue of the printed editions of Holy Scripture in the Library of the British and Foreign Bible Society," by T. H. Darlow and H. F. Moule.

As no Subject-Index was prepared for the former catalogue, the titles of all the works in that catalogue have been included in the Subject-Index of this volume, those of works entered only in the catalogue of 1886 being indicated by an asterisk, and those of editions of the same work which appear in both catalogues being marked by a dagger.

The English, or other European, title of a book is entered in the General Index when it has no Bengali title. Works with both English and Bengali titles are shown under the Bengali title only, except newspapers and other periodicals. In the case of a work having an alternative title, both are entered in the General Index, and only the principal title in the Subject-Index, with the other printed in brackets.

J. F. BLUMHARDT.

LONDON,
August 8, 1910.

SUPPLEMENTARY CATALOGUE

OF

BENGALI BOOKS.

ĀBĀJĪ VISHṆU KĀTHAVAṬE. Report on the search for Sanskrit [and Vernacular] manuscripts in the Bombay Presidency during the years 1891-92, 1892-93, 1893-94, and 1894-95. pp. 21, 121. *Bombay,* 1901. 8°. **14096. cc. 12.**

'ABBĀS 'ALĪ. *See* MUHAMMAD 'ABBĀS 'ALĪ.

'ABD al-AGHFAR. তরফের ইতিহাস। [Taraper itihāsa. An historical account of Tarap in the District of Sylhet.] pp. viii. 114. কলিকাতা ১২৯৪ [*Calcutta,* 1887.] 12°. **14127. a.**

'ABD al-'AZĪZ. মায়াদানোল ওলূম। [Maidān al-'ulūm. A treatise on Muhammadan social and religious observances. Second edition.] pp. 14, 344, 8. করটীয়া ১২৯৮ [*Karatia,* 1892.] 8°. **14129. d. 30.(2.)**

'ABD al-GHANĪ. বড় আছরারচ্ছালাত। [Asrār al-ṣalāt. A treatise on prayer, in Muhammadan Bengali verse.] pp. 180, 4. ঢাকা ১৩১০ [*Dacca,* 1904.] 8°. **14123. h. 34.(2.)**

—— কমলা পরির পুথী ও সাত দেওএর খেলা। [Kamalā parir puthī. A love story in Muhammadan Bengali.] pp. 108. ঢাকা ১৩০৯ [*Dacca,* 1903.] 8°. **14127. g. 15.(2.)**

—— নেয়ামতে দুনিয়া ও আখেরাত। [Ni'mat i dunyā. Advice on ethics and the observance of religious duties, in Muhammadan Bengali verse.] pp. 180, 4. ঢাকা ১৩১০ [*Dacca,* 1904.] 8°. **14123. h. 34.(1.)**

'ABD al-ḤAKK, *Dihlavī.* *See* ḤUSAIN ibn MAS'ŪD, *al-Farrā al-Baghawī.* হদিস-পূর্ব্ববিভাগ। *etc.* [Mishkāt al-maṣābiḥ. Translated into Bengali, together with notes from 'Abd al-Ḥakk's Persian commentary entitled Ashi''at al-lama'āt.] [1892, *etc.*] 8°. **14123. h. 21.**

'ABD al-ḤAKK (ABŪ MUḤAMMAD). *See* ḲUR'ĀN. বঙ্গানুবাদিত তফ্‌সীর হাক্কানী। [The Arabic text of the Koran, accompanied by a Bengali translation of the Hindustani version, and commentary of Abū Muḥammad 'Abd al-Ḥakk, entitled Tafsīr i ḥakkānī.] [1901, *etc.*] 8°. **14507. b. 34.**

'ABD al-ḤAMĪD II., *Sultan of the Turks.* সুলতান জুবিলী। [Sultān-jubilī. A poem in honour of the jubilee reign of Sultan 'Abd al-Ḥamīd.] pp. 18. রেঙ্গুন ১৯০০ [*Rangoon,* 1900.] 12°. **14129. a. 48.(5.)**

'ABD al-ḤĀMID KHĀN, *Yūsufzā'ī.* উদাসী। [Udāsī. "The Ascetic"; a collection of poems.] Pt. i. pp. xii. xxiv. 4, 504. টাঙ্গাইল ১৩০৭ [*Tangail,* 1901.] 8°. **14129. c. 52.**

'ABD al-JABBĀR, *Shaikh.* মদিনা-শরীফের ইতিহাস। [Madinā-sharīfer itihāsa. An historical account of the city of Medina.] pp. xii. 180. ময়মনসিংহ ১৩১৪ [*Mymensingh,* 1907.] 12°. **14127. aa. 40.**

'ABD al-ḲĀDIR, *of Sudampara.* *See* MUḤAMMAD ḲĀSIM, *Maulavi.* বড়পীর গুণাবলী। [Baṛa Pīrguṇāvalī. Translated by 'Abd al-Ḳādir from the Hindustani I'jāz i Ghauṣiyah.] [1899.] 8°. **14127. bb. 18.(1.)**

'ABD al-ḲĀDIR, *Shaikh.* *See* 'UBAID ALLĀH ibn MAS'ŪD. শরে বেকায়া। [Sharḥ i Wikāyah. A Bengali translation by Shaikh 'Abd al-Ḳādir.] [1902, *etc.*] 8°. **14125. a. 30.**

'ABD al-ḲĀDIR ibn MŪSĀ, *Jīlānī.* [*Life.*] *See* 'Alā al-Dīn Aḥmad, *Maulavī.* বড় পীর সাহেব জীবনচরিত। [Bara Pīr Sāheb.] [1899.] 12°. **14127. aa. 17.**

—— [*Life.*] *See* Muḥammad Ḳāsim, *Maulavī.* বড়পীর গুণাবলী। [Bara Pīr-guṇāvalī.] [1899.] 8°. **14127. bb. 18.(1.)**

'ABD al-KARĪM, *Assistant Inspector of Schools. See* Chharā. চট্টগ্রামী ছেলে-ভুলান ছড়া। [Chhele-bhulāna chharā. Nursery rhymes of Chittagong. Compiled by 'Abd al-Karīm.] [1902-1907.] 8°. **14133. f. 18.**

—— পুঁথির বিবরণ। (বাঙ্গালা পুঁথির বিবরণ) [Bāṅgālā punthir vivaraṇa. A descriptive catalogue of 433 Bengali manuscripts found in the District of Chittagong.] pp. 268. ১৩১০-১২ [1903-05.] *See* Academies, *etc.*—Calcutta.—*Bengal Academy of Literature.* সাহিত্য-পরিষৎ-পত্রিকা। [Sāhitya-parishat-patrikā.] Vol. ix., extra number; x., nos. 3 and 4; xii., no. 3. [1894, *etc.*] 8°. **14133. f. 18.**

—— A History of the Muhammadan Empire in India. Vol. I. ... ভারতবর্ষে মুসলমান রাজত্বের ইতিবৃত্ত। [Bhāratavarshe Musalmān rājatver itihāsa.] pp. iv. 154. *Calcutta*, 1898. 8°. **14127. bb. 11.**

'ABD al-KARĪM, *of Anwara, District Chittagong. See* Murtaẓā, *Saiyid, of Murshidabad.* মুসলমান বৈষ্ণব কবি সৈয়দ মর্ত্তজা। [Poems on the loves of Rādhā and Krishṇa. With a life of the author by 'Abd al-Karīm.] [1904.] 8°. **14129. cc. 11.**

'ABD al-KARĪM, *of Jaintiapur.* ওয়াজিবুল-আমল। [Wājib al-'amal. Muhammadan religious observances, in verse.] pp. 168. কলিকাতা ১৩১১ [*Calcutta*, 1905.] 8°. **14123. h. 36.**

Printed in Sylhet Nāgarī characters.

'ABD al-RAḤĪM, *of Bhawarkot.* আখ্লাকে আহাম্মদিয়া। [Akhlāk i Aḥmadiyah. A sketch of the life of Maulānā Ḥāfiẓ Aḥmad of Jaunpur. In Muhammadan Bengali.] pp. 68. নোয়াখালী ১৩০৬ [*Noakhali*, 1900.] 8°. **14127. bb. 18.(2.)**

'ABD al-RAḤĪM, *of Galachipa.* ঢাকার নবাব সাহেবের পুথি। [Ḍhākār Nawāb Sāheber puthī. A short account in verse of the Nawab of Dacca and his pedigree, with poems in praise of King Edward VII. and the Governor-General, and on the spread of cholera. In Muhammadan Bengali.] pp. 35. কলিকাতা ১৩১৩ [*Calcutta*, 1906.] 8°. **14127. bbb. 9.**

'ABD al-RAḤĪM, *Shāh.* অথর্ব্ব মহম্মদী বেদ। [Atharva Mahammadī veda. Religious rites of the Ḥanafī sect of Muhammadans, in verse.] pp. 58. কলিকাতা ১২৯৮ [*Calcutta*, 1891.] 8°. **14129. d. 30.(1.)**

—— মহম্মদী বেদ তত্ত্ব। [Mahammadī vedatattva. An inquiry into the principles of Muhammadan belief, in verse. Second edition.] Pt. i. pp. ii. 59. কলিকাতা ১৩১০ [*Calcutta*, 1904.] 8°. **14123. h. 32.**

'ABD al-RAḤĪM, *Shaikh.* ইসলাম *etc.* [Islām. A manual of instruction in the observance of prayers and other Muhammadan religious duties, designed for use in schools.] pp. ii. 116. কলিকাতা ১৩০৩ [*Calcutta*, 1896.] 16°. **14123. h. 24.**

'ABD al-SUBḤĀN. হিন্দু মোসলমান। [Hindu Mosalmān. An attack against Hindus, and the National Congress, in which the author cites numerous instances of wrong and injustice caused to the Muhammadan community by Hindu officials.] 3 pts. ঢাকা ১৮৮৯ [*Dacca*, 1889.] 12°. **14125. e. 23.**

Pts. 2 and 3, in one volume, are of the 2nd edition.

'ABD al-WAHHĀB, *Munshī, of Calcutta. See* Ghulām Nabī ibn 'Ināyat Allāh. সর্ব্বৃহৎ কাছাছল আম্বিয়া চারইয়ারী *etc.* [Ḳiṣaṣ al-anbiyā. Translated by 'Abd al-Wahhāb and others.] [1902.] 4°. **14123. hh. 1.**

ABHIRĀMA GOSVĀMĪ, *Vaishṇava saint.* [*Life.*] *See* Rāmadāsa, *Vaishṇava poet.* শ্রী অভিরামলীলামৃত। [Abhirāma-līlāmṛita.] [1891.] 8°. **14123. f. 46.**

ABŪ ḤANĪFAH. *See* Nu'mān ibn Ṣābit (Abu Ḥanīfah).

ABŪ al-ḤUSAIN, *Saiyid, M.A.* জীবন্ত-পুতুল কাব্য। [Jīvanta-putula. A romance in verse.] pp. 283. কলিকাতা ১৩১৪ [*Calcutta*, 1908.] 8°. **14128. c. 1.**

—— মোস্‌লেম-পতাকা বা হজ্‌রৎ-মোহাম্মদের জীবনী। [Moslem-patākā. A life of Muḥammad.] pp. xi. 218. কলিকাতা ১৯০৮ [*Calcutta*, 1908.] 12°. **14127. aaa. 1.**

—— যমজ-ভগিনী কাব্য বা সিরাজুদ্দৌলা উপন্যাস। [Yamaja bhaginī kāvya. An historical novel relating to Sirāj al-Daulah, in verse.] pp. 320. কলিকাতা ১৩১২ [*Calcutta*, 1905.] 12°. **14127. ee. 26.**

ABŪ MUḤAMMAD MUḤYĪ al-SUNNĀ. *See* Ḥusain ibn Masʿūd, *al-Farrā al-Baghawī.*

ABŪ WĀʿIẒ MUḤAMMAD. *See* Muʿiẓ al-Dīn (Abū Wāʿiẓ Muḥammad).

ABŪ al-WĀJID MUḤAMMAD IBRĀHĪM. সোরে-কেয়ামত। [Sūr i kiyāmat. An account in Muhammadan Bengali verse of recent earthquakes, cyclones, the plague, and other disasters, with an exhortation to Muhammadans to prepare for the resurrection-day.] pp. iv. 26. *Bogra,* [1898.] 8°. **14129. d. 32.**

ACADEMIES, *etc.*

Calcutta.

Asiatic Society of Bengal.

Catalogue of Printed books and Manuscripts in Sanskrit (and Bengali) belonging to the Oriental Library of the Asiatic Society of Bengal. Compiled by Paṇḍit Kunja Vihāri Nyāyabhūṣaṇa, under the supervision of Mahāmahopādhyāya Haraprasād S'hāstrī. *Calcutta,* 1899, *etc.* 4°. **14096. dd. 5.**

In progress.

Bengal Academy of Literature.

The Bengal Academy of Literature. [Proceedings.] *Calcutta,* 1893, *etc.* **14133. g. 18.**

সাহিত্য-পরিষৎ-পত্রিকা। [Sāhitya-parishat-patrikā. A quarterly journal of the Bengal Academy of Literature. Edited by Rajanīkānta Gupta and others.] কলিকাতা ১৩০১ [*Calcutta,* 1894, *etc.*] 8°. **14133. f. 18.**

The Bangiya-Sahitya-Parishad. A record of eleven years' work [of the Bengal Academy of Literature]. Published by the Honorary Secretary. pp. 61. *Calcutta,* 1905. 8°. **14125. ee. 41.**

London.

British Museum.

Catalogue of the Marathi, Gujarati, Bengali, Assamese, Oriya, Pushtu, and Sindhi Manuscripts in the Library of the British Museum. By J. F. Blumhardt. 5 pts. *London,* 1905. 4°. **Cat. Desk. A.**

Rangpur.

Bengal Academy of Literature.

রঙ্গপুর শাখা সাহিত্য-পরিষৎ-পত্রিকা। [Sāhitya-parishat-patrikā. A monthly magazine of the Rangpur branch of the Bengal Academy of Literature. Edited by Pañchānana Sarkār.] কলিকাতা ১৩১৩ [*Calcutta,* 1907, *etc.*] 8°. **14133. ff. 4.**

ACHYUTACHARAṆA CHAUDHURĪ. *See* Īṣāna Nāgara. শ্রী অদ্বৈত-প্রকাশ। [Advaita-prakāṣa. Edited, with a short account of the author, by Achyutacharaṇa Chaudhurī.] [1897.] 12°. **14129. a. 46.(1.)**

—— শ্রীমৎ হরিদাস ঠাকুরের জীবন-চরিত। [Haridāsa Ṭhākurer jīvanacharita. The life of Haridāsa Ṭhākura, son of Sumati Ṣarmā of Buran in the District of Jessore, a Vaishṇava devotee of the 15th century.] pp. ii. 113, iv. কলিকাতা ১৩০৩ [*Calcutta,* 1896.] 12°. **14127. a. 45.(2.)**

—— শ্রীমত রঘুনাথদাস গোস্বামীর জীবনচরিত। [Raghunāthadāsa Gosvāmīr jīvana-charita. The life and writings of Raghunāthadāsa Gosvāmī.] pp. ii. 64. কলিকাতা ১৩০০ [*Calcutta,* 1894.] 12°. **14127. aa. 2.(3.)**

—— শ্রীহট্টের ইতিহাস। প্রণয়ন কল্পে সংগৃহীত বিবরণাবলীর সুচি-পত্র। [Ṣrīhaṭṭer itihāsa. A table of contents to a projected history of Sylhet, giving the sources of information from which the work is to be compiled.] pp. 56. শ্রীহট্ট ১৩১৪ [*Sylhet,* 1907.] 8°. **14127. bb. 29.**

ADBHUTĀCHĀRYA. *See* Rajanīkānta Chakravartī. অদ্ভুতাচার্য্যের রামায়ণ। [Adbhutāchāryer Rāmāyaṇa. A paper on the Rāmāyaṇa of Adbhutāchārya.] [1907.] 8°. **14133. f. 18.**

ADHARACHANDRA DĀSA. ত্রিবেণী। [Triveṇī. A tale of domestic life.] pp. ii. 510. কলিকাতা [*Calcutta,* 1900.] 8°. **14127. cc. 16.**

ĀDITYAKUMĀRA CHAṬṬOPĀDHYĀYA. জীবন্ত ও মৃত ধর্ম্ম। [Jīvanta o mṛita dharma, or The living and the dead religion. A series of religious essays by members of the Brāhma Samāj, reprinted from the Tattvakaumudī. Compiled, with occasional alterations and additions, by Ādityakumāra Chaṭṭopādhyāya.] pp. ii. 146. কলিকাতা ১২৯৪ [*Calcutta,* 1888.] 12°. **14123. c. 23.(2.)**

ADVAITACHANDRA ĀDHYA. *See* Periodical Publications.—*Calcutta.* সংবাদ পূর্ণচন্দ্রোদয়। [Pūrṇachandrodaya. Edited by Advaitachandra Ādhya.] [1867.] Fol. **14003. e. 2.(9.)**

ADVAITĀCHĀRYA, *Disciple of Chaitanya.* *See* Īśāna Nāgara. শ্রী অদ্বৈত-প্রকাশ। [Advaita-prakāśa. A poem on the life of Advaitāchārya.] [1897.] 12°. **14129. a. 46.(1.)**

—— [*Life.*] *See* Vīreśvara Prāmāṇika. শ্রী অদ্বৈত-বিলাস। [Advaita-vilāsa.] [1899.] 12°. **14127. aa. 13.**

ĀDYĀPRASĀDA MIŚRA. *See* Mahābhārata.—*Bhagavadgītā.* শ্রী . . . The Illustrated Bhagwad Gita . . . Pandit Adya Prasada Misra, Editor. [1905, *etc.*] 8°. **14049. b. 47.**

ÆSOP. *See* Teacher. A key to Æsop's Fables . . . By a Teacher. [1889.] 12°. **14131. g.**

AGHORACHANDRA GHOSHA. সঙ্গীত সাগর। [Saṅgītasāgara. A collection of 9 poetical works, viz.: 1. Paramārthika gītāvalī; 2. Padāvalī, both by Rāmaprasāda Sena; 3. Padāvalī of Govindadāsa; 4. Ḍhapakīrtana; 5. Saṅgītamālā; 6. Vidyā Sundarer ṭappā; 7. Saṅgītahāra; 8. Saṅgītakalpadruma; and 9. Baul saṅgīta of Nirmalachandra Chaṭṭopādhyāya.] 2 vols. কলিকাতা ১২৯৬ [*Calcutta*, 1889.] 12°. **14129. b. 33.**

AGHORACHANDRA KĀVYATĪRTHA BHAṬṬĀCHĀRYA. মরুত্তযজ্ঞ। [Marutta-yajña. A mythological drama, based on the story of the Aśvamedha sacrifice made by king Marutta, as told in the Mahābhārata.] pp. ii. 182. কলিকাতা ১৩১৪ [*Calcutta*, 1907.] 8°. **14131. c. 20.(3.)**

AGHORANĀTHA CHAṬṬOPĀDHYĀYA. ভক্ত-চরিতামৃত। [Bhakta-charitāmṛita. The lives of 3 Vaishṇava saints and poets, viz. Rūpa Gosvāmī, Sanātana Gosvāmī, and Jīva Gosvāmī.] pp. iv. 164. কলিকাতা ১৩০০ [*Calcutta*, 1894.] 12°. **14127. aa. 2.(2.)**

AHALYĀBĀĪ, *Rani of Indore.* [*Life.*] *See* Yogīndranātha Vasu. অহল্যাবাই। [Ahalyābāi.] [1895.] 12°. **14127. a. 55.**

AHIBHŪSHAṆA BHAṬṬĀCHĀRYA. বোধনে বিসর্জ্জন। [Bodhane visarjana. A play on the vices prevalent in educated Hindu society.] pp. 48. কলিকাতা ১৩০৩ [*Calcutta*, 1896.] 12°. **14131. a. 38.(4.)**

AHMAD, *Ḥāfiẓ, of Jaunpur.* [*Life.*] *See* ʻAbd al-Raḥīm, *of Bhawarkot.* আখলাকে আহাম্মদিয়া। [Akhlāk i Aḥmadīyah.] [1900.] 8°. **14127. bb. 18.(2.)**

AHMAD KABĪR. রেঙ্গুন সহরে কল্বে বিয়ে॥ মুশলমান ধর্ম্ম যায় ডুবিয়ে॥ [Reṅgun shahare kalbe biye. A satire in verse on Burmese marriage and other social customs.] pp. 7. রেঙ্গুন ১৮৯৬ [*Rangoon*, 1896.] 16°. **14129. a. 17.(2.)**

Ā'IN. আইন! আইন!! আইন!!! [Ā'in. A protest against the Consent Bill, written by a Bengali lady.] pp. 12. *Dacca*, [1890.] 16°. **14123. e. 14.**

The Bengal Book List for March, 1891, gives "Induni Bhushan Devi" as the authoress.

AKSHAYACHANDRA SARKĀR. প্রাচীন কাব্য সংগ্রহ। [Prāchīna kāvya-saṅgraha. The works of old Bengali poets, in two parts. Pt. I. containing the poems of Chaṇḍīdāsa, Govindadāsa, and Vidyāpati with the Rāmeśvarī Satyanārāyaṇa; Pt. II., the poems of Mukundarāma Chakravartī, with variants. The whole edited with copious notes by Akshayachandra Sarkār.] কলিকাতা ১২৯১-৯২ [*Calcutta*, 1884-85.] 8°. **14129. g. 8.**

AKSHAYAKUMĀRA BARĀL. কনকাঞ্জলি। [Kanakāñjali. Miscellaneous short poems.] pp. iv. 90. কলিকাতা ১২৯২ [*Calcutta*, 1885.] 12°. **14129. a. 29.(1.)**

—— প্রদীপ গীতিকাব্য। [Pradīpa. Short poems. Second edition.] pp. 113. কলিকাতা ১৩০০ [*Calcutta*, 1894.] 8°. **14129. b. 39.**

AKSHAYAKUMĀRA CHAKRAVARTĪ. গুলির পিণ্ডী। [Gulir piṇḍī. A farce.] pp. 42. কলিকাতা ১৩১৩ [*Calcutta*, 1906.] 12°. **14131. aa. 5.(4.)**

—— বঙ্গীয় পুরোহিত ও মাহিষ্য সমালোচনা। [Vaṅgīya purohita o Māhishya samālochanā. A treatise on the origin and history of the Māhishya caste.] pp. vi. 40. কলিকাতা ১৩০৫ [*Calcutta*, 1900.] 12°. **14125. e. 31.(4.)**

AKSHAYAKUMĀRA DATTA. *Life.* *See* Nakuḍachandra Viśvāsa. অক্ষয়-চরিত। [Akshayacharita.] [1887.] 12°. **14131. d. 21.(1.)**

—— *See* Rajanīkānta Gupta. প্রতিভা। [Pratibhā. A review of the works of Akshayakumāra Datta.] [1896.] 12°. **14131. d. 35.**

—— The Religious Sects of the Hindus. ভারতবর্ষীয় উপাসক সম্প্রদায়। [Bhāratavarshīya upāsakasampradāya. Pt. i. Second edition.] pp. ii. iii. 315, iii. কলিকাতা ১৮৮৮ [*Calcutta*, 1888.] 8°. **14123. f. 38.**

—— Sea voyage and commerce of the ancient Hindus. প্রাচীন হিন্দুদিগের সমুদ্রযাত্রা ও বাণিজ্য-বিস্তার। [Prāchīna Hindudiger samudrayātrā. Edited with notes by Rajanīnātha Datta, the son of the author.] pp. 209. *Calcutta*, 1901. 12°. **14125. e. 42.**

AKSHAYAKUMĀRA DE. মহাজন পদাবলী। চণ্ডীদাস ও বিদ্যাপতি। [Mahājana-padāvalī. The poems of Chaṇḍīdāsa and Vidyāpati. Edited, with notes and biographies of the poets, by Akshayakumāra De.] pp. vi. 152. কলিকাতা ১৩০৯ [*Calcutta*, 1903.] 8°. **14129. e. 26.**

—— —— [Fourth edition.] pp. vi. 160. কলিকাতা ১৩১১ [*Calcutta*, 1905.] 8°. **14129. e. 30.**

—— —— [Fifth edition.] pp. vi. 160. কলিকাতা ১৩১৪ [*Calcutta*, 1907.] 8°. **14129. e. 33.**

AKSHAYAKUMĀRA GOSVĀMĪ. কৌমার বিলাস গ্রন্থঃ। [Kaumāravilāsa. A treatise on Tantric rites.] pp. ii. 27. যশোহর ১৩০৭ [*Jessore*, 1900.] 12°. **14128. e. 28.(2.)**

—— Second edition.] pp. iv. 27. যশোহর ১৩১১ [*Jessore*, 1904.] 12°. **14123. e. 33.**

AKSHAYAKUMĀRA MAITREYA. *See* PERIODICAL PUBLICATIONS.—*Calcutta*. ঐতিহাসিক চিত্র। [Aitihāsika chitra. Edited by Akshayakumāra Maitreya.] [1899-1900.] 8°. **14127. bb. 14.**

AKSHAYAKUMĀRA SENA. শ্রীশ্রীরামকৃষ্ণ পুঁথি *etc.* [Rāmakṛishṇa-punthi. A metrical account of the life of Rāmakṛishṇa Paramahaṃsa, son of Khudirāma Chaṭṭopādhyāya, of Kamarpukar in the District of Hooghly.] pp. 579, ii. কলিকাতা [*Calcutta*, 1901.] 8°. **14127. bbb. 5.(2.)**

AKSHAYAKUMĀRA VIDYĀVINODA. বঙ্গীয়-সাহিত্য-সমালোচনী। [Vaṅgīya-sāhitya-samālochanī. A critical examination into the origin and gradual development of the Bengali language and literature.] Pt. i. pp. 122. কলিকাতা ১৮৯৫ [*Calcutta*, 1895.] 8°. **14131. d. 34.**

'ALĀ al-DĪN AḤMAD, *Maulavī.* বড় পীর সাহেব জীবনচরিত। [Baṛa Pīr Sāheb. A life of the Ṣūfī saint 'Abd al-Ḳādir Jīlānī.] Pt. i. pp. viii. 228. ফরিদপুর ১৮৯৯ [*Faridpur*, 1899.] 12°. **14127. aa. 17.**

ALĀOL, *Pandit.* *See* NIẒĀMĪ, *Ganjavī.* সপ্ত পয়কর। [Sapta paykar. A metrical version by Pandit Alāol of the Persian Haft paikar.] [1897.] 8°. **14127. g. 11.**

—— [1905.] 8°. **14127. ee. 27.**

ALBERT, *Prince Consort of Victoria, Queen of Great Britain and Ireland. Life.* *See* MARTIN (*Sir* T.). The Life of His Royal Highness, the Prince Consort . . . Translated into Bengali, *etc.* 1892. 8°. **14127. b. 46.**

'ALĪ ALLĀH, *Saiyid, of Bogra.* গাজীমিয়াঁর বস্তানী। [Gājīmiyār bastānī. A tale depicting life amongst Muhammadans in the North-Eastern districts of Bengal.] Pt. i. pp. viii. 400. কলিকাতা ১৩০৬ [*Calcutta*, 1900.] 8°. **14127. ee. 10.**

ALLEN (I.). *See* BIBLE.—*Genesis.* সটীক আদি-পুস্তক। Genesis, annotated in Bengali, by I. Allen and G. H. Rouse. 1895. 8°. **14123. bb. 1.**

AMARENDRANĀTHA DATTA. অমর গ্রন্থাবলী। [Amara-granthāvalī. The complete works of Amarendranātha Datta.] কলিকাতা ১৩০৯- [*Calcutta*, 1902- .] 8°. **14127. g. 13.**
In progress.

AMBASHṬHA. অম্বষ্ঠ কোন্ বর্ণ। [Ambashṭha kon varṇa? A treatise in proof of the assertion that the Ambashṭhas belong to the Brahman caste.] pp. 24. কলিকাতা ১৩০০ [*Calcutta*, 1893.] 8°. **14125. ee. 28.(1.)**

AMBIKĀCHARAṆA BRAHMACHĀRĪ BHAṬṬĀCHĀRYA. বঙ্গ-রত্ন। [Vaṅgaratna. A short sketch of the life of the Bengali poet Ghanarāma Chakravartī, the author of the Dharmamaṅgala.] Pt. i. pp. 42. কলিকাতা ১২৯৩ [*Calcutta*, 1886.] 12°. **14127. a.**

AMBIKĀCHARAṆA GUPTA. *See* CHHAṚĀ. ছড়া। [Chhaṛā. Nursery rhymes of Hooghly, compiled by Ambikācharaṇa Gupta.] [1896.] 8°. **14133. f. 18.**

—— জয় কৃষ্ণ-চরিত। [Jayakṛishṇa-charita. A life of Jayakṛishṇa Mukhopādhyāya.] pp. 176. কলিকাতা [*Calcutta*, 1901.] 8°. **14127. bb. 16.(2.)**

AMBIKĀCHARAṆA GUPTA (*continued*). কবি জয়কৃষ্ণ দাস। [Kavi Jayakṛishṇa Dāsa. An account of the poet Jayakṛishṇa Dāsa and his writings.] ১৩১৪ [1907.] *See* ACADEMIES, *etc.*—Calcutta.—*Bengal Academy of Literature.* সাহিত্য-পরিষৎ-পত্রিকা। [Sāhitya-parishat-patrikā.] Vol. xiv. no. 1. [1894, *etc.*] 8°. **14133. f. 18.**

—— কুসুমকুমারী। [Kusumakumārī. A tale of police oppression, and of female conjugal devotion.] pp. 41. কলিকাতা ১২৯৫ [*Calcutta*, 1888.] 12°. **14127. c. 37.(2.)**

—— পুরাণ-কাগজ। [Purāna kāgaj. A novel written in the form of a collection of letters and documents relating to the possession of a district of Bengal during the time of Sirāj al-Daulah.] pp. iv. 152. কলিকাতা [*Calcutta*, 1899.] 12°. **14127. cc. 21 (3.)**

—— সহদেব চক্রবর্ত্তীর ধর্ম্মমঙ্গল। [Sahadeva Chakravartīr Dharmamaṅgala. An article on the poet Sahadeva and his Dharmamaṅgala.] ১৩০৪ [1898.] *See* ACADEMIES, *etc.*—Calcutta.—*Bengal Academy of Literature.* সাহিত্য-পরিষৎ-পত্রিকা। [Sāhitya-parishat-patrikā.] Vol. iv., no. 4. [1894, *etc.*] 8°. **14133. f. 18.**

AMBUJĀ SUNDARĪ DĀSA-GUPTĀ. প্রীতি ও পূজা। [Prīti o pūjā. Devotional and lyrical poems.] pp. iv. 141. কলিকাতা ১৩০৪ [*Calcutta*, 1897.] 12°. **14129. a. 25.(2.)**

ĀMI, *pseud.* [i.e. **KUÑJAVIHĀRĪ DEVA**]. ঠেঙ্গাপ্যাথিক ভুঁইফোড় ডাক্টর নাটক। [Ṭheṅgāpyāthik Bhuiṇphoṛ Dākṭar nāṭaka. A drama on the adventures of a native quack doctor, much addicted to drunkenness.] pp. ii. 121. কলিকাতা ১২৯৩ [*Calcutta*, 1886.] 12°. **14131. a. 25.(1.)**

ĀMIN. আমিন প্রহসন। [Āmin-prahasana. A dramatised sketch of the experiences and hardships of a native surveyor engaged in Government settlement duties.] pp. xii. 185. ১৮২১ [*Calcutta*, 1900.] 8°. **14131. a. 42.**

ĀM-KĀNṬĀL. আম-কাঁটালের ঝগড়া ও রসরাজ আনারসের লেক্‌চার। [Ām-kāṇṭāler jhagṛā. The quarrel between the mango and the jack-fruit tree, and other poems.] pp. 29. কলিকাতা ১৯০২ [*Calcutta*, 1902.] 12°. **14129. bb. 13.(4.)**

AMṚITA. অমৃত। [Amṛita. A tract on national progress, social and religious.] pp. 14. কলিকাতা [*Calcutta*, 1895.] 8°. **14125. ee. 26.(2.)**

AMṚITALĀLA VASU. অবলাবালা। [Abalā bālā. A detective story relating to the murder of a Brahmist gentleman.] pp. 125. কলিকাতা ১৩০৩ [*Calcutta*, 1897.] 12°. **14127. cc. 4.(2.)**

—— আদর্শ-বন্ধু। [Ādarṣa-bandhu. The model friend; a domestic drama.] pp. 214. কলিকাতা ১৩০৭ [*Calcutta*, 1900.] 12°. **14131. a. 41.(6).**

—— অমৃত গ্রন্থাবলী। [Amṛita-granthāvalī. The complete works of Amṛitalāla Vasu, edited by Upendranātha Mukhopādhyāya.] কলিকাতা ১৩১৩- [*Calcutta*, 1906- .] 8°. **14127. g. 18.**
In progress.

—— অমৃত-মদিরা। [Amṛita-madirā. Miscellaneous poems.] pp. 4, 4, 290. কলিকাতা ১৩১০ [*Calcutta*, 1903.] 12°. **14129. bb. 24.**

—— চঞ্চলা। [Chañchalā. A detective story.] pp. 162. কলিকাতা ১৩০৩ [*Calcutta*, 1897.] 12°. **14127. cc. 4.(3.)**

—— একাকার। [Ekākāra.] Social chaos. [A comedy in two acts. Second edition.] pp. 94. কলিকাতা ১৩০২ [*Calcutta*, 1895.] 12°. **14131. a. 38.(3.)**

—— গ্রাম্য-বিভ্রাট। সামাজিক নক্সা। [Grāmya vibhrāṭa.] The rural sketches. A society satire. pp. 116. কলিকাতা ১৩০৪ [*Calcutta*, 1897.] 12°. **14127. c. 30.(2.)**

—— কালাপানি বা হিন্দুমতে সমুদ্র যাত্রা। [Kālāpāni. A farce, ridiculing the practice of Bengalis going to England. Second edition.] pp. 50. কলিকাতা ১২৯৯ [*Calcutta*, 1893.] 12°. **14131. a. 33.(5.)**

—— তাজ্জব ব্যাপার। [Tājjab byāpār. A farce, directed against female emancipation. Third edition.] pp. 30. কলিকাতা ১২৯৮ [*Calcutta*, 1890.] 12°. **14131. a. 32.(1.)**

—— তরুবালা। [Tarubālā. A drama illustrating social life amongst educated Bengali gentlemen.] pp. 147. কলিকাতা ১২৯৭ [*Calcutta*, 1891.] 12°. **14131. a. 31.(2).**

ANĀDINĀTHA MUKHOPĀDHYĀYA. চেৎমতী। [Chetmatī. An historical novel of Rajput prowess.] pp. 108. কাশিপুর [*Kasipur*, 1886.] 12°. **14127. c. 31.(1.)**

ĀNANDA BHAṬṬA, *Descendant of Ananta Bhaṭṭa. See* BALLĀLA SENA, *King of Bengal.* বল্লালচরিতম্। [Ballāla-charita. Continued in a third canto by Ānanda Bhaṭṭa.] [1889.] 8°. **14058. b. 25.**

—— *See* BALLĀLA SENA, *King of Bengal.* শ্রী... বল্লাল-চরিতের বঙ্গানুবাদ। [Ballāla-charita. Translated from the Sanskrit chronicle by Ānanda Bhaṭṭa, which was published by Haraprasāda Śāstrī at Calcutta in 1901.] 1904. 12°. **14127. a. 45.(3.)**

ĀNANDACHANDRA MITRA. ভারতমঙ্গল। [Bhārata-maṅgala. A poem in 19 *sargas* on the social and religious condition of India.] Pt. i. pp. 400. কলিকাতা ১৮৯৪ [*Calcutta*, 1894.] 8°. **14129. c. 47.**

—— মিত্রকাব্য। [Mitra-kāvya. Songs and poems, chiefly with reference to India. Third edition.] pp. 260. কলিকাতা ১৩০৪ [*Calcutta*, 1897.] 8°. **14129. a. 42.(2.)**

—— পরমার্থ-প্রসঙ্গ। [Paramārthaprasaṅga. Essays on religious topics.] pp. 179. কলিকাতা ১৩০৬ [*Calcutta*, 1900.] 12°. **14123. c. 30.**

—— প্রবন্ধসার ... Pravandhasar. [Miscellaneous essays.] Second edition. pp. 132. *Calcutta*, 1896. 12°. **14125. e. 27.(4.)**

—— প্রেমানন্দ-কাব্য। [Premānanda-kāvya. Devotional songs.] pp. 128. কলিকাতা ১৩০৩ [*Calcutta*, 1897.] 8°. **14129. a. 42.(1.)**

ĀNANDAKUMĀRA KĀVYATĪRTHA. পদ্যচন্দ্রিকা। [Padyachandrikā. A short series of rules on points of Sanskrit syntax in Sanskrit verse, with explanations in Bengali prose.] pp. 31. কুমিল্লা ১২৯৫ [*Comilla*, 1889.] 12°. **14098. b. 35.**

ĀNANDAMOHANA VASU. *Life. See* ŚARATKUMĀRA SENA GUPTA. A short sketch of the Life of Ananda Mohan Basu. [1907.] 12°. **14127. aa. 18.(3.)**

ĀNANDANĀTHA RĀYA. কবি লালা জয়নারায়ণ। [Kavi Lālā Jayanārāyaṇa. An article on the life and poems of Lālā Jayanārāyaṇa of Japsa.] ১৩০৭ [1900.] *See* ACADEMIES, *etc.*—Calcutta.—*Bengal Academy of Literature.* সাহিত্য-পরিষৎ-পত্রিকা। [Sāhitya-parishat-patrikā.] Vol. vii., no. 3. [1894, *etc.*] 8°. **14133. f. 18.**

ĀNANDAVEDA VĪJA. আনন্দবেদ বীজ বা স্বর্গসোপান। [Ānandaveda vīja, also called Svargasopāna. A work containing a collection of hymns, and religious treatises by various writers, on the teachings of the Theistic Church.] pp. viii. 258. যশোহর ১৮০৯ [*Jessore*, 1887.] 8°. **14123. f. 39.**

ANAṄGAMOHINĪ DEVĪ, *Princess of Tipperah.* কণিকা। [Kaṇikā. Short poems on miscellaneous subjects.] pp. viii. 51. আগরতলা ১৩১১ ত্রিপুরাব্দ। [*Agartala*, 1903.] 12°. **14129. bb. 19.**

ANDERSON (JAMES DRUMMOND). Some Chittagong Proverbs, compiled as an example of the Dialect of the Chittagong District. pp. 86. *Calcutta*, 1897. 8°. **14127. bbb. 3.**

Printed for private circulation.

AṄGIRAS. অঙ্গিরঃ সংহিতা। [Aṅgiraḥ-saṃhitā. A code of *dharma*, in 72 Sanskrit stanzas. With Bengali translation.] *See* PAÑCHĀNANA TARKARATNA BHAṬṬĀCHĀRYA. ঊনবিংশতি সংহিতা। [Ūnavimṣati saṃhitā.] pp. 264-268. [1903.] 8°. **14039. c. 20.**

AṄKĀBHIDHĀNA. অথ অঙ্কাভিধান। [Aṅkābhidhāna. With a Bengali translation.] *See* GOPĪRAMAṆA TARKARATNA. কোষচন্দ্রিকা। [Koshachandrikā.] pp. 49-57. [1893.] 12°. **14090. b. 44.(1.)**

ANNADĀCHARAṆA BHAṬṬĀCHĀRYA. সপ্রমাণ সানুবাদ তীর্থতত্ত্বপ্রদায়িনী। [Tīrthatattva-pradāyinī. A Sanskrit work on pilgrimages, compiled with a Bengali translation by Annadācharaṇa.] pp. vi. 460. কলিকাতা ১৩০১ [*Calcutta*, 1894.] *obl.* 4°. **14033. e. 38.**

ANNADĀCHARAṆA GHAṬAKA KULARATNA. ব্রহ্মবংশাবলী। [Brahma-vaṃśāvalī. A genealogical account of Brahmans of the Ṣāṇḍilya, Kāśyapa, Sāvarṇa, Vātsya, and Bharadvāja *gotras.*] কলিকাতা ১২৯৭ [*Calcutta*, 1890.] 8°. **14127. b. 42.**

Separate pagination.

ANNADĀPRASĀDA VASU. অনঙ্গরঙ্গিণী। [Anaṅga Raṅgiṇī. A drama in imitation of Shakspere's "As you like it."] pp. 132. কলিকাতা ১৩০৪ [*Calcutta*, 1897.] 12°. **14131. a. 40.(8.)**

ANUKŪLACHANDRA GUPTA KĀVYATĪRTHA. *See* SARVAVARMAN. কলাপ-ব্যাকরণম্ । [Kalāpavyākaraṇa. The section on Sandhi. Edited with Bengali annotations by Anukūlachandra Gupta.] [1895.] 8°. **14090. bb. 13.(4.)**

ANŪPAKṚISHṆA MITRA. *See* JĪVANAKṚISHṆA SENA. সমর্থকোষ । *etc.* [Samarthakosha. Continued from no. 53 by Anūpakṛishṇa Mitra and Lalitakṛishṇa Vasu.] [1884, *etc.*] 4°. **14133. c. 4.**

ĀPASTAMBA. আপস্তম্বসংহিতা । [Āpastamba-saṃhitā. A metrical code of *dharma*, in 10 *adhyāyas*. Sanskrit text, with Bengali translation.] *See* PAÑCHĀNANA TARKARATNA BHAṬṬĀCHĀRYA. ঊনবিংশতি সংহিতা । [Ūnaviṃṣati saṃhitā.] pp. 275-288. [1903.] 8°. **14039. c. 20.**

APOSTLES. ডিডাকি । [The Didache, or Teaching of the Twelve Apostles, translated into Bengali with notes.] *See* NITYAGOPĀLA MUKHOPĀDHYĀYA. Studies in Apostolic Fathers. No. 2. pp. 5-29. [1895.] 8°. **14123. b. 18.**

ARABIAN NIGHTS. তরজমা আলেফ লায়লা । [Alf lailā. The Arabian Nights' Tales, translated into Muhammadan Bengali verse by Roshan 'Alī.] pp. 596. [*Calcutta*, 1892.] 4°. **14127. h. 1.**

The pagination is irregular; the text, however, is complete.

—— সচিত্র আরব্য রজনী । [Ārabya rajanī. The Arabian Nights' Tales, translated from the English by Dīnendrakumāra Rāya.] 3 pts. কলিকাতা ১৩০৯ [*Calcutta*, 1902.] 8°. **14127. ee. 14.**

—— সচিত্র আরব্য-উপন্যাস । বা একাধিক সহস্র রজনী । [Ārabya upanyāsa. The Arabian Nights' Tales, translated from the English, with illustrations, by Yogendranātha De. Sixth edition.] pp. vi. 416. কলিকাতা ১৩০৮ [*Calcutta*, 1901.] 8°. **14127. ee. 13.(2.)**

—— [Ninth edition.] pp. vi. 416. কলিকাতা ১৩১৫ [*Calcutta*, 1908.] 8°. **14128. b. 2.**

—— আরব্যোপন্যাস সচিত্র গার্হস্থ্য সংস্করণ । [Ārabyopanyāsa. An abridged and expurgated translation of the Arabian Nights' Tales, for family use, by Rāmānanda Chaṭṭopādhyāya.] 2 pts. pp. ii. 243, 240. এলাহাবাদ ১৩০৯ [*Allahabad*, 1903.] 12°. **14127. cc. 40.**

ARUṆAKĀNTA RĀYA. প্রভাবতী । [Prabhāvatī. A drama in prose and verse.] pp. 79. ঢাকা [*Dacca*, 1907.] 12°. **14131. aa. 5.(5.)**

ARYAN PICTURES. Aryan Pictures, published by the Chitra Silpi Company. আর্য্য চিত্রাবলী । [Ārya chitrāvalī.] Pts. 1 and 2. *Calcutta*, 1890. Fol. **14133. gg. 6.**

ĀRYA SĀHITYA SAMITI. *See* CALCUTTA.—*Ārya Sāhitya Samiti.*

ARZĀN 'ALĪ AHMAD. সচিত্র নজ্জতন্নেছা । [Lazzat al-nisā. A description of different types of men and women, according to the Kāmaṣāstra, with anecdotes in verse of women's wiles.] pp. 120. কলিকাতা ১৩০৪ [*Calcutta*, 1897.] 12°. **14125. bb. 25.**

ASĀMĀNYĀ, *Daughter of Jagat Seṭh.* [*Life.*] *See* UPENDRAKUMĀRA GHOSHA. আর্য্য-মহিলা । [Ārya-mahilā.] 1895. 12°. **14127. aa. 2.(5.)**

'ĀSHIK 'ALĪ, *Saiyid.* গুরু সংখ্যা নর্জ্জুম নামার পুথি । [Guru-saṅkhyā. A treatise on divination and astrology, in Muhammadan Bengali verse.] pp. 93. বগুড়া ১২৯৯ [*Bogra*, 1893.] 8°. **14125. dd. 17.**

—— পিরের ছেজরা নামা । [Pīrer shajarah-nāmah. A genealogy of the author's *pīr*, or spiritual preceptor, in Muhammadan Bengali verse.] pp. 16. বগুড়া ১২৯৯ [*Bogra*, 1893.] 12°. **14129. d.**

ASHṬĀVAKRA. অষ্টাবক্র সংহিতা । [Ashṭāvakra-saṃhitā. Sanskrit text, with a Bengali paraphrase and preface by Prasādadāsa Gosvāmī.] pp. vi. 81. কলিকাতা ১২৯২ [*Calcutta*, 1886.] 12°. **14048. b. 21.**

—— অষ্টাবক্র-সংহিতা । [Ashṭāvakra-saṃhitā. Sanskrit text, with a Bengali translation.] *See* PRASANNAKUMĀRA BHAṬṬĀCHĀRYA. যোগাম্বুধি । [Yogāmbudhi.] [1896.] 32°. **14048. a. 19.**

AṢOKĀ. অশোকা । [Aṣokā. A tale of Rajput life, written by an anonymous authoress.] pp. 62, vi. ১২৯৬ *Calcutta*, [1890.] 12°. **14127. d. 39.**

ASSAM. আসামভ্রমণ । [Āsām-bhramaṇa. An account of a journey to Assam, with notes on its geography, history, antiquities, and present condition.] pp. 144. কলিকাতা ১২৯৬ [*Calcutta*, 1890.] 12°. **14127. a. 38.(3.)**

ĀŚUTOSHA GHOSHA. মাননীয় শ্রীযুক্ত রমেশচন্দ্র দত্ত ... সংক্ষিপ্ত জীবনী। [Rameśachandra Datter saṃkshipta jīvanī. The life and writings of Rameśachandra Datta.] pp. 54. কলিকাতা ১৩০২ [*Calcutta*, 1895.] 8°. **14127. aa. 3.(3.)**

ĀŚUTOSHA MUKHOPĀDHYĀYA. ছেলে-ভুলান-ছড়া। [Chhele bhulāna chhaṛā. A collection of Bengali nursery rhymes.] pp. 2, 93. *Calcutta*, 1899. 12°. **14129. bb. 7.**

ĀŚUTOSHA ŚĀSTRĪ, *of the Sanskrit College, Calcutta. See* PURĀṆAS.—*Selections.* হিন্দুশাস্ত্র। ... অষ্টাদশ পুরাণ। [Ashṭādaśa-purāṇa. Selections from the 18 Purāṇas, with Bengali translations, and a brief account of each. Compiled by Āśutosha Śāstrī and Hṛishīkeśa Śāstrī.] [1897.] 8°. **14085. c. 45.(vol. ii.)**

ĀŚUTOSHA TARKATĪRTHA BHAṬṬĀCHĀRYA. *See* BHAṬṬI. भट्टिकाव्यम्। [Bhaṭṭikāvya. Edited with construing paraphrases, notes, and Bengali translation by Āśutosha Tarkatīrtha.] [1902, *etc.*] 8°. **14070. dd. 24.**

ĀŚVALĀYANA. আশ্বলায়ন-শ্রৌতসূত্রম্। (গৃহ্যসূত্রম্।) [Selections from the Śrautasūtra and Gṛihyasūtra. Edited with Bengali translations, preface, and notes by Rameśachandra Datta and Satyavrata Sāmaśramī.] [1895.] *See* RAMEŚACHANDRA DATTA. হিন্দুশাস্ত্র। [Hindu-śāstra.] Pt. iii., pp. 15-19; 40-47. [1895 97.] 8°. **14085. c. 45.(vol. i.)**

AṬALAVIHĀRĪ DATTA. বীর-বালক। [Vīrabālaka. The brave youth; a martial poem.] pp. 128. কলিকাতা ১৩০৮ [*Calcutta*, 1901.] 12°. **14129. bb. 17.**

ATRI. অত্রিসংহিতা। [Atri-saṃhitā. A code of *dharma*, in 391 Sanskrit stanzas. With Bengali translation.] *See* PAÑCHĀNANA TARKARATNA BHAṬṬĀCHĀRYA. ঊনবিংশতি সংহিতা। [Ūnaviṃśati saṃhitā.] pp. 1-24. [1903.] 8°. **14039. c. 20.**

ATULACHANDRA MUKHOPĀDHYĀYA. কাশীর গুপ্ত কথা। [Kāśīr gupta kathā.] Mysteries of Benares. pp. 134. বেনারস ১৮৯৩ [*Benares*, 1893.] 8°. **14127. ee. 4.(1.)**

ATULAKṚISHṆA GOSVĀMĪ. *See* LOCHANADĀSA ṬHĀKURA. শ্রীচৈতন্যমঙ্গল। [Chaitanya-maṅgala. Edited with a preface and notes by Atulakṛishṇa.] [1902.] 8°. **14123. i. 13.**

ATULAKṚISHṆA GOSVĀMĪ (*continued*). *See* RŪPA GOSVĀMĪ. লঘুভাগবতামৃত। [Laghubhāgavatāmṛita. With a Sanskrit commentary and Bengali translation and notes. Edited by Balāichānd and Atulakṛishṇa.] [1897.] 8°. **14016. c. 58.**

—— *See* VṚINDĀVANA DĀSA. শ্রীচৈতন্যভাগবত। [Chaitanya-bhāgavata. Edited with notes by Atulakṛishṇa.] [1899, *etc.*] 8°. **14123. i. 12.**

ATULAKṚISHṆA MITRA. অতুল-গ্রন্থাবলী। [Atula-granthāvalī. The works of Atulakṛishṇa Mitra. Edited by Upendranātha Mukhopādhyāya.] pp. 251. কলিকাতা ১৩১১ [*Calcutta*, 1904.] 8°. **14127. ee. 24.**

—— অতুল-গ্রন্থাবলী। [Atula-granthāvalī. Another collection of the works of Atulakṛishṇa Mitra. Edited by Hārādhana Chaṭṭopādhyāya.] Pt. i. কলিকাতা ১৩১১ [*Calcutta*, 1904, *etc.*] 8°. **14127. ee. 25.**

In progress!

—— শিরী-ফরহাদ্। [Śirī-Pharhād. A dramatised version of the romance of Shīrīn and Farhād.] pp. 124. কলিকাতা ১৩১৩ [*Calcutta*, 1906.] 12°. **14131. aa. 5.(2.)**

AVANĪNDRANĀTHA ṬHĀKURA. *See* RAVĪNDRANĀTHA ṬHĀKURA. চিত্রাঙ্গদা। [Chitrāṅgadā. With sketches by Avanīndranātha Ṭhākura.] [1892.] 4°. **14131. cc. 1.**

AVINĀŚACHANDRA CHAKRAVARTĪ, *of Calcutta. See* VIHĀRĪLĀLA CHAKRAVARTĪ. গ্রন্থাবলী। [Granthāvalī. Edited with an introduction by Avināśachandra Chakravartī.] [1900.] 12°. **14129. bb. 5.**

AVINĀŚACHANDRA CHAKRAVARTĪ, *of Dhubri High School.* कविताकोरकम् [Kavitākoraka. A collection of Sanskrit poems for educational purposes, with Bengali metrical translations.] pp. vi. 35, 44. कलिकाता १९०० [*Calcutta*, 1900.] 12°. **14076. b. 28.(3.)**

AVINĀŚACHANDRA CHAṬṬOPĀDHYĀYA. পত্রাবলী। [Patrāvalī. Mythological stories, and events in the history of India, described in verse in the form of letters.] Pt. i. pp. 123. কলিকাতা ১৩০৪ [*Calcutta*, 1897.] 8°. **14127. cc. 3.**

AVINĀŚACHANDRA DĀSA. সীতা। [Sītā. The story of Rāma and Sītā, taken from the Rāmāyaṇa.] pp. ii. 228. কলিকাতা ১২৯৭ [*Calcutta*, 1891.] 12°. **14127. d. 41.(1.)**

—— [Second edition.] pp. xvi. 248. *Calcutta*, 1897. 12°. **14127. cc. 4.(4.)**

AVINĀṢACHANDRA GAṄGOPĀDHYĀYA. *See* GIRIṢACHANDRA GHOSHA. গিরিশ-গীতাবলী। [Giriṣa-gītāvalī. Edited with a life of the author by Avināṣachandra.] [1904.] 32°. **14129. aa. 1.**

—— প্রহেলিকা-রত্নমালা। [Prahelikā-ratnamālā. A collection of riddles.] pp. 60. কলিকাতা ১৩০৮ [*Calcutta*, 1902.] 12°. **14125. f. 35.(2.)**

AVINĀṢACHANDRA GHOSHA. প্রীতি-গীতি। [Prītigīti. A collection of love-songs by various poets, compiled, with an introduction, and a short account of some of the authors, by Avināṣachandra Ghosha.] pp. 54, 6, 46, 936, 9, 13. কলিকাতা ১৩০৫ [*Calcutta*, 1899.] 8°. **14129. c. 50.**

AVINĀṢACHANDRA KAVIRATNA. *See* SUṢRUTA. সুশ্রুতসংহিতা। [Suṣruta-saṃhitā. Edited and translated into Bengali by Avināṣachandra Kaviratna.] [1885, *etc.*] 8°. **14043. d. 40.**

AYODHYĀRĀMA RĀYA, called KAVICHANDRA. সত্যনারায়ণ কথা। [Satyanārāyaṇa-kathā. A poem in praise of the god Satyanārāyaṇa. Edited with an introduction by Vyomakeṣa Mustafī.] ১৩০৮ [1901.] *See* ACADEMIES, *etc.*—Calcutta.—*Bengal Academy of Literature.* সাহিত্য-পরিষৎ-পত্রিকা। [Sāhitya-parishat-patrikā.] Vol. viii., no. 1. [1894, *etc.*] 8°. **14133. f. 18.**

ĀYURVEDA-SĀRASAṄGRAHA. আয়ুর্বেদ-সারসংগ্রহম্। [Āyurveda-sārasaṅgraha. A medical compendium in Sanskrit verse. Edited, with a Bengali prose translation, by Gopālachandra Sena Gupta.] Pt. i. pp. 176. কলিকাতা ১২৭৮ [*Calcutta*, 1873.] 8°. **14043. b. 10.(1.)**

'AẒĪM al-DĪN, *Naṣīrābādī.* আসক নামা। ['Āshiknāmah. Anecdotes of lovers, in Muhammadan Bengali verse.] pp. 109. ঢাকা ১৩০৪ [*Dacca*, 1897.] 8°. **14127. g. 10.(3.)**

'AẒĪM al-DĪN MUḤAMMAD CHAUDHURĪ. জীবন চরিত। [Jīvanacharita. The autobiography of a Muhammadan Sub-Inspector of the Bengal Police.] Pt. i. pp. iv. 156. বরিশাল ১২৯৬ [*Barisal*, 1889.] 12°. **14127. a.**

'AZĪZ BĀRĪ, *Munshī.* *See* BIBLE.—*Psalms.* Bari's Psalms of David. A Bengali metrical version. 1875. 12°. **3070. bb. 52.**

—— *See* BIBLE.—*Song of Solomon.* Swarga dampatya bilas, or Bari's Song of Solomon. A Bengali metrical version. 1875. 12°. **3070. bb. 52.**

'AZĪZ al-NISĀ, *of Bansdoha.* *See* PARNELL (T.), *Archdeacon of Clogher.* হারমিট বা উদাসীন। [Udāsīna. Parnell's "Hermit," translated into verse by 'Azīz al-Nisā.] [1906.] 12°. **14129. bb. 28.(4.)**

BĀDARĀYAṆA. বেদান্তদর্শন। [Vedānta-darṣana, i.e. the Brahmasūtras. Sanskrit text, with an anonymous commentary called Govindabhāshya, and a commentary on this by Baladeva Vidyābhūshaṇa; also a Bengali translation of the *bhāshya* by Ṣyāmalāla Gosvāmī, and a further commentary (*vivṛiti*) on it in Bengali. Edited by Kṛishṇagopāla Bhakta.] কলিকাতা ১২৯৭-১৩০১ [*Calcutta*, 1891-94.] 8°. **14048. dd. 23.**

Imperfect: wanting pp. 129-136 of the main work.

—— বেদান্তসূত্র। [Vedāntasūtra. Sanskrit text, with a Bengali commentary by Yadunātha Majumdār.] যশোহর ১৯০৪ [*Jessore*, 1904, *etc.*] 8°. **14049. b. 27.**

In progress.

BAHURŪPĪ. বহুরূপী। [Bahurūpī, or the Chameleon. Short amusing anecdotes.] pp. 24. কলিকাতা ১২৯৯ [*Calcutta*, 1892.] 12°. **14127. c. 42.(1.)**

BAITĀLIKA. *See* UMEṢACHANDRA VAITĀLIKA.

BALADEVA VIDYĀBHŪSHAṆA. সিদ্ধান্তরত্নম্। [Siddhāntaratna. A Sanskrit tractate in confirmation of the author's Govindabhāshya, in exposition of the Chaitanya-Vaishṇava doctrine, with a Sanskrit commentary. Edited, with a Bengali translation, by Ṣyāmalāla Gosvāmī.] pp. ii. 333. কলিকাতা ১৩০৪ [*Calcutta*, 1897.] 8°. **14048. cc. 24.**

BALĀICHĀND GOSVĀMĪ. *See* LĀLADĀSA BĀBĀJĪ. শ্রীশ্রীভক্তমাল গ্রন্থ। [Bhaktamāla. Edited with an introduction, note, and translations of Sanskrit *ṣlokas* by Balāichānd.] [1898.] 8°. **14129. e. 20.**

—— *See* RŪPA GOSVĀMĪ. লঘুভাগবতামৃত। [Laghubhāgavatāmṛita. Edited by Balāichānd.] [1897.] 8°. **14016. c. 58.**

BALARĀMA CHAKRAVARTĪ. কাঁড়াদাসী গুরুপ্রসাদী কীর্ত্তন। [Kāṇṛādāsī kīrtana. An account of Kāṇṛā Dāsa, a devotee of Benares, and of his wonderful powers as a magician.] pp. ii. 48. বারাণসী ১৮৯৭ [*Benares*, 1897.] 8°. **14127. bb. 17.**

BALARĀMA DĀSA, *of Calcutta.* শ্রী প্রবোধানন্দ সরস্বতীর জীবন চরিত। [Prabodhānanda Sarasvatīr jīvanacharita. The life of Prabodhānanda Sarasvatī, a convert to Vaishnavism from the Non-dual theory of Ṣaṅkarāchārya, under which he was known by the name of Prakāṣānanda.] pp. ii. 40. কলিকাতা, শ্রীচৈতন্যাব্দ ৪০৪ [*Calcutta*, 1891.] 8°. **14127. b. 47.(1.)**

BALARĀMA DĀSA, *Son of Ātmārāma.* বলরামদাস। [Balarāma Dāsa. The poems of Balarāma, a noted Vaishṇava poet. Edited with notes and an introduction by Ramaṇīmohana Mallika.] pp. ii. vi. 210. কলিকাতা ১৩০৬ [*Calcutta*, 1899.] 8°. **14129. c. 54.**

BALARĀMA DĀSA GUPTA. ভক্তি-পুষ্পাঞ্জলি। [Bhakti-pushpāñjali. Hindu devotional hymns.] pp. x. 254, iii. কলিকাতা ১৩১৪ [*Calcutta*, 1907.] 12°. **14123. e. 38.**

BALARĀMA PĀLA and Co. Prakriti bibeca abhidhana, or An illustrated and etymological dictionary of the Sanskrit and Bengali languages, containing 53,828 words . . . By Bulloram Paul and Co. সচিত্র প্রকৃতিবিবেক অভিধান। pp. 1860. *Calcutta*, ১২৯৯ [1892.] 8°. **14133. b. 14.**

BALENDRANĀTHA ṬHĀKURA. স্বর্গীয় বলেন্দ্রনাথ ঠাকুরের গ্রন্থাবলী। [Balendranātha Ṭhākurer granthāvalī. The complete works of Balendranātha Ṭhākura, edited with a life of the author by Ṛitendranātha Ṭhākura, and an introduction by Rāmendrasundara Trivedī.] pp. vii. viii. vii. 735. কলিকাতা ১৩১৪ [*Calcutta*, 1907.] 8°. **14127. ee. 30.**

BALLĀLA SENA, *King of Bengal.* বল্লালচরিতম্। [Ballāla-charita. A Sanskrit poetical chronicle, in two cantos, of Ballāla Sena, ruler of Bengal in the 14th century, purporting to have been originally compiled by his tutor Gopāla Bhaṭṭa, and continued in a third canto by Ānanda Bhaṭṭa in the 16th century. Edited, with a Bengali prose translation, index, notes, and an introduction, by Ṣaṣibhūshaṇa Bhaṭṭāchārya. Revised by Hariṣchandra Kaviratna.] pp. vii. viii. 84. কলিকাতা ১৮৮৯ [*Calcutta*, 1889.] 8°. **14058. b. 25.**

—— শ্রীমদানন্দ ভট্ট-বিরচিত সংস্কৃত বল্লাল-চরিতের বঙ্গানুবাদ। [Ballāla-charita. A Bengali translation by Dīnanātha Dhara from the Sanskrit chronicle by Ānanda Bhaṭṭa, which was published, with an English translation, by Haraprasāda Ṣāstrī at Calcutta in 1901.] pp. iv. 114. *Calcutta*, 1904. 12°. **14127. a. 45.(3.)**

BĀMĀ CHARAN BASU. *See* VĀMĀCHARAṆA VASU.

BANERJEA (K. M.). *See* KṚISHṆAMOHANA VANDYOPĀDHYĀYA.

BANERJEE (G. D.). *See* GURUDĀSA VANDHYOPĀDHYĀYA.

BANERJI (K.). *See* KĀṢĪNDRANĀTHA VANDYOPĀDHYĀYA.

BAṄKAVIHĀRĪ SHĀH. গীত রত্নাবলী। [Gīta-ratnāvalī. A collection of Vaishṇava songs on the cult of Kṛishṇa.] pp. 360. বগুড়া ১৮১২ [*Bogra*, 1890.] 8°. **14129. c. 44.**

BAṄKIMCHANDRA CHAṬṬOPĀDHYĀYA. *See* DĀMODARA MUKHOPĀDHYĀYA. মৃণ্ময়ী। [Mṛiṇmayī. A tale; being a sequel to Baṅkimchandra's Kapālakuṇḍalā.] [1886 ?] 8°. **14127. g. 4.**

—— *See* DĪNABANDHU MITRA. রায় দীনবন্ধু মিত্রের গ্রন্থাবলী। [Granthāvalī. With a life of the author by Baṅkimchandra.] [1901.] 8°. **14127. ee. 16.**

—— *See* DURGĀDĀSA DE. স্বর্ণ গোলকের সঙ্গীত। [Suvarṇa-golaker saṅgīta. Songs adapted from those in Baṅkimchandra's Suvarṇa-golaka.] [1897.] 12°. **14129. a. 51.(1.)**

—— *See* GIRIJĀPRASANNA RĀYA CHAUDHURĪ. বঙ্কিমচন্দ্র। [Baṅkimchandra. An analysis and critical review of two of Baṅkimchandra's novels, viz. Kṛishṇakānter Will and Chandraṣekhara.] [1886.] 8°. **14131. d. 17.(1.)**

—— *See* GIRIJĀPRASANNA RĀYA CHAUDHURĪ. বঙ্কিমচন্দ্র। [Baṅkimchandra. An analysis and critical review of three of Baṅkimchandra's novels, viz. Durgeṣanandinī, Kapālakuṇḍalā, and Mṛiṇālinī.] [1890.] 8°. **14131. d. 17.(2.)**

BAṄKIMCHANDRA CHAṬṬOPĀDHYĀYA (*continued*). *See* GIRIJĀPRASANNA RĀYA CHAUDHURĪ. বঙ্কিমচন্দ্র । [Baṅkimchandra. A critical analysis of the novels of Baṅkimchandra.] [1901.] 8°.
14131. d. 42.

—— *See* HĀRĀṆACHANDRA RAKSHITA. বঙ্গসাহিত্যে বঙ্কিম । [Vaṅgasāhitya Baṅkim. A critical examination of the works of Baṅkimchandra, with a short life of the novelist.] [1899.] 12°.
14125. e. 36.

—— *See* ĪṢVARACHANDRA GUPTA. গ্রন্থাবলী । [Granthāvalī. The complete works of Īṣvarachandra Gupta, with a life of the poet by Baṅkimchandra.] [1901.] 8°. **14129. e. 24.**

—— *See* ĪṢVARACHANDRA GUPTA. কবিতাসংগ্রহ । [Kavitāsaṅgraha. Edited, with a life of the poet, by Baṅkimchandra.] [1885-86.] 12°.
14129. a. 27.

—— *See* KEDĀRANĀTHA VIṢVĀSA. ভবানী পাঠক । [Bhavānī Pāṭhaka. A sequel to Baṅkimchandra's Devī Chaudhurāṇī.] 1900. 12°. **14127. cc. 26.**

—— *See* MAHĀBHĀRATA.—*Bhagavadgītā.* হিন্দুশাস্ত্র । ... শ্রীমদ্ভগবদ্গীতা । [Bhagavadgītā. With a Bengali translation by Baṅkimchandra (Adh. i. and ii.) and Dāmodara Vidyānanda.] [1897.] 8°. **14085. c. 45.(vol. ii.)**

—— *See* MAHENDRACHANDRA MAJUMDĀR. সাহিত্য ও সমাজ । [Sāhitya o samāja. A severe criticism on the Vishavṛiksha of Baṅkimchandra.] [1896.] 16°. **14131. d. 36.**

—— *See* RAJANĪKĀNTA GUPTA. প্রতিভা । [Pratibhā. A review of the works of Baṅkimchandra.] [1896.] 12°. **14131. d. 35.**

—— *See* SAÑJĪVACHANDRA CHAṬṬOPĀDHYĀYA. সঞ্জীবনী সুধা । [Sañjīvanī-sudhā. With a life of the author by Baṅkimchandra.] 1893. 12°.
14127. c. 52.

—— *See* SURENDRAMOHANA BHAṬṬĀCHĀRYA. হেমচন্দ্র । [Hemachandra. A sequel to Baṅkimchandra's Mṛiṇālinī.] [1905.] 12°. **14128. a. 4.**

—— আনন্দ মঠ । [Ānanda-maṭha. A Bengali novel. Third edition.] pp. 201, ix. iii. কলিকাতা ১২৯২ [*Calcutta,* 1886.] 12°. **14127. c. 24.**

BAṄKIMCHANDRA CHAṬṬOPĀDHYĀYA (*continued*). The Abbey of Bliss. A translation of Bankim Chandra Chatterjee's Anandamath, by Nares Chandra Sen-Gupta. Fifth edition. pp. xii. 201, vii *Calcutta,* [1906.] 12°. **14128. a. 15**

—— ধর্ম্মতত্ত্ব । প্রথম ভাগ । অনুশীলন । [Anuṣīlana. A philosophical discussion, in the form of a dialogue between a Guru and his disciple, on moral, intellectual, and physical culture, and the attainment of true happiness.] pp. ix. 359. কলিকাতা ১২৯৫ [*Calcutta,* 1888.] 12°. **14125. e. 20.**
Apparently part i. of a series entitled "Dharmatattva."

—— বঙ্কিমচন্দ্রের গ্রন্থাবলী । [Baṅkimchandrer granthāvalī. The collected works of Baṅkimchandra. Edited by Upendranātha Mukhopādhyāya.] কলিকাতা ১৩১০ [*Calcutta,* 1904- .] 8°.
In progress. **14127. g. 14.**

—— Chandra Shekhar ... Translated by Manmatha Nath Ray Chowdhury. pp. viii. 318, vii. *London, Calcutta* printed, [1904.] 8°.
14127. cc. 37.

—— Chandrashekhar ... Translated ... by Debendra Chandra Mullick. pp. vii. 177. *Calcutta,* 1905. 8°. **14128. a. 21.**

—— Det giftiga Trädet. [A Swedish translation of the Vishavṛiksha.] En Hinduisk Roman. ... Öfversättning. pp. 171. *Stockholm,* 1894. 8°.
14127. cc. 1.

—— Durgesa Nandini, or The Chieftain's daughter ... Translated ... by Charu Chandra Mookerjee. Second edition. pp. ii. 276. *Calcutta,* 1903. 12°.
14127. cc. 24.

—— গদ্য পদ্য বা কবিতাপুস্তক । [Gadya-padya. Short pieces in prose and verse. Second edition.] pp. v. 144. *Calcutta,* 1891. 12°. **14127. c. 47.**

—— ইন্দিরা । [Indirā. A short tale of married life. Fourth edition.] pp. 45. *Calcutta,* 1886. 12°.
14127. c. 26.(1.)

—— কমলাকান্ত । [Kamalākānta. Humorous and satirical sketches. Second edition.] pp. 250, ii. কলিকাতা ১২৯২ [*Calcutta,* 1885.] 12°. **14127. c. 23.**

—— Kopal-Kundala ... von Bunkim Chandra Chattopâdhyâya. Deutsch von Curt Klemm. pp. 200. *Leipzig,* 1886. 8°. **14127. e. 27.**

BAṄKIMCHANDRA CHAṬṬOPĀDHYĀYA (*continued*). কৃষ্ণচরিত্র। [Kṛishṇa-charitra. An examination into the life and character of Kṛishṇa.] Pt. i. pp. vi. 198. *Calcutta*, 1886. 12°. **14127. c. 22.**

—— [Second edition.] pp. 14, 10, 492. *Calcutta*, 1892. 12°. **14127. c. 46.**

—— Krishna Kanta's Will ... Translated by M. S. Knight, with introduction, glossary, and notes by J. F. Blumhardt. pp. 264. *London*, 1895. 8°. **14127. e. 46.**

—— রাধারাণী। [Rādhārāṇī. A short love-story. Third edition.] pp. 38. *Calcutta*, 1886. 12°. **14127. c. 26.(2.)**

—— সীতারাম। [Sītārāma. A novel. Second edition.] pp. 300. কলিকাতা ১২৯৫ [*Calcutta*, 1888.] 12°. **14127. c. 32.**

—— বিবিধ প্রবন্ধ। [Vividha prabandha. Miscellaneous essays.] pp. 280. ১২৯৪ *Calcutta*, [1889.] 12°. **14127. c. 33.**

—— যুগলাঙ্গুরীয়। [Yugalāṅgurīya. A tale of domestic life. Fourth edition.] pp. 36. *Calcutta*, 1886. 12°. **14127. c. 26.(3.)**

—— The Two Rings ... Translated [from Baṅkimchandra's Yugalāṅguriya] by Rakhal Chandra Banerjee. pp. 43. *Calcutta*, 1897. 8°. **14127. cc. 8.**

BAṄKIMCHANDRA RĀYA. দুঃখিনী মাতা। উপন্যাস। [Duḥkhinī mātā. The sorrowful mother: a story of domestic life.] pp. 143. কলিকাতা ১৩১৪ [*Calcutta*, 1907.] 8°. **14128. b. 1.**

—— রাজরাণী। [Rājarāṇī. A story of domestic life in Bengal.] pp. iv. 192. কলিকাতা ১৩১৪ [*Calcutta*, 1908.] 12°. **14128. a. 20.**

—— কাকী-মা। গার্হস্থ উপন্যাস। [Kākī-mā. A domestic story.] pp. 163. *Calcutta*, [1907.] 12°. **14128. a. 22.**

BĀRĪ (ʻAzīz). *See* ʻAzīz Bārī, *Munshī*.

BARMA (M. N.). *See* Mathurānātha Varmā.

BĀSAR-GHAR. বাসর-ঘর। [Bāsar-ghar. A description of the amusements and jokes that take place in the bridal chamber amongst the female relatives of a newly-married Hindu couple.] pp. 14. কলিকাতা ১২৯৩ [*Calcutta*, 1886.] 12°. **14125. e. 19.(2.)**

BASU (R. K.). *See* Rajanīkānta Vasu.

BATABYAL (Bipin Bihari). *See* Vipinavihārī Vaṭavyāla.

BĀTĀSU SARKĀR. ছীলছত্র রাজার জঙ্গ। [Chhīlchhatra rājār jang. A legend in Muhammadan Bengali verse relating to the defeat of the demon king Chhīlchhatra in a trial of strength with the Caliph ʻAlī.] pp. 48. ১৩০৪ [*Calcutta*, 1897.] 8°. **14127. g. 10.(2.)**

BAṬUDĀSA GOSVĀMĪ. *See* Rūpa Gosvāmī. সটীক ... শ্রীস্তবপুষ্পাঞ্জলিঃ। [Stavapushpāñjali. Edited by Baṭudāsa.] [1902.] 8°. **14072. ccc. 34.**

BAUDDHA DHARMĀṄKURA SABHĀ. *See* Calcutta.—*Bauddha Dharmāṅkura Sabhā.*

BENGAL.—*Eastern Bengal and Assam.* Government Gazette, Eastern Bengal and Assam. Vernacular Edition. গবর্ণমেন্ট গেজেট, পূর্ববঙ্গ এবং আসাম। *Shillong*, 1905, *etc.* Fol. **14125. aa. 3.**

BENGAL ACADEMY OF LITERATURE. *See* Academies, *etc.*—*Calcutta.*

BENGALI LADY. ইংলণ্ডে বঙ্গমহিলা। [Imlaṇḍe Vaṅgamahilā. A Bengali lady's experiences of English life, manners, and customs.] pp. iv. 309. কলিকাতা [*Calcutta*,] 1885. 12°. **14127. c. 29.**

BENIMADHAV GANGULI. *See* Veṇīmādhava Gaṅgopādhyāya.

BHAGAVĀN-CHANDRA CHAUDHURĪ. ভক্ত-নির্যাণ। [Bhakta-niryāṇa. An account of the death of Dharmacharaṇa Chaudhurī, the father of the author, and a devout follower of Chaitanya.] pp. 26. কলিকাতা ১২৯৯ [*Calcutta*, 1892.] 12°. **14127. a. 37.(3.)**

BHĀGAVATA ĀCHĀRYA. *See* Purāṇas.—*Bhāgavatapurāṇa.* কৃষ্ণপ্রেমতরঙ্গিণী। [Kṛishṇapremataraṅgiṇī. A metrical version of the Bhāgavatapurāṇa, by Bhāgavata Āchārya.] [1906, *etc.*] 8°. **14133. ff. 2.**

BHAGAVATĪ. চিত্রিত দশমহাবিদ্যা মূর্ত্তি। [Daṣamahāvidyā-mūrti. Ten coloured pictures of the goddess Bhagavatī in her ten manifestations, with Sanskrit illustrative quotations, and descriptions in Bengali.] কলিকাতা ১২৯২ [*Calcutta*, 1885.] 4°. **14033. e. 4.**

BHAGAVATĪCHARAṆA MITRA. জুবিলি বা পরার্দ্ধ্য-উৎসব। [Parārddhya-utsava. A short sketch of the life of Queen Victoria, written on the occasion of her Jubilee.] pp. 30. *Calcutta*, 1887. 12°. **14127. a. 31.(2.)**

BHAGAVATĪCHARAṆA PRADHĀNA. মহিষাদল রাজবংশ। [Mahishādala-rājavaṃṣa. An historical account of the Mahishādal race of kings from the earliest times to the present day.] pp. 83. কলিকাতা ১৩০৪ [*Calcutta*, 1897.] 12°. **14127. a. 22.(2.)**

BHAGAVATĪCHARAṆA VANDYOPĀDHYĀYA. History of Cooch Behar. By Bhagavati Charan Banerjee. কোচবিহারের ইতিহাস [Kochbihārer itihāsa. Second edition.] pp. ix. 170. *Cooch Behar*, 1884. 8°. **14127. b. 39.**

BHĀGYAVĀN VIDYĀLAṄKĀRA. *See* VIDYĀPATI. শৈবসর্বস্ব-সার। [Ṣaivasarvasvasāra. Edited with Bengali translations by Bhāgyavān.] [1897.] 12°. **14028. d. 57.(2.)**

BHAKTIRASĀMṚITA. ভক্তি রসামৃত। [Bhaktirasāmṛita. An account of celebrated Vaishṇava devotees.] *See* KṚISHṆAPRASANNA SENA. ভক্তি ও ভক্ত [Bhakti o bhakta.] pp. 77-150. [1887.] 8°. **14028. c. 56.**

BHAKTIRASATARAṄGIṆĪ. ভক্তিরস-তরঙ্গিণী। [Bhaktirasataraṅgiṇī. Songs in praise of Kālī, Ṣiva, and Kṛishṇa.] pp. viii. 108. [*Calcutta*, 1903.] 12°. **14123. e. 31.**

BHAKTITATTVASĀRA. ভক্তিতত্ত্বসার। [A collection of Vaishṇava poems. Another edition.] pp. 60. কলিকাতা ১৩১০ [*Calcutta*, 1904.] 8°. **14123. f. 49.(3.)**

BHĀRATACHANDRA RĀYA. *See* VAṂṢĪVADANA CHAṬṬOPĀDHYĀYA. আসল নূতন বিদ্যাসুন্দর টপ্পা। [Vidyā-Sundara ṭappā. Based on the poem of Bhāratachandra.] [1886.] 12°. **14129. b.**

BHĀRATACHANDRA RĀYA (*continued*). রায় গুণাকর ভারতচন্দ্রের গ্রন্থাবলী। [Bhāratachandrer granthāvalī. The poetical works of Bhāratachandra. With a life of the poet, extensive notes, and a review of his works.] কলিকাতা ১২৯৩ [*Calcutta*, 1886.] 12°. **14129. b. 32.**

—— The Poetical Works of Bharutchunder Roy, with his life and notes. [Published] by Day Brothers. ভারতচন্দ্র রায় গুণাকরের গ্রন্থাবলী। pp. xvi. 616. কলিকাতা ১৩০৭ [*Calcutta*, 1902.] 12°. **14129. a. 53.**

—— রায় গুণাকর ভারতচন্দ্রের গ্রন্থাবলী। [Bhāratachandrer granthāvalī. Edited, with a life of the poet, by Pūrṇachandra Mukhopādhyāya.] pp. vi. 208. কলিকাতা ১৩১১ [*Calcutta*, 1904.] 8°. **14129. e. 29.**

BHĀRATAVARSHĪYA SABHĀ. *See* BRITISH INDIAN ASSOCIATION.

BHĀRAVI. Kiratarjunium . . . [Sargas 1 to 3]. Text . . . with translations into English and Bengali by a distinguished Graduate of the Calcutta University: revised by a Professor of the Presidency College. pp. 203. *Calcutta*, 1886. 8°. **14072. cc. 12.(2.)**

—— Kiratarjun . . . in Bengali verse. Cantos 1 to 5, with copious notes . . . by Nobin Chandra Das, Kavi-Gunākar . . . ভারবি কৃত কিরাতার্জ্জুন। pp. viii. 92. [*Calcutta*,] 1906. 8°. **14129. cc. 18.**

BHĀSKARA ĀCHĀRYA. সিদ্ধান্তশিরোমণিঃ গোলাধ্যায়ঃ বাসনাভাষ্যসহিতঃ। [Siddhāntaṣiromaṇi. A Sanskrit treatise on astronomy. The Golādhyāya, with the author's Vāsanābhāshya, and Bengali translations and notes.] [1891, *etc.*] *See* PERIODICAL PUBLICATIONS.—*Calcutta*. অরুণোদয়। [Aruṇodaya.] Pt. i., no. 6. [1890, *etc.*] 4°. **14133. g. 16.**

Extending only over 28 pages.

BHĀSKARĀNANDA SVĀMĪ. [*Life.*] *See* BHŪDHARA CHAṬṬOPĀDHYĀYA. সাধুদর্শন। [Sādhudarṣana.] Pt. i. [1888.] 12°. **14127. a. 35.**

—— [*Life.*] *See* GOPĀLACHANDRA CHAṬṬOPĀDHYĀYA. যতীন্দ্র চরিত। [Yatīndra-charita.] [1892.] 8°. **14127. b. 47.(3.)**

BHĀSKARĀNANDA SVĀMĪ (*continued*). যতীন্দ্র-জীবন-চরিতম্। [Yatīndra-jīvana-charita. A Sanskrit poem on the life of Bhāskarānanda, a famous *yati*, or ascetic, of Benares. With a Bengali prose translation by Sureșvara Nārāyaṇa Deva.] pp. v. 89. *Calcutta*, 1892. 8°. **14058. b. 26.(2.)**

BHAṬṬI. ভট্টিকাব্যম্ । [Bhaṭṭikāvya. Sanskrit text, with the glosses of Nārāyaṇa Vidyāvinoda and Bharatasena. Edited with construing, paraphrases, grammatical notes, and Bengali translation by Āșutosha Tarkatīrtha Bhaṭṭāchārya.] কলিকাতা [*Calcutta*, 1902, *etc.*] 8°. **14070. dd. 24.**

—— Bhatti . . . Cantos i.-v. Text with notes by Pundit Nobin Ch. Vidyaratna . . . With English and Bengali translations, and model questions with model answers. Second edition. pp. 576, 84. *Calcutta*, [1894.] 12°. **14070. c. 57.(1.)**

—— ভট্টিকাব্যম্ । [Bhaṭṭikāvya. Sargas i.-v., with the Sanskrit commentaries of Jayamaṅgala, Bharatasena, and Nārāyaṇa Vidyāvinoda, analyses, and a Bengali translation by Tārāpada Kāvyatīrtha.] pp. iv. 312. কলিকাতা [*Calcutta*, 1895-96.] 8°. **14076. d. 49.**

In 4 fasciculi. No more seems to have been published.

—— ভট্টিকাব্যম্ । প্রথমতশ্চতুর্থসর্গ পর্য্যন্তম্ । [Bhaṭṭikāvya. Cantos i.-iv. With a Sanskrit commentary, re-arrangement of words, etymological notes, and Bengali translation, by Haranātha Deva Șāstrī.] কলিকাতা ১৩১০ [*Calcutta*, 1903.] 12°. **14085. c. 53.(1.)**

—— Bhatti Kavyam. Cantos i. and ii. [With grammatical notes in Sanskrit and English, Bengali and English translations, and extracts from Jayamaṅgala's commentary.] Edited by Devendra Kumar Vidyaratna. pp. ii. i. 20, 269, vi. *Calcutta*, [1903.] 12°. **14085. b. 48.**

—— Bhatti-kavyam. Cantos i. and ii. Calcutta University F.A. Sanskrit Course, 1905. With the commentary of Jayamangala and an introduction in English, easy Sanskrit commentary called Sarala . . . English and Bengali translations, model questions with answers, University papers, *etc.* . . . by Pandit Upendra Nath Vidyabhushana. 2 pts. *Calcutta*, [1904.] 12°. **14085. b. 47.**

BHAṬṬI (*continued*). Bhatti Kavyam. Canto xii. [With Jayamaṅgala's Sanskrit commentary, grammatical and exegetical notes in Sanskrit and English, Sanskrit paraphrase, and English and Bengali translations. Edited by] Bidhubhushan Goswami. pp. ii. 256. *Calcutta*, 1907. 12°. **14072. b. 26.(4.)**

BHAVABHŪTI. *See* SATĪȘACHANDRA VIDYĀBHŪSHAṆA. Bhavabhuti and his drama, *etc.* 1899. 12°. **14131. d. 41.**

—— মালতী-মাধব । [Mālatīmādhava. Translated by Jyotirindranātha Ṭhākura.] pp. iii. 151. কলিকাতা ১৩০৭ [*Calcutta*, 1900.] 8°. **14131. a. 43.(2.)**

—— উত্তর-চরিত । [Uttaracharita. A translation of the Uttararāmacharita nāṭaka by Jyotirindranātha Ṭhākura.] pp. 152. কলিকাতা ১৩০৭ [*Calcutta*, 1900.] 8°. **14131. a. 43.(1.)**

BHAVADEVA BHAṬṬĀCHĀRYA. Analysis and Composition. [For the use of Bengalis studying English.] pp. 79. *Brahmanbaria*, 1895. 12°. **14131. e. 20.(4.)**

BHĀVA MIȘRA. Bháva Prakása . . . an Encyclopædia of Hindu medicine . . . [Sanskrit text] with Bengali translations by Kaviraj Russick Lal Gupta . . . ভাবপ্রকাশ। 2 vols. *Calcutta*, 1883-88. 8°. **14043. e. 19.**

Published in 8 parts, with separate covers, and also tables of contents for pts. 1-4 in Bengali. A general table of contents in Sanskrit for pts. 5-8 is given at the end of the book.

—— ভাবপ্রকাশ । [Bhāvaprakāșa. Sanskrit text, with a Bengali translation by Kālīșachandra Sena Gupta.] 2 vols. কলিকাতা ১২৯৪ [*Calcutta*, 1887.] 8°. **14043. d. 39.**

—— সানুবাদ-ভাবপ্রকাশঃ । [Bhāvaprakāșa. Edited with a Bengali translation by Kālīprasanna Kaviȿekhara.] pp. 76, 1000. *Calcutta*, [1901.] 8°. **14043. dd. 9.**

BHAVĀNĪ, *Rāṇī.* [*Life.*] *See* UPENDRAKUMĀRA GHOSHA. আর্য্যা-মহিলা । [Ārya-mahilā.] 1895. 12°. **14127. aa. 2.(5.)**

BHAVĀNĪPRASĀDA. দুর্গা-মঙ্গল । [Durgāmaṅgala. A poem on the myth of the goddess Durgā.] pp. 32. ১৩০৮-১০ [1901-03.] *See* PERIODICAL

PUBLICATIONS.—*Calcutta.* প্রাচীন বাঙ্গালা গ্রন্থাবলী। [Prāchīna Bāṅgālā granthāvalī.] Nos. 8-14. [1900, *etc.*] 8°. **14133. ff. 2.**
Incomplete.

BHAVAṢAṄKARA TANTRAVIṢĀRADA. সচিত্র দশমহাবিদ্যা। [Daṣamahāvidyā. An illustrated account, in verse, of the nature and worship of the goddess Pārvatī in her ten manifestations. Compiled from Tantric sources, with Bengali preface, notes, and other matter.] pp. 12, 14, 84. *Calcutta,* ১৩০৭ [1901.] 12°. **14033. a. 41.(2.)**
Imperfect; pp. 85 ff. are missing.

—— সর্ব্বসিদ্ধিপ্রদায়িনী মহাশক্তি তন্ত্র। [Mahāṣakti-tantra. A compilation from magical works, chiefly in Sanskrit. Second edition.] pp. 132. ১৩০৭ *Calcutta,* [1901.] 12°. **14033. a. 10.(2.)**

BHAVENDRANĀTHA DE. জন্মান্তর-রহস্য। [Janmāntara-rahasya. A theosophist treatise in support of the doctrine of metempsychosis.] pp. v. 117. কলিকাতা ১৩০৩ [*Calcutta,* 1896.] 12°. **14123. e. 18.(1.)**

BHOLĀNĀTHA BHAṬṬĀCHĀRYA. প্রসূনাঞ্জলি। [Prasūnāñjali. Miscellaneous songs.] pp. xii. 111, ii. কলিকাতা [*Calcutta,* 1907.] 12°. **14129. bb. 34.(2.)**

BHOLĀNĀTHA MUKHOPĀDHYĀYA. আপনার মুখ আপনি দেখ। [Āpanār mukh āpani dekha.] (Amusing sketches of life and manners.) [Another edition.] pp. 156. কলিকাতা ১৩১৪ [*Calcutta,* 1907.] 12°. **14128. a. 19.**

—— আয়ুর্ব্বেদোক্ত দ্রব্যগুণাভিধান। [Āyurvedokta dravyaguṇābhidhāna. A dictionary of medical terms used in the Hindu system of medicine.] pp. ii. 407. কলিকাতা ১২৯৮ [*Calcutta,* 1892.] 8°. **14125. c. 37.**

—— কবিতাদর্পণ। [Kavitādarpaṇa. A Sanskrit poetical anthology, with Bengali verse-translations. Compiled by Bholānātha Mukhopādhyāya. Pt. I. Second edition.] pp. xii. 94. কলিকাতা ১৮৭৯ [*Calcutta,* 1879.] 12°. **14085. b. 27.**

BHŪDEVA MUKHOPĀDHYĀYA. *See* RAJANĪKĀNTA GUPTA. প্রতিভা। [Pratibhā. A review of the works of Bhūdeva Mukhopādhyāya.] [1896.] 12°. **14131. d. 35.**

BHŪDEVA MUKHOPĀDHYĀYA (*continued*). সামাজিক প্রবন্ধ। [Sāmājika prabandha. A treatise on social organizations.] pp. vi. 319. হুগলী ১২৯৯ [*Hooghly,* 1892.] 8°. **14125. ee. 27.(2.)**

—— স্বপ্নলব্ধ ভারতবর্ষের ইতিহাস। [Svapnalabdha Bhāratavarsher itihāsa. An imaginary history of India under improved moral, social, and political conditions.] pp. 62. হুগলি ১৩০২ [*Hooghly,* 1895.] 8°. **14125. ee. 28.(2.)**

—— বিবিধ প্রবন্ধ। [Vividha prabandha. Miscellaneous essays.] 2 pts. হুগলি চুঁচুড়া ১৩০২, ১৩১১ [*Hooghly, Chinsurah,* 1896, 1905.] 8°. **14131. d. 47.**

BHŪDHARA CHAṬṬOPĀDHYĀYA. ধর্ম্মানুষ্ঠান। [Dharmānushṭhāna. A manual for the performance of Hindu religious rites and ceremonies, consisting of Sanskrit texts with Bengali commentaries, translations, and notes.] pp. ii. viii. 604. কলিকাতা ১৩০২ [*Calcutta,* 1896.] 12°. **14028. bb. 1.**

—— সাধুদর্শন। [Sādhudarṣana. Lives of Hindu holy men and ascetics.] Pt. i. pp. 138. কলিকাতা ১২৯৪ [*Calcutta,* 1888.] 12°. **14127. a. 35.**

—— শাস্ত্রাপবাদ নিরাকরণ। [Ṣāstrāpavāda nirākaraṇa. A refutation of arguments adduced against the authority of the Hindu sacred writings.] Pt. i. pp. 60. কলিকাতা ১২৯৪ [*Calcutta,* 1887.] 12°. **14123. e. 23.(1.)**

BHUṆIPHOṚ RAHASYA. ভুঁইফোড় রহস্য ও রংদার চাটনি। [Bhuṇiphoṛ rahasya. A collection of humorous anecdotes. Second edition.] pp. 36. কলিকাতা ১৩০০ [*Calcutta,* 1892.] 12°. **14127. c. 55.(1.)**

BHŪPATI GOSVĀMĪ. *See* RĀMADĀSA, *Vaishṇava poet.* অভিরামলীলামৃত। [Abhirāma-līlāmṛita. Edited by Bhūpati Gosvāmī.] [1891.] 8°. **14123. f. 46.**

BHŪPENDRANĀRĀYAṆA CHAUDHURĪ. শোভাময়ী। ঐতিহাসিক উপন্যাস। [Ṣobhāmayī. [An historical novel.] pp. 78. কোচবিহার ১৩০৬ [*Cooch Behar,* 1899.] 12°. **14127. cc. 12.(3.)**

BHŪTACHHĀṚĀNA. ভূতছাড়ানপ্রকরণ। [Bhūta-chhāṛāna-prakaraṇa. A Tantric treatise on the methods to be employed for exorcising evil spirits, consisting of selections from Sanskrit works, with Bengali translations.] pp. 18. [1894.] See PERIODICAL PUBLICATIONS.—*Calcutta*. অরুণোদয় । [Aruṇodaya.] Pt. i., no. 34. [1890, *etc.*] 4°. **14133. g. 16.**

BHŪTANĀTHA VIDYĀRATNA. *See* ŚAṄKARĀNANDA, *Disciple of Ānandātmā*. আত্মপুরাণম্ । [Ātmapurāṇa. With a Bengali translation by Bhūtanātha.] [1885.] 8°. **14048. e. 13.**

BHUVANACHANDRA BASĀK. *See* TULASĪ DĀSA. তুলসীদাসকৃত রামায়ণ । [Rāmāyaṇa. Hindi text, with a Bengali transliteration and translation by Bhuvanachandra Vasāka.] [1887, *etc.*] 8°. **14158. d. 27.**

BHUVANACHANDRA MUKHOPĀDHYĀYA. ভারতীয় রহস্য । [Bhāratiya rahasya, or The mysteries of India. A Bengali novel.] Pt. i. pp. 406. কলিকাতা ১২৯৪ [*Calcutta*, 1887.] 12°. **14127. d. 34.**

—— হরিদাসের গুপ্তকথা । [Haridāser guptakathā. A tale of modern Bengali social life, in four parts.] pp. ii. 644. কলিকাতা ১৩১০ [*Calcutta*, 1904.] 8°. **14127. ee. 22.**

—— যাত্রা-বিলাস । বঙ্গ যাত্রার আসরের নক্সা । [Yātrāvilāsa. A treatise on some of the defects in modern Bengali dramatic representations.] pp. 19. *Calcutta*, 1886. 12°. **14131. d. 20.**

BHUVANACHANDRA MUKHOPĀDHYĀYA and **KRISHṆADHANA VIDYĀPATI.** বঙ্কিম বাবুর গুপ্তকথা । [Baṅkim Bābur guptakathā. A sensational novel.] pp. 654. [*Calcutta*,] 1890. 8°. **14127. e. 40.**

BHUVANAMOHANA BHAṬṬĀCHĀRYA, *of Murshidabad*. যোগেন্দ্র মাহাত্ম্যম্ । [Yogendra-māhātmya. A Sanskrit poetical panegyric on Yogendra Nārāyaṇa Rāya, zamindar of Lalgola. With a Bengali prose translation.] pp. 20. মুর্শিদাবাদ ১৮২২ [*Murshidabad*, 1901.] 12°. **14072. b. 25.(2.)**

BHUVANAMOHANA DĀSA GUPTA. মণি ও মুক্তা । [Maṇi o muktā. Short poems.] pp. ii. 102. কলিকাতা ১৩০৫ [*Calcutta*, 1898.] 12°. **14129. a. 28.(3.)**

BHUVANAMOHANA MUKHOPĀDHYĀYA. অগ্নিকুমারী । [Agnikumārī. A tale describing the nefarious marriage practices formerly prevalent in Hindu society.] pp. 196. কলিকাতা ১৩০০ [*Calcutta*, 1894.] 12°. **14127. d. 42.(1.)**

BIBLE. ধর্ম্মপুস্তক *etc.* [Dharm... Bible translated by W. Car... pore Missionaries.] 5 vols. [*Serampore*, 1801-09.] 8°. **1410. i. 1-5.**

The books of the Old Testament are in 4 volumes, viz.:— 1. Pentateuch, 1801; 2. Joshua—Esther, 1809; 3. Job—Song of Solomon, 1804; 4. Isaiah—Malachi, 1805. According to the Serampore Memoirs the correct dates of publication are: 1. 1802; 2. 1809; 3. 1803; 4. 1807. The Psalter appears to have been issued separately in 1803.

The Holy Bible, translated from the original tongues into the Bengalee language by [W. Carey and] the Serampore Missionaries. ধর্ম্মপুস্তক *etc.* [A revised edition of the preceding.] *Serampore*, 1832. 8°. **3070. d. 24.**

The text, in double columns, is divided into 2 parts: 1. Genesis—Esther, pp. 504; 2. Job—Malachi and New Testament, pp. 623. The New Testament has a separate title-page, with the date 1832 in Bengali, and 1833 in English figures.

The Holy Bible ... Translated out of the original tongues by [Dr. William Yates and] the Calcutta Baptist Missionaries with native assistants. (ধর্ম্মপুস্তক ।) pp. 1144. *Calcutta*, 1845. 8°. **3070. dd. 1.**

With references.

The Holy Bible ... Translated ... by [W. Yates and] the Calcutta Baptist Missionaries. [Revised by J. Wenger.] pp. 1139. *Calcutta*, 1861. 8°. **3068. e. 13.**

A reprint in smaller size appeared in 1867, edited with slight alterations by C. B. Lewis.

[Another edition.] 2 pts. *Calcutta*, 1877. 8°. **3068. f. 25.**

Eighth edition. pp. 12, 800, 267. *Calcutta*, 1892. 8°. **14123. b. 17.**

The Holy Bible, in Bengali, with References. ধর্ম্মপুস্তক । ... Translated ... by the Calcutta Baptist Missionaries, with Bengali assistants. Revised edition [by G. H. Rouse]. pp. 815, 257. *Calcutta*, 1897. 8°. **14123. bbb. 1.**

Revised 9th edition. pp. 815, 257. *Calcutta*, 1897. 8°. **14123. b. 20.**

[Another edition.] pp. viii. 843, 266. *Calcutta*, 1902. 8°. **14123. b. 21.**

OLD TESTAMENT.

The Old Testament in the Bengáli language. Translated from the original Hebrew by [Dr. W.

ta Baptist Missionaries, (ধর্ম্মপুস্তকের আদিভাগ।) pp. 8°. **1108. k. 7.**

ENTATEUCH.

র সমস্ত বাক্য। ... মোশার ব্যবস্থা যা হইতে। [The Pentateuch, Carey.] শ্রীরামপুর ১৮০১ [Se- 8°. **1108. e. 11.**

on. *Another copy of vol.* 1 *of the Bible* Carey.

GENESIS.

আদিপুস্তক এবং যাত্রাপুস্তকের প্রথম ভাগ। Ge... part of Exodus [ch. i.-xx.] in Bengáli. Translated from the Hebrew by [W. Yates and] the Calcutta Baptist Missionaries. pp. 191. *Calcutta,* 1847. 12°. **3070. b. 35.**

মুসালিখিত আদিপুস্তক ... Genesis and part of Exodus [ch. i.-xx.] in Bengálí, *etc.* [Another edition.] pp. 212. *Calcutta,* 1858. 12°. **3070. aa. 13.**

সটীক আদিপুস্তক। Genesis, annotated in Bengali, by I. Allen and G. H. Rouse. pp. 94. *Calcutta,* 1895. 8°. **14123. bb. 1.**

Genesis i.—ix. Bengali. জগতের আদিরত্তান্ত। [With an appendix, containing select texts from the Bible.] pp. 32. *Calcutta,* 1908. 12°. **14123. a. 40.(4.)**

EXODUS.

মুসালিখিত আদিপুস্তক এবং যাত্রাপুস্তকের প্রথম ভাগ। Genesis and part of Exodus [ch. i.-xx.]. Translated ... by [W. Yates and] the Calcutta Baptist Missionaries. *See* above: *Genesis.* 1847. 12°. **3070. b. 35.**

[Another edition.] 1858. 12°. **3070. aa. 13.**

PSALMS.

The Psalms of David, translated ... by the Serampore Missionaries. দাউদের গীত বাঙ্গলা ভাষাতে তর্জ্জমা করা গেল। [Dāuder gīta.] pp. 202. *Serampore,* 1832. 12°. **1108. b. 17.**

ইব্রীয় ভাষাহইতে ভাষান্তরীকৃত দায়ুদের গীত। এবং স্থলেমান্ লিখিত হিতোপদেশ। The Psalms of David and the Proverbs of Solomon ... Translated from the original Hebrew by the Calcutta Baptist Missionaries. 3rd edition. pp. 184, 56. *Calcutta,* 1848. 12°. **3070. b. 28.**

5th edition. pp. 184. *Calcutta,* 1848. 12°. **3089. b. 22.**

The Book of Psalms, newly translated in Bengali and English [by W. K. and K. M. B., i.e. William Kay and Krishṇamohana Vandyopādhyāya]. (গীতসংহিতা।) [Gītasaṃhitā.] pp. xi. 681. *Calcutta,* 1858. 8°. **3089. cc.**

Printed for private circulation.

ইব্রানি জবানহইতে তর্জমা করা দায়ুদের জবুরের কেতাব। The Psalms of David in Musalmán Bengali. [Translated by S. J. Hill.] pp. 336. *Calcutta,* 1858. 8°. **3089. d. 33.**

Bari's Psalms of David. (Swarga dampatya-bilas, or Bari's Song of Solomon.) A Bengali metrical version. [Adapted to various Indian metres, together with some original Bengali hymns, and a short introduction to Bengali music.] 3 pts. *Calcutta,* 1875. 12°. **3070. bb. 52.**

Psalms of David. [In Muhammadan Bengali.] দায়ুদের জবুরের কেতাব। pp. 263. কলিকাতা ১৮৮০ [*Calcutta,* 1880.] 8°. **3070. h. 37.**

গীতসংহিতা। [Gītasaṃhitā.] The Psalms in Bengali. [Translated by J. W. Thomas.] pp. 208. *Calcutta,* 1881. 16°. **3070. aaa. 30.**

PROVERBS.

ইব্রীয় ভাষাহইতে ভাষান্তরীকৃত স্থলেমান লিখিত হিতোপদেশ। The Proverbs of Solomon ... Translated from the original Hebrew by the Calcutta Baptist Missionaries. pp. 51. *Calcutta,* 1842. 12°. **3070. b. 13.**

Proverbs of Solomon ... Translated ... by W. Morton. (হিতোপদেশ সংগ্রহ।) [Hitopadeṣa-saṅgraha.] pp. 76. [*Calcutta,*] 1843. 8°. **3070. aa. 8.**

ইব্রীয় ভাষাহইতে ... স্থলেমান্ লিখিত হিতোপদেশ। The Psalms of David and the Proverbs of Solomon ... Translated ... by the Calcutta Baptist Missionaries. *See* above: *Psalms.* 1848. 8°. **3070. b. 28**

[Another edition.] pp. 54. *Calcutta,* 1849. 12°. **3070. b. 25.**

BIBLE.

SONG OF SOLOMON.

Swarga dampatya bilas, or Bari's Song of Solomon. A Bengali metrical version. *See* above: *Psalms.* Bari's Psalms of David, *etc.* 1875. 12°. **3070. bb. 52.**

ISAIAH.

ইব্রীয় ও কল্দীয় ভাষাহইতে ভাষান্তরীকৃত যিশয়িয় ও দানিয়েল ভবিষ্যদ্বক্তৃ লিখিত পুস্তক। The Books of the Prophets Isaiah and Daniel . . . Translated . . . by the Calcutta Baptist Missionaries. pp. 176. *Calcutta,* 1842. 12°. **3070. a. 14.**

DANIEL.

ইব্রীয় . . . ভাষাহইতে . . . দানিয়েল ভবিষ্যদ্বক্তৃ লিখিত পুস্তক। The Books of the Prophets Isaiah and Daniel . . . Translated . . . by the Calcutta Baptist Missionaries. *See* above: *Isaiah.* 1842. 12°. **3070. a. 14.**

NEW TESTAMENT.

ধর্ম্ম পুস্তক তাহা ঈশ্বরের সমস্ত বাক্য। . . . মঙ্গল সমাচার তর্জ্জমা হইল গ্রীক ভাষা হইতে। [Maṅgala-samāchāra. The New Testament, translated by W. Carey.] শ্রীরামপুর ১৮০১ [*Serampore,* 1801.] 8°. **218. k. 13.**

Without pagination. Another copy of vol. 5. of the Bible translated by W. Carey, presented to King George III. by the Managers of the Baptist Missionary Society, with a letter written by Robert Bowyer, dated 19th Sept., 1803.

ধর্ম্ম পুস্তক . . . মঙ্গল সমাচার *etc.* [Another copy.] **1108. e. 12.**

জগত্তারক প্রভু যিশু খ্রীষ্টের মঙ্গল সমাচার বাঙ্গালা ভাষাতে রচিত *etc.* [Maṅgala-samāchāra. The New Testament, translated by J. F. Ellerton.] pp. 993. কলিকাতা ১৮১৯ [*Calcutta,* 1819.] 8°. **842. c. 11.**

The New Testament . . . in the Bengallee language. Translated from the Greek, by [W. Yates and] the Calcutta Baptist Missionaries. pp. iv. 548. *Calcutta,* 1833. 8°. **3068. aaa. 69.**

Dharmapustaker Antabbág. The New Testament, *etc.* [Translated by W. Yates.] Printed for the British and Foreign Bible Society. pp. 231, 302. *London,* 1839. 8°. **3068. cc. 17.**

In Roman characters. Vol. 1 (Gospels) was printed by Richard Watts, vol. 2 (Acts—Revelation) by W. McDowall. Bound in one volume.

BIBLE.

NEW TESTAMENT (*continued*).

The New Testament . . . Translated . . . by the Calcutta Baptist Missionaries, *etc.* Fourth edition. pp. 467. *Calcutta,* 1839. 8°. **1108. e. 14.**

Fifth edition. pp. 617. *Calcutta,* 1841. 12°. **3070. c. 18.**

Eighth edition. [Revised by J. Wenger.] pp. 488. *Calcutta,* 1846. **3070. bb. 27.**

[Another edition.] pp. 465. *Calcutta,* 1854. 16°. **3070. a. 44.**

[Another edition.] pp. 768. *Calcutta,* 1859. 8°. **3070. cc. 24.**

[Another edition.] pp. 452. *Calcutta,* 1880. 8°. **3068. aa. 58.**

The New Testament . . . With references, *etc.* [J. Wenger's revision of W. Yates' translation.] pp. 604. *Calcutta,* 1880. 12°. **3070. aaa. 27.**

[Another edition.] pp. 452. *Calcutta,* 1884. 12°. **3068. aa. 62.**

ত্রাণকর্ত্তা প্রভু যীশু খ্রীষ্টের নূতন ধর্ম্মনিয়ম সম্বন্ধীয় গ্রন্থসমূহ। The New Testament in Bengali, with references. Translated . . . by the Calcutta Baptist Missionaries with native assistants. pp. 712. *Calcutta,* 1895. 8°. **14123. a. 32.**

—— The New Testament . . . Translated from the Greek by Christian Bomwetsch. [With an appendix.] (প্রভু ঈশুখ্রীষ্টের নূতন নিয়ম।) pp. v. viii. 32, 765, 25. *Calcutta,* 1905. 8°. **14123. b. 23.**

MATTHEW.

The Gospels according to St. Matthew and St. John, in English and Bengalee. [Translated by J. F. Ellerton.] মঙ্গল সমাচার মাত্তিউ রচিত আর মঙ্গল সমাচার য়োহন রচিত। *Calcutta,* 1819. 8°. **842. e. 8.**

Without pagination; Bengali and English on opposite pages. Besides the general title each book has its own title. Matthew was printed by Philip Pereira at the Hindoostanee Press; John at the Mission Press.

মথিলিখিত সুসমাচার। Gospel of Matthew. [Translated by W. Yates and revised by J. Wenger.] pp. 96. [*Calcutta,* 1854.] 8°. **3070. bb. 1.**

BIBLE.

MATTHEW (*continued*).

সুসমাচার। সাধু ম্যাথু। [The Gospel according to St. Matthew, translated from the English, with notes, by the Ārya Sāhitya Samiti.] pp. 236. কলিকাতা ১৩০১ [*Calcutta*, 1895.] 8°. **14123. b. 19.**

Matthew. Musalmani Bengali. মথি লিখিত ইঞ্জীল। pp. 107. *Calcutta*, 1897. 12°. **14123. a. 36.**

মথি লিখিত ইঞ্জীল। Matthew. Mussulmani Bengali. 6th edition. pp. 87. *Calcutta*, 1899. 12°. **14123. a. 37.**

Matthew in Musalmani Bengali. (মথির ইঞ্জীল।) 7th edition. pp. 87. *Calcutta*, 1904. 12°. **14123. a. 42.**

খ্রীষ্ট-পুরাণ মথি। [Khrīshṭa-purāṇa. A metrical version of the Gospel of St. Matthew by Madhusūdana Sarkār.] pp. ii. ii. v. 203. কলিকাতা ১৩১৪ [*Calcutta*, 1907.] 12°. **14123. a. 47.**

MARK.

মার্কলিখিত সুসমাচার। Gospel of Mark. [Translated by W. Yates and revised by J. Wenger.] pp. 64. [*Calcutta*, 1854.] 8°. **3070. bb. 4.**

মার্কের লিখিত ইঞ্জীল. Mark. Musalmani Bengali. 2nd edition. pp. 67. *Calcutta*, 1900. 8°. **14123. a. 38.**

Mark. ·Bengali. মার্কলিখিত সুসমাচার। pp. 57. *Calcutta*, 1908. 12°. **14123. a. 40.(3.)**

LUKE.

লুকলিখিত সুসমাচার। Gospel of Luke. [Translated by W. Yates and revised by J. Wenger.] pp. 104. [*Calcutta*, 1854.] 8°. **3070. bb. 6.**

লূকের লেখা ইঞ্জীল। [Translated into Muhammadan Bengali by J. Paterson.] pp. 104. কলিকাতা ১৮৭৯ [*Calcutta*, 1879.] 8°. **3068. dd. 18.**

লূকের লেখা ইঞ্জীল। ইয়ানে খোদাবন্দ ইসা মসীহের বয়ান। [A translation in Muhammadan Bengali, differing from the preceding version.] pp. 140. কলিকাতা [*Calcutta*, 1879.] 8°. **3068. dd. 19.**

Luke in Musalmani Bengali. (লুকের ইঞ্জীল।) 10th edition. pp. 90. *Calcutta*, 1904. 12°. **14123. a. 43.**

BIBLE.

JOHN, *Gospel of*.

The Gospel of St. John, in Bengalee and English. [Translated by J. F. Ellerton.] মঙ্গল সমাচার য়োহন রচিত *etc. Calcutta*, 1819. 8°. **3068. bb. 3.**

Without pagination; Bengali and English on opposite pages.

[Another copy.] *See* above: *Matthew*. The Gospels according to St. Matthew and St. John, *etc*. 1819. 8°. **842. e. 8.**

যোহন লিখিত সুসমাচার। Gospel of John. [Translated by W. Yates and revised by J. Wenger.] pp. 80. [*Calcutta*, 1854.] 8°. **3070. bb. 7.**

প্রভু যীশু খ্রীষ্টের জীবনচরিত্রের বিষয়ে যোহন লিখিত সুসমাচার এবং তিন পত্র। [The Gospel and Epistles of St. John.] pp. 120. *Calcutta*, 1881. 16°. **3070. aaa. 28.**

John. M[usalmani] Bengali. যোহন্নার ইঞ্জীল। pp. 71. *Calcutta*, 1898. 12°. **14123. a. 35.**

যোহন্নার ইঞ্জীল। John. Musalmani Bengali. 2nd edition. pp. 71. *Calcutta*, 1899. 12°. **14123. a. 39.**

যোহন লিখিত সুসমাচারের টীকা। . . . Commentary on John's Gospel for Bengali readers, based on that of the Rev. Marcus Dods, D.D., by the Rev. W. McCulloch. [With the Bengali translation of the text.] pp. 279. *Calcutta*, 1903. 8°. **14123. bb. 2.**

ACTS

প্রভু যীশু খ্রীষ্টের প্রেরিতদের ক্রিয়ার বিবরণ। [Translated by W. Yates and revised by J. Wenger.] pp. 112. *Calcutta*, [1880.] 12°. **3070. aaa. 29.**

প্রেরিতদিগের কার্য্য-বিবরণ। Acts of the Apostles. New version. pp. 92. *Calcutta*, 1901. 8°. **14123. a. 40.**

ROMANS.

রোমীয়দের প্রতি প্রেরিত পৌলের পত্র। The Epistle of Paul the Apostle to the Romans. New version. pp. 37. *Calcutta*, 1902. 12°. **14123. a. 40.**

রোমীয়দের প্রতি পত্রের টীকা। [Romīyader prati patrer ṭīkā.] . . . Commentary on the Epistle to the Romans for Bengali readers, by the Rev. W. McCulloch. [With the Bengali translation of the text.] pp. xix. 273. *Calcutta*, 1907. 8°. **14123. bb. 3.**

BIBLE.

HEBREWS.

ইব্রিয়দিগের প্রতি ধর্ম্মপ্রণিধি পৌলের পত্র। বঙ্গভাষায় অনুবাদিত। [Translated by Svāmī Dharmānanda Mahābhāratī.] pp. 24. কলিকাতা [Calcutta,] 1903. 8°. **14123. b. 22.**

JOHN, *Epistles of.*

প্রভু যীশু খ্রীষ্টের জীবনচরিত্রের বিষয়ে যোহন লিখিত ... তিন পত্র। [The Epistles of St. John.] *See* above: *John, Gospel of.* প্রভু যীশু খ্রীষ্টের জীবন *etc.* [The Gospel and Epistles of St. John.] 1881. 16°. **3070. aaa. 28.**

BIDHUBHUSHAN GOSWAMI. *See* VIDHŪBHŪSHAṆA GOSVĀMĪ.

BIDHUBHUSHAN MUKERJEE. *See* VIDHUBHŪSHAṆA MUKHOPĀDHYĀYA.

BINOD LAL SEN. *See* VINODALĀLA SENA.

BISVESVAR CHAKRAVARTI. *See* VIṢVEṢVARA CHAKRAVARTĪ.

BISWAS (A. T. C.). স্বর্গীয় সুপ্রসিদ্ধ মহাত্মা ... বমওয়েচ্ সাহেবের সংক্ষিপ্ত জীবন-চরিত। [Mahātmā Bomwetsch. A short life of the Rev. C. Bomwetsch.] pp. i. 52, iii. ১৯০৬ [*Calcutta*, 1906.] 8°. **14127. bb. 31.**

BLUMHARDT (JAMES FULLER). *See* BAṄKIMCHANDRA CHAṬṬOPĀDHYĀYA. Krishna Kanta's Will ... Translated by M. S. Knight; with introduction, glossary, and notes by J. F. Blumhardt. 1895. 8°. **14127. e. 46.**

—— Catalogue of the ... Bengali ... Manuscripts in the Library of the British Museum. By J. F. Blumhardt. 1905. 4°. *See* ACADEMIES, *etc.*—London.—*British Museum.* **Cat. Desk A.**

—— Catalogue of the Library of the India Office. Vol. II.—Part IV. Bengali ... Books. By J. F. Blumhardt. 1905. 8°. *See* ENGLAND.—*India Office.—Library.* **Cat. Desk A.**

BOGRA.—*Kanyāpaṇa nivāriṇī Sabhā.* কন্যাপণ নিবারিণী সভার বিবরণ। [An account of the proceedings of the Kanyāpaṇa-nivāriṇī Sabhā, or Society for the prevention of the sale of daughters in marriage.] pp. 13. বগুড়া ১২৯৫ [*Bogra*, 1889.] 8°. **14125. ee. 25.(4.)**

BOMWETSCH (CHRISTIAN). *See* BIBLE.—*New Testament.* The New Testament ... Translated from the Greek by C. Bomwetsch. [With an appendix.] 1905. 8°. **14123. b. 23.**

—— [*Life.*] *See* BISWAS (A. T. C.). স্বর্গীয় ... মহাত্মা ... বমওয়েচ্ সাহেবের সংক্ষিপ্ত জীবন-চরিত। [Mahātmā Bomwetsch.] [1906.] 8°. **14127. bb. 31.**

BONERJEA (UPENDRO KRISHNA). *See* UPENDRAKṚISHṆA VANDYOPĀDHYĀYA.

BOSE (C. L.). *See* CHUNILĀLA VASU.

BOSE (CHUNDER NATH). *See* CHANDRANĀTHA VASU.

BOSE, *Manager of the Bengal Circus.* প্রোফেসর বোসের অপূর্ব্ব ভ্রমণ-বৃত্তান্ত। [Apūrva bhramaṇavṛittānta. An account of travels in India.] pp. ii. 196. কলিকাতা ১৩০৯ [*Calcutta*, 1902.] 12°. **14127. aa. 25.**

BRAHMAN. The Zenana opened, or a Brahmin advocating female emancipation. (ভারতবর্ষীয় স্ত্রীগণের বিদ্যা শিক্ষা।) [Bhāratavarshīya strīgaṇer vidyāṣikshā.] pp. 58. *Calcutta*, 1851. 12°. **14123. a. 26.**

BRAHMĀNANDA BHĀRATĪ. সন্ধ্যা-যোগরহস্য। [Sandhyā-yogarahasya. A treatise on the practice of *yoga*. Edited with an introduction by Vimalācharaṇa Chaṭṭopādhyāya.] pp. ii. 27, 96. কলিকাতা ১৩০৭ [*Calcutta*, 1901.] 12°. **14123. e. 27.(1.)**

BRAHMĀNANDA TATTVADARṢĪ. *See* ṢAṢIBHŪSHAṆA MITRA MUSTAUPHĪ.

BRĀHMA SAMĀJ. *See* VIJAYAKṚISHṆA GOSVĀMĪ. ব্রাহ্মসমাজের বর্ত্তমান অবস্থা [Brāhma Samājer vartamāna avasthā. An account of the various changes which have taken place in the teachings of the Brāhma Samāj.] [1885] 12°. **14123. c. 8.(6.)**

—— ब्राह्मधर्म्म-प्रतिपादक-श्लोकसंग्रह। [Brāhmadharma-pratipādaka-ṣlokasaṅgraha.] (ব্রাহ্মধর্ম্ম প্রতিপাদক শ্লোকসংগ্রহ। A compilation of Theistic texts [translated into Bengali] from the Hindu, Jewish, Christian, Mahomedan and Parsee Scriptures.) [Published for the Brāhma Samāj]. pp. 66. কলিকাতা ১৭৯১ [*Calcutta*, 1869.] 12°. **14123. c. 24.**

The selections from the Hindu scriptures are in the Sanskrit original, the rest in English.

—— [Fifth edition.] pp. 224. *Calcutta*, 1904. 12°. **14072. b. 33.**

BRĀHMA SAMĀJ (*continued*). Order of Service in the Brahma Samāj, for the congregation and family. Translated into English [from the Bengali Brahmopāsanā-pranāḷi.] pp. 8. *Allahabad*, [1890.] 8°. **14123. d. 15.(3.)**

—— The Report of the East Bengal Brahmo Somaj for 1883-84 (1884-85). পূর্ব্ববাঙ্গলা ব্রাহ্মসমাজের ১২৯০ (৯১) সনের বার্ষিক কার্য্যবিবরণ। ঢাকা ১২৯১-৯২ [*Dacca*, 1884-85.] 8°. **14123. d. 16.**

BRAHMA-SAṂHITĀ. ব্রহ্মসংহিতা। [Brahma-saṃhitā. A Sanskrit work on *Yoga*, accompanied by a Bengali translation.] *See* PRASANNAKUMĀRA BHAṬṬĀCHĀRYA. যোগাম্বুধি। [Yogāmbudhi.] [1896.] 32°. **14048. a. 19.**

The text is said to be in 100 adhyāyas, of which this work contains only 5.

BṚIHASPATI. বৃহস্পতিসংহিতা। [Bṛihaspati-saṃhitā. A code of *dharma*, in 80 Sanskrit stanzas. With Bengali translation.] *See* PAÑCHĀNANA TARKARATNA BHAṬṬĀCHĀRYA. ঊনবিংশতি সংহিতা। [Ūnaviṃṣati saṃhitā.] pp. 335-339. [1903.] 8°. **14039. c. 20.**

BRITISH INDIAN ASSOCIATION. [A circular to the members of the Association occasioned by a letter of Gurucharaṇa Dāsa on the suppression of dacoity. Signed by the Secretary, Raja Īṣvarachandra Siṃha.] *Eng. and Beng.* [*Calcutta*,] 1860. 4°. **14003. e. 2.(7.)**

—— ভারতবর্ষীয় সভা। ষাণ্মাসিক বিবরণ। [The proceedings of the half-yearly meeting of the British Indian Association, held on the 19th July, 1865, under the presidentship of Ramānātha Ṭhākura.] pp. 27. কলিকাতা ১৮৬৫ [*Calcutta*, 1865.] 8°. **14125. ee. 23.(1.)**

BROJENDRA LALL BHATTACHARJEE. *See* VRAJENDRALĀLA BHAṬṬĀCHĀRYA.

BROWN (CHARLES PHILIP). Bákyábalí, or Idiomatical exercises, English and Bengali; with dialogues . . . specimens of legal documents, letters, *etc.* Revised and improved by Gopee Kissen Mitter. বাক্যাবলী। pp. 267. *Calcutta*, 1877. 12°. **14131. f. 14.**

BUDDHA. [*Life.*] *See* KĀLINDĪ, *Rāṇī.* বৌদ্ধারঞ্জিকা। [Bauddhā-rañjikā.] [1890.] 12°. **14123. k. 2.**

BUDDHA (*continued*). [*Life.*] *See* KṚISHṆAKUMĀRA MITRA. বুদ্ধদেবচরিত *etc.* [Buddhadeva-charita.] [1900.] 12°. **14127. aa. 12.**

—— *See* KṚISHṆAPADA VIDYĀRATNA. একশৃঙ্গ নাটক। [Ekaṣṛiṅga nāṭaka.] A drama on the previous life of Buddha. 1897. 12°. **14131. a. 40.(5.)**

—— [*Life.*] *See* NAVĪNACHANDRA SENA. অমিতাভ। [Amitābha.] [1895.] 12°. **14123. k. 3.**

—— [*Life.*] *See* PRAMATHANĀTHA RĀYA CHAUDHURĪ. গৌরাঙ্গ। [Gaurāṅga.] [1903.] 8°. **14123. k. 8.**

—— [*Life and teachings.*] *See* RĀMADĀSA SENA. Buddhadeva. [1891.] 12°. **14127. a. 41.**

BULLORAM PAUL. *See* BALARĀMA PĀLA.

BUNYAN (JOHN). যাত্রিকের গতি [Yātriker gati.] . . . The Pilgrim's Progress from this world to that which is to come. [Translated into Bengali.] pp. x. 452. *Calcutta*, 1854. 8°. **14123. a. 41.**

BURHĀN al-DĪN AḤMAD, *Maulavī.* সহজ পারসীশিক্ষা। [Sahaj Pārsī-ṣikshā. The elements of Persian grammar.] pp. 27. কলিকাতা ১৩০৭ [*Calcutta*, 1901.] 8°. **14131. e. 32.**

BYRON (GEORGE GORDON NOEL), *Baron Byron.* *See* HEMACHANDRA MITRA, *B.L.* নরসিংহ। [Narasiṃha. A metrical adaptation of Byron's 'Manfred.'] [1888.] 12°. **14129. bb. 13.(1.)**

CALCUTTA.—*Ārya Sāhitya Samiti.* *See* BIBLE.—*Matthew.* সুসমাচার। মাথু ম্যাথ্যু। [The Gospel according to St. Matthew, translated, with notes, by the Ārya Sāhitya Samiti of Calcutta.] [1895.] 8°. **14123. b. 18.**

—— *Bauddha Dharmāṅkura Sabhā.* বৌদ্ধ ধর্ম্মাঙ্কুর সভার কার্য্যবিবরণী। [Proceedings of the tenth annual meeting of the Bauddha Dharmāṅkura Sabhā.] pp. ii. 40. [*Calcutta*, 1902.] 12°. **14123. k. 4.(3.)**

—— *Board of Examiners.* Specimens of Examination Papers in Oriental languages with manuscripts in facsimile, set by the Board of Examiners, Fort William, 1905-06, *etc.* *Calcutta*, 1906, *etc.* 8°. **14117. bb. 13.**

In progress. The specimens of manuscripts are lithographed.

CALCUTTA (*continued*). *Sāvitrī Library.* সাবিত্রী। [Sāvitrī. A collection of papers on various social topics which were read at the Calcutta Sāvitrī Library, during a course of six years.] pp. iii. 260. কলিকাতা ১২৯৩ [*Calcutta*, 1886.] 8°. **14125. ee. 21.**

—— *University.* Subjects of Examination in the Bengali language appointed by the Syndicate of the Calcutta University for the Entrance Examination of 1900. Edited by Sris Chandra Chaudhuri. pp. ii. 139. *Calcutta*, 1898. 8°. **14131. d. 38.**

CAREY (William), *D.D.* *See* Bible. ধর্ম্মপুস্তক *etc.* [Dharmapustaka. The Holy Bible translated by W. Carey.] [1801-09.] 8°. **1410. i. 1-5.**

—— The Holy Bible, translated . . . by [W. Carey and] the Serampore Missionaries. 1832. 8°. **3070. d. 24.**

—— A Dictionary of the Bengalee Language. Vol. I. Bengalee and English. Abridged from Dr. Carey's quarto Dictionary. Revised and edited by Brojendra Nath Ghosal. Eleventh edition. pp. 637. *Calcutta*, 1890. 8°. **12907. cc. 31.**

—— A Dictionary of the Bengali Language. Vol. I. Bengali and English . . . Revised and edited by Rasamay Mitra . . . and Brojendra Nath Ghosal. Twelfth edition. pp. 648. *Calcutta*, 1902. 8°. **14133. b. 19.**

CATALOGUES. List of Bengali and Sanskrit books, pamphlets, *etc.*, published at native presses in Calcutta, in 1865. pp. 16. [*Calcutta*, 1865 ?] 8°. **14131. d. 18.**

CATECHISMS. প্রশ্নোত্তরমালা অর্থাৎ কাটিকিজম্ *etc.* [Praṣnottaramālā. A Catechism for the use of Roman Catholics in the diocese of Dacca.] pp. 42. *Dacca*, 1907. 12°. **14123. a. 46.**

CHAITANYA. [*Life.*] *See* Jagadīṣvara Gupta. চৈতন্যলীলামৃত। [Chaitanya-lilāmṛita.] [1890.] 8°. **14127. b. 44.**

—— [*Life.*] *See* Jayānanda. শ্রীচৈতন্যমঙ্গল। [Chaitanya-maṅgala.] [1900, *etc.*] 8°. **14133. ff. 2.**

CHAITANYA (*continued*). [*Life.*] *See* Kavikarṇapūra. শ্রীচৈতন্যচরিতামৃত মহাকাব্যং। [Chaitanya-charitāmṛita.] [1885-92.] 8°. **14058. b. 28.**

—— [*Life.*] *See* Lochanadāsa Ṭhākura. শ্রী-চৈতন্যমঙ্গল। [Chaitanya-maṅgala.] [1902.] 8°. **14123. i. 13.**

—— [*Life.*] *See* Navīnachandra Mukhopādhyāya. অপূর্ব্ব নদের চাঁদ *etc.* [Apūrva Nader Chāṇd.] [1887.] 12°. **14127. a. 33.(1.)**

—— [*Life and doctrines.*] *See* Prasannakumāra Vidyāratna. শ্রীগৌরাঙ্গ-তত্ত্ব সহ শ্রীগৌরাঙ্গ-চরিত। [Gaurāṅgatattva, and Gaurāṅgacharita.] [1899.] 8°. **14127. bb. 13.**

—— [*Life.*] *See* Purushottama Miṣra, called Premadāsa. শ্রীচৈতন্যচন্দ্রোদয় নাটক। [Chaitanya-chandrodaya nāṭaka.] [1886.] 8°. **14123. i. 9.**

—— *See* Rāmaprasanna Ghosha. শ্রীশ্রীগৌর-চন্দ্রোদয়। [Gaura-chandrodaya. An anthological work on Chaitanya and his religious teachings.] [1901.] 8°. **14123. ff. 5.**

—— [*Life.*] *See* Ṣiṣirakumāra Ghosha. শ্রীঅমিয়-নিমাই চরিত। [Amiya-Nimāi-charita.] [1904, *etc.*] 12°. **14127. aa. 31.**

—— *See* Stursberg (O.). Das Caitanyacaritāmṛta des Kṛṣṇadāsa Kavirāja. Eine altbengalische Lebensgeschichte Caitanyas. Inaugural-Dissertation . . . von Otto Stursberg. [1907.] 8°. **14123. ff. 17.**

—— [*Life.*] *See* Ṣyāmalāla Gosvāmī. শ্রীশ্রীগৌর-সুন্দর *etc.* [Gaura-sundara.] [1907.] 8°. **14127. bb. 26.**

—— [*Life.*] *See* Upendrakumāra Ghosha. শ্রী-চৈতন্য-চরিত। [Chaitanya-charita.] [1895.] 12°. **14127. aa. 3.(4.)**

—— [*Life.*] *See* Vṛindāvana Dāsa. শ্রীশ্রীচৈতন্য ভাগবত। [Chaitanya-bhāgavata.] [1886.] 8°. **14123. i. 10.**

—— শ্রীশ্রীচৈতন্যচরিত। [Chaitanya-charita. An anonymous life of Chaitanya. Fourth edition.] pp. 108. কলিকাতা ১৩১৪ [*Calcutta*, 1907.] 12°. **14127. aa. 39.**

CHAMPAKA-KALIKĀ. চম্পক-কলিকা। [Champaka-kalikā. An anonymous poem on the tenets of sectarian Vaishṇavas. Edited with critical notes by Rāmendrasundara Trivedī.] ১৩০৭ [1900.] *See* ACADEMIES, *etc.*—Calcutta.—*Bengal Academy of Literature.* সাহিত্য-পরিষৎ-পত্রিকা। [Sāhitya-parishat-patrikā.] Vol. vii., no. 1. [1894, *etc.*] 8°. **14133. f. 18.**

CHAṆḌĪCHARAṆA BASĀK. বঙ্গের বৈঠকী-রহস্য। [Vaṅger baiṭhakī-rahasya. Humorous sketches of modern Bengali life.] pp. 130. কলিকাতা ১৩০২ [*Calcutta,* 1895.] 8°. **14127. ee. 4.(2.)**

CHAṆḌĪCHARAṆA GHOSHA. Bishakosa Manchitra. বিশ্বকোষ মানচিত্র। [A Pauranic description of the creation and constitution of the world.] pp. 28. With a map. কলিকাতা [*Calcutta,* 1895.] 8°. **14123. f. 50. and 14003. e. 2.(22.)**

—— স্ত্রীপ্রকৃতি [Strīprakṛiti. A poem on the various stages of a Hindu woman's existence. With coloured representations.] *Calcutta,* [1887.] *s.sh.* Fol. **14003. e. 2.(1.)**

CHAṆḌĪCHARAṆA SENA. অযোধ্যার বেগম। [Ayodhyār Begam. An historical novel on the cruelties and indignities to which the Begams of Oudh were subjected, during the time of Sirāj al-Daulah and Warren Hastings.] 2 pts. কলিকাতা ১৮৮৬ [*Calcutta,* 1886.] 8°. **14127. f. 36.(1.)**

—— দেওয়ান গঙ্গাগোবিন্দ সিংহ। [Dīwān Gaṅgāgovinda Siṃha. An historical novel of the time of Warren Hastings.] pp. 188, xiv. কলিকাতা ১২৯৩ [*Calcutta,* 1886.] 8°. **14127. e. 22.(2.)**

—— এই কি রামের অযোধ্যা। [Ei ki Rāmer Ayodhyā. An historical romance on the condition of Oudh at the beginning of the present century.] pp. 264. কলিকাতা ১৮৯৫ [*Calcutta,* 1895.] **14127. c. 56.(1.)**

—— Liberator of the Indian Press. মুদ্রাযন্ত্রের স্বাধীনতা প্রদাতা লর্ড মেটকাফের সংক্ষিপ্ত জীবনী। [Mudrā-yantrer svādhīnatā-pradātā. An account of the Indian career of Sir Charles Metcalfe.] pp. 236, xxiv. কলিকাতা ১৮৮৭ [*Calcutta,* 1887.] 8°. **14127. b. 36.**

—— মহারাজ নন্দকুমার *etc.* [Mahārāja Nandakumāra. An historical novel showing the political and social condition of Bengal a century ago, and denouncing the execution of Nandakumāra as a judicial murder.] pp. 392, xvi. কলিকাতা ১২৯২ [*Calcutta,* 1885.] 8°. **14127. e. 22.(1.)**

—— Rani of Jhansi. An historical romance. ঝান্সীর রাণী ঐতিহাসিক উপন্যাস। [Jhānsīr rāṇī.] pp. 380, ii. কলিকাতা ১৮৮৮ [*Calcutta,* 1888.] 8°. **14127. e. 26.**

CHAṆḌĪCHARAṆA SMṚITIBHŪSHAṆA. *See* RAGHUNANDANA BHAṬṬĀCHĀRYA, *Son of Harihara.* স্মৃতিশাস্ত্রং। আহ্নিকতত্ত্বম। [Āhnikatattva. Edited by Chaṇḍīcharaṇa.] [1908.] 8°. **14033. bbb. 45.**

—— *See* ŚAṄKARĀNANDA, *Disciple of Ānandātmā.* আত্মপুরাণম্। [Ātmapurāṇa. With a Bengali translation by Chaṇḍīcharaṇa.] [1885.] 8°. **14048. e. 13.**

—— *See* ŚRĪNIVĀSA ĀCHĀRYA, *Astrologer.* শুদ্ধিদীপিকা। [Śuddhidīpikā. Edited with Bengali translation by Chaṇḍīcharaṇa.] [1901.] 8°. **14053. ccc. 33.**

—— *See* ŚŪLAPĀṆI. প্রায়শ্চিত্তবিবেকঃ। [Prāyaśchittaviveka. Edited with Bengali notes by Chaṇḍīcharaṇa.] [1903.] 8°. **14033. aa. 31.**

CHAṆḌĪCHARAṆA VANDYOPĀDHYĀYA. *See* ŚAMBHUCHANDRA VIDYĀRATNA. ভ্রমনিরাস। [Bhramanirāsa. A criticism on Chaṇḍīcharaṇa's life of Īśvarachandra Vidyāsāgara.] [1895.] 8°. **14131. d. 31.**

—— কমলকুমার। [Kamalakumāra. A dramatised story of domestic life.] pp. iv. 226. কলিকাতা ১৩০৪ [*Calcutta,* 1897.] 8°. **14131. b. 25.**

—— বিদ্যাসাগর। [Vidyāsāgara. The life of Pandit Īśvarachandra Vidyāsāgara.] pp. xii. 542, xxi. *Calcutta,* 1895. 8°. **14127. bb. 1.**

CHAṆḌĪDĀSA. চণ্ডীদাস। [The poems of Chaṇḍīdāsa.] *See* AKSHAYACHANDRA SARKĀR. প্রাচীন কাব্য সংগ্রহ। [Prāchīna kāvya-saṅgraha.] Pt. i. [1884-1885.] 8°. **14129. g. 8.**

—— আদি কবি চণ্ডীদাস ঠাকুর প্রণীত। মহাজনপদাবলী অর্থাৎ পদ-সংগ্রহ। [Mahājana-padāvalī. A collection of *padas* by Chaṇḍīdāsa, edited, with an introductory life of the poet, by Kuñjavihārī Vaṇik.] Pt. i. pp. xxii. 111. ১৮৮৮ *Dacca,* [1888.] 12°. **14129. b. 34.**

CHAṆḌĪDĀSA (*continued*). আদি কবি চণ্ডীদাস ঠাকুর প্রণীত। মহাজন পদাবলী। [Mahājana-padāvalī. Another collection of *padas* by Chaṇḍīdāsa, with occasional notes.] pp. 116. *Dacca*, 1890. 12°. **14129. b. 35.(1.)**

—— চণ্ডীদাস। [The poems of Chaṇḍīdāsa, with notes and a biography of the poet.] *See* AKSHAYAKUMĀRA DE. মহাজন পদাবলী। চণ্ডীদাস ও বিদ্যাপতি। [Mahājana-padāvalī.] [1903.] 8°. **14129. e. 26.**

—— [Fourth edition.] [1905.] 8°. **14129. e. 30.**

—— [Fifth edition.] [1907.] 8°. **14129. e. 33.**

—— চণ্ডীদাসের অপ্রকাশিত পদাবলী। [Unpublished poems of Chaṇḍīdāsa.] ১৩০৬ [1898.] *See* ACADEMIES, *etc.*—Calcutta.—*Bengal Academy of Literature.* সাহিত্য-পরিষৎ-পত্রিকা। [Sāhitya-parishat-patrikā.] Vol. v., nos. 2, 3. [1894, *etc.*] 8°. **14133. f. 18.**

CHAṆḌĪPRASĀDA GHOSHA. *See* SHAKSPERE (W.). হ্যাম্‌লেট। [Hamlet. Translated by Chaṇḍīprasāda Ghosha.] 1894. 12°. **14131. a. 36.(1.)**

CHANDRAKĀNTA GUHA MAULIKA. কায়স্থ বংশাবলী। [Kāyastha vaṃṣāvalī. A genealogy of the Kāyasthas of Bengal, with an account of the origin of the caste.] pp. v. 126, xi. কলিকাতা ১২৯৫ [*Calcutta*, 1888.] 4°. **14127. bbb. 1.**

CHANDRAKĀNTA NYĀYĀLAṄKĀRA. *See* SARVAVARMĀ. কলাপ-ব্যাকরণম্। [Kalāpa-vyākaraṇa. Section i., with notes and a Bengali translation by Chandrakānta. Third edition.] [1889.] 8°. **14090. c. 36.**

—— [Fourth edition.] [1895.] 12°. **14090. b. 45.(3.)**

CHANDRAKĀNTA SENA. বামাসুন্দরী বা আদর্শনারী। [Ādarṣa-nārī, or "The model woman." The life of Vāmā Sundarī, a much-esteemed Hindu lady.]. pp. ii. 8, 124. কলিকাতা ১৩০৩ [*Calcutta*, 1896.] 12°. **14127. aa. 6.(5.)**

CHANDRAKĀNTA TARKĀLAṄKĀRA. হিন্দুদর্শন। [Hindudarṣana.] Lectures on Hindu Philosophy, by Mahámahopádhyáya Chandrakánta Tarkálankára. 4 pts. *Calcutta*, 1899-1901. 8°. **14123. ff. 1.**

CHANDRAKĀNTA TARKĀLAṄKĀRA (*continued*). Lectures on Hindu Philosophy, *etc.* Second edition. pp. ii. ix. xii. xiii. 231. কলিকাতা ১৮২৬ [*Calcutta*, 1904.] 8°. **14123. ff. 15.**

CHANDRAKĀNTA VASU. কঃ পন্থাঃ [Kaḥ panthāḥ. The superiority of the spiritualism of Hinduism over the materialism of Western civilization.] pp. 68. ১৮৯৮ *Calcutta*, [1898.] 12°. **14123. e. 24.(1.)**

—— বর্ত্তমান বাঙ্গালা সাহিত্যের প্রকৃতি। [Vartamāna Bāṅgālā sāhityer prakṛiti. The prevailing defects of Bengali literature, with suggestions for its improvement.] pp. 59. কলিকাতা ১৩০৬ [*Calcutta*, 1899.] 12°. **14131. d. 39.(1.)**

CHANDRAKĀNTA VIDYĀRATNA. অনুবাদ শিক্ষা। [Anuvāda-ṣikshā,] or How to translate English and Bengali into Sanskrit. pp. 85. *Chittagong*, 1892. 8°. **14131. g.**

CHANDRAKUMĀRA KAVIBHŪSHAṆA, *Kavirāja.* *See* GOVINDADĀSA, *Kavirāja.* সানুবাদ ভৈষজ্য-রত্নাবলী। [Bhaishajya-ratnāvalī. With a Bengali translation by Chandrakumāra Kavibhūshaṇa.] [1893.] 8°. **14043. e. 31.**

CHANDRAKUMĀRA TARKĀLAṄKĀRA. *See* KṚISHṆĀNANDA VĀGĪṢA BHAṬṬĀCHĀRYA. তন্ত্রসারঃ [Tantrasāra. Accompanied by a translation by Chandrakumāra Tarkālaṅkāra.] [1879-86.] 4°. **14033. bb. 22.**

CHANDRANĀTHA VASU, *Government Translator.* *See* INDIA.—*Legislative Council.* Bengali version [by Chandranātha Vasu] of the Assam Labour and Emigration Act, Act vi. of 1901. [1901.] 8°. **14125. a. 31.**

—— *See* INDIA.—*Legislative Council.* India Act . . . ভারতবর্ষের গবর্ণমেন্ট। [A collection of Acts passed by the Governor-General of India in Council from 1897 to 1902. Translated by Chandranātha Vasu.] [1897-1902.] 8°. **14125. a. 32.**

—— *See* INDIA.—*Legislative Council.* Bengal Act . . . বঙ্গদেশের গবর্ণমেন্ট। [A collection of Acts passed by the Lieutenant-Governor of Bengal from 1897 to 1900. Translated by Chandranātha Vasu.] [1897-1900.] 8°. **14125. a. 33.**

CHANDRANĀTHA VASU, *M.A.* *See* SAÑJĪVACHANDRA CHAṬṬOPĀDHYĀYA. সঞ্জীবনী সুধা। [Sañjivanī-sudhā. With a criticism by Chandranātha Vasu.] 1893. 12°. **14127. c. 52.**

—— *See* SOMADEVA. কথা-সরিৎসাগর। [Kathāsaritsāgara. Translated by Chandranātha Vasu.] [1903, *etc.*] 8°. **14127. ee. 18.**

—— *See* VĀLMĪKI. অদ্ভুত রামায়ণ। [Adbhuta Rāmāyaṇa. A prose version of the Rāmāyaṇa by Chandranātha Vasu.] [1902.] 8°. **14129. ee. 9.**

—— হিন্দুত্ব। [Hindutva. A treatise on the principles of Hinduism.] pp. vi. 405. কলিকাতা ১৮৯২. [*Calcutta*, 1892.] 8°. **14123. e. 19.**

—— সাহিত্য পুস্তক। [Sāhitya-pustaka. A selection of descriptive pieces from the works of various authors, in elegant Bengali prose.] pp. iv. 128. কলিকাতা ১২৯৯ [*Calcutta*, 1893.] 12°. **14131. d. 22.(2.)**

—— শকুন্তলাতত্ত্ব। অর্থাৎ অভিজ্ঞান শকুন্তলের সমালোচনা। [Ṣakuntalā-tattva. A criticism on the Ṣakuntalā, or Sanskrit drama of Kālidāsa. Second edition.] pp. 159. কলিকাতা ১২৯৬ [*Calcutta*, 1890.] 8°. **14131. d. 25.**

—— সাবিত্রীতত্ত্ব। [Sāvitrī-tattva. A critical analysis of the Mahābhārata story of Sāvitrī, specially in connection with its bearings on the duties of domestic life.] pp. 215. কলিকাতা ১৯০০ [*Calcutta*, 1900.] 8°. **14131. d. 39.(2.)**

CHANDRANĀTHA VIDYĀRATNA. কোকশাস্ত্র। [Kokaṣāstra. Sexual physiology, translated from Sanskrit sources.] pp. v. 230. কলিকাতা ১৩১৪ [*Calcutta*, 1907.] 12°. **14125. b. 24.**

CHANDRAṢEKHARA DEVA. *See* RĀMACHANDRA VIDYĀVĀGĪṢA. Second discourse on the spiritual worship of God ... Translated ... [into English] by Chundrushekhur Dev. 1844. 8°. **14123. d. 15.(1.)**

CHANDRAṢEKHARA KARA. অনাথ বালক। [Anātha bālaka. A domestic novel.] pp. 160. *Calcutta*, 1891. 12°. **14127. c. 44.(1.)**

CHANDRAṢEKHARA MUKHOPĀDHYĀYA. রস-গ্রন্থাবলী। [Rasa-granthāvalī. A collection of amusing poems by various authors. Compiled by Chandraṣekhara Mukhopādhyāya.] pp. 133. কলিকাতা ১৩১২ [*Calcutta*, 1905.] 8°. **14129. e. 23.(2.)**

—— সারস্বতকুঞ্জ। [Sārasvata-kuñja. Essays and reviews, reprinted from the Vaṅgadarṣana, a monthly journal.] pp. 127. কলিকাতা ১২৯২ [*Calcutta*, 1885.] 8°. **14133. h. 11.**

—— উদ্‌ভ্রান্ত প্রেম। [Udbhrānta prema. Thoughts on human existence. Fifth edition.] pp. 112. কলিকাতা ১২৯৯ [*Calcutta*, 1892.] 12°. **14125. e. 24.(2.)**

CHANDRAṢEKHARA SENA, called **PARIVRĀJAKA.** Shanne's Tour round the world ... পরিব্রাজক শ্রীচন্দ্রশেখর সেনের ভূ-প্রদক্ষিণ ও পশ্চিমাঞ্চল পরিদর্শন। [Bhū-pradakshiṇa.] pp. viii. 767, 12. *Calcutta*, [1897.] 8°. **14127. aa. 4.**

CHANDRODAYA VIDYĀVINODA BHAṬṬĀCHĀRYA. *See* JĀNAKĪNĀTHA BHAṬṬĀCHĀRYA. প্রবেশিকার ভ্রমসংশোধনীর ভ্রমপ্রদর্শনী। Bhrama-pradarsani. [A reply to the Bhrama-saṃṣodhanī of Chandrodaya Vidyāvinoda.] [1887.] 12°. **14131. d. 23.(2.)**

—— পণ্ডিত শ্রীযুক্ত মহেশচন্দ্র ন্যায়রত্ন ... মহাশয়ের প্রবেশিকার ভ্রমসংশোধনী। [Bhrama-saṃṣodhanī. Mistakes, grammatical and otherwise, in the Sanskrit Entrance Examination Course, which was edited by Maheṣachandra Nyāyaratna.] pp. iii. 44. কলিকাতা [*Calcutta*, 1887.] 12°. **14131. d. 23.(1.)**

—— চিন্তা-লহরী। [Chintālaharī. Short essays on various topics.] pp. viii. 180. কলিকাতা ১৩০৪ [*Calcutta*, 1897.] 12°. **14125. e. 35.**

—— শিলালিপি-সংগ্রহ। [Ṣilālipi-saṅgraha. A collection of inscriptions, chiefly Sanskrit, found in the District of Tippera, with Bengali explanations.] pp. i. 45. আগরতলা ১৩১৪ [*Agartala*, 1904.] 8°. **14058. cc. 6.**

—— সংস্কৃত ব্যাকরণের সোপান। [Sopāna. The rules of Sanskrit grammar explained in Bengali.] pp. 92. *Calcutta*, 1892. 12°. **14131. e. 23.(2.)**

CHARAKA. চরক-সংহিতা। মূল ও বঙ্গানুবাদ। [Charaka-saṃhitā. Sanskrit text, edited with a Bengali translation by Satīṣachandra Ṣarmā Kavibhūshaṇa.] pp. xxii. xxviii. 576, 888. কলিকাতা ১৩১১ [*Calcutta*, 1905.] 8°. **14043. dd. 12.**

CHĀRUCHANDRA ĀCHĀRYA. সভ্যতা-সঙ্কট। [Sabhyatāsaṅkaṭa.] Fatal civilization. [A drama directed against female education and emancipation.] pp. 123. কলিকাতা ১৩০৭ [*Calcutta*, 1900.] 12°. **14131. a. 41.(7.)**

CHĀRUCHANDRA MITRA. নীলাঞ্জনা। [Nilāñjanā. An historical drama.] pp. 112. কলিকাতা ১৩০২ [*Calcutta*, 1896.] 12°. **14131. a. 32.(4.)**

CHĀRUCHANDRA MUKHOPĀDHYĀYA. *See* BAṄKIMCHANDRA CHAṬṬOPĀDHYĀYA. Durgesa Nandini ... Translated ... by Charu Chandra Mookerjee. Second edition. 1903. 12°. **14127. cc. 24.**

—— রোহিণী। [Rohiṇī. A tale of domestic life in Bengal.] pp. 298. কলিকাতা ১৩০৪ [*Calcutta*, 1898.] 8°. **14127. ee. 8.**

CHĀRUCHANDRA VASU. *See* SUTTAPIṬAKA. ধম্মপদ। [Dhammapada. Pali text, with construing, Sanskrit version, and Bengali translation by Chāruchandra Vasu.] [1901-02.] 8°. **14133. ff. 1.**

—— [1904.] 12°. **14098. a. 43.**

CHHAṚĀ. ছড়া। [Chhaṛā. Nursery rhymes of Burdwan, compiled by Kuñjalāla Rāya; also of Hooghly, compiled by Ambikācharaṇa Gupta.] ১৩০৩ [1896.] *See* ACADEMIES, *etc.*—Calcutta.—*Bengal Academy of Literature.* সাহিত্য-পরিষৎ-পত্রিকা। [Sāhitya-parishat-patrikā.] Vol. iii., no. 1. [1894, *etc.*] 8°. **14133. f. 18.**

—— ছেলে ভুলানো ছড়া। [Chhele-bhulāna chhaṛā. Nursery rhymes of Calcutta. Compiled by Ravīndranātha Ṭhākura.] ১৩০১ [1895.] *See* ACADEMIES, *etc.*—Calcutta.—*Bengal Academy of Literature.* সাহিত্য-পরিষৎ-পত্রিকা। [Sāhitya-parishat-patrikā.] Vol. i., no. 3. [1894, *etc.*] 8°. **14133. f. 18.**

—— ছেলে ভুলানো ছড়া। [Chhele-bhulāna chhaṛā. Another collection of nursery rhymes, from Bankura, Midnapore, and the Santal Parganas.] ১৩০২ [1895.] *See* ACADEMIES, *etc.*—Calcutta.—*Bengal Academy of Literature.* সাহিত্য-পরিষৎ-পত্রিকা। [Sāhitya-parishat-patrikā.] Vol. ii., no. 3. [1894, *etc.*] 8°. **14133. f. 18.**

—— চট্টগ্রামী ছেলে-ভুলান ছড়া। [Chhele-bhulāna chhaṛā. Nursery rhymes of Chittagong. Compiled by ʻAbd al-Karīm.] ১৩০৯-১৩১৩ [1902-1907.] *See* ACADEMIES, *etc.*—Calcutta.—*Bengal Academy of Literature.* সাহিত্য-পরিষৎ-পত্রিকা। [Sāhitya-parishat-patrikā.] Vol. ix., no. 2; x., no. 2; xii., no. 4; xiii., no. 1. [1894, *etc.*] 8°. **14133. f. 18.**

CHIRAÑJĪVA ŚARMĀ. ব্রহ্মগীত। [Brahmagīta. Discourses on the principles of the Brahmist religion, in 3 parts, viz., Karmayoga, Jñānayoga, and Bhaktiyoga.] 3 pts. কলিকাতা ১৩০৮-০৯ [*Calcutta*, 1901-02.] 8°. **14123. d. 18.(2.)**

—— গীতরত্নাবলী। [Gītaratnāvalī. A collection of Brahmist hymns.] 2 pts. কলিকাতা ১৮০৬-০৮ [*Calcutta*, 1885-87.] 12°. **14123. e. 20.**

—— বিংশ শতাব্দী আশা-কাব্য। [Viṃśa śatābdī. A tale containing a forecast of Brahmism at the end of the twentieth century.] pp. ii. 329. কলিকাতা ১২৯৮ [*Calcutta*, 1891.] 8°. **14127. e. 43.**

—— যুগল মিলন অর্থাৎ দাম্পত্য প্রেম নাটক। [Yugala milana. A drama in four acts on conjugal affection.] pp. 75. কলিকাতা ১২৯৩ [*Calcutta*, 1886.] 8°. **14131. c. 17.**

CHITTASPANDANA. চিত্তস্পন্দন। [Chittaspandana. A collection of sonnets.] pp. 151. কলিকাতা ১৩১১ [*Calcutta*, 1904.] 12°. **14129. bb. 26.**

CHOONEY LALL DASS. *See* CHUNILĀLA DĀSA.

CHOWDHURY (MANMATHA NATH RAY). *See* MANMATHANĀTHA RĀYA CHAUDHURĪ.

CHUNDER NATH BOSE. *See* CHANDRANĀTHA VASU.

CHUNILĀLA DĀSA. নিদান এবং রুগ্নদেহ সূক্ষ্মতত্ত্ব। [Nidāna.] The Student's hand-book of Pathology and Morbid Anatomy ... Compiled from various English authors by Chooney Lall Dass. Second edition, revised and enlarged. pp. ii. xviii. 330. *Calcutta*, 1905. 8°. **14125. cc. 5.**

CHUNILĀLA VASU, *Assistant Surgeon.* Rasayanasutra, being a treatise on elementary Physics and Chemistry in Bengali ... By Asst. Surgn. Chuni Lal Bose. Parts I. and II. রসায়ন-সূত্র। pp. ii. viii. 200, 109. *Calcutta*, 1897. 8°. **14125. c. 41.**

CHURĪ. চুরী জুয়াচুরী জাল ও খুন। [Churī, juyāchurī jāl o khun, or Theft, cheating, forgery, and murder.] A sensational novel. pp. 200. কলিকাতা ১২৯৮ [*Calcutta*, 1891.] 12°. **14127. c. 43.(1.)**

CLEMENT I., *Saint, Pope.* প্রাচীন ধর্ম-প্রবন্ধ। [Prāchīna dharma-prabandha. Clement's Second Epistle to the Corinthians, translated into Bengali, with notes.] *See* NITYAGOPĀLA MUKHOPĀDHYĀYA. Studies in Apostolic Fathers. No. 2, pp. 30-54. [1895.] 8°. **14123. b. 16.**

COLLECTION. Collection de contes et chansons populaires. (Vol. 6. Contes Indiens. Les Trente-deux Récits . . . traduits du Bengali . . . par L. Feer.) *Paris, Le Puy* [printed], 1881, *etc.* 16°. **2348. a.**

COOCH BEHAR.—*Punyāh Exhibition Melā.* The Reports and Proceedings of the Cooch Behar Pooneah Exhibition Mela, 1893. [Partly in English, and partly in Bengali.] pp. 17, 23. *Cooch Behar*, 1894. Fol. **14133. g. 17.**

COPPÉE (FRANÇOIS ÉDOUARD JOACHIM). *See* JYOTIRINDRANĀTHA ṬHĀKURA. ফরাসী-প্রসূন। [Pharāsī-prasūna. Selections from the writings of François Coppée, and other French authors, translated into Bengali.] [1904.] 12°. **14131. d. 48.**

COWELL (EDWARD BYLES). *See* MUKUNDARĀMA CHAKRAVARTĪ. Three episodes from the old Bengali poem "Caṇḍī," translated into English by E. B. Cowell. 1902. 8°. **Ac. 8826/11.**

CUNNINGHAM (JOSEPH DAVEY). শিখ-ইতিহাস। [Şikh-itihāsa. A Bengali translation of Cunningham's History of the Sikhs, by Pramathanātha Sānyāla, with additional chapters on the Second Sikh war by the editor Durgādāsa Lāhiṛī.] pp. v. lv. 707, 124. কলিকাতা ১৩১৪ [*Calcutta*, 1907.] 12°. **14127. aa. 47.**

CYPRIAN, *Saint, Bishop of Carthage.* প্রভুর প্রার্থনা বিষয়ক উপদেশ। [Prabhur Prārthanā vishayaka upadeṣa. An exposition of the Lord's Prayer, translated from the Latin tract of St. Cyprian by G. Ch. M., *i.e.* Gopālachandra Mitra.] pp. 29. ১৮৫৪ [*Calcutta*, 1854.] 12°. **14123. a. 26.(2.)**

DACCA.—*Mahomedan Friends' Association.* The First Annual Report of the Dacca Mahomedan Friends' Association. ঢাকা মুসলমান সুহৃদ সম্মিলনীর . . . কার্য্যবিবরণ। ১৮৮৩। [For 1883.] (১৮৮৬-৮৭ সনের অনুষ্ঠান পত্র।) [For 1886-87.] 2 pts. ঢাকা ১৮৮৪ [*Dacca*, 1884, 1887.] 8°. **14123. h. 18.**

DADHIBHŪSHAṆA KAVIRATNA BHAṬṬĀCHĀRYA. টাকী-রায়চতুর্দ্ধুরীণ-বংশ। [Ṭākī Rāya Chaturdhurī-vamṣa. A Sanskrit poem in 9 *sargas*, giving an account of the Rāya Chaturdhuriṇa or Rāya Chaudhurī family of Kāyasthas in Taki, a town in the District of the 24 Parganas. Accompanied by a Bengali prose translation.] pp. iv. iv. 85, 18. কলিকাতা ৭৫১৮ [*Calcutta*, 1896.] 8°. **14076. c. 66.**

DĀ'IM 'ALĪ LASHKAR. আজায়েব বাহরে আলম। ['Ajā'ib bahār i 'ālam. A story of love and adventure, in Muhammadan Bengali verse.] pp. 111. কলিকাতা ১৩০৩ [*Calcutta*, 1896.] 8°. **14129. d. 31.**

ḌĀK. ডাকপুরুষের বচন। [Ḍākpurusher vachana. A collection of maxims and witty sayings, in verse, written in an old provincial dialect.] pp. 39. কলিকাতা ১২৯৫ [*Calcutta*, 1888.] 16°. **14125. f. 41.**

DAKSHA. দক্ষসংহিতা। [Daksha-saṃhitā. A code of *dharma*, in 7 *adhyāyas*. Sanskrit text, with Bengali translation.] *See* PAÑCHĀNANA TARKARATNA BHAṬṬĀCHĀRYA. ঊনবিংশতি সংহিতা। [Ūnaviṃṣati saṃhitā.] pp. 421-434. [1903.] 8°. **14039. c. 20.**

DAKSHIṆĀCHARAṆA RĀYA. *See* TĀRAKANĀTHA GAṄGOPĀDHYĀYA. Svarnalata. . . . Translated into English by D. C. Roy, *etc.* 1906. 8°. **14128. a. 14.**

DAKSHIṆĀCHARAṆA SENA. ঐকতানিক স্বরসংগ্রহ। [Aikatānika svarasaṅgraha.] . . . A collection of airs for concert. 2 pts. কলিকাতা ১২৯২ [*Calcutta*, 1886.] 8°. **D. 838.**

—— [Pt. i. Third edition.] pp. 56. কলিকাতা ১৩০১ [*Calcutta*, 1894.] 8°. **14125. d. 24.**

—— চুন্টার সেন বংশ। [Chunṭār Sena-vamṣa. A history of the Vaidya caste and their advent to Eastern Bengal, with an account of the Senas of Chunta in the district of Tippera.] pp. 19. শ্রীহট্ট ১৩১৫ [*Sylhet*, 1908.] 8°. **14125. ee. 40.(2.)**

ḌALLAṆA MIṢRA. *See* SUṢRUTA. সুশ্রুতসংহিতা। [Suṣruta-saṃhitā. With Ḍallaṇa's commentary, translated into Bengali.] [1885, *etc.*] 8°. **14043. d. 40.**

DALVAṆA ĀCHĀRYA. *See* ḌALLAṆA MIṢRA.

DAMIEN, *Father* [*i.e.* JOSEPH DE VENSTER]. *See* VENSTER (J. DE).

DĀMODARA MUKHOPĀDHYĀYA. *See* ṢĀNTIMAYA. শান্তিময় । [Ṣāntimaya. A sequel to Dāmodara Mukhopādhyāya's Dui bhagnī, or "The two sisters."] [1899.] 12°. **14127. c. 30.(5.)**

—— কর্ম্মক্ষেত্র । [Karmakshetra. A Bengali novel illustrating the virtue of philanthropy.] pp. 379. *Calcutta,* ১৩০৮ [1901.] 12°. **14127. cc. 30.**

—— Ma-o-meye, or The Mother and Daughter. A Bengali romance of Damodar Mukerji, Vidyananda, translated into English by R. P. De. pp. iii. 203. *Calcutta,* 1906. 12°. **14128. a. 10.**

—— মৃণ্ময়ী । [Mṛiṇmayī. A tale; being a sequel to the Kapālakuṇḍalā of Baṅkimchandra Chaṭṭopādhyāya. Fourth edition.] pp. 133. কলিকাতা [*Calcutta,* 1886 ?] 8°. **14127. g. 4.**

—— [Tenth edition.] pp. x. 349. *Calcutta,* ১৩০৮ [1901.] 12°. **14127. cc. 28.**

—— নবাব-নন্দিনী । [Nabāb-nandinī. A novel in imitation of Baṅkimchandra's Durgeṣanandinī.] pp. ii. 293. ১৩০৮ *Calcutta,* [1901.] 12°. **14127. cc. 29.**

—— সোণার কমল । [Soṇār kamala, or The golden lotus. A novel.] pp. 438. ১৩০৮ *Calcutta,* [1901.] 12°. **14127. cc. 25.**

—— যোগেশ্বরী । [Yogeṣvarī. The story of a Brahman youth of Benares.] pp. ii. 604. কলিকাতা ১৩০৪ [*Calcutta,* 1898.] 12°. **14127. cc. 6.**

DĀMODARA VIDYĀNANDA. *See* MAHĀBHĀRATA.—*Bhagavadgītā.* হিন্দুশাস্ত্র । . . . শ্রীমদ্ভগবদ্গীতা । [Bhagavadgītā. With a Bengali translation by Baṅkimchandra (Adh. i. and ii.) and Dāmodara Vidyānanda (iii.-xviii.).] [1897.] 8°. **14085. c. 45.(vol. ii.)**

—— *See* MAHĀBHĀRATA.—*Bhagavadgītā.* শ্রীমদ্ভগবদ্গীতা । [Bhagavadgītā. Sanskrit text, with word-for-word interpretation, paraphrase and commentary in Bengali, Sanskrit commentaries and notes. Edited by Dāmodara Vidyānanda.] [1897-1905.] 8°. **14049. bb. 11.**

—— হিন্দুশাস্ত্র । . . . মহাভারত । [Mahābhārata. A summary of the Sanskrit epic, with quotations.] pp. i. 157. [1896.] *See* RAMEṢACHANDRA DATTA. হিন্দুশাস্ত্র । [Hindu-ṣāstra.] Pt. vii. [1895-97.] 8°. **14085. c. 45.(vol. ii.)**

DANḌĪ. A Complete Key to the Sanskrit Course দশকুমারচরিতম্ [Daṣakumāracharita, Chapter viii. and other selections] for F.A. Examination for 1889. Containing Bengali and English translations . . . Edited by Tárá Kumár Kaviratna. Second edition. *Calcutta,* 1888. 12°. **14072. cc. 36.**

DĀSA GOSVĀMĪ. *See* RAGHUNĀTHA DĀSA GOSVĀMĪ.

DĀṢARATHĪ RĀYA. পাঁচালী । [Pāṇchālī. Poems, chiefly on the life of Krishṇa. Pt. 9. Second edition.] pp. 125. কলিকাতা ১২৮৯ [*Calcutta,* 1882.] 16°. **14129. c. 34.**

Imperfect; wanting the first sheet.

—— দাশুরায়ের পাঁচালী । মাথুর । [Pāṇchālī. Poems on the sports of Krishṇa at Muttra.] pp. 5. কলিকাতা ১৩০৮ [*Calcutta,* 1901.] 8°. **14129. cc. 1.(3.)**

—— দাশরথি রায়ের পাঁচালী । ষাটটী পালায় সম্পূর্ণ । [Pāṇchālī. A complete collection in 60 *pālās.* Edited with an introduction, life of the author, and notes, by Harimohana Mukhopādhyāya.] pp. 22, 57, 2190, 59. কলিকাতা ১৩০৯ [*Calcutta,* 1902.] 12°. **14129. bb. 15.**

DATTĀTRAYA BALAVANTA PĀRASNĪS. *See* JYOTIRINDRANĀTHA ṬHĀKURA. ঝাঁশির রাণী । [Jhāṇṣir rāṇī. Translated and compiled from the Marathi of Dattātraya Pārasnīs.] [1903.] 12°. **14127. aa. 29.**

DAULAT AḤMAD. সাহারঙ্গ বাদশা ও তোলাপতি কন্যার পুথি । [Sāhāraṅga bādshā o Tolāpati kanyār puthi. The romance of Sāhāraṅga and Tolāpati, princess of Kashmīr. In Muhammadan Bengali verse.] pp. 306, 6. কুমিল্লা [*Comilla,* 1903.] 8°. **14127. g. 15.(1.)**

DAULAT AḤMAD and MUḤAMMAD 'UMAR. কক্বরমা । অং ত্রিপুরা-ব্যাকরণ । [Kakbarmā. A grammar of the Tippera language, with a vocabulary and short sentences with Bengali equivalents.] pp. iv. 100. কুমিল্লা ১৩০৭ [*Comilla,* 1898.] 12°. **14131. e. 33.(3.)**

DAY (LAL BEHARI), *Rev.* *See* LĀLAVIHĀRĪ DE.

DAYĀLCHANDRA SOMA, *M.B.* See GIRĪṢACHANDRA BĀGCHHĪ. Diseases of women ... Revised and corrected by Rai Doyal Chandra Shome Bahadur. 1899. 8°. **14125. b. 15.**

DAYĀMAYĪ SENA. [*Life.*] See ṢARACHCHANDRA DATTA. দয়াময়ী সেনের সংক্ষিপ্ত জীবন চরিত। [Dayāmayī Sener saṃkshipta jīvanacharita.] [1890.] 12°. **14127. a. 37.(1.)**

DAYĀNANDA SARASVATĪ, *Svāmī*. দয়ানন্দের স্বরচিত জীবনবৃত্ত। উল্লিখিত ও লিখিত। [Dayānander svarachita jīvanavṛitta. The autobiography of Svāmī Dayānanda; consisting of an address delivered at Poona on the 15th August, 1875, and articles published in "The Theosophist" (1879-1880). Translated into Bengali and edited by Devendranātha Mukhopādhyāya from English versions of the author's Hindi original.] pp. 24, 48. কলিকাতা ১৩১৫ [*Calcutta*, 1908.] 12°. **14127. aaa. 2.**

—— পঞ্চ মহাযজ্ঞবিধিঃ [Pañcha-mahāyajña-vidhi. The ritual of the five great sacrifices, as modified and commented on by Dayānanda Sarasvatī. Edited for the Paropakāriṇī Sabhā of Ajmere, with a Bengali translation, by Satyacharaṇa Rāya.] pp. xii. v. 122, ii. কলিকাতা, আজমীর ১৮২০ [*Calcutta* printed, *Ajmere*, 1898.] 16°. **14028. a. 26**

—— সত্যার্থপ্রকাশ। [Satyārthaprakāṣa. A treatise on the interpretation and teachings of the Vedas. Translated into Bengali from the Hindi of Dayānanda Sarasvatī.] pp. v. ix. 829. কলিকাতা ১৩০৮ [*Calcutta*, 1901.] 8°. **14123. gg. 1.**

DE (R. P.). See DĀMODARA MUKHOPĀDHYĀYA. Ma-o-meye ... Translated into English by R. P. De. 1906. 12°. **14128. a. 10.**

DEBENDRA CHANDRA MULLICK. See DEVENDRACHANDRA MALLIKA.

DE FOE (DANIEL). রবিন্‌সন্ ক্রুশো। [Robinson Crusoe. Translated into Bengali by J. Robinson. Fourth edition.] pp. ii. 327. কলিকাতা ১৮৭০ [*Calcutta*, 1870.] 12°. **14127. f. 43.**

DENONATH BANERJEE. See DĪNANĀTHA VANDYOPĀDHYĀYA.

DEVAKĪNANDANA, *Kavivallabha, Son of Gopāla.* See VYOMAKEṢA MUSTAFĪ. শীতলা-মঙ্গল। [Ṣītalā-maṅgala. A critical examination of a poem in praise of the goddess Ṣītalā, with a biographical notice of the author.] [1898.] 8°. **14133. f. 18.**

DEVAPRATIPĀLAKA. সিদ্ধান্ত বিন্দু। [Siddhānta-vindu. A popular exposition of Vedānta philosophy.] Pt. i. pp. vi. 194. বৰ্দ্ধমান ১৩০৪ [*Burdwan*, 1898.] 8°. **14123. g. 5.**

DEVENDRACHANDRA MALLIKA. See BAṄKIMCHANDRA CHAṬṬOPĀDHYĀYA. Chandrashekhar ... Translated ... by Debendra Chandra Mullick. 1905. 8°. **14128. a. 21.**

DEVENDRAKIṢORA ĀCHĀRYA CHAUDHURĪ. গায়ত্রী। [Gāyatrī. A tale, illustrating the rascality of the native officials employed by landlords.] pp. 216. কলিকাতা ১২৯৯ [*Calcutta*, 1892.] 12°. **14127. c. 44.(2.)**

DEVENDRAKUMĀRA VIDYĀRATNA. See BHAṬṬI. Bhatti Kavyam. Cantos i. and ii. [With grammatical notes in Sanskrit and English, and Bengali and English translations.] Edited by Devendra Kumar Vidyaratna. [1903.] 12°. **14085. b. 48.**

DEVENDRANĀTHA GOSVĀMĪ. See ĪṢVARA KṚISHṆA. The Sánkhya Káriká ... Translated [text and commentary] by Debendra Nath Goswami. 1887. 8°. **14048. bb. 40.**

DEVENDRANĀTHA MUKHOPĀDHYĀYA. See DAYĀNANDA SARASVATĪ, *Svāmī*. দয়ানন্দের স্বরচিত জীবনবৃত্ত। [Dayānander svarachita jīvanavṛitta. The autobiography of Svāmī Dayānanda, translated from the English, and edited, by Devendranātha Mukhopādhyāya.] [1908.] 12°. **14127. aaa. 2.**

—— জাতীয় সাহিত্যের আবশ্যকতা ও উন্নতি। [Jātīya sāhityer āvaṣyakatā o unnati. A lecture on the necessity, and the improvement, of national literature.] pp. 81. কলিকাতা ১৮৯৫ [*Calcutta*, 1895.] 12°. **14125. e. 26.(4.)**

DEVENDRANĀTHA RĀYA. ভৈষজ্য-সূত্র ও ব্যবহার। [Bhaishajya-sūtra o vyavahāra.] The Principles and Practice of Medicine. By Devendra Nath Roy. pp. xvi. 1058. *Calcutta*, 1895. 8°. **14125. c. 40.**

DEVENDRANĀTHA SENA. অশোক-গুচ্ছ। [Aṣoka-guchchha. Poems on various subjects.] pp. 144. কলিকাতা ১৩০৭ [*Calcutta*, 1900.] 12°.
14129. a. 38.(6.)

DEVENDRANĀTHA SENA GUPTA and UPENDRANĀTHA SENA GUPTA. আয়ুর্ব্বেদ-সংগ্রহ। [Âyurveda-saṅgraha. A manual of medical practice, comprising Sanskrit extracts compiled from the works of chief authority, with Bengali interpretations. Fifth edition.] pp. iii. xl. 1224, xlviii. কলিকাতা [*Calcutta*, 1908.] 4°. **14043. ddd. 4.**

DEVENDRANĀTHA ṬHĀKURA. [*Life.*] *See* ĪṢĀNACHANDRA VASU. শ্রীমন্মহর্ষি দেবেন্দ্রনাথ ঠাকুর *etc.* [Ṣrīmanmaharshi Devendranātha Ṭhākura.] 1902. 12°. **14127. aa. 24.**

—— ব্রাহ্মধর্ম্মের ব্যাখ্যান। [Brāhmadharmer vyākhyāna. Brahmist sermons.] 2 pts. কলিকাতা ১৮০৭ [*Calcutta*, 1885.] 8°. **14123. d. 5.(2.)**

—— পরলোক ও মুক্তি। [Paraloka o mukti. A Brahmist tract on salvation and a future existence, based on the teachings of the Upanishads.] pp. 40. কলিকাতা ১৮১৭ [*Calcutta*, 1895.] 16°.
14123. c. 25.(2.)

—— প্রধান আচার্য্যের উপদেশ। [Upadeṣa. A series of Brahmist discourses, delivered monthly during the Saṃvat year 1785.] pp. 87. কলিকাতা ১৭৮৬ [*Calcutta*, 1864.] 12°. **14123. c. 26.**

DEVENDRANĀTHA VASU. বেজায় আওয়াজ। [Bejāy āwāj] or Royal salute. [A drama, ridiculing Bengali valour and patriotism.] pp. 39. *Calcutta*, 1893. 12°. **14131. a. 37.(1.)**

DEVENDRAVIJAYA VASU. *See* GOPĀLACHANDRA CHAṬṬOPĀDHYĀYA. কবিতামালা। [Kavitāmālā. Edited, with a life of the poet, by Devendravijaya Vasu.] [1896.] 12°. **14129. a. 39.(3.)**

DEVĪPRASANNA RĀYA CHAUDHURĪ. অপরাজিতা। [Aparājitā. A novel, depicting social life in Bengal. Second edition.] কলিকাতা ১৩১১ [*Calcutta*, 1904.] 8°. **14127. f. 19.(2.)**

—— ভিখারী। [Bhikhārī. A novel, advocating social reform in Bengal. Second edition.] pp. 128. কলিকাতা ১২৯৫ [*Calcutta*, 1888.] 8°.
14127. e. 27.(1.)

DEVĪPRASANNA RĀYA CHAUDHURĪ (*continued*). ভ্রমণ-বৃত্তান্ত। [Bhramaṇa-vṛittānta. Travels in India. Part I. Orissa.] pp. 96. কলিকাতা ১৩০২ [*Calcutta*, 1895.] 8°. **14127. bb. 6.**

—— দ্যুতি। বিবিধ প্রবন্ধ। [Dyuti. Essays on literary, social, and religious topics.] pp. 148. কলিকাতা ১৩০২ [*Calcutta*, 1895.] 8°.
14125. ee. 28.(1.)

—— মুরলা। [Muralā. A novel, showing the temptations to which a Hindu child-widow is exposed.] pp. 164. কলিকাতা ১২৯৯ [*Calcutta*, 1892.] 8°. **14127. e. 38.(2.)**

—— নবলীলা উপন্যাস। [Navalīlā. A novel, advocating a reformed state of Hindu society.] pp. ii. 168. কলিকাতা ১২৯২ [*Calcutta*, 1885.] 8°.
14127. f. 35.(2.)

—— পুণ্যপ্রভা। [Puṇyaprabhā. A tale on the oppressions of zamindars and native police officers.] pp. ii. 234. কলিকাতা ১৩০৩ [*Calcutta*, 1896.] 8°.
14127. ee. 5.(1.)

—— বিরাজমোহন। [Virājamohana. A tale of social life in Bengal. Third edition.] pp. 148. কলিকাতা ১২৯৬ [*Calcutta*, 1889.] 8°.
14127. e. 27.(1.)

—— বিবাহ-সংস্কার। [Vivāha-saṃskāra. A series of essays on the reformation of the Indian marriage system.] pp. ii. 126. কলিকাতা ১২৯৫ [*Calcutta*, 1889.] 8°. **14125. ee. 22.(3.)**

—— বিবেকবাণী [Vivekavāṇī. A collection of essays on moral and social subjects.] Pt. i. pp. ii. 92. কলিকাতা ১২৯১ [*Calcutta*, 1885.] 8°.
14125. f. 29.

DEVĪPŪJĀ. দেবীপূজা অথবা কোচবিহার রাজ্যে দুর্গোৎসব। [Devī-pūjā. A brief description of the annual festival held at Cooch Behar in honour of the goddess Devī, with an account of its origin and religious significance.] pp. 23. কোচবিহার ১২৯৭ [*Cooch Behar*, 1890.] 12°. **14123. e. 15.(1.)**

DHAMMAPADA. *See* SUTTAPIṬAKA.

DHANAKṚISHṆA ADHIKĀRĪ. শ্রীল শ্রীযুক্ত সনাতন গোস্বামী ও শ্রীরূপ গোস্বামীর জীবন চরিত্র। [Sanātana Gosvāmī o Rūpa Gosvāmīr jīvana-charitra. The lives of the two brothers and Vaishṇava teachers,

Sanātana Gosvāmī and Rūpa Gosvāmī.] pp. ii. 149. কলিকাতা ১২৯৮ [*Calcutta*, 1892.] 8°.
14127. b. 47.(2.)

DHANAVALLABHA SET. How to translate idiomatically from Bengali into English. By Dhan Ballabh Set . . . Second edition. pp. 118. *Calcutta*, 1889. 12°. **12901. ccc. 9.(3.)**

—— Fourth edition . . . improved. pp. 178. *Calcutta*, 1895. 12°. **14131. e. 27.**

ḌHAPAKĪRTANA. ঢপকীর্ত্তন। [Ḍhapakīrtana. A collection of Vaishṇava songs.] *See* AGHORACHANDRA GHOSHA. সঙ্গীত সাগর। [Saṅgītasāgara.] Vol. i. [1889.] 12°. **14129. b. 33.**

DHARMADĀSA. বিদগ্ধ-মুখমণ্ডনম্। [Vidagdha-mukhamaṇḍana. A series of riddles in Sanskrit verse. Edited with Sanskrit interpretations and Bengali translations by Şyāmācharaṇa Kaviratna.] pp. 92. কলিকাতা ১৩১১ [*Calcutta*, 1905.] 8°.
14072. b. 21.(2.)

DHARMĀNANDA MAHĀBHĀRATĪ. *See* BIBLE.—*Hebrews.* ইব্রিয়দিগের প্রতি ধর্মপ্রণিধি পৌলের পত্র। [Translated by Svāmī Dharmānanda Mahābhāratī.] 1903. 8°. **14123. b. 22.**

—— সিদ্ধান্ত-সমুদ্র। [Siddhāntasamudra. Social and statistical accounts of certain Hindu castes in Bengal.] Pts. 2-5. কলিকাতা ১৩১০ [*Calcutta*, 1903.] 12°. **14125. e. 47.**

DHARMARĀJA BARUYĀ. Hastasar, or Bauddha Mahaparitran. A Collection of Buddhist Hymns, Precepts, *Karmasthanas* and *Parittas* in Pali text, with Bengali interpretations and translation in prose and poetry. By Dharma Raj Barhuya. (হস্তসার বা বৌদ্ধ মহাপরিত্রাণ।) Pt. i. pp. iii. vi. ii. 342. *Calcutta*, 1893. 12°. **14098. a. 28.**

DHĪRENDRANĀTHA PĀLA. অদ্ভুত গুপ্তকথা। [Adbhuta guptakathā. A Bengali novel.] pp. 143. কলিকাতা ১২৯৫ [*Calcutta*, 1888.] 12°.
14127. d. 33.(2.)

—— বাঙ্গালীর লীলা। [Bāṅgālīr līlā. A tale of social life in Bengal.] pp. 70. কলিকাতা ১২৯২ [*Calcutta*, 1885.] 8°. **14127. f. 35.(1.)**

—— কলিকাতা রহস্য। . . . [Kalikātā-rahasya.] Mystries [*sic*] of Calcutta. Completed in three parts. pp. 378. কলিকাতা ১২৯৫ [*Calcutta*, 1888.] 8°. **14127. e. 25.**

DHĪRENDRANĀTHA PĀLA (*continued*). কলির ভুষণ্ডি। [Kalir bhūshaṇḍi. Humorous sketches of social life and manners amongst Bengali Babus of the present day.] Pt. i. pp. 53. কলিকাতা ১২৯৫ [*Calcutta*, 1888.] 12°. **14125. e.**

—— লক্ষ টাকা বা যক্ষের ধন। [Laksha ṭākā. One lakh of rupees; an amusing tale.] pp. 32. *Calcutta*, [1904.] 12°. **14127. d. 19.(3.)**

—— শাস্ত্র-মহিমা। [Şāstra-mahimā. A critical examination of the sacred works of the Hindus.] pp. 22, 186, viii. কলিকাতা ১২৯৮ [*Calcutta*, 1891.] 12°. **14131. d. 27.**

—— শতগল্প। [Şata galpa. A collection of 100 short tales.] Nos. 1—4. কলিকাতা ১৮৯১ [*Calcutta*, 1891.] 12°. **14127. c. 45.**

—— স্বর্ণ বাই। [Svarṇa Bāi. A tale on the experiences of a prostitute.] pp. 100, vi. কলিকাতা ১২৯৫ [*Calcutta*, 1888.] 12°. **14127. c. 37.(6.)**

DHĪREŞVARA ĀCHĀRYA. Leelamanjari. [A poem on the life of Kṛishṇa] in Sanscrit and vernacular [*i.e.* with a Bengali prose translation]. Edited [or rather composed] by Dhiresvar Acharyaj. Pt. i. pp. 20. *Jarhah*, 1880. 16°. **14070. a. 6.**

DHULĪP SINGH, *Maharaja.* *See* ŞIKH-YUDDHA. শিখযুদ্ধের ইতিহাস, *etc.* [Şikh-yuddher itihāsa. A history of the Sikh wars, and an account of the life of Dhulīp Singh.] [1893.] 8°.
14127. bb. 3.

DHŪRJAṬI. *See* YOGENDRANĀTHA VASU, called DHŪRJAṬI.

DICTIONARIES. সংক্ষিপ্ত বাঙ্গালা অভিধান। [Saṃkshipta Bāṅgālā abhidhāna. An abridged Bengali dictionary in Bengali.] pp. 273. কলিকাতা [*Calcutta*, 1902.] 8°. **14133. b. 17.**

DĪNABANDHU GHAṬAKA KULABHŪSHAṆA. কায়স্থ-কারিকা ও বংশাবলি। [Kāyastha-kārikā. A history of the Kāyastha families in Bengal, with genealogical tables showing how they are connected by marriage. Compiled by Dīnabandhu Ghaṭaka with the assistance of Īşānachandra Ghaṭaka Rājaşiromaṇi and Vijayakṛishṇa Ghaṭaka Chūḍāmaṇi.] 3 vols. in 87 parts. কলিকাতা [*Calcutta*, 1886-91.] 4°. **14123. i. 11.**

DĪNABANDHU MITRA. রায় দীনবন্ধু মিত্রের গ্রন্থাবলী। [Granthāvalī. The collected works of Dīnabandhu Mitra. With a life of the author by Bankimchandra Chaṭṭopādhyāya. Edited by Upendranātha Mukhopādhyāya.] pp. 29, 730. কলিকাতা ১৩০৮ [*Calcutta*, 1901.] 8°. **14127. ee. 16.**

DĪNABANDHU SENA. The Records of the Moslem Emperors. বাদসাহী দপ্তর *etc.* [Bādshāhī daftar. A series of historical tales.] Pt. i. pp. 40. *Calcutta*, শ্রীচৈতন্যাব্দ ৪১৫ [1900.] 12°. **14127. cc. 22.**

DĪNADAYĀLA DĀSA PRĀMĀṆIKA. *See* KOKILADŪTA. সংস্কৃত কোকিলদূতং। [Kokiladūta. With a Bengali translation by Dīnadayāla Dāsa of a Sanskrit commentary by Kālidāsa Sena.] [1862.] 8°. **14072. cc. 50.**

DĪNANĀTHA DHARA. *See* BALLĀLA SENA, *King of Bengal.* শ্রী ... বল্লাল-চরিতের বঙ্গানুবাদ। [Ballāla-charita. Translated by Dīnanātha Dhara from the Sanskrit chronicle by Ānanda Bhaṭṭa.] 1904. 12°. **14127. a. 45.(3.)**

DĪNANĀTHA GANGOPĀDHYĀYA. হিন্দুধর্মের আন্দোলন ও সংস্কার। [Hindu dharmer āndolana. Suggestions on the reformation of the Hindu religious system.] pp. 57. কলিকাতা ১৩০০ [*Calcutta*, 1893.] 12°. **14123. e. 16.(1.)**

DĪNANĀTHA KAVIRATNA ŚĀSTRĪ. বৈদ্য রহস্য। [Vaidyarahasya. A treatise illustrated from Sanskrit texts to prove that Vaidyas are of the Śūdra class, and quite distinct from the Ambashṭhas; being a reply to a work entitled Ambashṭha kon varṇa.] pp. 118. কলিকাতা [*Calcutta*, 1899.] 8°. **14125. ee. 33.(1.)**

DĪNANĀTHA SĀNYĀLA. *See* MADHUSŪDANA DATTA (MICHAEL). মেঘনাদবধ কাব্য। [Meghanādavadha kāvya. Edited with notes by Dīnanātha Sānyāla.] [1907.] 8°. **14129. e. 31.**

DĪNANĀTHA VANDYOPĀDHYĀYA. তত্ত্বনির্ণয়। ... Tattva nirnaya ... [A series of essays in the form of dialogues "containing examinations of the latest theories advanced by English philosophers"] by Denonath Banerjee. 2 pts. *Calcutta*, 1879, 86. 12°. **14125. f. 32.**

DĪNANĀTHA VIDYĀRATNA, *of Baraipur.* দিননাথ-পদাবলী। [Dinanātha-padāvalī. Miscellaneous songs.] Pt. i. pp. viii. 64. *Contai*, ১৩১২ [1906.] 8°. **14129. cc. 1.(4.)**

DĪNENDRAKUMĀRA RĀYA. *See* ARABIAN NIGHTS. সচিত্র আরব্য রজনী। [Ārabya rajanī. Translated from the English by Dīnendrakumāra Rāya.] [1902.] 8°. **14127. ee. 14.**

DĪNEŚACHANDRA SENA. *See* PERIODICAL PUBLICATIONS.—*Calcutta.* প্রাচীন বাঙ্গালা গ্রন্থাবলী। [Prāchīna Bāṅgālā granthāvalī. Edited in part by Dīneśachandra Sena.] [1900, *etc.*] 8°. **14133. ff. 2.**

—— বেহুলা। [Behulā. The legendary story of Behulā and the merchant Chānd, taken from old poems containing the myth of Manasā the serpent-goddess. Second edition.] pp. viii. 138. কলিকাতা [*Calcutta*, 1907.] 16°. **14128. aa. 2.**

—— ধর্মমঙ্গল। [Dharmamaṅgala. An article on the Dharmamaṅgala, a poem by Māṇik Gāṅgulī.] ১৩১৩ [1907.] *See* ACADEMIES, *etc.*—Calcutta.—*Bengal Academy of Literature.* সাহিত্য-পরিষৎ-পত্রিকা। [Sāhitya-parishat-patrikā.] Vol. xiii., no. 1. [1894, *etc.*] 8°. **14133. f. 18.**

—— জড়ভরত। [Jaḍabharata. A mythological story.] pp. iv. 141. কলিকাতা [*Calcutta*, 1908.] 32°. **14128. aa. 4.**

—— ফুল্লরা। [Phullarā. The story of Phullarā, taken from the Chaṇḍī of Mukundarāma Chakravartī.] pp. iv. 120. কলিকাতা [*Calcutta*, 1907.] 16°. **14128. aa. 3.**

—— সতী। [Satī. The mythological story of Satī, the wife of Śiva, who destroyed herself by fire at the sacrifice made by her father Daksha.] pp. iv. viii. 102. কলিকাতা ১৩১৩ [*Calcutta*, 1907.] 16°. **14128. aa. 1.**

—— বঙ্গভাষা ও সাহিত্য। [Vaṅgabhāshā o sāhitya. Bengali language and literature. Second edition.] pp. xx. 10, 646, 12, 11. কলিকাতা [*Calcutta*, 1901.] 8°. **14131. d. 43.**

DĪNEŚACHARAṆA VASU. দীনেশ-গ্রন্থাবলী। [Dīneśa-granthāvalī. The collected works of Dīneśacharaṇa Vasu.] pp. 264. কলিকাতা ১৩১০ [*Calcutta*, 1903.] 8°. **14127. ee. 20.**

DIOGNETUS. ডাইওগ্নিটাসের প্রতি। [The Epistle to Diognetus, translated into Bengali with notes.]

See NITYAGOPĀLA MUKHOPĀDHYĀYA. Studies in Apostolic Fathers. No. 2, pp. 55-77. [1895.] 8°.
14123. b. 18.

—— দিয়গ্নীতসের প্রতি পত্র। [Diyagnītaser prati patra.] The Epistle to Diognetus ... Translated into Bengali by M. N. Nath [i.e. Mathurānātha Nātha.] pp. ii. 14. *Calcutta*, 1908. 12°.
14123. a. 46.(2.)

DODS (MARCUS), *the Younger*. *See* BIBLE.—*John, Gospel of*. যোহন লিখিত সুসমাচারের টীকা। ... Commentary on John's Gospel ... based on that of the Rev. Marcus Dods, *etc.* 1903. 8°.
14123. bb. 2.

DOST MUḤAMMAD. *See* KHAIBAR, *City of*. খয়বরের জঙ্গনামা। [Khaibarer jang-nāmā. Translated from the Persian by Dost Muḥammad.] [1889.] 8°. **14129. d. 27.**

DOYAL CHANDRA SHOME. *See* DAYĀLCHANDRA SOMA.

DUḤKHĪṢYĀMA DĀSA. গোবিন্দমঙ্গল। [Govinda-maṅgala. An account in verse of the life of Kṛishṇa, based on the 10th chapter of the Bhāgavatapurāṇa. Edited, with a life of the author, by Īṣānachandra Vasu.] pp. vi. vii. 269. কলিকাতা ১৮০৮ [*Calcutta*, 1886.] 8°. **14129. c. 37.**

DUNCAN (JONATHAN). *See* ENGLAND.—*Parliament*. Summary of clauses of the Act of Parliament of the 18th of May 1784. Translated by J. Duncan. 1785. 8°. **14125. a.**

DURGĀCHARAṆA GUPTA. Gupta Press Avidhan, or a Dictionary containing almost all the Bengali and Sanskrit words with their appropriate Bengali and English equivalents ... Compiled by Durga Charan Gupta ... গুপ্তপ্রেশ অভিধান। [New and enlarged edition.] Pt. I. pp. ii. 960. [*Calcutta*, 1905.] 16°. **14133. a. 17.**

Apparently no more was published.

DURGĀCHARAṆA RAKSHITA. তাম্বুল বণিক্ বা বঙ্গীয় তাম্বুলী বৈশ্যজাতির ইতিহাস। [Tāmbūla vaṇik, or Vaṅgīya Tāmbūlī Vaiṣya. A treatise on the Tāmbūla Vaiṣya caste.] pp. vi. 206, 40. ১৩১০ [*Calcutta*, 1903.] 8°. **14125. ee. 38.**

DURGĀDĀSA DE. গল্প-গুজব। [Galpa-gujab. Sketches of Bengali female life.] pp. 44. কলিকাতা ১৩০২ [*Calcutta*, 1895.] 12°. **14127. c. 43.(2.)**

DURGĀDĀSA DE (*continued*). জুবিলী যজ্ঞ। [Jubilī-yajña. A dramatic composition on the Diamond Jubilee of the reign of Queen Victoria, with special reference to her rule in India.] pp. 15. কলিকাতা [*Calcutta*, 1897.] 12°. **14131. a. 40.(9.)**

—— গল্প-গুজব। সামাজিক সরস নক্সা। কালো বউ। [Kālo bau, or The black wife. A tale of domestic life amongst Hindus of the present time.] pp. 48. কলিকাতা ১৩০৩ [*Calcutta*, 1896.] 12°.
14127. c. 57.(3.)

No. 3 of a series entitled Galpa-gujab.

—— সুবর্ণ গোলকের সঙ্গীত। [Suvarṇa-golaker saṅgīta. Songs adapted from those in the farce Suvarṇa-golaka of Baṅkimchandra Chaṭṭopādhyāya. Second edition.] pp. 10. কলিকাতা ১৩০৪ [*Calcutta*, 1897.] 12°. **14129. a. 51.(1.)**

DURGĀDĀSA LĀHIṚĪ. *See* CUNNINGHAM (J. D.). শিখ-ইতিহাস। [Ṣikh-itihāsa. A Bengali translation of Cunningham's History of the Sikhs, with additional chapters on the Second Sikh war by the editor Durgādāsa Lāhiṛī.] [1907.] 12°.
14127. aa. 47.

—— আদর্শ-চরিত। [Ādarṣa-charita. A biographical notice of Kṛishṇamohana Vandyopādhyāya.] pp. ii. 70. কলিকাতা ১২৯২ [*Calcutta*, 1886.] 12°. **14127. a. 29.**

—— বাঙ্গালীর গান। [Bāṅgālīr gāna. Songs by Bengali poets. Compiled with an introduction, alphabetical index containing the first line of each poem, a list of poets and a biographical notice of each, by Durgādāsa Lāhiṛī.] pp. xi. iii. 75, 1048. কলিকাতা ১৩১২ [*Calcutta*, 1905.] 8°.
14129. cc. 13.

—— দ্বাদশ নারী বা আর্য্য-মহিলা। [Dvādaṣa nārī. Short notices of twelve celebrated Hindu women.] pp. 228. কলিকাতা ১২৯১ [*Calcutta*, 1885.] 12°.
14127. a. 26.

DURGĀDĀSA RĀYA. *See* NAROTTAMA DĀSA. প্রেমভক্তিচন্দ্রিকা। [Premabhakti-chandrikā. Edited, with an introductory preface, and notes, by Durgādāsa Rāya.] [1890.] 16°. **14123. e. 13.(2.)**

—— ṢAṄKARA ĀCHĀRYA. मोह-मुद्गरः [Mohamudgara.] ... Edited ... with Bengali, Hindi and English translations by Durga Das Ray. 1888. 32°. **14048. a. 11.**

DURGĀDĀSA VASU. নববিধান তত্ত্ব। [Navavidhāna-tattva. The doctrines of the Theistic Church, in the form of questions and answers.] pp. 43. টাঙ্গাইল ১২৯৪ [*Tangail*, 1887.] 12°.
14123. c. 23.(1.)

DURGĀMOHANA DĀSA. প্রফুল্ল। [Praphulla. Short poems.] pp. ii. 68. *Calcutta*, 1907. 12°.
14129. bb. 28.(8.)

DURGĀMOHANA SMRITITĪRTHA. *See* VIṢVADEVA ĀCHĀRYA. রাঘব দীপিকা। [Rāghava-dīpikā. Edited, with an introduction, a prose translation, and additional matter in Bengali by Durgāmohana.] [1892.] 8°. **14028. d. 48.(2.)**

DURGĀVATĪ, *Rāṇī of Garmandal.* [*Life.*] *See* UPENDRAKUMĀRA GHOSHA. আর্য্য-মহিলা। [Ārya-mahilā.] 1895. 12°. **14127. aa. 2.(5.)**

DURLABHA MALLIKA. গোবিন্দচন্দ্র গীত। প্রাচীন কবি দুর্লভ মল্লিক কৃত। [Govindachandragīta. An ancient historical poem. Edited with an introduction and critical notes by Ṣivachandra Ṣīla.] pp. xxxi. 144. কলিকাতা ১৩০৮ [*Calcutta*, 1901.] 8°. **14129. cc. 4.**

DUTT (MICHAEL M. S.). *See* MADHUSŪDANA DATTA (MICHAEL).

DUTT (R. C.). *See* RAMEṢACHANDRA DATTA.

DUTT (U. K.), *M.D., of Aberdeen.* *See* UPENDRAKRISHṆA DATTA.

DVĀRAKĀNĀTHA DATTA. দীনভারতের অনুনয়। [Dīna Bhārater anunaya. A series of articles on the social, educational, and commercial progress of India.] pp. iii. ii. 114. কলিকাতা ১৯০৫ [*Calcutta*, 1905.] 8°. **14125. ee. 30.(2.)**

DVĀRAKĀNĀTHA MITRA, *Judge of the High Court at Calcutta.* [*Life.*] *See* KĀLĪPRASANNA DATTA. বিচারপতি দ্বারকানাথ মিত্রের জীবনী। [Dvārakānātha Mitrer jivanī.] [1892.] 12°. **14127. a. 37.(4.)**

DVĀRAKĀNĀTHA VASU. *See* RĀMAPRASĀDA SENA. কবিরঞ্জন রামপ্রসাদের গ্রন্থাবলী। [Rāmaprasāder granthāvalī. Edited, with notes and a life of the poet, by Dvārakānātha Vasu.] [1895.] 12°. **14129. a. 37.**

—— Hints on [English] composition and translation [for Bengali students]. pp. 93. *Calcutta*, 1891. 12°. **14131. e. 25.(1.)**

DVĀRAKĀNĀTHA VASU (*continued*). জীবনী-কোষ। [Jīvanī-kosha. A dictionary of Hindu mythology and biography.] pp. 316. কলিকাতা ১৮৯৪ [*Calcutta*, 1894.] 12°. **14133. d. 3.**

—— প্রবাদ-পুস্তক। [Pravāda-pustaka. Bengali proverbs, alphabetically arranged, with an essay on the uses of proverbs in determining the characteristics of a nation.] pp. vi. 131. কলিকাতা ১৮৯৩ [*Calcutta*, 1893.] 12°. **14125. f. 34.(2.)**

DVĀRAKEṢA KĀVYATĪRTHA. *See* PURĀṆAS.—*Dharmapurāṇa.* বৃহদ্ধর্ম্মপুরাণম্। [Bṛihad-dharma-purāṇa. With a Bengali translation by Dvārakeṣa Kāvyatīrtha and others.] [1908.] 8°.
14016. dd. 28.(1.)

DVĀRIKĀNĀTHA, *Zamindar of Singur.* [*Life.*] *See* PRAMATHANĀTHA VARMĀ. সিঙ্গুরের স্বর্গীয় জমিদার দ্বারিকানাথ বাবু *etc.* [Dvārikānātha Bābu.] [1887.] 12°. **14127. a. 33.(2.)**

DVIJENDRALĀLA RĀYA. এক ঘরে। [Ek ghare. A protest against the refusal of orthodox Hindus to re-admit into their society any native gentleman returning from England, except on the performance of certain expiatory ceremonies.] pp. 35. *Calcutta*, [1889.] 12°. **14125. e. 19.(5.)**

—— কল্কি-অবতার। [Kalki-avatāra. A farce describing the vicious habits of educated Bengali Bābus.] pp. 8, 103. কলিকাতা ১৩০২ [*Calcutta*, 1895.] 12°. **14131. a. 37.(6.)**

—— নুরজাহান। নাটক। [Nūrjahān. An historical drama on the life of the empress Nūrjahān.] pp. iii. 176. কলিকাতা [*Calcutta*, 1908.] 12°.
14131. aa. 10.

—— পাষাণী। [Pāshāṇī. A mythological drama.] pp. iv. 122. কলিকাতা ১৩০৭ [*Calcutta*, 1900.] 12°.
14131. aa. 9.(1.)

DVIJENDRANĀTHA ṬHĀKURA. অদ্বৈত মতের সমালোচনা। [Advaita mater samālochanā. A review of the *advaita*, or non-dual teachings of Hindu philosophy.] pp. 44, 8. কলিকাতা ১৩০৩ [*Calcutta*, 1896.] 8°. **14123. f. 49.(2.)**

—— অদ্বৈত মতের প্রথম ও দ্বিতীয় সমালোচনা। [Revised edition, with the addition of a second part.] pp. 70. কলিকাতা ১৩০৪ [*Calcutta*, 1897.] 8°.
14123. ff. 6.(1.)

DVIJENDRANĀTHA ṬHĀKURA (*continued*). আর্য্যামি এবং সাহেবিআনা। [Āryāmi evaṃ Sāhebiānā. A satire on the effect of an Anglicising influence on Hindus of the present time.] pp. 31. কলিকাতা ১২৯৭ [*Calcutta*, 1890.] 8°. **14125. ee. 26.(1.)**

EASTERN BENGAL and ASSAM. [For the Government Gazette and other publications of the Province of Eastern Bengal and Assam.] *See* INDIA.—*Eastern Bengal and Assam.*

EDWARD VII., *King of Great Britain and Ireland.* *See* YOGEṢVARA GHOSHA. A short poem in Bengali, with an English translation, on the Coronation of His Most Gracious Majesty Edward VII., *etc.* 1902. 12°. **14129. bb. 13.(3.)**

—— The Coronation Song. Composed on the occasion of the coronation of... King Edward VII., Emperor of India. (অভিষেক-গীত) [Abhishekagīta.] pp. 7, 8, *Beng.* and *English. Calcutta*, [1902.] 12°. **14129. bb. 18.(3.)**

In the Calcutta Book-list, Sept. 1902, the name "Ananda Chandra Mitra" appears under the heading "Author, translator, or editor."

ELLERTON (J. F.). *See* BIBLE.—*New Testament.* জগত্তারক প্রভু যিশু খ্রীষ্টের মঙ্গল সমাচার *etc.* [Maṅgalasamāchāra. The New Testament, translated by J. F. Ellerton.] [1819.] 8°. **842. c. 11.**

—— *See* BIBLE.—*Matthew.* The Gospels according to St. Matthew and St. John, in English and Bengalee. [Translated by J. F. Ellerton.] 1819. 8°. **842. e. 8.**

—— *See* BIBLE.—*John, Gospel of.* The Gospel of St. John, in Bengalee and English. [Translated by J. F. Ellerton.] 1819. 8°. **3068. bb. 3.**

EMERSON (RALPH WALDO). এমার্সন সন্দর্ভ। Emerson sandarva, or Translations from the essays of Mr. R. W. Emerson of America. By a Villager [signing himself in the preface, য, ন, ম। *i.e.* Y. N. M.] Pt. i. pp. vi. 170. *Cooch Behar*, 1890. 8°. **14125. ee. 24.**

ENGLAND.—*India Office.*—*Library.* Catalogue of the Library of the India Office. Vol. II.—Part iv. Bengali, Oriya, and Assamese Books. By J. F. Blumhardt. pp. viii. 353. *London*, 1905. 8°. **Cat. Desk A.**

ENGLAND.—*Parliament.* Summary of such of the clauses of the Act of Parliament of the 18th May 1784, as relate to the natives of India. Translated into the Bengal language by J. Duncan. pp. 14. [*Calcutta*,] 1785. 8°. **14125. a.**

ENGLISH LANGUAGE. A self-guide to the knowledge of the English language, in English and Bengalee, containing words of one to seven syllables, with their pronunciation and meaning. To which is added a short English grammar. pp. viii. 152. *Calcutta*, 1822. 8°. **12906. b. 5.**

ENGLISH SPELLING-BOOK. The English spelling-book. No. I. With Bengali pronunciation and meaning . . . and reading lessons, *etc.* (ইংরেজী বর্ণমালা) [Imrejī varṇamālā.] pp. 102. *Calcutta*, 1854. 12°. **12906. aaa. 9.**

EPHEMERIDES. নূতন পঞ্জিকা। শকাব্দাঃ ১৭৮৮ . . . ইং ১৮৬৬-৬৭ [Nūtana pañjikā. An almanac for the Saṃvat year 1788, corresponding to A.D. 1866-67.] কলিকাতা [*Calcutta*, 1866.] 8°. **14133. e. 8.**

—— সন ১৩০৬ সালের বৃহৎ মহম্মদীয় পঞ্জিকা। [Mahammadīya pañjikā. A Muhammadan almanac for the year 1306 B.S. By Muḥammad Riyāẓ al-Dīn Aḥmad.] pp. 72, 70, 72. কলিকাতা [*Calcutta*, 1899.] 12°. **14133. e. 10.**

—— মহাম্মদীয় পঞ্জিকা। [Mahammadīya pañjikā. A Muhammadan almanac for B.S. 1309, *i.e.* A.D. 1902-03.] pp. 108, 193. ১৩০৮ [*Calcutta*, 1902.] 12°. **14133. e. 11.**

—— নূতন পঞ্জিকা সন ১৩০৬ সাল ডাইরেক্টারি (P. M. Bagchi's illustrated Directory of India for 1899 or 1306 B.S.) pp. viii. 48, 240, 280, 24, 248, 16, 432, 216. *Calcutta*, 1899. 8°. **14133. e. 9.**

EPICTETUS. এপিক্‌টেটসের উপদেশ। [Epikṭeṭaser upadeṣa. Selections from the Discourses of Epictetus, translated by Jyotirindranātha Ṭhākura.] pp. viii. 80. কলিকাতা ১৩১৪ [*Calcutta*, 1907.] 12°. **14123. a. 46.(3.)**

ESHAN CHUNDER BOSE. *See* ĪṢĀNACHANDRA VASU.

FAKĪRDĀS CHAṬṬOPĀDHYĀYA. *See* RĀMACHANDRA VANDYOPĀDHYĀYA, *Kavivara.* শ্রীধর্ম্মমঙ্গল। [Dharmamaṅgala. Edited, with a life of the author, by Fakīrdās Chaṭṭopādhyāya.] [1906.] 8°. **14133. ff. 1.**

FARĪD al-DĪN 'AṬṬĀR. *See* GIRIṢACHANDRA SENA. তত্ত্বরত্নমালা। [Tattvaratnamālā. A collection of Ṣūfī anecdotes taken from the Manṭiḳ al-ṭair of Farīd al-Dīn 'Aṭṭār.] [1907.] 8°. **14123. h. 40.**

—— Tapasmala, or Lives of Mahomedan Saints. Compiled from Tejkaratuloulia, a Persian work [by Farīd al-Dīn 'Aṭṭār]. Translated into Bengali [by Giriṣachandra Sena.] তাপসমালা। 6 pts. *Calcutta*, 1880-95. 8°. **14123. h. 14.**

al-FARRĀ al-BAGHAWĪ. *See* ḤUSAIN ibn MAS'ŪD, *al-Farrā al-Baghawī.*

FAṢĪḤ al-DĪN. مصباح الاسلام আদি ও আসল ॥ মেছবাহল এছলাম ॥ [Miṣbāḥ al-Islām. A treatise on Muhammadan religious obligations, in Muhammadan Bengali verse.] pp. 136. ঢাকা ১৯০২ [*Dacca*, 1902.] 8°. **14123. h. 29.(3.)**

FEER (LÉON). *See* VIKRAMĀDITYA, *King of Ujjayinī.* Contes Indiens. Les Trente-deux Récits du Trône . . . traduits . . . et augmentés d'une étude et d'un index par Léon Feer. 1883. 12°. **2348. aa. 34.**

FIRDAUSĪ. [*Life.*] *See* MUZAMMAL ḤAḲḲ. ফেরদৌসী-চরিত। . . . Ferdausi charita, *etc.* 1898. 16°. **14127. aa. 15.**

—— ছহি সাহানামা। [Shāh-nāmah. Translated into Muhammadan Bengali verse by Muḥammad Khāṭir. Second edition.] pp. 345. ১২৯২ [*Calcutta*, 1886.] 4°. **14129. g. 7.**

GADĀDHARA DĀSA. শ্রীনাথধর্ম। [Śrīnātha-dharma. An account in verse of the worship of God, under the name Śrīnātha, as taught by Rādhākṛishṇa of Naopāṛā.] pp. 16. ঢাকা ১৩০৩ [*Dacca*, 1896.] 16°. **14123. e. 18.(2.)**

GADA SIṂHA. নানার্থমঞ্জরী। [Nānārthamañjarī. A Sanskrit vocabulary of synonymns in verse, with a Bengali translation.] *See* GOPĪRAMAṆA TARKARATNA. কোষচন্দ্রিকা। [Koshachandrikā.] pp. 1-20. [1893.] 12°. **14090. b. 44.(1.)**

GAGANACHANDRA RĀYA, *of Ghazipur.* মহাত্মা পওহারী বাবা। [Mahātmā Paohārī Bābā. An account of the life and teachings of Paohārī Bābā, *i.e.* Harabhajana Dāsa, a Hindu saint of Ghazipur, born in A.D. 1840.] pp. ii. 60. *Calcutta*, 1899. 12°. **14127. aa. 14.(3.)**

GALPA-BHĀṆḌĀRA. সচিত্র গল্প-ভাণ্ডার। [Galpa-bhāṇḍāra. A collection of witticisms and humorous anecdotes.] pp. 108. *Calcutta*, 1895. 12°. **14127. c. 55.(4.)**

GAṆEṢACHANDRA MUKHOPĀDHYĀYA. A Bengalee Dictionary of Court Terms. Compiled by G. C. Mukerjee. pp. 38. *Calcutta*, [1902.] 8°. **14133. a. 15.**

—— জীবনী-সংগ্রহ। [Jīvanī-saṅgraha. Lives of eminent Indian saints.] pp. iii. 168. কলিকাতা ১৯০৭ [*Calcutta*, 1907.] 12°. **14127. aa. 46.**

GAṄGĀDĀSA, *Son of Gopāladāsa.* ছন্দোমঞ্জরী। [Chhandomañjarī. A Sanskrit treatise on poetical metres, in 6 *stabakas*, with 2 Sanskrit commentaries, and a Bengali translation by Rāmanārāyaṇa Vidyāratna. Edited by Rāmadeva Miṣra. Second edition.] pp. ii. 302, viii. মুর্শিদাবাদ ১৩১৩ [*Murshidabad*, 1907.] 8°. **14055. b. 5.**

GAṄGĀDHARA NYĀYARATNA. *See* KṚISHṆA MIṢRA. প্রবোধচন্দ্রোদয় নাটক। [Prabodhachandrodaya nāṭaka. With a Bengali translation by Gaṅgādhara Nyāyaratna and others.] [1855.] 16°. **14079. a. 4.**

GAṄGĀDHARA VANDYOPĀDHYĀYA. *See* RĀMACHANDRA VANDYOPĀDHYĀYA. The First Collection of English synonyms explained in Bengali . . . Revised by Babu Gangadhar Banerji. 1902. 8°. **14131. g. 33.**

—— Translation and Retranslation. Sixth edition. pp. ii. 223. *Calcutta*, 1885. 12°. **14131. f. 30.**

GAṄGĀGATI DĀSA. *See* ṢARACHCHANDRA DATTA and GAṄGĀGATI DĀSA. আসাম প্রদেশের বিশেষ বিবরণ। [Āsām pradeṣer viṣesha vivaraṇa.] [1906.] 12°. **14131. f. 34.**

GAṄGĀNĀRĀYAṆA CHAKRAVARTĪ. জ্ঞানাম্বুধি। [Jñānāmbudhi. A compilation of Sanskrit texts bearing on various points of Hindu religion, domestic and social duties, with translations and occasional notes in Bengali. Pt. i. entitled Saṃsāra-tattva; Pt. ii. entitled Brahma-tattva.] 2 pts. কলিকাতা ১২৯৬-৯৭ [*Calcutta*, 1890-91.] 8°. **14033. bb. 33.**

GAṄGĀRĀMA, *Kavi.* কবি গঙ্গারাম ও মহারাষ্ট্রপুরাণ। [Mahārāshṭra-purāṇa. A poem on the Maratha invasion of Bengal during the time of the Nawab 'Alī Virdī Khān, in the middle of the 18th century. The first Canto only, edited with an historical introduction by Vyomakeṣa Mustafī.] ১৩১৪ [1907.] *See* ACADEMIES, *etc.*—Calcutta.—*Bengal Academy of Literature.* সাহিত্য-পরিষৎ-পত্রিকা। [Sāhitya-parishat-patrikā.] Vol. xiii., no. 4. [1894, *etc.*] 8°. **14133. f. 18.**

GANGULI (T. N.). *See* TĀRAKANĀTHA GAṄGOPĀDHYĀYA.

GAUḌAPĀDA ĀCHĀRYA. *See* ĪṢVARA KṚISHṆA. The Sánkhya Káriká ... also the commentary of Gaurapada ... translated into Bengali. 1887. 8°. **14048. ff.**

—— গৌড়পাদীয় আগম। [Āgama, or Āgama-ṣāstra. An epitome of the Māṇḍukyopanishad. Chapters ii. to iv. only of the Sanskrit text, with a Bengali prose version by Mahendranātha Ghoshāl.] pp. 76. বারাণসী ১২৯৬ [*Benares*, 1890.] 8°. **14010. c. 52.(4.)**

GAURADĀSA VAIRĀGĪ. আদিব্রহ্মাণ্ড ভাণ্ডার বা তন্ত্র মন্ত্র সংগ্রহ। [Ādi-Brahmāṇḍa-bhāṇḍāra. A collection of Sanskrit verses, containing charms, medicinal recipes, astrological and other omens and prognostications, compiled by Gauradāsa from various Tantric and other sources. With Bengali prose translations. Fourth edition.] pp. 158. ১২৯৬ *Calcutta*, [1890.] 8°. **14003. c. 1.(1.)**

Forms part of a series entitled Gauradāsa-granthāvali.

—— লম্পটের নাকেখৎ। [Lampaṭer nākekhat. A farce. Third edition.] ১২৯৭ *Calcutta*, [1890.] 8°. **14003. c. 1.(4.)**

Forms part of a series entitled Gauradāsa-granthāvali.

GAURAGOVINDA RĀYA. হিন্দুধর্ম্মের পুনরুত্থান। [Hindudharmer punarutthāna. A tract on the revival of Hinduism.] pp. 30. কলিকাতা [*Calcutta*, 1896.] 12°. **14123. e. 16.(2.)**

—— কেশবচন্দ্র। [Keṣavachandra. A brief account of Keṣavachandra Sena, and other leaders of the Brāhma Samāj.] pp. 28. কলিকাতা ১৮১৪ [*Calcutta*, 1893.] 12°. **14127. a. 37.(5.)**

—— কেশবচন্দ্রের অন্তর্বাহ্য। [Keṣavachandrer antarbāhya. An abstract of a lecture on the teachings of Keṣavachandra Sena.] pp. 33. কলিকাতা [*Calcutta*, 1896.] 12°. **14123. c. 28.(2.)**

GAURAGOVINDA RĀYA (*continued*). কেশবচন্দ্রের উপাস্য। [Keṣavachandrer upāsya. A lecture on the aim of Keṣavachandra's religious worship.] pp. 20. কলিকাতা [*Calcutta*, 1895.] 12°. **14123. c. 28.(1.)**

—— শ্রীকৃষ্ণের জীবন ও ধর্ম্ম। [Ṣrī Kṛishṇer jīvana o dharma. The life and religion of Kṛishṇa.] pp. viii. 286. কলিকাতা ১৮১১ [*Calcutta*, 1889.] 8°. **14123. f. 40.**

—— [Second edition.] pp. viii. 286. কলিকাতা ১৮১৪ [*Calcutta*, 1892.] 8°. **14123. f. 44.**

GAURAMOHANA CHANDRA. স্বধর্ম্মত্যাগীর সামাজিক অব্যবহার্য্যতা বিষয়ে শাস্ত্রীয় ব্যবস্থা। [Svadharmatyāgīr ... vyavasthā. Decisions of pandits of the Suvarṇavaṇik caste, refusing to re-admit a Hindu convert to Christianity into their community.] pp. 8. কলিকাতা ১৩০১ [*Calcutta*, 1895.] 8°. **14125. ee. 28.(5.)**

GAUTAMA. গৌতমীয়-ধর্ম্মসূত্রম্। [Dharmasūtra. *Adhyāyas* iii., viii., xi. Sanskrit text, with Bengali translations and notes.] [1895.] *See* RAMEṢACHANDRA DATTA. হিন্দুশাস্ত্র। [Hindu-ṣāstra.] Pt. iii., pp. 48-58. [1895-97.] 8°. **14085. c. 45.(vol. i.)**

—— গৌতমসংহিতা। [Gautama-saṃhitā. A code of *dharma*, in 29 *adhyāyas*. Sanskrit text, with Bengali translation.] *See* PAÑCHĀNANA TARKARATNA BHAṬṬĀCHĀRYA. ঊনবিংশতি-সংহিতা। [Ūnaviṃṣati saṃhitā.] pp. 435-464. [1903.] 8°. **14039. c. 20.**

GHANARĀMA CHAKRAVARTĪ. [*Life.*] *See* AMBIKĀCHARAṆA BRAHMACHĀRĪ BHAṬṬĀCHĀRYA. বঙ্গ-রত্ন। [Vaṅgaratna.] [1886.] 12°. **14127. a.**

—— শ্রীধর্ম্ম মঙ্গল। [Dharma-maṅgala. A religious poem.] pp. iii. 335. কলিকাতা ১২৯৫ [*Calcutta*, 1888.] 8°. **14129. e. 16.**

GHATAK (A.). Bengali made easy for Englishmen and English knowing people. pp. ii. iii. 101. *Calcutta*, 1903. 12°. **14131. e. 35.(2.)**

GHAZZĀLĪ. *See* MUHAMMAD ibn MUHAMMAD, *Ghazzālī*.

GHERAṆḌA. যোগরত্নম ঘেরণ্ডসংহিতা। [Yogaratna, also called Gheraṇḍa-saṃhitā. A work on the Yoga, mainly on the bodily postures and other Tantric aspects of the system, in the form of seven lectures in verse, delivered to a pupil. Sanskrit text, with a Bengali prose translation by Kālīprasanna Vidyāratna.] pp. iv. 122. কলিকাতা ১২৯৩ [*Calcutta*, 1886.] 8°. **14048. b. 35.**

—— যোগশাস্ত্রঃ। ঘেরণ্ডসংহিতা অন্যান্য প্রমাণসহ। [Yogaṣāstra. The Gheraṇḍa-saṃhitā, with selections from other works on *yoga*. Sanskrit text, with Bengali translations and preface.] pp. 414. [1891, *etc.*] *See* PERIODICAL PUBLICATIONS.—*Calcutta*. অরুণোদয়। [Aruṇodaya.] Pt. i., no. 10. [1890, *etc.*] 4°. **14133. g. 16.**

—— ঘেরণ্ড-সংহিতা। [Gheraṇḍa-saṃhitā. Sanskrit text, with a Bengali translation.] *See* PRASANNAKUMĀRA BHAṬṬĀCHĀRYA. যোগাম্বুধি। [Yogāmbudhi.] [1896.] 32°. **14048. a. 19.**

GHOSE (G. C.). *See* GIRIṢACHANDRA GHOSHA.

GHOSH (H. H.). হস্ত-তন্ত্র বয়ন। [Hastatantravayana. A treatise on native hand-loom weaving.] কলিকাতা ১৩১৩ [*Calcutta*, 1906.] 12°. **14125. ddd. 3.**

GHOSH (P.). *See* PAÑCHĀNANA GHOSHA.

GHULĀM NABĪ ibn 'INĀYAT ALLĀH. সর্ব্বরহৎ কাছাছল আম্বিয়া চারইয়ারী *etc.* [Ḳiṣaṣ al-anbiyā. A history of the saints from Adam to Muḥammad; being an enlarged version in Muhammadan Bengali verse, of Ghulām Nabī's Hindustani translation of the Persian Ḳiṣaṣ al-anbiyā of Isḥāḳ al-Nishāpūrī, by Tāj al-Dīn Muḥammad, Muḥammad Khāṭir, and 'Abd al-Wahhāb.] pp. iv. ii. 920. কলিকাতা ১৩০৭ [*Calcutta*, 1902.] 4°. **14123. hh. 1.**

GHULĀM RABBĀNĪ. মোরশেদ-বিলাপ। [Murshid-vilāp. Verses in memory of the late Maulavī Ṭālib Allāh, the author's religious perceptor.] pp. 31. কলিকাতা ১৩০৬ [*Calcutta*, 1900.] 12°. **14129. a. 48.(4.)**

GHULĀM SARWAR. *See* ḲUR'ĀN. কোরাণ শরিফ। [Koran. Arabic text, with a Bengali translation and commentary by Na'īm al-Dīn, assisted by Ghulām Sarwar.] [1887, *etc.*] 8°. **14509. b. 18.**

—— *See* MUḤAMMAD ibn ISMĀ'ĪL, *Bukhārī*. সহি বোখারী শরিফ। [Ṣaḥīḥ. Arabic text, with a Bengali translation, commentary, and notes, by Na'īm al-Dīn, assisted by Ghulām Sarwar.] [1898, *etc.*] 8°. **14522. b. 17.**

GHULĀM SARWAR (*continued*). *See* NA'ĪM al-DĪN, *Maulavī*. জোব্দাতল মসায়েল। [Zubdat al-masā'il. Compiled with the assistance of Ghulām Sarwar.] [1887.] 8°. **14123. h. 19.**

—— *See* NIẒĀM, *Shaikh*. ফতওয়ায় আলমগিরী। [Fatāwā i 'Ālamgīrī. Translated with the assistance of Ghulām Sarwar.] [1884, *etc.*] 8°. **14123. h. 22.**

GIRIDHARA. *See* JAYADEVA, *Son of Bhojadeva*. মহাকবি জয়দেবের গীতগোবিন্দের প্রাকৃত পদ্যানুবাদ। [Gītagovinda. A metrical translation by Giridhara.] [1889.] 12°. **14129. a. 21.(2.)**

GIRIJĀBHŪSHAṆA BHAṬṬĀCHĀRYA. পশ্চিমে বাঙ্গালী। [Paṣchime Bāṅgālī. A tale showing the vices to which Bengali Babus are addicted when in service away from their homes.] pp. 115. কলিকাতা ১২৯৫ [*Calcutta*, 1888.] 12°. **14127. d. 35.(2.)**

—— প্রবাসী বাঙ্গালী। [Pravāsī Baṅgālī. Short sketches, exposing some of the vicious habits to which Bengalis are addicted when away from their native country, and free from social restraints.] pp. ii. 96. কলিকাতা ১২৯৫ [*Calcutta*, 1888.] 8°. **14125. e. 22.(2.)**

GIRIJĀPRASANNA RĀYA CHAUDHURĪ. বঙ্কিমচন্দ্র। [Baṅkimchandra. An analysis and critical review of two of Baṅkimchandra's novels, viz.:—Kṛishṇakānter Will, and Chandraṣekhara.] pp. vii. 106, 36. কলিকাতা ১২৯৩ [*Calcutta*, 1886.] 8°. **14131. d. 17.(1.)**

—— বঙ্কিমচন্দ্র। [Baṅkimchandra. An analysis and critical review of three of Baṅkimchandra's novels, viz.:—Durgeṣanandinī, Kapālakuṇḍalā, and Mṛiṇālinī.] pp. 28, 68, 78. কলিকাতা ১২৯৭ [*Calcutta*, 1890.] 8°. **14131. d. 17.(2.)**

—— বঙ্কিমচন্দ্র। [Baṅkimchandra. A critical analysis and examination of the novels of Baṅkimchandra Chaṭṭopādhyāya.] 3 pts. কলিকাতা [*Calcutta*, 1901.] 8°. **14131. d. 42.**

GIRĪNDRANĀTHA VANDYOPĀDHYĀYA. মীরা বাই। [Mīrā Bāi. An historical novel narrating the incidents which led to the British conquest of the Panjab.] pp. 196. কলিকাতা ১৩০৫ [*Calcutta*, 1898.] 12°. **14127. c. 30.(7.)**

GIRĪṢACHANDRA BĀGCHHĪ. Diseases of women in Bengali. By Girish Chandra Bagchee . . . Revised and corrected by Rai Doyal Chandra Shome Bahadur. (স্ত্রী-রোগ।) [Strīroga.] pp. 4, 4, 39, 636. *Calcutta*, 1899. 8°. **14125. b. 15.**

GIRIṢACHANDRA DĀSA. লোকনাথ-চরিত। [Lokanātha-charita. A short account of the life of Lokanātha Brahmachārī, a famous devotee of Baradi in the district of Dacca, who is said to have lived to the age of 160.] pp. 31. ঢাকা ১২৯৭ [*Dacca*, 1890.] 12°. **14127. a. 37.(2.)**

GIRIṢACHANDRA GHOSHA. *See* SHAKSPERE (W.). ম্যাক্‌বেথ। [Macbeth. Translated by Giriṣachandra Ghosha.] [1900.] 8°. **14131. aa. 4.(1.)**

—— আবু হোসেন। [Abū Ḣusain. A comedy.] pp. 67. কলিকাতা ১৩০০ [*Calcutta*, 1893.] 12°. **14131. a. 37 (2.)**

—— বলিদান। [Balidāna. A social drama on the evils of selling girls in marriage. Second edition.] pp. 202. কলিকাতা ১৩১৪ [*Calcutta*, 1907.] 12°. **14131. aa. 8.(2.)**

—— চন্দ্রা [Chandrā. A tale of the Indian mutiny.] pp. 164. কলিকাতা ১২৯৪ [*Calcutta*, 1887.] 12°. **14127. d. 36.(1.)**

—— ছত্রপতি শিবাজী। ঐতিহাসিক নাটক। [Chhatrapati Ṣivājī. An historical drama on the life of Ṣivājī.] pp. vi. 235. কলিকাতা ১৩১৪ [*Calcutta*, 1907.] 12°. **14131. aa. 8.(1.)**

—— গিরিশ-গীতাবলী। [Giriṣa-gītāvalī. A collection of poems and songs by Giriṣachandra Ghosha. Edited with a life of the author by Avināṣachandra Gaṅgopādhyāya.] pp. 26, 448, 31. কলিকাতা ১৩১০ [*Calcutta*, 1904.] 32°. **14129. aa. 1.**

—— গিরীশ-গ্রন্থাবলী। [Giriṣa-granthāvalī. The complete works of Giriṣachandra Ghosha.] 3 vols. কলিকাতা ১২৯৯ *etc.* [*Calcutta*, 1892-93.] 8°. **14127. g. 8.**

—— গিরীশ-গ্রন্থাবলী। [Giriṣa-granthāvalī. The complete works of Giriṣachandra Ghosha, edited by Upendranātha Mukhopādhyāya.] কলিকাতা ১৩১২ [*Calcutta*, 1905- .] 8°. **14127. g. 17.**
In progress.

GIRIṢACHANDRA GHOSHA (*continued*). হারানিধি। [Hārānidhi. A social drama.] pp. 166. কলিকাতা ১২৯৭ [*Calcutta*, 1890.] 12°. **14131. a. 30.(2.)**

—— কালাপাহাড়। [Kālāpāhāṛ. A drama on the conquest of Orissa during the time of Sulaimān, Nawab of Bengal.] pp. 204. *Calcutta*, ১৮৯৬ [1896.] 12°. **14132. a. 32.(8.)**

—— মায়াবসান। [Māyāvasāna. A domestic drama.] pp. 171. কলিকাতা ১৩০৪ [*Calcutta*, 1898.] 12°. **14131. a. 41.(2.)**

—— প্রফুল্ল। [Praphulla. A drama in 5 acts, exposing the vices of modern Bengali life.] pp. 176. কলিকাতা ১২৯৬ [*Calcutta*, 1889.] 12°. **14131. a. 30.(1.)**

—— পূর্ণচন্দ্র নাটক। [Pūrṇachandra nāṭaka. A dramatical version of Kāñchanamālā, a Bengali tale founded on a Buddhist legend.] pp. 128. কলিকাতা [*Calcutta*, 1888.] 12°. **14131. a. 27.(3.)**

—— সভ্যতার পাণ্ডা। [Sabhyatār pāṇḍā. A farce, directed against the introduction of Western civilization.] pp. 50. ১৩০১ [*Calcutta*, 1894.] 12°. **14131. a. 37.(4.)**

GIRĪṢACHANDRA LĀHIRĪ. প্রাতঃস্মরণীয়া ৺ মহারাণী শরৎসুন্দরীর জীবন-চরিত। [Mahārāṇī Ṣarat Sundarīr jīvana-charita. A biography of Mahārāṇī Ṣarat Sundarī.] pp. 139. কলিকাতা ১৩০১ [*Calcutta*, 1894.] 8°. **14127. aa. 3.(2.)**

—— ঋতুবিহার। [Ṛituvihāra. A description of the seasons of the year, in verse.] pp. iv. 117. কলিকাতা ১২৯৯ [*Calcutta*, 1892.] 8°. **14129. c. 41.(4.)**

—— স্বর্গ ও নরক। [Svarga o naraka. Heaven and hell; an allegorical poem.] pp. 58. রঙ্গপুর ১৩০৬ [*Rangpur*, 1900.] 12°. **14129. a. 38.(4.)**

GIRIṢACHANDRA SENA. *See* FARĪD al-DĪN 'AṬṬĀR. Tapasmala, or Lives of Mahomedan Saints . . . Translated into Bengali [by Giriṣachandra Sena]. 1880-95. 8°. **14123. h. 14.**

—— *See* ḤĀFIẒ, *Shīrāzī*. হাফেজ। *etc.* [Dīwān of Hāfiẓ, translated from the Persian, with notes, by Giriṣachandra Sena.] [1891.] 16°. **14129. aa. 2.**

—— *See* ḤUSAIN ibn MAS'ŪD, *al-Farrā al-Baghawī*. হদিস-পূর্ব্ববিভাগ। *etc.* [Mishkāt al-

HĀRĀṆACHANDRA RAKSHITA. *See* SHAKSPERE (W.). সেক্সপিয়র। [The Plays of Shakspere, translated by Hārāṇachandra Rakshita.] [1896-1898.] 8°. **14131. b. 24.**

—— —— [1900-02.] 8°. **14131. b. 26.**

—— হেম-হার। [Hemahāra. Ten short stories.] pp. 107. কলিকাতা ১৩০২ [*Calcutta*, 1896.] 12°. **14127. c. 54.(4.)**

—— কামিনী ও কাঞ্চন। [Kāminī o kāñchana. Woman and gold: a story illustrating the religious teachings of Rāmakṛishṇa Paramahaṃsa. Second edition.] pp. 347. কলিকাতা ১৩১৪ [*Calcutta*, 1908.] 12°. **14128. a. 28.**

—— প্রতিভাসুন্দরী। [Pratibhāsundarī. A tale of Ujjayini and the astrologer Mihira, son of Varāha.] pp. iv. 374. কলিকাতা ১৩১১ [*Calcutta*, 1904.] 12°. **14127. cc. 41.**

—— বঙ্গসাহিত্য বঙ্কিম। [Vaṅgasāhitya Baṅkim. A critical examination of the works of Baṅkimchandra, and their influence on Bengali literature, with a short life of the novelist. Second edition.] pp. 35, 223. কলিকাতা ১৩০৬ [*Calcutta*, 1899.] 12°. **14125. e. 36.**

—— বঙ্গের শেষবীর [Vaṅger ṣesha-vīra. An historical novel dealing with incidents in the life of Raja Pratāpāditya. Second edition.] pp. ii. 298. কলিকাতা ১৩০৫ [*Calcutta*, 1898.] 12°. **14127. cc. 12.(2.)**

HĀRĀṆACHANDRA VANDYOPĀDHYĀYA. *See* UPANISHADS. অথ শান্তিপাঠঃ ॥ [Ṣāntipātha. With a Bengali translation by Hārāṇachandra.] 1892. 8°. **14010. c. 43.(vol. 2.)**

HARANĀTHA DEVA ṢĀSTRĪ. *See* BHAṬṬI. ভট্টিকাব্যম্। প্রথমতশ্চতুর্থসর্গপর্য্যন্তম্। [Bhaṭṭikāvya. Cantos 1—4. With a Sanskrit commentary, etymological notes, and Bengali translation by Haranātha.] [1903.] 12°. **14085. c. 53.(1.)**

HARANĀTHA GHOSHA. পত্র-দলিল শিক্ষা। [Patra-dalil-ṣikshā. A letter-writer, with specimens of zamindari accounts and documents. Ninth edition.] pp. 160. ঢাকা ১৩১৪ [*Dacca*, 1907.] 12°. **14131. f. 32.(2.)**

HARAPRASĀDA ṢĀSTRĪ. *See* ACADEMIES, *etc.*—Calcutta.—*Asiatic Society of Bengal.* Catalogue of Printed books and Manuscripts in Sanskrit (and Bengali) . . . Compiled . . . under the supervision of Mahāmahopādhyāya Haraprasād S'hāstrī. 1899, *etc.* 4°. **14096. dd. 5.**

—— *See* PERIODICAL PUBLICATIONS.—*Calcutta.* প্রাচীন বাঙ্গালা গ্রন্থাবলী। [Prāchīna Bāṅgālā granthāvalī. Edited by Haraprasāda Ṣāstrī.] [1900, *etc.*] 8°. **14133. ff. 2.**

—— ভারত মহিলা। [Bhārata-mahilā. The social duties of Hindu women, exemplified by the lives of famous women of ancient Sanskrit literature. Third edition.] pp. 76. *Calcutta*, 1891. 12°. **14125. e. 27.(1.)**

—— Discovery of Living Buddhism in Bengal. By Haraprasád S'ástri. pp. 31. *Calcutta*, 1897. 4°. **14123. k. 5.**

—— মেঘদূত ব্যাখ্যা। [Meghadūta-vyākhyā. An examination of the Sanskrit poem of Kālidāsa.] pp. v. 88. কলিকাতা ১৩০৯ [*Calcutta*, 1902.] 12°. **14131. d. 41.(2.)**

—— রমাই পণ্ডিতের ধর্ম্মমঙ্গল। [Ramāi Paṇḍiter Dharmamaṅgala. An article on the poet Ramāi Paṇḍita and his Dharmamaṅgala.] ১৩০৪ [1897.] *See* ACADEMIES, *etc.*—Calcutta.—*Bengal Academy of Literature.* সাহিত্য-পরিষৎ-পত্রিকা। [Sāhitya-parishat-patrikā.] Vol. iv., no. 1. [1894, *etc.*] 8°. **14133. f. 18.**

—— বাল্মীকির জয়। [Vālmīkir jaya.] The Three Forces, physical, intellectual, and moral. pp. 94. *Calcutta*, 1886. 12°. **14125. e.**

—— [Another edition.] pp. 84, 11. কলিকাতা ১৩০৯ [*Calcutta*, 1902.] 12°. **14125. e. 39.(2.)**

—— Vernacular Literature of Bengal before the introduction of English education. pp. 16. *Calcutta*, [1891.] 8°. **14131. d. 24.**

HARBOLĀ BHĀṆṚ. হরবোলা ভাঁড়। [Harbolā bhāṇṛ, or The professional jester. A collection of witty anecdotes.] pp. 60. কলিকাতা [*Calcutta*, 1892.] 12°. **14127. c. 42.(2.)**

HARDING (H. JANE). *See* ĪṢVARACHANDRA VIDYĀSĀGARA. The Exile of Sītā. Translated . . . by H. J. Harding. [1904.] 8°. **14127. ee. 21.**

HAREKRISHṆA GOSVĀMĪ. আলাপ-কৌমুদী। [Ālāpa kaumudī. Thoughts on the decay of Hinduism, and the evil results of British rule.] pp. 30. কলিকাতা [*Calcutta*, 1887.] 8°. **14125. ee. 20.(3.)**

HARICHARAṆA MAJUMDĀR, *of Gayhat, Mymensingh.* ঘটপূজা। [Ghaṭapūjā. A Sanskrit ritual for the ceremony of worshipping consecrated pots. With some appended matter in Bengali.] pp. iv. 68. গয়হাটা, কলিকাতা ১৩০৮ [*Gayhat, Calcutta printed,* 1901.] *obl.* 8°. **14028. dd. 10.(3.)**

—— পুরোহিত-দর্পণ। [Purohitadarpaṇa. A manual for the use of priests in the performance of daily rites. Sanskrit text, with Bengali notes, rubrics, and translations.] Pt. i. pp. vi. 243. কলিকাতা ১৩০৬ [*Calcutta,* 1899.] 8°. **14028. d. 72.**

No more has been registered.

HARIDĀSA, *Vaishṇava saint.* [*Life.*] *See* KĀLĪPRASANNA GHOSHA. ভক্তির জয় *etc.* [Bhaktir jaya.] [1895.] 12°. **14127. a. 52.**

HARIDĀSA GHOSHA, *Pleader.* বীণা। [Vīṇā. Lyrical poems.] pp. iv. 168. কলিকাতা ১৩০৬ [*Calcutta,* 1900.] 8°. **14129. bb. 6.**

HARIDĀSA ŚĀSTRĪ. বেদ বিবাদ সমালোচনা। [Vedavivāda-samālochanā. A review of the controversy arising from Rameśachandra Datta's Bengali translation of the Vedas.] pp. 25. *Calcutta,* 1885. 12°. **14131. d. 14.(1.)**

—— বেদ বিবাদ বিচার। [Vedavivāda-vichāra. Another pamphlet on the same subject as the preceding.] pp. 20. [*Calcutta,* 1885.] 12°. **14131. d. 14.(2.)**

HARIDĀSA ṬHĀKURA, *Son of Sumati Śarmā.* [*Life.*] *See* ACHYUTACHARAṆA CHAUDHURĪ. শ্রীমৎ হরিদাস ঠাকুরের জীবন-চরিত। [Haridāsa Ṭhākurer jīvanacharita.] [1896.] 12°. **14127. a. 45.(2.)**

HARIDĀSA VANDYOPĀDHYĀYA. হেমচন্দ্র। [Hemachandra. A tale of domestic life.] pp. 232. কলিকাতা [*Calcutta,* 1896.] 8°. **14127. d. 41.(3.)**

—— কুলীনকাহিনী। [Kulīnakāhinī. A tale showing the evil results of polygamy amongst Kulin Brahmans.] pp. 44. কলিকাতা [*Calcutta,* 1885.] 12°. **14127. d. 29.(3.)**

HARIGOPĀLA VASU. *See* MAHĀBHĀRATA.—*Bhagavadgītā.* পদ্যগীতা। [Padyagītā. A metrical version of the Bhagavadgītā by Harigopāla Vasu.] [1905.] 8°. **14133. ff. 1.**

HARIHARĀNANDA, *Sāṅkhyayogāchārya.* *See* SUTTAPIṬAKA. श्रीमद्-भगवद्-गौतमबुद्ध-भाषितं धम्मपदम् . . . The Dharmapada . . . Rendered in Sanskrit verse [together with a Bengali translation] by Svámí Hariharánanda Áraṇya. 1905. 8°. **14099. bb. 13.**

—— सांख्यतत्त्वालोकः तत्त्वनिदिध्यासनगाथा-महायोगेश्वरस्तोत्रादि-समेतः . . . সানুবাদ সাংখ্যতত্ত্বালোক *etc.* [Sāṅkhyatattvāloka. A Sanskrit treatise on the Sāṅkhya philosophy. Followed by Tattvanididhyāsanagāthā, and Mahāyogeśvarastotra, short philosophical hymns. Edited with Bengali translations, notes, and appendices by Sachchidānanda.] pp. 160. কলিকাতা ১৯০৩ [*Calcutta,* 1903.] 8°. **14049. b. 14.**

HARIHARA SĀDHAKENDRA. *See* TANTRAS. গুপ্তসাধনতন্ত্রম্। [Guptasādhanatantra. Edited with a Bengali translation by Harihara Sādhakendra.] [1886.] 8°. **14028. d. 29.(2.)**

HARIJĪVANA PRĀMĀṆIKA. সঙ্গীতসূত্রসার। [Saṅgīta-sūtrasāra. The principles of Hindu music, compiled from Sanskrit and other sources.] Pt. i. pp. ii. 60. রাণাঘাট ১২৯৯ [*Ranaghat,* 1892.] 12°. **14125. d. 20.**

HARIKIṄKARA MUKHOPĀDHYĀYA. প্রমোদিনী নাটক। [Pramodinī. A social drama.] pp. 148. বেনারস ১২৯৯ [*Benares,* 1892.] **14131. c.**

HARIKṚISHṆA ADHIKĀRĪ. First Lessons in translation from Bengali into English. By Hari Krishna Adhikari . . . Second edition . . . enlarged. pp. iii. 200. *Calcutta,* 1893. 12°. **14131. e. 20.(3.)**

HARILĀLA CHAṬṬOPĀDHYĀYA. বৈষ্ণব-ইতিহাস। [Vaishṇava-itihāsa. An account of the lives and works of ancient Vaishṇava teachers and poets, Vaishṇava festivals and places of pilgrimage.] pp. ii. 104. কলিকাতা ১৩১২ [*Calcutta,* 1906.] 12°. **14123. e. 34.(2.)**

HARILĀLA GUPTA KAVIRATNA. আয়ুর্বেদ-চন্দ্রিকা। [Āyurveda-chandrikā. A dictionary of Sanskrit words used in medical literature, with Bengali equivalents.] pp. viii. 856. কলিকাতা ১৮২৮ [*Calcutta,* 1906.] 8°. **14043. dd. 14.**

HARILĀLA VANDYOPĀDHYĀYA. আড়কাটী নাটক। [Āṛkāṭī. A drama on the methods by which coolies are recruited for work in foreign countries.] pp. 89. কলিকাতা ১৩০৪ [*Calcutta,* 1897.] 12°. **14131. a. 41.(1.)**

—— কলিকাতা-রহস্য বা নেপাল ডাক্তারের ডায়েরী। [Kalikātā-rahasya. A story, depicting life in Calcutta.] pp. iv. 615. কলিকাতা ১৩০৪ [*Calcutta,* 1897.] 8°. **14127. ee. 6.**

HARILĀLA VANDYOPĀDHYĀYA (*continued*). যুবরাজ টীকেন্দ্রজিৎ বা লোমহর্ষণ মণিপুর কাণ্ড। [Yuvarāja Ṭīkendrajit. A drama on the Manipur insurrection.] Pt. i. pp. 128. *Calcutta*, 1896. 12°. **14131. a. 39.**

HARIMOHANA BASĀK, *of Mahajanpur*. গৃহ-মুষ্টিযোগ চিকিৎসা সংগ্রহ। [Gṛihamushṭiyoga. A collection of domestic *mushṭiyoga* remedies for ordinary diseases and ailments.] pp. ii. 38. ঢাকা ১৩০৬ [*Dacca*, 1900.] 8°. **14125. c. 43.**

HARIMOHANA MUKHOPĀDHYĀYA. *See* DĀSARATHĪ RĀYA. দাশরথি রায়ের পাঁচালী। [Pāñchālī. Edited with an introduction, life of the author, and notes by Harimohana.] [1902.] 12°. **14129. bb. 15.**

—— কমলাদেবী। [Kamalā Devī. An historical novel of the time of Akbar.] pp. 236. কলিকাতা ১২৯৩ [*Calcutta*, 1886.] 12°. **14127. c. 31.(2.)**

HARIMOHANA PRĀMĀṆIKA. কমলাকরুণাবিলাসো নাম শুভাঙ্কঃ [Kamalā karuṇāvilāsa. An *aṅka* or Sanskrit drama in one act, with Bengali translation. Edited with notes by Yaśodānanda Prāmāṇika.] pp. v. v. 96. কলিকাতা [*Calcutta*, 1899.] 8°. **14079. c. 42.(2.)**

—— কোকিলদূতম্। [Kokiladūta. A Sanskrit poem in 100 stanzas on the loves of Rādhā and Kṛishṇa, in imitation of the Meghadūta. With Sanskrit commentary and Bengali paraphrase. Edited by Sudhāmaya Prāmāṇika. Second edition.] pp. viii. 169. কলিকাতা ১৩১১ [*Calcutta*, 1905.] 8°. **14070. dd. 22.(2.)**

HARIMOHANA VANDYOPĀDHYĀYA. ভরত-কাহিনী। [Bhārata-kāhinī. An inquiry into the economic condition of India under the British rule, with suggestions for its social and political improvement.] pp. iv. 350. দ্বারভাঙ্গা ১৩০৭ [*Darbhanga*, 1900.] 8°. **14125. ee. 34.**

HARIMOHANA VIDYĀBHŪSHAṆA. *See* JAYADEVA, *Son of Bhojadeva*. গীতগোবিন্দ। [Gītagovinda. With a translation, and introductory essay, by Harimohana.] [1887.] 8°. **14070. c. 46.**

HARINĀRĀYAṆA JYOTĪRATNA. *See* SĀMUDRIKA. সানুবাদ বৃহৎ সামুদ্রিক। [Bṛihat sāmudrika. Sanskrit text, with Bengali introduction, and translation. Edited by Harinārāyaṇa.] [1902.] 8°. **14053. eee. 4.(4.)**

HARINĀRĀYAṆA MIŚRA. *See* TULASĪ DĀSA. রামায়ণ [Rāmāyaṇa. A metrical translation by Harinārāyaṇa Miśra.] [1905.] 8°. **14129. cc. 14.**

HARINĀTHA MAJUMDĀR, called KĀṄGĀL. কাঙ্গাল-ফিকিরচাঁদ ফকীরের বাউল সংগীত *etc.* [Bāul saṅgita. Devotional songs.] pp. x. 204, 24, iv. কুমারখালী ১৩১০ [*Kumarkhali*, 1904.] 12°. **14129. bb. 12.(3.)**

—— হরিনাথ গ্রন্থাবলী। [Harinātha-granthāvalī. The collected works of Harinātha, edited by Jaladhara Sena.] Pt. i. pp. iv. 332. কলিকাতা ১৩০৮ [*Calcutta*, 1901.] 8°. **14127. ee. 17.**

—— কাঙ্গাল-সংগীত। [Kāṅgāl-saṅgīta. Religious and devotional songs. Edited, with a biography of the author, by Satīśachandra Majumdār.] pp. ii. 64. কুমারখালী ১৩০৩ [*Kumarkhali*, 1897.] 12°. **14129. a. 49.**

HARINĀTHA SMṚITIBHŪSHAṆA. *See* VIŚVANĀTHA TARKABHŪSHAṆA. বিশ্বনাথ রামায়ণ। [Viśvanātha Rāmāyaṇa. Edited by Harinātha.] [1890.] 8°. **14123. f. 41.**

HARIPADA CHAṬṬOPĀDHYĀYA. দুর্গাসুর। পৌরাণিক নাটক। [Durgāsura. A Pauranic drama.] pp. ii. 276. কলিকাতা ১৯০৮ [*Calcutta*, 1908.] 12°. **14131. aa. 6.**

—— নন্দকুমারের ফাঁসী। [Nandakumārer phāṅsī. A drama on the trial and execution of Nandakumāra. Fourth edition.] ১২৯৬ [*Calcutta*, [1890.] 8°. **14003. c. 1.(2.)**

Forms part of the 2nd edition of vol. i. *of a series of works published by Gauradāsa Vairāgī, under the title* Gauradāsa-granthāvali. *The several works have a continuous pagination.*

HARIPADA MUKHOPĀDHYĀYA. ধর্ম্ম ষোড়শকং নাম শ্রীশ্রীজামালপুরেশ্বর বুড়ারাজমহাস্তোত্রম। [Dharma-shoḍaśaka, or Jāmālpureśvara-burārājastotra. A Sanskrit poem of 16 stanzas in praise of Śiva, preceded by a *maṅgalācharaṇa* of 8 stanzas, and accompanied by a Sanskrit commentary, and Bengali translations.] pp. 28. দাইহাট [*Daihat*, 1901.] *obl.* 12°. **14028. b. 68.(2.)**

HARIPRABHĀ TĀKEDĀ. কেদার-নলিনী। [Kedāra-Nalinī. A biographical account of Nalinībālā, an orphan girl who was rescued from the house of a prostitute by the Dacca Rescue Home, her marriage with Kedāranātha Sāhā of Bogra, and subsequent widowhood.] pp. 90. ঢাকা [*Dacca*, 1908.] 12°. **14127. aa. 39.(2.)**

HARIPRASĀDA CHAKRAVARTĪ. ডাক্তরি অভিধান ... [Ḍāktarī abhidhāna.] A glossary of medical terms in Bengali. pp. 204, 67. ঢাকা ১২৯৬ [*Dacca*, 1890.] 8°. **14125. c. 35.**

—— [Second edition.] pp. iii. 274. ঢাকা ১৯০১ [*Dacca*, 1901.] 12°. **14125. b. 16.**

HARIPRASĀDA MUKHOPĀDHYĀYA. বিচিত্র বঙ্গচিত্র। [Vichitra Vaṅgachitra. A tale, containing sketches of life in Bengal, and exposing the pernicious customs and vices prevalent in modern Hindu society.] pp. iii. 205. কলিকাতা ১২৯৪ [*Calcutta*, 1888.] 8°. **14127. f. 39.**

HARIPRIYA KONCH. তাম্বুল বণিকের উপবীত। [Tāmbūla baṇiker upavīta. An account of the Tāmbūla, or Betel-seller, caste.] pp. 14. কলিকাতা [*Calcutta*, 1907.] 8°. **14125. ee. 33.(2.)**

HARIRĀMA DHARA. ছাত্রবোধ-অভিধান। [Chhātrabodha-abhidhāna. Students' Bengali dictionary. pp. 449. ঢাকা ১৩১৩ [*Dacca*, 1907.] 12°. **14133. a. 16.**

HARIṢCHANDRA, *King of Oudh.* [*Life.*] *See* LOKANĀTHA DATTA. Harish-chandra-charita. 1893. 8°. **14127. b. 38.(4.)**

HARIṢCHANDRA, *of Benares.* The Intellectual Offering, or a collection of poems in honour of the visit of His Royal Highness the Prince of Wales to this country, written by several gentlemen in various languages. Compiled by late Babu Harishchandra. (শ্রীমান যুবরাজের ভারতবর্ষে আগমোপলক্ষে কবিতাবলী।) *Bankipur*, 1889. 8°. **14076. d. 52.**

Separate pagination for each language.

HARIṢCHANDRA BHAṬṬĀCHĀRYA KAVIRATNA. जरावैराग्यम्। [Jarāvairāgya. A Sanskrit poem in 77 stanzas on the disillusionment produced by age; with a commentary by the author. Edited with a preface and metrical version in Bengali by Govinalāla Vandyopādhyāya.] pp. iv. 78. কলিকাতা ১৩০৫ [*Calcutta*, 1898.] 12°. **14072. b. 20.(2.)**

HARIṢCHANDRA DATTA. A treatise on the science of Hindu music. Edited [*i.e.* compiled] by Harishchandra Datta. সঙ্গীত তানসেন। [Saṅgīta Tāna Sena.] pp. 8, 12, 224, 88. কলিকাতা ১২৯৯ [*Calcutta*, 1892.] 8°. **14125. d. 19.**

HARIṢCHANDRA KAVIRATNA. *See* BALLĀLA SENA, *King of Bengal.* বল্লালচরিতম্। [Ballāla-charita. Sanskrit text, with a Bengali translation, notes, *etc.* Revised by Hariṣchandra Kaviratna.] [1889.] 8°. **14058. b. 25.**

HARIṢCHANDRA MUKHOPĀDHYĀYA, *Editor of "The Hindoo Patriot."* [*Life.*] *See* RĀMAGOPĀLA SĀNNYĀLA. হিন্দু পেট্রিয়টের ভূতপূর্ব্ব সম্পাদক হরিশ্চন্দ্র মুখোপাধ্যায়ের জীবনী। The life of Babu Harish Chandra Mukerjee. 1890. 8°. **14127. b. 36.**

HARIṢCHANDRA NIYOGĪ. মালতী-মালা। [Mālatī-mālā. Lyrical poems.] pp. vi. 267. কলিকাতা ১৩০৬ [*Calcutta*, 1899.] 12°. **14129. bb. 2.**

HĀRĪTA. হারীতসংহিতা। [Hārīta-saṃhitā. A code of *dharma* in the shorter recension of 7 *adhyāyas.* Sanskrit text with Bengali translation.] *See* PAÑCHĀNANA TARKARATNA BHAṬṬĀCHĀRYA. ঊনবিংশতি সংহিতা। [Ūnaviṃṣati saṃhitā.] pp. 122-134. [1903.] 8°. **14039. c. 20.**

HARSHADEVA, *King of Thanesar.* Nagananda ... [A Sanskrit drama.] Text with notes by Pundit Nobin Chandra Vidyaratna, and with translations into English and Bengali by a Professor of the Presidency College. नागानन्दम्। pp. 324. *Calcutta*, 1887. 12°. **14079. b. 38.**

—— নাগানন্দ। [Nāgānanda. Translated by Jyotirindranātha Ṭhākura.] pp. 87. কলিকাতা ১৩০৯ [*Calcutta*, 1902.] 12°. **14131. aa. 9.(3.)**

—— প্রিয়দর্শিকা। [Priyadarṣikā. A drama, translated from the Sanskrit by Jyotirindranātha Ṭhākura.] pp. 54. কলিকাতা ১৩১১ [*Calcutta*, 1904.] 12°. **14131. aa. 3.(4.)**

—— The Ratnavali. A Sanskrit drama by Sriharsha. रत्नावली नाटिका।... Edited with English and Bengali translations, a Sanskrit commentary, and Anglo-Sanskrit notes by Sris Chandra Chakravarti. 2 pts. *Dacca, Calcutta* printed, 1902. 12°. **14080. b. 12.**

—— Notes on Ratnávalí. With English and Bengali translations by Satíśa Chandra Vidyábhúshana. pp. 8, xx. 79, 81, 69. *Calcutta*, 1903. 8°. **14085. c. 54.**

HASTĀMALAKA ĀCHĀRYA. हस्तामलकम्। [Hastāmalaka. A Sanskrit philosophical poem, with a commentary ascribed to Ṣaṅkara Āchārya, and a

Bengali translation.] *See* MAHEŚACHANDRA PĀLA. বেদান্তরত্নাবলী [Vedānta-ratnāvalī.] Pt. i., pp. 1-15. [1883, *etc.*] 8°. **14048. bb. 15.**

HĀSYAVADANA GOSVĀMĪ. *See* NAROTTAMA DĀSA. হাটপত্তনের টিকা *etc.* [Hāṭapattana and Prārthanā. With commentaries by Hāsyavadana Gosvāmī.] [1892.] 8°. **14129. c. 41.(3.)**

HEMACHANDRA, *Disciple of Devachandra.* সানুবাদ অভিধানচিন্তামণিঃ। [Abhidhāna-chintāmaṇi. Followed by Jinadeva's Ṣiloñchha and index.. Sanskrit text, edited with a Bengali translation by Nārāyaṇachandra Bhaṭṭāchārya Vidyābhūshaṇa.] pp. ii. ii. 747, iv. *Calcutta,* ১৩১৪ [1907.] 12°. **14092. a. 34.**

HEMACHANDRA DATTA. মহৎ জীবন। [Mahat jīvana. Biographical sketches of eminent Bengali gentlemen and families.] Pt. i. pp. 68. কলিকাতা [*Calcutta,* 1893.] 12°. **14127. a. 54.**

HEMACHANDRA KUṆḌA. সরোজ-বালা। [Sarojabālā. A tale in verse describing a Hindu girl-marriage.] pp. 126. বেনারস [*Benares,* 1891.] 16°. **14127. cc. 5.**

HEMACHANDRA MITRA. নরসিংহ। [Narasiṃha. A metrical adaptation of Byron's 'Manfred.'] pp. 84. কলিকাতা ১২৯৫ [*Calcutta,* 1888.] 12°. **14129. bb. 13.(1.)**

—— বীরাঙ্গনা পত্রোত্তর কাব্য। [Vīrāṅganā-patrottara kāvya. A poem in blank verse, purporting to contain replies to the letters which form the subject of Michael Madhusūdana Datta's poem Vīrāṅganā.] pp. 74. কলিকাতা ১৩০৫ [*Calcutta,* 1898.] 8°. **14129. cc. 1.(1.)**

HEMACHANDRA MUKHOPĀDHYĀYA. *See* MADHUSŪDANA DATTA (M.). সটীক মেঘনাদবধ কাব্য। [Meghanādavadha. Edited, with notes, and a critical and biographical introduction, by Hemachandra Mukhopādhyāya.] [1890.] 8°. **14129. c. 42.**

HEMACHANDRA SENA, *M.D.* A Hand-book of Materia Medica in Bengali. By Hem Chandra Sen. pp. 411, 16. *Calcutta,* 1903. 8°. **14125. cc. 3.**

HEMACHANDRA VANDYOPĀDHYĀYA. হেমচন্দ্রের গ্রন্থাবলী। [Hemachandrer granthāvalī. The complete works of Hemachandra.] pp. 466, 34. কলিকাতা ১৩০৬ [*Calcutta,* 1900.] 8°. **14129. cc. 5.**

HEMACHANDRA VANDYOPĀDHYĀYA (*continued*). হেমচন্দ্রের গ্রন্থাবলী। [Hemachandrer granthāvalī. The complete works of Hemachandra, edited by Upendranātha Mukhopādhyāya.] pp. ii. 431. কলিকাতা ১৩১৪ [*Calcutta,* 1906.] 8°. **14127. g. 16.**

—— Kabitabalee. A poetical selection by Babu Hem Chandra Banerji . . . কবিতাবলী। pp. 36, 91. *Calcutta,* 1898. 12°. **14129. a. 28.(5.)**

—— রোমিও-জুলিয়েত। [Romio-Juliyet. A play based on Shakspere's "Romeo and Juliet."] pp. 8, 189. কলিকাতা ১৩০১ [*Calcutta,* 1895.] 8°. **14131. a. 36.(2.)**

HEMACHANDRA VIDYĀRATNA. *See* MAHĀBHĀRATA.—*Bhagavadgītā.* শ্রীমদ্ভগবদ্গীতা। [Bhagavadgītā. With a Bengali translation by Hemachandra Vidyāratna.] [1895.] 16°. **14060. b. 15.**

—— *See* VĀLMĪKI. হিন্দুশাস্ত্র। . . . রামায়ণ। [Rāmāyaṇa. A prose version by Hemachandra Vidyāratna.] [1896.] 8°. **14085. c. 45.(vol. ii.)**

HEMENDRANĀTHA SIṂHA. প্রেম। [Prema. A treatise on love, worldly and religious.] pp. iii. 182. কলিকাতা ১৩০২ [*Calcutta,* 1895.] 12°. **14125. e. 26.(5.)**

HEMENDRAPRASĀDA GHOSHA. অধঃপতন উপন্যাস। [Adhaḥpatana. A tale describing the gradual downfall of an educated Bengali youth through an unfortunate marriage.] pp. 275. *Calcutta,* ১৩০৬ [1899.] 12°. **14127. cc. 14.**

HILL (SAMUEL JOHN). *See* BIBLE.—*Psalms.* ইব্রানি জবানহইতে তরজমা করা জব্বুরের কেতাব। The Psalms of David in Musalmán Bengali. [Translated by S. J. Hill.] 1858. 8°. **3089. d. 33.**

HINDU SACRED PICTURES. হিন্দুধর্ম্ম সম্বন্ধীয় চিত্রাবলী। [Hindudharma sambandhīya chitrāvalī.] . . . Hindu Sacred Pictures. [With verses descriptive of each.] Series A. Nos. 1-12. *Calcutta,* 1884-1886. 4°. **14133. gg. 7.**

HINDU WORSHIP. An Apology for the present system of Hindoo worship. Written in the Bengali language [by Rādhākānta Deva] and accompanied by an English translation [by Sir W. H. Macnaghten]. pp. 50. *Calcutta,* 1817. 8°. **14123. f. 51.**

The English translation only.

HĪRĀLĀL ḌHOL. *See* Nāga Bhaṭṭa. কামরত্ন তন্ত্রম্। [Kāmaratna tantra. Edited by Hīrālāl Ḍhol.] [1885.] 8°. **14033. bb. 21.**

—— *See* Sadānanda Yogīndra. সটীক সানুবাদ বেদান্ত-সার। [Vedāntasāra. Sanskrit text and commentary, with a Bengali translation. Edited by Hīrālāl Ḍhol.] [1903.] 12°. **14048. b. 41.**

HĪRENDRANĀTHA DATTA. *See* Vālmīki. কৃত্তিবাসী রামায়ণ। [Rāmāyaṇa. Translated by Kṛittivāsa. Collated from ancient manuscripts, and edited with a glossary and index of obsolete words by Hīrendranātha Datta.] [1904, *etc.*] 8°. **14129. cc. 15.**

—— গীতায় ঈশ্বরবাদ। [Gītāy Īśvaravāda. The philosophy of the Bhagavadgītā on the worship of Īśvara, and its relationship with the various schools of Hindu philosophy.] pp. ii. 398. কলিকাতা ১৩১২ [*Calcutta,* 1906.] 12°. **14123. e. 36.**

HITOPADEŚA. হিতোপদেশ [Hitopadeśa. Another edition of the Bengali translation by Mṛityuñjaya Śarmā, with occasional Sanskrit verse.] pp. 345. কলিকাতা ১৭৪৫ [*Calcutta,* 1824.] 8°. **14127. e. 39.**

—— Hitopadesha .... [Sanskrit text] with English and Bengali translations. Selected and compiled with elaborate notes [in Sanskrit], by Barada Kanta Vidyaratna. Fourth edition. হিতোপদেশঃ। pp. ii. 145, 38, 66. *Calcutta,* 1883. 8°. **14072. ccc. 6.**

—— হিতোপদেশঃ [Hitopadeśa. Sanskrit text, with a Bengali translation in prose and verse, notes, prefatory remarks, and appendices, by Tārākumāra Kaviratna.] pp. xii. vi. x. 276, 25, 34. কলিকাতা ১২৯৫ [*Calcutta,* 1889.] 8°. **14076. d. 43.**

—— হিতোপদেশীয় সুবৃহৎ মিত্রলাভঃ [Hitopadeśa. Mitralābha, or Book I. Sanskrit text, with grammatical analyses and notes, Bengali interpretations, *etc.* Edited by Gurunātha Vidyānidhi. Second edition.] pp. 335. কলিকাতা ১৩১২ [*Calcutta,* 1906.] 8°. **14085. e. 57.**

Wanting pp. 1-12.

HOLLE (Martin). *See* Śaratkumāra Ghosha. Sarath Kumar Gosh Indische Nächte. [Translated into German by Martin Holle.] [1906.] 8°. **14128. a. 7.**

HOMER. হেক্টর-বধ। [Hekṭar-vadha. The death of Hector, translated into Bengali by Michael Madhusūdana Datta from the Greek text of Homer's Iliad.] pp. 106. কলিকাতা ১৩১৪ [*Calcutta,* 1907.] 12°. **14128. a. 27.**

HOOGHLY.—*Public Library.* হুগলিস্থ সাধারণ পুস্তকাগারের কার্য্য নির্ব্বাহার্থ নিয়ম। [Rules for the management of the Public Library at Hooghly.] pp. 7. [*Hooghly,* 1870 ?] 8°. **14125. ee. 25(1.)**

HṚISHĪKEŚA ŚĀSTRĪ. *See* Purāṇas.—*Selections.* হিন্দুশাস্ত্র। ... অষ্টাদশ পুরাণ। [Ashṭādaśa-purāṇa. Selections from the 18 Purāṇas, with Bengali translations, and a brief account of each. Compiled by Āśutosha Śāstrī and Hṛishīkeśa Śāstrī.] [1897.] 8°. **14085. c. 45.(vol. ii.)**

—— *See* Śāṇḍilya. শাণ্ডিল্যসূত্রম্। [Śāṇḍilya-sūtra. Edited with a Bengali translation by Hṛishīkeśa Śāstrī.] [1906.] 8°. **14049. b. 41.**

—— বাঙ্গালা ব্যাকরণ। [Bāṅgālā vyākaraṇa. A grammar of the Bengali language.] pp. 210. কলিকাতা ১৩০৭ [*Calcutta,* 1900.] 12°. **14131. e. 35.**

HUGO (Victor Marie), *Viscount.* *See* Jyotirindranātha Ṭhākura. ফরাসী-প্রসূন। [Pharāsī-prasūna. Selections from the writings of Victor Hugo and other French authors, translated into Bengali.] [1904.] 12°. **14131. d. 48.**

ḤUSAIN ibn MAS'ŪD, *al-Farrā al-Baghawī.* হদিস-পূর্ব্ববিভাগ। ... মেশ্‌কাত মসাবিহ হইতে অনুবাদিত *etc.* [Mishkāt al-maṣābīḥ. A collection of Muhammadan traditions by al-Farrā al-Baghawī, redacted by Muḥammad al-Khaṭīb. Translated into Bengali from the Arabic original, together with notes selected from 'Abd al-Ḥaḳḳ's Persian commentary entitled Ashi'at al-lama'āt, by Giriśachandra Sena.] কলিকাতা ১৮১৩ [*Calcutta,* 1892, *etc.*] 8°. **14123. h. 21.**

IMDĀD al-ḤAḲḲ. আঁখি-জল। [Āṅkhijal. Lyrics.] pp. 41.] কলিকাতা ১৩০৬ [*Calcutta,* 1900.] 12°. **14129. bb. 8.(4.)**

'INĀYAT ḤUSAIN ibn NAWĀZISH AḤMAD. ফতুহশাম। [Futūḥ al-Shām. The conquest of Syria by the Muhammadans, translated into verse from 'Ināyat Ḥusain's Hindustani version of the Arabic history of Wāḳidī by Munshī Pīr Muḥammad and Maulavī Muḥammad 'Abbās 'Alī.] 3 pts. কলিকাতা ১৩১০-১১ [*Calcutta,* 1905.] Fol. **14127. bbb. 6.**

INDIA.—*Eastern Bengal and Assam.* Government Gazette.—Eastern Bengal and Assam. Vernacular Edition. গবর্ণমেন্ট গেজেট, পূর্ব্ববঙ্গ এবং আসাম। *Shillong*, 1905, *etc.* Fol. **14125. aa. 3.**

In progress. Wanting No. 10 *of* 1907.

—— *Government of India.* হেজাজের তীর্থযাত্রিদের নিমিত্ত সাধারণ উপদেশ। [Rules and Regulations of the Government of India regarding the transport of pilgrims to Arabia.] pp. 109. কলিকাতা ১৮৯৮ [*Calcutta*, 1898.] 8°. **14125. a. 28.(1.)**

—— *Legislative Council.* India Act ... ভারতবর্ষের গবর্ণমেন্ট। [A collection of Acts passed by the Governor-General of India in Council from 1897 to 1902. Translated by Chandranātha Vasu.] [*Calcutta*, 1897-1902.] 8°. **14125. a. 32.**

—— Bengal Act. বঙ্গদেশের গবর্ণমেন্ট। [A collection of Acts passed by the Lieutenant-Governor of Bengal from 1897 to 1900. Translated by Chandranātha Vasu.] [*Calcutta*, 1897-1900.] 8°. **14125. a. 33.**

—— Bengali version of the Indian Penal Code, Act xlv. of 1860, as modified up to the end of the year 1899. ভারতবর্ষের দণ্ডবিধির আইন। pp. 42, 198. কলিকাতা ১৯০০ [*Calcutta*, 1900.] 8°. **14125. a. 28.(4.)**

—— Bengali version of the Indian Court-Fees Act, Act vii. of 1870, as modified up to the 1st October, 1899. ভারতবর্ষের আদালতের রসুমবিষয়ক আইন। pp. 6, 77. কলিকাতা ১৯০০ [*Calcutta*, 1900.] 8°. **14125. a. 28.(2.)**

—— Bengali version of the Indian Evidence Act, Act i. of 1872, as modified up to the 1st April, 1899. ভারতবর্ষের সাক্ষ্য বিষয়ক আইন। pp. 13, 83. কলিকাতা ১৮০০ [*Calcutta*, 1900.] 8°. **14125. a. 28.(3.)**

—— Bengali version [by Chandranātha Vasu] of the Assam Labour and Emigration Act, Act vi. of 1901. আসামে মজুরীকরণ ও মজুরদের গমনবিষয়ক আইন। pp. 18, 110. কলিকাতা ১৯০১ [*Calcutta*, 1901.] 8°. **14125. a. 31.**

—— *Linguistic Survey.* Linguistic Survey of India. Vol. v. Indo-Aryan Family. Eastern Group. Part i. Specimens of the Bengali and Assamese Languages. Compiled and edited by G. A. Grierson. pp. iv. 446. *Calcutta*, 1903. 4°. **759. k. 2.**

INDRAJĀLA. ইন্দ্রজালং। [Indrajāla. A Sanskrit work on magic, with a Bengali translation and appendix.] pp. 26. [1891.] *See* PERIODICAL PUBLICATIONS.—*Calcutta.* অরুণোদয়। [Aruṇodaya.] Pt. i., no. 11. [1890, *etc.*] 4°. **14133. g. 16.**

INDUMĀDHAVA MALLIKA. চীন ভ্রমণ। [Chīnbhramaṇa. Travels in China.] pp. ii. 187. [*Calcutta*, 1906.] 12°. **14127. aa. 36.**

INDUPRABHĀ, *Ṣrīmatī.* বৈভ্রাজিকা। [Vaibhrājikā. Miscellaneous poems.] pp. v. 278. কলিকাতা ১৩১০ [*Calcutta*, 1903.] 12°. **14129. a. 35.**

ĪṢĀNACHANDRA GHAṬAKA RĀJAṢIROMAṆI. *See* DĪNABANDHU GHAṬAKA KULABHŪSHAṆA. কায়স্থ-কারিকা ও বংশাবলি। [Kāyastha-kārikā. Compiled with the assistance of Īṣānachandra Ghaṭaka.] [1886, *etc.*] 4°. **14123. i. 11.**

ĪṢĀNACHANDRA RĀYA CHAUDHURĪ. আর্য্যধর্ম্ম-তত্ত্ব। [Āryadharmatattva. An exposition of the principles of the Hindu religion.] pp. iv. 291. কলিকাতা ১৩০৫ [*Calcutta*, 1898.] 12°. **14123. e. 24.(2.)**

ĪṢĀNACHANDRA VASU. *See* DUḤKHĪṢYĀMA DĀSA. গোবিন্দমঙ্গল। [Govindamaṅgala. Edited, with a life of the author, by Īṣānachandra Vasu.] [1886.] 8°. **14129. c. 37.**

—— *See* RĀJANĀRĀYAṆA VASU. Brahmo Catechism ... Translated into English by Babu Eshan Chunder Bose. 1890. 16°. **14123. c.**

—— শ্রীমন্মহর্ষি দেবেন্দ্রনাথ ঠাকুর মহোদয়ের জীবন বৃত্তান্তের স্বল্প পরিচয়। [Ṣrīmanmaharshi Devendranātha Ṭhākura. A life of the Brahmist preacher Devendranātha Ṭhākura.] pp. 128. *Calcutta*, 1902. 12°. **14127. aa. 24.**

ĪṢĀNA NĀGARA. শ্রী অদ্বৈত-প্রকাশ। [Advaita-prakāṣa. A poem in 22 *adhyāyas* on the life of Advaitāchārya, written by his companion and disciple Īṣāna Nāgara, in Ṣaka 1490. Edited, with a short account of the author, by Achyutacharaṇa Chaudhurī.] pp. xii. 261. কলিকাতা, গৌরাব্দ ৪১২ [*Calcutta*, 1897.] 12°. **14129. a. 46.(1.)**

ISMĀ'ĪL, *Munshī.* নুরল এছলাম। [Nūr al-Islām. The principles of Muhammadan belief and ceremonial observances, in verse.] pp. 400. ঢাকা ১৩১৪ [*Dacca*, 1907.] 8°. **14123. h. 37.**

ĪṢVARACHANDRA GUPTA. ঈশ্বরচন্দ্র গুপ্তের গ্রন্থাবলী [Granthāvalī. The poems of Īṣvarachandra Gupta, edited by Kālīprasanna Vidyāratna.] pp. vi. 170. কলিকাতা ১৩০৬ [*Calcutta*, 1900.] 8°. **14129. e. 23.(1.)**

—— গ্রন্থাবলী। [Granthāvalī. Another, and more complete, collection of the works of Īṣvarachandra Gupta, with a life of the poet by Bankimchandra Chaṭṭopādhyāya. Edited by Muṇīndrakṛishṇa Gupta.] 2 vols. কলিকাতা ১৩০৮ [*Calcutta*, 1901.] 8°. **14129. e. 24.**

—— কবিতাসংগ্রহ। [Kavitāsaṅgraha. The poetical works of Īṣvarachandra Gupta. Edited, with a life of the poet, by Baṅkimchandra Chaṭṭopādhyāya.] 2 pts. কলিকাতা ১২৯২-৯৩ [*Calcutta*, 1885-86.] 12°. **14129. a. 27.**

ĪṢVARACHANDRA VIDYĀRATNA. মুক্তিপ্রদীপঃ। [Muktipradīpa. Opinions of learned Hindu pandits on the surest plan of securing salvation, consisting chiefly of quotations from Sanskrit works, with accompanying Bengali prose translations. Compiled by Īṣvarachandra Vidyāratna with the aid of Jānakīnātha Ṣukla.] pp. 25. মুর্শিদাবাদ ১৮০৯ [*Murshidabad*, 1888.] 8°. **14123. f. 33.(3.)**

ĪṢVARACHANDRA VIDYĀSĀGARA. [*Life.*] *See* CHAṆḌĪCHARAṆA VANDYOPĀDHYĀYA. বিদ্যাসাগর। [Vidyāsāgara.] 1895. 8°. **14127. bb. 1.**

—— *See* KĀLIDĀSA. শকুন্তলা। [Ṣakuntalā. A prose adaptation of the Sanskrit drama by Īṣvarachandra Vidyāsāgara.] [1907.] 8°. **14131. b. 27.**

—— *See* KĀLĪSAHĀYA RĀYA CHAUDHURĪ. Rijubyākhyá, or A complete key to [Īṣvarachandra Vidyāsāgara's] Rijupatha. 1879. 12°. **14085. b.**

—— [*Life.*] *See* NĀRĀYAṆA VANDYOPĀDHYĀYA. বিদ্যাসাগর চরিত। [Vidyāsāgara-charita.] 1893. 12°. **14127. b. 49.(2.)**

—— *See* RAJANĪKĀNTA GUPTA. প্রতিভা। [Pratibhā. A review of the works of Īṣvarachandra Vidyāsāgara.] [1896.] 12°. **14131. d. 35.**

—— *See* ṢAMBHUCHANDRA VIDYĀRATNA. ভ্রমনিরাস। [Bhramanirāsa. A criticism on Chaṇḍīcharaṇa's life of Īṣvarachandra Vidyāsāgara, pointing out inaccurate statements made in that biography.] [1895.] 8°. **14131. d. 31.**

ĪṢVARACHANDRA VIDYĀSĀGARA (*continued*). [*Life.*] *See* ṢAMBHUCHANDRA VIDYĀRATNA. বিদ্যাসাগর-জীবনচরিত। [Vidyāsāgara-jīvanacharita.] [1891.] 8°. **14127. b. 49.(1.)**

—— [*Life.*] *See* VIHĀRĪLĀLA SARKĀR. বিদ্যাসাগর। [Vidyāsāgara.] [1895.] 12°. **14127. a. 50.**

—— *See* YADUNĀTHA CHAṬṬOPĀDHYĀYA. Riju britti, or A complete key to the Rijupatha [of Īṣvarachandra Vidyāsāgara.] 1880. 12°. **14085. b.**

—— The Exile of Sītā. Translated from the elegant Bengali [Sītār vanavāsa] ... by H. Jane Harding. pp. 96. *London*, [1904.] 8°. **14127. ee. 21.**

ĪṢVARA KRISHṆA. The Sánkhya Káriká ... also the ... commentary of Gaurapada translated [into English] and illustrated ... by H. H. Wilson ... and translated into Bengali [text and commentary] by Debendra Nath Gosvami. 2 pts. *Sansk. Eng.* and *Beng. Calcutta*, 1887. 8°. **14048. bb. 40.**

—— সাংখ্য-দর্শনম্। মহর্ষি-কপিল-মতম। ঈশ্বরকৃষ্ণাচার্য্য-প্রণীত কারিকাত্মকম্। [Sāṅkhyadarṣana. The Sanskrit text of the Sāṅkhyakārikā with the commentary Tattvakaumudī of Vāchaspati Miṣra. Edited with a supercommentary called Pūrṇimā, and Bengali translations and explanations of the text by Pañchānana Tarkaratna.] pp. iv. 229. কলিকাতা ১৩১০ [*Calcutta*, 1903.] 8°. **14049. b. 17.**

—— সাংখ্যতত্ত্ব-কৌমুদী। [Sāṅkhyatattvakaumudī. The Sanskrit text of the Sāṅkhyakārikā, and the commentary of Vāchaspati Miṣra. Edited with Sanskrit grammatical explanations, and Bengali translations and notes, by Pūrṇachandra Vedāntachuñchu.] pp. ii. iii. iii. 254, 3. সৈদাবাদ ১৯০১ [*Saidabad*, 1901.] 8°. **14048. dd. 34.(1.)**

ĪṢVARA SARKĀR. সাগর যাত্রা। [Sāgara-yātrā. A humorous sketch, in verse, of a visit by a woman and her niece to a place of pilgrimage on the seashore.] pp. 16. ১৭৮৬ [*Calcutta*, 1869.] 16°. **14129. b.**

JAGADĀNANDA, *Vaishṇava poet. See* KĀLIDĀSA NĀTHA. বৈষ্ণব কবি জগদানন্দ। [Vaishṇava kavi Jagadānanda. An account of the poet Jagadānanda and his writings.] [1898.] 8°. **14133. f. 18.**

—— শ্রীজগদানন্দ-পদাবলী। [Jagadānanda-padāvalī. The poems of Jagadānanda, a Vaishṇava poet of the 18th century. Edited with notes and a life of the author by Kālidāsa Nātha.] pp. ii. 12, 82. কলিকাতা ১৩০৬ [*Calcutta*, 1899.] 12°. **14129. a. 45.**

Wanting pp. 77-80: pp. 65-68 are in duplicate.

JAGADBANDHU MAITRA. মহাত্মা কেশব চন্দ্র সেনের সংক্ষিপ্ত জীবনী। [Mahātmā Keṣavachandra Sener saṃkshipta jīvanī. A short account of the life of Keṣavachandra Sena.] pp. xviii. 72. কলিকাতা ১২৯৩ [*Calcutta*, 1886.] 12°. **14127. a. 29.(2.)**

JAGADĪṢVARA GUPTA. চৈতন্যলীলামৃত। [Chaitanya-līlāmṛita. The life of Chaitanya, compiled from Sanskrit and Bengali works.] 2 pts. pp. iv. 324; viii. 304. কলিকাতা ১২৯৭ [*Calcutta*, 1890.] 8°. **14127. b. 44.**

JAGADRĀMA RĀYA. *See* PAÑCHKAṚI GHOSHA. জগৎরাম রায়ের রামায়ণ। [Jagadrāma Rāyer Rāmāyaṇa. A paper on the Rāmāyaṇa of Jagadrāma Rāya.] [1895.] 8°. **14133. f. 18.**

—— দুর্গা-পঞ্চরাত্রি। বা শ্রীরামচন্দ্রের দুর্গোৎসব। [Durgā-pañcharātrī, or Rāmachandrer durgotsava. A poem on the worship of Durgā, being an excerpt from the Rāmāyaṇa of Jagadrāma. Edited by Kāṣīvilāsa Vandyopādhyāya.] pp. ii. 105. *Calcutta*, ১৩০৮ [1901.] 8°. **14129. e. 25.(1.)**

—— অষ্ট কাণ্ডে সম্পূর্ণ জগদ্রামী-রামায়ণ। [Rāmāyaṇa. A metrical version of the Sanskrit epic. Edited by Kāṣīvilāsa Vandyopādhyāya.] pp. vii. 587. কলিকাতা ১৩১৩ [*Calcutta*, 1906.] 8°. **14129. e. 32.**

JAGANMOHANA TARKĀLAṄKĀRA. *See* ṢAṄKARĀNANDA, *Disciple of Ānandātmā*. আত্মপুরাণ। [Ātmapurāṇa. With a Bengali translation by Jaganmohana Tarkālaṅkāra.] [1835.] 8°. **14048. e. 13.**

JAGANNĀRĀYAṆA MUKHOPĀDHYĀYA. নূতন অভিধান। [Nūtana abhidhāna. A small Bengali dictionary.] pp. 435. কলিকাতা ১২৪৫ [*Calcutta*, 1838.] 12°. **14133. a. 12.**

JAGANNĀTHA ṢUKLA. *See* TULASĪ DĀSA. তুলসীদাস কৃত রামায়ণ। [Rāmāyaṇa. Hindi text, with a Bengali translation and notes by Jagannātha Ṣukla.] [1884, *etc.*] 8°. **14158. f. 23.**

JAGANNĀTHA VIDYĀRṆAVA. *See* PURĀṆAS.—*Dharmapurāṇa*. বৃহদ্ধর্মপুরাণম্। [Bṛihad-dharma-purāṇa. With a Bengali translation by Jagannātha and others.] [1908.] 8°. **14016. dd. 28.(1.)**

—— *See* PURĀṆAS.—*Padmapurāṇa*. পদ্মপুরাণম্। পাতালখণ্ডম্। [Pātālakhaṇḍa. With a Bengali translation by Jagannātha and others.] [1903.] 8°. **14018. f. 20.**

JAGATTĀRIṆĪ DĀSĪ. লাট কর্জ্জন। [Lāṭ Karjan. A poem in eulogy of the administration of Lord Curzon.] pp. 27. কলিকাতা ১৩১২ [*Calcutta*, 1906.] 12°. **14129. bb. 17.(4.)**

JAHARLĀL DHARA. শঙ্কর-বিজয় নাটক। [Ṣaṅkara-vijaya nāṭaka. A drama dealing with the main incidents of the life and teachings of Ṣaṅkara Āchārya.] pp. 116. কলিকাতা ১৩০৪ [*Calcutta*, 1897.] 12°. **14131. a. 40.(7.)**

JALADHARA SENA. *See* HARINĀTHA MAJUMDĀR, called KĀṄGĀL. হরিনাথ গ্রন্থাবলী। [Granthāvalī. Edited by Jaladhara Sena.] [1901, *etc.*] 8°. **14127. ee. 17.**

JALĀL al-DĪN, *Rūmī*. *See* GIRIṢACHANDRA SENA. তত্ত্বরত্নমালা। [Tattvaratnamālā. A collection of Ṡūfī anecdotes taken from the Maṣnawī of Jalāl al-Dīn, Rūmī.] [1907.] 8°. **14123. h. 40.**

JAMĪDĀR. জমীদার ও রায়তের গল্প। [Jamīdār o rāyater galpa, or The story of the landlord and his tenant. A Christian allegory.] pp. 18. কলিকাতা ১৮৭২ [*Calcutta*, 1872.] 16°. **14123. a. 23.(2.)**

JANĀB 'ĀLĪ, *Son of Amīr, of Dhasa*. *See* MUḤAMMAD 'ABD al-RAḤMĀN KHĀN. আখলাকল আওলীয়া *etc.* [Akhlāk al-auliyā. Translated into verse by Munshī Janāb 'Ālī.] [1901.] 8°. **14123. h. 29.(2.)**

JĀNAKĪNĀTHA BASĀK. মণিপুর-প্রহেলিকা। [Maṇipura-prahelikā. An account of Manipur and the outbreak of 1890.] pp. vi. 166. কলিকাতা ১২৯৮ [*Calcutta*, 1892.] 8°. **14127. b. 48.(2.)**

JĀNAKĪNĀTHA BHAṬṬĀCHĀRYA. প্রবেশিকার ভ্রমসংশোধনীর ভ্রমপ্রদর্শনী। Bhrama-pradarsani. [A defence of Maheṣachandra Nyāyaratna's Sanskrit Entrance Examination Course, being a reply to the Bhrama-saṃṣodhanī of Chandrodaya Bhaṭṭāchārya.] pp. 88. কলিকাতা [*Calcutta*, 1887.] 12°. **14131. d. 23.(2.)**

JĀNAKĪNĀTHA PĀLA, *B.L.*, *Vāchaspati*. শ্রীরূপ-সনাতন। জীবনী ও শিক্ষা। [Ṣrīrūpa-Sanātana. The lives of Rūpa Gosvāmī and Sanātana Gosvāmī.] pp. iv. 138. কুমারখালী ১৩১১ [*Kumarkhali*, 1904.] 12°. **14127. a. 45.(4.)**

JĀNAKĪNĀTHA ŚUKLA. *See* ĪŚVARACHANDRA VIDYĀRATNA. মুক্তিপ্রদীপঃ। [Muktipradīpa. Compiled with the aid of Jānakīnātha Śukla.] [1888.] 8°. **14128. f. 33.(3.)**

JĀNAKĪNĀTHA VASU. নাট্য-বিকার [Nāṭya-vikāra] or The Dramatic delirium. [A drama.] pp. 48. কলিকাতা ১২৯৮ [*Calcutta*, 1891.] 12°. **14131. a. 33.(1.)**

JĀNAKĪVALLABHA SENA, *of Rangpur.* [*Life.*] *See* RAJANĪKĀNTA BHAṬṬĀCHĀRYA. জানকীবল্লভ চরিত। [Jānakīvallabha-charita.] [1891.] 8°. **14127. b. 38.(2.)**

JATINDRA NATH SEN. *See* YATĪNDRANĀTHA SENA.

JAYADEVA, *Son of Bhojadeva.* [*Life.*] *See* RAJANĪKĀNTA GUPTA. জয়দেবচরিত। [Jayadeva-charita.] [1889.] 12°. **14131. d. 21.(2.)**

—— [*Life.*] *See* VANAMĀLĪ DĀSA. জয়দেব-চরিত। [Jayadeva-charita.] [1900.] 8°. **14133. ff. 2.**

—— গীতগোবিন্দ। [Gītagovinda. Sanskrit text and commentary, with a Bengali translation, and introductory essay by Harimohana Vidyābhūshaṇa.] pp. xxvi. 90, 62. কলিকাতা ১২৯৩ [*Calcutta*, 1887.] 8°. **14070. c. 46.**

—— মহাকবি জয়দেবের গীতগোবিন্দের প্রাকৃত পদ্যানুবাদ। [Gītagovinda. A metrical translation by Giridhara. Edited, with notes and an account of the life and works of Jayadeva, by Śyāmalāla Basāk.] pp. xiii. 87, iv. কলিকাতা ১৮১০ [*Calcutta*, 1889.] 12°. **14129. a. 21.(2.)**

—— শ্রীশ্রীগীতগোবিন্দম্। [Gītagovinda. Sanskrit text, with an anonymous Sanskrit commentary styled Bālabodhinī, and a Bengali introduction and translation of the text.] pp. 390. *Calcutta*, [1901.] 16°. **14076. a. 27.**

—— শ্রীশ্রীগীতগোবিন্দ। [Gītagovinda. A metrical translation by Pārvatīcharaṇa Mukhopādhyāya.] pp. v. 61. কলিকাতা ১৩১২ [*Calcutta*, 1906.] 12°. **14129. bb. 28.(2.)**

JAYAGOPĀLA GOSVĀMĪ. রত্নযুগল। [Ratnayugala. A novel, depicting Bengali social life.] pp. ii. 300. কলিকাতা ১৩০৮ [*Calcutta*, 1901.] 8°. **14127. ee. 15.(1.)**

JAYAGOPĀLA TARKĀLAṄKĀRA. [*Life.*] *See* VISHṆUCHANDRA BHAṬṬĀCHĀRYA. ৺ জয় গোপাল তর্কালঙ্কার মহাশয়ের জীবনচরিত। [Jayagopāla Tarkālaṅkāra-jīvanacharita.] [1901.] 12°. **14127. aa. 21.**

JAYAKṚISHṆA DĀSA, *Kavi.* *See* AMBIKĀCHARAṆA GUPTA. কবি জয়কৃষ্ণ দাস। [Kavi Jayakṛishṇa Dāsa. An account of the poet Jayakṛishṇa Dāsa and his writings.] [1907.] 8°. **14133. f. 18.**

JAYAKṚISHṆA MUKHOPĀDHYĀYA. [*Life.*] *See* AMBIKĀCHARAṆA GUPTA. জয় কৃষ্ণ-চরিত। [Jayakṛishṇa-charita.] [1901.] 8°. **14127. bb. 16.(2.)**

JAYĀNANDA MIŚRA, *Son of Subuddhi Miśra.* *See* NAGENDRANĀTHA VASU. কবি জয়ানন্দ ও চৈতন্য-মঙ্গল। [Kavi Jayānanda o Chaitanya-maṅgala. An account of the poet Jayānanda and his Chaitanya-maṅgala; with copious extracts from the poem.] [1897.] 8°. **14133. f. 18.**

—— শ্রীচৈতন্যমঙ্গল। [Chaitanya-maṅgala. A poem on the life of Chaitanya.] pp. 152. ১৩০৭-১০ [1901-04.] *See* PERIODICAL PUBLICATIONS.—*Calcutta.* প্রাচীন বাঙ্গালা গ্রন্থাবলী। [Prāchīna Bāṅgālā granthāvalī.] Nos. 2-14. [1900, *etc.*] 8°. **14133. ff. 2.**

JAYANĀRĀYAṆA, *Lālā.* *See* ĀNANDANĀTHA RĀYA. কবি লালা জয়নারায়ণ। [Kavi Lālā Jayanārāyaṇa. An article on the life and poems of Lālā Jayanārāyaṇa.] [1900.] 8°. **14133. f. 18.**

JAYANĀRĀYAṆA, *Rājakavi, of Benares.* *See* VYOMAKEŚA MUSTAFĪ. রাজকবি জয়নারায়ণ। [Rājakavi Jayanārāyaṇa. The life and poems of Jayanārāyaṇa.] [1900.] 8°. **14133. f. 18.**

JAYANĀTHA CHAUDHURĪ. রাজা রামমোহন রায়ের ধর্ম্মমত। [Rājā Rāmamohana Rāyer dharmamata.] . . . The religious views of Raja Ram Mohan Roy. pp. viii. 306. ময়মনসিংহ ১৮৯২ [*Mymensingh*, 1892.] 12°. **14123. c. 27.**

JĪMŪTAVĀHANA. জীমূতবাহনকৃত দায়ভাগঃ। [Dāyabhāga. Sanskrit text, with Kṛishṇa Tarkālaṅkāra's commentary. Edited, with a Bengali translation of the text, by Nīlakamala Vidyānidhi.] pp. 276. কলিকাতা ১৩০৪ [*Calcutta*, 1898.] 8°. **14038. c. 49.**

JĪVA GOSVĀMĪ. [*Life.*] *See* AGHORANĀTHA CHAṬṬOPĀDHYĀYA. ভক্ত-চরিতামৃত। [Bhakta-charitāmṛita.] [1894.] 12°. **14127. aa. 2.(2.)**

JĪVA GOSVĀMĪ (*continued*). গোপালচম্পূঃ। [Gopāla-champū. A Sanskrit work in prose and verse on the life of Kṛishṇa, with a short Sanskrit commentary by Vīrachandra Gosvāmī. Edited, with a Bengali prose translation, by Rāmanārāyaṇa Vidyāratna.] 6 pts. মুর্শিদাবাদ। ৪০৫ চৈতন্যাব্দ ১৩০০ [*Murshidabad*, 1890-93.] 8°. **14076. d. 45.**

Incomplete: breaking off at p. 474.

—— হরিনামামৃতম্। [Harināmāmṛita. A Sanskrit Vaishṇava work on Sanskrit grammar, with a commentary. Edited, with a Bengali translation, by Rāmanārāyaṇa Vidyāratna.] 12 pts. মুরশিদাবাদ ১২৯১-৯৯ [*Murshidabad*, 1884-94.] 8°. **14093. b. 12.**

Incomplete: breaking off at p. 800.

JĪVANAKṚISHṆA MUKHOPĀDHYĀYA. হরিদাসী। [Haridāsī. A tale, describing the evils of drink.] pp. 61. কলিকাতা ১৩০২ [*Calcutta*, 1896.] 12°. **14127. d. 42.(3.)**

—— সত্য-সরলা নাটক। [Satya-Saralā nāṭaka. A social drama.] pp. 161. কলিকাতা ১২৯৭ [*Calcutta*, 1890.] 12°. **14131. a. 31.(1.)**

JĪVANAKṚISHṆA SENA. সমর্থকোষ। বাঙ্গালা অভিধান। [Samarthakosha. A Bengali-English and English and Bengali Dictionary. [With a dictionary of Materia Medica, and a Pauranic encyclopædia. Compiled by Jīvanakṛishṇa Sena as far as no. 52, and continued from no. 53 (p. 833) by Anupakṛishṇa Mitra and Lalitakṛishṇa Vasu.] কলিকাতা [*Calcutta*, 1884, *etc.*] 4°. **14133. c. 4.**

In progress. Wanting pp. 829-832.

JÑĀNACHANDRA BASĀK. সুরাপান বা বিষপান।... [Surāpāna.] A hand-book of temperance. pp. vi. 245. কলিকাতা ১৮৮৮ [*Calcutta*, 1888.] 12°. **14125. e. 22.**

JÑĀNADĀSA. নিকুঞ্জ-সাজান। [Nikuñja-sājān. A poem on Rādhā and Kṛishṇa. Edited by Tārakeśvara Bhaṭṭāchārya.] ১৩০২ [1902.] *See* ACADEMIES, *etc.*—Calcutta.—*Bengal Academy of Literature.* সাহিত্য-পরিষৎ-পত্রিকা। [Sāhitya-parishat-patrikā.] Vol. ix., no. 2. [1894, *etc.*] 8°. **14133. f. 18.**

JÑĀNĀNANDA DEVA, *Yogāchārya, Avadhūta.* সিদ্ধান্তদর্শন। [Siddhāntadarśana. A series of studies tending to reconcile dualism with monism by an examination of numerous passages from Sanskrit authors. Preceded by the Ānanda-laharī of Śaṅkara Āchārya.] pp. 22, 275. কলিকাতা নবদ্বীপ ১৩০৪ [*Calcutta* printed, *Nadia*, 1898.] 12°. **14048. b. 33.(5.)**

JÑĀNANIDHI BHAṬṬĀCHĀRYA. কৌতুক কথা অর্থাৎ হাস্য রসোদ্দীপক গল্প। [Kautuka-kathā. A collection of amusing tales and anecdotes, illustrative of Bengali wit and humour.] Pt. i. pp. 194. কলিকাতা ১২৯১ [*Calcutta*, 1884.] 12°. **14127. d. 31.**

JÑĀNĀRTHĪ ŚARMĀ. থিওসফি বা তত্ত্ববিদ্যা। [Tattva-vidyā. A treatise on theosophy, showing how the teachings of modern theosophists are in accord with the teachings of the different systems of Hindu philosophy.] pp. viii. 129. কলিকাতা ১২৯৩ [*Calcutta*, 1886.] 12°. **14125. f. 31.(1.)**

JÑĀNENDRAKUMĀRA RĀYA CHAUDHURĪ. অশ্ব-তত্ত্ব। [Aśva-tattva. A treatise on the horse and its diseases.] pp. 258. *Calcutta*, ১২৯২ [1886.] 12°. **14125. bb. 20.(4.)**

Forms pt. 5 of a series entitled Jiva-tattva.

—— গো-তত্ত্ব। [Go-tattva. A treatise on the cow and its diseases.] pp. 115. কলিকাতা ১২৯০ [*Calcutta*, 1884.] 12°. **14125. bb. 20.(1.)**

Forms pt. 2 of a series entitled Jiva-tattva.

—— মার্জ্জার-তত্ত্ব। [Mārjāra-tattva. A treatise on the cat and its diseases.] pp. 77. কলিকাতা ১২৯২ [*Calcutta*, 1886.] 12°. **14125. bb. 20.(3.)**

Forms pt. 4 of a series entitled Jiva-tattva.

—— সারমেয়-তত্ত্ব। [Sārameya-tattva. A treatise on the dog and its diseases.] pp. iv. 288. কলিকাতা ১২৯১ [*Calcutta*, 1884.] 12°. **14125. bb. 20.(2.)**

Forms pt. 3 of a series entitled Jiva-tattva.

JÑĀNENDRALĀLA RĀYA. প্রবন্ধ-লহরী। [Prabandha-laharī. Essays on literary, scientific, and social subjects.] pp. 223, vii. কলিকাতা ১৩০৩ [*Calcutta*, 1896.] 12°. **14125. e. 27.(3.)**

JÑĀNENDRAMOHINĪ DATTA, *Śrīmatī.* ধূলিরাশি। [Dhūlirāśi.] A heap of dust. [Miscellaneous short poems] pp. x. 121. *Calcutta*, 1894. 12°. **14129. b. 40.**

JÑĀNENDRANĀTHA TANTRARATNA BHAṬṬĀCHĀRYA. রহস্যপূজা-পদ্ধতি। [Rahasyapūjā-paddhati. A mystic supplementary ritual in

Sanskrit. With Bengali introductions, rubrics and notes, and an appendix of Sanskrit and Bengali hymns.] pp. iv. 37, 78. কলিকাতা ১৩০৮ [*Calcutta*, 1901.] 8°. **14033. bb. 42.(3.)**

JÑĀNENDRAṢAṢĪ GUPTA. উপকথা। [Upakathā. Bengal Folk-tales.] 2 pts. pp. iv. 184, 154. কলিকাতা ১৩১৪ [*Calcutta*, 1907.] 12°. **14128. a. 25.**

JOGGESHUR GHOSE. *See* YOGEṢVARA GHOSHA.

JOGINDRA NATHA TARKACHUDAMANI. *See* YOGĪNDRANĀTHA TARKACHŪḌĀMAṆI.

JOHNSON (SAMUEL), *LL.D.* রাসেলাস। [Rasselas. Translated into Bengali by Tārāṣaṅkara Tarkaratna. Another edition.] pp. vi. 195. কলিকাতা ১৩১৩ [*Calcutta*, 1907.] 12°. **14128. a. 16.**

JYOTIRINDRANĀTHA ṬHĀKURA. *See* BHAVABHŪTI. মালতী-মাধব। [Mālatīmādhava. Translated by Jyotirindranātha Ṭhākura.] [1900.] 8°. **14131. a. 43.(2.)**

—— *See* BHAVABHŪTI. উত্তর-চরিত। [Uttaracharita. A translation of the Uttararāmacharita by Jyotirindranātha Ṭhākura.] [1900.] 8°. **14131. a. 43.(1.)**

—— *See* EPICTETUS. এপিক্‌টেটসের উপদেশ। [Epikṭeṭaser upadeṣa. Selections from the Discourses of Epictetus, translated by Jyotirindranātha Ṭhākura.] [1907.] 12°. **14123 a. 46.(3.)**

—— *See* HARSHADEVA, *King of Thanesar.* নাগানন্দ। [Nāgānanda. Translated by Jyotirindranātha Ṭhākura.] [1902.] 12°. **14131. aa. 9.(3.)**

—— *See* HARSHADEVA, *King of Thanesar.* প্রিয়দর্শিকা। [Priyadarṣikā. Translated by Jyotirindranātha Ṭhākura.] [1904.] 12°. **14131. aa. 3.(4.)**

—— *See* KĀLIDĀSA. মালবিকাগ্নিমিত্র। [Mālavikāgnimitra. Translated by Jyotirindranātha Ṭhākura.] [1901.] 12°. **14131. a. 48.(4.)**

—— *See* KĀLIDĀSA. বিক্রমোর্ব্বশী। [Vikramorvaṣī. Translated by Jyotirindranātha Ṭhākura.] [1901.] 12°. **14131. a. 48.(3.)**

—— *See* KRISHṆA MIṢRA. প্রবোধ-চন্দ্রোদয় নাটক। [Prabodhachandrodaya nāṭaka. Translated by Jyotirindranātha Ṭhākura.] [1902.] 12°. **14131. aa. 9.(4.)**

JYOTIRINDRANĀTHA ṬHĀKURA (*continued*). *See* PERIODICAL PUBLICATIONS.—*Calcutta.* বীণা-বাদিনী। [Vīṇā-vādinī. Edited by Jyotirindranātha Ṭhākura.] [1897-99.] 12°. **14125. d. 27.**

—— *See* RĀJAṢEKHARA, *Son of Durduka.* কর্পূরমঞ্জরী। [Karpūramañjarī. Translated by Jyotirindranātha Ṭhākura.] [1904.] 12°. **14131. aa. 3.(3.)**

—— *See* RĀJAṢEKHARA, *Son of Durduka.* বিদ্ধশালভঞ্জিকা। [Viddhaṣālabhañjikā. Translated by Jyotirindranātha Ṭhākura.] [1903.] 12°. **14131. aa. 3.(2.)**

—— *See* SHAKSPERE (W.). জুলিয়াস্ সীজার। [Julius Caesar. Translated by Jyotirindranātha Ṭhākura.] [1907.] 12°. **14131. a. 46.**

—— *See* SŪDRAKA, *Raja of Magadha.* মৃচ্ছকটিক। [Mṛichchhakaṭika. Translated by Jyotirindranātha Ṭhākura.] [1901.] 12°. **14131. a. 43.(4.)**

—— *See* VIṢĀKHADATTA. মুদ্রা-রাক্ষস। [Mudrārākshasa. Translated by Jyotirindranātha Ṭhākura.] [1901.] 12°. **14131. a. 43.(3.)**

—— অলীক বাবু। [Alīka Bābu. A social farce.] pp. 94. কলিকাতা ১৩০৭ [*Calcutta*, 1900.] 12°. **14131. a. 45.**

—— চণ্ডকৌশিক। [Chaṇḍakauṣika. A mythological drama.] pp. 88. কলিকাতা [*Calcutta*, 1901.] 8°. **14131. aa. 9.(2.)**

—— ঝাঁশির রাণী। [Jhāṇsir rāṇī. An account of the life and heroism of Lakshmībāī, Rāṇī of Jhansi, translated and compiled from the Marathi of Dattātraya Balavanta Pārasnīs.] pp. 73. কলিকাতা ১৩১০ [*Calcutta*, 1903.] 12°. **14127. aa. 29.**

—— মহাবীর-চরিত। [Mahāvīra-charita. A drama on the legend of Rāma.] pp. 185. কলিকাতা ১৩০৮ [*Calcutta*, 1901.] 12°. **14131. a. 48.(2.)**

—— ফরাসী-প্রসূন। [Pharāsī-prasūna. Selections from the writings of François Coppée, Victor Hugo, and other French authors. Translated in prose and verse by Jyotirindranātha Ṭhākura.] pp. ii. 256. কলিকাতা ১৩১১ [*Calcutta*, 1904.] 12°. **14131. d. 48.**

—— প্রবন্ধ-মঞ্জরী। [Prabandha-mañjarī. Miscellaneous essays.] pp. iii. 598. কলিকাতা ১৩১২ [*Calcutta*, 1905.] 8°. **14131. d. 46.**

JYOTIRINDRANĀTHA ṬHĀKURA (*continued*). রজত-গিরি। ব্রহ্মদেশীয় নাটক। [Rajata-giri. A drama translated from the Burmese, with an introductory description of the Burmese theatre.] pp. 59. কলিকাতা ১৩১০ [*Calcutta*, 1904.] 12°. **14131. a. 44.(2.)**

—— স্বপ্নময়ী। [Svapnamayī. An historical novel.] pp. 189. কলিকাতা ১৩০৯ [*Calcutta*, 1902.] 8°. **14127. ee. 15.(2.)**

—— বসন্ত-লীলা। [Vasantalīlā. A drama on the sports of Kṛishṇa with the milkmaids of Brindaban.] pp. 32. কলিকাতা ১৩০৬ [*Calcutta*, 1900.] 12°. **14131. a. 44.(1.)**

JYOTISHĀNANDA BHĀGAVATA. প্রেমতত্ত্ব-পদাবলী। [Prematattva-padāvalī. Poems on the loves of Rādhā and Kṛishṇa, and occasional Sanskrit texts with translations and commentary.] pp. 200. কলিকাতা ১৩১০ [*Calcutta*, 1904.] 8°. **14129. cc. 7.**

JYOTISHI (T. P.). *See* TĀRIṆĪPRASĀDA JYOTISHĪ.

KABĪR. *See* VAISHṆAVACHARAṆA BASĀK. দোহাবলী। [Dohāvalī. A collection of Hindi *dohās* by Kabīr and other poets, with Bengali translations, and a life of the poet.] [1899.] 12°. **14158. c. 44.**

—— *See* YOGENDRANĀTHA SARKĀR. কবির *etc.* [Kabīr. A biography of the Hindi poet, with selections from his poems, accompanied by a Bengali translation.] [1893.] 12°. **14127. a. 37.(6.)**

—— কবির। হিন্দি ভাষায় মূল বাঙ্গালা ও আধ্যাত্মিক ব্যাখ্যা সহ। [Kabīr. A collection of the poems of Kabīr. Hindi text in Bengali character, with a Bengali translation, and commentary, by Pañchānana Bhaṭṭāchārya.] Pt. i. pp. iii. 160. কলিকাতা ১২৯৭ [*Calcutta*, 1890.] 8°. **14158. d. 37.**

KAIKOBĀD, *pseud.* অশ্রু-মালা। [Aṣrumālā. Miscellaneous poems.] pp. viii. 100. ঢাকা ১৩০২ [*Dacca*, 1896.] 12°. **14129. b. 44.(4.)**

KAILĀSACHANDRA GHOSHA. বাঙ্গালা সাহিত্য [Bāṅgālā sāhitya. An account of the gradual development of Bengali literature up to the time of Raja Rāmamohana Rāya.] pp. ii. 147. কলিকাতা ১২৩২ [*Calcutta*, 1885.] 12°. **14131. d. 15.**

KAILĀSACHANDRA MITRA. আদর্শ-জীবন। [Ādarṣa-jīvana. A short sketch of the life of Kailāsachandra Mitra, a convert to Christianity, and a native missionary of the Baptist Society.] pp. 23. *Calcutta*, 1800. 32°. **14123. a. 23.(3.)**

KAILĀSACHANDRA SIṂHA. রাজমালা বা ত্রিপুরার ইতিহাস। [Rājamālā. An historical account of the district of Tippera and its rulers.] pp. xiii. 60, 596. ১৩০৩ [*Comilla*, 1896.] 12°. **14127. aa. 7.**

—— সাধক সঙ্গীত। [Sādhaka saṅgīta. Songs in praise of the goddess Kālī by Rāmaprasāda Sena and other poets. Edited by Kailāsachandra Siṃha, with a sketch of the life of Rāmaprasāda Sena, and a brief account of the Rajas of Nadia.] 2 pts. কলিকাতা [*Calcutta*, 1885.] 12°. **14123. e. 10.**

—— সেনরাজগণ। [Sena-rājagaṇa. A history of the kings of the Sena dynasty.] pp. 26. কলিকাতা ১২৯১ [*Calcutta*, 1885.] 8°. **14127. b. 35.**

—— [Second edition.] pp. 59. কলিকাতা ১২৯৩ [*Calcutta*, 1886.] 12°. **14127. a. 31.(1.)**

—— শ্রীদারুব্রহ্ম। [Ṣrīdāru Brahma. A treatise on the temple and worship of Jagannātha in Orissa.] pp. 62. কলিকাতা ১২৯৩ [*Calcutta*, 1886.] 8°. **14123. f. 33.(2.)**

KĀLĪCHARAṆA MITRA. কাপ্তেন বাবু। সামাজিক নাট্যরঙ্গ। [Kāpten Bābu. A social drama.] pp. 43. কলিকাতা ১৩০৪ [*Calcutta*, 1897.] 12°. **14131. a. 40.(3.)**

KĀLIDĀSA. মহাকবি কালিদাসের গ্রন্থাবলী। [Granthāvalī. The complete works of Kālidāsa. Sanskrit text, with commentaries and Bengali translations. Edited by Kālīpada Vidyāratna.] pp. 2375, 390, 217, 21, 15, 6. কলিকাতা ১৩০২ [*Calcutta*, 1895.] 8°. **14070. d. 34.**

—— কালিদাস-সূক্তয়ঃ। [Kālidāsa-sūktayaḥ.] Kalidas's Apothegms [*sic*]. [Selected, with English and Bengali paraphrases], by Rai Radhanath Rai Bahadur. . . . Bengal-edition. pp. iii. 102. *Calcutta*, [1903.] 12°. **14085. b. 23.(2.)**

—— Abhijñānaṣakuntala. *See* below: Ṣakuntalā.

—— Kumarasambhabam . . . Cantos i.-vii. Text with notes by Pundit Nobin Ch. Vidyaratna . . .

With English and Bengali translations and model questions with model answers. pp. 764. *Calcutta*, [1894.] 12°. **14070. c. 57.(2.)**

—— Málabikágnimitra ... translated into Bengali by Sourindro Mohun Tagore. Second edition. pp. ii. 166. *Calcutta*, 1877. 16°. **14131. a. 26.**

A reimpression, in smaller size, with a new preface, of the edition of **1859.**

—— মালবিকাগ্নিমিত্র। [Mālavikāgnimitra. An anonymous Bengali translation.] ১৩০৭-১৩০৯ [1900-02.] *See* PERIODICAL PUBLICATIONS.—*Calcutta*. সাহিত্য-সংহিতা। [Sāhitya-saṃhitā.] Vol. i. no. 7—iii. no. 12. [1900, *etc.*] 8°. **14133. ff. 1.**

—— মালবিকাগ্নিমিত্র। [Mālavikāgnimitra. Translated by Jyotirindranātha Ṭhākura.] pp. 95. কলিকাতা ১৩০৮ [*Calcutta*, 1901.] 12°. **14131. a. 48.(4.)**

—— Kalidasa's Meghadutam [I. 1-38]. Containing ... Mallinatha's commentary ... Bengali and English translations, Anglo Sanskrit notes... grammatical, rhetorical, and explanatory notes ... by Pandit Nabin Chandra Vidyaratna. New edition. pp. 168. *Calcutta*, [1901.] 8°. **14085. c. 49.(1.)**

—— *See* HARAPRASĀDA ŚĀSTRĪ, *M.A.* মেঘদূত ব্যাখ্যা। [Meghadūta-vyākhyā. An explanation of the Sanskrit poem of Kalidāsa.] [1902.] 12°. **14131. d. 41.(2.)**

—— Raghubamsam. Cantos i.-vi. Containing prose version, paraphrase ... Sanjivani ... Bengali and English translations of all the slokas, grammatical and explanatory notes both in English and Sanskrit ... Edited by Pandit Nabin Chandra Vidyaratna. Thoroughly revised and enlarged edition. 2 pts. *Calcutta*, 1901. 8°. **14085. c. 50.**

—— अभिज्ञानशकुन्तलम्। (Kalidasa's Abhijnana Sakuntalam. Edited with an introduction, glossary, English and Bengali translations, various readings, and the commentary Sarala by Pandit Nabin Chandra Vidyaratna. New edition.) pp. ix. 12, 418, 352, viii. कलिकातायां १८२२ [*Calcutta*, 1901.] 8°. **14080. c. 41.**

—— শকুন্তলা। [Ṣakuntalā. A prose adaptation of the Sanskrit drama by Īṣvarachandra Vidyāsāgara.] pp. 60. ঢাকা ১৩১৪ [*Dacca*, 1907.] 8°. **14131. b. 27.**

KĀLIDĀSA (*continued*).

—— *See* CHANDRANĀTHA VASU, *M.A.* শকুন্তলাতত্ত্ব। [Ṣakuntalātattva. A criticism on the Sanskrit drama of Kālidāsa.] [1890.] 8°. **14131. d. 25.**

—— *See* PĀRVATĪCHARAṆA BHAṬṬĀCHĀRYA. সচিত্র শকুন্তলা উপন্যাস। [Ṣakuntalā. Adapted from the drama of Kālidāsa.] [1907.] 12°. **14128. a. 11.**

—— *See* YOGĪNDRANĀTHA TARKACHŪḌĀMAṆI. The minute essay on Abhijnana Sacuntalam of Calidasa. 1890. 12°. **14131. d. 27.**

—— বিক্রমোর্ব্বশী। [Vikramorvaṣī. Translated by Jyotirindranātha Ṭhākura.] pp. 4, 84. কলিকাতা ১৩০৮ [*Calcutta*, 1901.] 12°. **14131. a. 48.(3.)**

—— সঞ্জীবনী কালিদাসের কবিতা। [Kālidāser kavitā. A cycle of stanzas ascribed to Kālidāsa, with Bengali translations and notes, preceded by a biography of the poet in Bengali. To which are added a selection of Sanskrit stanzas by various authors, and some Hindi *dohās* by Tulasī Dāsa, with Bengali translations. Compiled and edited by Vaishṇavacharaṇa Basāk.] pp. 132, 46. কলিকাতা ১৩০৩ [*Calcutta*, 1897.] 12°. **14127. aa. 14.(1.)**

—— কালিদাসের কবিতা। [Kālidāser kavitā. Two series of Sanskrit stanzas ascribed to Kālidāsa. Compiled and edited with a Bengali translation and biography of the poet by Ṣaratkumāra Sena.] pp. 178. কলিকাতা ১৩০৮ [*Calcutta*, 1901.] 12°. **14076. b. 26.(2.)**

—— চতুর্থ অধ্যায়। [Miscellaneous Sanskrit stanzas, purporting to be by Kālidāsa and other poets. With Bengali translation and additional matter.] *See* NĪLAMAṆI VIDYĀLAṄKĀRA BHAṬṬĀCHĀRYA. উদ্ভট কবিতা-কৌমুদী। [Udbhaṭa kavitākaumudī.] Pt. i., pp. 42-70. [1890.] 8°. **14085. c. 43.**

KĀLIDĀSA MUKHOPĀDHYĀYA. যদুরায়। [Yadu Rāya. The story of Yadu Rāya and Mādhava Bāgchī, two rival zamindars.] pp. 278. কলিকাতা ১৮৯৯ [*Calcutta*, 1899.] 8°. **14127. c. 50.(2.)**

KĀLIDĀSA NĀTHA. *See* GOVINDA DĀSA, *Vaishṇava poet.* গোবিন্দদাস-পদাবলী। [Govindadāsa-padāvalī. Edited with notes by Kālidāsa Nātha.] [1901, *etc.*] 8°. **14129. cc. 6.**

—— *See* JAGADĀNANDA ṬHĀKURA, *Vaishṇava poet.* শ্রীজগদানন্দ-পদাবলী। [Jagadānanda-padāvalī. Edited with notes and a life of the author by Kālidāsa Nātha.] [1899.] 12°. **14129. a. 45.**

—— শ্রীশ্রীকীর্ত্তন-গীত-রত্নাবলী। [Kīrtana-gītaratnāvalī. A collection of Vaishṇava songs, compiled from various sources and edited by Kālidāsa Nātha. Second edition.] pp. iv. 408. কলিকাতা ১৩১৩ [*Calcutta*, 1907.] 8°. **14123. ff. 16.**

—— বৈষ্ণবকবি জগদানন্দ। [Vaishṇava kavi Jagadānanda. An account of the Vaishṇava poet Jagadānanda and his writings.] ১৩০৪ [1899.] *See* ACADEMIES, *etc.*— Calcutta.—*Bengal Academy of Literature.* সাহিত্য-পরিষৎ-পত্রিকা। [Sāhitya-parishat-patrikā.] Vol. v., no. 4. [1894, *etc.*] 8°. **14133. f. 18.**

KĀLĪKIṄKARA YAṢA. গয়াসুরের হরিপাদপদ্ম লাভ গীতাভিনয়। [Gayāsurer Haripādapadmalābha. A dramatised version of the Pauranic story of the demon Gayā.] pp. 175. *Calcutta*, 1896. 8°. **14131. c. 18.(2.)**

KĀLĪKṚISHṆA DĀSA. রস রত্নাকরান্তর্গত কামিনী কুমার নামক কাব্য। [Kāminī Kumāra. A love-tale in verse.] pp. xiv. 242. কলিকাতা ১২৪০ [*Calcutta*, 1833.] 8°. **14129. c. 39.**

KĀLĪKṚISHṆA DEVA, *Raja.* চন্দ্র ও সূর্য্যগ্রহণের সামান্য বিবরণ। [Chandra o sūrya grahaṇer vivaraṇa. A diagram explanatory of the eclipses of the sun and moon.] *Sansk.* and *Beng.* কলিকাতা ১২৪২ [*Calcutta*, 1835.] *s.sh.* **14003. e. 2.(4.)**

—— A short system of polite learnig [*sic*]: being an introduction to the arts and sciences, and other branches of useful knowledge. Compiled and translated by Maha-raja Kalee-Krishna Behadur .... সংক্ষিপ্ত সদ্বিদ্যাবলী। [Saṃkshipta sadvidyāvalī.] pp. 122. *Engl.* and *Beng.* [*Calcutta*,] 1833. 8°. **14125. f. 30.(4.)**

Imperfect: wanting pp. 16-23.

—— [Another copy.] **T. 1607.(2.)**

KĀLĪKUMĀRA BHAṬṬĀCHĀRYA NYĀYARATNA. নবকালী পুরাণ। [Nava Kālīpurāṇa. Hymns in praise of Hindu deities, and on mythological subjects, written in a semi-Sanskrit style.] pp. 113. বারাণসী ১২৯৭ [*Benares*, 1891.] 8°. **14123. ff. 8.**

KĀLĪKUMĀRA MAJUMDĀR. হরিপুর-মজুমদার-বংশাবলী। [Haripura-Majumdār-vaṃṣāvalī. The genealogy of the Haripur Majumdār family.] pp. 16, 50. সিরাজগঞ্জ ১৩০২ [*Śirajganj*, 1895.] 8°. **14127. bb. 4.(1.)**

KĀLĪKUMĀRA MUKHOPĀDHYĀYA. বাপ্‌রে-কলি! (সামাজিক-প্রহসন) [Bāpre kali.] Society comedietta, in two acts. pp. 28. কলিকাতা ১২৯২ [*Calcutta*, 1886.] 12°. **14131. a. 24.(1.)**

KĀLĪKUMĀRA ṢARMĀ. An abridgment of Vyakaranadarsha [or Grammar of the Sanskrit language]. ব্যাকরণাদর্শের সংক্ষেপ। [Vyākaraṇādarṣer saṃkshepa.] pp. 116. উত্তরপাড়া ১৮৯০ [*Uttarpara*, 1890.] 12°. **14131. e. 23.(1.)**

KĀLĪMAYA GHAṬAKA. শর্ব্বাণী। [Ṣarvāṇī. A tale of dacoity in Bengal 30 years ago.] pp. 192. কলিকাতা ১২৯৬ [*Calcutta*, 1890.] 12°. **14127. d. 38.(1.)**

KĀLĪMOHANA RĀYA CHAUDHURĪ. ছন্দোবোধ শব্দসাগর। [Chhandobodha ṣabdasāgara. A dictionary of rhyming words, designed as an aid to poetical composition.] 3 pts. রঙ্গপুর ১৩০০ [*Rangpur*, 1883.] 12°. **14133. a. 12.**

KĀLĪNĀRĀYAṆA GUPTA, *of Bhatpara.* ভাবসঙ্গীত। [Bhāvasaṅgīta. Brahmist hymns. Sixth edition.] pp. 18, 228. ঢাকা ১৩০১ [*Dacca*, 1901.] 16°. **14123. c. 31.**

KĀLĪNĀTHA CHAUDHURĪ. রাজসাহীর সংক্ষিপ্ত ইতিহাস। [Rājshāhīr saṃkshipta itihāsa. An historical and geographical account of the District of Rajshahi from the time of the establishment of British government.] pp. ii. iv. 346. কলিকাতা ১৩০৮ [*Calcutta*, 1901.] 8°. **14127. bb. 15.**

KĀLINDĪ, *Rāṇī.* বৌদ্ধা-রঞ্জিকা। অর্থাৎ বৌদ্ধদিগের মূল ধর্ম্মগ্রন্থ। [Bauddhā-rañjikā. The life of Buddha translated in verse by Rāṇī Kālindī from a Pali work, the name of which is stated in the preface to be 'Thāduttāng.'] Pt. i. pp. iv. 236. চট্টগ্রাম ১৮৯০ [*Chittagong*, 1890.] 12°. **14123. k. 2.**

KĀLĪPADA MUKHOPĀDHYĀYA. Notes on Sakuntala [in Sanskrit, Bengali and English.] By Kalipada Mukerjee, *etc.* pp. 323. *Calcutta*, 1895. 12°. **14072. b. 22.**

KĀLĪPADA VIDYĀRATNA, *of Bhatpalli.* *See* KĀLIDĀSA. মহাকবি কালিদাসের গ্রন্থাবলী। [Granthāvalī. Edited by Kālīpada Vidyāratna.] [1895.] 8°. **14070. d. 34.**

—— *See* PURĀṆAS.—*Mārkaṇḍeyapurāṇa.* শ্রীশ্রীচণ্ডী। [Chaṇḍī. Edited with a Bengali version by Kālīpada Vidyāratna.] [1900.] 16°. **14028. a. 29.**

—— *See* ŚĀTĀTAPA. শাতাতপীয়-কর্ম্মবিপাকঃ। [Śātātapīya-karmavipāka. Edited and revised by Kālīpada Vidyāratna.] [1902.] 8°. **14033. aa. 28.(3.)**

KĀLĪPRASANNA CHAṬṬOPĀDHYĀYA. *See* SHAKSPERE (W.). ওথেলো। ["Othello," translated by Kālīprasanna Chaṭṭopādhyāya.] [1894.] 12°. **14131. a. 34.**

—— The Mode of studying and teaching languages. Translated and compiled from the original texts, French and English, by Kali Prasanna Chatterjee. (ভাষা-শিক্ষা) [Bhāshāśikshā.] pp. ii. 304. *Calcutta*, 1894. 8°. **14131. g. 30.(2.)**

—— সর্ব্বাণী। [Sarvāṇī. A drama, the scene of which is laid at the palace in Manipur.] pp. 112. কলিকাতা ১৩০৩ [*Calcutta*, 1896.] 12°. **14131. a. 32.(5.)**

—— শত-গল্প পরীর উপন্যাস। [Śata galpa. One hundred fairy-tales, compiled and translated from English and other sources.] pp. v. 380. কলিকাতা ১৩০৪ [*Calcutta*, 1898.] 12°. **14127. cc. 4.(5.)**

KĀLĪPRASANNA DATTA. বিচারপতি দ্বারকানাথ মিত্রের জীবনী। [Dvārakānātha Mitrer jīvanī. A life of Dvārakānātha Mitra, late Judge of the High Court at Calcutta.] pp. xii. 216, 40. কলিকাতা ১২৯৯ [*Calcutta*, 1892.] 12°. **14127. a. 37.(4.)**

KĀLĪPRASANNA GHOSHA. *See* PERIODICAL PUBLICATIONS.—*Dacca.* বান্ধব। [Bāndhava. Edited by Kālīprasanna Ghosha.] [1901, *etc.*] 8°. **14133. ff. 3.**

KĀLĪPRASANNA GHOSHA (*continued*). *See* RĀMANĀRĀYAṆA GHOSHA, *Kavivara.* নৈষধ-কাব্য। [Naishadha kāvya. Edited with an introduction by Kālīprasanna Ghosha.] [1890.] 12°. **14127. cc. 23.(2.)**

—— ভক্তির জয় অথবা হরিদাসের জীবন-যজ্ঞ। [Bhaktir jaya. The story of the life and teachings of Haridāsa, the associate of Chaitanya.] pp. iv. 222. কলিকাতা ১৩০২ [*Calcutta*, 1895.] 12°. **14127. a. 52.**

—— গোপ জাতীয় জ্ঞানদায়িনী বা জাতিমালা। [Gopajātīya-jñānadāyinī. A treatise on the Gopa, or cow-herd caste; with proofs of its being of Vaiśya origin.] pp. 23. যশোহর ১৩০৬ [*Jessore*, 1900.] 12°. **14125. e. 31.(5.)**

—— প্রমোদলহরী অথবা বিবাহ-রহস্য। [Pramodalaharī. Humorous articles on Hindu marriages.] pp. iv. 183. ঢাকা ১৩০১ [*Dacca*, 1895.] 8°. **14125. e. 28.**

KĀLĪPRASANNA KAVIŚEKHARA, *Kavirāja.* *See* BHĀVA MIŚRA. সানুবাদ-ভাবপ্রকাশঃ। [Bhāvaprakāśa. Edited with a Bengali translation by Kālīprasanna.] [1901.] 8°. **14043. dd. 9.**

—— *See* SUŚRUTA. সুশ্রুত-সংহিতা। [Suśrutasaṃhitā. Edited with a Bengali translation by Kālīprasanna.] [1898.] 8°. **14043. dd. 8.**

—— রত্নপ্রভা। অর্থাৎ-সানুবাদ-দ্রব্যগুণাভিধানম্। [Ratnaprabhā. A Sanskrit metrical compilation on Materia Medica, in 18 *adhyāyas*, with a Bengali translation.] pp. xvi. 268. *Calcutta*, [1901.] 8°. **14043. cc. 21.**

KĀLĪPRASANNA KĀVYAVIŚĀRADA. *See* VIDYĀPATI. The Poets of Bengal. Bidyapati. A comprehensive collection of his Bengali songs, compiled ... with copious notes and an introduction by Kaliprasanna Kavyabisharad. [1894.] 8°. **14129. cc. 10.**

KĀLĪPRASANNA MUKHOPĀDHYĀYA. পণ্ডিত রত্ন মেলাবলী। [Paṇḍitaratna-melāvalī. Genealogical tables of the various *gotras* of the Brahmans of the Paṇḍitaratna class.] pp. ii. vi. 68. কলিকাতা ১৩১৩ [*Calcutta*, 1907.] 4°. **14127. bbb. 7.(2.)**

KĀLĪPRASANNA SENA GUPTA. বঙ্গীয় কবি। অষ্টম খণ্ড। [Vaṅgīya kavi. The poets of Bengal; their lives and works. Part i. Ambashṭha khaṇḍa. Poets of the Vaidya caste.] pp. xlii. v. 676, iii. আগরতলা ১৩১৩ [*Agartala*, 1906.] 12°.. **14127. aa. 43.**

KĀLĪPRASANNA SIṂHA. *See* MAHĀBHĀRATA. মহাভারত। [Mahābhārata. Translated into prose by Kālīprasanna Siṃha.] [1898, *etc.*] 8°. **14129. f. 7.**

KĀLĪPRASANNA VANDYOPĀDHYĀYA. বাঙ্গলার ইতিহাস অষ্টাদশ শতাব্দী নবাবী আমল। [Bāṅgalār itihāsa. History of Bengal under the Muhammadan rule of the 18th century.] pp. iv. 528, 31. কলিকাতা ১৩০৮ [*Calcutta*, 1901.] 8°. **14127. bb. 19.**

KĀLĪPRASANNA VIDYĀRATNA BHAṬṬĀCHĀRYA, *of Mallikpur, Jessore.* *See* GHERAṆḌA. যোগরত্নম ঘেরণ্ডসংহিতা। [Yogaratna. With a Bengali translation by Kālīprasanna Vidyāratna.] [1886.] 8°. **14048. b. 35.**

—— *See* ĪŚVARACHANDRA GUPTA. ঈশ্বরচন্দ্র গুপ্তের গ্রন্থাবলী। [Granthāvalī. Edited by Kālīprasanna Vidyāratna.] [1900.] 8°. **14129. e. 23.**

—— *See* MAHĀBHĀRATA. — *Aśvamedhaparva.* জৈমিনি-ভারত। [Aśvamedhaparva. Translated into verse by Kālīprasanna Vidyāratna.] [1902.] 8°. **14129. e. 28.**

—— *See* NĀGA BHAṬṬA. কামরত্নম্। [Kāmaratna. With a Bengali translation by Kālīprasanna Vidyāratna.] [1894.] 8°. **14033. bb. 43.**

—— *See* PARĀŚARA. সানুবাদ পরাশরসংহিতা। [Parāśara-saṃhitā. Edited with a Bengali translation by Kālīprasanna Vidyāratna.] [1903.] 8°. **14039. b. 15.(3.)**

—— *See* PAVANAVIJAYA. পবনবিজয়স্বরোদয়ঃ। Pavanavijaya-svarodaya. Edited with a Bengali translation by Kālīprasanna Vidyāratna.] [1892.] 12°. **14028. b. 72.(2.)**

—— *See* PURĀṆAS.—*Kalkipurāṇa.* সানুবাদ কল্কি-পুরাণম্। [Kalkipurāṇa. With a Bengali translation by Kālīprasanna Vidyāratna.] [1899.] 8°. **14016. d. 36.(2.)**

—— *See* PURĀṆAS.—*Skandapurāṇa.* সানুবাদ উৎকলখণ্ড। [Utkalakhaṇḍa. Edited with a Bengali translation by Kālīprasanna Vidyāratna.] [1905.] 8°. **14016. dd. 15.(2.)**

KĀLĪPRASANNA VIDYĀRATNA BHAṬṬĀCHĀRYA, *of Mallikpur, Jessore (continued).* *See* RATIMAÑJARĪ. রতিমঞ্জরী বা রমণীরঙ্গ। [Ratimañjarī. Edited, with a Bengali translation, by Kālīprasanna Vidyāratna.] [1901.] 12°. **14053. b. 41.**

—— *See* RATIŚĀSTRA. সচিত্র শিবোক্ত রতিশাস্ত্র। [Ratiśāstra. With a Bengali translation by Kālīprasanna Vidyāratna.] [1895.] 12°. **14053. b. 28.**

—— *See* SĀMUDRIKA. সানুবাদ বৃহৎ সামুদ্রিক। [Sāmudrika. Enlarged and edited with a Bengali translation by Kālīprasanna Vidyāratna.] [1892.] 8°. **14053. cc. 66.**

—— *See* ŚAṄKARA ĀCHĀRYA. শঙ্করাচার্য্যের গ্রন্থমালা। [Śaṅkarāchāryer granthamālā. Edited with Bengali translations by Kālīprasanna Vidyāratna.] [1903.] 8°. **14033. aa. 30.**

—— *See* TANTRAS. কালীতন্ত্রম্। [Kālītantra. With a Bengali translation by Kālīprasanna Vidyāratna.] 1892. 8°. **14033. bb. 44.**

—— *See* TANTRAS. সানুবাদ মহানির্ব্বাণ-তন্ত্র *etc.* [Mahānirvāṇa-tantra. Sanskrit text, with a Bengali translation by Kālīprasanna Vidyāratna.] [1907.] 8°. **14028. dd. 18.**

—— *See* TANTRAS. সানুবাদ-রাধাতন্ত্রম্। [Rādhātantra. Edited with a Bengali version by Kālīprasanna Vidyāratna.] [1906.] 8°. **14033. bbb. 42.**

—— *See* VṚINDĀVANA DĀSA. শ্রীচৈতন্যভাগবত। [Chaitanya-bhāgavata. Edited by Kālīprasanna Vidyāratna.] [1903.] 8°. **14123. ff. 11.**

—— সানুবাদ বৃহত্তন্ত্রকোষঃ। [Bṛihat tantrakosha. A Thesaurus of Tantric ritual, in nine chapters. Compiled and translated into Bengali by Kālīprasanna Vidyāratna.] pp. x. 191. কলিকাতা ১২৯৩ [*Calcutta*, 1887.] 8°. **14028. d. 32.**

—— শ্রীদুর্গাভক্তি-চিন্তামণি। [Durgābhakti-chintāmaṇi. A collection of Pauranic and Tantric accounts of the goddess Durgā and her worship.] pp. 4, 189. কলিকাতা ১৩০৬ [*Calcutta*, 1899.] 8°. **14123. ff. 6.(2.)**

—— হিন্দু-তীর্থতরঙ্গিণী। যাবতীয় তীর্থকৃত্যাসম্বলিত। [Hindu tīrthataraṅgiṇī. A handbook for pilgrims visiting holy places, comprising Sanskrit texts on the various legends and rites, with Bengali

translations and notes on ritual.] pp. ii. iv. 184. কলিকাতা ১৩১০ [*Calcutta*, 1903.] 8°.
14039. b. 15.(4.)

—— কবির ঝঙ্কার। বিচিত্র বিচিত্র উদ্ভট শ্লোকাবলী। [Kavir jhankāra. 717 miscellaneous Sanskrit stanzas compiled from various sources, with Bengali translation and notes.] pp. xvii. 306. কলিকাতা ১৩০৯ [*Calcutta*, 1902.] 12°.
14076. a. 28.

—— নিত্যতন্ত্রম্। [Nityatantra. A work on Tantric practices of religion. Compiled from Sanskrit sources, with a Bengali version by Kālīprasanna Vidyāratna.] pp. 2, 140. *Calcutta*, 1900. 8°. **14033. aa. 18.**

—— পাচন-সংগ্রহ ও কবিরাজী-শিক্ষা। [Pāchana-saṅgraha. A collection of native medical prescriptions, compiled by Kālīprasanna Vidyāratna.] pp. x. 144. কলিকাতা ১৩১৩ [*Calcutta*, 1906.] 12°.
14125. b. 21.(3.)

—— যোগাঙ্কুর। [Yogāṅkura. A collection of tracts on the Yoga, comprising the Shaṭchakra of Pūrṇānanda Gosvāmī, the Kshurikopanishad, the Rāmagītā from the Adhyātmarāmāyaṇa, and the Pañcharatnastotra from the Muṇḍamālātantra. Sanskrit text and commentaries, with Bengali translations.] pp. ii. 159. কলিকাতা ১৩০০ [*Calcutta*, 1894.] 12°. **14046. b. 28.(2.)**

KĀLĪṢACHANDRA SENA GUPTA. *See* BHĀVA MIṢRA. ভাবপ্রকাশ। [Bhāvaprakāṣa. With a Bengali translation by Kālīṣachandra Sena Gupta.] [1887.] 8°. **14043. d. 39.**

KĀLĪSAHĀYA RĀYA CHAUDHURĪ. Rijubyákhyá, or A complete key to [Īṣvarachandra Vidyāsāgara's] Rijupatha. ঋজুব্যাখ্যা। Pt. i. pp. 246. *Sansk., Beng.* and *Engl. Calcutta*, 1879. 12°.
14085. b.

—— Rijubyákhyá. [Fourth edition.] pp. 245. *Calcutta*, 1881. 12°. **14085. b.**

KĀLĪṢAṄKARA DĀSA. হিন্দু বিবাহ ও কন্যাবিক্রয়। [Hindu-vivāha o kanyā-vikraya. Hindu marriages as enjoined by the Ṣāstras, exposing the evil practice of selling daughters in marriage.] pp. 48. কলিকাতা ১৮০৯ [*Calcutta*, 1885.] 12°.
14125. e. 17.(5.)

—— প্রেরিত কালীশঙ্কর দাস কবিরাজ। [Prerita Kālīṣaṅkara Dāsa. The life of Kālīṣaṅkara Dāsa, a Brahmist preacher.] pp. 195. কলিকাতা ১৮২৫ [*Calcutta*, 1903.] 12°. **14127. aa. 21.(5.)**

KĀLĪVARA VEDĀNTAVĀGĪṢA. *See* GOTAMA, surnamed AKSHAPĀDA. গৌতম ... ন্যায়দর্শন। [Nyāya-darṣana, Adhyāya 1, with Vātsyāyana's commentary. Edited with a Bengali translation by Kālīvara Vedāntavāgīṣa.] [1906.] 8°. **14049. bb. 18.**

—— *See* KAPILA. সাঙ্খ্যসূত্রম্ ... Sankhya sutra, *etc.* [Edited, with a Bengali translation by Kālīvara Vedāntavāgīṣa.] [1886.] 8°. **14048. bb. 34.**

—— *See* SADĀNANDA YOGĪNDRA. সটীক সানুবাদ বেদান্ত-সার। [Vedāntasāra. With a Bengali translation by Kālīvara Vedāntavāgīṣa.] [1903.] 12°.
14048. b. 41.

—— *See* SĀYAṆA ĀCHĀRYA. পঞ্চদশী। [Pañchadaṣī. Translated by Kālīvara Vedāntavāgīṣa.] [1884.] 8°. **14123. f. 37.**

—— *See* YOGAVĀSISHṬHARĀMĀYAṆA. বাশিষ্ঠমহা-রামায়ণম্। [Edited with a Bengali translation by Kālīvara Vedāntavāgīṣa.] [1893, *etc.*] 8°.
14048. dd. 16.

—— হিন্দুশাস্ত্র। ... ষড়্দর্শন। [Shaḍdarṣana. An exposition of the 6 great philosophical systems, illustrated by Sanskrit quotations. Followed by the Vedāntasāra, with a Bengali translation.] pp. i. 205. [1895.] *See* RAMEṢACHANDRA DATTA. হিন্দুশাস্ত্র। [Hindu-ṣāstra.] Pt. v. [1895-97.] 8°.
14085. c. 45.(vol. i.)

KĀMĀKHYĀCHARAṆA VANDYOPĀDHYĀYA. স্ত্রী-শিক্ষা। [Strīṣikshā. An essay on female education.] pp. 103. ঢাকা ১৩০৪ [*Dacca*, 1898.] 12°.
14125. e. 38.(1.)

KĀMĀKHYĀNĀTHA TARKAVĀGĪṢA. বেদান্ত বিষয়ক প্রবন্ধ। [Vedānta vishayaka prabandha. An essay on the Vedānta.] pp. vi. 29. কলিকাতা [*Calcutta*,] 1906. 12°. **14123. e. 34.**

KAMALĀKĀNTA. কামধেনু। [Kāmadhenu. A collection of riddles, puzzles, and useful recipes.] Pt. i. pp. vi. 96. কলিকাতা ১৮৮৫ [*Calcutta*, 1885.] 12°. **14133. h. 10.**

KAMALĀKĀNTA BHAṬṬĀCHĀRYA. কমলাকান্ত-পদাবলী। [Padāvalī. Songs on Ṣakti-worship.] pp. viii. 99. কলিকাতা ১২৯২ [*Calcutta*, 1885.] 12°.
14123. f. 33.

KAMALĀKĀNTA BRAHMADĀSA. তত্ত্বোপনিষদ্। [Tattvopanishad. Teachings of the Brāhma Samāj.] Pt. i. pp. 132. কলিকাতা ১৩০২ [*Calcutta*, 1896.] 12°. **14123. c. 29.**

KAMALAKṚISHṆA SIṂHA. *See* RĀJA SIṂHA, *Mahārāja*. রাগ-মালা ও সংক্ষিপ্ত মনসা পাঁচালী। [Rāgamālā and Manasā pāñchālī. Edited by Kamalakṛishṇa Siṃha.] [1891.] 12°. **14129. a.**

KAMALALOCHANA, *of Rangpur.* চণ্ডিকা-বিজয় কাব্য। [Chaṇḍikā-vijaya, also called Kālīyuddha. An ancient poem on the myth of the goddess Kālī. Edited with an introduction by Haragopāla Dāsa Kuṇḍu.] [1907, *etc.*] *See* ACADEMIES, *etc.*—Rangpur.—*Bengal Academy of Literature.* রঙ্গপুর শাখা সাহিত্য-পরিষৎ-পত্রিকা। [Sāhitya-parishat-patrikā.] Vol. i., no. 1, *etc.* [1907, *etc.*] 8°. **14133. ff. 4.**

KĀMINĪ SENA. আলো ও ছায়া। [Ālo o chhāyā, or Lights and shadows. A collection of lyrics and ballads. Second edition.] pp. vi. 185. কলিকাতা ১২৯৮ [*Calcutta*, 1892.] 12°. **14129. a. 33.**

KAṆĀDA. বৈশেষিক-দর্শনম্। [Vaiṣeshikadarṣana, *i.e.* the Vaiṣeshikasūtra. Sanskrit text, with Ṣaṅkara Miṣra's commentary Upaskāra. Edited with a Sanskrit commentary called Parishkāra, and a Bengali translation and commentary by Pañchānana Tarkaratna Bhaṭṭāchārya.] pp. iv. iii. 474. কলিকাতা ১৩১৩ [*Calcutta*, 1906.] 8°. **14049. b. 43.**

KĀṆĀILĀL GHOSHĀL. প্রবাদ সংগ্রহ বিস্তৃত ব্যাখ্যা সহিত। [Pravāda-saṅgraha.] A collection of Bengali and Hindi proverbs, with explanatory notes. pp. 138. *Calcutta*, 1890. 12°. **14125. f.**

KĀṆĀILĀL MUKHOPĀDHYĀYA. প্রায়শ্চিত্তান্তে অব্যবহার্য্যতা বিচার। [Prāyaṣchittānte avyavahāryatāvichāra. An inquiry into the question whether a Hindu who has become a pervert, or who has eaten unclean food, or journeyed to foreign lands, may, on expiation, be re-admitted to caste.] 3 pts. [*Calcutta*, 1898.] 8°. **14125. e. 34.**

KANDARPAMOHANA VIDYĀRATNA. স্বর্ণ বণিকের কুলজী। [Suvarṇa baṇiker kulajī. A genealogical account of the Sonār baniyā caste.] pp. ii. 84. হুগলি ১৮০৯ [*Hooghly*, 1887.] 8°. **14127. b. 37.**

KĀṄGĀL. *See* HARINĀTHA MAJUMDĀR.

KĀṄGĀLĪCHARAṆA SENA. ব্রহ্মসঙ্গীত-স্বরলিপি। [Brahmasaṅgīta-svaralipi. A collection of Brahmist songs, with musical notation.] Pt. i. pp. xi. 245. কলিকাতা ১৮২৬ [*Calcutta*, 1905.] 8°. **14123. d. 22.**

KANHAIYĀ LĀLA ṢĀSTRĪ. সংস্কৃত ব্যাকরণ-বোধ। . . . Vyakaranabodha. A treatise on Sanskrit grammar in Bengali. pp. 15, 288. *Calcutta*, 1899. 8°. **14131. e. 30.**

KĀṆṚĀ DĀSA, *of Benares.* *See* BALARĀMA CHAKRAVARTĪ. কাঁড়াদাসী গুরুপ্রসাদী কীর্ত্তন। [Kāṇṛādāsī kīrtana. An account of Kāṇṛā Dāsa and of his wonderful powers as a magician.] [1897.] 8°. **14127. bb. 17.**

KĀNTICHANDRA RĀṚHĪ. নবদ্বীপমহিমা। [Navadvīpa-mahimā. An account of the ancient city of Navadvīpa, the modern Nadia, and of its Sanskrit *ṭolas.*] pp. 4, 192. হুগলী ১২৯৮ [*Hooghly*, 1891.] 12°. **14127. a. 42.(1.)**

KANYĀPAṆA-NIVĀRIṆĪ SABHĀ. *See* BOGRA.—*Kanyāpaṇa-nivāriṇī Sabhā.*

KAPILA. মহর্ষিকপিল-প্রণীত-সাংখ্যদর্শনম্। [Sāṅkhyadarṣana. The Sanskrit text of the Aphorisms of Sāṅkhya Philosophy of Kapila, with Vijñāna Bhikshu's Sanskrit commentary, and an explanatory translation in Bengali. Edited and compiled by Maheṣachandra Pāla.] pp. 472. কলিকাতা ১৮০৭ [*Calcutta*, 1885.] 8°. **14048. bb. 22.**

—— সাঙ্খ্যসূত্রম্ . . . Sankhya sutra by Kapila. With the commentaries of Anirudha Bhatta. [Edited, with a Bengali translation, by Kālīvara Vedāntavāgīṣa Bhaṭṭāchārya.] pp. ii. 173. কলিকাতা ১৮০৮ [*Calcutta*, 1886.] 8°. **14048. bb. 34.**

KĀRTTIKEYACHANDRA RĀYA, *Diwān of Nadia.* স্বর্গীয় দেওয়ান কার্ত্তিকেয়চন্দ্র রায়ের আত্মজীবনচরিত। [Kārttikeyachandra Rāyer ātmajīvanacharita. Autobiography, with memoirs of the Rajas of Nadia.] pp. iv. ii. 186. কলিকাতা [*Calcutta*, 1904.] 8°. **14127. bb. 21.**

KĀṢIDĀSA MUSTAUPHĪ. শান্তিগীতা। [Ṣāntigītā. A Sanskrit poem on resignation and the supreme truths of religion, accompanied by an extensive Bengali commentary by the author's nephew Ṣaṣibhūshaṇa Mitra Mustauphī, also known as Brahmānanda Tattvadarṣī.] pp. viii. 215. *Calcutta*, 1897. 8°. **14076. b. 32.**

KĀṢĪNĀTHA SMĀRTAVĀGĪṢA. রত্নবিভ্রম। [Ratnavibhrama. An exposure of errors contained in Madhusūdana Smṛitiratna's commentary on the Dattakamīmaṃsā, and the Dattaka-chandrikā, two Sanskrit treatises on the law of inheritance.] pp. ii. 26. কলিকাতা ১২৯৫ [*Calcutta*, 1888.] 8°. **14125. a. 19.(1.)**

KĀṢĪNĀTHA TARKAPAÑCHĀNANA. *See* KṚISHṆA MIṢRA. প্রবোধচন্দ্রোদয় নাটক। [Prabodhachandrodaya nāṭaka. With a Bengali translation by Kāṣīnātha and others.] [1855.] 16°. **14079. a. 4.**

KĀṢĪNDRANĀTHA VANDYOPĀDHYĀYA. Popular Tales of Bengal. By Kasindranath Banerji. pp. ii. 224. *Calcutta*, 1905. 12°. **14128. a. 5.**

KĀṢĪRĀMA DĀSA. *See* MAHĀBHĀRATA. The Mohabharut . . . Translated . . . by Kaseeram Dass Mohanubhaba, *etc.* [1903.] 8°. **14129. e. 27.**

—— —— প্রতিমূর্ত্তির সহিত মহাভারত অষ্টাদশ পর্ব্ব। [Mahābharata. Translated by Kāṣīrāma Dāsa.] [1907.] 8°. **14129. e. 34.**

—— —— কাশীরাম দাস বিরচিত মহাভারত। দান পর্ব্ব। [Dānaparva. A hitherto unpublished canto of Kāṣīrāma Dāsa's translation of the Mahābhārata.] [1908.] 12°. **14129. bbb. 1.**

KĀṢĪVILĀSA VANDYOPĀDHYĀYA. *See* JAGADRĀMA. দুর্গা-পঞ্চরাত্রি। *etc.* [Durgā-pañcharātri. Edited by Kāṣīvilāsa Vandyopādhyāya.] [1901.] 8°. **14129. e. 25.**

—— *See* JAGADRĀMA. অষ্ট কাণ্ডে সম্পূর্ণ জগদ্রামী-রামায়ণ। [Rāmāyaṇa. Edited by Kāṣīvilāsa Vandyopādhyāya.] [1906.] 8°. **14129. e. 32.**

KĀṬIRĀMA ṬHĀKURA. আটাকাটি। সমাজ সংস্কারক সন্দর্ভ। [Āṭākāṭi. An exposure of some of the evil habits and manners of educated Bengalis.] pp. 102. *Calcutta*, 1885. 12°. **14125. e. 17.(6.)**

KĀTYĀYANA. কাত্যায়ন সংহিতা। [Kātyāyana-saṃhitā, or Karmapradīpa. Sanskrit text, with Bengali translation.] *See* PAÑCHĀNANA TARKARATNA BHAṬṬĀCHĀRYA. ঊনবিংশতি সংহিতা। [Ūnaviṃṣati saṃhitā.] pp. 303-334. [1903.] 8°. **14039. c. 20.**

KAVIBHŪSHAṆA (R. K.). Kayastha-tattwam. (কায়স্থ-তত্ত্বম্)। [A Sanskrit work in 208 stanzas, compiled to prove the descent of the Kāyastha caste from the Kshatriyas. With Bengali notes and translations.] pp. 3, 56. কুমারখালী ১৩০৬ [*Kumarkhali*, 1899.] 12°. **14058. a. 13.(3.)**

Forms no. 1 *of the* Tattvāmbudhi *series.*

KAVICHANDRA. *See* AYODHYĀRĀMA RĀYA.

KAVIKAṄKAṆA. *See* MUKUNDARĀMA CHAKRAVARTĪ.

KAVIKARṆAPŪRA, *Son of Ṣivānandasena.* অলঙ্কারকৌস্তুভঃ। [Alaṅkārakaustubha. A Sanskrit treatise on rhetoric in 10 *kiraṇas*, with a commentary by Viṣvanātha Chakravartī. Edited with a Bengali translation of the text by Rāmanārāyaṇa Vidyāratna.] pp. i. 834, xx. মুর্শিদাবাদ ১৩০৫ [*Murshidabad*, 1899.] 8°. **14053. ccc. 25.**

—— শ্রীচৈতন্যচরিতামৃত মহাকাব্যং। [Chaitanya-charitāmṛita. A Sanskrit poem in 20 *sargas* on the life of Chaitanya. Edited, with a Bengali prose translation, by Rāmanārāyaṇa Vidyāratna.] pp. 704, ii. মুর্শিদাবাদ ১২৯২ [*Murshidabad*, 1885-1892.] 8°. **14058. b. 28.**

KAVIRAÑJANA. *See* RĀMAPRASĀDA SENA.

KAVIVALLABHA, *Son of Rājavallabha.* *See* TĀRAKEṢVARA BHAṬṬĀCHĀRYA. কবিবল্লভের রসকদম্ব। [Kavivallabher rasakadamba. An article on the Vaishṇava poet Kavivallabha and his poem Rasakadamba.] [1902.] 8°. **14133. f. 18.**

KAY (WILLIAM), *D.D.* *See* BIBLE.—*Psalms.* The Book of Psalms, newly translated in Bengali and English [by William Kay and Kṛishṇamohana Vandyopādhyāya]. 1858. 8°. **3089. cc.**

KEDĀRANĀTHA, *Zamindar.* গ্রহবিপ্র। [Grahavipra. A tract on the functions of astrologers, illustrated by Sanskrit quotations.] pp. 8. উলুবেড়িয়া ১২৯৯ [*Uluberia*, 1893.] 8°. **14053. c. 56.(3.)**

KEDĀRANĀTHA DATTA. দত্তবংশমালা। [Dattavaṃṣamālā. Genealogies of the Datta families. With a Sanskrit poem on the same subject, entitled Dattavaṃṣa. Second edition.] pp. iv. 232. কলিকাতা ১৩০৬ [*Calcutta*, 1900.] 16°. **14053. a. 16.**

KEDĀRANĀTHA MAJUMDĀR. ময়মনসিংহের ইতিহাস। [Maymansiṃher itihāsa. A history of the District of Mymensingh.] pp. ii. iv. 234. কলিকাতা ১৯০৬ [*Calcutta*, 1906.] 12°. **14127. aa. 32.(2.)**

—— [Second edition.] pp. iv. 204. কলিকাতা ১৯০৭ [*Calcutta*, 1907.] 12°. **14127. aa. 49.**

—— ময়মনসিংহের বিবরণ। [Maymansiṃher vivaraṇa. An account of the District of Mymensingh. With a map.] pp. 171. কলিকাতা ১৯০৪ [*Calcutta*, 1904.] 12°. **14127. aa. 32.**

KEDĀRANĀTHA MAṆḌALA. বেহদ্দ-বেহায়া। [Behadd be-hāyā. A comedy, directed against female emancipation in Bengal.] pp. 39. ১৩০০ *Calcutta*, [1894.] 12°. **14131. a. 37.(3.)**

KEDĀRANĀTHA SARKĀR. নব-শিল্প। [Nava ṣilpa.] A short essay on some useful fibrous plants of India. pp. 33. কলিকাতা ১৩০৪ [*Calcutta*, 1898.] 12°. **14125. bb. 29.**

KEDĀRANĀTHA VIṢVĀSA. ভবানী পাঠক। [Bhavānī Pāṭhaka. A sequel to Bankimchandra's Devī Chandhurāṇī.] pp. 322. *Calcutta*, 1900. 12°. **14127. cc. 26.**

KEṢAVACHANDRA ĀCHĀRYA. Hasti-chikitsa. A practical treatise on the treatment of diseases of elephants . . . by Keshab Chandra Acharya. . . . হস্তী-চিকিৎসা ও হস্তীদেহের সংক্ষিপ্ত বিবরণ। pp. ii. ii. 97. *Calcutta*, 1886. 8°. **14125. c. 34.**

KEṢAVACHANDRA RĀYA KARMAKĀRA. শব্দার্থ-প্রকাশিকা। [Ṣabdārthaprakāṣikā. A Bengali dictionary, with derivations and Sanskrit notes. Tenth edition.] pp. vi. 658. কলিকাতা ১২৯৪ [*Calcutta*, 1887.] 4°. **14133. c. 7.**

KEṢAVACHANDRA SENA. [*Life.*] *See* GAURAGOVINDA RĀYA. কেশবচন্দ্র। [Keṣavachandra.] [1893.] 12°. **14127. a. 37.(5.)**

—— [*Life.*] *See* JAGADBANDHU MAITRA. মহাত্মা কেশব চন্দ্র সেনের সংক্ষিপ্ত জীবনী। [Mahātmā Keṣavachandra Sener saṃkshipta jīvanī.] [1886.] 12°. **14127. a. 29.(2.)**

—— আচার্য্য কেশবচন্দ্র। [Āchārya Keṣavachandra. A full account of the life of Keṣavachandra Sena, and of the development of the Brāhma Samāj since the time of Raja Rāmamohana Rāya.] কলিকাতা ১৮১৩ [*Calcutta*, 1892, *etc.*] 8°. **14123. d. 20.**

Imperfect, wanting all after pt. 3 of vol. ii.

—— আচার্য্যের উপদেশ। [Āchāryer upadeṣa. A collection of sermons preached by Keṣavachandra Sena.] Pts. i.-ii.; iv.-vi. কলিকাতা ১৮১৮-১৯ [*Calcutta*, 1896-97.] 12°. **14123. a. 34.**

—— ব্রহ্মগীতোপনিষৎ [Brahma gītopanishat. The teachings of Keṣavachandra Sena on *Yoga* and *Bhakti.*] 2 pts. কলিকাতা ১৮০৮-০৯ [*Calcutta*, 1887-88.] 12°. **14123. c. 21.**

—— ব্রহ্মমন্দিরের উপদেশ। [Brahma mandirer upadeṣa. Brahmist sermons.] Pt. i. pp. 59. কলিকাতা ১৮০৭ [*Calcutta*, 1885.] 8°. **14123. d. 14.**

—— ব্রাহ্মিকাদিগের প্রতি শ্রীমদাচার্য্য কেশবচন্দ্র সেনের উপদেশ। [Brāhmikādiger prati upadeṣa. Discourses on the religions and social duties of female members of the Brāhma Samāj. Another edition.] 2 pts. কলিকাতা ১৮০৯ [*Calcutta*, 1888.] 8°. **14123. d. 17.**

—— জীবন-বেদ। [Jīvana-veda. An autobiography, containing an account of the growth and gradual development of the author's religious beliefs. Second edition.] pp. 168. কলিকাতা ১৮০৮ [*Calcutta*, 1885.] 12°. **14123. c. 18.**

—— Keshub Chunder Sen. Correct statement of some disputed facts in his life. [Consisting of letters, some of which are in English, and various articles.] pp. 83. *Calcutta*, [1904.] 8°. **14127. bb. 24.(2.)**

—— নবসংহিতা। [Nava-saṃhitā. A Bengali translation of Keṣavachandra Sena's English work entitled "The New Dispensation, or the Minister's Exposition of it." Third edition.] pp. iv. 173. কলিকাতা ১৩১৩ [*Calcutta*, 1907.] 12°. **14123. c. 28.(5.)**

—— সাধু-সমাগম। [Sādhusamāgama, or Communion with holy men. Religious meditations.] pp. 85. কলিকাতা ১৩০৯ [*Calcutta*, 1888.] 12°. **14123. c. 22.(2.)**

—— সামাজিক ব্রহ্মোপাসনা প্রণালী। [Sāmājika Brahmopāsanā-praṇālī. The mode of conducting public worship in the Brāhma Samāj, with

a selection of prayers. Fifth edition.] pp. 36. কলিকাতা ১৮০৯ [*Calcutta*, 1888.] 12°.
14123. c. 22.(1.)

KEṢAVACHANDRA VANDYOPĀDHYĀYA. *See* PURĀṆAS.—*Bhāgavatapurāṇa.* পদ্য শ্রীমদ্ভাগবত। [Bhāgavatapurāṇa. A metrical translation by Keṣavachandra Vandyopādhyāya.] [1906.] 8°.
14123. gg. 4.

KHAGENDRANĀTHA ṢĀSTRĪ. *See* PURĀṆAS.—*Brahmāṇḍapurāṇa.* অধ্যাত্মরামায়ণম্। [Adhyātma-rāmāyaṇa. Edited, with Sanskrit analyses, and Bengali translations and paraphrases, by Khagendranātha.] [1901, *etc.*] 8°. **14016. d. 61.**

KHAIBAR, *City of.* খয়বরের জঙ্গনামা। [Khaibarer jang-nāmā. An historical romance, in Muhammadan Bengali verse, on the capture of Khaibar from the Jews by Muhammad. Translated from the Persian by Dost Muhammad. Second edition.] pp. 236, iv. কলিকাতা ১২৯৬ [*Calcutta*, 1889.] 8°.
14129. d. 27.

KHANĀ. [*Life.*] *See* UPENDRAKUMĀRA GHOSHA. আর্য্য-মহিলা। [Ārya-mahilā.] 1895. 12°.
14127. aa. 2.(5.)

—— *See* YOGEṢACHANDRA RĀYA, *M.A.* খনা। [Khanā. A paper on Khanā and her astrological sayings.] [1903.] 8°. **14133. f. 18.**

—— খনার বচন। [Khanār vachana. A collection of the sayings of Khanā, in old Bengali verse, on astrological, domestic, and agricultural matters. Edited, with explanations, by Madhusūdana Bhaṭṭāchārya.] pp. 52. *Calcutta*, 1889. 12°. **14125. dd. 15.**

al-**KHAṬĪB.** *See* MUHAMMAD ibn 'ABD ALLĀH, *al-Khaṭīb.*

KHOSĀLACHANDRA RĀYA. বাখরগঞ্জের ইতিহাস। [Bākhargañjer itihāsa.] History of Backerganj. pp. 210. *Barisal*, 1895. 12°. **14127. a. 51.(3.)**

KIRANABĀLĀ GĀṄGULĪ, *Srīmatī.* আধ্যাত্মীক [*sic*] কিরণ-প্রকাশ। [Ādhyātmika kiraṇaprakāṣa. A Christian treatise on leading a spiritual life; with hymns.] pp. ii. 138. কানপুর [*Cawnpore*, 1902.] 12°. **14123. a. 14.(2.)**

KĪRTTIVĀSA, *Author of the Rāmāyaṇa.* *See* KṚITTIVĀSA.

KIṢORĪLĀLA RĀYA. মন্ত্রার্থ সম্বলিত তান্ত্রিক অভিধান। . . . Tantrik abbidhan. [A dictionary of Tantric terms and symbols.] Pt. i. pp. xviii. 42. বগুড়া ১৩০২ [*Bogra*, 1895.] 8°. **14133. b. 16.**

KLEMM (CURT). *See* BAṄKIMCHANDRA CHAṬṬOPĀDHYĀYA. Kopal-Kundala . . . Deutsch von C. Klemm. 1886. 8°. **14127. c. 27.**

KNIGHT (MIRIAM S.), *Mrs.* *See* BAṄKIMCHANDRA CHAṬṬOPĀDHYĀYA. Krishna Kanta's Will . . . Translated by M. S. Knight, *etc.* 1895. 8°.
14127. e. 46.

—— *See* PYĀRĪCHĀṆD MITRA, called ṬEKCHĀṆD ṬHĀKURA. The Spoilt Boy. [A translation of Ālāler gharer dulāl by Narendranātha Mitra, with the aid of M. S. Knight.] 1882-83. 8°.
P.P. 1423. ld.

—— *See* ṢIVANĀTHA ṢĀSTRĪ. The Second Daughter-in-law; or the History of Pramada, *etc.* [Translated from the Bengali by M. S. Knight.] 1882. 8°. **P.P. 1423. ld.**

—— *See* TĀRAKANĀTHA GAṄGOPĀDHYĀYA. Lalita and Saudamini . . . Translated by Mrs. J. B. Knight. 1891. 8°. **P.P. 1423. ld.**

—— *See* TĀRAKANĀTHA GAṄGOPĀDHYĀYA. Shornalata: a tale of Hindu life. By Tarak Nath Ganguli. [Translated by M. S. Knight.] 1883-1884. 8°. **P.P. 1423. ld.**

KOKILADŪTA. সংস্কৃতকোকিলদূতং। [Kokiladūta. A Sanskrit poem in 104 stanzas in imitation of Kālidāsa's Meghadūta. Accompanied by a Sanskrit commentary by Kālidāsa Sena, and its Bengali translation by Dīnadayāla Dāsa Prāmāṇika.] pp. xi. 195. শান্তিপুর ১৭৮৫ [*Santipur*, 1862.] 8°. **14072. cc. 50.**

KONNAGAR.—*Public Library.* Rules of the Konnuggur Public Library. কোন্নগর সাধারণ পুস্তকালয়ের নিয়মাবলী। pp. 7. [*Calcutta*, 1870?] 8°.
14125. ee. 25.(2.)

KRAMADĪṢVARA. সংক্ষিপ্ত সারব্যাকরণ। [Saṃkshipta sāra-vyākaraṇa. A Sanskrit grammar, being an abridgment of the sūtras of Kramadīṣvara. Edited with a Sanskrit commentary, and a Bengali translation by Upendranātha Chakravartī.] pp. 28. কলিকাতা [*Calcutta*,] 1891. 8°.
14090. c. 38.(1.)

Selections from the Sandhi-pāda only.

KṚIKALĀSADĪPIKĀ. বিবিধসাধন। কৃকলাসদীপিকা। [Kṛikalāsadīpikā. A work on Tantric magic. Sanskrit text, with a Bengali translation.] pp. 20. [1893, *etc.*] *See* PERIODICAL PUBLICATIONS.—*Calcutta.* অরুণোদয়। [Aruṇodāya.] Pt. i., no. 31. [1890, *etc.*] 4°. **14133. g. 16.**

KṚIPĀNĀTHA ṢARMĀ VIṢVĀSA. অকলঙ্ক যোগ। [Akalaṅka yoga. Miscellaneous writings in prose and verse, with occasional Sanskrit stanzas.] pp. iv. iii. 276. কলিকাতা ১৩১০ [*Calcutta*, 1903.] 12°. **14131. d. 45.**

KṚISHṆABANDHU MUKHOPĀDHYĀYA. Mode of translation [from Bengali into English]. By Krishna Bandhu Mukerjee. pp. 135. *Serajgunge*, 1891. 12°. **14131. e. 21.(1.)**

KṚISHṆA-CHAITANYA. *See* CHAITANYA.

KṚISHṆACHANDRA RĀYA, *of Calcutta.* Phrases and Idioms, with explanations in English and Bengali, and illustrative sentences from standard English works. By Krishna Chandra Roy. Fifth edition. Revised and enlarged. pp. iv. 592. *Calcutta*, 1904. 8°. **14131. g. 34.**

KṚISHṆACHANDRA TĀLAVIṢĀRADA. সঙ্গীত-ব্যাকরণ। [Saṅgīta-vyākaraṇa. A treatise on the Hindu system of musical notation.] pp. 136. ঢাকা ১৩০৬ [*Dacca*, 1900.] 8°. **14125. d. 28.**

KṚISHṆACHANDRA VASU MALLIKA. মনস্তাপ। [Manastāpa. Patriotic songs.] pp. vi. 70. *Calcutta*, ১৩১৩ [1907.] 12°. **14129. bb. 33.**

KṚISHṆACHARAṆA MAJUMDĀR. *See* YADUNANDANA, *Kavi.* মূল ঢাকুর ও সমালোচনা *etc.* [Ḍhākura. Edited, with an introduction and notes, by Kṛishṇacharaṇa Majumdār, and followed by a criticism on a treatise by Govindamohana Rāya Vidyāvinoda.] [1891.] 12°. **14127. a. 20.**

KṚISHṆADĀSA, *Disciple of Rūpa Gosvāmī.* শ্রীশ্রী-গোপী-উপাসনা গ্রন্থ। [Gopī-upāsanā. A poem on the sports of Kṛishṇa with the milkmaids of Brindaban.] pp. 72. *Calcutta*, 1896. 8°. **14129. e. 49.**

Published for the first time from a MS. *dated* 1257 B.S.

KṚISHṆADĀSA KAVIRĀJA, *Gosvāmī.* *See* STURSBERG (O.). Das Caitanyacaritāmṛta des Kṛsṇadāsa Kavirāja. . . . Inaugural-Dissertation . . . von Otto Stursberg. [1907.] 8°. **14123. ff. 17.**

KṚISHṆADĀSA KAVIRĀJA, *Gosvāmī (continued).* বাল্য-বিলাস। [Bālyavilāsa. A poem on the sports of Kṛishṇa when a boy.] *See* VAISHṆAVA GRANTHĀVALĪ. বৈষ্ণব গ্রন্থাবলী। [1900.] 12°. **14123. e. 20.(3.)**

—— বৃহৎ আশ্রয় নির্ণয় গ্রন্থ অর্থাৎ ভাব আশ্রয়। [Bṛihat āṣraya-nirṇaya. A treatise in verse on different modes of Vaishṇava worship. Fifth edition.] pp. 12. ঢাকা [*Dacca*, 1894.] *obl.* 8°. **14123. f. 49.(1.)**

—— শ্রীশ্রীচৈতন্যচরিতামৃত। [Chaitanya-charitāmṛita. The life of Chaitanya, in verse. Edited with copious notes, and translations of Sanskrit quotations accompanied by Sanskrit commentaries, by Madanagopāla Gosvāmī.] কাল্না ১৮১৩ [*Kalna*, 1891, *etc.*] 4°. **14123. i. 8.**

—— শ্রীশ্রীচৈতন্যচরিতামৃত। [Chaitanya-charitāmṛita. With the Sanskrit commentary of Viṣvanātha Chakravartī, and a Bengali interpretation, styled Sudhāsañchāriṇī by the editor, Mākhanlāla Dāsa Bhāgavatabhūshaṇa.] 3 vols. কলিকাতা ১৩১৫ [*Calcutta*, 1908.] 8°. **14123. g. 24.**

—— কৃষ্ণকর্ণামৃত। [Kṛishṇakarṇāmṛita. A poem on the sports of Kṛishṇa at Brindaban, being a metrical translation by Yadunandana Dāsa of Kṛishṇadāsa's Sanskrit commentary, entitled Sāraṅgaraṅgadā, on the Kṛishṇakarṇāmṛita of Vilvamaṅgala Gosvāmī.] *See* VAISHṆAVA GRANTHĀVALĪ. বৈষ্ণব গ্রন্থাবলী। [1900.] 12°. **14123. e. 20.(3.)**

—— প্রেমাঙ্কুর। [Premāṅkura. Vaishṇava hymns and poems, some few of which are in Sanskrit. Second edition.] pp. 15. বহরমপুর [*Berhampore*, 1887.] 12°. **14123. e. 12.(1.)**

KṚISHṆADĀSA PĀLA, *Editor of "The Hindoo Patriot."* [*Life.*] *See* RĀMAGOPĀLA SĀNNYĀLA. কৃষ্ণদাস পালের জীবনী। The life of Kristo Das Pal, *etc.* **14127. b. 45.(2.)**

KṚISHṆADĀSA ṢĀSTRĪ. *See* PURĀṆAS.—*Garuḍapurāṇa.* গরুড়পুরাণম্। [Garuḍapurāṇa. With a Bengali translation by Kṛishṇadāsa.] [1907.] 8°. **14016. dd. 26.**

—— *See* PURĀṆAS.—*Padmapurāṇa.* পদ্মপুরাণম্। স্বর্গ-খণ্ডম্। [Padmapurāṇa. The Svarga-khaṇḍa. With a Bengali translation by Kṛishṇadāsa.] [1906.] 8°. **14016. dd. 24.(1.)**

KRISHṆADEVĀCHĀRYA. নৃসিংহপরিচর্য্যা। [Nṛisiṃha-paricharyā. An authoritative work in verse on Vaishṇava tenets. Sanskrit text, edited, with a Bengali prose translation, by Rāmanārāyaṇa Vidyāratna.] pp. 313, iv. মুর্শিদাবাদ। ৪০৫ চৈতন্যাব্দ [*Murshidabad*, 1890.] 8°. **14033. b. 56.**

KRISHṆADHANA VANDYOPĀDHYĀYA. *See* KSHETRAMOHANA GOSVĀMĪ. বঙ্গৈকতান। [Vaṅgaikatāna.] The Bengali Concert. [A collection of Bengali airs, set to music, according to the English system of notation. Edited by Kṛishṇadhana Vandyopādhyāya.] 1867. Fol. **M. F. 636. q.(6.)**

—— A Comprehensive Grammar of vocal music, or a theoretical and practical treatise on the art of singing. By Krishna Dhan Banerjee. গীতসূত্রসার। [Gītasūtrasāra.] 2 pts. কোচবিহার ১৮৮৬ [*Cooch Behar*, 1886.] 8°. **14125. d. 13.**

—— Part I. Second edition. কোচবিহার ১৮৯৭ [*Cooch Behar*, 1897.] 8°. **14125. d. 25.**

—— A Self-instructor for the Harmonium. By Krishnadhan Banerjee. হার্ম্মোনিয়ম শিক্ষা। [Hārmoniyam-śikshā.] pp. vi. 80. কোচবিহার ১৮৯৯ [*Cooch Behar*, 1899.] 8°. **14125. d. 96.**

KRISHṆADHANA VIDYĀPATI. *See* BHUVANACHANDRA MUKHOPĀDHYĀYA and KRISHṆADHANA VIDYĀPATI. বঙ্কিম বাবুর গুপ্তকথা। [Baṅkim Bābur guptakathā.] 1890. 8°. **14127. e. 40.**

—— কৌতুক চতুরঙ্গ বা সৎরঞ্জ-বিজ্ঞান। [Kautuka-chaturaṅga, also called Satranj-vijñāna. A treatise on chess, with numerous problems.] pp. v. 234, ii. কলিকাতা ১২৯৩ [*Calcutta*, 1886.] 8°. **14125. dd. 14.**

KRISHṆAGOPĀLA BHAKTA. *See* BĀDARĀYAṆA. বেদান্তদর্শন। [Vedānta-darśana. Edited with notes by Kṛishṇagopāla Bhakta.] [1891, *etc.*] 8°. **14048. dd. 23.**

KRISHṆAGOPĀLA CHAKRAVARTĪ. অঞ্জলি। কাব্য। [Añjalī. Love songs.] Pt. i. pp. 60. *Kumarkhali*, [1898]. 12°. **14129. a. 52.(2.)**

KRISHṆAKAMALA BHAṬṬĀCHĀRYA. *See* MANU. হিন্দুশাস্ত্র। . . . ধর্ম্মশাস্ত্র। [Selections from the Dharmaśāstra of Manu. Edited with Bengali translations, preface, and notes by Kṛishṇakamala and Kṛishṇapada Vidyāratna.] 1895. 8°. **14085. c. 45.(vol. i.)**

KRISHṆAKAMALA GOSVĀMĪ. কৃষ্ণকমল-গ্রন্থাবলী। [Kṛishṇakamala-granthāvalī. The Collected works of Kṛishṇakamala Gosvāmī. Edited, with a life of the author, by Kāminīkumāra Gosvāmī. Second edition.] pp. ii. 30, 307, 20. শ্রীচৈতন্যাব্দ ৪১৯ *Calcutta*, [1904.] 12°. **14131. aa. 2.**

—— কৃষ্ণকমল-গ্রন্থাবলী অর্থাৎ স্বপ্নবিলাস, দিব্যোন্মাদ, বিচিত্র বিলাস। [Svapnavilāsa, Divyonmāda, and Vichitravilāsa. Three dramatic compositions in prose and verse on the sports of Kṛishṇa with the milkmaids of Brindaban. With a biography of the author.] pp. 30, 76, 78, 74. *Calcutta*, ১৩০২ [1896.] 12°. **14131. a. 38.(5.)**

KRISHṆAKĀNTA BHĀDURĪ, called RASASĀGARA. Life of Rasha Sagur and some of his ex-tempore poems. Collected by Shyamadhuba Roy. শ্রীকবি রসসাগরের জীবন চরিত এবং তাঁহার কতকগুলি উপস্থিত পাদপূরণ। [Rasasāgarer jīvanacharita.] Second edition. pp. iii. 47. *Calcutta*, 1898. 12°. **14127. aa. 14.(2.)**

KRISHṆAKIŚORA RĀYA. দুর্গালীলাতরঙ্গিণী। [Durgālīlā-taraṅgiṇī. Poems on the mythology of the goddess Durgā.] pp. vii. 255. কলিকাতা ১৩১২ [*Calcutta*, 1906.] 12°. **14129. bb. 31.**

KRISHṆAKUMĀRA MITRA. ভিক্টোরিয়া-চরিত সচিত্র। [Bhikṭoriyā-charita. A life of Queen Victoria.] pp. 70. কলিকাতা ১৮৯৮ [*Calcutta*, 1898.] 8°. **14127. bb. 12.**

—— বুদ্ধদেব-চরিত ও বৌদ্ধধর্ম্মের সংক্ষিপ্ত বিবরণ। [Buddhadeva-charita. The life of Buddha, and an account of Buddhism. Fourth edition.] pp. 227. কলিকাতা ১৩০৬ [*Calcutta*, 1900.] 12°. **14127. aa. 12.**

—— মহম্মদ-চরিত ও মুসলমান ধর্ম্মের সংক্ষিপ্ত বিবরণ। [Mahammad-charita. A life of the Prophet Muḥammad, from a Brahmist stand-point; with a brief sketch of the Muhammadan religion, which is compared to the monotheism of the Vedānta philosophy.] pp. 264. কলিকাতা ১২৯৩ [*Calcutta*, 1886.] 12°. **14127. a. 30.**

KRISHṆALĀLA MOHANALĀLA JHAVERĪ. *See* RAMEŚACHANDRA DATTA. Shivaji . . . A novel translated . . . by Krishnalal Mohanlal Jhaveri. 1899. 8°. **14127. ee. 19.**

KRISHṆA MIŚRA. প্রবোধচন্দ্রোদয় নাটক। [Prabodhachandrodaya nāṭaka. A Sanskrit allegorical drama, with a Bengali translation by Kāśīnātha Tarkapañchānana, Gaṅgādhara Nyāyaratna and Rāmakiṅkara Śiromaṇi.] pp. 190. কলিকাতা ১২৬২ [*Calcutta*, 1855.] 16°. **14079. a. 4.**

—— প্রবোধ-চন্দ্রোদয় নাটক। [Prabodhachandrodaya nāṭaka. Translated by Jyotirindranātha Ṭhākura.] pp. ii. 117. কলিকাতা ১৩০৮ [*Calcutta*, 1902.] 12°. **14131. aa. 9.(4.)**

KṚISHṆAMOHANA DHARA. Raja-bhakti, or A poem giving vent to the loyal feelings of the people of Assam at the approaching retirement of the Hon'ble H. J. S. Cotten, Chief Commissioner of the Province ... রাজ-ভক্তি। pp. 41. ঢাকা ১৯০২ [*Dacca*, 1902.] 12°. **14129. bb. 18.(2.)**

KṚISHṆAMOHANA VANDYOPĀDHYĀYA, *Rev.* *See* BIBLE.—*Psalms.* The Book of Psalms, newly translated in Bengali and English [by W. Kay and Kṛishṇamohana Vandyopādhyāya]. 1858. 8°. **3089. cc.**

—— [*Life.*] *See* DURGĀDĀSA LĀHIṚĪ. আদর্শ-চরিত [Ādarṣa-charita.] [1886.] 12°. **14127. a. 29.**

—— Ordination sermon, preached by command of the Right Revd. the Lord Bishop of Calcutta, at Trinity Church, Amherst Street, by Revd. K. M. Banerjea. pp. 20. *Chinsurah*, 1870. 12°. **14123. a. 26.(3.)**

KṚISHṆĀNANDA VĀGĪṢA BHAṬṬĀCHĀRYA. বৃহৎ তন্ত্রসার। [Bṛihat Tantrasāra. An epitome of the Tantras, with a Bengali translation by Prasannakumāra Ṣāstrī Bhaṭṭāchārya.] pp. vi. 374, 198; 17 *plates.* কলিকাতা ১৩০৩ [*Calcutta*, 1896.] 4°. **14033. c. 39.**

—— ষট্‌কর্ম্মদীপিকা। [Shaṭkarmadīpikā. A Sanskrit work treating of six modes of magic. With a Bengali translation.] *See* TANTRAS.—*Dattātreyatantra.* দত্তাত্রেয়ঃ, pp. 40-93. [1885.] 4°. **14033. bb. 24.(1.)**

—— ষট্‌কর্ম্মদীপিকা। [Shaṭkarmadīpikā. With a Bengali version.] pp. 40. [1890, *etc.*] *See* PERIODICAL PUBLICATIONS.—*Calcutta.* অরুণোদয়। [Aruṇodaya.] Pt. i., no. 2. [1890, *etc.*] 4°. **14133. g. 16.**

—— তন্ত্রসারঃ [Tantrasāra. Sanskrit text, with a Bengali translation by Chandrakumāra Tarkāaṅkāra, and, as far as p. 195, with an anonymous Sanskrit commentary. Edited by Rasikamohana Chaṭṭopādhyāya.] pp. v. 750. কলিকাতা ১২৮৫ [*Calcutta*, 1879-86.] 4°. **14033. bb. 22.**

KṚISHṆAPADA VIDYĀRATNA. *See* MANU. হিন্দু-শাস্ত্র। ... ধর্ম্মশাস্ত্র। [Selections from the Dharmaṣāstra of Manu. Edited with Bengali translations, preface, and notes by Kṛishṇakamala Bhaṭṭāchārya and Kṛishṇapada Vidyāratna.] 1895. 8°. **14085. c. 45.(vol. i.)**

—— একশৃঙ্গ নাটক বা ভগবান্ বুদ্ধদেবের পূর্ব্ব জীবনী। [Ekaṣriṅga nāṭaka.] A drama on the previous life of Buddha, with his noble doctrines. pp. vi. 98. *Chittagong*, 1897. 12°. **14131. a. 40.(5.)**

KṚISHṆAPRASANNA SENA. ভক্তি ও ভক্ত [Bhakti o bhakta. A compilation of Sanskrit texts, with Bengali translations and explanations, and of Bengali works in prose and verse, bearing on *bhakti*, or Vaishṇava devotion. Second edition.] pp. 154. বারাণসী ১৮০৮ [*Benares*, 1887.] 8°. **14028. c. 56.**

KṚISHṆARĀMA DĀSA, *Son of Bhagavatīcharaṇa Dāsa.* রায়মঙ্গল। [Rāyamaṅgala. A poem in honour of Dakshiṇarāya, the local god of the Sunderban, with critical notes by Vyomakeṣa Mustafī.] ১৩০৩ [1896-97.] *See* ACADEMIES, *etc.*—Calcutta.—*Bengal Academy of Literature.* সাহিত্য-পরিষৎ-পত্রিকা। [Sāhitya-parishat-patrikā.] Vol. iii., nos. 3 and 4. [1894, *etc.*] 8°. **14133. f. 18.**

KṚISHṆARĀMA DATTA. রাধিকামঙ্গল। [Rādhikāmaṅgala. A poem on the lives of Rādhā and Kṛishṇa.] pp. 31. ১৩০৯ [1902.] *See* PERIODICAL PUBLICATIONS.—*Calcutta.* প্রাচীন বাঙ্গালা গ্রন্থাবলী। [Prāchīna Bāṅgālā granthāvalī.] no. 12. [1900, *etc.*] 8°. **14133. ff. 2.**

KṚISHṆA SĀRVABHAUMA. পদাঙ্কদূতম্। [Padāṅkadūta. A Sanskrit poem on the legend of Kṛishṇa and Rādhā, in imitation of the Meghadūta. Edited, with grammatical analyses, translation, and commentary in Bengali by Ṣyāmācharaṇa Kaviratna.] pp. xiv. 95. *Calcutta*, ১৮২৬ [1904.] 12°. **14060. b. 17.(2.)**

KṚISHṆENDRA RĀYA. স্বভাব-নীতি। [Svabhāvanīti. Useful lessons from nature.] pp. 143. কলিকাতা ১৩০২ [*Calcutta*, 1896.] 8°. **14131. g. 31.**

KṚITTIVĀSA. *See* VĀLMĪKI. কৃত্তিবাসী রামায়ণ। [Rāmāyaṇa. Translated by Kṛittivāsa. Collated from ancient manuscripts.] [1904, *etc.*] 8°. **14129. cc. 15.**

—— —— রামায়ণ। [Rāmāyaṇa. With an extensive introduction, and life of Kṛittivāsa.] [1906.] 8°. **14129. cc. 18.**

—— —— কৃত্তিবাসী রামায়ণ *etc.* [Rāmāyaṇa. Edited, with a life of the poet, by Subalachandra Mitra.] [1908.] 8°. **14129. e. 35.**

—— সরল কৃত্তিবাস। [Sarala Kṛittivāsa. A simplified metrical version of the Rāmāyaṇa of Kīrttivāsa, with illustrations, and an introduction containing an account of the author and his poem, by Yogīndranātha Vasu.] pp. xvii. 220, vii. কলিকাতা ১৩১৪ [*Calcutta*, 1907.] 4°. **14129. f. 8.**

KSHEMĀNANDA BRAHMACHĀRĪ. সচিত্র সম্ভোগ-রত্নাকর ও ঐন্দ্রজালিকবশীকরণ বিদ্যা। কামরত্নসমুচ্চয়ঃ। [Sambhogaratnākara, or Kāmaratnasamuchchaya. A treatise on the psychology and physiology of love, chiefly in Sanskrit verses compiled from divers sources, with metrical Bengali paraphrases.] pp. 224. *Calcutta*, 1902. 12°. **14053. b. 41.(2.)**

—— সচিত্র লজ্জতন্নেছা বা কামরত্ন-সমুচ্চয়। [Sambhogaratnākara. Another issue of the preceding work, under the title of Lazzat al-nisā, with an appended chapter in Bengali.] pp. 229. *Calcutta*, 1902. 12°. **14053. b. 41.(3.)**

KSHETRAGOPĀLA RĀYA. ইন্দ্রকুমারী। [Indrakumārī. An historical tale.] pp. 118. *Calcutta*, 1891. 8°. **14127. f. 42.(4.)**

KSHETRAMOHANA GHOSHA. প্রভাত-কুমারী। [Prabhāta-kumārī. A tale of Bengali social life.] pp. 104. কলিকাতা ১৩০৪ [*Calcutta*, 1898.] 12°. **14127. cc. 10.(3.)**

KSHETRAMOHANA GOSVĀMĪ. আশুরঞ্জনীতত্ত্ব।... Asuranjanitatwa, or a treatise on Esrar, by Kshetra Mohan Goswami. pp. ii. 77. কলিকাতা ১২৯২ [*Calcutta*, 1885.] 8°. **14125. d. 11.**

—— বঙ্গৈকতান। [Vaṅgaikatāna.] The Bengali Concert. [A collection of Bengali airs, by Kshetramohana Gosvāmī, set to music according to the English system of notation, and edited by Krishnadhana Vandyopādhyāya.] *Lith.* যোধপুর [*Jodhpur*,] 1867. Fol. **M.F. 636. q.(6.)**

Without pagination.

KSHETRAMOHANA GUPTA. প্রাইভেট টিউটরের দুঃস্বপ্ন। [Prāibheṭ ṭiuṭarer duḥsvapna. The unprincipled conduct of a private tutor in a Bengali family. A story of domestic life.] pp. 30. কলিকাতা ১৩০৬ [*Calcutta*, 1899.] 12°. **14127. c. 30.(4.)**

KSHETRAMOHANA SENAGUPTA VIDYĀRATNA. সচিত্র বয়ন-বিদ্যা বা তাঁত-শিক্ষা। [Vayana-vidyā. A treatise on the native art of weaving.] pp. 72. কলিকাতা ১৩১৩ [*Calcutta*, 1906.] 12°. **14125. ddd. 1.**

KSHETRAMOHANA VANDYOPĀDHYĀYA. The Translator's Friend, or a Dictionary of Law terms . . . Part i. Bengali-English-Roman Urdu. By Kshetra Mohan Banerjee. Revised by Purna Chandra Dutta. pp. 94, 8, 32, 19. *Calcutta*, 1898. 8°. **14125. a. 27.**

KSHĪRODĀPRASĀDA CHAṬṬOPĀDHYĀYA. *See* PLAYFAIR (W. S.). ধাত্রীবিদ্যা। [Dhātrīvidyā.] ... A treatise on the science and practice of midwifery. [Translated by Kshīrodāprasāda Chaṭṭopādhyāya.] 1901. 8°. **14125. c. 42.**

KSHĪRODAPRASĀDA VIDYĀVINODA. দাদা ও দিদি। রঙ্গনাট্য। [Dādā o didi. A farce.] pp. 55. কলিকাতা ১৩১৪ [*Calcutta*, 1908.] 12°. **14131. aa. 7.(3.)**

—— পদ্মিনী। [Padminī. An historical drama on the siege of Chitor, by ʿAlā al-Dīn, king of Delhi.] pp. ii. 201. কলিকাতা ১৩১৩ [*Calcutta*, 1906.] 12°. **14131. aa. 5.(1.)**

KSHITĪNDRANĀTHA ṬHĀKURA. *See* MAHĀBHĀRATA.—*Bhagavadgītā.* শ্রীমদ্ভগবদ্গীতা। [Bhagavadgītā. Sanskrit text and Bengali translation. Edited with an index and introduction by Kshitīndranātha Ṭhākura.] [1895.] 16°. **14065. b. 15.**

—— আর্য্যরমণীর শিক্ষা ও স্বাধীনতা। [Ārya ramaṇīr ṣikshā o svādhīnatā. A treatise on the education and independence of Hindu women.] pp. xii. 270. কলিকাতা ১৩০৭ [*Calcutta*, 1901.] 12°. **14125. e. 38.(3.)**

—— ব্রাহ্মসমাজ ও তাহার কার্য্য। [Brāhma Samāj o tāhār kārya. A tract on the services rendered to the Hindu community by the Âdi Brâhma Samāj.] pp. 26. কলিকাতা ১৮১৭ [*Calcutta*, 1895.] 12°. **14123. c. 28.(3.)**

—— রাজা হরিশ্চন্দ্র। [Rājā Hariśchandra. A dissertation on the legend of Hariśchandra, king of Oudh, who became an ascetic.] pp. ii. 100, iii. কলিকাতা [*Calcutta*, 1897.] 12°. **14131. d. 44.**

KUDRAT ALLĀH. জাওয়াহেরল এছলাম। [Jawāhir al-Islām. Religious and ethical advice, in Muhammadan Bengali verse.] pp. 120. কলিকাতা ১৩১১ [*Calcutta*, 1904.] 8°. **14123. h. 26.(2.)**

KULACHANDRA DE DĀSA. *See* VIPINAVIHĀRĪ VANDYOPĀDHYĀYA and KULACHANDRA DE DĀSA. হুঁকাপুরাণ মাহাত্ম্য। [Huṇkā-purāṇa-māhātmya.] [1892.] 8°. **14072. b. 21.**

KULACHANDRA GUPTA. সংক্ষিপ্ত উর্দ্দো-ভাষাভিধান। [Urdū-bhāshābhidhāna. An Urdu-Bengali vocabulary.] pp. ii. 42. ব্রাহ্মণবাড়িয়া ১৩০১ [*Brahmanbaria*, 1894.] 8°. **14133. b. 15.**

The Urdu is in Bengali characters.

KULIKĀHINĪ. কুলিকাহিনী [Kulikāhinī.] Sketches from Cooly life. pp. 181. *Calcutta*, 1888. 8°. **14127. f. 37.(2.)**

KUMUDINĪ, *Wife of Rāmachandra Siṃha.* A brief sketch of the life of Srimati Kumudinee, the wife of R. C. Sinha, of the New Dispensation Brahma Somaj of India. কুমুদিনী-চরিত্র। [Kumudinī-charitra.] pp. vi. 128. *Cooch Behar*, 1890. 12°. **14127. a. 36.**

KUMUDINĪ VASU, *Śrīmatī.* আভা। [Ābhā. Miscellaneous poems.] pp. viii. 228. কুমিল্লা ১৩১২ [*Comilla*, 1905.] 8°. **14129. cc. 12.**

KUÑJALĀLA RĀYA. *See* CHHAṚĀ. ছড়া। [Chhaṛā. Nursery rhymes of Burdwan, compiled by Kuñjalāla Rāya.] [1896.] 8°. **14133. f. 18.**

KUÑJAVIHĀRĪ BĀGCHĪ. বাঙ্গালির প্রকৃতি। [Bāṅgālir prakṛiti. A sketch of life in Bengal thirty years ago.] Pt. i. pp. 77. কলিকাতা ১২৮৫ [*Calcutta*, 1888.] 12°. **14127. e. 36.**

KUÑJAVIHĀRĪ BAṆIK. *See* CHAṆḌĪDĀSA. আদি কবি চণ্ডীদাস ঠাকুর প্রণীত মহাজন-পদাবলী [Mahājana padāvalī. A collection of *padas* by Chaṇḍīdāsa, edited, with an introductory life of the poet, by Kuñjavihārī Baṇik.] [1888.] 12°. **14129. b. 34.**

KUÑJAVIHĀRĪ BHAṬṬĀCHĀRYA. অনঙ্গ-মঞ্জরী। [Anaṅgamañjarī. The marriage of the daughter of Raja Jayachandra. An historical drama in 5 acts.] pp. 118. ঢাকা ১২৯৪ [*Dacca*, 1887.] 12°. **14131. c. 17.(2.)**

KUÑJAVIHĀRĪ DEVA. *See* ÂMI, *pseud.* [i.e. KUÑJAVIHĀRĪ DEVA.]

KUÑJAVIHĀRĪ GAṄGOPĀDHYĀYA. মাতৃপূজা বা স্বর্গোদ্ধার। [Mātṛipūjā, also called Svargoddhāra. A mythological drama.] pp. iii. 278. হাওড়া [*Howrah*,] 1908. 8°. **14131. aa. 11.**

KUÑJAVIHĀRĪ NYĀYABHŪSHAṆA. *See* ACADEMIES, *etc.*—Calcutta.—*Asiatic Society of Bengal.* Catalogue of Printed books and Manuscripts in Sanskrit (and Bengali) . . . Compiled by Paṇḍit Kunja Vihāri Nyāyabhūṣaṇa, *etc.* 1899, *etc.* 4°. **14096. dd. 5.**

KUR'ĀN. কোরাণ শরিফ। قرآن مجيد فرقان حميد ব্যাখ্যা ও টীকা সহ বঙ্গানুবাদিত। [The Koran, Arabic text, accompanied by a Bengali translation and commentary by Na'īm al-Dīn, assisted by Ghulām Sarwar.] করটীয়া ১৮৯১ [*Karatia*, 1891, *etc.*] 8°. **14509. b. 18.**

Pp. 1-112 were published tentatively during 1887-90, being afterwards withdrawn and reprinted with corrections.

—— [Second edition.] করটীয়া ১৩০৬ [*Karatia*, 1899, *etc.*] 8°. **14509. b. 22.**

—— বঙ্গানুবাদিত তফসীর হাক্কানী। [The Koran. Arabic text, accompanied by a Bengali translation by Madhu Miyān of the Hindustani version, and commentary of Abū Muhammad 'Abd al-Ḥakk, entitled Tafsīr i ḥakkānī.] কলিকাতা [*Calcutta*, 1901, *etc.*] 8°. **14507. b. 34.**

—— قرآن مجيد مترجم কোরাণ শরীফ। [The Koran. Arabic text, with Shāh Rafī' al-Dīn's interlineary Hindustani translation, and marginal notes from various sources. Edited, with a Bengali interlineary translation of the text and of the Hindustani notes by Muhammad 'Abbās 'Alī.] কলিকাতা ১৩১৪ [*Calcutta*, 1907, *etc.*] Fol. **14509. d. 21.**

In progress.

—— কোরাণ শরিফ। [The Koran, translated from the Arabic, with notes, by Girisachandra Sena. Third edition.] pp. viii. iv. x. 720. কলিকাতা ১৮২৯ [*Calcutta*, 1908.] 8°. **14123. h. 39.**

KUR'ĀN (*continued*). কোর-আন। সংক্ষিপ্ত ব্যাখ্যা সহ সবিস্তার অনুবাদ। তবারকল্লজী নামক পারা। [The 29th Section of the Koran, Surahs 67-77, translated into Bengali with notes, by Taslīm al-Dīn Ahmad.] pp. 101. কলিকাতা ১৩১৪ [*Calcutta*, 1907.] 8°. **14123. h. 38.**

—— قرآن مجيد مترجم ... কোরাণ শরীফ। আমপারা। [The 30th, or last Section of the Koran, Surahs 78-114, preceded by the Surah Fātihah, Arabic text, with Shāh Rafīʿ al-Dīn's interlineary Hindustani translation. Edited, with a Bengali interlineary translation of the text, and of Hindustani marginal notes, compiled from various sources, by Muhammad ʿAbbās ʿAlī.] pp. 48. কলিকাতা ১৩১৫ [*Calcutta*, 1908.] 8°. **14509. b. 22.**

LAKSHMAṆA MAJUMDĀR. চট্টগ্রামী-ভাষা। [Chaṭṭagrāmī bhāshā. Specimens of the Chittagong dialect in prose and verse.] pp. ii. 11. চট্টগ্রাম [*Chittagong*, 1905.] 12°. **14125. f. 42.**

LAKSHMĪBĀĪ, *Rāṇī of Jhansi*. *See* JYOTIRINDRANĀTHA ṬHĀKURA. ঝাঁশির রাণী। [Jhāṇsir rāṇī. An account of the life and heroism of Lakshmībāī, Rāṇī of Jhansi.] [1903.] 12°. **14127. aa. 29.**

LAKSHMĪNĀRĀYAṆA CHAKRAVARTĪ. শক-দুহিতা বা দুর্গোদ্ধার। [Śakaduhitā. An historical novel on the defeat of the Śakas under Mihirakula by Vikramāditya, king of Ujjain.] pp. 236. কলিকাতা ১৩০৬ [*Calcutta*, 1899.] 12°. **14127. c. 30.(6.)**

LĀLADĀSA BĀBĀJĪ. শ্রীশ্রীভক্তমাল গ্রন্থ। [Bhaktamāla. The lives of Vaishṇava saints, in verse, based on the Hindi Bhaktamāla of Nābhājī. With quotations from Sanskrit works, and extracts from the Hindi text of Nābhājī, and the commentary thereon by Priyā Dāsa. Edited with an introduction, notes, and translations of Sanskrit *ślokas* by Balāichānd Gosvāmī.] pp. iv. viii. 483. কলিকাতা ১৩০৫ [*Calcutta*, 1898.] 8°. **14129. e. 20.**

LĀLĀ JAYANĀRĀYAṆA. *See* JAYANĀRĀYAṆA, *Lālā, of Japsa.*

LĀLAMOHANA VIDYĀNIDHI BHAṬṬĀCHĀRYA. ভারতীয় আর্য্যজাতির আদিম অবস্থা। [Bhāratīya Āryajātir ādima avasthā.] . . . The Primitive State of Indian Aryans. pp. xiii. 291. কলিকাতা ১৮৯১ [*Calcutta*, 1891.] 12°. **14125. e. 25.**

LĀLAMOHANA VIDYĀNIDHI BHAṬṬĀCHĀRYA. (*continued*). Kávya-nirnaya, or A treatise on rhetorical composition in Bengali . . . Seventh edition. Revised and enlarged. pp. ii. iv. viii. 356, vi. হুগলী [*Hooghly*,] 1898. 12°. **14131. d. 37.**

—— Sambandhanirṇaya, or A social history of the principal Hindu castes in Bengal . . . (সম্বন্ধ-নির্ণয়।). Second edition . . . enlarged. pp. xxvi. 607. *Calcutta*, 1896. 8°. **14125. e. 29.**

—— Supplement to the Sambandhanirṇaya . . . Genealogy and Classification. By Lalmohan Vidyanidhi. pp. xii. 424, 96, xii. *Calcutta*, 1900. 12°. **14125. e. 45.**

LALANĀ-MUKURA. ললনা-মুকুর। [Lalanā-mukura. A tale of social life in a Bengali family, by an anonymous authoress.] pp. 233. কলিকাতা ১২৯৫ [*Calcutta*, 1889.] 12°. **14127. e. 35.**

LĀLAVIHĀRĪ DE, *Rev.* Folk-tales of Bengal. [Translated orally from tales told by Bengali story-tellers] by the Rev. Lal Behari Day. pp. xii. 284. *London*, 1883. 8°. **2348. e. 17.**

LĀLAVIHĀRĪ SIṂHA KSHATRĪ, *of Bhagalpur*. *See* NĀNAK, *Bābā*. জপজিসাহেব। [Japjī. With a Bengali translation by Lālavihārī Siṃha.] [1901.] 8°. **14162. bb. 7.(2.)**

LALITACHANDRA MITRA, *M.A.* *See* NALINĪBĀLĀ, *Daughter of Devendravijaya Vasu*. নলিনী-গাথা। [Nalinīgāthā. Edited by Lalitachandra Mitra, with a life of the poetess.] [1898.] 12°. **14129. a. 44.**

LALITAKṚISHṆA VASU. *See* JĪVANAKṚISHṆA SENA. সমর্থকোষ। [Samarthakosha. Continued from no. 53 by Anupakṛishṇa Mitra and Lalitakṛishṇa Vasu.] [1884, *etc.*] 4°. **14133. c. 4.**

LECTURES. অবিদ্বানের নিমিত্ত পরমার্থবিদ্যা বিষয়ক পাঠসমূহ। [Paramārthavidyā.] Lectures on Theology for the illiterate. pp. vi. 684. *Calcutta*, 1860. 8°. **14123. a. 44.**

LETHBRIDGE (*Sir* ROPER), *K.C.I.E.* *See* ŚIVANĀTHA ŚĀSTRĪ. Ramtanu Lahiri . . . [Translated] from the Bengali . . . Edited by Sir Roper Lethbridge. 1907. 8°. **10606. i. 19.**

LIKHITA. লিখিতসংহিতা। [Likhita-saṃhitā. A code of *dharma*, in 92 Sanskrit stanzas. With Bengali translation.] *See* PAÑCHĀNANA TARKARATNA BHAṬṬĀCHĀRYA. ঊনবিংশতি সংহিতা। [Ūnaviṃśati saṃhitā.] pp. 414-420. [1903.] 8°. **14039. c. 20.**

LITURGIES.—ENGLAND, *Church of.* A Form of Prayer and Thanksgiving to Almighty God, in Bengali, to be used on Thursday, the 28th July, 1859 . . . in commemoration of the restoration of peace. (প্রার্থনা ও ধন্যবাদের প্রণালী।) [Prārthanā o dhanyavāder praṇālī.] pp. 7. *Calcutta*, 1859. 8°. **14123. b. 17.**

—— ROME, *Church of.* ধর্ম্মগ্রন্থ। Dharmagrantha. [Manual of prayers for congregational use by Bengali converts.] pp. 136. *Calcutta*, 1895. 12°. **14123. a. 31.**

LOCHANADĀSA ṬHĀKURA. শ্রীচৈতন্যমঙ্গল। [Chaitanya-maṅgala. The life of Chaitanya, in verse. Edited, with a preface and notes, by Atulakṛishṇa Gosvāmī.] pp. ii. x. 199. কলিকাতা ১৩০৮ [*Calcutta*, 1902.] 8°. **14123. i. 13.**

—— শ্রীশ্রীচৈতন্যমঙ্গল। [Chaitanya-maṅgala. With a biographical sketch of the author.] pp. xiv. 119. কলিকাতা, গৌরাব্দ ৪১৭ [*Calcutta*, 1903.] 8°. **14123. g. 21.**

LOHĀRĀMA ŚIRORATNA. Grammar of the Bengali language . . . Twenty-seventh edition. pp. iv. 287. *Calcutta*, 1892. 12°. **14131. e. 24.**

LOKANĀTHA BRAHMACHĀRĪ. [*Life.*] *See* GIRIŚACHANDRA DĀSA. লোকনাথ-চরিত। [Lokanātha-charita.] [1890.] 12°. **14127. a. 37.(2.)**

LOKANĀTHA DATTA. Harish-chandra-charita. [The life of Hariśchandra, king of Oudh, compiled from various Sanskrit sources] by Lokenath Datta. (হরিশ্চন্দ্র-চরিত।) pp. 76. *Calcutta*, 1893. 8°. **14127. b. 38.(4.)**

LOKANĀTHA VANDYOPĀDHYĀYA. যমের মায়ের গঙ্গাস্নান। [Yamer māyer gaṅgāsnāna. A humorous sketch, in prose and verse.] pp. 7. কলিকাতা ১২৬৯ [*Calcutta*, 1863.] 12°. **14127. f. 42.(2.)**

LONG (JAMES), *Rev.* Analysis of the Bengali poem Ráj Málá, or Chronicles of Tripura. By the Rev. J. Long. (Journal of the Asiatic Society of Bengal. Vol. xix. pp. 533-557.) *Calcutta*, 1850. 8°. **Ac. 8826/11.**

—— [Another edition.] pp. 41. *Dacca* [1901.] 8°. **14125. f. 39.**

McCULLOCH (WILLIAM), *Rev.* *See* BIBLE.—*John, Gospel of.* যোহন লিখিত সুসমাচারের টীকা। . . . Commentary on John's Gospel . . . by the Rev. W. McCulloch. 1903. 8°. **14123. bb. 2.**

—— *See* BIBLE.—*Romans.* রোমীয়দের প্রতি পত্রের টীকা। . . . Commentary on the Epistle to the Romans . . . by the Rev. W. McCulloch. 1907. 8°. **14123. bb. 3.**

MACNAGHTEN (*Sir* WALTER HAY), *Bart.* *See* HINDU WORSHIP. An apology for the present system of Hindoo worship . . . accompanied by an English translation [by Sir W. H. Macnaghten]. 1817. 8°. **14123. f. 51.**

MADANAGOPĀLA GOSVĀMĪ. *See* KṚISHṆADĀSA KAVIRĀJA, *Gosvāmī.* শ্রীশ্রীচৈতন্যচরিতামৃত। [Chaitanya-charitāmṛita. Edited with copious notes by Madanagopāla Gosvāmī.] [1891, *etc.*] 4°. **14123. i. 8.**

—— *See* RŪPA GOSVĀMĪ. লঘুভাগবতামৃত। [Laghubhāgavatāmṛita. With a Bengali translation and notes by Madanagopāla Gosvāmī.] [1897.] 8°. **14016. c. 58.**

MADANAMOHANA HĀLDĀR. বসুক। . . . Basuka, or The Determination and Exposition of the caste of which 'Basaka' is the initial patronymic name. The Merchants in Ancient India. Part i. pp. iv. 220. *Calcutta*, 1895. 8°. **14125. ee. 29.(1.)**

MAḌEL BHRĀTĀ. মডেল ভ্রাতা। [Maḍel bhrātā, or The model brother. A tale, exposing the vices of educated Bengali Babus.] Pt. i. pp. 123. কলিকাতা ১২৯৩ [*Calcutta*, 1887.] 12°. **14127. c. 30.(1.)**

MĀDHAVA, *Son of Indukara.* নিদান। [Nidāna. A treatise on pathology. Translated from the Sanskrit by Kavirāja Sāradācharaṇa Sena Kaviratna.] pp. vi. 146. *Rajshahi*, [1903.] 8°. **14125. c. 43.(2.)**

MĀDHAVACHANDRA DĀSA. [Mythological drawings printed from wood-blocks.] 3 sheets. [*Calcutta*, 1860 ?] Fol. **14133. gg. 7.(2.)**

MĀDHAVACHANDRA TARKACHŪḌĀMAṆI. শ্রী-শ্রীগৌরগোপীবল্লভার্চ্চন চন্দ্রিকা। [Gauḍagopīvallabhārchana-chandrikā. A manual of devotion to Kṛishṇa, compiled by Mādhavachandra. Sanskrit text, with rubrics and occasional translations of prayers in Bengali. Third edition.] pp. 39. ঢাকা ১২৯৯ [*Dacca*, 1892.] 8°. **14028. d. 59.(2.)**

MĀDHAVĀCHĀRYA. জাগরণ। [Jāgaraṇa. A Bengali poem in honour of the goddess Chaṇḍī, written in the 16th century.] pp. 294. চট্টগ্রাম ১২৯৯ [*Chittagong*, 1892.] *obl.* 8°. **14129. g. 9.**

—— শ্রীকৃষ্ণমঙ্গল। [Kṛishṇa-maṅgala. The life of Kṛishṇa, in verse. New and revised edition.] pp. iv. iv. 319. কলিকাতা ১৩১০ [*Calcutta*, 1903.] 8°. **14123. g. 22.**

MADHU MIYĀN. *See* Kur'ān. বঙ্গানুবাদিত তফ্সীর হাক্কানী। [The Koran. Arabic text, accompanied by a Bengali translation by Madhu Miyān of the Hindustani version, and commentary entitled Tafsīr i ḥakkānī.] [1901, *etc.*] 8°. **14507. b. 34.**

MADHUSŪDANA, *Āchārya of the Nigamāgama Maṇḍalī, Muttra.* Sri Madhusudana Sanhitá. A key to understand the system of Hinduism, the universal religion. (শ্রীশ্রীমধুসূদন সংহিতা।) [Sanskrit text, with a Bengali translation and notes.] pp. iv. vi. iv. iii. 305. *Calcutta*, [1899.] 8°. **14028. d. 73.**

MADHUSŪDANA BHAṬṬĀCHĀRYA. *See* Khanā. খনার বচন। [Khanār vachana. Edited, with explanations, by Madhusūdana Bhaṭṭāchārya.] 1889. 12°. **14125. dd. 15.**

MADHUSŪDANA DĀSA. *See* Upanishads. চৈতন্যোপনিষদ্। [Chaitanyopanishad. Sanskrit text, with a Bengali translation, called Amṛitavindu, by Madhusūdana Dāsa.] [1885.] 12°. **14010. b. 7.(1.)**

MADHUSŪDANA DATTA (Michael). *See* Hemachandra Mitra. বীরাঙ্গনা পত্রোত্তর কাব্য। [Vīrāṅganā-patrottara kāvya. A poem in blank verse, purporting to contain replies to the letters which form the subject of Michael Madhusūdana Datta's Vīrāṅganā.] [1898.] 8°. **14129. cc. 1.(1.)**

—— *See* Homer. হেক্টর-বধ। [Hekṭar-vadha. The death of Hector, translated by Michael Madhusūdana Datta from the Greek text of Homer's Iliad.] [1907.] 12°. **14128. a. 27.**

MADHUSŪDANA DATTA (Michael) (*continued*). *See* Rajanīkānta Gupta. প্রতিভা। [Pratibhā. A series of the works of Michael Madhusūdana Datta.] [1896.] 12°. **14131. d. 35.**

—— *See* Yogīndranātha Tarkachūḍāmaṇi. The essay on Meghanada badha of Michael Madhusudana Datta, *etc.* 1887. 8°. **14131. d. 19.**

—— [*Life.*] *See* Yogīndranātha Vasu. মাইকেল মধুসূদন দত্তের জীবন-চরিত। [Māikel Madhusūdana Datter jīvana-charita.] [1893.] 8°. **14127. bb. 2.**

—— বুড়ো শালিকের ঘাড়ে রোঁ। [Buṛo sāliker ghāṛe roṅ, or Feathers on the neck of the old parrot. A humorous sketch of Hindu social life. Another edition.] pp. 36. কলিকাতা [*Calcutta*, 1905.] 12°. **14131. aa. 4.(5.)**

—— মধুসূদন গ্রন্থাবলী। [Madhusūdana-granthāvalī. The collected works of Michael Madhusūdana Datta.] কলিকাতা ১৩১১ [*Calcutta*, 1904, *etc.*] 8°.
In progress. **14127. ee. 23.**

—— মায়াকানন। [Māyākānana. A drama in 5 acts.] pp. 103. কলিকাতা ১৩১৪ [*Calcutta*, 1907.] 12°. **14131. aa. 7.(2.)**

—— সটীক মেঘনাদবধ কাব্য। [Meghanādavadha kāvya. An epic poem, in blank verse, based on Hindu mythology. Edited, with notes, and a critical and biographical introduction, by Hemachandra Mukhopādhyāya. Twelfth edition.] pp. 46, 320. কলিকাতা ১৮৯০ [*Calcutta*, 1890.] 8°. **14129. c. 42.**

—— মেঘনাদবধ কাব্য। [Meghanādavadha kāvya. Edited with notes by Dīnanātha Sānyāla.] pp. iv. 266, 7. কলিকাতা ১৩১৩ [*Calcutta*, 1907.] 8°. **14129. e. 31.**

—— Ratnavali: a Drama in four Acts. Translated from the Bengali by [the author] Michael M. S. Dutt. pp. 71. *Calcutta*, 1904. 12°. **14131. aa. 4.(3.)**

A reprint of the original edition of 1858.

—— Sermiṣtá: a Drama in five Acts. Translated from the Bengali by the author Michael M. S. Dutt. pp. 73. *Calcutta*, 1859. 8°. **14131. cc. 2.**

—— [Another edition.] pp. 90. *Calcutta*, 1904. 12°. **14131. a. 4.(2.)**

MADHUSŪDANA PĀLA. সংসার লীলা। [Saṃsāra-līlā. An historical story of the latter part of the 16th century.] pp. 458. কলিকাতা ১৩০৫ [*Calcutta*, 1898.] 12°. **14127. cc. 9.**

MADHUSŪDANA SARKĀR. *See* BIBLE.—*Matthew.* খ্রীষ্ট-পুরাণ মথি। [Khrīshṭa-purāṇa. A metrical version of the Gospel of St. Matthew by Madhusūdana Sarkār.] [1907.] 12°. **14123. a. 47.**

MADHUSŪDANA SENA GUPTA. বরিশাল। [Bariṣāl. A poem on the distress and poverty of the inhabitants of the district of Barisal.] pp. 16. কলিকাতা [*Calcutta*, 1906.] 12°. **14129. bb. 28.(3.)**

MADHUSŪDANA SMṚITIRATNA. *See* KĀṢĪNĀTHA SMĀRTAVĀGĪṢA. রত্নবিভ্রম। [Ratnavibhrama. An exposure of errors contained in Madhusūdana's commentary on the Dattaka-mīmāṃsā, and the Dattaka-chandrikā.] [1888.] 8°. **14125. a. 19.(1.)**

MAEZUDDIN ABO WAEZ MOHAMMAD. *See* MU'IZZ al-DĪN (ABŪ WĀ'IẒ MUḤAMMAD).

MĀGHA. Sisupalabadha. Cantos i. and ii. [Sanskrit text, with paraphrase and Mallinātha's commentary.] Edited [with translations into English and Bengali] by Pundit Nobin Ch. Vidyaratna. (শিশুপালবধম্ ।) Second edition. pp. 206. *Calcutta*, [1891.] 8°. **14072. cc. 51.**

—— Magha's Shishupal badham. [Sarga i.] Containing an introduction in English . . . paraphrase . . . Mallinatha's Sarbankasa, Bengali and English translations . . . Anglo Sanskrit notes . . . with exhaustive grammatical notes . . . by Pandit Nabin Chandra Vidyaratna. New edition. pp. iv. 236. *Calcutta*, [1901.] 8°. **14085. c. 49.(2.)**

MAHĀBHĀRATA. *See* CHANDRANĀTHA VASU. সাবিত্রীতত্ত্ব। [Sāvitrī-tattva. A critical analysis of the Mahābhārata story of Sāvitrī.] [1900.] 8°. **14131. d. 39.(2.)**

—— *See* DĀMODARA VIDYĀNANDA. হিন্দুশাস্ত্র। ... মহাভারত। [Mahābhārata. A summary of the Sanskrit epic, with quotations.] [1896.] 8°. **14085. c. 45.(vol. ii.)**

—— *See* RĀMACHANDRA MUKHOPĀDHYĀYA, *of Harinabhi.* দুর্গামঙ্গল। [Durgāmangala. A metrical version of the Mahābhārata story of Nala and Damayantī.] 1898. 12°. **14129. a. 26.(2.)**

MAHĀBHĀRATA (*continued*). *See* SURENDRANĀTHA ṬHĀKURA. মহাভারত। মূল আখ্যান। [Mahābhārata. The incidents of the epic poem translated in narrative form.] [1906.] 8°. **14129. ff. 2.**

—— মহাভারত। [Mahābhārata. With the Harivaṃṣa. Translated into prose by Kālīprasanna Siṃha. Sixth edition.] কলিকাতা ১৩০৫ [*Calcutta*, 1898, *etc.*] 8°. **14129. f. 7.**

In progress. Part of a series entitled Purāṇa-saṅgraha.

—— মহাভারত। [Mahābhārata. A metrical version by Vijaya Paṇḍita of the Sanskrit epic. Edited by Nagendranātha Vasu.] 2 pts. *Calcutta*, [1899-1906.] 8°. **14129. ff. 1.**

One of the Sāhityaparishat-granthāvali *series.*

—— মহাভারত। [Mahābhārata. Translated from the Sanskrit into Bengali verse by Rājakṛishṇa Rāya.] কলিকাতা ১৩০৮ [*Calcutta*, 1901.] 4°. **14129. g. 10.**

Separate pagination for each book.

—— The Mohabharut . . . Translated into Bengalee . . . by Kaseeram Dass Mohanubhaba. সচিত্র ও সমগ্র মহাভারত অষ্টাদশপর্ব্ব। pp. xiv. 1048. কলিকাতা ১৩১০ [*Calcutta*, 1903.] 8°. **14129. e. 27.**

—— প্রতিমূর্ত্তির সহিত মাহাভারত অষ্টাদশ পর্ব্ব। [Mahābhārata. Translated by Kāṣīrāma Dāsa. Another edition.] pp. x. ii. 1080. With 8 plates. কলিকাতা ১৩১৪ [*Calcutta*, 1907.] 8°. **14129. e. 34.**

—— মহাভারত। [Mahābhārata. A prose translation made by order of Mahtāb Chand, Maharaja of Burdwan.] 2 vols. কলিকাতা ১৩১৪ [*Calcutta*, 1907.] 4°. **14129. g. 11.**

—— ছুটিখানের মহাভারত। অশ্বমেধ পর্ব্ব। [Aṣvamedhaparva. A metrical translation of the redaction ascribed to Jaimini, composed for Chhuṭi Khān of Chittagong by Ṣrīkara Nandī.] pp. 120. *See* PERIODICAL PUBLICATIONS.—*Calcutta.* প্রাচীন বাঙ্গালা গ্রন্থাবলী। [Prāchīna Bāṅgālā granthāvalī.] nos. 1-15. [1900, *etc.*] 8°. **14133. ff. 2.**

Incomplete; no more published.

—— জৈমিনি-ভারত। [Aṣvamedhaparva. Translated into verse by Kālīprasanna Vidyāratna. Second edition.] pp. iii. 329. কলিকাতা [*Calcutta*, 1902.] 8°. **14129. e. 26.**

MAHĀBHĀRATA (*continued*). কাশীরাম দাস বিরচিত মহাভারত। দানপর্ব্ব। [Dānaparva. A hitherto unpublished canto of Kāṣīrāma Dāsa's translation of the Mahābhārata, apparently containing an amplified version of part of the Āṣramavāsikaparva. Edited, with an introduction and life of Kāṣīrāma, by Ṣrīṣachandra Chaṭṭopādhyāya.] pp. 24, 144. কলিকাতা ১৪১৫ [*Calcutta*, 1908.] 12°. **14129. bbb. 1.**

—— পাণ্ডবগীতা। [Pāṇḍavagītā. Eighty stanzas from the Mahābhārata in praise of Vishṇu. Sanskrit text, with Bengali translation.] *See* PAÑCHA GĪTĀ. পঞ্চগীতা। [Pancha gītā.] pp. 287-323. [1906.] 16°. **14028. a. 33.**

—— পরাশরগীতা। [Parāṣaragītā. An exposition of polity, morals, *etc.*, forming the Sanskrit text of Ṣāntiparva ccxci.-ccxcix., with Bengali translation.] *See* PAÑCHA GĪTĀ. পঞ্চগীতা। [Pañcha gīta.] pp. 324-502. [1906.] 16°. **14028. a. 33.**

—— BHAGAVADGĪTĀ.—*See* HĪRENDRANĀTHA DATTA. গীতায় ঈশ্বরবাদ। [Gītāy Īṣvaravāda. The philosophy of the Bhagavadgītā on the worship of Īṣvara.] [1906.] 12°. **14123. e. 36.**

—— শ্রীমদ্ভগবদ্গীতা। [Bhagavadgītā. Sanskrit text, and commentary by Ṣrīdharasvāmī, with a Bengali translation of the text by Hemachandra Vidyāratna. Edited with an index and introduction by Kshitindranātha Ṭhākura.] pp. i. iv. xv. 143, 574. কলিকাতা ১৮১৬ [*Calcutta*, 1895.] 16°. **14065. b. 15.**

—— হিন্দুশাস্ত্র। . . . শ্রীমদ্ভগবদ্গীতা। [Bhagavadgītā. Sanskrit text, with a Bengali translation by Bankimchandra Chaṭṭopādhyāya (Adh. i. and ii.) and Dāmodara Vidyānanda (iii.-xviii.).] pp. i. 121. [1897.] *See* RAMEṢACHANDRA DATTA. হিন্দুশাস্ত্র। [Hindu-ṣāstra.] Pt. viii. [1895-97.] 8°. **14085. c. 45.(vol. ii.)**

—— শ্রীমদ্ভগবদ্গীতা। [Bhagavadgītā. Sanskrit text, with a word-for-word interpretation, paraphrase and commentary in Bengali, the Sanskrit commentaries of Ṣankara, Rāmānuja, Hanumān and Baladeva Vidyābhūshaṇa, Ānandagiri, Ṣrīdhara, Madhusūdana, Nīlakaṇṭha, and Viṣvanātha, notes, *etc.* Edited by Dāmodara Mukhopādhyāya Vidyānanda.] Pts. 19-26, 29-33. কলিকাতা ১৮১৯-১৮২৭ [*Calcutta*, 1897-1905.] 8°. **14049. bb. 11.**

MAHĀBHĀRATA (*continued*). শ্রীমদ্ভগবদ্গীতা। [Bhagavadgītā. A Bengali prose translation.] *See* PURĀṆAS.—*Bhāgavatapurāṇa.* শ্রীকৃষ্ণলীলা। [Kṛishṇalīlā.] pp. 1229-1298. [1904.] 8°. **14016. dd. 10.**

—— পদ্যগীতা। [Padyagītā. A metrical version of the Bhagavadgītā by Harigopāla Vasu.] ১৩১২ [1905.] *See* PERIODICAL PUBLICATIONS.—*Calcutta.* সাহিত্য-সংহিতা। [Sāhitya-saṃhitā.] Vol. vi., no. 2. [1900, *etc.*] 8°. **14133. ff. 1.**

—— গীতাকাব্য। [Gītākāvya. A metrical translation of the Bhagavadgītā by Ṣaivalinī Devī.] pp. vi. 186. কলিকাতা ১৯০১ [*Calcutta*, 1901.] 12°. **14129. bb. 11.**

—— **श्रीमद्भगवद्गीता नवपीयूषप्रवाह भाष्य।** The Illustrated Bhagwad Gita . . . Containing:—Text. . . . Translations in:—Hindi. Urdu. Persian. Bengali. English. Commentaries . . . Short history of the Bhagwad Gita. Chronological table of Lunar dynasty, and copious notes . . . Paudit Adya Prasada Misra, Editor. *Benares*, १९०५ [1905, *etc.*] 8°. **14049. b. 47.**

In progress. The Bengali is in Nagari characters.

MAHĀNANDA CHAKRAVARTĪ, *Jyotishī.* অবধৌতিক চিকিৎসা। [Avadhautika chikitsā. The cure of diseases by the *avadhautika* system of treatment.] pp. 33. কালনা ১৩০৭ [*Kalna*, 1901.] 12°. **14125. b. 18.(1.)**

MAHENDRACHANDRA MAJUMDĀR. রণ-রাও। [Raṇa Rāo. A poem in blank verse on the story of Raṇa Rāo of Mandowar, taken from Tod's "Rajasthan."] pp. v. 181. কলিকাতা ১৩০৩ [*Calcutta*, 1897.] 12°. **14129. a. 48.(1.)**

—— সাহিত্য ও সমাজ। [Sāhitya o samāja. A severe criticism on the Vishavṛiksha of Bankimchandra Chaṭṭopādhyāya.] pp. 64. কলিকাতা ১৩০৩ [*Calcutta*, 1896.] 16°. **14131. d. 36.**

MAHENDRALĀL KHĀN, *Raja of Narajol, Midnapore.* *See* PURĀṆAS.—*Brahmāṇḍapurāṇa.* অধ্যাত্ম রামায়ণম্। [Adhyātmarāmāyaṇa. With a Bengali metrical version by Raja Mahendralāl Khān.] [1908.] 4°. **14018. a. 3.**

MAHENDRANĀTHA ĀDHYA, called MUNIṚISHI ṢARMĀ. পশু শাস্ত্রম্। [Paṣu-ṣāstra. The peculiarities of various Hindu castes likened to the habits of different animals.] pp. 12. কলিকাতা [*Calcutta*, 1896.] 12°. **14125. e. 31 (2.)**

MAHENDRANĀTHA BHAṬṬĀCHĀRYA. *See* SARVAVARMĀ. কলাপ-ব্যাকরণম্। [Kalāpa-vyākaraṇa. The Sanskrit text of Kātantra, Chapter I., and commentary, with a Bengali translation by Mahendranātha Bhaṭṭāchārya.] [1900.] 8°. **14090. b. 32.(2.)**

MAHENDRANĀTHA CHAṬṬOPĀDHYĀYA. সচিত্র সমাজরহস্য স্বপ্নদর্শন। [Samāja-rahasya. A description of the corrupt social customs of certain Hindu castes.] pp. 82. *Calcutta*, 1897. 12°. **14125. e. 39.**

MAHENDRANĀTHA GHOSHĀL. *See* GAUḌAPĀDA ĀCHĀRYA. গৌড়পাদীয় আগম। [Āgama-śāstra, Chapters ii., iii., iv. With a Bengali translation by Mahendranātha Ghoshāl.] [1890.] 8°. **14010. c. 52.(4.)**

MAHENDRANĀTHA RĀYA VIDYĀNIDHI. An historical sketch of the Aryan-Hindu women of the Vedic, Upanishadic and Puranic period. . . . প্রাচীন আর্য্যরমণীগণের ইতিবৃত্ত [Prāchīna Ārya ramaṇīgaṇer itivṛitta.] pp. 108. ১২৯৪ *Calcutta*, [1887.] 12°. **14127. a. 31.(3.)**

MAHENDRANĀTHA VIDYĀNIDHI. *See* PERIODICAL PUBLICATIONS.—*Calcutta*. অনুশীলন। [Anuśilana. Edited by Mahendranātha Vidyānidhi.] [*Calcutta*, 1894.] 8°. **14133. f. 15.**

—— *See* UDDHAVĀNANDA. রাধিকা-মঙ্গল। [Rādhikā-maṅgala. With an account of the author and his writings by Mahendranātha Vidyānidhi.] [1896.] 8°. **14133. f. 18.**

MAHEŚACHANDRA BHAṬṬĀCHĀRYA. The Pharmaceutist's Manual: a companion to the German and American homœopathic pharmacopœias. ভেষজ-বিধান। [Bheshaja-vidhāna.] pp. 85, 144. *Calcutta*, 1892. 8°. **14125. c. 36.**

MAHEŚACHANDRA DĀSA DE. বিজয় বসন্ত যাত্রা। [Vijaya-Vasanta yātrā. A drama in six acts. Sixth edition.] pp. 48. কলিকাতা ১২৯৩ [*Calcutta*, 1886.] 12°. **14131. a. 22.(2.)**

MAHEŚACHANDRA NYĀYARATNA. *See* CHANDRODAYA BHAṬṬĀCHĀRYA. পণ্ডিত শ্রীযুক্ত মহেশচন্দ্র ন্যায়রত্ন ... মহাশয়ের প্রবেশিকার ভ্রমসংশোধনী। [Bhramasaṃśodhanī. Mistakes in the Sanskrit Entrance Examination Course, which was edited by Maheśachandra Nyāyaratna.] [1887.] 12°. **14131. d. 23.(1.)**

—— *See* GOSAIṆ-DĀS SARKĀR. মহেশ-মাহাত্ম্য। [Maheśa-māhātmya. A eulogy in verse of Maheśachandra Nyāyaratna.] [1893.] 12°. **14129. b. 35.(5.)**

—— *See* JĀNAKĪNĀTHA BHAṬṬĀCHĀRYA. প্রবেশিকার ভ্রমসংশোধনীর ভ্রমপ্রদর্শনী। Bhrama-pradarsani. [A defence of Maheśachandra Nyāyaratna's Sanskrit Entrance Examination Course.] [1887.] 12°. **14131. d. 23.(2.)**

—— প্রবেশিকা-সমালোচনার ভ্রমদর্শিনী প্রকৃত কথা। [Prakṛita kathā.] . . . A review of criticisms on the Sanskrit Selections for the Entrance examination, 1891. pp. 210. *Calcutta*, 1889. 12°. **14131. d. 23.(3.)**

—— বর্ত্তমান বর্ষের সন্ধিপূজার সময় নির্ণয় ও পঞ্জিকার ইতিবৃত্ত। [Sandhi-pūjār samaya-nirṇaya. A treatise on the determination of the exact time for the celebration of the Sandhi-pūjā in the Bengali year 1298.] pp. iii. 60. কলিকাতা ১২৯৮ [*Calcutta*, 1891.] 8°. **14133. e. 7.**

MAHEŚACHANDRA PĀLA. *See* KAPILA. মহর্ষি-কপিল-প্রণীত-সাংখ্যদর্শনম্। [Sāṅkhyadarśana. Edited by Maheśachandra Pāla.] [1885.] 8°. **14048. bb. 22.**

—— *See* UPANISHADS. ঋগ্বেদীয়-ঐতরেয়োপনিষৎ [A series of Upanishads, compiled with Bengali translations by Maheśachandra Pāla.] [1881, *etc.*] 8°. **14007. cc. 8.**

—— বেদান্তরত্নাবলী। [Vedānta-ratnāvalī. A collection of Sanskrit treatises of the Vedānta school, compiled with Sanskrit commentaries, and Bengali translations, by Maheśachandra Pāla.] Pts. 1 and 2. কলিকাতা ১৮০৫-০৬ [*Calcutta*, 1805-1806.] 8°. **14048. bb. 15.**

MAHEŚACHANDRA SENA. আদর্শ কবি। [Ādarśa kavi. An essay on Bengali songs, and dramatic representations.] pp. 78, iv. কলিকাতা ১২৯৫ [*Calcutta*, 1888.] 12°. **14131. d. 20.**

MAHEŚACHANDRA TARKACHŪḌĀMAṆI. The Cabinet of Poesy, or A series of detatched [*sic*] Sanskrit stanzas, each giving in itself a pithy saying and a complete poetical idea. [With commentary and a Bengali metrical version.] . . .

Third edition. Composed by Mahesh Chandra Tarkachurhamani. (কাব্যপেটিকা) [Kāvyapeṭikā.] 2 pts; 1 *plate.* *Chinsurah,* [1902-06.] 8°.
14072. ccc. 35.

MAHIMĀCHANDRA MAJUMDĀR. গৌড়ে ব্রাহ্মণ। [Gauṛe Brāhmaṇa. An account of the different classes of Bengali Brahmans, their families and subdivisions, from the time of Ādiṣūra.] pp. viii. 315. *Calcutta,* 1886. 8°. **14127. b. 33.**

MAHĪNDRALĀLA ṢĪLA. Catechism of Hindu Music. By Mohindro Lall Seal. (বঙ্গ-সঙ্গীতের প্রশ্নোত্তর-মালা।) [Vaṅga saṅgīter praṣnottara-mālā.] pp. iv. 90, x. *Calcutta,* 1890. 12°.
14125. d. 17.

MAHOMEDAN FRIENDS' ASSOCIATION. *See* DACCA.—*Mahomedan Friends' Association.*

MAHTĀB CHANDRA SIṂHA, *of Maheshpur.* পারিজাত-হরণ গীতাভিনয়। [Pārijāta-haraṇa. A drama on Kṛishṇa's theft of the *pārijāta* tree from paradise.] pp. 228. কলিকাতা ১৩১২ [*Calcutta,* 1905.] 8°. **14131. b. 25.(3.)**

MAJLISI-RAṄGILĀ. মজ্‌লিসি রঙ্গিলা ও বৈঠকী খাতা। [Majlisi-raṅgilā. A collection of amusing anecdotes.] pp. 24. কলিকাতা ১২৯৯ [*Calcutta,* 1892.] 12°. **14127. c. 42.(3.)**

MAJUMDAR (S. C.). *See* ṢAILEṢACHANDRA MAJUMDĀR.

MĀKHANLĀLA DĀSA BHĀGAVATABHŪSHAṆA. *See* KṚISHṆADĀSA KAVIRĀJA, *Gosvāmī.* শ্রীশ্রীচৈতন্য-চরিতামৃত। [Chaitanya-charitāmṛita. With a Bengali interpretation, styled Sudhāsañchāriṇī, by Mākhanlāla Dāsa.] [1908.] 8°. **14123. g. 24.**

MĀLĀDHARA VASU, called GUṆARĀJA KHĀN. শ্রী শ্রীকৃষ্ণ বিজয়। বঙ্গ ভাষার আদি কাব্য। [Ṣrī-kṛishṇavijaya. A Vaishṇava poem on the life of Kṛishṇa, said to be the oldest Bengali poem extant, and written in the Ṣaka year 1405, or 1483 A.D.] pp. iv. 217. কলিকাতা [*Calcutta,* 1887.] 8°. **14129. c. 35.**

MALDAH.—*Ādi Kaivarta Samāj.* আদি কৈবর্ত্ত ইতিহাস। [Ādi Kaivarta-itihāsa. An account of the origin and status of the Kaivarta caste.] pp. 26. মালদহ ১৩০৯ [*Maldah,* 1903.] 12°.
14125. e. 31.(7.)

MĀNAKUMĀRĪ DĀSĪ. কনকাঞ্জলি। [Kanakāñjali. Miscellaneous poems.] pp. viii. 260. কলিকাতা ১৩০৩ [*Calcutta,* 1896.] 12°. **14129. a. 30.**

—— বীরকুমার-বধ-কাব্য। [Vīrakumāravadha. A poem on the death of Abhimanyu.] pp. x. 235. *Calcutta,* ১৩১০ [1904.] 12°. **14129. bb. 22.**

MAṄGALACHAṆḌĪ. মঙ্গলচণ্ডীর পাঁচালী। [Maṅgala-chaṇḍīr pāñchālī. A poem in praise of the goddess Maṅgalachaṇḍī. Edited by Tārakeṣvara Bhaṭṭā-chārya.] ১৩০৯ [1902.] *See* ACADEMIES, *etc.*—Calcutta.—*Bengal Academy of Literature.* সাহিত্য-পরিষৎ-পত্রিকা। [Sāhitya-parishat-patrikā.] Vol. ix., no. 1. [1894, *etc.*] 8°. **14133. f. 18.**

MĀṆIK CHANDRA. The song of Mánik Chandra. [A Bengali poem in the Rangpur dialect, printed in Devanagari characters, with an English translation and introductory remarks.] By G. A. Grierson. (Journal of the Asiatic Society of Bengal. Vol. xlvii., pt. i., pp. 135-238.) *Calcutta,* 1878. 8°. **2098. b.**

MĀṆIK GĀṄGULĪ, *Son of Gadādhara. See* DĪNEṢA-CHANDRA SENA. ধর্ম্মমঙ্গল। [Dharmamaṅgala. An article on the Dharmamaṅgala, a poem by Māṇik Gāṅgulī.] [1907.] 8°. **14133. f. 18.**

—— *See* VRAJASUNDARA SĀNNYĀLA. মাণিক গাঙ্গুলী ও ধর্ম্মমঙ্গল। [Māṇik Gāṅgulī o Dharmamaṅgala. An account of the poet Māṇik Gāṅgulī and his Dharmamaṅgala.] [1906.] 8°. **14133. f. 18.**

—— শ্রীধর্ম্মমঙ্গল। [Dharmamaṅgala. An old Bengali legendary poem.] pp. 227. ১৩০৭-০৯ [1901-03.] *See* PERIODICAL PUBLICATIONS.—*Calcutta.* প্রাচীন বাঙ্গালা গ্রন্থাবলী। [Prāchīna Bāṅgālā granthāvalī.] nos. 3-11. [1900, *etc.*] 8°.
14133. ff. 2.

MAṆIMOHANA DEVANĀTHA. যোগিতত্ত্ব-সার। [Yogītattvasāra. An inquiry into the position of the Yogī caste. Second edition.] pp. 24. কলিকাতা ১৩১০ [*Calcutta,* 1903.] 8°.
14125. ee. 36.(3.)

MAṆĪNDRAKRISHṆA GUPTA. *See* ĪṢVARACHANDRA GUPTA. গ্রন্থাবলী। [Granthāvalī. The complete works of Īṣvarachandra Gupta, edited by Maṇīndrakṛishṇa Gupta.] [1901.] 8°. **14129. e. 24.**

MAṆĪNDRALĀLA GHOSHA. *See* PURĀṆAS.— *Padmapurāṇa.* সচিত্র রতিশাস্ত্র। [Ratiṣāstra. Edited and translated by Maṇīndralāla Ghosha.] [1901.] 12°. **14053. b. 42.**

MAṆĪNDRANĀTHA CHAṬṬOPĀDHYĀYA. *See* PRABHĀVATĪ DEVĪ. অমল-প্রসূন। [Amalaprasūna. Edited, with a life of the authoress, by Maṇīndranātha Chaṭṭopādhyāya.] [1900.] 12°. **14129. a. 50.**

MANMATHANĀTHA RĀYA CHAUDHURĪ. *See* BAṄKIMCHANDRA CHAṬṬOPĀDHYĀYA. Chandra Shekhar . . . Translated by Manmatha Nath Ray Chowdhury. [1904.] 8°. **14127. cc. 37.**

MANMATHANĀTHA VIDYĀRATNA BHAṬṬĀCHĀRYA. কামরূপ তন্ত্রমন্ত্র। [Kāmarūpa-tantramantra. A collection of Sanskrit magic charms, compiled with a Bengali translation by Manmathanātha Vidyāratna.] pp. ii. 56. কলিকাতা ১৩০৯ [*Calcutta*, 1902.] 8°. **14028. c. 52.(2.)**

MANOHARA DĀSA. অনুরাগ-বল্লী। [Anurāgavallī. A poem in 8 cantos on the life of the Chaitanya apostle Ṣrīnivāsa Āchārya, with quotations from Sanskrit works, and a Sanskrit laudatory poem in 10 *ṣlokas* by the author. Followed by an appendix containing a Bengali translation of the Sanskrit verses.] pp. 7, 134. কলিকাতা শ্রীগৌরাব্দ ৪১৩ [*Calcutta*, 1898.] 12°. **14129. a. 46.(2.)**

—— দিনমণিচন্দ্রোদয়। [Dinamaṇi-chandrodaya. A Vaishṇava poem in 21 chapters.] *See* VAISHṆAVA GRANTHĀVALĪ. বৈষ্ণব গ্রন্থাবলী। [1900.] 12°. **14123. e. 20.(3.)**

MANOMATADHANA DE. Sangita suttra, or An abstract grammar of vocal and instrumental music. Part I. By Manomata Dhan Dey. (সঙ্গীত সূত্র) pp. ii. 64. *Calcutta*, 1888. 8°. **14125. d. 14.**

MANOMOHANA GOSVĀMĪ. পৃথ্বিরাজ। ঐতিহাসিক নাটক। [Pṛithvirāja. An historical drama, relating to Pṛithvirāja king of Delhi.] pp. 184. কলিকাতা ১৩১২ [*Calcutta*, 1905.] 12°. **14131. aa. 4.(7.)**

—— [Another edition.] pp. 66. কলিকাতা ১৩১২ [*Calcutta*, 1906.] 8°. **14131. cc. 3.**

MANOMOHANA RĀYA. ঐতিহাসিক প্রবন্ধ। প্রথম খণ্ড। [Aitihāsika prabandha. Historical essays. Part i. The life of Raja Pratāpa Siṃha. Second edition.] pp. 61. কলিকাতা ১২৯৪ [*Calcutta*, 1887.] 12°. **14127. a.**

—— রিজিয়া। বিয়োগান্ত দৃশ্যকাব্য। [Rijiyā. An historical drama.] pp. 164. কলিকাতা ১৩০৫ [*Calcutta*, 1899.] 12°. **14131. a. 41.(4.)**

MANOMOHANA VANDYOPĀDHYĀYA. First Book in English and Bengali. By Bábu Monmohun Banerji. pp. 20, *lith. Lahore*, 1889. 16°. **14131. e.**

MANOMOHANA VASU. দুলীন। [Dulīn. An historical novel.] pp. 440. কলিকাতা ১২৯৮ [*Calcutta*, 1891.] 8°. **14127. e. 41.**

—— হিন্দুমেলার উদ্দেশ্য বিষয়ক বক্তৃতা। [Hindumelār uddeṣya. A lecture on the observance of Hindu festivals.] pp. 29. ১৭৯০ [*Calcutta*, 1868.] 8°. **14123. f. 33.(4.)**

—— পদ্যমালা। [Padyamālā. A Bengali primer, in verse. Another edition.] 2 pts. কলিকাতা ১৮৮৩-৮৪ [*Calcutta*, 1886-84.] 12°. **14131. f. 31.**

Pt. i. *is of the 14th, and pt.* ii. *of the 2nd edition.*

MANORAÑJANA GUHA. আশা-প্রদীপ। [Āṣāpradīpa. Experiences in mesmerism and spiritualism.] pp. vii. 114. কলিকাতা ১২৯৪ [*Calcutta*, 1887.] 12°. **14125. dd. 16.**

MANU. হিন্দুশাস্ত্র। . . . ধর্মশাস্ত্র। [Selections from the Dharmaṣāstra of Manu, followed by extracts from other Dharmaṣāstras. Edited with Bengali translations, preface, and notes by Kṛishṇakamala Bhaṭṭāchārya and Kṛishṇapada Vidyāratna.] pp. i. 95. 1895. *See* RAMEṢACHANDRA DATTA. হিন্দুশাস্ত্র। [Hindu-ṣāstra.] Pt. iv. [1895-97.] 8°. **14085. c. 45.(vol. i.)**

MARTIN (CAULFIELD AYLMER). Key to the system of transliteration to be used by the Bengal Educational Service. pp. ii. 34. *Calcutta*, 1898. 8°. **14131. g. 32.**

MARTIN (*Sir* THEODORE). The Life of His Royal Highness, the Prince Consort . . . Condensed and translated into Bengali . . . by J. Rudd Rainey. (রাজকুমার আলবার্টের জীবনী।) pp. viii. ii. 438. কলিকাতা [*Calcutta*,] 1892. 8°. **14127. b. 46.**

MATHURĀDĀSA GOSVĀMĪ, *Disciple of Mukundadāsa.* শ্রীশ্রীচৈতন্য কারিকাগ্রন্থঃ। [Chaitanya-kārikā

grantha. A treatise on the principles and practice of the Chaitanya church, comprising an anthology of Sanskrit texts, chiefly in verse, with Bengali translations, and Bengali metrical extracts.] pp. 102. কলিকাতা ১৩১১ [*Calcutta*, 1904.] 8°.
14123. ff. 14.

MATHURĀNĀTHA NĀTHA. *See* DIOGNETUS. দিয়গ্নীতসের প্রতি পত্র। [Diyagnītaser prati patra.] The Epistle to Diognetus . . . Translated by M. N. Nath. 1908. 12°. **14123. a. 46.(2.)**

MATHURĀNĀTHA VARMĀ. A Handbook of English Composition in Bengali. By Mathuranath Barma. pp. iii. 231. *Calcutta*, 1894. 12°.
14131. e. 26.

—— [Another edition.] pp. iv. 161. *Calcutta*, 1900. 12°. **14131. e. 31.**

MATILĀLA GHOSHA. *See* ṢIṢIRAKUMĀRA GHOSHA. কালাচাঁদ-গীতা। [Kālāchānd-gītā. Edited with an introduction and notes by Matilāla Ghosha.] [1896.] 8°. **14129. b. 42.(2.)**

MATILĀLA RĀYA. গয়াসুরের হরিপাদপদ্মলাভ গীতাভিনয়। [Gayāsurer Haripādapadmalābha. A drama on the mythological story of the demon Gaya.] pp. 8, 165. কলিকাতা ১৩০৪ [*Calcutta*, 1897.] 8°.
14131. c. 19.(1.)

MEGHANĀTHA BHAṬṬĀCHĀRYA. আর্য্যনারী গাথা। [Āryanārī gāthā. An account in verse of the lives of celebrated Hindu women.] pp. 228. কলিকাতা [*Calcutta*, 1885?] 8°. **14129. c. 36.**

—— সত্যনারায়ণ ব্রতকথা। [Satyanārāyaṇa-vratakathā. A poem on the worship of the god Satyanārāyaṇa.] pp. 23. কলিকাতা ১৩০৬ [*Calcutta*, 1899.] 12°. **14129. a. 46.(4.)**

MEM SĀHEB. মেম সাহেব। ব্যাঙ্গোপন্যাস। [Mem Sāheb. The story of an Anglicized Bengali lady who deceived and illtreated her husband.] pp. 70. কলিকাতা ১২৯৩ [*Calcutta*, 1886.] 12°.
14127. c. 37.(1.)

METCALFE (*Sir* CHARLES THEOPHILUS), *Baron Metcalfe.* [*Indian career.*] *See* CHAṆḌĪCHARAṆA SENA. Liberator of the Indian Press, *etc.* [1887.] 8°.
14127. b. 36.

MEYE PARLIAMENT. মেয়ে পার্লেমেন্ট বা দ্বিতীয় ভাগ ভারত উদ্ধার। [Meye Parliament. A satire on the measures being taken for bringing about female emancipation, being a sequel to the Bhārata-uddhāra.] pp. 65. কলিকাতা [*Calcutta*, 1886.] 8°.
14125. ee. 20.(2.)

MICHAEL MADHUSUDAN DATT. *See* MADHUSŪDANA DATTA (MICHAEL).

MIDNIGHT TRAVELLER, *pseud.* *See* NIṢĀCHARA, *pseud.*

MILL (JOHN STUART). [*Life.*] *See* YOGENDRANĀTHA VANDYOPĀDHYĀYA VIDYĀBHŪSHAṆA. জন্ ষ্টুয়ার্ট মিলের জীবন-বৃত্ত। [Jan Shṭuyārṭ Miler jīvana-vṛitta.] 1884. 12°. **14127. aa. 5.**

MILTON (JOHN). ত্রিদিব-চ্যুতি। [Tridiva-chyuti. A prose translation of Milton's Paradise Lost, by Nanīgopāla Mukhopādhyāya.] Pt. i. pp. 22. কলিকাতা ১৩০০ [*Calcutta*, 1893.] 12°.
14129. a. 38.(1.)

—— প্রাসাদ। [Prāsāda.] . . . Milton's Paradise Lost, Book I. [Translated into verse with notes by Ṣaṣāṅkanātha Rāya.] pp. v. 56. [*Calcutta*, 1906.] 12°. **14123. a. 45.**

MĪRĀBĀĪ. [*Life.*] *See* UPENDRAKUMĀRA GHOSHA. আর্য্য-মহিলা। [Ārya-mahilā.] 1895. 12°.
14127. aa. 2.(5.)

MITRA (J. N.). *See* YOGENDRANATHA MITRA.

MOHINĪMOHANA CHAṬṬOPĀDHYĀYA. পরম হংস শিবনারায়ণ স্বামীর ভ্রমণ বৃত্তান্ত। [Bhramaṇa-vṛittānta. An account of the life, travels, and teachings of Paramahaṃsa Ṣivanārāyaṇa Svāmī.] pp. 173, 31. কলিকাতা ১৮১৪ [*Calcutta*, 1892.] 8°.
14127. b. 47.(4.)

—— [Third edition, enlarged.] pp. iv. 158. কলিকাতা ১৮১৩ [*Calcutta*, 1902.] 8°. **14127. bb. 20.**

MOHINĪMOHANA DĀSA GUPTA. History of Sylhet. By Mohini Mohon Das Gupta. শ্রীহট্টের ইতিহাস। [Ṣrīhaṭṭer itihāsa.] pp. ii. 28. ঢাকা [*Dacca*,] 1903. 12°. **14127. aa. 28.**

MOKSHADĀCHARAṆA SĀMĀDHYĀYĪ. *See* PATAÑJALI. পাণিনীয় মহাভাষ্য। মূল ও বঙ্গানুবাদ। [Mahābhāshya. With a Bengali translation by Mokshadācharaṇa.] [1907, *etc.*] 8°. **14090. bb. 28.**

MONMOHUN BANERJI. *See* MANOMOHANA VANDYOPĀDHYĀYA.

MORTON (WILLIAM), *Missionary.* *See* BIBLE.—*Proverbs.* Proverbs of Solomon . . . Translated . . . by W. Morton. 1843. 8°. **3070. aa. 8.**

MṚINĀLINĪ, *Śrīmatī.* মনোবীণা। [Manoviṇā. Miscellaneous poems, partly adapted from works of English poets.] pp. 14, 259. *Calcutta,* 1900. 8°. **14129. bb. 1.**

MṚITYUÑJAYA VIDYĀLAṄKĀRA. *See* HITOPADEŚA. হিতোপদেশ [Hitopadeśa. Translated by Mṛityuñjaya Vidyālaṅkāra.] [1824.] 8°. **14127. e. 39.**

—— *See* VIKRAMĀDITYA, *King of Ujjayini.* শ্রী বিক্রমাদিত্যের বত্রিশ সিংহাসন সংগ্রহ *etc.* [Siṃhāsana battiṣī. Translated by Mṛityuñjaya Vidyālaṅkāra.] [1816.] 8°. **14127. e. 42.**

—— Contes Indiens. Les Trente-deux Récits du Trône . . . traduits du Bengali (de Mrityunjaya), *etc.* 1883. 12°. **2348. a.**

—— The Prabodh Chandriká. [A collection of Bengali prose compositions.] Compiled by the late Mrityunjay Bidyálankár. pp. 8, 188. *Calcutta,* 1862. 8°. **14127. ee. 7.**

—— রাজাবলী। [Rājāvalī. A history of India from the earliest times to the arrival of Warren Hastings. Another edition.] pp. 2, 158. কলিকাতা ১৩১২ [*Calcutta,* 1905.] 12°. **14127. aa. 28.(2.)**

MUBĀRAK 'ALĪ, *Saiyid.* অপূর্ব্ব কাহিনী। [Apūrva kāhinī. A romance, translated by Rādhānātha Mitra from a Hindustani work by Munshī Saiyid Mubārak 'Alī.] pp. 274, 2. *Calcutta,* 1898. 12°. **14127. cc. 21.(2.)**

MUDGARADHĀRĪ HĀSYABHŪSHAṆA, *pseud.* ভোটমঙ্গল বা দেবাসুরের মিউনিসিপাল-বিভ্রাট। [Bhoṭmaṅgala. A farcical representation of election scandals and squabbles in Bengal.] pp. ii. 46. কলিকাতা [*Calcutta,* 1889.] 12°. **14131. a. 28.(4.)**

MUFAẒẒAL al-RAḤMĀN, *Saiyid.* احسان المومنين [Iḥsān al-mūminīn. A treatise on religious observations, in Arabic characters.] pp. 420, *lith.* كلكته ١٩٠٤ [*Calcutta,* 1904.] 8°. **14123. h. 30.**

MUḤAMMAD, *the Prophet.* [*Life.*] *See* ABŪ al-ḤUSAIN, *Saiyid.* মোস্লেম-পতাকা *etc.* [Moslem-patākā.] [1908.] 12°. **14127. aaa. 1.**

MUḤAMMAD, *the Prophet (continued).* [*Life.*] *See* GIRIŚACHANDRA SENA. মহাপুরুষ মোহম্মদের জীবনচরিত। [Mohammader jīvanacharita.] [1885-87.] 8°. **14123. h. 17.**

—— [*Life.*] *See* KṚISHṆAKUMĀRA MITRA. মহম্মদ-চরিত *etc.* [Mahammad charita.] [1886.] 12°. **14127. a. 30.**

—— [*Life.*] *See* MUḤAMMAD 'ABD al-'AZĪZ. সংক্ষিপ্ত মহম্মদ-চরিত। [Saṃkshipta Mahammad-charita.] [1901.] 12°. **14127. aa. 21.(2.)**

MUḤAMMAD ibn 'ABD ALLĀH, *al-Khaṭīb.* *See* ḤUSAIN ibn MAS'ŪD, *al-Farrā al-Baghawī.* হদিস-পূর্ব্ববিভাগ। *etc.* [Mishkāt al-maṣābīḥ. Redacted by Muḥammad al-Khaṭīb.] [1892, *etc.*] 8°. **14123. h. 21.**

MUḤAMMAD ibn ISMĀ'ĪL, *Bukhārī.* সহি বোখারী শরিফ। [Ṣaḥīḥ. A work on traditions, consisting of the Arabic text of Bukhārī's Ṣaḥīḥ, with a Bengali translation, commentary, and notes, by Na'īm al-Dīn, assisted by Maulavī Ghulām Sarwar.] করটীয়া ১৩০৪ [*Karatia,* 1898, *etc.*] 8°. **14522. b. 17.**

MUḤAMMAD ibn MUḤAMMAD, *Ghazzālī.* সৌভাগ্য-স্পর্শমণি। [Saubhāgya-sparśamaṇi. A work on Muhammadan religious duties; being a translation by Mirzā Muḥammad Yūsuf 'Alī of the Kīmiyā i sa'ādat, a Persian abridgment of Ghazzālī's Arabic Iḥyā 'ulūm al-dīn.] Pt. i. pp. 31. কলিকাতা ১৮৯৫ [*Calcutta,* 1895.] 8°. **14123. h. 23.**

MUḤAMMAD ibn 'UMAR, *Wāḳidī.* *See* 'INĀYAT ḤUSAIN ibn NAWĀZISH AḤMAD. ফতুহশাম। [Futūḥ al-Shām. Translated into verse from 'Ināyat Ḥusain's Hindustani version of the Arabic history of Wāḳidī.] [1905.] Fol. **14127. bbb. 6.**

MUḤAMMAD 'ABBĀS (ABŪ al-ḤASAN). মাছাএলে জরুরিয়া ও তরিকায় নববিয়া। [Masā'il i ẓarūriyah. Religious precepts and observances compiled from Arabic sources, in Muhammadan Bengali verse.] Pt. i. pp. 200. কলিকাতা ১৩০২ [*Calcutta,* 1896.] 8°. **14123. h. 26.(1.)**

MUḤAMMAD 'ABBĀS 'ALĪ. *See* 'INĀYAT ḤUSAIN ibn NAWĀZISH AḤMAD. ফতুহশাম। [Futūḥ al-Shām. Translated into verse by Munshī Pīr Muḥammad and Maulavī Muḥammad 'Abbās 'Alī.] [1905.] Fol. **14127. bbb. 6.**

MUḤAMMAD 'ABBĀS 'ALĪ *(continued)*. See Ḳur'ān. قرآن مجيد مترجم কোরাণ শরীফ। [The Koran. Edited with a Bengali interlinear translation of the text and of the Hindustani notes by Muḥammad 'Abbās 'Alī.] [1907, *etc.*] Fol. **14509. d. 21.**

—— See Ḳur'ān. قرآن مجيد مترجم ... আমপারা। [The 30th Section of the Koran, with Shāh Rafī' al-Dīn's Hindustani interlinear translation. Edited, with a Bengali interlinear translation of the text, and of Hindustani marginal notes, by Muḥammad 'Abbās 'Alī.] [1908.] 8°. **14509. b. 22.**

MUḤAMMAD 'ABD al-'AZĪZ. সংক্ষিপ্ত মহম্মদ-চরিত। [Saṃkshipta Mahammad-charita. A short account of the life of Muḥammad.] pp. 6, 152. কুমারখালী ১৯০১ [*Kumarkhali*, 1901.] 12°. **14127. aa. 21.(2.)**

MUḤAMMAD 'ABD al-GHANĪ. See 'Abd al-Ghanī.

MUḤAMMAD 'ABD al-ḲĀDIR, *of Mymensingh*. See Sa'dī. گلستان ... পুষ্পোদ্যান অর্থাৎ ... গোলেস্তান। [Pushpodyāna. The Gulistān translated from the Persian in prose and verse by Muḥammad 'Abd al-Ḳādir.] [1901.] 8°. **14129. d. 33.**

—— See Sa'dī. গোলেস্তাঁর বঙ্গানুবাদ। [Gulistān. Chapters 5 to 7, translated by Muḥammad 'Abd al-Ḳādir.] [1905.] 12°. **Pers. 1657.**

MUḤAMMAD 'ABD al-RAḤMĀN KHĀN. আখলাকল আওলীয়া তরজমা মকাচ্ছাদছালেহিন। [Akhlāḳ al-auliyā. Anecdotes of Muhammadan saints, being a translation in Muhammadan Bengali verse by Munshī Janāb 'Ālī of the Maḳāṣid al-ṣāliḥīn, a Hindustani version of the Persian Ḥikāyāt al-ṣāliḥīn.] pp. 216. কলিকাতা ১৩০৮ [*Calcutta*, 1901.] 8°. **14123. h. 29.(2.)**

MUḤAMMAD AFẒAL. মুজমা রাগ হরিবংশ। [Mujmā rāg harivaṃṣa. A collection of religious poems, in Muhammadan Bengali.] Pt. ii. pp. 104. শ্রীহট্ট ১৩১৩ [*Sylhet*, 1907.] 8°. **14123. h. 42.**

In Sylhet Nagari characters.

MUḤAMMAD ḲĀSIM, *Maulavī*. বড়পীর গুণাবলী। [Baṛa Pīr-guṇāvalī. An account of the life and miracles of 'Abd al-Ḳādir Jīlānī, translated by 'Abd al-Ḳādir into Muhammadan Bengali from the Hindustani I'jāz i Ghauṣīyah of Muḥammad Ḳāsim.] pp. 72. কলিকাতা ১৩০৬ [*Calcutta*, 1899.] 8°. **14127. bb. 18.(1.)**

MUḤAMMAD KHĀṬIR. See Firdausī. ছহি সাহা-নামা। [Shāh-nāmah. Translated into Muhammadan Bengali verse by Muḥammad Khāṭir.] [1886.] 4°. **14129. g. 7.**

—— See Ghulām Nabī ibn 'Ināyat Allāh. সর্ব্বরহৎ কাছাছল আম্বিয়া চারইয়ারী *etc.* [Ḳiṣaṣ al-anbiyā. Translated by Muḥammad Khāṭir and others.] [1902.] 4°. **14123. hh. 1.**

MUḤAMMAD NA'ĪM al-DĪN. See Na'īm al-Dīn.

MUḤAMMAD NI'MAT ALLĀH. হুজ্জতল মোমেনিন। অর্থাৎ ফিরদ্দে জেরারল মাছাজেদল মফছেদিন। [Ḥujjat al-Mūminīn. A compilation, in Muhammadan Bengali verse, of authoritative traditions on the illegality of erecting new mosques in the vicinity of existing ones, to the detriment of the latter.] pp. 19. করটীয়া ১২৯৭ [*Karatia*, 1890.] 8°. **14123. h. 28.(1.)**

MUḤAMMAD RIYĀẒ al-DĪN AḤMAD. See Ephemerides. সন ১৩০৬ সালের বৃহৎ মহম্মদীয় পঞ্জিকা। [Mahammadīya pañjikā. A Muhammadan almanac for the year 1306 B.S. By Muḥammad Riyāẓ al-Dīn Aḥmad.] [1899.] 12°. **14133. e. 10.**

MUḤAMMAD ROSHAN 'ALĪ. আরবি শিক্ষা। [Ārabi-ṣikshā. Lessons in Arabic.] Pt. i. pp. 80. কলিকাতা ১৩১৪ [*Calcutta*, 1907.] 8°. **14131. g. 35.**

MUḤAMMAD 'UMAR. See Daulat Aḥmad and Muḥammad 'Umar. কক্বরমা। *etc.* [Kakbarmā.] [1898.] 12°. **14131. e. 33.(3.)**

MUḤAMMAD WA'Ẓ al-DĪN. এছলামিয় মন্ত্র। [Islāmīya mantra. A collection of Muhammadan charms and incantations.] Pt. i. pp. 31. কলিকাতা ১৩০৩ [*Calcutta*, 1895.] 8°. **14123. h. 25.**

MUḤAMMAD YŪSUF 'ALĪ, *Mirzā*. See Muḥammad ibn Muḥammad, *Ghazzālī*. সৌভাগ্য-স্পর্শমণি। [Saubhāgya-sparṣamaṇi. A translation by Muḥammad Yūsuf 'Alī of the Kīmiyā i sa'ādat.] [1895.] 8°. **14123. h. 23.**

MU'IZ al-DĪN (Abū Wā'iẓ Muḥammad), *Muwā'iẓ*. قواعد پارسی [Kawā'id i Pārsī.] ... A Persian grammar in Bengalee, by Maezuddin Abo Waez-Mohammad Mawaez. pp. 31. *Calcutta*, 1902. 12°. **14131. e. 33.(2.)**

MUKADDAS 'ALĪ. তামাকের জন্মকথা। [Tāmāker janmakathā. A satire, in Muhammadan Bengali verse, directed against the Wahhābīs for their absurd scruples regarding the use of tobacco.] pp. 14. করটীয় ১২৯৪ [*Karatia*, 1887.] 8°. **14129. d.**

MUKERJEE (G. C.). *See* GAṆEŚACHANDRA MUKHOPĀDHYĀYA.

MUKHERJEE (UPENDRA CHANDRA). *See* UPENDRACHANDRA MUKHOPĀDHYĀYA.

MUKHLIṢ al-RAHMĀN CHAUDHURĪ. Shoka Bharati, or The melancholy condolence of H. G. M. Queen Empress Victoria. By Mowlvi Md. Mukhlisurrahman Chowdrisahib, B.A. শোক ভারতী। pp. v. 27. দিনাজপুর [*Dinajpur*, 1902.] 16°. **14129. a. 1.**

MUKHOPĀDHYĀYA (FRANCIS XAVIER). Differences in idiom between Bengali and English . . . By Francis Xavier Mukerji. pp. ii. 95. *Calcutta*, 1889. 8°. **14131. g. 27.**

MUKTAKEŚĪ, *Devī*. [*Life.*] *See* PRASANNAKUMĀRA BHAṬṬĀCHĀRYA. স্বর্গীয় দেবী মুক্তকেশীর চরিতামৃত। [Devī Muktakeṣīr charitāmṛita.] [1891.] 12°. **14127. a. 40.**

MUKUNDA, *Kavi*. *See* RASIKACHANDRA VASU. জগন্নাথ-বিজয় ও কবি মুকুন্দ। [Jagannātha-vijaya o Kavi Mukunda. An article on the Jagannātha-vijaya, a poem in praise of the god Jagannātha, and its author Kavi Mukunda, with extracts from the poem.] [1901.] 8°. **14133. f. 18.**

MUKUNDACHANDRA RĀYA CHAUDHURĪ. মণিপুরের ইতিহাস। [Maṇipurer itihāsa. An account of the Native State of Manipur, with a detailed narrative of the outbreak of 1890.] pp. iv. 238, 98. কলিকাতা ১২৯৮ [*Calcutta*, 1891.] 12°. **14127. a. 42.(2.)**

MUKUNDADAYĀLA VASU. *See* PĀṆINI. লিঙ্গানুশাসনম্। [Liṅgānuṣāsana. Edited with Bengali notes by Mukundadayāla Vasu.] [1894.] 12°. **14090. b. 43.(2.)**

—— *See* UṆĀDISŪTRA. উণাদিসূত্রম্। [Uṇādisūtra. Selections, with a commentary in Sanskrit and Bengali by Mukundadayāla Vasu.] [1893.] 12°. **14092. a. 17.(2.)**

MUKUNDARĀMA CHAKRAVARTĪ, called KAVIKAṄKAṆA. *See* DĪNEṢACHANDRA SENA. ফুল্লরা। [Phullarā. The story of Phullarā, taken from the Chaṇḍī of Mukundarāma.] [1907.] 16°. **14128. aa. 3.**

—— কবিকঙ্কণ চণ্ডী। [Chaṇḍī. The poems of Mukundarāma Chakravartī, with variants.] [1885.] *See* AKSHAYACHANDRA SARKĀR. প্রাচীন কাব্য সংগ্রহ। [Prāchīna kāvya-saṅgraha.] Pt. ii. [1884, *etc.*] 8°. **14129. g. 8.**

—— শ্রীকবিকঙ্কণ চণ্ডী। [Chaṇḍī. Another edition of the poems of Mukundarāma, with an introduction on the language and style of the poet, and a glossary of difficult words.] pp. vi. xiii. iii. vii. 314. কলিকাতা ১৩০৯ [*Calcutta*, 1902.] 8°. **14129. cc. 2.**

—— কবিকঙ্কণ চণ্ডী। [Chaṇḍī. With an introductory notice of the author and his writings, and a glossary. Second edition.] pp. vi. xii. ii. vii. 314. কলিকাতা ১৩১৩ [*Calcutta*, 1907.] 8°. **14129. cc. 16.**

—— Three episodes from the old Bengali poem "Caṇḍī," translated into English by E. B. Cowell. (Journal of the Asiatic Society of Bengal. Vol. lxxi. Part i., extra No. 2.) pp. viii. 46. *Calcutta*, 1902. 8°. **Ac. 8826/11.**

MULLENS (HANNAH CATHERINE). The history of Phulmani and Karuna... Translated from the Bengali of Mrs. Mullens. pp. 138. *Calcutta*, 1853. 8°. **14123. b. 11.**

MULLICK (DEBENDRA CHANDRA). *See* DEVENDRACHANDRA MALLIKA.

MUNAUWAR 'ALĪ, *of Kanchanpur*. আলমাছ ও গোলরায়হান। [Almās o Gul-raihān. A tale of love and adventure in Muhammadan Bengali verse.] pp. 222. ঢাকা ১৩০৪ [*Dacca*, 1897.] 8°. **14127. g. 10.(1.)**

MUNIRISHI SARMĀ. *See* MAHENDRANĀTHA ĀḌHYA.

MURALĪ. মুরলী। [Muralī. Phonographic records in use by the Indian Elysian Entertainment Company, with the words of the Bengali and Hindi songs and pieces.] pp. iv. 35. *Puthia, Rajshahi*, [1903.] 12°. **14125. d. 20.(2.)**

MURĀRIMOHANA GUPTA. Sangita Pravesika, or A complete course of Hindu music. Treating chiefly of Vadya-kanda. (সঙ্গীত-প্রবেশিকা) 2 pts. *Calcutta*, 1889-91. 8°. **14125. d. 15.**

MURTAZĀ, *Saiyid, of Murshidabad.* মুসলমান বৈষ্ণব কবি সৈয়দ মর্ত্তুজা। [Poems on the loves of Rādhā and Krishṇa. With an account of the author by 'Abd al-Karīm.] pp. vi. 16. রাজসাহী ১৩১১ [*Rajshahi*, 1904.] 8°. **14129. cc. 11.**

MUSHARRAF HUSAIN, *Mīr.* বিষাদ-সিন্ধু ... Bishad-sindhu, or The history of the Moharam. 2 pts. ময়মনসিংহ *Calcutta* [*Mymensingh*], 1885-87. 8°. **14123. h. 20.**

Pt. ii. was published at Mymensingh.

—— [Fifth edition.] pp. 528. কলিকাতা ১৩১১ [*Calcutta*, 1905.] 12°. **14123. h. 35.**

—— হজরত বেলালের জীবনী। [Hajrat Belāler jīvanī. The story of the devotion of the mu'azzin Bilāl to Muḥammad; in verse.] pp. 32, 10. কলিকাতা ১৩১২ [*Calcutta*, 1905.] 12°. **14128. a. 9.**

MUZAMMAL HAKK. ফেরদৌসী-চরিত। ... Ferdausi charita, or The life of Ferdausi, the poet laureate of Ghizni. By Mozammel Huque. pp. 88. কলিকাতা [*Calcutta*,] 1898. 16°. **14127. aa. 15.**

—— প্রেম-হার। [Premahāra. Love poems.] pp. 96. *Calcutta*, 1898. 12°. **14129. a. 48.(2.)**

NĀBHĀJĪ. *See* LĀLADĀSA BĀBĀJĪ. শ্রীশ্রীভক্তমাল গ্রন্থ। [Bhaktamāla. Based on the Hindi Bhaktamāla of Nābhājī, with extracts therefrom.] [1898.] 8°. **14129. e. 20.**

NABIN CHANDRA VIDYARATNA. *See* NAVĪNACHANDRA VIDYĀRATNA.

NĀGA BHAṬṬA. কামরত্ন তন্ত্রম্। [Kāmaratna. A Sanskrit work on magic, with a Bengali translation. Edited by Hīrālāl Ḍhol.] pp. iv. 88, 101. কলিকাতা ১২৯২ [*Calcutta*, 1885.] 8°. **14033. bb. 21.**

—— কামরত্নম্। [Kāmaratna. Sanskrit text, with a Bengali translation.] pp. 70. [1891.] *See* PERIODICAL PUBLICATIONS. — *Calcutta.* অরুণোদয়। [Aruṇodaya.] Pt. i., no. 18. [1890, *etc.*] 4°. **14133. g. 16.**

NĀGA BHAṬṬA (*continued*). কামরত্নম্। [Kāmaratna. Sanskrit text, somewhat expurgated. Edited with a Bengali translation by Kālīprasanna Vidyāratna.] pp. 116. কলিকাতা ১৩০১ [*Calcutta*, 1894.] 8°. **14033. bb. 43.**

NĀGĀRJUNA, *Siddha.* সিদ্ধনাগার্জ্জুনকক্ষপুটম্। [Kakshapuṭa. A manual of the black art. Sanskrit text, with a Bengali translation.] pp. 71. [1891, *etc.*] *See* PERIODICAL PUBLICATIONS.—*Calcutta.* অরুণোদয়। [Aruṇodaya.] Pt. i., no. 16. [1890, *etc.*] 4°. **14133. g. 16.(vol. i.)**

NAGENDRABĀLĀ SARASVATĪ. অমিয়গাথা। [Amiyagāthā. Short poems. Edited, with a life of the authoress, by Rādhānātha Rāya.] pp. x. v. 210. কলিকাতা ১৩০৮ [*Calcutta*, 1902.] 12°. **14129. a. 34.**

—— কণা। [Kaṇā. Short poems.] pp. 60. কলিকাতা ১৩১২ [*Calcutta*, 1905.] 12°. **14129. bb. 17.(3.)**

—— কুসুম-গাথা। [Kusumagāthā. Short poems.] pp. viii. 91. কলিকাতা ১৩১২ [*Calcutta*, 1905.] 12°. **14129. bb. 16.(2.)**

—— মর্ম্মগাথা। [Marmagāthā. Short poems.] pp. ii. iii. 170. হুগলী ১৩০৩ [*Hughli*, 1896.] 12°. **14129. b. 44.(6.)**

—— প্রেম-গাথা। [Premagāthā. Lyrical poems.] pp. iii. 155. ১৩০৫ [*Calcutta*, 1898.] 12°. **14129. a. 28.(6.)**

NAGENDRACHANDRA MITRA. কার্লাইল ও বর্ত্তমান যুগধর্ম্ম। [Kārlāil o vartamāna yugadharma. A lecture on Carlyle and the religion of the present age.] pp. 36. কলিকাতা ১৮৯৪ [*Calcutta*, 1894.] 12°. **14131. d. 32.**

NAGENDRALĀLA BARUYĀ, *Kavirāja.* *See* SAṄKHĀRA BHĀJANI. বৌদ্ধ-কাহিনী সংগ্রহ। [Bauddha-kāhinī-saṅgraha. Translated from the Burmese Saṅkhāra bhājani by Nagendralāla Baruyā.] [1903.] 12°. **14123. k. 4.(2.)**

NAGENDRANĀTHA CHAṬṬOPĀDHYĀYA. মহাত্মা থিওডোর পার্কারের জীবনচরিত। [Thioḍor Pārkārer jīvanacharita. A life of Theodore Parker.] pp. 201. কলিকাতা ১২৯২ [*Calcutta*, 1886.] 8°. **14127. bb. 9.**

NAGENDRANĀTHA GHOSHA. দান-যজ্ঞ। [Dānayajña. A drama on the celebration of a sacrifice by the father of Kṛishṇa.] pp. 106. ভবানীপুর ১৩০৩ [*Bhawanipur*, 1897.] 12°. **14131. a. 40.(6.)**

NAGENDRANĀTHA GUPTA. লীলা। [Lilā. A tale of Hindu society, describing the sufferings of a Hindu widow. Second edition.] pp. 274. কলিকাতা ১৩০৬ [*Calcutta*, 1899.] 8°. **14127. cc. 17.**

—— তমস্বিনী। [Tamasvinī. A tale of domestic life in Bengal.] pp. 237. কলিকাতা ১৩০৭ [*Calcutta*, 1900.] 12°. **14127. cc. 18.**

NAGENDRANĀTHA ṢĀSTRĪ, *of Kandi, Murshidabad.* Naya Shastra or Elements of Sanskrit logic in Bengali with full notes . . . ন্যায়শাস্ত্র। pp. iv. 96. কলিকাতা [*Calcutta*, 1903.] 12°. **14125.f.40.(2.)**

NAGENDRANĀTHA SENA GUPTA, *Kavirāja.* দ্রব্যগুণ-শিক্ষা। [Dravyaguṇaṣikshā. Materia Medica, compiled from native and European works. Fourth edition.] pp. vi. 510. কলিকাতা ১৯০২ [*Calcutta*, 1902.] 8°. **14125. cc. 1.**

—— [Fifth edition.] pp. v. 510. কলিকাতা ১৯০৫ [*Calcutta*, 1905.] 8°. **14125. cc. 6.**

—— কবিরাজি-শিক্ষা। [Kavirāji-ṣikshā. A comprehensive treatise on Hindu medicine, surgery, and Materia Medica. Eighth edition.] 2 vols. কলিকাতা ১৩০৯ [*Calcutta*, 1902.] 8°. **14125. cc. 2.**

—— সচিত্র সুশ্রুত-সংহিতা। [Suṣruta-saṃhitā. A treatise on medicine based on Sanskrit and English works. Second edition.] pp. viii. 50, 726, ii. কলিকাতা ১৩০৯ [*Calcutta*, 1903.] 8°. **14125. cc. 4.**

NAGENDRANĀTHA VASU. *See* ACADEMIES, *etc.*—Calcutta.—*Bengal Academy of Literature.* সাহিত্য-পরিষৎ-পত্রিকা। [Sāhitya-parishat-patrikā. Edited in part by Nagendranātha Vasu.] [1894, *etc.*] 8°. **14133. f. 18.**

—— *See* MAHĀBHĀRATA. মহাভারত। [Mahābhārata. A metrical version by Vijaya Paṇḍita. Edited by Nagendranātha Vasu.] [1899, *etc.*] 8°. **14129. ff. 1.**

—— *See* NARAHARI CHAKRAVARTĪ. ব্রজ-পরিক্রমা [Vraja-parikramā. Edited, with notes and a life of the author, by Nagendranātha Vasu.] [1905.] 12°. **14129. bb. 30.**

NAGENDRANĀTHA VASU (*continued*). *See* PERIODICAL PUBLICATIONS.—*Calcutta.* প্রাচীন বাঙ্গালা গ্রন্থাবলী। [Prāchīna Bāṅgālā granthāvalī. Edited in part by Nagendranātha Vasu.] [1900, *etc.*] 8°. **14133. ff. 2.**

—— *See* PURĀṆAS.—*Brahmāṇḍapurāṇa.* ব্রহ্মাণ্ড-পুরাণম্। [Brahmāṇḍapurāṇa. Edited, with a prose translation and notes, by Nagendranātha Vasu.] [1891-94.] 8°. **14016. c. 46.**

—— *See* RĀMĀI PAṆḌITA. শূন্যপুরাণ। [Ṣūnyapurāṇa. Edited, with an introduction and glossary, by Nagendranātha Vasu.] [1908.] 12°. **14129. bbb. 3.**

—— *See* RAṄGALĀLA MUKHOPĀDHYĀYA. বিশ্বকোষ। [Viṣvakosha. Edited in part by Nagendranātha Vasu.] [1885, *etc.*] 4°. **14133. c. 5.**

—— The Castes and Sects of Bengal. By Nagendra Nath Vasu. . . . বঙ্গের জাতীয় ইতিহাস। [Vaṅger jātīya itihāsa.] [*Calcutta*, 1900, *etc.*] 8°. **14125. ee. 32.**

In progress.

—— Curtain lecture. মশারি-রহস্য। [Maṣāri rahasya. Short sketches of life in Bengal, in proof of the superiority of Hindu over European social institutions.] pp. 82. কলিকাতা ১২৯৪ [*Calcutta*, 1887.] 12°. **14125. ee. 22.(1.)**

—— কবি জয়ানন্দ ও চৈতন্য-মঙ্গল। [Kavi Jayānanda o Chaitanya-maṅgala. An account of the poet Jayānanda and his Chaitanya-maṅgala, a work on the life of Chaitanya; with copious extracts from the poem.] ১৩০৪ [1897.] *See* ACADEMIES, *etc.*—Calcutta.—*Bengal Academy of Literature.* সাহিত্য-পরিষৎ-পত্রিকা। [Sāhitya-parishat-patrikā.] Vol. iv., no. 3. [1894, *etc.*] 8°. **14133. f. 18.**

—— Kayastha Ethnology . . . কায়স্থের বর্ণ-নির্ণয়। [Kāyasther varṇanirṇaya.] pp. iii. ii. 146. *Calcutta*, [1901.] 8°. **14125. ee. 35.**

—— বিজয় পণ্ডিতের মহাভারত। [Vijaya Paṇḍiter Mahābhārata. A paper on the Mahābhārata of Vijaya Paṇḍita, with extracts from the poem.] ১৩০৩ [1896.] *See* ACADEMIES, *etc.*—Calcutta.—*Bengal Academy of Literature.* সাহিত্য-পরিষৎ-পত্রিকা। [Sāhitya-parishat-patrikā.] Vol. iii., no. 2. [1894, *etc.*] 8°. **14133. f. 18.**

NA'ĪM al-DĪN. *See* KUR'ĀN. কোরাণ শরিফ। [The Koran. Arabic text, accompanied by a Bengali translation and commentary by Na'īm al-Dīn.] [1887, *etc.*] 8°. **14509. b. 18.**

—— —— [1899, *etc.*] 8°. **14509. b. 22.**

—— *See* MUHAMMAD ibn ISMĀ'ĪL, *Bukhārī*. সহি বোখারী শরিফ। [Ṣaḥīḥ. Arabic text, with a Bengali translation, commentary, and notes, by Na'īm al-Dīn.] [1898, *etc.*] 8°. **14522. b. 17.**

—— *See* NIẒĀM, *Shaikh*. ফতওয়ায় আলমগিরী। [Fatāwā i 'Ālamgīrī. Translated from the Arabic by Na'īm al-Dīn.] 1884, *etc.* 8°. **14123. h. 22.**

—— আদেল্লায় হানিফীয়া। রদ্দে লামজহাবীয়া। [Adillah i Ḥanafīyah. Proofs of the orthodoxy of Ḥanafī tenets, in the form of arguments with an apostate Maulavī of Bhagalpur. Second edition.] Pt. i. pp. 180. করটীয়া ১৯০৪ [*Karatiya*, 1904.] 8°. **14123. h. 33.**

—— জোব্দাতোল মাসায়েল। [Zubdat al-masā'il. A treatise on Muhammadan ceremonial observances, compiled from Arabic sources in the form of a catechism by Na'īm al-Dīn with the assistance of Ghulām Sarwar. Second edition.] pp. iv. 256, 24. সেরপুর ১২৯৮ হিজরি [*Sherpur*, 1881.] 8°. **14123. f. 31.**

—— [Fourth edition.] pp. iv. 246. করটীয়া ১২৯৪ [*Karatia*, 1887.] 8°. **14123. h. 19.**

—— [Sixth edition.] pp. vi. 240. করটীয়া ১৮৯৬ [*Karatia*, 1896.] 8°. **14123. h. 27.**

NAKSHATRAKOSHA. অথ নক্ষত্রকোষ। [Nakshatrakosha. A Sanskrit list of synonyms for the lunar mansions in verse, with a Bengali translation.] *See* GOPĪRAMAṆA TARKARATNA. কোষচন্দ্রিকা। [Koshachandrikā.] pp. 40-45. [1893.] 12°. **14090. b. 44.(1.)**

NAKUḌACHANDRA VIŚVĀSA. অক্ষয়-চরিত। . . . [Akshayacharita,] or an illustrated life of the late Babu Aksay Kumar Dutta. pp. ii. 68. কলিকাতা ১২৯৪ [*Calcutta*, 1887.] 12°. **14131. d. 21.(1.)**

NAKULEŚVARA VIDYĀBHŪSHAṆA. আকবর। [Akbar. A story of domestic life.] pp. 109. কলিকাতা ১৮৯৮ [*Calcutta*, 1898.] 12°. **14127. cc. 10.(6.)**

NAKULEŚVARA VIDYĀBHŪSHAṆA (*continued*). ভাষাবোধ বাঙ্গালা ব্যাকরণ। [Bāṅgālā vyākaraṇa. A grammar of the Bengali language.] pp. vi. 205. *Calcutta*, 1898. 12°. **14131. e. 34.**

—— কুমুদানন্দ ঐতিহাসিক উপন্যাস। [Kumudānanda. An historical tale.] pp. 262. কলিকাতা ১৩১৪ [*Calcutta*, 1907.] 12°. **14128. a. 18.**

—— সন্ন্যাস। [Sannyāsa. A Bengali novel.] pp. 202. কলিকাতা ১৮৯২ [*Calcutta*, 1892.] 8°. **14127. e. 38.(3.)**

NALINĪBĀLĀ, *Daughter of Devendravijaya Vasu.* নলিনী-গাথা। [Nalinīgāthā. Miscellaneous poems. Edited by Lalitachandra Mitra, with a life of the late poetess, who died at the age of 20.] pp. xi. 363, vi. কলিকাতা [*Calcutta*, 1898.] 12°. **14129. a. 44.**

NALINĪBĀLĀ, *of Dacca.* [*Life.*] *See* HARIPRABHĀ TAKEDĀ. কেদার-নলিনী। [Kedāra-Nalinī.] [1908.] 12°. **14127. aa. 39.(2.)**

NĀMDĀR. বনগাঁয়ে শিয়াল রাজা। [Bangāṅye śiyāl rājā, or The jackal king of the village. A farce.] pp. 16. কলিকাতা ১২৭৪ [*Calcutta*, 1868.] 16°. **14131. a.**

NĀNAK, *Bābā.* জপজিসাহেব। [Japjī. The introductory prayer of the Ādi Granth. Panjabi text, in Bengali characters, with a Bengali translation by Lālavihārī Siṃha Kshatrī of Bhagalpur.] pp. iv. 28. মুর্শিদাবাদ ১৩০৭ [*Murshidabad*, 1901.] 8°. **14162. bb. 7.(2.)**

—— নানক প্রকাশ। [Nānak-prakāśa. An account of the life of Bābā Nānak.] Pt. i. pp. xiii. 91. কলিকাতা ১৮০৭ [*Calcutta*, 1885.] 8°. **14123. f. 1.(3.)**

NANDAKUMĀRA, *Maharaja.* [*Life.*] *See* SATYACHARAṆA ŚĀSTRĪ. মহারাজ-নন্দকুমার-চরিত। [Mahārāja Nandakumāra-charita.] [1899.] 12°. **14127. aa. 11.**

NANDAKUMĀRA KAVIRATNA BHAṬṬĀCHĀRYA. *See* ŚIVASAṂHITĀ. শিবসংহিতা। [Śivasaṃhitā. With a Bengali translation by Nandakumāra Kaviratna.] [1886.] 8°. **14028. d. 20.**

NANDALĀLA RĀYA. ভেকাশ্রিত তত্ত্ববোধঃগ্রন্থঃ। [Bhekāśrita tattvabodha. A philosophical treatise of the Vaishṇava school, in verse, Sanskrit text, with a Bengali prose translation. Compiled by Nandalāla Rāya.] pp. 25. কলিকাতা ১২৯৪ Calcutta, [1887.] *obl.* 8°. **14048. bb.**

—— নূতন পাঁচালী। [Pāñchālī. A collection of ballads on mythological subjects. Second edition.] Pt. i.-iv. pp. 476. কলিকাতা ১২৯৫ [*Calcutta*, 1888.] 16°. **14129. a. 31.**

NANĪGOPĀLA MUKHOPĀDHYĀYA. *See* MILTON (J.). ত্রিদিব-চ্যুতি। [Tridiva-chyuti. A prose translation of Milton's Paradise Lost, by Nanīgopāla Mukhopādhyāya.] [1893.] 12°. **14129. a. 38.(1.)**

NĀRADA. নারদকৃত ভক্তিসূত্র। [Bhaktisūtra. A collection of 83 aphorisms on Vaishṇava devotion, attributed to the sage Nārada. Sanskrit text, with a Bengali translation and commentary.] *See* KṚISHṆAPRASANNA SENA. ভক্তি ও ভক্ত [Bhakti o bhakta.] pp. 1-41. [1887.] 8°. **14028. c. 56.**

—— ভক্তিসূত্রম্ দেবর্ষি নারদ প্রোক্তম্ [Bhaktisūtra. Sanskrit text, with a Bengali exposition by Śyāmalāla Gosvāmī.] pp. 120. কলিকাতা ১৩১১ [*Calcutta*, 1904.] 16°. **14028. bb. 15.**

—— নারদ ও ভক্তি মার্গ। [Nārada o bhakti-mārga.] Narada and the doctrine of faith. [A Christian tract.] pp. 4. *Calcutta*, 1892. 12°. **14123. a. 27.(1.)**

NARAHARI CHAKRAVARTĪ. ব্রজ-পরিক্রমা [Vraja-parikramā. A poem describing the district of Braj and the local cult of Kṛishṇa, illustrated by verses from Sanskrit works. Edited, with notes and a biography of the author, by Nagendranātha Vasu.] pp. 77, 345. ১৩১২ [*Calcutta*, 1905.] 12°. **14129. bb. 30.**

NARAHARI DĀSA. শ্রীশ্রীনরোত্তমবিলাস। [Narottama-vilāsa. An account, in verse, of the life of Narottama Dāsa, the author's preceptor.] pp. 170. কলিকাতা ১২৯৬ [*Calcutta*, 1890.] 8°. **14127. b.**

NARASIṂHACHANDRA HĀLDĀR. Language. Illustrated by upwards of one hundred select expressions [in Bengali and English] and 20 syllogisms. Part I. [By] Nursing Chunder Halder. pp. 24. [*Calcutta*,] 1886. 12°. **7410. dg. 54.(3.)**

NĀRĀYAṆACHANDRA BHAṬṬĀCHĀRYA VIDYĀBHŪSHAṆA. *See* HEMACHANDRA, *Disciple of Devachandra.* সানুবাদ অভিধানচিন্তামণিঃ *etc.* [Abhidhāna-chintāmaṇi. Sanskrit text, edited with a Bengali translation by Nārāyaṇachandra.] [1907.] 12°. **14092. a. 34.**

NĀRĀYAṆACHANDRA PĀLA. নাটাপোল। [Nāṭāpol. A metrical description of Natapol, a town in the District of the 24 Parganas, as it was 30 years ago.] pp. 11. উলুবেড়িয়া ১২৯৯ [*Uluberia*, 1894.] 12°. **14127. a. 51.(1.)**

NĀRĀYAṆA DĀSA, *Author of the Bhaktamāla.* *See* NĀBHĀJĪ.

NĀRĀYAṆADĀSA KAVIRĀJA. [For editions of the Sanskrit work entitled Rājavallabhīya-dravyaguṇa, Dravyaguṇa, Rājavallabha-nighaṇṭu, or Rājavallabha, in the redaction of Nārāyaṇadāsa:] *See* RĀJAVALLABHA.

NĀRĀYAṆA VANDYOPĀDHYĀYA. বিদ্যাসাগর চরিত স্বরচিত। [Vidyāsāgara-charita. A life of Pandit Īśvarachandra Vidyāsāgara, compiled from autobiographical notes. Second edition.] pp. iii. 53. *Calcutta*, 1893. 12°. **14127. b. 49.(2.)**

NARENDRAKṚISHṆA ŚIROMAṆI. ধর্ম্মজীবন। [Dharmajīvana. A compendium of rules for the practice of religion, copiously illustrated from Sanskrit texts.] pp. ii. viii. 313. কলিকাতা ১৩০৬ [*Calcutta*, 1899.] 12°. **14028. bb. 2.**

NARENDRANĀTHA DATTA. *See* VIVEKĀNANDA SVĀMĪ.

NARENDRANĀTHA MITRA. *See* PYĀRĪCHĀND MITRA, called ṬEKCHĀND ṬHĀKUR. The Spoilt Boy. [A translation of Ālāler gharer dulāl by Narendranātha Mitra, with the aid of M. S. Knight.] 1882-83. 8°. **P.P. 1423. ld.**

NAREŚACHANDRA SENA GUPTA. *See* BAṄKIMCHANDRA CHAṬṬOPĀDHYĀYA. The Abbey of Bliss. A translation of . . . Anandamath by Nares Chandra Sen-Gupta. [1906.] 12°. **14128. a. 15.**

NAROTTAMA DĀSA. [*Life.*] *See* NARAHARI DĀSA. শ্রীশ্রীনরোত্তমবিলাস। [Narottama-vilāsa.] [1890.] 8°. **14127. b.**

—— [*Life.*] *See* ŚIŚIRAKUMĀRA GHOSHA. শ্রীনরোত্তম চরিত। [Narottama-charita.] [1891.] 12°. **14127. a. 39.**

NAROTTAMA DĀSA (*continued*). দেহ-কড়চ। [Deha-karcha. A metaphysical tract, printed literatim, with notes, from a MS. dated Śaka 1603. With a life of the author.] ১৩০৪ [1897.] *See* ACADEMIES, *etc.*—Calcutta.—*Bengal Academy of Literature.* সাহিত্য-পরিষৎ-পত্রিকা। [Sāhitya-parishat-patrikā.] Vol. iv., no. 1. [1894, *etc.*] 8°. **14133. f. 18.**

—— হাটপত্তনের টিকা ও প্রার্থনার শব্দ অর্থ টিকা। [Hāṭapattana, and Prārthanā. Two Vaishṇava religious tracts in verse, accompanied by commentaries by Hāsyavadana Gosvāmī.] pp. 36. কলিকাতা ১২৯৯ [*Calcutta*, 1892.] 8°. **14129. c. 41.(3.)**

—— নরোত্তমদাস। [Narottama Dāsa. A collection of Vaishṇava songs. Edited, with annotations, and a critical account of the life and works of the poet, by Ramaṇīmohana Mallika.] pp. 71, 129. কলিকাতা ১৩০৯ [*Calcutta*, 1903.] 8°. **14123. ff. 10.(3.)**

—— প্রেমভক্তিচন্দ্রিকা। [Premabhakti-chandrikā. A Vaishṇava poem. Edited, with an introductory preface containing a sketch of the life of the author, and notes, by Durgādāsa Rāya.] pp. xx. 41. দার্জ্জিলিং ১৮৯০ [*Darjeeling*, 1890.] 16°. **14123. e. 13.(2.)**

—— শ্রীশ্রীপ্রেমভক্তিচন্দ্রিকা। [Premabhakti-chandrikā. Edited by Rāmadayāla Ghosha, with a Sanskrit commentary by Viśvanātha Chakravartī, and Bengali explanatory notes by Rādhikānātha Gosvāmī.] pp. iv. 161. কলিকাতা [*Calcutta*, 1896.] 12°. **14123. e. 20.(1.)**

NĀṢIR 'ALĪ KHĀN, *Yūsufzai.* বঙ্গীয় মুসলমান। [Vaṅgīya Musalmān. An account of the present condition of Muhammadans in Bengal.] pp. iv. 78. কলিকাতা ১২৯৭ [*Calcutta*, 1891.] 12°. **14125. e. 24.(1.)**

NATH (M. N.). *See* MATHURĀNĀTHA NĀTHA.

NAVADVĪPACHANDRA VIDYĀRATNA GOSVĀMĪ. শ্রীগৌরাঙ্গ-মঙ্গল-সঙ্গীত লীলা-রস-তত্ত্ব-সার-সংগ্রহ। [Gaurāṅga-maṅgalasaṅgīta. A compilation of religious writings of the Chaitanya sect, with supplements from the Sanskrit literature of the school. Third edition.] Pt. i. pp. viii. 287. কলিকাতা ১৩০৮ [*Calcutta*, 1902.] 12°. **14123. e. 30.**

—— শ্রীশ্রীসনাতন-বৈষ্ণব-ব্রত-দিন ও উৎসব সময় প্রভৃতির নির্ণয় পুস্তক। [Sanātana Vaishṇava-vrata-dina. A treatise on the dates of the ancient festivals of the Eastern Vaishṇavas.] pp. 264. কলিকাতা ১৩০৭-০৮ [*Calcutta*, 1900-01.] 8°. **14123. ff. 4.**
In two parts; incomplete.

—— বৈষ্ণবাচারদর্পণ। বৈষ্ণবসর্ব্বস্ব। [Vaishṇavāchāradarpaṇa. An anthological summary of Vaishṇava doctrine of the Chaitanya school, composed chiefly of Bengali verse, and Sanskrit texts, mostly in verse. Third edition.] Pt. i. pp. xx. 372. কলিকাতা ১৮২৩ [*Calcutta*, 1901.] 8°. **14123. f. 56.**

NAVAKĀNTA CHAṬṬOPĀDHYĀYA. ভারতীয় সঙ্গীত-মুক্তাবলী। [Bhāratīya saṅgītamuktāvalī. A collection of 1580 songs by Bengali poets, with short biographical sketches. Fourth edition.] Vol. i. pp. xlvi. 916. ঢাকা ১৯০১ [*Dacca*, 1901.] 12°. **14129. bb. 4.**

NAVAKIŚORA GUPTA. সাধু-সঙ্গীত বা সাধক-সঙ্গীত। [Sādhu-saṅgīta. Hindu devotional songs.] Pt. i. pp. 90. কলিকাতা ১২৯৮ [*Calcutta*, 1891.] 12°. **14125. d. 21.**

NAVAKṚISHṆA SIṂHA. গীতাষ্টক। [Gītāshṭaka. Eight Vaishṇava songs.] *See* KṚISHṆAPRASANNA SENA. ভক্তি ও ভক্ত [Bhakti o bhakta.] pp. 151-154. [1887.] 8°. **14028. c. 56.**

NAVAKUMĀRA DEVA ŚARMĀ. মীমাংসাতত্ত্ব। [Mīmāṃsātattva. A discussion of five questions relating to Hindu religion, specially with reference to the antiquity of Śiva-worship.] pp. 201. ঢাকা ১৩০৪ [*Dacca*, 1897.] 8°. **14123. ff. 3.**

NAVALĪLĀ. নবলীলা। [Navalīlā. A drama, embodying the teachings of the Theistic Church.] pp. 31. ঢাকা ১৮০৯ [*Dacca*, 1888.] 12°. **14131. a. 27.(1.)**

NAVARĀJA BARUYĀ. শিক্ষাসার। [Śikshāsāra. Buddhist ritual explained in Bengali verse.] Pt. i. pp. 20. চট্টগ্রাম ২৪৩৬ বুদ্ধাব্দ [*Chittagong*, 1893.] 12°. **14123. k. 4.**

NAVĪNACHANDRA DĀSA. *See* BHĀRAVI. Kiratarjun ... in Bengali verse. Cantos 1 to 5, with copious notes ... By Nobin Chandra Das. 1906. 8°. **14129. cc. 18.**

—— Soka-giti. [Elegiac poems.] Including Gray's Elegy in Bengali. By Nobin Chandra Das. (শোক-গীতি।) pp. iii. 28. *Calcutta*, 1900. 8°. **14129. cc. 1.(2.)**

NAVĪNACHANDRA MUKHOPĀDHYĀYA. অপূর্ব্ব নদের চাঁদ বা শ্রীকৃষ্ণ চৈতন্য অবতারের জীবনচরিত। [Apūrva Nader Chāṇd. A sketch of the life of Chaitanya, showing that the chief events of his life and doctrines have been borrowed from the Bible.] pp. xv. 63. কলিকাতা ১৮৮৭ [*Calcutta*, 1887.] 12°. **14127. a. 33.(1.)**

—— আর্য্যসঙ্গীত। [Āryasaṅgīta. Aryan Lays. Pt. i. Draupadīnigraha. Pt. ii. Jātīyanigraha.] কলিকাতা ১২৮৬, ১৩০৯ [*Calcutta*, 1880, 1902.] 8°. **14129. c. 13.(6.)**

NAVĪNACHANDRA SENA. *See* VĪRESVARA PĀṆḌE. ঊনবিংশ শতাব্দীর মহাভারত। [Ūnaviṃśa śatābdīr Mahābhārata. An adverse criticism on Navīnachandra Sena's poems Raivataka, Kurukshetra, and Prabhāsa.] 1897. 12°. **14131. d. 6.(2.)**

—— আমার জীবন। [Āmār jīvana. My life; an autobiography.] কলিকাতা ১৩১৪ [*Calcutta*, 1908, *etc.*] 12°. **14127. aa. 45.**

In progress.

—— অমিতাভ। [Amitābha. The life and teachings of Buddha, in verse.] pp. x. 201. কলিকাতা [*Calcutta*, 1895.] 12°. **14123. k. 3.**

—— [Second edition.] pp. x. 201. কুমিল্লা ১৩০৮ [*Comilla*, 1901.] 12°. **14123. k. 6.**

—— কুরুক্ষেত্র। কাব্য। [Kurukshetra. A mythological poem.] pp. 344. কলিকাতা ১৩০০ [*Calcutta*, 1894.] 12°. **14129. c. 46.**

—— পলাশির যুদ্ধ। কাব্য। [Palāśir yuddha. A metrical account of the battle of Plassey. Ninth edition.] pp. 171, ii. 32. কলিকাতা ১৩১০ [*Calcutta*, 1903.] 8°. **14129. bb. 20.**

—— [Tenth edition.] pp. 171, ii. 33. কলিকাতা ১৩১৪ [*Calcutta*, 1907.] 12°. **14129. bb. 35.**

—— প্রবাসের পত্র। [Pravāser patra. Travels in the North-West Provinces and Bombay; being a series of letters from the author, written during his travels, to his wife.] pp. 118. কলিকাতা ১২৯৯ [*Calcutta*, 1892.] 12°. **14127. a. 42.(4.)**

—— রৈবতক। [Raivataka. An epic poem, in 20 cantos, based on mythology, according to modern Hindu phases of religious thought.] pp. vi. 380. কলিকাতা ১২৯৬ [*Calcutta*, 1890.] 8°. **14129. c. 43.**

NAVĪNACHANDRA VIDYĀRATNA. *See* BHAṬṬI. Bhatti. . . . Cantos i.-v. Text with notes by Pundit Nobin Ch. Vidyaratna . . . with English and Bengali translations, *etc.* [1894.] 12°. **14070. c. 57.(1.)**

—— *See* KĀLIDĀSA. অভিজ্ঞানশকুন্তলম্। (Kalidasa's Abhijnana Sakuntalam. Edited with an introduction, glossary, English and Bengali translations, various readings, and the commentary Sarala by Nabin Chandra Vidyaratna.) [1901.] 8°. **14080. c. 41.**

—— *See* KĀLIDĀSA. Kumarasambhabam . . . Cantos i.-vii. Text with notes by Pundit Nobin Ch. Vidyaratna . . . With English and Bengali translations, *etc.* [1894.] 12°. **14070. c. 57.(2.)**

—— *See* KĀLIDĀSA. Kalidasa's Meghadutam. [I. 1—38.] Containing . . . Mallinatha's commentary . . . Bengali and English translations . . . notes . . . by Pandit Nabin Chandra Vidyaratna. [1901.] 8°. **14085. c. 49.(1.)**

—— *See* KĀLIDĀSA. Raghubamsam. Cantos i.-vi. Containing prose version, paraphrase . . . Bengali and English translations . . . notes both in English and Sanskrit . . . Edited by Nabin Chandra Vidyaratna. 1901. 8°. **14085. c. 50.**

—— *See* MĀGHA. Sisupalabadha . . . Edited [with a Bengali translation] by Nobin Ch. Vidyaratna. 1891. 8°. **14072. cc. 51.**

—— —— Magha's Shishupal badham. [Sarga i.]. Containing an introduction in English . . . paraphrase . . . Mallinatha's Sarbankasa, Bengali and English translations . . . with . . . notes . . . By Pandit Nabin Chandra Vidyaratna. [1901.] 8°. **14085. c. 49.(2.)**

—— A key to [Rajanīkānta Gupta's] Sahityasangraha by Nabin Chundra Vidyaratna. pp. 508. *Sansk. Beng.* and *Eng. Calcutta*, 1883. 12°. **14090. b. 31.**

Published in two fasciculi, of which the first is of the 3rd, and the second of the 2nd, edition.

NAVĪNAKṚISHṆA LĀHĀ. *See* PURĀṆAS.—*Bhavishyapurāṇa.* ভবিষ্যপুরাণ। [Bhavishyapurāṇa. Sanskrit text, edited with a Bengali translation by Navīnakṛishṇa Lāhā.] [1886.] 8°. **14018. b. 15.**

NAVĪNAKṚISHṆA LĀHĀ (*continued*). *See* TANTRAS. সিদ্ধিশঙ্করতন্ত্র। [Siddhisaṅkaratantra. Sanskrit text, edited with a translation by Navīnakṛishṇa Lāhā.] [1886.] 12°. **14033. a. 41.(1.)**

NAWĀB al-DĪN AḢMAD. মহাত্মা হজরত এমাম-আবুহানীফা সাহেবের জীবন চরিত। [Abū Ḣanīfah jīvanacharita. A life of Abū Ḣanīfah, the Arabic writer on Muhammadan Law.] pp. vi. 97. কলিকাতা ১৩০৫ [*Calcutta*, 1899.] 8°. **14127. bb. 16.(1.)**

NAY-ṢO RŪPEYĀ. নয়শো রুপেয়া। [Nay-ṣo rūpeyā, or Nine hundred rupees. A social drama directed against the evil practice of Brahmans selling their daughters in marriage. Second edition.] pp. 80. কলিকাতা ১৩০৪ [*Calcutta*, 1898.] 8°. **14131. c. 19.(3.)**

NĀẒIR ʻALĪ. মন মহিনীর কবিতা। [Man-mohinīr kavitā. Love songs, in Muhammadan Bengali.] pp. 13. রেঙ্গুন [*Rangoon*, 1903.] 8°. **14129. d. 31.(2.)**

—— রেঙ্গুনের কাব্য কবিতা। [Reṅguner kāvya-kavitā. A description of Rangoon, in Muhammadan Bengali verse.] pp. 13. কলিকাতা ১৩১০ [*Calcutta*, 1903.] 8°. **14127. bb. 25.**

NIDHIRĀMA MUKHOPĀDHYĀYA. মৎস্যের চাষ। [Matsyer chāsh. A treatise on] pisciculture. বা ধনাগমের একটি সহজ উপায়। pp. iv. 130. কলিকাতা ১২৯৪ [*Calcutta*, 1887.] 12°. **14125. bb. 21.**

NIGAMĀNANDA PARAMAHAṂSA. জ্ঞানীগুরু বা জ্ঞান ও সাধন পদ্ধতি। [Jñānīguru. Religious and philosophical teachings in 3 parts, viz.: Nānākāṇḍa, Jñānakāṇḍa, and Sādhanakāṇḍa.] pp. v. ii. ii. 460. কুমিল্লা ১৩১৫ [*Comilla*, 1908.] 8°. **14123. e. 39.**

NIKHILANĀTHA RĀYA. মুর্শিদাবাদের ইতিহাস। [Murshidābāder itihāsa. A history of Murshidabad.] কলিকাতা ১৩০৯ [*Calcutta*, 1902, *etc.*] 8°. *In progress.* **14127. aa. 23.**

—— মুর্শিদাবাদ-কাহিনী। [Murshidābād-kāhinī. Historical sketches in connection with Murshidabad, the last seat of the Muhammadan rule in Bengal.] pp. v. 552, 36. বহরমপুর ১৩০৪ [*Berhampore*, 1897.] 8°. **14127. aa. 8.**

—— [Second edition.] pp. xviii. 637. কলিকাতা ১৩১০ [*Calcutta*, 1903.] 8°. **14127. aa. 26.**

NĪLAKAMALA VIDYĀNIDHI BHAṬṬĀCHĀRYA. *See* JĪMŪTAVĀHANA. জীমূতবাহনকৃত দায়ভাগঃ। [Dāyabhāga. Edited, with a Bengali translation, by Nīlakamala Vidyānidhi.] [1898.] 8°. **14038. c. 49.**

—— *See* RAGHUNANDANA BHAṬṬĀCHĀRYA. সটীক-সানুবাদ-উদ্বাহতত্ত্বং। [Udvāhatattva. Edited, with a Bengali translation, by Nīlakamala Vidyānidhi.] [1896.] 8°. **14033. bb. 42.**

—— *See* RĀMAṢAṄKARA DEVA ṢARMĀ. সানুবাদ বৃহৎ জাতকচন্দ্রিকা। [Bṛihat jātakachandrikā. Edited, with a Bengali translation, by Nīlakamala Vidyānidhi.] [1892.] 8°. **14053. c. 63.**

—— *See* ṢRĪNIVĀSA ĀCHĀRYA, *Astrologer.* দীপিকা বা শুদ্ধিদীপিকা। [Dīpikā. With a Bengali translation by Nīlakamala Vidyānidhi.] [1901.] 8°. **14053. ccc. 23.**

—— সটীক-সানুবাদ-জ্যোতিষতত্ত্ববারিধিঃ। [Jyotisha-tattva-vāridhi. A manual of astrology, consisting of a compilation of Sanskrit texts, notes and commentary, and Bengali translations of the text.] pp. ii. xii. 568. কলিকাতা ১৩০০ [*Calcutta*, 1894.] 8°. **14053. ccc. 1.**

NĪLAKĀNTA GOSVĀMĪ. *See* RĀJAVALLABHA GOSVĀMĪ. শ্রীমুরলী-বিলাস। [Muralī-vilāsa. Edited, with notes, by Nīlakānta Gosvāmī.] [1894.] 12°. **14129. b. 41.**

NĪLAKAṆṬHA, *Vaishṇava poet.* নীলকণ্ঠ-গীতাবলী। [Nīlakaṇṭha-gītāvalī. Religious songs by Nīlakaṇṭha and other Vaishṇava poets.] pp. 84. *Calcutta*, 1903. 12°. **14129. bb. 12.(2.)**

NĪLAKAṆṬHA MAJUMDĀR. *See* ROWE (F. J.) and NĪLAKAṆṬHA MAJUMDĀR. Examples and Exercises in translation. Bengali-English. 1902. 12°. **14131. e. 36.**

—— বিবাহ ও নারীধর্ম। [Vivāha o nārīdharma. A treatise on marriage, and the duties of women, illustrated from Sanskrit texts.] pp. iv. ii. 306. কলিকাতা [*Calcutta*, 1901.] 12°. **14125. e. 43.**

NĪLAKAṆṬHA MUKHOPĀDHYĀYA. বাল্য-কাহিনী। [Bālyakāhinī. A poem on the childhood of the Raja of Hatampur, and the efforts made by his grandmother and others to prevent the management of the estate by the Court of Wards.] pp. xi. 532. রামপুর ১৩১১ [*Rampur*, 1906.] 8°. **14129. cc. 19.**

NĪLAMAṆI MUKHOPĀDHYĀYA. সঙ্গীত-সন্দর্ভ। [Saṅgīta-sandarbha. A collection of songs to Hindu deities. Compiled, with an introduction and a short account of the most noted of the authors, by Nīlamaṇi Mukhopādhyāya.] Pt. i. pp. vi. x. 149. কলিকাতা [*Calcutta*, 1900.] 16°. **14129. a. 16.(2.)**

NĪLAMAṆI VIDYĀLAṄKĀRA BHAṬṬĀCHĀRYA. উদ্ভট কবিতা-কৌমুদী। [Udbhaṭa kavitā-kaumudī. Select Sanskrit verses, with Bengali translations.] Pt. i. pp. ii. 70, ii. কলিকাতা ১২৯৭ [*Calcutta*, 1890.] 8°. **14085. c. 43.**

NĪLARATNA MUKHOPĀDHYĀYA. রামমোহনের রামায়ণ। [Rāmamohaner Rāmāyaṇa. An article on the Rāmāyaṇa of Rāmamohana Vandyopādhyāya, with extracts from his poem.] ১৩০২ [1895.] *See* ACADEMIES, *etc.*—Calcutta.—*Bengal Academy of Literature.* সাহিত্য-পরিষৎ-পত্রিকা। [Sāhitya-parishat-patrikā.] Vol. ii., no. 1. [1894, *etc.*] 8°. **14133. f. 18.**

NIMĀICHĀṆD ṢĪLA. সুবর্ণবণিক্। [Suvarṇa-baṇik. A treatise on the origin and social status of the Suvarṇa or trading caste of Bengal.] pp. v. xii. 180. কলিকাতা ১৮৮৫ [*Calcutta*, 1885.] 8°. **14127. b. 41.**

NINĀJ MOHINĪ. নিনাজমোহিনী। উপন্যাস। [Nināj Mohinī. A tale of Western Bengal during the Mahratta invasion.] pp. 87. কলিকাতা ১৮৮৭ [*Calcutta*, 1887.] 8°. **14127. f. 40.(1.)**

NIRMALACHANDRA CHAṬṬOPĀDHYĀYA. বৃহৎ বাউল সঙ্গীত। [Bāul saṅgīta. A collection of *Bāul* songs, or ballads.] pp. 292. কলিকাতা ১২৯৩ [*Calcutta*, 1886.] 12°. **14129. a. 29.(2.)**

NIṢĀCHARA, *pseud.* সমাজ-কুচিত্র। [Samāja-kuchitra.] The Evils of our society. By a Midnight Traveller. [Second edition.] pp. ii. 72. কলিকাতা ১২৯৪ [*Calcutta*, 1888.] 12°. **14125. e. 19.(3.)**

NITYAGOPĀLA MUKHOPĀDHYĀYA. Handbook of Sericulture by Nitya Gopal Mukerji. [Translated into English by the author from his Bengali original.] pp. ii. ii. 298. *Calcutta*, 1899. 8°. **14125. dd. 19.**

—— Studies in Apostolic Fathers, No. 2. প্রাচীন ধর্ম-শিক্ষা। [Prāchīna dharma-ṣikshā. Compiled and translated from the English, with notes, by Nityagopāla Mukhopādhyāya.] pp. ii. 82. কলিকাতা ১৮৯৫ [*Calcutta*, 1895.]. 8°. **14123. b. 18.**

NITYAKARMA. আহ্নিককৃত্যম্। বিশুদ্ধ-নিত্যকর্ম। [Āhnikakṛitya. A manual of daily religious duties, in Sanskrit. Edited with a Bengali introduction, translation and notes by Ṣyāmācharaṇa Kaviratna. Fifth edition.] pp. 154. কলিকাতা ১৩০৮ [*Calcutta*, 1902.] 12°. **14033. a. 49.**

—— নিত্য কর্মানুষ্ঠান পদ্ধতি, কর্মলোচন ও পরিশিষ্ট। [Nityakarmānushṭhāna-paddhati. A manual of daily ritual, with Bengali rubrics, interpretations, and notes. Followed by 2 appendices—viz. Karmalochana, a compendium of rules for conduct, and an excursus on Tantric worship.] pp. x. 2, 408. কলিকাতা ১৩০৫ [*Calcutta*, 1898.] 8°. **14028. bb. 7.**

NITYĀNANDA CHAKRAVARTĪ. *See* VYOMAKEṢA MUSTAFĪ. শীতলা-মঙ্গল। [Ṣītalāmaṅgala. A critical examination of a poem in praise of the goddess Ṣītalā, with a biographical notice of the author.] [1898.] 8°. **14133. f. 18.**

NITYĀNANDA DĀSA. *See* RĀYA ṢEKHARA. শ্রীরায় শেখরের অষ্টকালীয় দণ্ডাত্মিকা পদাবলী। [Ashṭakālīya daṇḍātmikā. Edited with an introduction by Nityānanda Dāsa.] [1901.] 8°. **14123. ff. 10.(1.)**

—— [*Life.*] *See* VṚINDĀVANA DĀSA. শ্রীশ্রীনিত্যানন্দচরিতামৃত। [Nityānanda-charitāmṛita.] [1902.] 8°. **14127. bb. 24.**

—— প্রেমবিলাস। [Premavilāsa. An old Bengali Vaishṇava poem, in 20 cantos or *vilāsas*, containing an account of the life of Ṣrīnivāsa Āchārya and other Vaishṇava teachers. Edited, with an introductory account of the work and its author, by Rāmanārāyaṇa Vidyāratna.] মুর্শিদাবাদ ১২৯৮-১২৯৯ [*Murshidabad*, 1892-93.] 8°. **14129. e. 17.(2.)**

NITYASAKHĀ MUKHOPĀDHYĀYA. *See* PERIODICAL PUBLICATIONS.—*Brindaban.* শ্রীবৈষ্ণব-সন্দর্ভ। [Vaishṇava-sandarbha. Edited by Nityasakhā Mukhopādhyāya.] [1903, *etc.*] 8°. **14123. ff. 13.**

—— লীলা-বিলাস। [Līlā-vilāsa. A semi-mythological drama, introducing Vaishṇava tenets.] pp. 167. কলিকাতা ১৮৯৩ [*Calcutta*, 1893.] 12°. **14131. a. 38.(1.)**

NIVĀRAṆACHANDRA DĀSA. মহাত্মা ত্রৈলিঙ্গ স্বামির জীবনচরিত। [Trailiṅga Svāmīr jīvana-charita. The life of Trailiṅga Svāmī, a devotee of Benares, who is said to have died in the Bengali year 1809, at the age of 250 years.] pp. 82. কাশী [*Benares*, 1893.] 12°. **14127. aa. 2.(1.)**

NIVĀRAṆACHANDRA MUKHOPĀDHYĀYA. সুর-সঙ্গীত। [Sura-saṅgīta. A poem describing the creation of the world, the scientific attainments of man, his spiritual decay, and the consequent destruction of the universe.] pp. ii. 122, vi. কলিকাতা [*Calcutta*, 1899.] 8°. **14129. bb. 8.(3.)**

NIẒĀM, *Shaikh*. ফতওয়ায় আলমগিরী। [Fatāwā i 'Ālamgīrī. A collection of decisions on Muhammadan law, according to the Ḥanafī school, compiled by Shaikh Niẓām and other learned men. Translated from the Arabic by Na'īm al-Dīn, assisted by Ghulām Sarwar.] 4 pts. কলিকাতা। করটীয়া ১৮৮৪-৯২ [*Karatia*, 1884-92.] 8°. **14123. h. 22.**

No more appears to have been published.

NIẒĀMĪ, *Ganjavī*. সপ্ত পয়কর। [Sapta paykar. A metrical version by Pandit Alāol of the Persian Haft paikar, or Seven tales told by the seven favourites of king Bahrāmgor. Second edition.] pp. 204, ii. কলিকাতা ১৩০৪ [*Calcutta*, 1897.] 8°. **14127. g. 11.**

—— [Third edition.] pp. ii. 205. কলিকাতা ১৩১১ [*Calcutta*, 1905.] 8°. **14127. ee. 27.**

NOBIN CHANDRA DAS. *See* NAVĪNACHANDRA DĀSA.

NṚISIṂHACHANDRA MUKHOPĀDHYĀYA. *See* PERIODICAL PUBLICATIONS.—*Calcutta*. সাহিত্য-সংহিতা। [Sāhityasaṃhitā. Edited by Nṛisiṃhachandra Mukhopādhyāya.] [1900, *etc.*] 8°. **14133. ff. 1.**

NU'MĀN ibn ṢĀBIT (ABŪ ḤANĪFAH). [*Life.*] *See* NAWĀB al-DĪN AḤMAD. মহাত্মা হজরত এমাম আবুহানীফা সাহেবের জীবন চরিত। [Abū Ḥanīfah jīvana-charita.] [1899.] 8°. **14127. bb. 16.(1.)**

NŪR MUḤAMMAD, *Maulavī*. কলির শ্বশুর। [Kalir ṣvaṣura. A poem on the vices consequent on injudicious marriages amongst Muhammadans.] pp. 40. কলিকাতা ১৩০০ [*Calcutta*, 1893.] 8°. **14129. d. 30.(3.)**

NURSING CHUNDER HALDER. *See* NARASIṂHACHANDRA HĀLDĀR.

OCHTERLONY (*Sir* DAVID), *Monument of*. অক্টার্লনি হইতে কুতব পর্য্যন্ত। [Akṭārlani haite kutab paryanta. A diary of a fortnight's trip from the Ochterlony Monument at Calcutta to Delhi and back, giving a description of places of interest on the East Indian Railway.] pp. xii. 209. কলিকাতা ১৮৯২ [*Calcutta*, 1892.] 16°. **14127. a. 43.**

OLCOTT (HENRY STEELE). বৌদ্ধধর্ম-প্রশ্নোত্তর। [Bauddhadharma-praṣnottara. "A Catechism of the Buddhist religion," translated into Bengali.] pp. 44. বহরমপুর ১৮৯৩ [*Berhampore*, 1893.] 8°. **14123. k. 1.**

OSWELL (G. D.). *See* PYĀRĪCHĀṆD MITRA, called ṬEKCHĀṆD ṬHĀKUR. The Spoilt Child . . . Translated by G. D. Oswell. pp. 14, 234. *Calcutta*, 1893. 8°. **14127. c. 53.**

PADAKALPATARU. শ্রীশ্রীপদ-কল্প-তরু। [Padakalpataru. A collection of poems from the works of famous Vaishṇava poets. A new edition, edited by Satīṣachandra Rāya.] 2 pts. কলিকাতা ১৩০৪ [*Calcutta*, 1897.] 8°. **14129. a. 40.**

—— [Another edition.] 4 pts. pp. 1062. কলিকাতা [*Calcutta*, 1905.] 12°. **14129. bb. 25.**

PĀGALER KATHĀ. পাগলের কথা। [Pāgaler kathā. Strictures on the present state of Hindu society and education.] pp. 29. কলিকাতা ১২৯২ [*Calcutta*, 1885.] 12°. **14125. e. 17.(4.)**

—— [Second edition.] pp. 48. কলিকাতা ১২৯৪ [*Calcutta*, 1887.] 12°. **14125. e. 21.(2.)**

PAL (S. B.). *See* SATYENDRABHŪSHAṆA PĀLA.

PAÑCHA GĪTĀ. পঞ্চগীতা। [Pañcha gītā. Five Sanskrit poems on religious, philosophic and ethical subjects, viz.: Rāmagītā, Uttaragītā, Ṣāntigītā, Pāṇḍavagītā and Parāṣaragītā. With Bengali translations and notes by Prasannakumāra Ṣāstrī Bhaṭṭāchārya.] pp. 502. কলিকাতা ১৩১৩ [*Calcutta*, 1906.] 16°. **14028. a. 33.**

PAÑCHĀNANA BHAṬṬĀCHĀRYA. *See* KABĪR. কবির। *etc.* [Kabīr. A collection of the poems of Kabīr. Edited, with a Bengali translation and commentary, by Pañchānana Bhaṭṭāchārya.] [1890, *etc.*] 8°. **14158. d. 37.**

PAÑCHĀNANA DĀSA. চারিজন্ম তত্ত্ব নিরূপণ। [Chārijanma-tattvanirūpaṇa. Esoteric Vaishṇavism, in verse.] pp. vi. 276. কলিকাতা ১৩০৪ [*Calcutta*, 1898.] *obl.* 8°. **14123. ff. 2.**

PAÑCHĀNANA GHOSHA. Mensuration in Bengali, by P. Ghosh . . . পরিমিতি। [Parimiti.] pp. ii. 260. *Calcutta*, 1898. 12°. **14125. bb. 24.**

PAÑCHĀNANA RĀYA CHAUDHURĪ. *See* PRĀṆAHARI YOGAVIṢĀRADA. কামশাস্ত্র বা মোহিনীতন্ত্র। [Kāmaṣāstra. Sanskrit text, with a Bengali translation by Pañchānana Rāya Chaudhurī.] [1901.] 12°. **14053. b. 40.**

—— কুল-কলঙ্কিনী বা কলিকাতার গুপ্তকথা। [Kulakalañkinī, also called Kalikātār guptakathā. The story of a Calcutta prostitute.] pp. 244. *Calcutta*, 1900. 8°. **14127. ee. 11.**

—— পাশকরা মাগ। [Pās-karā māg. The Bengali lady-graduate. A farce.] pp. 36. কলিকাতা ১৩০৮ [*Calcutta*, 1902.] 12°. **14131. aa. 1.(2.)**

PAÑCHĀNANA SARKĀR. *See* ACADEMIES, *etc.*—Rangpur.—*Bengal Academy of Literature.* রঙ্গপুর শাখা সাহিত্য-পরিষৎ-পত্রিকা। [Sāhitya-parishat-patrikā. Edited by Pañchānana Sarkār.] [1907, *etc.*] 8°. **14133. ff. 4.**

PAÑCHĀNANA TARKARATNA BHAṬṬĀCHĀRYA, *of Bhatpalli.* *See* ĪṢVARA KṚISHṆA. সাংখ্য-দর্শনম্। *etc.* [Sāṅkhyadarṣana. Being the Sāṅkhyakārikā with commentary of Vāchaspati. Edited with a supercommentary, called Pūrṇimā, and Bengali translations and explanations of the text by Pañchānana Tarkaratna.] [1903.] 8°. **14049. b. 17.**

—— *See* KABĪR. কবির। *etc.* [Kabīr. A collection of the poems of Kabīr, with a Bengali translation, and commentary, by Pañchānana Tarkaratna.] [1890.] 8°. **14158. d. 37.**

—— *See* KAṆĀDA. বৈশেষিক-দর্শনম্। [Vaiṣeshika-darṣana. Edited with a Sanskrit commentary, called Parishkāra, and a Bengali translation and commentary by Pañchānana Tarkaratna.] [1906.] 8°. **14049. b. 43.**

—— *See* PURĀṆAS.—*Agnipurāṇa.* অগ্নিপুরাণম্। [Agnipurāṇa. Sanskrit text, with a Bengali translation. Edited by Pañchānana Tarkaratna.] [1907.] 8°. **14016. dd. 29.**

—— *See* PURĀṆAS.—*Brahmāṇḍapurāṇa.* ব্রহ্মাণ্ড-পুরাণম্। *etc.* [Brahmāṇḍapurāṇa. Sanskrit text and Bengali translation. Edited by Pañchānana Tarkaratna.] [1908.] 8°. **14018. b. 22.(1.)**

—— *See* PURĀṆAS.—*Brahmavaivartapurāṇa.* ব্রহ্মবৈবর্ত্ত পুরাণ। [Brahmavaivartapurāṇa. Translated by Pañchānana Tarkaratna.] [1904.] 8°. **14123. g. 20.**

—— *See* PURĀṆAS.—*Bṛihan-nāradīyapurāṇa.* বৃহন্নারদীয়পুরাণম্। [Bṛihan-nāradīyapurāṇa. Sanskrit text, with a Bengali translation by Pañchānana Tarkaratna.] [1895.] 12°. **14016. b. 19.**

—— *See* PURĀṆAS.—*Devībhāgavatapurāṇa.* দেবী-ভাগবত। [Devībhāgavatapurāṇa. Translated by Pañchānana Tarkaratna.] [1908.] 8°. **14123. ff. 20.**

—— *See* PURĀṆAS.—*Devīpurāṇa.* দেবীপুরাণম্। [Devīpurāṇa. Sanskrit text, with a Bengali translation. Edited by Pañchānana Tarkaratna.] [1905.] 8°. **14016. dd. 15.(3.)**

—— *See* PURĀṆAS.—*Dharmapurāṇa.* বৃহদ্ধর্ম্মপুরাণম্। [Bṛihad-dharmapurāṇa. Sanskrit text, edited by Pañchānana Tarkaratna, with a Bengali translation by the latter and others.] [1908.] 8°. **14016. dd. 28.(1.)**

—— *See* PURĀṆAS.—*Garuḍapurāṇa.* গরুড়পুরাণম্। [Garuḍapurāṇa. Sanskrit text with a Bengali translation. Edited by Pañchānana Tarkaratna.] [1907.] 8°. **14016. dd. 26.**

—— *See* PURĀṆAS.—*Kalkipurāṇa.* কল্কিপুরাণম্। *etc.* [Kalkipurāṇa. Sanskrit text and Bengali translation. Edited by Pañchānana Tarkaratna.] [1908.] 8°. **14018. b. 22.(2.)**

—— *See* PURĀṆAS.—*Kūrmapurāṇa.* কূর্ম্মপুরাণম্। সানুবাদম্। [Kūrmapurāṇa. Sanskrit text, with a Bengali translation. Edited by Pañchānana Tarkaratna.] [1904.] 8°. **14016. dd. 15.(1.)**

—— *See* PURĀṆAS.—*Padmapurāṇa.* পদ্মপুরাণম্। পাতালখণ্ডম্। [Padmapurāṇa. The Pātāla-khaṇḍa, Sanskrit text, with a Bengali translation. Edited by Pañchānana Tarkaratna.] [1903.] 8°. **14018. b. 20.**

PAÑCHĀNANA TARKARATNA BHAṬṬĀCHĀRYA, *of Bhatpalli (continued)*. *See* PURĀṆAS.—*Padmapurāṇa.* পদ্মপুরাণম্। স্বর্গ-খণ্ডম্। [Padmapurāṇa. The Svarga-khaṇḍa, Sanskrit text, with a Bengali translation by Kṛishṇadāsa Ṣāstrī. Edited by Pañchānana Tarkaratna.] [1906.] 8°. **14016. dd. 24.(1.)**

—— *See* PURĀṆAS.—*Ṣivapurāṇa.* শিবপুরাণ। [Ṣivapurāṇa. Translated into Bengali. Edited by Pañchānana Tarkaratna.] [1905.] 8°. **14123. i. 16.**

—— —— শিবপুরাণম্। [Ṣivapurāṇa. Sanskrit text, with a Bengali translation. Edited by Pañchānana Tarkaratna.] [1907.] 8°. **14016. dd. 30.**

—— *See* PURĀṆAS.—*Skandapurāṇa.* কাশীখণ্ড। [Kāṣī-khaṇḍa. A section of the Skandapurāṇa, translated by Pañchānana Tarkaratna.] [1902.] 8°. **14123. ff. 9.**

—— —— উৎকলখণ্ডম্। [Utkala-khaṇḍa. A section of the Skandapurāṇa. Sanskrit text, edited with a Bengali translation by Pañchānana Tarkaratna.] [1902.] 8°. **14016. dd. 5.**

—— *See* PURĀṆAS.—*Vāmanapurāṇa.* বামনপুরাণম্। [Vāmanapurāṇa. Sanskrit text, with a Bengali translation. Edited by Pañchānana Tarkaratna.] [1908.] 8°. **14016. dd. 28.(2.)**

—— *See* PURĀṆAS.—*Varāhapurāṇa.* বরাহ পুরাণম্। [Varāhapurāṇa. Sanskrit text, with a Bengali translation by Tārākānta Kāvyatīrtha. Edited by Pañchānana Tarkaratna.] [1906.] 8°. **14016. dd. 23.**

—— *See* PURĀṆAS.—*Vishṇupurāṇa.* বিষ্ণু পুরাণম্। [Vishṇupurāṇa. Sanskrit text, with a Bengali translation. Edited by Pañchānana Tarkaratna.] [1907.] 8°. **14016. dd. 24.(2.)**

—— *See* SĀYAṆA ĀCHĀRYA. পঞ্চদশী। [Pañchadaṣī. Edited, with a Bengali translation of the text, by Pañchānana Tarkaratna.] [1904.] 8°. **14049. b. 31.**

—— *See* VĀLMĪKI. রামায়ণম্। [Rāmāyaṇa. Sanskrit text, with a Bengali prose translation. Edited by Pañchānana Tarkaratna.] [1904.] 8°. **14068. c. 18.**

—— *See* VIDYĀPATI. বিদ্যাপতি . . . পদাবলী। [Padāvalī. Edited, with notes and a short life of the poet, by Pañchānana Tarkaratna.] [1895.] 12°. **14129. b. 44.(3.)**

—— *See* YOGAVĀSISHṬHA-RĀMĀYAṆA. যোগবাশিষ্ঠ-রামায়ণ। [Yogavāsishṭha-rāmāyaṇa. Translated into prose by Pañchānana Tarkaratna.] [1905.] 4°. **14123. i. 15.**

—— উগ্রক্ষত্রিয়-বিবরণ। [Ugrakshetriya-vivaraṇa. A treatise on the Ugrakshetriya, or Āgurī, caste; containing some account of their origin, settlement in Bengal, and manners and customs.] pp. 89, vi. কলিকাতা ১২৯৭ [*Calcutta*, 1890.] 8°. **14127. b. 43.**

—— ঊনবিংশতি সংহিতা। [Ūnavimṣati-saṃhitā. The Sanskrit text of the Dharmaṣāstras or Codes of Atri, Vishṇu, Hārīta, Yājñavalkya, Uṣanas, Aṅgiras, Yama, Āpastamba, Saṃvarta, Kātyāyana, Bṛihaspati, Parāṣara, Vyāsa, Ṣaṅkha, Likhita, Daksha, Gautama, Ṣātātapa, and Vasishṭha, with Bengali translations. Edited by Pañchānana Tarkaratna.] pp. 509. কলিকাতা ১৩১০ [*Calcutta*, 1903.] 8°. **14039. c. 20.**

—— বিশুদ্ধ নিত্যকর্ম্ম। [Viṣuddha nityakarma. A treatise on the daily religious duties of Hindus. Second edition.] Pt. i. pp. 52. কলিকাতা ১৩০১ [*Calcutta*, 1895.] 8°. **14123. e. 17.**

PAÑCHĀNANDA, *pseud.* পঞ্চানন্দ। [Pañchānanda. Humorous sketches of domestic life in Bengal.] Pt. i. pp. 322. কলিকাতা ১৩০৫ [*Calcutta*, 1898.] 12°. **14127. cc. 20.(1.)**

PAÑCHATANTRA. পঞ্চতন্ত্র। [Pañchatantra. Translated from the Sanskrit by Tārākānta Kāvyatīrtha Bhaṭṭāchārya.] . pp. ii. 376. কলিকাতা ১৩১২ [*Calcutta*, 1906.] 12°. **14128. a. 12.**

PĀṆCHKAṚI DE. জীবন্মৃত-রহস্য উপন্যাস। [Jīvanmṛita-rahasya. A sensational novel on hypnotism.] pp. 318, 13. *Calcutta*, [1903.] 12°. **14127. cc. 36.**

—— মায়াবী। [Māyāvī. A sensational novel.] pp. 318. *Calcutta*, 1901. 12°. **14127. cc. 27.**

PĀṆCHKAṚI GHOSHA. জগদ্রাম রায়ের রামায়ণ। [Jagadrāma Rāyer Rāmāyaṇa. A paper on the Rāmāyaṇa of Jagadrāma Rāya.] ১৩০২ [1895.] *See* ACADEMIES, *etc.*—Calcutta.—*Bengal Academy of Literature.* সাহিত্য-পরিষৎ-পত্রিকা। [Sāhitya-parishat-patrikā.] Vol. ii., no. 3. [1894, *etc.*] 8°. **14133. f. 18.**

PĀṆḌAVAGĪTĀ. পাণ্ডব-গীতা বা প্রপন্ন-গীতা [Pāṇḍavagītā, also called Prapannagītā. A selection of Sanskrit verses on the Vaishṇava cult, taken from the Mahābhārata and the Purāṇas. Edited with a Bengali metrical version by Pūrṇachandra De Kāvyaratna Udbhaṭasāgara.] pp. vi. 56. কলিকাতা ১৯০৪ [*Calcutta*, 1904.] 12°. **14033. a. 29.(2.)**

PĀṆINI. [For the Mahābhāshya, an exposition of the Sūtras of Pāṇini:] *See* PATAÑJALI.

—— লিঙ্গানুশাসনম্। [Liṅgānuṣāsana, or Sūtras on Gender. Edited with Bengali notes by Mukundadayāla Vasu.] pp. 30. কোচবিহার ১৩০১ [*Cooch Behar*, 1894.] 12°. **14090. b. 43.(2.)**

—— সিদ্ধান্তকৌমুদী। ... Siddhanta Kaumudi ... with a commentary entitled the "Tattwabodhini" by Jnanendra Saraswati, and with a Bengali translation. Edited ... by Kaviraj Binod Lal Sen. 2 vols. ১৮১২-১৪ *Calcutta*, [1890-92.] 8°. **14090. d. 29.**

—— অথ বৈদিকং ব্যাকরণম্॥ [Siddhāntakaumudī. The section on Vedic grammar, with Bengali notes, and an appendix on Vedic metres.] pp. 31. *See* ṢYĀMACHARAṆA KAVIRATNA. স্বপরিশুদ্ধ-সটীক ত্রিবেদীয়-ক্রিয়াকাণ্ড-পদ্ধতিঃ। [Trivedīya kriyākāṇḍa-paddhati.] 1906. *obl.* 8°. **14033. bbb. 44.**

—— সিদ্ধান্তসন্দীপনী *etc.* [Siddhāntasandīpanī. A re-arrangement of the Aphorisms, with a Bengali commentary by Vasantakumāra Rāya. Part 3, containing the sections on *Kāraka* and *Samāsa.*] pp. 179. কলিকাতা ১৩০৮ [*Calcutta*, 1901.] 12°. **14092. a. 17.(3.)**

PANTAINOS, *of Alexandria.* ভারতবর্ষের ধর্ম-প্রবর্ত্তক প্যান্টিনাসের লিপিবিশেষের অন্তভাগ। [The latter portion of a letter of Pantainos, translated into Bengali with notes.] *See* NITYAGOPĀLA MUKHOPĀDHYĀYA. Studies in Apostolic Fathers. No. 2, pp. 77-82. **14123. b. 18.**

PAOHĀRĪ BĀBĀ. *See* HARABHAJANA DĀSA, *of Ghazipur.*

PARĀṢARA. পরাশরসংহিতা। [Parāṣara-saṃhitā. A code of *dharma,* in 12 *adhyāyas.* Sanskrit text with Bengali translation.] *See* PAÑCHĀNANA TARKARATNA BHAṬṬĀCHĀRYA. ঊনবিংশতি সংহিতা। [Ūnaviṃṣati saṃhitā.] pp. 340-376. [1903.] 8°. **14039. c. 20.**

PARĀṢARA (*continued*). সানুবাদ পরাশরসংহিতা। [Parāṣara-saṃhitā. Sanskrit text, edited with a Bengali translation by Kālīprasanna Vidyāratna.] pp. ii. ii. v. 100. কলিকাতা ১৩১০ [*Calcutta*, 1903.] 8°. **14039. b. 15.(3.)**

PAREṢACHANDRA VANDYOPĀDHYĀYA. বাঙ্গালার পুরাবৃত্ত। [Bāṅgālār purāvṛitta. A history of Bengal from ancient times.] *Calcutta*, ১৩১৪ [1907, *etc.*] 12°. **14127. aa. 44.**

In progress.

PARIVRĀJAKA. *See* CHANDRAṢEKHARA SENA.

PARKER (THEODORE). [*Life.*] *See* NAGENDRANĀTHA CHAṬṬOPĀDHYĀYA. মহাত্মা থিওডোর পার্কারের জীবনচরিত। [Thiodor Pārkārer jīvanacharita.] [1885.] 8°. **14127. bb. 9.**

PARNELL (THOMAS), *Archdeacon of Clogher.* হারমিট বা উদাসীন। [Udāsīna. Parnell's "Hermit" translated into verse by ʿAzīz al-Nisā. Third edition.] pp. 12. কলিকাতা ১৩১৩ [*Calcutta*, 1906.] 12°. **14129. bb. 28.(4.)**

PĀRVATĪCHARAṆA BHAṬṬĀCHĀRYA. কুলীন কুমারী। [Kulīna kumārī, or The high-caste maiden. A farce. Third edition.] ১২৯৬ [*Calcutta*, [1890.] 8°. **14003. c. 1.(3.)**

Forms part of a series entitled Gauradāsa-granthāvali.

—— সচিত্র শকুন্তলা উপন্যাস। [Ṣakuntalā. The story of Ṣakuntalā, adapted from the Sanskrit drama of Kālidāsa. Fourth edition.] pp. 95. কলিকাতা ১৩১৪ [*Calcutta*, 1907.] 12°. **14128. a. 11.(1.)**

—— *See* JAYADEVA, *Son of Bhojadeva.* শ্রীশ্রীগীতগোবিন্দ। [Gītagovinda. A metrical translation by Pārvatīcharaṇa Mukhopādhyāya.] [1906.] 12°. **14129. bb. 28.(2.)**

PAṢUPATI MITRA. বিবাহ-সঙ্কট নাটক। [Vivāha-saṅkaṭa nāṭaka. A drama depicting the evils of Hindu marriage customs.] pp. vi. 126. কলিকাতা [*Calcutta*, 1896.] 12°. **14131. a. 32.(6.)**

PATAÑJALI. পাণিনীয় মহাভাষ্য। মূল ও বঙ্গানুবাদ। [Mahābhāshya. An exposition of the Sūtra of Pāṇini; Sanskrit text with a Bengali translation by Mokshadācharaṇa Sāmādhyāyī.] *Calcutta*, ১৩১৩ [1907, *etc.*] 8°. **14090. bb. 28.**

In progress.

PATAÑJALI (*continued*). পাতঞ্জলদর্শনম্। [Pātañjala-darṣana. Comprising the Aphorisms, the *bhāshya* ascribed to Vyāsa, the *vṛitti* of Bhojarāja, the *ṭīkās* of Vāchaspati Miṣra and Rāmānanda Sarasvatī, and occasional Bengali translations.] [1891, *etc.*] *See* PERIODICAL PUBLICATIONS.—*Calcutta.* অরুণোদয়। [Aruṇodaya.] Pt. i., no. 25. [1890, *etc.*] 4°. **14133. g. 16.**

Extending only to Sūtra xxxii.

—— পাতঞ্জলদর্শন। [Pātañjala-darṣana. The Aphorisms with a brief commentary, and the *bhāshya* ascribed to Vyāsa. Edited, with a Bengali translation of the *bhāshya*, and explanations of the same, by Pūrṇachandra Vedāntachuñchu Ṣarmā.] pp. vii. 349. কলিকাতা ১৮৯৮ [*Calcutta*, 1898.] 8°. **14048. cc. 23.**

—— পাতঞ্জল যোগসূত্র . . . Patanjal Joga Sutra. Text and its explanation [with a preface] in Bengalee. pp. iv. 144. কলিকাতা ১৮০৬ [*Calcutta*, 1884.] 12°. **14048. b. 18.**

PATERSON (J.), *Rev.* *See* BIBLE.—*Luke.* লূকের লেখা ইঞ্জীল। [Translated into Muhammadan Bengali by J. Paterson.] [1879.] 8°. **3068. dd. 18.**

PAVANAVIJAYA. পবনবিজয়স্বরোদয়ঃ। [Pavanavijaya-svarodaya. A Sanskrit Tantric treatise in 324 verses on the suppression of the breath. With a Bengali translation.] pp. 35. [1891, *etc.*] *See* PERIODICAL PUBLICATIONS.—*Calcutta.* অরুণোদয়। [Aruṇodaya.] Pt. i., no. 13. [1890, *etc.*] 4°. **14133. g. 16.**

—— পবনবিজয়স্বরোদয়ঃ। [Pavanavijaya-svarodaya. A similar Sanskrit treatise, in 21 *adhyāyas*. Edited with a Bengali prose translation by Kālīprasanna Vidyāratna Bhaṭṭāchārya. Second edition.] pp. 116. কলিকাতা ১২৯৮ [*Calcutta*, 1892.] 12°. **14028. b. 72.(2.)**

—— পবন-বিজয় স্বরোদয় শাস্ত্রম্। [Pavanavijaya-svarodaya. Sanskrit text, in 36 *adhyāyas*, with Bengali translation and notes.] pp. 118. *Calcutta*, [1901.] 12°. **14033. a. 41.(4.)**

PERIODICAL PUBLICATIONS.

BARANAGAR.

ভারত-শ্রমজীবী। [Bhārata-ṣramajīvī. A monthly newspaper.] Vol. vi. Nos. 4 and 7. বরাহনগর ১২৮৬ [*Baranagar*, 1879.] Fol. **14133. g. 15.(7.)**

PERIODICAL PUBLICATIONS (*continued*).

BRINDABAN.

শ্রীবৈষ্ণব-সন্দর্ভ। [Vaishṇava-sandarbha. A monthly magazine of Bengali and Sanskrit Vaishṇava literature. Edited by Nityasakhā Mukhopādhyāya.] শ্রীবৃন্দাবন শ্রীচৈতন্যাব্দ ৪১৮ [*Brindaban*, 1903, *etc.*] 8°. **14123. ff. 13.**

CALCUTTA.

ঐতিহাসিক চিত্র। [Aitihāsika chitra. A quarterly journal devoted to Indian historical research. Edited by Akshayakumāra Maitreya.] Vol. i., nos. 1-3. রাজসাহী ১৮৯৯ [*Rajshahi*, 1899-1900.] 8°. **14127. bb. 14.**

অনুশীলন মাসিক পত্র ও সমালোচন। [Anuṣīlana. A monthly literary journal, edited by Mahendranātha Vidyānidhi.] Vol. i., nos. 1-7. কলিকাতা ১৩০১ [*Calcutta*, 1894.] 8°. **14133. f. 15.**

অরুণোদয় মাসিক পত্রিকা। [Aruṇodaya. A monthly magazine chiefly devoted to astrology and the occult sciences, in which are published divers Sanskrit texts bearing on these subjects, with commentaries and Bengali translations. Edited by Rasikamohana Chaṭṭopādhyāya.] Vols. i.-v. no. 3. কলিকাতা ১২৯৭ [*Calcutta*, 1890, *etc.*] 4°. **14133. g. 16.**

No numbers have been registered since 1897.

ভারতী। [Bhāratī. A monthly literary magazine. Vol. i., no. 1, edited by Dvijendranātha Ṭhākura; vol. xxii., by Ravīndranātha Ṭhākura; vols. xxiv.-xxxi., by Ṣrīmatī Saralā Devī; vols. xxxii., *etc.*, by Ṣrīmatī Svarṇakumārī Devī.] কলিকাতা ১২৮৪ [*Calcutta*, 1877, *etc.*] 8°. **14133. f. 6.**

মহিলা বান্ধব। [Mahilā-bāndhava, or Woman's friend. A bi-monthly periodical for women.] Vol. ii., no. 14. কলিকাতা ১৮৮৭ [*Calcutta*, 1887.] 4°. **14133. g. 14.(6.)**

পাক্ষিক সংবাদ। [Pākshika saṃvāda. A bi-monthly Christian journal.] Vol. i., no. 17. কলিকাতা ১৮৭১ [*Calcutta*, 1871.] Fol. **14133. g. 15.(6.)**

প্রাচীন বাঙ্গালা গ্রন্থাবলী। [Prāchīna Bāṅgālā granthāvalī. A bi-monthly journal devoted to the publication of ancient Bengali works. Edited by Haraprasāda Ṣāstrī and others.] nos. 1-17. ১৩০৭-১৯১২ [*Calcutta*, 1900-06.] 8°. **14133. ff. 2.**

No more numbers appear to have been issued. The publication of other works was taken up by the Vaṅgīya Sāhitya-parishat, or Bengal Academy of Literature.

PERIODICAL PUBLICATIONS.

CALCUTTA (*continued*).

সংবাদ পূর্ণচন্দ্রোদয়। [Pūrṇachandrodaya. A daily newspaper, edited by Advaitachandra Āḍhya. No. 8429. 2nd April, 1867.] ১৮৬৭ [*Calcutta*, 1867.] Fol. **14003. e. 2.(9.)**

রহস্য-সন্দর্ভ। Rahasya sandarbha: a monthly magazine of literature, science and art. [Edited by Rājendralāla Mitra.] Vol. iv., nos. 44, 45. *Calcutta*, 1868. Fol. **14133. g. 15.(3.)**

সাধনা। মাসিক পত্রিকা। [Sādhanā. A monthly literary magazine, edited (vols. 1-3) by Sudhīndranātha Ṭhākura, and (vol. 4) by Ravīndranātha Ṭhākura.] Vols. i.-iv., no. 2. কলিকাতা ১২৯৮ *etc.* [*Calcutta*, 1891-95.] 12°. **14133. f. 11.**

সাহিত্য। মাসিক পত্র ও সমালোচন। [Sāhitya. A monthly literary journal and review, edited by Sureṣachandra Samājapati.] Vols. i., ii. কলিকাতা ১২৯৭-৯৮ [*Calcutta*, 1890-91.] 8°. **14133. f. 10.**

সাহিত্য-সংহিতা। [Sāhitya-saṃhitā. A monthly literary journal, edited by Nṛisiṃhachandra Mukhopādhyāya and Subalachandra Mitra.] কলিকাতা ১৩০৭ [*Calcutta*, 1900, *etc.*] 8°. **14133. ff. 1.**

In progress.

সমালোচনী। [Samālochanī. A monthly review, edited by Ṣaileṣachandra Majumdār.] Vols. i.-iii. কলিকাতা ১৩০৮ [*Calcutta*, 1902-1905.] 12°. **14133. ee. 1.**

Wanting nos. 11 *and* 12 *of vol.* ii. *and no.* 10 *of vol.* iii.

সাপ্তাহিক সংবাদ। [Sāptāhika saṃvāda. A Christian newspaper, published weekly.] Vol. i., no. 36. কলিকাতা ১৮৬৯ [*Calcutta*, 1869.] Fol. **14133. g. 15.(5.)**

শিক্ষা-পরিচর। [Ṣikshā-parichara. A monthly periodical for the spread of education, edited by Ṣarachchandra Chaudhurī.] Vols. i.-iii. কলিকাতা ১২৯৬-৯৮ [*Calcutta*, 1889-91.] 8°. **14133. f. 12.**

No more was published.

उषा। वैदिकपत्रिका। [Ushā. A journal of Vedic and general criticism, consisting of Sanskrit texts with commentaries, reviews, and other articles, both in Sanskrit and in Bengali. Edited by Satyavrata Sāmaṣrami Bhaṭṭāchārya.] कलिकाता १८११ [*Calcutta*, 1889, *etc.*] 8°. **14010. c. 43.**

In progress.

PERIODICAL PUBLICATIONS.

CALCUTTA (*continued*).

বামাবোধিনী পত্রিকা। [Vāmābodhinī patrikā. A monthly magazine for women.] Vol. ii., no. 2. ১২৭৩ [*Calcutta*, 1867.] 8°. **14133. g. 15.(1.)**

[Vaṅga-darṣana.] *See* CHANDRAṢEKHARA MUKHOPĀDHYĀYA. সারস্বতকুঞ্জ। [Sārasvata-kuñja. Essays and reviews, reprinted from the Vaṅgadarṣana.] [1855.] 8°. **14133. h. 11.(1.)**

—— *See* RĀJAKṚISHṆA MUKHOPĀDHYĀYA. নানা প্রবন্ধ। [Nānā prabandha. Miscellaneous essays, reprinted from the Vaṅgadarṣana.] 1885. 8°. **14133. h. 11.(2.)**

বঙ্গ-জীবন। [Vaṅga-jīvana. A monthly literary magazine and review, edited by Tāriṇīcharaṇa Sena.] Vol. i. কলিকাতা ১৩০২ [*Calcutta*, 1896.] 8°. **14133. f. 14.**

Wanting nos. 3 *and* 4.

বিজ্ঞান। [Vijñāna. A monthly scientific newspaper] ... Under the patronage of the Indian Industrial Association. Vol. i., no. 1. কলিকাতা ১৩০১ [*Calcutta*, 1894.] 8°. **14133. f. 17.**

বীণা-বাদিনী। [Vīṇā-vādinī. A monthly musical journal. Edited by Jyotirindranātha Ṭhākura.] 2 vols. কলিকাতা [*Calcutta*, 1897-99.] 12°. **14125. d. 27.**

CHINSURAH.

বাসনা। [Vāsanā. A monthly journal and review.] Vol. ii., nos. 7, 8; iii., nos. 4, 5. চুঁচুড়া ১৩০২ [*Chinsurah*, 1896.] 8°. **14133. f. 16.**

DACCA.

বান্ধব। [Bāndhava. A monthly literary journal and review. Edited by Kālīprasanna Ghosha.] ঢাকা ১৩০৮ [*Dacca*, 1901, *etc.*] 8°. **14133. ff. 3.**

In progress.

পল্লী-বিজ্ঞান। [Pallī-vijñāna. A monthly newspaper.] Vol. i., nos. 10, 11; vol. ii., no. 4. ঢাকা ১৮৯৭-৯৮ [*Dacca*, 1867-68.] Fol. **14133. g. 15.(2.)**

Incomplete; wanting pp. 5-12 *of vol.* i., *no.* 10.

বঙ্গবন্ধু। [Vaṅga-bandhu. A bi-monthly newspaper.] Vol. vi., no. 3. ঢাকা ১৭৯৭ [*Dacca*, 1875.] Fol. **14133. g. 15.(4.)**

PERSIAN TALES. সচিত্র পারস্য-উপন্যাস। [Pārasya upanyāsa. The Persian Tales, translated into Bengali from an English version.] pp. 272. কলিকাতা ১৩১৩ [*Calcutta*, 1906.] 8°. **14127. f. 46.**

PHAṬIKACHANDRA DĀSA GUPTA. [*Life.*] *See* VAIKUṆṬHACHANDRA DĀSA GUPTA. ফটিকচন্দ্রদাস গুপ্তের সংক্ষিপ্ত জীবন চরিত। [Phaṭikachandra Dāsa Gupter jīvanacharita.] [1896.] 12°. **14127. aa. 6.(2.)**

PĪR MUḤAMMAD, also called PĪR BAKHSH. *See* ʻINĀYAT ḤUSAIN ibn NAWĀZISH AḤMAD. ফতুহশাম। [Futūḥ al-Shām. Translated into verse by Munshī Pīr Muḥammad and Maulavī Muḥammad ʻAbbās ʻAlī.] [1905.] Fol. **14127. bbb. 6.**

PĪTĀMBARACHANDRA CHANDA. ভাদু পুরাণ। [Bhādu-purāṇa. An account of the worship of Bhādu, a form of the goddess Durgā; with songs.] pp. 50. বাঁকুড়া [*Bankura*, 1897.] 24°. **14123. e. 21.**

PĪTĀMBARA DĀSA. পীতাম্বরদাসের রস-মঞ্জরী। [Rasa-mañjarī. An old Bengali poem on the erotic element of composition, with an introduction and notes.] ১৩০৬ [1899.] *See* ACADEMIES, *etc.*—Calcutta.—*Bengal Academy of Literature.* সাহিত্য-পরিষৎ-পত্রিকা। [Sāhitya-parishat-patrikā.] Vol. vi., no. 1. [1894, *etc.*] 8°. **14133. f. 18.**

PLAYFAIR (WILLIAM SMOULT). ধাত্রীবিদ্যা। [Dhātrīvidyā.] . . . A treatise on the science and practice of midwifery. [Translated by Kshīrodāprasāda Chaṭṭopādhyāya. Third edition.] pp. xxvi. 817. *Calcutta*, 1901. 8°. **14125. c. 42.**

P. M. BĀGCHI. *See* EPHEMERIDES. নূতন পঞ্জিকা সন ১৩০৬ সাল (P. M. Bagchi's illustrated Directory of India for 1899 or 1305 B.S.) 1899. 8°. **14133. e. 9.**

POONEAH EXHIBITION MELA. *See* COOCH BEHAR.—*Puṇyāh Exhibition Melā.*

PRABHĀSACHANDRA MITRA. লেখা। [Lekhā. Short poems.] pp. viii. 114. কলিকাতা ১৩১৩ [*Calcutta*, 1906.] 12°. **14129. bb. 36.**

PRABHĀSACHANDRA RĀYA. পার্ব্বত্য-কাহিনী। [Pārvatya-kāhinī. An account of the Santal Parganas, its administration and the manners and customs of the Santals.] pp. xi. 131. কলিকাতা ১৩১৪ [*Calcutta*, 1908.] 12°. **14125. e. 52.**

PRABHĀTACHANDRA KĀVYATĪRTHA VIDYĀVINODA. অনুবাদ-চন্দ্রিকা। . . . Anubada chandrika. [Useful vocabularies and dialogues.] *Eng., Sansk.* and *Beng.* pp. 40. *Dacca*, 1893. 8°. **14133. b.**

PRABHĀTAKUMĀRA MUKHOPĀDHYĀYA. নবকথা। [Navakathā. Twelve short stories.] pp. 234. কলিকাতা ১৩০৬ [*Calcutta*, 1899.] 8°. **14127. cc. 15.**

PRABHĀVATĪ DEVĪ. অমল-প্রসূন বা প্রভাবতী-কবিতাবলী। [Amalaprasūna. A collection of poems by Prabhāvatī Devī. Edited, with a life of the authoress, by Maṇīndranātha Chaṭṭopādhyāya.] pp. ii. 33, 174. যশোহর ১৩০৭ [*Jessore*, 1900.] 12°. **14129. a. 50.**

PRABODHACHANDRA DE. কৃষিক্ষেত্র। [Krishikshetra. A treatise on Indian agriculture.] 2 pts. কলিকাতা [*Calcutta*, 1895.] 12°. **14125. bb. 7.(2.)**

—— ফুলওয়ারি বা মালঞ্চ। [Phulwārī. A treatise on gardening and floriculture.] pp. iii. iii. 191. কলিকাতা ১৩০৬ [*Calcutta*, 1899.] 12°. **14125. bb. 26.**

PRABODHACHANDRA SARKĀR. শালফুল। [Śālaphula. An historical novel relating to the rebellion of the Naiks in the Midnapore district in the beginning of the present century.] pp. iv. 170. বাঁকুড়া ১৩০৪ [*Bankura*, 1897.] 12°. **14127. cc. 12.(1.)**

PRABODHĀNANDA SARASVATĪ, *Vaishṇava teacher.* *See* PRAKĀŚĀNANDA, afterwards called PRABODHĀNANDA SARASVATĪ.

PRABODHAPRAKĀŚA SENA GUPTA. A Dictionary of Proverbs [Bengali and English]. By Prabodh Prakas Sen Gupta. pp. 245. *Calcutta*, 1899. 12°. **14125. f. 36.**

PRAJĀPATI, *pseud.* ঠাকুরপো। সামাজিক প্রহসন। [Ṭhākurpo. A farce, explaining the vices of modern social life among the Brahmans.] A reformation of the day! pp. 74. *Howrah*, 1886. 12°. **14131. a. 25.(2.)**

PRAKĀŚĀNANDA, afterwards called PRABODHĀNANDA SARASVATĪ. [*Life.*] *See* BALARĀMA DĀSA. শ্রী প্রবোধানন্দ সরস্বতীর জীবন চরিত। [Prabodhānanda Sarasvatīr jīvanacharita.] [1891.] 8°. **14127. b. 47.(1.)**

PRAKĀṢĀNANDA, afterwards called PRABODHĀNANDA SARASVATĪ. [*Life.*] (*continued*). *See* ṢIṢIRAKUMĀRA GHOSHA. শ্রী প্রবোধানন্দ ও শ্রীগোপাল ভট্ট। [Prabodhānanda o Gopāla Bhaṭṭa.] [1896.] 12°. **14123. e. 16.(3.)**

—— মাহিষ্যদীধিতি। [Māhishyadīdhiti. A treatise on the Māhishya, or Kaivarta caste.] pp. 48. কলিকাতা [*Calcutta*, 1903.] 12°. **14125. e. 31.(9.)**

PRAMATHANĀTHA KĀVYATĪRTHA. *See* ṢRĪPATI KAVIRATNA and PRAMATHANĀTHA KĀVYATĪRTHA. সন্দর্ভহার। (Sandarbhahar.) 1896. 12°. **14125. e. 27.(5.)**

PRAMATHANĀTHA MITRA. যোগী। ঐতিহাসিক উপন্যাস। [Yogī, or The devotee. An historical novel of the time of the siege of Udaipur by the Mugals.] pp. 259. কলিকাতা ১৮৮৬ [*Calcutta*, 1886.] 8°. **14127. f. 36.(2.)**

PRAMATHANĀTHA RĀYA CHAUDHURĪ. গৌরাঙ্গ। [Gaurāṅga. The life of Buddha, in verse.] pp. ii. 192. ১৩০৯ [*Calcutta*, 1903.] 8°. **14123. k. 8.**

—— গীতিকা। [Gītikā. A collection of lyrics.] pp. vi. 168. [*Calcutta*, 1900.] 8°. **14129. c. 51.**

—— পদ্মা। [Padmā. Lyrical poems.] pp. viii. 155. কলিকাতা ১৩০৫ [*Calcutta*, 1899.] 8°. **14129. bb. 14.**

PRAMATHANĀTHA SĀNYĀLA. *See* CUNNINGHAM (J. D.). শিখ-ইতিহাস। [Ṣikh-itihāsa. A Bengali translation, by Pramathanātha Sānyāla, of Cunningham's History of the Sikhs.] [1907.] 12°. **14127. aa. 47.**

PRAMATHANĀTHA VARMĀ. সিঙ্গুরের স্বর্গীয় জমিদার দ্বারিকানাথ বাবু ও তাঁহার বংশাবলীর জীবনচরিত। [Dvārikānātha Bābu o tāṇhār jīvanacharita. A biography of Dvārikānātha, a wealthy zamindar of Singur in the district of Hooghly.] pp. 71. কলিকাতা ১২৯৪ [*Calcutta*, 1887.] 12°. **14127. a. 33.(2.)**

PRAMATHANĀTHA VASU. বিবিধ প্রবন্ধ। [Vividha prabandha. A collection of articles reprinted from the Navajīvana and Bhāratī. Compiled by Pramathanātha Vasu.] pp. 99. ১২৯৯ [*Calcutta*, 1893.] 12°. **14125. e. 26.(3.)**

PRAMATHEṢVARA KĀVYARATNA. Stepping-stone to Sanskrit composition . . . সংস্কৃত-ভাষা-শিক্ষা। [Saṃskṛita bhāshāṣikshā.] pp. 121, xxviii. *Calcutta*, 1896. 12°. **14131. e. 29.**

PRAMODAKĀNTA VASU. সৌরভ। [Saurabha. Miscellaneous short poems.] pp. ii. 82. কলিকাতা ১৩০৬ [*Calcutta*, 1899.] 12°. **14129. bb. 8.(1.)**

PRĀṆAHARI YOGAVIṢĀRADA. কামশাস্ত্র বা মোহিনীতন্ত্র। [Kāmaṣāstra, or Mohinītantra. A treatise on erotics, and magic in connexion therewith, in 4 parts. Preceded by verses on the Daṣamahāvidyā of Devī, *etc.* Sanskrit text, and Bengali translations by Pañchānana Rāya Chaudhurī.] pp. xiv. 188. কলিকাতা ১৩০৭ [*Calcutta*, 1901.] 12°. **14053. b. 40.**

PRĀṆAKṚISHṆA DATTA. বৈরাগী রঘুনাথ দাস। [Vairāgī Raghunātha Dāsa. A life of Raghunātha Dāsa, son of Govardhana Dāsa of Saptagram, in the District of Hooghly, a famous Vaishṇava of the 16th century, A.D.] pp. 68. *Calcutta*, 1903. 12°. **14127. aa. 21.(4.)**

PRĀṆAKṚISHṆA GAṄGOPĀDHYĀYA. কেরাণি-চরিত। [Kerānī-charita, or The Bengali clerk.] . . . A society comedietta in two acts. কলিকাতা ১২৯২ [*Calcutta*, 1885.] 12°. **14131. a. 24.(2.)**

PRAṆAYA-YĀTRĪ. প্রণয়-যাত্রী। [Praṇaya-yātrī. A fairy tale.] pp. 86. কলিকাতা ১২৯৯ [*Calcutta*, 1892.] 12°. **14127. c. 42.(4.)**

PRASĀDADĀSA GOSVĀMĪ. *See* ASHṬĀVAKRA. অষ্টাবক্র সংহিতা। [Ashṭāvakra-saṃhitā. Sanskrit text, with a paraphrase and preface by Prasādadāsa Gosvāmī.] [1886.] 12°. **14048. b. 21.**

—— *See* TANTRAS.—*Viṣvasāratantra.* গুরুগীতা। [Gurugītā-stotra. With a paraphrase and prefatory notes on the practice of Yoga by Prasādadāsa Gosvāmī.] [1885.] 12°. **14033. a. 12.(2.)**

PRASĀDAKUMĀRA MUKHOPĀDHYĀYA. চিকিৎসা-কোষ। [Chikitsākosha. A dictionary of medical terms explained in Bengali.] pp. ii. 628. *Calcutta*, 1894. 12°. **14125. b. 13.**

—— প্রাচীন কলিকাতা। [Prāchīna Kalikātā. A tale of life in Calcutta, and the detection of crime half a century ago. Second edition.] pp. iii. 136. কলিকাতা ১২৯৪ [*Calcutta*, 1888.] 12°. **14127. d. 35.(3.)**

PRASĀDAKUMĀRA MUKHOPĀDHYĀYA (*continued*). সাহিত্য শোভা। [Sāhitya-śobhā. A collection of twenty miscellaneous pieces, containing different specimens of Bengali composition.] pp. xxii. 396. কলিকাতা ১৮৯০ [*Calcutta*, 1890.] 8°. **14127. f. 44.**

—— সোণার সংসার। [Soṇār saṃsāra. A tale of Bengali life.] pp. 228. কলিকাতা ১২৯৪ [*Calcutta*, 1887.] 12°. **14127. d. 35.(1.)**

PRASANNACHANDRA VIDYĀRATNA. পত্র লিখিবার পাঠ। [Patra likhibār pāṭha. A Bengali letter-writer. Sixteenth edition.] pp. 56. ঢাকা [*Dacca*, 1900.] 12°. **14131. f. 32.**

PRASANNAKUMĀRA BHAṬṬĀCHĀRYA. স্বর্গীয় দেবী মুক্তকেশী চরিতামৃত। [Devī Muktakeśīr charitāmṛita. The life of Muktakeśī, the wife of Bābu Śarachchandra Chaudhurī, a Brahmist lady of extraordinary abilities.] pp. 104, 37. কলিকাতা ১২৯৮ [*Calcutta*, 1891.] 12°. **14127. a. 40.**

PRASANNAKUMĀRA GHOSHA. হারাণী ওরফে চারুহাসিনী। [Hārāṇī. A story of domestic life.] pp. 122. বগুড়া ১৩০৩ [*Bogra*, 1896.] 8°. **14127. ee. 5.(3.)**

PRASANNAKUMĀRA GOSVĀMĪ. *See* RĀMADĀSA, *Vaishṇava poet.* শ্রীঅভিরামলীলামৃত। [Abhirāma-līlāmṛita. Edited by Prasannakumāra Gosvāmī.] [1894.] 8°. **14129. f. 6.(1.)**

PRASANNAKUMĀRA NĀGA. রাজপুতাঙ্গনা কাব্য। [Rājputāṅganā kāvya. A poem describing the siege of Chitor by Sultan ʻAlā al-Dīn Khiljī, and the heroism of its female defenders.] pp. 184. [*Calcutta*, 1904.] 12°. **14129. bb. 18.(4.)**

PRASANNAKUMĀRA RĀYA, *Pleader.* *See* YADUNANDANA, *Kavi.* বারেন্দ্র ঢাকুর। [Ḍhākur. With a supplementary part on Vārendra Kāyarthas of modern times. By Prasannakumāra Rāya.] [1908.] 12°. **14127. aa. 40.(2.)**

PRASANNAKUMĀRA SĀHĀ BAṆIKYA. তবলা-তরঙ্গিণী। [Tablā-taraṅgiṇī. Instruction on the *tablā*, or Indian drum. Second edition.] pp. ix. 142. কলিকাতা ১৩০৮ [*Calcutta*, 1901.] 8°. **14125. d. 29.(1.)**

PRASANNAKUMĀRA ŚĀSTRĪ BHAṬṬĀCHĀRYA. *See* KRISHṆĀNANDA BHAṬṬĀCHĀRYA. বৃহৎ তন্ত্রসার। [Bṛihat-Tantrasāra. With a Bengali translation by Prasannakumāra.] [1896.] 4°. **14033. c. 39.**

—— *See* PAÑCHA GĪTĀ. পঞ্চগীতা। [Pañcha gītā. With Bengali translations and notes by Prasannakumāra.] [1906.] 16°. **14028. a. 33.**

—— *See* UPANISHADS. উপনিষদাবলী। [Upanishadāvalī. A collection of 10 Upanishads. Edited with Bengali translations by Prasannakumāra.] [1896.] 12°. **14010. b. 12.**

—— সটীক পুরোহিত-সর্ব্বস্ব। [Purohita-sarvasva. A manual of the 10 Vedic domestic rites and other ceremonies, with various rituals and prayers from other sources, with Sanskrit texts.] pp. ii. viii. 576, 103. কলিকাতা ১৩১৩ [*Calcutta*, 1906.] 8°. **14123. g. 23.**

—— যোগাম্বুধি। [Yogāmbudhi. A collection of 6 Sanskrit works on Yoga: viz., Gheraṇḍa-saṃhitā, Śiva-saṃhitā, Shaṭchakra-nirūpaṇa, Ashṭāvakra-saṃhitā, Yogī-yājñavalkya, and Brahma-saṃhitā. Edited with Bengali translations by Prasannakumāra Bhaṭṭāchārya.] কলিকাতা ১৩০৩ [*Calcutta*, 1896.] 32°. **14048. a. 19.**

Each work has a separate pagination.

PRASANNAKUMĀRA SENA. A Dictionary of Court Terms in use in Bengal. Compiled by P. C. Sen. pp. 26. *Konnagar*, 1895. 8°. **14125. a. 19.(3.)**

PRASANNAKUMĀRA VIDYĀRATNA, *Smārta-chuḍāmaṇi.* শ্রীগৌরাঙ্গ-তত্ত্ব সহ শ্রীগৌরাঙ্গ-চরিত। [Gaurāṅgatattva. A treatise on the religious teachings of Chaitanya; also Gaurāṅgacharita, a life of Chaitanya. Illustrated by Sanskrit texts.] pp. 270. কলিকাতা [*Calcutta*, 1899.] 8°. **14127. bb. 13.**

PRASANNAKUMĀRA VIDYĀRATNA BHAṬṬĀ-CHĀRYA. ভাবসিন্ধু। [Bhāvasindhu. Poems embodying the teachings of ancient Hindu sages, with notes.] pp. xxiv. 264. কলিকাতা ১৩১৪ [*Calcutta*, 1907.] 12°. **14129. bb. 37.**

PRASANNAMAYĪ DĀSĪ. বিভূতি প্রভা নাটক। [Vibhūti-Prabhā nāṭaka. A drama depicting female domestic life in Bengal.] pp. 57. ফরিদপুর [*Faridpur*, 1905.] 12°. **14131. aa. 4.(6.)**

PRATĀPACHANDRA GHOSHA. বঙ্গাধিপ-পরাজয়। [Vaṅgādhipa-parājaya. An historical novel on the conquest of Bengal under Raja Pratāpāditya by the Emperor Akbar in 1576.] pp. vi. iii. 599, ii. কলিকাতা ১৭৯১ [*Calcutta*, 1869.] 8°. **14127. b. 18.**

—— —— [Another edition.] pp. iv. iii. 606. কলিকাতা ১৩১৫ [*Calcutta*, 1908.] 8°. **14127. ee. 31.**

PRATĀPACHANDRA MAJUMDĀR. স্ত্রীচরিত্র। [Strīcharitra. Moral lessons for female readers. Second edition.] pp. ii. 164. কলিকাতা ১৩০৫ [*Calcutta*, 1899.] 12°. **14125. e. 38.(2.)**

PRATĀPACHANDRA RĀYA. *See* PURĀṆAS.—*Bhāgavatapurāṇa.* শ্রীমদ্ভাগবত। [Bhāgavatapurāṇa. Translated into Bengali, and edited by Pratāpachandra Rāya.] [1885-87.] 8°. **14123. g. 17.**

PRATĀPĀDITYA, *Raja.* [*Life.*] *See* SATYACHARAṆA ŚĀSTRĪ. প্রতাপাদিত্যের জীবন-চরিত। [Pratāpādityer jīvanacharita.] [1896.] 12°. **14127. aa. 6.(4.)**

PRATĀPA SIṂHA, *Raja.* [*Life.*] *See* MANOMOHANA RĀYA. ঐতিহাসিক প্রবন্ধ। [Aitihāsika prabandha. Pt. i.] [1887.] 12°. **14127. a.**

PREMACHANDRA TARKAVĀGĪŚA, *Professor of Rhetoric.* [*Life.*] *See* RĀMĀKSHAYA CHAṬṬOPĀDHYĀYA. ৺ প্রেমচন্দ্র তর্কবাগীশের জীবনচরিত। [Premachandra Tarkavāgīśer jīvanacharita.] [1892.] 8°. **14127. b. 38.(3.)**

—— [1896.] 8°. **14127. bb. 4.(2.)**

—— [1901.] 8°. **14127. aa. 16.**

—— [1906.] 12°. **14127. aa. 34.**

PREMADĀSA. *See* PURUSHOTTAMA MIŚRA.

PREMADĀSA MIŚRA. শ্রীশ্রীবংশী-শিক্ষা। [Vaṃśīśikshā. Vaishṇava songs.] pp. 243. কলিকাতা ১২৯৯ [*Calcutta*, 1893.] *obl.* 8°. **14129. c. 45.**

PREMAKUÑJA. সচিত্র প্রেমকুঞ্জ। [Premakuñja. A collection of love stories, taken from Sanskrit, English and other sources.] pp. 622. *Calcutta*, [1898.] 12°. **14127. cc. 11.**

PREMALATĀ. প্রেমলতা। সামাজিক উপন্যাস। [Premalatā. A novel describing Hindu social life. Second edition.] pp. ii. 344. কলিকাতা ১৩০০ [*Calcutta*, 1894.] 8°. **14127. d. 41.(2.)**

PREMA-NĀṬAKA. *Begin.* জয় ২ গজানন বিঘ্ন বিনাশন *etc.* [Prema-nāṭaka. A love-tale, in prose and verse.] pp. 23. [*Calcutta*, 1865.] 8°. **14127. f. 42.(1.)**

PRIVATE TUTOR. The Private Tutor, or a Book for the million. প্রাইভেট টিউটার ইংরেজী শিক্ষার সহজ উপায়। [Lessons on English grammar.] pp. 132. কলিকাতা ১২৯৯ [*Calcutta*, 1893.] 12°. **14131. e. 20.(2.)**

PRIYAṂVADĀ DEVĪ. রেণু। [Reṇu. A collection of sonnets.] pp. iv. 69. কলিকাতা [*Calcutta*, 1900.] 12°. **14129. bb. 18.(1.)**

PRIYANĀTHA CHAKRAVARTĪ. জীবন-পরীক্ষা ভীষণ স্বপ্ন-চতুষ্টয়। [Jīvana-parīkshā. Spiritual and ethical instruction, in the form of four allegories. Fourth edition.] pp. 36, 344. কলিকাতা ১৩১৫ [*Calcutta*, 1908.] 8°. **14123. ff. 19.**

PRIYANĀTHA MUKHOPĀDHYĀYA. Detective Stories. দারোগার দপ্তর। [Dārogār daptar.] Nos. 1-4, 13-56, 61-100. কলিকাতা ১৮৯২-১৩০৭ [*Calcutta*, 1892-1900.] 12°. **14128. a. 1.**

—— মানিনী। গার্হস্থ্য উপন্যাস। [Māninī. A story of Hindu domestic life, showing the evils of Western civilization.] pp. 52. *Calcutta*, 1896. 12°. **14127. c. 57.(4.)**

One of the author's "Detective Stories."

PRIYANĀTHA RĀYA. স্বর-বিন্যাস। . . . [Svaravinyāsa.] Indian music in European notation. Part i. By Priya Nath Roy. pp. ii. 24. *Darjeeling*, 1889. 8°. **14125. d. 22.**

—— শ্যামানন্দ প্রকাশ। [Śyāmānanda-prakāśa. An account in verse of the life of Śyāmānanda, the disciple of Jīva Gosvāmī.] pp. iv. 56. ঘাঁটাল ১৩০২ [*Ghantal*, 1895.] 12°. **14129. b. 44.(1.)**

PRIYANĀTHA SENA. অদ্বৈতবাদ-বিচার। [Advaitavādavichāra. A dissertation on the Vedānta teachings on the philosophy of monism.] pp. 179. ঢাকা ১৩০৪ [*Dacca*, 1897.] 8°. **14123. f. 53.**

PUṆYĀH EXHIBITION MELĀ. *See* COOCH BEHAR.—*Puṇyāh Exhibition Melā.*

PURĀṆAS.—*Selections.* হিন্দুশাস্ত্র। . . . অষ্টাদশ পুরাণ। [Ashṭādaśa-purāṇa. Selections from the 18 Purāṇas, with Bengali translations, and a brief account of each. Compiled by Āśutosha Śāstrī and Hṛishīkeśa Śāstrī.] pp. i. 325. [1897.]

See RAMEṢACHANDRA DATTA. হিন্দুশাস্ত্র। [Hindu-ṣāstra.] Pt. ix. [1895-97.] 8°. **14085. c. 45. (vol. ii.)**

—— ĀDIPURĀNA. আদিপুরাণ। মূল ও বাঙ্গালা-গদ্যানুবাদ। [Ādipurāṇa. Sanskrit text, accompanied by a Bengali prose translation.] 2 pts. pp. 182, 254. *Calcutta*, 1891. 8°. **14016. c. 47.**

—— AGNIPURĀṆA. অগ্নিপুরাণম্। [Agnipurāṇa. Sanskrit text, with a Bengali translation by Tārākānta Kāvyatīrtha. Edited by Pañchānana Tarkaratna.] pp. vi. 779. কলিকাতা ১৩১৪ [*Calcutta*, 1907.] 8°. **14016. dd. 29.**

—— BHĀGAVATAPURĀṆA. *See* DUḤKHĪṢYĀMA DĀSA. গোবিন্দমঙ্গল। [Govindamaṅgala. A poem, based on the 10th chapter of the Bhāgavatapurāṇa.] [1886.] 8°. **14129. c. 37.**

—— ভাগবত নির্ণয়। [Bhāgavata-nirṇaya. An examination into the contents of the Bhāgavatapurāṇa, and a discussion as to whether it should be regarded as forming one of the 18 Purāṇas.] pp. 15. [*Calcutta?* 1860?] 12°. **14123. e.**

—— শ্রীমদ্ভাগবত। [Bhāgavatapurāṇa. Translated into Bengali, and edited by Pratāpachandra Rāya.] কলিকাতা ১২৯১-৯৩ [*Calcutta*, 1885-87.] 8°. **14123. g. 17.**

Each book has a separate pagination.

—— শ্রীমদ্ভাগবতম্ [Bhāgavatapurāṇa. Sanskrit text, with three Sanskrit commentaries and a Bengali translation by Rāmanārāyaṇa Vidyāratna.] মুর্শিদাবাদ ১২৯২ [*Murshidabad*, 1885-95.] 4°. **14016. dd. 3.**

As far as Skandha xi. adhy. 27.

—— পদ্য শ্রীমদ্ভাগবত। [Bhāgavatapurāṇa. A metrical translation by Keṣavachandra Vandyopādhyāya.] কলিকাতা [*Calcutta*, 1906.] 8°. **14123. gg. 4.**

—— শ্রীকৃষ্ণলীলা। [Kṛishṇalīlā. The Sanskrit text of Bk. x., i.-li., of the Bhāgavata with glosses, Bengali paraphrases, and additional chapters in Bengali upon Vaishṇava doctrine and ritual, including a version of the Bhagavadgītā. Compiled and edited by Ṣyāmalāla Gosvāmī.] pp. 1298. কলিকাতা ১৩১০ [*Calcutta*, 1904.] 8°. **14016. dd. 10.**

—— কৃষ্ণপ্রেমতরঙ্গিণী। [Kṛishṇaprematarangiṇī. A metrical version of the Bhāgavatapurāṇa, by Bhāgavata Āchārya.] pp. 419. ১৩০৮-১২ [1901-06.] *See* PERIODICAL PUBLICATIONS.—*Calcutta.* প্রাচীন বাঙ্গালা গ্রন্থাবলী। [Prāchīna Bāṅgālā granthāvalī.] Nos. 3-17. [1900, *etc.*] 8°. **14133. ff. 2.**

—— শ্রীমদ্ভাগবতান্তর্গত নবযোগেন্দ্রোপাখ্যান ও উদ্ধবগীতা। [Navayogendropākhyāna, and Uddhavagītā. The Sanskrit text of Skandha xi. of the Bhāgavata, with analysis, translation and commentary in Bengali. Edited by Ṣyāmalāla Gosvāmī.] pp. 2, 512. [*Calcutta*, 1900.] 8°. **14018. b. 19.**

—— BHAVISHYAPURĀṆA. ভবিষ্যপুরাণ। [Bhavishyapurāṇa. Sanskrit text, edited with a Bengali translation by Navīnakṛishṇa Lāhā.] 3 pts. কলিকাতা ১২৯২ [*Calcutta*, 1886.] 8°. **14018. b. 15.**

As far as the middle of adhy. 7.

—— BRAHMĀṆḌAPURĀṆA. ব্রহ্মাণ্ড-পুরাণম্। [Brahmāṇḍapurāṇa. Sanskrit text, edited with a Bengali prose translation and notes by Nagendranātha Vasu.] Pts. 1-23. pp. xvi. 728. কলিকাতা ১২৯৮-১৩০১ [*Calcutta*, 1891-94.] 8°. **14016. c. 46.**

No more has been registered.

—— ব্রহ্মাণ্ডপুরাণম্। . . . সংস্কৃত মূল ও বঙ্গানুবাদ সমেত। [Brahmāṇḍapurāṇa. Sanskrit text, with a Bengali translation by Tārākānta Kāvyatīrtha. Edited by Pañchānana Tarkaratna.] pp. i. ii. 355. কলিকাতা ১৩১৫ [*Calcutta*, 1908.] 8°. **14018. b. 22. (1.)**

—— অধ্যাত্মরামায়ণম্। [Adhyātma-rāmāyaṇa. Sanskrit text, with the commentary of Rāma Varmā. Edited with analyses and Bengali translations and paraphrases by Khagendranātha Ṣāstrī.] কলিকাতা ১৩০৮ [*Calcutta*, 1901.] 8°. **14016. d. 61.**

In progress.

—— অধ্যাত্ম রামায়ণম্। [Adhyātma-rāmāyaṇa. Sanskrit text, with Rāma Varmā's Sanskrit commentary, and a Bengali metrical version by Raja Mahendralāl K͟hān of Narajol.] pp. ii. 462, 291. কলিকাতা ১৮২৯ [*Calcutta*, 1908.] 4°. **14018. a. 3.**

—— শ্রীশ্রীরামগীতা। [Rāmagītā. A poem of 62 stanzas from the Uttarakāṇḍa, *sarga* v., of the Adhyātma-rāmāyaṇa. Sanskrit text and commentary, with a Bengali translation.] *See* KĀLĪPRASANNA VIDYĀRATNA BHAṬṬĀCHĀRYA. যোগাঙ্কুর। [Yogāṅkura.] pp. 97-156. [1894.] 12°. **14048. b. 28.(2.)**

—— শ্রীরামগীতা। [Rāmagītā. Sanskrit text, with Bengali translation.] *See* PAÑCHA GĪTĀ. পঞ্চগীতা [Pañcha gītā.] pp. 1-34. [1906.] 16°. **14028. a. 33.**

—— BRAHMAVAIVARTAPURĀṆA. ব্রহ্মবৈবর্ত্ত পুরাণ। [Brahmavaivartapurāṇa, translated into verse by Tinkaṛi Viṣvāsa.] pp. vii. 758. কলিকাতা ১২৯২ [*Calcutta*, 1885.] 8°. **14123. g. 16.**

—— ব্রহ্মবৈবর্ত্ত পুরাণ। [Brahmavaivartapurāṇa. Translated into prose by Pandit Pañchānana Tarkaratna and others. Second edition.] pp. viii. 645. কলিকাতা ১৩১০ [*Calcutta*, 1904.] 8°. **14123. g. 20.**

—— BṚIHAN-NĀRADĪYAPURĀṆA. বৃহন্নারদীয়পুরাণম্। [Bṛihan-nāradīyapurāṇa. Sanskrit text, with a Bengali translation by Pañchānana Tarkaratna.] pp. 122, 152. কলিকাতা ১৩০১ [*Calcutta*, 1895.] 12°. **14016. b. 19.**

—— বৃহন্নারদীয়পুরাণ। [Bṛihan-nāradīyapurāṇa. Translated by Yajñeṣvara Vandyopādhyāya.] pp. 327. কলিকাতা ১৩০৭ [*Calcutta*, 1901.] 8°. **14123. e. 25.**

—— বৃহন্নারদীয় পুরাণ। [Bṛihan-nāradīyapurāṇa. A metrical translation made by order of Govinda Māṇikya, Maharaja of Tippera. With a preface containing a short account of the Rajas of Tippera.] pp. xviii. ix. 464. আগরতলা ১৩১৬ [*Agartalah*, 1908.] 12°. **14123. e. 37.**

—— DEVĪBHĀGAVATAPURĀṆA. দেবী-ভাগবত। [Devībhāgavatapurāṇa. Translated by Pañchānana Tarkaratna. Second edition.] pp. ii. vi. 775, কলিকাতা ১৩১৫ [*Calcutta*, 1908.] 8°. **14123. ff. 20.**

—— DEVĪPURĀṆA. দেবীপুরাণম্। [Devīpurāṇa. Sanskrit text, with a Bengali translation. Edited by Pañchānana Tarkaratna.] pp. 428. কলিকাতা ১৩১১ [*Calcutta*, 1905.] 8°. **14016. dd. 15.(3.)**

—— DHARMAPURĀṆA. বৃহদ্ধর্ম্মপুরাণম। [Bṛihaddharmapurāṇa. Sanskrit text, edited by Pañchānana Tarkaratna, with a Bengali translation by the latter, Rāmānuja Vidyārṇava, Jagannātha Vidyārṇava, and Dvārakeṣa Kāvyatīrtha. Second edition.] pp. i. ii. 372. কলিকাতা ১৩১৪ [*Calcutta*, 1908.] 8°. **14016. dd. 28.(1.)**

—— GARUḌAPURĀṆA. অষ্টাদশপুরাণম্। (গরুড়পুরাণম্।) [Garuḍapurāṇa. Sanskrit text, with a Bengali translation by Rasikamohana Chaṭṭopādhyāya.] 2 pts. কলিকাতা ১২৮৯ [*Calcutta*, 1883.] 4°. **14016. e. 39.**

The first of a projected edition and translation of the 18 Purāṇas. No more appears to have been published.

—— গরুড়পুরাণম্। [Garuḍapurāṇa. Sanskrit text, with a Bengali translation by Kṛishṇadāsa Ṣāstrī. Edited by Pañchānana Tarkaratna.] pp. i. v. 776. কলিকাতা ১৩১৪ [*Calcutta*, 1907.] 8°. **14016. dd. 26.**

—— KALKIPURĀṆA. সানুবাদ কল্কিপুরাণম্। [Kalkipurāṇa. Sanskrit text, with a Bengali translation by Kālīprasanna Vidyāratna.] pp. vi. 247. কলিকাতা ১৩০৬ [*Calcutta*, 1899.] 8°. **14016. d. 36.(2.)**

—— কল্কিপুরাণম্। . . . সংস্কৃত মূল ও বঙ্গানুবাদসমেত। [Kalkipurāṇa. Sanskrit text, with a Bengali translation by Tārākānta Kāvyatīrtha. Edited by Pañchānana Tarkaratna.] pp. i. ii. 122. কলিকাতা ১৩১৫ [*Calcutta*, 1908.] 8°. **14018. b. 22.(2.)**

—— KŪRMAPURĀṆA. কূর্ম্মপুরাণম্। সানুবাদম্। [Kūrmapurāṇa. Sanskrit text, with a Bengali translation. Edited by Pañchānana Tarkaratna.] pp. ii. 422. কলিকাতা ১৩১১ [*Calcutta*, 1904.] 8°. **14016. dd. 15.(1.)**

—— MĀRKAṆḌEYAPURĀṆA. শ্রীমার্কণ্ডেয় পুরাণম্। [Mārkaṇḍeyapurāṇa. Sanskrit text, with a Bengali translation by Rohiṇīnandana Sarkār.] Pts. 1-8. কলিকাতা ১২৯১-৯৩ [*Calcutta*, 1885-87.] 8°. **14016. c. 37.**

As far as adhy. 36.

—— শ্রীশ্রীচণ্ডী। [Chaṇḍī, also called Devīmāhātmya, or Durgāpāṭha. Sanskrit text, and commentary by Gopālachandra Chakravartī. Edited with a Bengali version by Kālīpada Vidyāratna.] pp. iv. xviii. 488. কলিকাতা [Calcutta, 1900.] 16°. **14028. a. 29.**

—— PADMAPURĀṆA. শ্রীশ্রীপদ্ম-পুরাণ। [Padmapurāṇa. An abridged metrical version by Tārāpada Vidyālaṅkāra.] pp. vi. 160. কলিকাতা ১৩১০ [Calcutta, 1904.] 8°. **14123. gg. 3.**

—— শ্রীশ্রীপদ্মপুরাণ। [Padmapurāṇa. Translated into verse by Vaṃṣīdāsa.] pp. viii. 380. ঢাকা [Dacca, 1904.] obl. 12°. **14123. gg. 2.**

—— পদ্মপুরাণম্। পাতালখণ্ডম্। অনুবাদ সমেতম। [Pātāla-khaṇḍa. Sanskrit text, with a Bengali translation by Jagannātha Vidyārṇava, Vīreṣanātha Kāvyatīrtha, and others. Edited by Pañchānana Tarkaratna.] pp. iii. 743. কলিকাতা ১৩১০ [Calcutta, 1903.] 8°. **14018. b. 20.**

—— সচিত্র রতিশাস্ত্র। [Ratiṣāstra. A treatise on the Ars Amoris, purporting to be compiled from the Padmapurāṇa. Sanskrit text, edited and translated into Bengali by Maṇīndralāla Ghosha. Third edition.] pp. 135. কলিকাতা ১৩০৮ [Calcutta, 1901.] 12°. **14053. b. 42.**

—— পদ্মপুরাণম্। স্বর্গ-খণ্ডম্। [Svarga-khaṇḍa. Sanskrit text, with Bengali translation by Kṛishṇadāsa Ṣāstrī. Edited by Pañchānana Tarkaratna.] pp. ii. ii. 274. কলিকাতা ১৩১৩ [Calcutta, 1906.] 8°. **14016. dd. 24.(1.)**

—— পদ্মপুরাণম্। উত্তরখণ্ডম্। [Uttara-khaṇḍa. Sanskrit text, with Bengali translation by Rāmanārāyaṇa Vidyāratna.] Pts. 1-12. মুর্শিদাবাদ ১৩০৫-০৯ [Murshidabad, 1899-1903.] 4°. **14016. e. 45.**

—— বৃন্দাবন প্রাপ্ত্যুপায়। [Vṛindāvana-prāptyupāya. The Sanskrit text of *adhyāyas* 99-108 of the Pātālakhaṇḍa, containing an account of Kṛishṇa's amours, and cognate legends, with a Bengali metrical paraphrase by Viṣvambhara Pāṇi.] pp. ii. 244. কলিকাতা ১৩০৬ [Calcutta, 1900.] 8°. **14076. c. 75.(1.)**

Different from the editions of the Sanskrit Pātālakhaṇḍa.

—— ṢIVAPURĀṆA. শিবপুরাণ। [Ṣivapurāṇa. Translated into Bengali by various Pandits. Edited by Pañchānana Tarkaratna.] pp. 6, 518. কলিকাতা ১৩১২ [Calcutta, 1905.] 8°. **14123. i. 16.**

PURĀṆAS (*continued*). শিবপুরাণম্। [Ṣivapurāṇa. Sanskrit text, with a Bengali translation. Edited by Pañchānana Tarkaratna.] pp. i. i. viii. 1325. কলিকাতা ১৩১৪ [Calcutta, 1907.] 8°. **14016. dd. 30.**

—— SKANDAPURĀṆA. *See* ṢIVAPRASANNA MAITREYA VIDYĀBHŪSHAṆA. কাশী দর্শন। [Kāṣī-darṣana. An account of the city of Benares, taken chiefly from the Kāṣī-khaṇḍa of the Skandapurāṇa.] [1897.] 8°. **14123. f. 55.**

—— কাশীখণ্ড। বঙ্গানুবাদ। [Kāṣī-khaṇḍa. A section of the Skandapurāṇa, translated into prose by Pañchānana Tarkaratna. Second edition.] pp. ii. 433. কলিকাতা ১৩০৮ [Calcutta, 1902.] 8°. **14123. ff. 9.**

—— উৎকলখণ্ডম্। [Utkala-khaṇḍa. The Sanskrit text of a section of the Skandapurāṇa treating of the legends of Orissa. Edited with a Bengali translation by Pañchānana Tarkaratna.] pp. ii. ii. 305. কলিকাতা ১৩০৯ [Calcutta, 1902.] 8°. **14016. dd. 5.**

—— সানুবাদ উৎকলখণ্ড। [Utkala-khaṇḍa. Sanskrit text, edited with a Bengali translation by Kālīprasanna Vidyāratna.] pp. iv. 556. কলিকাতা ১৩১১ [Calcutta, 1905.] 8°. **14016. dd. 15.(2.)**

—— VĀMANAPURĀṆA. বামনপুরাণং। [Vāmanapurāṇa. Sanskrit text, edited with a Bengali prose translation by Ṭhākuradāsa Chūḍāmaṇi.] pp. iv. 725. কলিকাতা ১২৯৩ [Calcutta, 1886.] 8°. **14018. b. 16.**

—— বামনপুরাণম্। [Vāmanapurāṇa. Sanskrit text, with a Bengali translation by Tārākānta Kāvyatīrtha. Edited by Pañchānana Tarkaratna.] pp. i. ii. 439. কলিকাতা ১৩১৪ [Calcutta, 1908.] 8°. **14016. dd. 28.(2.)**

—— VARĀHAPURĀṆA. বরাহ পুরাণম্। [Varāhapurāṇa. Sanskrit text, with a Bengali translation by Tārākānta Kāvyatīrtha. Edited by Pañchānana Tarkaratna.] pp. ii. iv. 724. কলিকাতা ১৩১৩ [Calcutta, 1906.] 8°. **14016. dd. 23.**

—— VISHṆUPURĀṆA. বিষ্ণুপুরাণম্। [Vishṇupurāṇa. Sanskrit text, with a Bengali translation. Edited by Pañchānana Tarkaratna.] pp. i. iv. 448. কলিকাতা ১৩১৪ [*Calcutta*, 1907.] 8°. **14016. dd. 24.(2.)**

PŪRṆACHANDRA CHAKRAVARTĪ. গানবাজনা। [Gān-bājnā. An elementary treatise on music, both vocal and instrumental.] pp. xii. 189. কলিকাতা ১২৯৭ [*Calcutta*, 1890.] 12°. **14125. d. 16.**

PŪRṆACHANDRA DATTA. *See* KSHETRAMOHANA VANDYOPĀDHYĀYA. The Translator's Friend, or a Dictionary of Law Terms . . . Revised by Purna Chandra Dutta. 1898. 8°. **14125. a. 27.**

—— পারিবারিক ইতিহাস। [Pārivārika itihāsa. A short sketch of the family history of the author, during the last 100 years.] pp. 26. *Calcutta*, [1894.] 12°. **14127. aa. 2.(4.)**

PŪRṆACHANDRA DE, *Kāvyaratna Udbhaṭasāgara. See* PĀṆḌAVAGĪTĀ. পাণ্ডব-গীতা বা প্রপন্ন-গীতা। [Pāṇḍavagītā. Edited, with a Bengali metrical version, by Pūrṇachandra De.] [1904.] 12°. **14033. a. 29.(2.)**

—— উদ্ভট-শ্লোক-মালা। [Udbhaṭa-ṣlokamālā. An anthology of Sanskrit verses, classified according to subject. Compiled, with Bengali metrical rendering and notes, by Pūrṇachandra De.] pp. xvi. 239. কলিকাতা ১৯০৪ [*Calcutta*, 1904.] 8°. **14072. ccc. 42.**

PŪRṆACHANDRA GUPTA. Bangali bau, or The instructive lessons on the career of life of the native females . . . বাঙ্গালী বউ। pp. 60. *Calcutta*, 1885. 12°. **14125. e. 17.(2.)**

—— ছায়া। [Chhāyā. A tale, in two parts, giving a picture of domestic life in a Hindu joint-family.] pp. viii. 250, 207. কলিকাতা ১২৯৬ [*Calcutta*, 1890.] 12°. **14127. d. 37.**

PŪRṆACHANDRA MUKHOPĀDHYĀYA. *See* BHĀRATACHANDRA RĀYA. রায় গুণাকর ভারতচন্দ্রের গ্রন্থাবলী। [Bhāratachandrer granthāvalī. Edited, with a life of the poet, by Pūrṇachandra Mukhopādhyāya.] [1904.] 8°. **14129. e. 29.**

PŪRṆACHANDRA SARKĀR. হাল আমলের সভ্যতা! . . . [Hāl āmaler sabhyatā], or Civilization of the day in Bengal. pp. 46. ঢাকা ১৮৮৫ [*Dacca*, 1885.] 12°. **14125. e. 17.(3.)**

PŪRṆACHANDRA VASU. সাহিত্য-চিন্তা। [Sāhitya-chintā. Essays, illustrating the characteristic features of ancient Hindu literature.] pp. iv. v. ii. 188. কলিকাতা ১৩০৩ [*Calcutta*, 1896.] 12°. **14125. e. 27.(2.)**

PŪRṆACHANDRA VEDĀNTACHUÑCHU SĀṄKHYABHŪSHAṆA. *See* ĪṢVARA KṚISHṆA. সাংখ্যতত্ত্ব-কৌমুদী। [Sāṅkhyatattvakaumudī. The Sanskrit text of the Sāṅkhyakārikā and commentary. Edited, with Sanskrit grammatical explanations, and Bengali translations and notes, by Pūrṇachandra.] [1901.] 8°. **14048. dd. 34.(1.)**

—— *See* PATAÑJALI. পাতঞ্জলদর্শন। [Pātañjala-darṣana. Edited, with a Bengali translation of the Sanskrit *bhāshya*, and explanations of the same, by Pūrṇachandra.] [1898.] 8°. **14048. cc. 23.**

PŪRṆĀNANDA. *See* UPANISHADS. কৈবল্যোপনিষৎ। [Kaivalya-upanishad. With a prose translation by Pūrṇānanda.] [1870?] 12°. **14010. b. 8.(1.)**

PŪRṆĀNANDA GOSVĀMĪ, *Disciple of Brahmānanda.* ষট্চক্র-নিরূপণং। [Shaṭchakra-nirūpaṇa. A Yogic tract of 57 stanzas on the action of the Ṣakti, or cosmic energy, in the six centres of the microcosm. Sanskrit text and commentary, with a Bengali translation.] *See* KĀLĪPRASANNA VIDYĀRATNA BHAṬṬĀCHĀRYA. যোগাঙ্কুর। [Yogāṅkura.] pp. 1-84. [1894.] 12°. **14048. b. 28.(2.)**

—— ষট্চক্র-নিরূপণম্। [Shaṭchakra-nirūpaṇa. Sanskrit text, with a different Bengali translation.] *See* PRASANNAKUMĀRA BHAṬṬĀCHĀRYA. যোগাম্বুধি। [Yogāmbudhi.] [1896.] 32°. **14048. a. 19.**

PURUSHOTTAMA ĀCHĀRYA, called SVARŪPA-DĀMODARA. [*Life.*] *See* RASIKAMOHANA CHAKRAVARTĪ. শ্রীস্বরূপদামোদর। [Svarūpa-Dāmodara.] [1904, *etc.*] 12°. **14127. aa. 30.**

PURUSHOTTAMA DEVA, *Grammarian.* একাক্ষর-কোষ। [Ekāksharakosha. A Sanskrit vocabulary of synonyms in verse. With a Bengali translation.] *See* GOPĪRAMAṆA TARKARATNA. কোষচন্দ্রিকা। [Koshachandrikā.] pp. 25-37. [1893.] 12°. **14090. b. 44.(1.)**

PURUSHOTTAMA MIṢRA, called PREMADĀSA. শ্রী-চৈতন্য চন্দ্রোদয় নাটক। [Chaitanya-chandrodaya nāṭaka. The life of Chaitanya in verse, interspersed with Sanskrit ṣlokas.] pp. viii. 252. কলিকাতা ১২৯২ [Calcutta, 1886.] 8°. **14123. i. 9.**

PYĀRĪCHĀND MITRA, called ṬEKCHĀND ṬHĀKUR. আলালের ঘরের দুলাল। [Ālāler gharer dulāl. A tale of Hindu domestic life. Revised edition.] pp. iii. i. v. 212. কলিকাতা ১৩১০ [Calcutta, 1904.] 12°. **14131. aa. 1.(3.)**

—— The Spoilt Boy. By Tekchand Thakur. [A translation of Ālāler gharer dulāl, by Narendranātha Mitra, with the aid of M. S. Knight.] (Journal of the National Indian Association, nos. 139-148.) *London*, 1882-83. 8°. **P.P. 1423. ld.**

—— The Spoilt Child: a tale of Hindu domestic life, by Peary Chand Mitter (Tek Chand Thakur). Translated by G. D. Oswell. pp. 14, 234. *Calcutta*, 1893. 8°. **14127. c. 53.**

—— লুপ্তরত্নোদ্ধার। [Lupta-ratnoddhāra.] . . . Gems recovered from the deep, or The works in Bengali of Peary Chand Mittra. কলিকাতা ১২৯৯ [Calcutta, 1892.] 8°. **14127. g. 9.**

Each work has a separate title-page and pagination.

—— রামারঞ্জিকা ও যাত্রা সমালোচনা। [Rāmārañjikā. Dialogues on the moral and intellectual training of Hindu women. Another edition. Also Yātrā-samālochanā, a review of the native drama, by Sañjīvachandra Chaṭṭopādhyāya.] pp. 128. কলিকাতা ১৩১৪ [Calcutta, 1907.] 12°. **14125. e. 49.**

PYĀRĪMOHANA DĀSA. কলিকাতা-পথ-প্রদর্শক ও ডাইরেক্টরী পঞ্জিকা সহ। [Kalikātā-pathapradarṣaka. Calcutta Street guide and Directory.] pp. 22, 116, 4, 438. *Calcutta*, [1893.] 12°. **14133. h. 12.**

PYĀRĪMOHANA MAJUMDĀR. বার্‌মিজ্ শিক্ষা। [Bārmij-ṣikshā. A Burmese vocabulary and primer for Bengalis.] Pt. i. pp. 140. কলিকাতা ১৩১৪ [Calcutta, 1907.] 12°. **14131. e. 33.(4.)**

PYĀRĪṢAṄKARA DĀSA GUPTA. মহারাণা প্রতাপ সিংহ। [Mahārāṇā Pratāpa Siṃha. A poem narrating the exploits of Pratāpa Siṃha of Chitor.] pp. 56. কলিকাতা ১৩০৬ [Calcutta, 1900.] 12°. **14129. a. 38.(5.)**

—— রত্নাকর। [Ratnākara. The legendary story of Ratnākara, the robber, who eventually became the sage Vālmiki, and author of the Sanskrit Rāmāyaṇa.] pp. 46. কলিকাতা ১৩১৫ [Calcutta, 1908.] 12°. **14128. a. 29.**

Forms pt. 1 of a series of the author's works, styled Āmār granthāvalī.

RĀDHĀGOVINDA KARA. *See* SCHAEFFER (O.). স্ত্রীরোগের চিত্রাবলী ও সংক্ষিপ্ত-তত্ত্ব। [Strīroger chitrāvalī.] . . . Authorized translation by Radha Gobinda Kar. [1907.] 12°. **14125. b. 25.**

RĀDHĀGOVINDA PĀLA, *of Midnapore.* কুরুকলঙ্ক-কাব্য। [Kurukalaṅka. A poem dealing with the Mahābhārata story of the defeat of the Kauravas.] pp. ii. 207. *Calcutta*, 1901. 12°. **14129. bb. 10.**

RĀDHĀKĀNTA DEVA, *Raja.* An apology for the present system of Hindoo worship. Written in the Bengali language [by Rādhākānta Deva], *etc.* 1817. 8°. *See* HINDU WORSHIP. **14123. f. 51.**

RĀDHĀKṚISHṆA DĀSA VAIRĀGĪ. গোসানী-মঙ্গল। [Gosānīmaṅgala. A poem narrating the exploits of Kānteṣvara, an ancient king of Cooch Behar.] pp. ii. 110. কলিকাতা ১৩০৬ [Calcutta, 1899.] 12°. **14129. a. 38.(2.)**

RĀDHĀMĀDHAVA GHOSHA. বৃহৎ সারাবলি। [Bṛihat sārāvali. A metrical version of the substance of the Purāṇas from a Vaishṇava point of view.] Pts. 1-29. বাঁকুড়া ১২৯৮-১৩০১ [Bankura, 1891-99.] 8°. **14129. e. 18.**

RĀDHĀMATI. রাধামতি উপন্যাস। [Rādhāmati. A tale illustrating some of the temptations and vices of modern Bengali society.] pp. iv. 296, ii. *Calcutta*, [1889.] 12°. **14127. c. 38.**

RĀDHĀMOHANA DEVA VARMĀ. কক্-বরক্-মা। (Kok-barak-ma. The Grammar of Tripura Language. By Radha Mohan Deo Barman Thakur.) pp. iv. 42. কুমিল্লা ১৩০১ [Comilla, 1900.] 12°. **14131. e. 33.**

RĀDHĀMOHANA TARKĀLAṄKĀRA. সত্যনারায়ণ ব্রত কথা। [Satyanārāyaṇa-vratakathā. A poem on the worship of the god Satyanārāyaṇa.] pp. 21. কলিকাতা ১৮১৯ [Calcutta, 1898.] 12°. **14129. a. 46.(3.)**

RĀDHĀNĀTHA MITRA. *See* MUBĀRAK ʻALĪ, *Saiyid.* অপূর্ব্ব কাহিনী। [Apūrva kāhinī. Translated from the Hindustani by Rādhānātha Mitra.] 1898. 12°. **14127. cc. 21.(2.)**

RĀDHĀNĀTHA MITRA (*continued*). আকাশ-কুসুম। ভারত স্বাধীন। [Ākāṣakusuma. A dramatic composition in verse, ridiculing the idea of the emancipation of India from British rule.] pp. 16, xii. কলিকাতা [*Calcutta*, 1888.] 32°. **14131. a.**

RĀDHĀNĀTHA RĀYA, *Inspector of Schools*. *See* KĀLIDĀSA. কালিদাস-সূক্তয়:। Kalidas's Apothegms [*sic*]. [Selected, with English and Bengali paraphrases], by Rai Radhanath, *etc.* [1903.] 8°. **14085. b. 23.(2.)**

—— *See* NAGENDRABĀLĀ SARASVATĪ. অমিয়গাথা। [Amiyagāthā. Edited, with a life of the authoress, by Rādhānātha Rāya.] [1902.] 12°. **14129. a. 34.**

RĀDHĀPRASĀDA RĀYA. বিজ্ঞান-নীতি-প্রসূন। [Vijñāna-nītiprasūna. Essays on moral and social topics, interspersed with anecdotes.] 3 pts. কলিকাতা ১২৯৬ [*Calcutta*, 1889-]1891. 8°. **14125. f. 19.**

RĀDHĀRAMAṆA KARA. সরোজা। [Sarojā. A drama of social life in Bengal. Second edition.] pp. 78. *Calcutta*, 1889. 12°. **14131. a. 29.**

RĀDHĀSVĀMĪ. রাধাস্বামীমতসন্দেশ। [Rādhāsvāmīmatasandeṣa. An exposition of the tenets of the Rādhāsvāmī cult of Vedantism.] pp. 75. হাওড়া ১৮৯৫ [*Howrah*, 1895.] 8°. **14123. f. 52.**

RĀDHĀVINODA HĀLDĀR. পাসকরা মাগ। [Pāskarā māg, or The graduate wife. A farce, directed against the introduction of English manners, and a high class English education given to Bengali ladies.] pp. 42. *Calcutta*, 1888. 12°. **14131. a. 28.(1.)**

RĀDHEṢACHANDRA DĀSA. *See* VṚINDĀVANA DĀSA. শ্রীশ্রীভজননির্ণয় গ্রন্থ। [Bhajananirṇaya. Edited by Rādheṣachandra.] [1901.] 12°. **14129. bb. 12.**

RĀDHIKĀ. রাধিকার মানভঙ্গ। [Rādhikār mānabhaṅga. An old Bengali anonymous poem on the amours of Rādhā and Krishṇa.] pp. 26. ১৩০৮ [1901.] *See* PERIODICAL PUBLICATIONS.—*Calcutta*. প্রাচীন বাঙ্গালা গ্রন্থাবলী। [Prāchīna Bāṅgālā granthāvalī.] nos. 6-8. [1900, *etc.*] 8°. **14133. ff. 2.**

RĀDHIKĀNĀTHA GOSVĀMĪ, *of Brindaban*. *See* NAROTTAMA DĀSA. শ্রীশ্রীপ্রেমভক্তিচন্দ্রিকা। [Prema-bhakti-chandrikā. With explanatory notes by Rādhikānātha Gosvāmī.] [1896.] 12°. **14123. e. 20.(1.)**

—— *See* VIṢVANĀTHA CHAKRAVARTĪ, *Vaishṇava poet*. শ্রীকৃষ্ণভাবনামৃত মহাকাব্য। [Krishṇa-bhāvanāmṛita. A prose translation of a poem by Viṣvanātha, with a brief account of the poet, and a list of his works. By Rādhikānātha Gosvāmī.] [1902.] 8°. **14123. ff. 10.(2.)**

RĀDHIKĀNĀTHA VANDYOPĀDHYĀYA. দুর্ভিক্ষ ও দরিদ্রতা। [Durbhiksha o daridratā. Remedies for the prevention of famine and poverty in Bengal.] pp. ii. 109. ১৮১৮ *Calcutta*, [1896.] 8°. **14125. ee. 30.**

RĀDHIKĀRAMAṆA CHAṬṬOPĀDHYĀYA. Encyclopædia of India in Bengali. Edited by Radhika Raman Chatterji. ভারত-দর্পণ। [Bhārata-darpaṇa.] *Calcutta*, 1895, *etc.* 8°. **14133. f. 13.**

In progress.

RĀGHAVĀNANDA, *Astronomer*. দিনচন্দ্রিকামতে পঞ্চাঙ্গসাধন। অর্থাৎ পঞ্জিকাগণনা। [Pañchāṅgasādhana, or Pañjikāgaṇanā. A treatise on the calculation of the calendar, comprising Rāghavānanda's Dinachandrikā, with a Bengali version, and notes.] pp. 22. [1890, *etc.*] *See* PERIODICAL PUBLICATIONS.—*Calcutta*. অরুণোদয়। [Aruṇodaya.] Pt. i., no. 3. [1890, *etc.*] 4°. **14133. g. 16.**

RĀGHAVA RĀMA, *of Mitara*. [*Life.*] *See* VIṢVADEVA ĀCHĀRYA. রাঘব দীপিকা। [Rāghava-dīpikā.] [1892.] 8°. **14028. d. 46.(2.)**

RAGHUNANDANA BHAṬṬĀCHĀRYA, *Son of Harihara*. স্মৃতিশাস্ত্রম্। আহ্নিকতত্ত্বম্। [Āhnikatattva. Part 3 of the Smṛititattva, treating of the daily rituals. Accompanied by the commentary of Madhusūdana Smṛitiratna, and followed by a Bengali translation. Edited by Chaṇḍīcharaṇa Smṛitibhūshaṇa.] pp. i. 297, 32. কলিকাতা [*Calcutta*, 1908.] 8°. **14033. bbb. 45.**

—— সটীক-সানুবাদ-উদ্বাহতত্ত্বং। [Udvāhatattva. A treatise on Hindu marriages, being the Sanskrit text of the 9th Tattva of the Smṛititattva, with a Sanskrit commentary by Kāṣīrāma Vāchaspati. Edited, with a Bengali translation of the text, by Nīlakamala Vidyānidhi.] pp. ii. 140. কলিকাতা ১৩০২ [*Calcutta*, 1896.] 8°. **14033. bb. 42.**

RAGHUNANDANA GOSVĀMĪ. শ্রীশ্রীমদ্রামরসায়ন। [Rāmarasāyana. A metrical version of the Rāmāyaṇa, embodying Vaishṇava teachings, especially on the subject of *bhakti.*] pp. viii. 959. কলিকাতা ১২৯৬ [*Calcutta*, 1889.] 8°. **14127. e. 37.**

—— শ্রীরামরসায়ন। [Rāmarasāyana. Another edition.] pp. iii. iii. 939. কলিকাতা ১৩০৮ [*Calcutta*, 1902.] 8°. **14129. cc. 3.**

RAGHUNĀTHA DĀSA GOSVĀMĪ, *Son of Govardhana Dāsa.* [*Life.*] *See* ACHYUTACHARAṆA CHAUDHURĪ. শ্রীমৎ রঘুনাথদাস গোস্বামীর জীবনচরিত। [Raghunātha Dāsa Gosvāmīr jīvana-charita.] [1894.] 12°. **14127. aa. 2.(3.)**

—— [*Life.*] *See* PRĀṆAKṚISHṆA DATTA. বৈরাগী রঘুনাথ দাস। [Vairāgī Raghunātha Dāsa.] 1903. 12°. **14127. aa. 21.(4.)**

—— [*Life.*] *See* RASIKAMOHANA CHAKRAVARTĪ. শ্রীমৎ দাসগোস্বামী। [Srīmat Dāsa Gosvāmī.] [1906.] 12°. **14127. aa. 16.(2.)**

—— *See* RŪPA GOSVĀMĪ. সটীক . . . শ্রীস্তবপুষ্পাঞ্জলিঃ। [Stavapushpāñjali. A series of Vaishṇava lyrics compiled from the Stavamālā of Rūpa Gosvāmī, and Stavāvali of Raghunātha Dāsa.] [1902.] 8°. **14072. ccc. 3A.**

RAGHUNĀTHA SĀRVABHAUMA. বিশ্ববিজ্ঞানং। পৌরাণিক ব্রহ্মাণ্ড বিবরণং গদ্যানুবাদ সহিতং। [Visvavijñāna. A Sanskrit treatise on cosmogony, according to the Purāṇas, with a Bengali translation.] Pt. i. pp. 32, 28. ময়মনসিংহ ১৮০১ [*Mymensingh*, 1880.] 8°. **14053. cc. 30.**

RAHASYA-BHĀṆḌĀRA. রহস্য-ভাণ্ডার [Rahasya-bhāṇḍāra. A collection of amusing anecdotes, containing specimens of Bengali wit and humour. Second edition.] pp. 152. কলিকাতা ১২৯৭ [*Calcutta*, 1891.] 12°. **14127. d. 40.(2.)**

RAINEY (J. RUDD). *See* MARTIN (*Sir* T.). The life of His Royal Highness, the Prince Consort . . . condensed and translated into Bengali . . . by J. R. Rainey. 1892. 8°. **14127. b. 46.**

RĀJAKṚISHṆA MUKHOPĀDHYĀYA. নানা প্রবন্ধ। [Nānā prabandha. Miscellaneous essays reprinted from the Vaṅgadarṣana.] pp. 206. *Calcutta*, 1885. 8°. **14133. h. 11.(2.)**

RĀJAKṚISHṆA RĀYA, *Dramatist.* চন্দ্রহাস। [Chandrahāsa. A Pauranic tale, dramatized in four acts.] pp. 115. কলিকাতা ১২৯৫ [*Calcutta*, 1888.] 12°. **14131. a.**

—— হীরে মলিনী। . . . Heera malini. A comic opera. pp. 29. কলিকাতা ১২৯৭ [*Calcutta*, 1891.] 12°. **14131. a. 32.(2.)**

—— কাণা কড়ি। [Kāṇā kaṛi. A farce, exposing the conceited airs of worthless Bengali pleaders, doctors, and clerks.] pp. 22. কলিকাতা ১২৯৫ [*Calcutta*, 1888.] 12°. **14131. a. 28.(2.)**

—— লক্ষহীরা। [Lakshahīrā. The story of the prostitute Lakshahīrā, and of her becoming a devotee.] pp. 90. কলিকাতা ১২৯৭ [*Calcutta*, 1891.] 12°. **14131. a. 32.(3.)**

—— নবমেধ যজ্ঞ। [Navamedha-yajña. A mythological drama.] pp. 111. কলিকাতা ১২৯৮ [*Calcutta*, 1891.] 12°. **14131. a. 33.(2.)**

RĀJAKṚISHṆA RĀYA, *Kavivara.* *See* MAHĀBHĀRATA. মহাভারত। [Mahābhārata. Translated into verse by Rājakṛishṇa Rāya.] [1901.] 4°. **14129. g. 10.**

RĀJAKUMĀRA SENA GUPTA KAVIRATNA. *See* RĀJAVALLABHA. রাজবল্লভীয় দ্রব্যগুণঃ। [Dravyaguṇa. Edited, with a Bengali translation, by Rājakumāra Sena Gupta.] [1891.] 8°. **14043. c. 42.(1.)**

RĀJAMĀLĀ. *See* LONG (J.). Analysis of the Bengali poem Ráj Málá, or Chronicles of Tripura. 1850. 8°. **2098. a.**

RĀJANĀRĀYAṆA DĀSA. লিখন-পত্র-দলিল-শিক্ষা। [Likhana-patra dalil-ṣikshā. A Bengali Primer, with a letter-writer and specimens of zamindari documents and accounts. Fifth edition.] pp. 134. *Dacca*, ১৩১৪ [1907.] 12°. **14131. f. 32.(3.)**

—— [Sixth edition.] pp. 134. *Dacca*, ১৩১৪ [1907.] 12°. **14131. f. 35.**

—— [Seventh edition.] pp. 152. *Dacca*, ১৩১৪ [1907.] 12°. **14131. f. 36.**

RĀJANĀRĀYAṆA VASU. Brahmo Catechism. By Babu Raj Narain Bose. Translated into English [apparently from the Bengali] by Babu Eshan Chunder Bose. pp. 18. *Allahabad*, 1890. 16°. **14123. c.**

RĀJANĀRĀYAṆA VASU (*continued*). ধর্ম্মতত্ত্বদীপিকা। [Dharmatattva-dīpikā. Brahmist discourses in 2 parts, entitled Dharmatattvaviveka, and Dharmatattva-vyākhyāna.] কলিকাতা ১৮৬৬ [*Calcutta*, 1866.] 8°. **14123. d. 19.(1.)**

—— সেকাল আর একাল। [Se-kāl ār e-kāl. An essay on some of the evil effects of Western civilization on Hindu society.] pp. ii. 82. কলিকাতা ১৭৯৬ [*Calcutta*, 1874.] 8°. **14125. ee. 27.(1.)**

RĀJANĀTHA GUHA. স্তবকাবলী [Stavakāvalī. A poem in honour of the Jubilee reign of Queen Victoria.] pp. 24. কোচবিহার ১২৯৩ [*Cooch Behar*, 1886.] 8°. **14129. c. 41.**

RAJANĪCHANDRA CHAKRAVARTĪ, *Sub-Inspector of Police.* A Pocket book of Descriptive Roll Writers . . . By Rajani Chandra Chakraverty. pp. iv. 24. *Beng.* and *Engl.* *Calcutta*, [1898.] 16°. **14125. bb. 28.**

RAJANĪKĀNTA BHAṬṬĀCHĀRYA. জানকীবল্লভ চরিত। [Jānakīvallabha-charita. The life of Jānakīvallabha Sena, a leading zamindar of the Rangpur district.] pp. vii. 126. কলিকাতা ১২৯৭ [*Calcutta*, 1891.] 8°. **14127. b. 38.(2.)**

RAJANĪKĀNTA CHAKRAVARTĪ. অদ্ভুতাচার্য্যের রামায়ণ। [Adbhutāchāryer Rāmāyaṇa. A paper on the Rāmāyaṇa of Adbhutāchārya.] ১৩১৩ [1907.] *See* ACADEMIES, *etc.*—Calcutta.—*Bengal Academy of Literature.* সাহিত্য-পরিষৎ-পত্রিকা। [Sāhitya-parishat-patrikā.] Vol. xiii., no. 1. [1894, *etc.*] 8°. **14133. f. 18.**

RAJANĪKĀNTA GUPTA. *See* ACADEMIES, *etc.*—Calcutta.—*Bengal Academy of Literature.* সাহিত্য-পরিষৎ-পত্রিকা। [Sāhitya-parishat-patrikā. Vols. i.-iii., no. 1. Edited by Rajanīkānta Gupta.] [1894, *etc.*] 8°. **14133. f. 18.**

—— ঐতিহাসিক পাঠ। [Aitihāsika pāṭha. Studies in history, showing the origin and gradual development of the Hindu religion in India. Second edition.] pp. iv. 168. কলিকাতা ১২৯১ [*Calcutta*, 1885.] 12°. **14127. a. 28.**

—— আমাদের জাতীয় ভাব। [Āmāder jātīya bhāva, or Our national feeling. An essay.] pp. 26. কলিকাতা ১২৯৮ [*Calcutta*, 1891.] 12°. **14125. e. 26.(1.)**

RAJANĪKĀNTA GUPTA (*continued*). আমাদের বিশ্ববিদ্যালয়। [Āmāder viṣvavidyālaya. A pamphlet urging the necessity of a closer study of vernacular languages and literature by students of the Universities.] pp. 32. *Calcutta*, [1894.] 8°. **14131. d. 31.(2.)**

—— আর্য্যকীর্ত্তি। [Āryakīrti. Sketches of the lives of great and patriotic Hindu men and women. Fourth edition.] pp. ii. 296. কলিকাতা ১৮৮৬ [*Calcutta*, 1886] 12°. **14127. a. 25.**

—— ভারতপ্রসঙ্গ। [Bhārata-prasaṅga. Historical essays on the occupation of Bengal by the English.] pp. 247. কলিকাতা ১২৯৪ [*Calcutta*, 1888.] 12°. **14127. a. 34.**

—— জয়দেব চরিত। [Jayadeva-charita. An account of the life and writings of Jayadeva. Second edition.] pp. 61. কলিকাতা ১২৯৬ [*Calcutta*, 1889.] 12°. **14131. d. 21.(2.)**

—— প্রতিভা। [Pratibhā. A review of the works of five eminent Bengali authors, viz.—Īṣvarachandra Vidyāsāgara, Akshayakumāra Datta, Bhūdeva Mukhopādhyāya, Michael Madhusūdana Datta, and Baṅkimchandra Chaṭṭopādhyāya.] pp. ii. 210. কলিকাতা ১৩০৩ [*Calcutta*, 1896.] 12°. **14131. d. 35.**

—— সিপাহি যুদ্ধের ইতিহাস। [Sipāhī yuddher itihāsa. A history of the Indian Mutiny, compiled chiefly from English sources.] 5 pts. কলিকাতা ১৮৮৬-১৩০৭ [*Calcutta*, 1886-1902.] 8°. **14127. bb. 8.**

Pts. 1 and 2 are of the second edition.

RAJANĪKĀNTA MUKHOPĀDHYĀYA. Idiomatic phrases . . . Containing upwards of four thousands of phrases in English and Bengali. By Rajanikanta Mukerji. Second edition . . . enlarged and improved. pp. 169. *Calcutta*, 1889. 12°. **14131. g. 25.**

RAJANĪKĀNTA VASU. Grammar and composition. A help for beginners, compiled from many English grammars, with copious exercises. By R. K. Basu. pp. 84. *Calcutta*, 1885. 12°. **14131. e. 14.(2.)**

The author's name has been supplied in manuscript.

RAJANĪKĀNTA VIDYĀVINODA. বঙ্গীয়-শব্দসিন্ধু। [Vaṅgīya ṣabdasindhu. A dictionary of Bengali,

Urdu, Hindi, and other words in ordinary colloquial use.] pp. iii. 474. *Calcutta*, ১৯০৭ [1907.] 12°. **14133. b. 21.**

RAJANĪNĀTHA DATTA. *See* AKSHAYAKUMĀRA DATTA. Sea voyage and commerce of the ancient Hindus. [Edited, with notes, by Rajanīnātha Datta.] 1901. 12°. **14125. e. 42.**

RĀJAŚEKHARA, *Son of Durduka.* কর্পূর-মঞ্জরী। [Karpūramañjarī. A drama, translated from the Sanskrit by Jyotirindranātha Ṭhākura.] pp. 64. কলিকাতা ১৩১১ [*Calcutta*, 1904.] 12°. **14131. aa. 3.(3.)**

—— বিদ্ধ-শালভঞ্জিকা। [Viddhaśālabhañjikā. A drama, translated from the Sanskrit by Jyotirindranātha Ṭhākura.] pp. 72. কলিকাতা ১৩১০ [*Calcutta*, 1903.] 12°. **14131. aa. 3.(2.)**

RĀJA SIṂHA, *Mahārāja.* রাগ-মালা ও সংক্ষিপ্ত মনসা পাঁচালী। [Rāgamālā and Manasā-pāṇchālī. Two poetical works, the former on the personification of the various *rāgas* and *rāginīs*, or modes in Hindu music; the latter on the legendary story of the goddess Manasā. Edited by Kamalakṛishṇa Siṃha, the great-grandson of the author.] pp. vi. 30, 12. কলিকাতা ১২৯৭ [*Calcutta*, 1891.] 12°. **14129. a. 39.(1.)**

RĀJAVALLABHA. রাজবল্লভীয় দ্রব্যগুণঃ। [Rājavallabhīya-dravyaguṇa, also called Dravyaguṇa, Rājavallabha-nighaṇṭu or Rājavallabha. A Sanskrit metrical treatise on Materia Medica, in six *parichchhedas*, ascribed to a legendary Rājavallabha, and redacted by Nārāyaṇadāsa Kavirāja. Edited, with a Bengali translation, by Rājakumāra Sena Gupta Kaviratna.] pp. ii. 160. কলিকাতা ১২৯৮ [*Calcutta*, 1891.] 8°. **14043. c. 42.(1.)**

—— রাজবল্লভীয় দ্রব্যগুণঃ। [Rājavallabhīya-dravyaguṇa. Edited, with a Bengali translation, by Rājendranātha Sena Kaviratna.] pp. xxii. 192. কলিকাতা ১৯৫৮ [*Calcutta*, 1901.] 12°. **14043. b. 14.(3.)**

RĀJAVALLABHA GOSVĀMĪ. শ্রীমুরলী-বিলাস। [Muralī-vilāsa. An old Vaishṇava poem, containing an account of the author's family history. Edited, with notes, and translations of Sanskrit *ślokas*, by Nīlakānta Gosvāmī and Vinodavihārī Gosvāmī.] pp. ix. 436, 7, 12. কলিকাতা ১৩০১ [*Calcutta*, 1894.] 12°. **14129. b. 41.**

RĀJENDRACHANDRA ŚĀSTRĪ. *See* ACADEMIES, *etc.*—Calcutta.—*Bengal Academy of Literature.* সাহিত্য-পরিষৎ-পত্রিকা। [Sāhitya-parishat-patrikā. Vol. iii., nos. 2 and 3. Edited by Rājendrachandra Śāstrī.] 1894, *etc.* 8°. **14133. f. 18.**

RĀJENDRALĀLA GHOSHA. সইএর পাঁচালী। [Saier pāṇchālī. Songs on the custom of keeping *sais*, or female friends, to ward off dangers of snake-bites, cholera and smallpox.] pp. 11. [*Calcutta*, 1897.] 12°. **14129. a. 51.(2.)**

RĀJENDRALĀLA MITRA. *See* PERIODICAL PUBLICATIONS.—*Calcutta.* রহস্য-সন্দর্ভ। Rahasya sandarbha. [Edited by Rājendralāla Mitra.] 1868. Fol. **14133. g. 15.(3.)**

—— পাপীর পাগলামী বা মনের কথা। [Pāpīr pāglāmī, or The ravings of a sinner. Thoughts on the frailty of life, and the sinfulness of human nature.] pp. viii. 26. কলিকাতা ১২৯৪ [*Calcutta*, 1887.] 12°. **14125. e. 21.(3.)**

RĀJENDRALĀLA SIṂHA. নির্ম্মলা। [Nirmalā. A tale of Hindu domestic life.] pp. 57. কলিকাতা ১৮১৭ [*Calcutta*, 1895.] 12°. **14127. ee. 4.(3.)**

RĀJENDRALĀLA SŪRA. A Medical Dictionary with Latin-Bengali and English. By Dr. Rajendra Lal Sur. pp. 120. *Calcutta*, 1897. 12°. **14125. b. 14.**

—— বৈশ্য জাতিমালা। Vaisya jatiyamala. [A tract on the Vaiśya caste.] By Dr. Rajendra Lal Sur. pp. 32. *Beng.* and *Eng.* *Calcutta*, 1893. 12°. **14125. e. 30.(1.)**

RĀJENDRANĀRĀYAṆA KAVIRATNA. বঙ্গ-ভাষা আশ্রয়ভিক্ষা। [Vaṅga-bhāshā āśrayabhikshā. An article advocating a closer study by Bengalis of the language and literature of their country. Reprinted from the Śikshā-parichara.] pp. 10. কলিকাতা [*Calcutta*, 1891.] 8°. **14125. ee. 26.(2.)**

RĀJENDRANĀTHA SENA KAVIRATNA. *See* RĀJAVALLABHA. রাজবল্লভীয় দ্রব্যগুণঃ। [Rājavallabhīya-dravyaguṇa. Edited, with a Bengali translation, by Rājendranātha.] [1901.] 12°. **14043. b. 14.(3.)**

RĀJEŚVARA GUPTA. বর্ণ-বিন্যাস। [Varṇa-vinyāsa. Etymological rules of grammar. Second edition.] pp. 51. ঢাকা ১৮৮৭ [*Dacca*, 1887.] 12°. **14131. e. 14.(3.)**

RĀJYESVARA GOSVĀMĪ. বর্ণ-দর্পণ। [Varṇa-darpaṇa. A short sketch of Hindu castes, chiefly of the Yogī Brahmans of Sylhet.] 4 pts. ব্রাহ্মণবাড়িয়া ১৩০০ [*Brahmanbaria*, 1894.] 12°.
14125. e. 31.(1.)

RĀKHĀLACHANDRA VANDYOPĀDHYĀYA. *See* BAṄKIMCHANDRA CHAṬṬOPĀDHYĀYA. The Two Rings . . . Translated [from Baṅkimchandra's Yugalāṅgurīya] by Rakhal Chandra Banerjee. 1897. 8°.
14127. cc. 8.

RĀKHĀLADĀSA BHAṬṬĀCHĀRYA. স্বাধীন জেনানা। Female emancipation. [Svādhīna jenānā. A farce, showing the evil effects of the abolition of the Hindu custom of keeping women in seclusion. Second edition.] pp. 34. কলিকাতা ১২৯৩ [*Calcutta*, 1886.] 12°. **14125. e. 17.(9.)**

—— বঙ্গের অধোনতি। [Vaṅger adhonati, or The decline of Bengal. An unfavourable criticism on English rule in Bengal.] Pt. i. pp. 24. কলিকাতা ১৮৮৬ [*Calcutta*, 1886.] 12°. **14125. e. 16.**

RĀKHĀLADĀSA KAVIRATNA. পারমার্থিক গীতাবলী। [Pāramārthika gītāvalī. Religious songs. Pt. i. Poems by Rāmaprasāda Sena.] pp. xxii. 119. কলিকাতা ১২৯৩ [*Calcutta*, 1886.] 12°.
14129. a. 25.

RĀKHĀLADĀSA VIDYĀRATNA. A Manual of Sanskrit composition and translation. pp. iv. 105. *Calcutta*, 1891. 12°. **14092. a. 13.(2.)**

RĀMABHADRA, *Dvija.* সত্যদেব-সংহিতা। [Satyadeva-saṃhitā. A poem in praise of the god Satyanārāyaṇa. Edited by Vyomakeśa Mustafī.] ১৩০৮ [1901.] *See* ACADEMIES, *etc.*—Calcutta.—*Bengal Academy of Literature.* সাহিত্য-পরিষৎ-পত্রিকা। [Sāhitya-parishat-patrikā.] Vol. viii., no. 2. [1894, *etc.*] 8°. **14133. f. 18.**

RĀMACHANDRA, *Disciple of Rāmakrishṇa Paramahaṃsa. See* RĀMAKṚISHṆA PARAMAHAṂSA. তত্ত্ব-প্রকাশিকা। *etc.* [Tattva-prakāṣikā. A collection of 300 teachings of Rāmakṛishṇa, compiled and explained by Rāmachandra.] [1908.] 8°.
14123. ff. 18.

RĀMACHANDRA, *Son of Rāmadhana, of Harinabhi. See* ṢARACHCHANDRA ṢĀSTRĪ. দ্বিজ রামচন্দ্রের দুর্গামঙ্গল কাব্য। [Rāmachandrer Durgāmaṅgala. An article on the Durgāmaṅgala of Rāmachandra.] [1898.] 8°. **14133. f. 18.**

RĀMACHANDRA DATTA. শ্রীশ্রীরামকৃষ্ণ পর[মহংস] দেবের জীবন বৃত্তান্ত। [Rāmachandra-jīvana-vṛitt[ānta.] The biography of Rāmakṛishṇa Paramaham[sa.] pp. 210. কলিকাতা ১২৯৭ [*Calcutta*, 1890.] 8°.
14127. b. 45.(

—— লীলামৃত। [Līlāmṛita. A religious drama.] pp. 132. কলিকাতা ১৩০৭ [*Calcutta*, 1900.] 12°.
14131. a. 48.(1.)

RĀMACHANDRA MALLIKA. ঊনবিংশ শতাব্দি। পাচক পুরাণ। [Ūnaviṃṣa ṣatābdi. A humorous tale representing the Hindu gods and goddesses as British subjects, and creating a new class of Brahmans as cooks. Second edition.] pp. 19. কলিকাতা ১২৯৫ [*Calcutta*, 1888.] 12°. **14127. c. 37.(3.)**

RĀMACHANDRA MUKHOPĀDHYĀYA, *of Harinabhi.* দুর্গামঙ্গল। [Durgāmaṅgala. A metrical version of the Mahābhārata story of Nala and Damayantī. Edited, with a short account of the author, by Ṣarachchandra Ṣāstrī.] pp. vii. 138. *Calcutta*, 1898. 12°. **14129. a. 28.(2.)**

RĀMACHANDRA ṢARMĀ, *Āchārya.* দিনকৌমুদী। [Dinakaumudī. A Sanskrit treatise on the calculation of the calendar. Edited, with a Bengali preface and translation, by Viṣvambhara Jyotishārṇava. Part i., treating of the *tithis.*] pp. 10, 37. কলিকাতা ১৮২০ [*Calcutta*, 1898.] 12°.
14053. b. 31.(3.)

The editor states that the author wrote this work in 1664 A.D.

RĀMACHANDRA TARKĀLAṄKĀRA. *See* ṢĀTĀTAPA. শাতাতপীয়-কর্ম্মবিপাক। [Ṣātātapīya-karmavipāka. With a Bengali translation by Rāmachandra Tarkālaṅkāra.] [1880.] 16°. **14028. b. 106.(1.)**

—— —— [1902.] 8°. **14033. aa. 28.(3.)**

RĀMACHANDRA VANDYOPĀDHYĀYA, *Bābu.* The First Collection of English synonyms explained in Bengali with illustrations. By Ram Chandra Banerji. Revised by Babu Gangadhar Banerji. pp. iii. 85. *Calcutta*, 1902. 8°. **14131. g. 33.**

RĀMACHANDRA VANDYOPĀDHYĀYA, *Kavivara, Son of Manohara.* শ্রীধর্ম্মমঙ্গল [Dharmamaṅgala. An ancient Vaishṇava religious poem. Edited, with a life of the author, by Fakīrdās Chaṭṭopādhyāya.] ১৩১৩ [1906.] *See* PERIODICAL PUBLICATIONS.—*Calcutta,* সাহিত্য-সংহিতা। [Sāhitya-saṃhitā.] Vol. vii., no. 7. [1900, *etc.*] 8°. **14133. ff. 1.**

HANDRA VIDYĀVĀGĪṢA. Second discourse spiritual worship of God, delivered by Ramu Shurma at the Brahma Sumaj . . . Transfrom Bengallee [into English] by Chundru-ur Dev. pp. 6. *Calcutta*, 1844. 8°. 14123. d. 15 (1.)

— Sixth discourse . . . delivered by Ramandru Shurma . . . Translated . . . [into English] f Tarachand Chukruvurtee. pp. 4. *Calcutta*, 844. 8°. 14123. d. 15.(2.)

RĀMACHARAṆA NĀTHA. The house I live in, or the Human body. আমার বাসগৃহ অর্থাৎ মানব দেহ বিবরণ। [Āmār vāsagṛiha.] pp. 58. কলিকাতা ১৮৬৯ [*Calcutta*, 1869.] 12°. 14125. b.

RĀMACHARAṆA ṢIRORATNA. *See* VIJAYA GUPTA, *the Poet.* মনসা মঙ্গল বা পদ্মাপুরাণ। [Manasā-maṅgala. Edited, with an introduction, by Rāmacharaṇa Ṣiroratna.] [1896.] 8°. 14129. f. 6.(3.)

RĀMACHARAṆA VASU. [*Life.*] *See* SHOḌAṢĪBĀLĀ DĀSĪ. স্বর্গীয় মহাত্মা রামচরণ বসুর জীবন চরিত। [Rāmacharaṇa Vasur jīvanacharita.] [1903.] 12°. 14127. aa. 21.(3.)

RĀMADĀSA, *Vaishṇava poet.* অভিরামলীলামৃত। [Abhirāma-līlāmṛita. A poem on the life of Abhirāma Gosvāmī, a Vaishṇava saint. Edited, with a preface, by BhūpatiGosvāmī.] Pt. i. pp. কলিকাতা ১২৯৮ [*Calcutta*, 1891.] 8°. 14123. f. 46.

—— শ্রীঅভিরামলীলামৃত। [Abhirāma-līlāmṛita. Edited by Prasannakumāra Gosvāmī.] pp. iv. 158. কলিকাতা [*Calcutta*, 1894.] 8°. 14129. f. 6.(1.)

RĀMADĀSA SENA. Bharat rahasya, or Essays on the ancient religion and warfares of India . . . ভারত-রহস্য। Pt. i. pp. iv. 301. কলিকাতা ১২৯২ [*Calcutta*, 1886.] 12°. 14127. a. 27.

—— Buddhadeva. His life and teachings. By . . . Ram Das Sen. বুদ্ধদেব। pp. 12, 283. কলিকাতা [*Calcutta*, 1891.] 12°. 14127. a. 41.

Pp. 257—272 are wrongly numbered as 157—172.

—— কবিতালহরী। [Kavitālaharī. Miscellaneous poems. Second edition.] pp. vi. 117. কলিকাতা ১২৭৫ [*Calcutta*, 1869.] 12°. 14129. a. 23.(1.)

—— রামদাস-গ্রন্থাবলী। [Rāmadāsa-granthāvalī.] (Works of Dr. Ramdas Sen. Vol. I. Aitihasika rahasya, or Essays on the history, philosophy, arts and sciences of ancient India. Third edition, revised and enlarged.) pp. xxiv. 453, 18. *Calcutta*, 1902. 8°. 14127. bb. 22.

RĀMADAYĀLA BHAKTIRATNA. সঙ্কীর্ত্তন-তরণী। [Saṅkīrtana-taraṇī. A collection of *kīrtanas*, or Vaishṇava songs. Compiled by Rāmadayāla. With wood-cuts.] pp. 18, 139. কলিকাতা ১২৯৮ [*Calcutta*, 1892.] 12°. 14129. b. 35.(3.)

RĀMADAYĀLA DĀSA. শাস্ত্রীয় হালিক দাস। বা মাহিষ্য জাতি। [Māhishya jāti. A short account of the origin and customs of the Māhishya or Kaivarta caste.] pp. 18. কলিকাতা [*Calcutta*, 1903.] 12°. 14125. e. 31.(8.)

RĀMADAYĀLA GHOSHA. *See* NAROTTAMA DĀSA. শ্রীশ্রীপ্রেমভক্তিচন্দ্রিকা। [Premabhakti-chandrikā. Edited by Rāmadayāla Ghosha, with a Sanskrit commentary by Viṣvanābha Chakravartī, and Bengali explanatory notes by Rādhikānātha Gosvāmī.] [1896.] 12°. 14123. e. 20.(1.)

RĀMADAYĀLA MAJUMDĀR. শ্রীবিচার চন্দ্রোদয় ও . . . পঞ্চদেবতা ধ্যান ও স্তোত্র। [Vichārachandrodaya. An exposition, in catechetical form, of the Vedānta system. Preceded and followed by a selection of Vedantic hymns, by Ṣaṅkara Āchārya and others.] pp. xvi. 3, 266. কলিকাতা ১৩০৮ [*Calcutta*, 1901.] 12°. 14123. e. 22.

RĀMADEVA MIṢRA. *See* GAṄGĀDĀSA, *Son of Gopāladāsa.* ছন্দোমঞ্জরী। [Chhandomañjarī. Edited by Rāmadeva Miṣra.] [1907.] 8°. 14055. b. 5.

RĀMAGATI NYĀYARATNA. ইলছোবা। অথবা স্বপ্নলব্ধ উপাখ্যান। [Ilchhobā. An historical novel.] pp. 144. চুঁচুড়া ১২৯৪ [*Chinsurah*, 1888.] 8°. 14127. f. 40.(2.)

RĀMAGOPĀLA GHOSHA. [*Life.*] *See* SATĪṢACHANDRA MUKHOPĀDHYĀYA. মহাত্মা রামগোপাল ঘোষ। [Mahātmā Rāmagopāla Ghosha.] 1905. 12°. 14127. aa. 18.(2.)

RĀMAGOPĀLA JOYĀRDĀR. গোপাল-গীতাবলী। [Gopāla-gītāvalī. Philosophical poems.] Pt. i. কলিকাতা ১৯০৬ [*Calcutta*, 1906.] 12°. 14129. bb. 28.

RĀMAGOPĀLA SĀNNYĀLA. হিন্দু পেট্রিয়টের ভুতপূর্ব্ব সম্পাদক হরিশ্চন্দ্র মুখোপাধ্যায়ের জীবনী। [Hariṣchandra Mukhopādhyāyer jīvanī.] The life of Babu Harish Chandra Mukerjee, the founder of the Hindoo Patriot. pp. viii. 56. কলিকাতা ১৮৮৭ [*Calcutta*, 1887.] 8°. **14127. b. 38.**

—— কৃষ্ণদাস পালের জীবনী। [Kṛishṇadāsa Pāler jīvanī.] The life of Kristo Das Pal, the late editor of the Hindoo Patriot. pp. 64. *Calcutta*, 1890. 8°. **14127. b. 45.(2.)**

RAMĀI PAṆḌITA. *See* HARAPRASĀDA ŚĀSTRĪ. রমাই পণ্ডিতের ধর্ম্মমঙ্গল। [Ramāi Paṇḍiter Ḋharmamaṅgala. An article on the poet Ramāi Paṇḍita and his Dharmamaṅgala.] [1897.] 8°. **14133. f. 18.**

—— শূন্যপুরাণ। [Śūnyapurāṇa. An ancient Pauranic poem, edited, with an extensive introduction and glossary, by Nagendranātha Vasu.] pp. iii. 71, 176. কলিকাতা ১৩১৪ [*Calcutta*, 1908.] 12°. **14129. bbb. 3.**

RĀMAKAMALA VIDYĀLAṄKĀRA. The Prakritibáda, or an Illustrated Etymological Dictionary of the Sanskrit and Bengali languages . . . Fourth edition, thoroughly revised, improved and enlarged by Ramesha Chandra Bandyopadhyaya. pp. x. 1678, 16. *Calcutta*, ১২৯৫ [1888.] 8°. **14133. b. 13.**

RĀMAKIṄKARA ŚIROMAṆI. *See* KṚISHṆA MIŚRA. প্রবোধচন্দ্রোদয় নাটক। [Prabodhachandrodaya nāṭaka. With a Bengali translation by Rāmakṛishṇa Śiromaṇi and others.] [1855.] 16°. **14079. a. 4.**

RĀMAKṚISHṆA GAṄGOPĀDHYĀYA. প্রভাবতী। সামাজিক উপন্যাস। [Prabhāvatī. A story of domestic life.] pp. 130. কলিকাতা ১৩০৩ [*Calcutta*, 1897.] 12°. **14127. cc. 10.(1.)**

RĀMAKṚISHṆA PARAMAHAṂSA, *Son of Khudirāma.* [*Life.*] *See* AKSHAYAKUMĀRA SENA. শ্রীশ্রীরামকৃষ্ণ পুঁথি *etc.* [Rāmakṛishṇa-punthi.] [1901.] 8°. **14127. bbb. 5.(2.)**

—— [*Life.*] *See* BHŪDHARA CHAṬṬOPĀDHYĀYA. সাধুদর্শন। [Sādhudarśana.] Pt. i. [1888.] 12°. **14127. a. 35.**

—— *See* HĀRĀṆACHANDRA RAKSHITA. কামিনী ও কাঞ্চন। [Kāminī o kāñchana. A story, illustrating the religious teachings of Rāmakṛishṇa.] [1908.] 12°. **14128. a. 28.**

RĀMAKṚISHṆA PARAMAHAṂSA, *Son of Khudirāma (continued).* [*Life.*] *See* RĀMACHANDRA DATTA. শ্রীশ্রীরামকৃষ্ণ পরমহংসদেবের জীবন বৃত্তান্ত। [Rāmakṛishṇa-jīvana-vṛittānta.] [1890.] 8°. **14127. b. 45.(1.)**

—— তত্ত্ব-প্রকাশিকা। অর্থাৎ শ্রীশ্রীরামকৃষ্ণদেবের উপদেশ। [Tattva-prakāśikā. A collection of 300 teachings of Rāmakṛishṇa, compiled and explained by his disciple Rāmachandra. Third edition.] pp. ii. vii. 450. কলিকাতা ১৩১৪ [*Calcutta*, 1908.] 8°. **14123. ff. 18.**

RĀMAKṚISHṆA VIDYĀBHŪSHAṆA. *See* SĀYAṆA ĀCHĀRYA. শঙ্করবিজয়ম্। [Śaṅkaravijaya. Sanskrit text, with a Bengali translation and preface by Rāmakṛishṇa Vidyābhūshaṇa.] [1882-86.] 4°. **14048. e. 11.**

RĀMĀKSHAYA CHAṬṬOPĀDHYĀYA. ৺ প্রেমচন্দ্র তর্কবাগীশের জীবনচরিত ও কবিতাবলী। [Premachandra Tarkavāgīśer jīvanacharita. A life cf Premachandra Tarkavāgīśa, Professor of Rhetoric at the Calcutta Sanskrit College.] pp. ii. 116, x. কলিকাতা ১৮৯২ [*Calcutta*, 1892.] 8°. **14127. b. 38.(3.)**

—— [Second edition.] pp. iv. 168. কলিকাতা ১৮৯৬ [*Calcutta*, 1896.] 8°. **14127. bb. 4.(2.)**

—— [Third edition.] pp. 7, 215. কলিকাতা ১৩০৬ [*Calcutta*, 1901.] 8°. **14127. aa. 16.**

—— ৺ প্রেমচন্দ্র তর্কবাগীশের জীবনচরিত ও কবিতাবলী। . . . Life and Slokas of Prem Chandra Tarkavagisa. By Rai Ramakhoy Chatterji Bahadoor. [Fourth edition.] pp. ix. 319. কলিকাতা [*Calcutta*, 1906.] 12°. **14127. aa. 34.**

—— পুলিস ও লোকরক্ষা। [Pulis o lokarakshā. A history of Police administration in Bengal from the commencement of the British rule.] pp. ii. 157. *Calcutta*, 1892. 12°. **14125. a. 20.**

RĀMAKUMĀRA CHAKRAVARTĪ. ঠাকুরদাদার পরিত্রাণ। [Ṭhākuradādār paritrāṇa. A social tale.] pp. 187. কলিকাতা ১৩০৩ [*Calcutta*, 1896.] 8°. **14127. ee. 5.(2.)**

RĀMAKUMĀRA DĀSA. কশ্যপ-তন্ত্র। [Kaśyapa-tantra. A collection of incantations and prescriptions for the cure of various ailments, and the averting of various calamities. Compiled and translated from Sanskrit sources by Rāmakumāra Dāsa.] pp. ix. 156. কলিকাতা ১৩০৬ [*Calcutta*, 1899.] 12°. **14123. e. 28.(1.)**

—— [Second edition.] pp. 10, 183. কলিকাতা ১৩০৮ [*Calcutta*, 1901.] 12°. **14123. e. 29.**

RĀMAKUMĀRA LASKAR. পথিক বা যতোধর্মস্ততো জয়ঃ। [Pathika. A novel.] Pt. i. pp. ii. 208. কলিকাতা ১৩০২ [*Calcutta*, 1896.] 8°. **14127. ee. 2.**

RĀMAMOHANA RĀYA, *Raja.* *See* JAYANĀTHA CHAUDHURĪ. রাজা রামমোহন রায়ের ধর্মমত। [Rājā Rāmamohana Rāyer dharma-mata.] ... The religious views of Raja Ram Mohan Roy. [1892.] 12°. **14123. c. 27.**

—— [*Life.*] *See* RAVĪNDRANĀTHA ṬHĀKURA. রামমোহন রায় [Rāmamohana Rāya.] [1885.] 12°. **14123. c. 8.(4.)**

—— The complete works of Raja Ram Mohun Roy. Vol. i. Sanskrit and Bengali. (রাজা রামমোহন রায়-প্রণীত গ্রন্থাবলি।) কলিকাতা ১৭৯৫ [*Calcutta*, 1873.] 8°. **14127. g. 7.**

—— রাজা রামমোহন রায়ের সংস্কৃত ও বাঙ্গালা গ্রন্থাবলী। [Sanskrit and Bengali works. A reprint.] pp. iv. 836. এলাহাবাদ কলিকাতা ১৩১২ [*Allahabad, Calcutta* printed, 1905.] 12°. **14128. a. 2.**

—— রাজা রামমোহন রায়ের সঙ্গীতাবলী। [Saṅgītāvalī. Brahmist hymns.] pp. vii. 54. কলিকাতা ১৮১০ [*Calcutta*, 1889.] 12°. **14123. c. 19.(2.)**

RĀMAMOHANA VANDYOPĀDHYĀYA, *of Matiyari.* *See* NĪLARATNA MUKHOPĀDHYĀYA. রামমোহনের রামায়ণ। [Rāmamohaner Rāmāyaṇa. An article on the Rāmāyaṇa of Rāmamohana, with extracts from his work.] [1895.] 8°. **14133. f. 18.**

RAMAṆAKṚISHṆA CHAṬṬOPĀDHYĀYA. সামুদ্রিক রেখাদি বিচার। [Sāmudrika rekhādi-vichāra. A treatise on palmistry, in the form of question and answer between a Guru and his disciple. With 48 diagrams.] pp. 20, 129, 14. কলিকাতা ১৩০২ [*Calcutta*, 1895.] 8°. **14125. dd. 18.**

—— Samudrika siksha: or Lessons on Palmistry. Illustrated with 18 diagrams. [Compiled in English] by Roman Kristo Chatterjee. pp. 30, 106. *Calcutta*, 1896. 12°. **14125. bb. 23.**

Partly translated from the author's Bengali work bearing the same title.

RĀMĀNANDA CHAṬṬOPĀDHYĀYA. *See* ARABIAN NIGHTS. আরব্যোপন্যাস *etc.* [Ārabyopanyāsa. An abridged and expurgated translation of the Arabian Nights by Rāmānanda Chaṭṭopādhyāya.] [1903.] 12°. **14127. cc. 40.**

RĀMANĀRĀYAṆA GHOSHA, *Kavivara.* নৈষধকাব্য। [Naishadha kāvya. The story of Nala and Damayantī, in verse. Edited, with an introduction, by Kālīprasanna Ghosha.] pp. xii. 133. [*Dacca*, 1896.] 12°. **14127. cc. 23.(2.)**

The last page is wanting.

RĀMANĀRĀYAṆA VIDYĀRATNA. *See* GAṄGĀDĀSA, *Son of Gopāladāsa.* ছন্দোমঞ্জরী। [Chhandomañjarī. With a Bengali translation by Rāmanārāyaṇa Vidyāratna.] [1907.] 8°. **14055. b. 5.**

—— *See* JĪVA GOSVĀMĪ. গোপালচম্পূঃ। [Gopālachampū. Edited, with a Bengali prose translation, by Rāmanārāyaṇa Vidyāratna.] [1890, *etc.*] 8°. **14076. d. 45.**

—— *See* JĪVA GOSVĀMĪ. হরিনামামৃতম্ [Harināmāmṛita. Edited, with a Bengali translation, by Rāmanārāyaṇa Vidyāratna.] [1884, *etc.*] 8°. **14093. b. 12.**

—— *See* KAVIKARṆAPŪRA. অলঙ্কারকৌস্তুভঃ। [Alaṅkārakaustubha. Edited, with a Bengali translation, by Rāmanārāyaṇa Vidyāratna.] [1899, *etc.*] 8°. **14053. ccc. 25.**

—— *See* KAVIKARṆAPŪRA. শ্রীচৈতন্যচরিতামৃত মহাকাব্যং। [Chaitanya-charitāmṛita. Edited, with a prose translation, by Rāmanārāyaṇa Vidyāratna.] [1885, *etc.*] 8°. **14058. b. 28.**

—— *See* KṚISHṆADEVĀCHĀRYA. নৃসিংহপরিচর্যা। [Nṛisiṁha-paricharyā. Edited, with a Bengali prose translation, by Rāmanārāyaṇa Vidyāratna.] [1890.] 8°. **14033. b. 56.**

—— *See* NITYĀNANDA DĀSA. প্রেমবিলাস। [Premavilāsa. Edited by Rāmanārāyaṇa Vidyāratna.] [1892-93.] 8°. **14129. e. 17.(2.)**

RĀMANĀRĀYAṆA VIDYĀRATNA (*continued*). *See* PURĀṆAS.—*Bhāgavatapurāṇa.* শ্রীমদ্ভাগবতম্। [With a Bengali translation by Rāmanārāyaṇa Vidyāratna.] [1885, *etc.*] 4°. **14016. dd. 3.**

—— *See* PURĀṆAS.—*Padmapurāṇa.* পদ্মপুরাণম্। উত্তরখণ্ডম্। [Uttarakhaṇḍa, with a Bengali translation by Rāmanārāyaṇa Vidyāratna.] [1899, *etc.*] 4°. **14016. e. 45.**

—— *See* RŪPA GOSVĀMĪ. উজ্জ্বলনীলমণিঃ। [Ujjvalanīlamaṇi. Edited, with a prose translation, by Rāmanārāyaṇa Vidyāratna.] [1892, *etc.*] 8°. **14053. d. 49.**

—— *See* VILVAMAṄGALA GOSVĀMĪ. কৃষ্ণকর্ণামৃত। [Kṛishṇakarṇāmṛita. Edited, with a prose translation, by Rāmanārāyaṇa Vidyāratna.] [1890, *etc.*] 8°. **14076. d. 44.**

RAMAṆĪMOHANA GHOSHA. মঞ্জরী। [Mañjarī. Lyrical poems.] pp. ii. 109. কলিকাতা [*Calcutta*, 1907.] 12°. **14129. bb. 34.(1.)**

—— মুকুর। [Mukura. Short poems on various subjects.] pp. ii. 102. কলিকাতা ১৩০৬ [*Calcutta*, 1899.] 12°. **14129. bb. 8.(2.)**

RAMAṆĪMOHANA MALLIKA. *See* BALARĀMA DĀSA, *Son of Ātmārāma.* বলরামদাস। [Balarāma Dāsa. Edited, with notes and an introduction, by Ramaṇīmohana Mallika.] [1899.] 8°. **14129. c. 54.**

—— *See* NAROTTAMA DĀSA. নরোত্তমদাস। [Narottama Dāsa. A collection of Vaishṇava songs. Edited, with annotations, and a critical account of the life and works of the poet, by Ramaṇīmohana Mallika.] [1903.] 8°. **14123. ff. 10.(3.)**

—— প্রাচীনা স্ত্রী-কবি। [Prāchīnā strī-kavi. A collection of short poems by old Bengali poetesses on the amours of Kṛishṇa.] pp. 14. কলিকাতা ১৩০৫ [*Calcutta*, 1899.] 12°. **14129. bb. 16.(1.)**

RĀMĀNUJA VIDYĀRṆAVA. *See* PURĀṆAS.—*Dharmapurāṇa.* বৃহদ্ধর্মপুরাণম্ [Bṛihad-dharmapurāṇa. With a Bengali translation by Rāmānuja Vidyārṇava and others.] [1908.] 8°. **14016. dd. 28.(1.)**

RĀMAPRASĀDA SENA, called KAVIRAÑJANA. *See* KAILĀSACHANDRA SIṂHA. সাধক সঙ্গীত। [Sādhaka saṅgīta. Songs in praise of the goddess Kālī by Rāmaprasāda Sena and other poets. With a sketch of the life of Rāmaprasāda Sena.] [1885.] 12°. **14123. e. 10.**

—— *See* RĀKHĀLADĀSA KAVIRATNA. পারমার্থিক গীতাবলী। [Pāramārthika gītāvalī. Religious songs. Pt. i. By Rāmaprasāda Sena.] **14129. a. 25.**

—— [*Life.*] *See* ṢĀNTIRĀMA DE. কবিরঞ্জন রামপ্রসাদ সেনের জীবন-বৃত্তান্ত। [Rāmaprasāda Sener jīvana-vṛittānta.] [1889.] 12°. **14131. d. 21.(3.)**

—— কবিরঞ্জন কাব্যসংগ্রহ। [Kāvyasaṅgraha. The poetical works of Rāmaprasāda Sena.] pp. vi. iv. 187, 2, 30, 113, 3. কলিকাতা ১২৯২ [*Calcutta*, 1885.] 12°. **14129. a. 26.**

—— পদাবলী। [Padāvalī. Devotional songs, chiefly in praise of the goddess Kālī, by Rāmaprasāda Sena and other poets. Second edition.] pp. 70. কলিকাতা ১২৯২ [*Calcutta*, 1886.] 12°. **14129. a. 24.(1.)**

—— পদাবলী। [Padāvalī. Another collection of songs by Rāmaprasāda Sena and other poets.] pp. 72. কলিকাতা ১২৯২ [*Calcutta*, 1886.] 12°. **14129. a. 24.(2.)**

—— কবিরঞ্জন রামপ্রসাদের গ্রন্থাবলী। [Rāmaprasāder granthāvalī. The poetical works of Rāmaprasāda Sena. Edited, with notes and a life of the poet, by Dvārakānātha Vasu.] pp. 16, 332. *Calcutta*, ১৮৯৫ [1895.] 12°. **14129. a. 37.**

—— বিদ্যাসুন্দর। [Vidyā-Sundara. The story of Vidyā and Sundara in verse, with copious notes, a life of the author and a criticism of the work.] pp. iv. 51, 181, 123, iv. কলিকাতা ১২৯৩ [*Calcutta*, 1886.] 12°. **14129. b. 31.**

RĀMAPRASANNA GHOSHA. শ্রীশ্রীগৌরচন্দ্রোদয়। [Gaurachandrodaya. An anthological work on Chaitanya and his religious teachings. With copious Sanskrit quotations.] pp. ii. 216, iv. বহরমপুর ১৩০৮ [*Berhampore*, 1901.] 8°. **14123. ff. 5.**

RĀMAPRASANNA VANDYOPĀDHYĀYA, *Saṅgītāchārya.* সঙ্গীত-মঞ্জরী। [Saṅgīta-mañjarī. Airs set in the Bengali system of musical notation.] pp. xxiv. 728. কলিকাতা ১৩১৪ [*Calcutta*, 1907.] 4°. **14125. d. 30.**

RĀMAṢAṄKARA DEVA. সানুবাদ বৃহৎ জাতকচন্দ্রিকা। [Bṛihat jātakachandrikā. A Sanskrit treatise on nativities. Edited, with a Bengali translation, by Nīlakamala Vidyānidhi.] pp. xii. 408. কলিকাতা ১৮১৩ [*Calcutta*, 1892.] 8°. **14053. c. 63.**

RĀMAṢARAṆA TARKAVĀGĪṢA. পণ্ডিত রামশরণ তর্কবাগীশ। [Paṇḍita Rāmaṣaraṇa Tarkavāgīṣa. A short life of Pandit Rāmaṣaraṇa of Bansbaria, in the District of Hooghly.] pp. 10. বাঁশবেড়িয়া ১৩১৪ [*Bansbaria*, 1907.] 8°. **14127. bb. 30.**

RĀMATANU CHAṬṬOPĀDHYĀYA. [*Life.*] *See* ṢRĪMANTA CHAṬṬOPĀDHYĀYA. বংশ-তরু। [Vaṃṣa-taru.] [1891.] 12°. **14127. a. 45.**

RĀMATANU LĀHIRĪ. [*Life.*] *See* ṢIVANĀTHA ṢĀSTRĪ. Ramtanu Lahiri, *etc.* 1907. 8°. **10606. i. 19.**

RĀMATĀRAKA SENA. ଦ୍ୱିଭାଷା ବର୍ଣ୍ଣପରିଚୟ [Dvi-bhāshā varṇaparichaya.] অর্থাৎ বঙ্গোৎকল বর্ণপরিচয়। [A Bengali-Oriya primer.] pp. 12. *Balasore*, 1885. 12°. **14131. e. 20.**

RAMCHUNDRU SHURMA. *See* RĀMACHANDRA VIDYĀVĀGĪṢA.

RĀMENDRASUNDARA TRIVEDĪ. *See* ACADEMIES, *etc.*—Calcutta.—*Bengal Academy of Literature.* সাহিত্য-পরিষৎ-পত্রিকা। [Sāhitya-parishat-patrikā. Vols. vi., no. 2—x., no. 2. Edited, in part, by Rāmendrasundara Trivedī.] [1894, *etc.*] 8°. **14133. f. 18.**

—— *See* BALENDRANĀTHA ṬHĀKURA. স্বর্গীয় বলেন্দ্রনাথ ঠাকুরের গ্রন্থাবলী। [Balendranātha Ṭhākurer granthāvalī. With an introduction by Rāmendrasundara Trivedī.] [1907.] 8°. **14127. ee. 30.**

—— *See* CHAMPAKA-KALIKĀ. চম্পক-কলিকা। [Champaka-kalikā. Edited, with critical notes, by Rāmendrasundara Trivedī.] [1900.] 8°. **14133. f. 18.**

—— *See* VĀLMĪKI. রামায়ণ-তত্ত্ব। [Rāmāyaṇa-tattva. Published under the editorship of Rāmendrasundara Trivedī.] [1902, *etc.*] 8°. **14133. f. 18.**

—— *See* VAṂṢĪVADANA ṢARMĀ. পুণ্ডরীককুলকীর্ত্তি পঞ্জিকা *etc.* [Puṇḍarīkakulakīrtti pañjikā. Edited, with a Bengali translation and appendices, by Rāmendrasundara Trivedī.] [1901.] 8°. **14058. b. 47.**

RĀMENDRASUNDARA TRIVEDĪ (*continued*). *See* YOGĪNDRANĀTHA SARKĀR. খুকুমণির ছড়া। [Khukumaṇir chhaṛā. Edited, with an introduction, by Rāmendrasundara Trivedī.] [1899.] 12°. **14129. a. 43.**

RAMEṢACHANDRA, *Bhikshu, of Chittagong.* বৌদ্ধালঙ্কার। [Bauddhālaṅkāra. A lectionary of short Pali texts on Buddhist religion. With translations and explanations in Bengali.] pp. ii. 34. চট্টগ্রাম ১৪৩৪ বুদ্ধাব্দ [*Chittagong*, 1891.] 12°. **14098. a. 22.(2.)**

RAMEṢACHANDRA DĀSA. সুলভ ছাত্র-সহচর-অভিধান। [Chhātra-sahachara-abhidhāna. Students' dictionary of Bengali synonyms.] pp. 115. কলিকাতা ১৩০২ [*Calcutta*, 1895.] 12°. **14133. a. 13.**

RAMEṢACHANDRA DATTA. [*Life.*] *See* ĀṢUTOSHA GHOSHA. মাননীয় শ্রীযুক্ত রমেশচন্দ্র দত্ত ... সংক্ষিপ্ত জীবনী। [Rameṣachandra Datta saṃkshipta jīvanī.] [1895.] 8°. **14127. aa. 3.(3.)**

—— *See* VEDAS.—*Ṛigveda.* ঋগ্বেদ সংহিতা। [Ṛig-veda-saṃhitā. Translated, with notes, by Rameṣachandra Datta.] [1885-87.] 8°. **14123. f. 35.**

—— হিন্দুশাস্ত্র। [Hindu-ṣāstra. Selections from Sanskrit literature, with Bengali translations. Edited, with prefaces, by Rameṣachandra Datta.] 2 vols. কলিকাতা ১৩০২-০৩ [*Calcutta*, 1895-97.] 8°. **14085. c. 45.**

—— ইয়ুরোপে তিন বৎসর। [Iyurope tin batsar, or Three years in Europe. Translated from the English of Rameṣachandra Datta. Third edition.] pp. 87. কলিকাতা ১২৯৬ [*Calcutta*, 1899.] 12°. **14127. a. 38.(2.)**

—— মহারাষ্ট্র জীবন-প্রভাত। [Jīvanaprabhāta. An historical novel on the exploits of Ṣivājī. Fourth edition.] pp. 262. কলিকাতা [*Calcutta*, 1897.] 12°. **14127. cc. 2.**

—— Shivaji, or the Morning of Maratha life. A novel, translated from [the] Bengali [Jīvanaprabhāta], by Krishnalal Mohanlal Jhaveri. pp. 339. *Ahmedabad*, 1899. 8°. **14127. ee. 19.**

—— রাজপুত জীবন-সন্ধ্যা। [Jīvanasandhyā, or The Evening of life. An historical romance of the time of Jahāṅgīr. Fifth edition.] pp. 200. কলিকাতা [*Calcutta*, 1896.] 8°. **14127. c. 51.**

RAMEṢACHANDRA DATTA (*continued*). The Literature of Bengal . . . By Romesh Chunder Dutt. Revised edition: with portraits. pp. v. 250. *Calcutta*, 1895. 8°. **14131. d. 29.**

—— সমাজ। [Samāja. A tale, advocating social reform in Hindu society.] pp. 202. কলিকাতা [*Calcutta*, 1894.] 12°. **14127. d. 42.(2.)**

—— সংসার। [Saṃsāra. A story of Bengali domestic life.] pp. 212. কলিকাতা ১২৯৩ [*Calcutta*, 1886.] 8°. **14127. e. 23.**

—— The Lake of Palms. A story of Indian domestic life. Translated into English [from his original Bengali Saṃsāra], by Romesh Dutt, C.I.E. pp. viii. 256. *London*, 1902. 8°. **14127. d. 44.**

RAMEṢACHANDRA SIṂHA. গাথা। [Gāthā. Short poems.] pp. iii. 139. কলিকাতা ১৩১০ [*Calcutta*, 1903.] 12°. **14129. bb. 13.(5.)**

RAMEṢACHANDRA VANDYOPĀDHYĀYA. *See* Rāmakamala Vidyālaṅkāra. The Prakritibáda. . . . Fourth edition, thoroughly revised, improved and enlarged, by Ramesha Chandra Bandyopadhyaya. [1888.] 8°. **14133. b. 13.**

RĀMEṢVARA TARKĀLAṄKĀRA. বঙ্গ ভাষাভিধান [Abhidhāna. A dictionary of the Bengali language.] pp. 473. কলিকাতা [*Calcutta*, 1830 ?] 8°. **14133. b. 11.**

RAMKHE (M.), *Rev.* বাঙ্গালা-গারো অভিধান। [Bāṅgālā-Gāro abhidhāna.] . . . Bengali-Garo Dictionary. pp. 884. *Tura, Assam*, 1887. 8°. **14133. b. 12.**

RAṆAGHAT.—*Sanātana Dharmotsāhinī Sabhā.* রাণাঘাট সনাতন ধর্ম্মোৎসাহিনী সভার তৃতীয় অধিবেশন। [An account of the proceedings at the third meeting of the Sanātana Dharmotsāhinī Sabhā of Ranaghat.] pp. 16. কলিকাতা ১৯২৬ [*Calcutta*, 1869.] 8°. **14125. ee. 23.(2.)**

RAṄGALĀLA MUKHOPĀDHYĀYA and others. বিশ্বকোষ। [Viṣvakosha. A Bengali dictionary, and general encyclopædia, compiled by Raṅgalāla Mukhopādhyāya, Trailokyanātha Mukhopādhyāya, Nagendranātha Vasu, and Upendrachandra Vasu.] রাহুতা কলিকাতা ১২৯২ [*Rahuta, Calcutta*, 1885, *etc.*] 4°. **14133. c. 5.**

In progress.

RASAMAYA MITRA. *See* Carey (W.), *D.D.* A Dictionary of the Bengali Language. Vol. i. Bengali and English . . . Revised and edited by Rasamay Mitra . . . and Brojendra Nath Ghosal. 1902. 8°. **14133. b. 19.**

RASASĀGARA. *See* Krishṇakānta Bhādurī.

RĀSAVIHĀRĪ SĀṄKHYATĪRTHA. *See* Rūpa Gosvāmī. নাটক-চন্দ্রিকা। [Nāṭaka-chandrikā. Edited, with a Bengali translation, by Rāsavihārī.] [1907.] 8°. **14055. b. 3.**

RASIKACHANDRA VASU. দুর্গামঙ্গল ও কবি রূপনারায়ণ। [Durgāmaṅgala. An article on the Durgāmaṅgala, a poem in praise of the goddess Durgā, and its author Rūpanārāyaṇa.] ১৩০৪ [1897.] *See* Academies, *etc.*—Calcutta.—*Bengal Academy of Literature.* সাহিত্য-পরিষৎ-পত্রিকা। [Sāhitya-parishat-patrikā.] Vol. iv., no. 2. [1894, *etc.*] 8°. **14133. f. 18.**

—— জগন্নাথ-বিজয় ও কবি মুকুন্দ। [Jagannātha-vijaya o Kavi Mukunda. An article on the Jagannātha-vijaya, a poem in praise of the god Jagannātha, and its author Kavi Mukunda, with extracts from the poem.] ১৩০৭ [1901.] *See* Academies, *etc.*—Calcutta.—*Bengal Academy of Literature.* সাহিত্য-পরিষৎ-পত্রিকা। [Sāhitya-parishat-patrikā.] Vol. vii. no. 4. [1894, *etc.*] 8°. **14133. f. 18.**

RASIKACHANDRA VASU, *of Barisal.* রত্নোদ্ধার। [Ratnoddhāra. A poem on the legend and cult of the god Satyanārāyaṇa. With the Sanskrit text of the Satyanārāyaṇa-vratakathā, from the Revākhaṇḍa of the Skandapurāṇa.] pp. 83. বরিশাল ১৩০৬ [*Barisal*, 1899.] 12°. **14028. b. 66.(4.)**

RASIKALĀLA GUPTA. *See* Bhāva Miṣra. Bháva Prakása . . . with Bengali translations by . . . Russick Lal Gupta. 1883, *etc.* 8°. **14043. e. 19.**

—— Hindu Practice of Medicine. By Kaviraj Russick Lal Gupta. [A treatise in English, with the Bengali names of drugs and diseases.] pp. 202, xv. *Calcutta*, 1892. 8°. **14125. c. 39.(2.)**

RASIKAMOHANA CHAKRAVARTĪ. শ্রীমৎ দাসগোস্বামী। [Ṣrīmat Dāsa Gosvāmī. A biography of the Vaishṇava teacher, Raghunātha Dāsa Gosvāmī, including several of his Sanskrit hymns, with Bengali translations of some of them.] pp. iv. xvi. 240. কলিকাতা ৪২৬ [*Calcutta*, 1906.] 12°. **14127. aa. 16.(2.)**

—— শ্রীস্বরূপদামোদর। [Svarūpa-Dāmodara. An account of the life of Purushottama Āchārya and other intimate companions of Chaitanya.] Pt. i. pp. iv. 278. কলিকাতা ৪১৯ গৌরাব্দ [*Calcutta*, 1904.] 12°. **14127. aa. 30.**

RASIKAMOHANA CHAṬṬOPĀDHYĀYA. *See* KṚISHṆĀNANDA VĀGĪSA BHAṬṬĀCHĀRYA. তন্ত্রসারঃ [Tantrasāra. Edited, with a Bengali translation, by Rasikamohana Chaṭṭopādhyāya.] [1879-86.] 4°. **14033. bb. 22.**

—— *See* PERIODICAL PUBLICATIONS.—*Calcutta*. অরুণোদয়। [Aruṇodaya. Edited by Rasikamohana Chaṭṭopādhyāya.] [1890, *etc.*] 4°. **14133. g. 16.**

—— *See* PURĀṆAS.—*Garuḍapurāṇa*. অষ্টাদশ-পুরাণম্ (গরুড়পুরাণম্) [Garuḍapurāṇa. With a Bengali translation by Rasikamohana Chaṭṭopādhyāya.] [1883.] 4°. **14016. e. 39.**

—— *See* SIBLY (E.), *M.D.* যাবনিক জীন্ আদি সাধন। [Extracts from Sibly's "Illustration of the celestial science of astrology," with a preface by Rasikamohana Chaṭṭopādhyāya.] [1885.] 4°. **14125. dd. 13.**

—— *See* TANTRAS.—*Dattātreyatantra*. দত্তাত্রেয়ঃ [Dattātreyatantra. Followed by the Shaṭkarma-dīpikā. Edited, with a Bengali translation, by Rasikamohana Chaṭṭopādhyāya.] [1885.] 4°. **14033. bb. 24.(1.)**

—— লুপ্তগুপ্ত শাস্ত্রের সূচীপত্র। [Luptagupta śāstrer sūchipatra. An index to the astrological and Tantric publications, both Sanskrit and Bengali, of Rasikamohana Chaṭṭopādhyāya. With a Bengali and English preface.] Pt. i. pp. vi. xl. 176. কলিকাতা ১৩০২ [*Calcutta*, 1894.] 8°. **14033. bbb. 2.**

—— প্রেত-তত্ত্ব। [Pretatattva. A work on necromancy.] pp. 13. [1894.] *See* PERIODICAL PUBLICATIONS.—*Calcutta*. অরুণোদয়। [Aruṇodaya.] Pt. i., no. 33. [1890, *etc.*] 4°. **14133. g. 16.**

—— বশ্যতন্ত্র-মেস্মেরিজম্। [Vaśyatantra. A treatise on hypnotism.] pp. 33. [1893, *etc.*] *See* PERIODICAL PUBLICATIONS.—*Calcutta*. অরুণোদয়। [Aruṇodaya.] Pt. i., no. 32. [1890, *etc.*] 4°. **14133. g. 16.**

—— যন্ত্রসারতন্ত্রম্। [Yantrasāra-tantra. A collection of magical diagrams and illustrations, taken from the author's compilation Tantrasāra, explained in Bengali, with extracts from Sanskrit works.] pp. v. 48, v. কলিকাতা ১২৯২ [*Calcutta*, 1885.] 4°. **14033. bb. 24.(2.)**

RASIKĀNANDA, *Disciple of Śyāmānanda.* [*Life.*] *See* GOPĪJANAVALLABHA DĀSA. রসিকমঙ্গল। [Rasikamaṅgala.] [1898.] 8°. **14127. bbb. 5.**

RĀŚIKOSHA. অথ রাশিকোষ। [Rāśikosha. A Sanskrit vocabulary of synonyms for the signs of the zodiac, in verse. With a Bengali translation.] *See* GOPĪRAMAṆA TARKARATNA. কোষচন্দ্রিকা। [Koshachandrikā.] pp. 38, 39. [1893.] 12°. **14090. b. 44.(1.)**

RATIMAÑJARĪ. রতিমঞ্জরী বা রমণীরঙ্গ। [Ratimañjarī, or Ramaṇīraṅga. A Sanskrit poetical manual of the Art of Love. Edited, with a Bengali translation, chiefly in verse, by Kālīprasanna Vidyāratna.] pp. iv. 88. কলিকাতা ১৩০৮ [*Calcutta*, 1901.] 12°. **14053. b. 41.**

RATIŚĀSTRA. সচিত্র শিবোক্ত রতিশাস্ত্র। [Ratiśāstra. An Ars Amoris in 17 cantos, in Sanskrit. With a Bengali translation by Kālīprasanna Vidyāratna Bhaṭṭāchārya. Second edition.] pp. 4, 176. কলিকাতা ১৩০১ [*Calcutta*, 1895.] 12°. **14053. b. 28.**

RATNEŚVARA RĀYA. তেরছদী। [Tera-śadī, or The thirteenth century. A Muhammadan poem on the decline of religion and morality in the present age.] pp. 14. ঢাকা [*Dacca*, 1868 ?] 12°. **14129. a.**

RAVĪNDRANĀTHA ṬHĀKURA. *See* CHHAṚĀ. ছেলে ভুলানো ছড়া। [Chhele-bhulāna chhaṛā. Nursery rhymes of Calcutta. Compiled by Ravīndranātha Ṭhākura.] [1895.] 8°. **14133. f. 18.**

—— *See* PERIODICAL PUBLICATIONS.—*Calcutta*. ভারতী। [Bhāratī. Vol. xxii. edited by Ravīndranātha Ṭhākura.] [1877, *etc.*] 12°. **14133. f. 6.**

—— *See* PERIODICAL PUBLICATIONS.—*Calcutta*. সাধনা। [Sādhanā. Edited (vol. 1-3) by Sudhīndranātha Ṭhākura, and (vol. 4) by Ravīndranātha Ṭhākura.] [1891-95.] 12°. **14133. f. 11.**

—— আধুনিক সাহিত্য। [Ādhunika sāhitya. Modern literature; a series of articles showing the gradual development of modern Bengali literature.] pp. i. 160. কলিকাতা [*Calcutta*, 1907.] 12°. **14131. d. 49.(4.)**

—— ঔপনিষদ ব্রহ্ম। [Aupanishad-brahma. An essay on the Deity of the Upanishads.] pp. 42. ১৩০৮ [*Calcutta*, 1901.] 12°. **14125. e. 40.(2.)**

—— বাউল। [Bāul songs.] pp. ii. 32. কলিকাতা [*Calcutta*, 1905.] 12°. **14129. bb. 17.(2.)**

—— ভারতবর্ষ। [Bhāratavarsha. Ten articles on subjects connected with India, reprinted from the Vaṅgadarṣana.] pp. 154. কলিকাতা ১৩১২ [*Calcutta*, 1906.] 12°. **14125. e. 32.**

—— ছোট গল্প। [Chhoṭa galpa. A collection of short stories on social topics.] pp. 189. কলিকাতা ১৩০০ [*Calcutta*, 1894.] 12°. **14127. d. 43.(2.)**

—— চিত্রা। [Chitrā. Miscellaneous poems, chiefly descriptive.] pp. ii. 151. কলিকাতা ১৩০২ [*Calcutta*, 1896.] 8°. **14129. b. 43.(3.)**

—— চিত্রাঙ্গদা। [Chitrāṅgadā. A drama on the story of Chitrāṅgadā, adapted from the Mahābhārata. With sketches by Avanīndranātha Ṭhākura, reproduced by chromo-lithography.] pp. 41. কলিকাতা ১২৯৯ [*Calcutta*, 1892.] 4°. **14131. cc. 1.**

—— চোখের বালি। [Chokher bāli. A tale of modern Bengali life.] pp. 338. কলিকাতা [*Calcutta*, 1903.] 8°. **14127. cc. 38.**

—— গল্প দশক। [Galpa-daṣaka. A collection of ten short tales.] pp. 220. কলিকাতা ১৩০২ [*Calcutta*, 1895.] 12°. **14127. c. 54.(2.)**

—— গল্পগুচ্ছ। [Galpa-guchchha. Short stories of social and domestic life.] 2 pts. কলিকাতা ১৩০৭ [*Calcutta*, 1900.] 12°. **14127. cc. 19.**

—— গানের বহি ও বাল্মীকি-প্রতিভা। [Gāner bahi. A collection of miscellaneous songs. Followed by Vālmīki-pratibhā, a drama in verse.] pp. 26, 407. কলিকাতা ১৮১৫ [*Calcutta*, 1893.] 16°. **14129. a. 23.**

RAVĪNDRANĀTHA ṬHĀKURA (*continued*). গোড়ায় গলদ্। [Goṛāy galad. A social farce.] pp. 136. কলিকাতা ১২৯৯ [*Calcutta*, 1892.] 12°. **14131. a. 33.(3.)**

—— হাস্য-কৌতুক। [Hāsya-kautuka. Short pieces on the model of English charades.] pp. 85. কলিকাতা [*Calcutta*, 1907.] 12°. **14125. f. 43.**

—— কড়ি ও কোমল। [Kaṛi o komala. Short poems. Second edition.] pp. 4, 188. কলিকাতা ১৩০১ [*Calcutta*, 1895.] 12°. **14129. b. 43.(1.)**

—— কথা। [Kathā. Short moral and religious poems.] pp. 2, 110. কলিকাতা ১৩০৬ [*Calcutta*, 1900.] 12°. **14129. a. 46.(5.)**

—— কথা-চতুষ্টয়। [Kathā-chatushṭaya. Four short stories on every-day life in Bengal.] pp. 130. কলিকাতা ১৩০১ [*Calcutta*, 1894.] 12°. **14127. c. 54.(1.)**

—— কাব্য-গ্রন্থ। [Kāvya-grantha. The poems of Ravīndranātha Ṭhākura, edited by Saileṣa-chandra Majumdār.] 9 pts. কলিকাতা ১৩১০ [*Calcutta*, 1904.] 12°. **14129. bb. 23.**

—— কাব্য গ্রন্থাবলী। [Kāvya-granthāvalī. A complete collection of the author's poetical works.] pp. viii. 476. কলিকাতা ১৩০৩ [*Calcutta*, 1896.] 4°. **14129. ccc. 1.**

—— খেয়া। [Kheyā. Short poems.] pp. iii. iii. 174. কলিকাতা [*Calcutta*, 1906.] 8°. **14129. c. 49.**

—— ক্ষণিকা। [Kshaṇikā. Miscellaneous short poems.] pp. iv. 225. [*Calcutta*, 1900.] 16°. **14129. a. 47.**

—— লোক সাহিত্য। [Loka-sāhitya. Popular literature.] pp. i. 87. কলিকাতা [*Calcutta*, 1907.] 12°. **14131. d. 49.(2.)**

—— নৈবেদ্য। [Naivedya. A century of sonnets.] pp. 200. ১৩০৮ [*Calcutta*, 1901.] 12°. **14129. bb. 13.**

—— প্রভাত-সঙ্গীত। [Prabhāta-saṅgīta, or Songs of sunrise. Second edition.] pp. ix. 96. কলিকাতা ১৮১৩ [*Calcutta*, 1891.] 12°. **14129. a. 32.(1.)**

—— প্রাচীন সাহিত্য। [Prāchīna sāhitya. Ancient literature.] pp. 87. কলিকাতা [*Calcutta*, 1907.] 12°. **14131. d. 49.(1.)**

RAVĪNDRANĀTHA ṬHĀKURA (*continued*). প্রহসন। [Prahasana. Two social farces, viz. Goṛāy galad and Vaikuṇṭher khātā.] pp. 99, 41. কলিকাতা [*Calcutta*, 1908.] 12°. **14131. aa. 12.**

—— প্রজাপতির নির্ব্বন্ধ। [Prajāpatir nibandha. A tale of social life.] pp. 189. কলিকাতা [*Calcutta*, 1908.] 12°. **14128. a. 17.**

—— রাজা ও রাণী। [Rājā o rāṇī. A drama in prose and verse.] pp. 149. কলিকাতা ১২৯৬ [*Calcutta*, 1889.] 8°. **14131. b. 21.**

—— রাজা প্রজা। [Rājā-prajā. Essays on polity, with special reference to the government of India.] pp. 162. কলিকাতা [*Calcutta*, 1908.] 12°. **14125. e. 53.(2.)**

—— রামমোহন রায়। [Rāmamohana Rāya. The life and teachings of Raja Rāmamohana Rāya.] pp. 34. কলিকাতা [*Calcutta*, 1885.] 12°. **14123. c. 8.(4.)**

—— সাহিত্য। [Sāhitya. A review of modern Bengali literature.] pp. i. 163. কলিকাতা [*Calcutta*, 1907.] 12°. **14131. d. 49.(3.)**

—— সমাজ। [Samāja. Essays on modern Hindu society.] pp. 158. কলিকাতা [*Calcutta*, 1908.] 12°. **14125. e. 53.(4.)**

—— সমূহ। [Samūha. Essays and addresses on the *svadeṣī* agitation in Bengal.] pp. 121. কলিকাতা [*Calcutta*, 1908.] 12°. **14125. e. 53.(1.)**

—— সন্ধ্যা-সঙ্গীত। [Sandhyā-saṅgīta, or Songs of sunset. Second edition.] pp. 105. কলিকাতা ১৮১৩ [*Calcutta*, 1891.] 12°. **14129. a. 32.(2.)**

—— শারদোৎসব নাটিকা। [Ṣāradotsava. A short dramatic composition to be acted by students of the Brahmacharyāṣrama at Bolpur.] pp. 167. কলিকাতা [*Calcutta*, 1908.] *obl.* 12°. **14131. aa. 13.**

—— সোনার তরী। [Sonār tarī. Miscellaneous poems. Second edition.] pp. viii. 209. কলিকাতা ১৩০১ [*Calcutta*, 1895.] **14129. b. 43.(2.)**

—— স্বদেশ। [Svadeṣa. Essays on certain phases of social condition in Bengal.] pp. 119. কলিকাতা [*Calcutta*, 1908.] 12°. **14125. e. 53.(3.)**

—— বৈকুণ্ঠের খাতা। [Vaikuṇṭher khātā. A tale of domestic life, in the form of a drama.] pp. 55. কলিকাতা ১৩০৩ [*Calcutta*, 1897.] 12°. **14131. a. 40.(2.)**

RAVĪNDRANĀTHA ṬHĀKURA (*continued*). বিচিত্র গল্প। [Vichitra galpa. A collection of amusing stories.] 2 pts. কলিকাতা ১৩০১ [*Calcutta*, 1894.] 12°. **14127. c. 55.(3.)**

—— ব্যঙ্গকৌতুক। [Vyaṅga-kautuka. Humorous pieces and farces.] pp. 99. কলিকাতা [*Calcutta*, 1907.] 12°. **14131. aa. 8.(3.)**

—— য়ুরোপ যাত্রীর ডায়ারি। [Yūrop yātrīr ḍāyāri. An account of travels in Europe. Pt. i. Introduction.] pp. 78. কলিকাতা ১২৯৮ [*Calcutta*, 1891.] 12°. **14127. c. 40.**

RAVĪNDRANĀTHA ṬHĀKURA and **ṢRĪṢACHANDRA MAJUMDĀR.** পদরত্নাবলী। [Padaratnāvali. A collection of Vaishṇava songs from the works of famous Bengali poets.] pp. vi. xx. 108. কলিকাতা ১২৯২ [*Calcutta*, 1885.] 12°. **14129. a. 23.(3.)**

RĀYA ṢEKHARA. শ্রীরায় শেখরের অষ্টকালীয় দণ্ডাত্মিকা পদাবলী। [Ashṭakālīya daṇḍātmikā. Poems on the sports of Kṛishṇa. Edited, with an introduction, by Nityānanda Dāsa.] pp. ii. vi. 139. বৃন্দাবন ১৯৫৮ [*Brindaban*, 1901.] 8°. **14123. f. 10.(1.)**

REMFRY (Henry H.). ব্রিটীশ ভারতে আইনের উন্নতি ও সংহিতাকরণ বিষয়। [Briṭīs Bhārate āiner unnati. A Bengali translation of H. H. Remfry's "Codification and Improvement of Law in British India."] pp. 17. কলিকাতা ১২৯৭ [*Calcutta*, 1891.] 8°. **14125. a. 19.(2.)**

ṚITENDRANĀTHA ṬHĀKURA. *See* Balendranātha Ṭhākura. স্বর্গীয় বলেন্দ্রনাথ ঠাকুরের গ্রন্থাবলী। [Balendranātha Ṭhākurer granthāvalī. Edited, with a life of the author, by Ṛitendranātha Ṭhākura.] [1907.] 8°. **14127. ee. 30.**

ROBINSON (John). *See* De Foe (D.). রবিন্‌সন্ ক্রুশো। [Robinson Crusoe. Translated by J. Robinson.] [1870.] 12°. **14127. f. 43.**

ROHIṆĪKĀNTA MUKHOPĀDHYĀYA. কুলসার সংগ্রহ। [Kulasāra-saṅgraha. Genealogical tables of Rāḍhīya Brahman families.] 5 pts. কলিকাতা ১২৯২ [*Calcutta*, 1886.] 8°. **14127. b. 34.**

ROHIṆĪKUMĀRA SENA GUPTA. চণ্ডবিক্রম। [Chaṇḍavikrama. A tale of Rajput valour.] pp. 346. কলিকাতা ১২৯৩ [*Calcutta*, 1888.] 8°. **14127. f. 41.**

ROHIṆĪKUMĀRA SENA GUPTA (*continued*). কনকলতা। [Kanakalatā. A tale of love and adventure during the time of Raja Pratāpāditya, in the latter part of the 16th century. Second edition.] pp. ii. 162. ১৩০৫ *Barisal*, [1898.] 12°. **14127. cc. 4.(6.)**

ROHIṆĪNANDANA SARKĀR. *See* PURĀṆAS.—*Mārkaṇḍeyapurāṇa.* শ্রীমার্কণ্ডেয় পুরাণম্। [Mārkaṇḍeyapurāṇa. Sanskrit text, with a Bengali translation by Rohiṇīnandana Sarkār.] [1885, *etc.*] 8°. **14016. c. 37.**

—— *See* UPANISHADS. শিবোপনিষৎ। [Śiva-upanishad. A Sanskrit poem, with a Bengali prose translation, by Rohiṇīnandana Sarkār.] [1890.] 8°. **14028. c. 59.**

ROMAN KRISTO CHATTERJEE. *See* RAMAṆA-KṚISHṆA CHAṬṬOPĀDHYĀYA.

ROMESH CHUNDER DUTT. *See* RAMEŚACHANDRA DATTA.

ROSHAN 'ALĪ. *See* ARABIAN NIGHTS. তরজমা আলেফ লায়লা। [Alf lailā. Translated into Muhammadan Bengali verse by Roshan 'Alī.] [1892.] 4°. **14127. h. 1.**

ROUSE (G. H.). *See* BIBLE. The Holy Bible ... Translated ... by the Calcutta Baptist Missionaries ... Revised edition [by G. H. Rouse]. 1897. 4°. **14123. bbb. 1.**

—— —— 1897. 8°. **14123. b. 20.**

—— *See* BIBLE.—*Genesis.* সটীক আদিপুস্তক। Genesis, annotated in Bengali, by I. Allen and G. H. Rouse. 1895. 8°. **14123. bb. 1.**

—— Tracts for Muhammadans ... Translated from the Bengali. pp. viii. 112. *Madras*, 1893. 12°. **14123. a. 33.**

ROWE (FREDERICK JAMES) and **NĪLAKAṆṬHA MAJUMDĀR.** Examples and Exercises in translation—Bengali-English. pp. viii. 339. *Calcutta*, 1902. 12°. **14131. e. 36.**

ROY (D. C.). *See* DAKSHIṆĀCHARAṆA RĀYA.

ROY (DEVENDRA NATH). *See* DEVENDRANĀTHA RĀYA.

ROY (KRISHNA CHANDRA). *See* KṚISHṆACHANDRA RĀYA.

RŪPA GOSVĀMĪ. [*Life.*] *See* AGHORANĀTHA CHAṬṬOPĀDHYĀYA. ভক্ত-চরিতামৃত। [Bhakta-charitāmṛita.] [1894.] 12°. **14127. aa. 2.(2.)**

—— [*Life.*] *See* DHANAKṚISHṆA ADHIKĀRĪ. শ্রীল শ্রীযুক্ত সনাতন গোস্বামী ও শ্রীরূপ গোস্বামীর জীবন চরিত্র। [Sanātana ... o Rūpa Gosvāmīr jīvana-charitra.] [1892.] 8°. **14127. b. 47.(2.)**

—— [*Life.*] *See* JĀNAKĪNĀTHA PĀLA, *B.L.* শ্রীরূপ-সনাতন। [Śrīrūpa-Sanātana.] [1904.] 12°. **14127. a. 45.(4.)**

—— হংসদূত। [Haṃsadūta, or Goose-Messenger. A Sanskrit poem in 101 stanzas, modelled on Kālidāsa's Meghadūta. Edited, with a Bengali translation, by Yogendranātha De.] pp. 46. কলিকাতা ১৩০৫ [*Calcutta*, 1898.] 12°. **14060. b. 17.**

—— লঘুভাগবতামৃত। [Laghu-bhāgavatāmṛita. An exposition of the Vaishṇava doctrine of Chaitanya, as set forth in the Bhāgavata and cognate Sanskrit works, and consisting of two parts styled Kṛishṇāmṛita and Bhaktāmṛita. With a Sanskrit commentary by Baladeva Vidyābhūshaṇa, and Bengali translation and notes by Madanagopāla Gosvāmī. Edited by Balāichāṇd Gosvāmī and Atulakṛishṇa Gosvāmī.] pp. viii. xxxii. iv. 184, 97. কলিকাতা ১৩০৪ [*Calcutta*, 1897.] 8°. **14016. c. 58.**

—— নাটক-চন্দ্রিকা। [Nāṭaka-chandrikā. A Sanskrit treatise on the art of dramatic poetry, as illustrated in the religious plays of the Chaitanya church. Edited, with a Bengali translation, by Rāsavihārī Sāṅkhyatīrtha.] pp. vi. 226, ii. কাশীমবাজার ১৩১৩ [*Cossimbazar*, 1907.] 8°. **14055. b. 3.**

—— সটীক ও সানুবাদ শ্রীস্তবপুষ্পাঞ্জলিঃ। [Stava-pushpāñjali. A series of Sanskrit Vaishṇava devotional lyrics of the Chaitanya sect, compiled from the Stavamālā of Rūpa Gosvāmī, as arranged by Jīva Gosvāmī, and from Raghunāthadāsa Gosvāmī's Stavāvali. With a Sanskrit commentary, and a Bengali translation. Edited by Baṭudāsa Gosvāmī.] pp. ii. ii. 538. বৃন্দাবন ১৯৫৮ [*Brindaban*, 1902.] 8°. **14072. ccc. 3 A.**

—— উজ্জ্বলনীলমণিঃ। [Ujjvala-nīlamaṇi. A Sanskrit work on the art of Poetics, especially as applied to the legend of Kṛishṇa. With the commentary called Lochanarochanī by Jīva Gosvāmī, and that called Ānandachandrikā by Viṣvanātha Chakravartī. Edited, with a Bengali translation, by Rāmanārāyaṇa Vidyāratna. Second edition.] pp. i. i. ii. x. 992. মুর্শিদাবাদ ১২৯৫ [*Murshidabad*, 1889.] 8°. **14053. d. 49.**

RŪPANĀRĀYAṆA, *Son of Jagannātha Ghosha. See* RASIKACHANDRA VASU. দুর্গামঙ্গল ও কবি রূপনারায়ণ। [Durgāmaṅgala. An article on the poem and its author Rūpanārāyaṇa.] [1897.] 8°. **14133. f. 18.**

RUSSICK LAL. *See* RASIKALĀLA.

SĀBITRĪ LIBRARY. *See* CALCUTTA.—*Sāvitrī Library.*

SACHCHIDĀNANDA ARAṆYA. *See* HARIHARĀNANDA, *Sāṅkhyayogāchārya.* सांख्यतत्त्वालोकः *etc.* [Sāṅkhyatattvāloka. Edited, with Bengali translations, notes, and appendices, by Sachchidānanda.] [1903.] 8°. **14049. b. 14.**

SADĀNANDA YOGĪNDRA. বেদান্তসারঃ [Vedāntasāra. Elements of Vedānta philosophy. Sanskrit text, preceded by the Hastāmalaka and Nirañjanāshṭaka of Ṣaṅkara Āchārya, and the Siddhāntabindusāra of Madhusūdana Sarasvatī, with Bengali translations, and followed by the Sanskrit commentaries entitled Subodhinī and Vidvanmanorañjinī.] *See* MAHEṢACHANDRA PĀLA. বেদান্তরত্নাবলী। [Vedānta-ratnāvalī.] Pt. i. [1805-06.] 8°. **14048. bb. 15.**

—— বেদান্তসারঃ। [Vedānta-sāra. Sanskrit text, with a Bengali translation and introduction.] [1895.] *See* RAMEṢACHANDRA DATTA. হিন্দুশাস্ত্র। [Hindu-ṣāstra.] Pt. v., pp. 153-205. [1895-97.] 8°. **14065. c. 45.(vol. i.)**

—— সটীক সানুবাদ বেদান্ত-সার। [Vedānta-sāra. Sanskrit text, with the commentary Subodhinī of Nṛisiṃha Sarasvatī, and a Bengali translation by Kālīvara Vedāntavāgīṣa. Edited by Hīrālāl Ḍhol. Third edition.] pp. iv. 80, 53. কলিকাতা ১৩০৯ [*Calcutta*, 1903.] 12°. **14048. b. 41.**

Forms section 3 of the series Vidyākalpadruma.

SA'DĪ. গোলেস্তাঁর বঙ্গানুবাদ। [Gulistān. Chapters 5 to 7, translated in prose and verse by Maulavī Muḥammad 'Abd al-Ḳādir. With the Persian text and transliteration of the portions in verse.] pp. viii. 182. কলিকাতা ১৩১২ [*Calcutta*, 1905.] 12°. **Pers. 1657.**

SA'DĪ (*continued*). گلستان ... পুষ্পোদ্যান অর্থাৎ... গোলেস্তান। [Pushpodyāna. The Gulistān of Sa'dī, translated from the Persian in prose and verse by Shaikh Muḥammad 'Abd al-Ḳādir.] Pt. i. pp. ii. 144. [*Calcutta*, 1901.] 8°. **14129. d. 33.**

ṢADR al-DĪN, *of Mecca.* মেপ্তাহোলকাবা। [Miftāḥ al-ka'bah. A guide to the pilgrimage of Mecca and Medina, in Muhammadan Bengali verse.] pp. 177. নোয়াখালী ১৩০৯ [*Noakhali*, 1903.] 8°. **14129. d. 34.**

SAHADEVA CHAKRAVARTĪ. *See* AMBIKĀCHARAṆA GUPTA. সহদেব চক্রবর্তীর ধর্মমঙ্গল। [Sahadeva Chakravartīr Dharmamaṅgala. An article on the poet Sahadeva and his Dharmamaṅgala.] [1898.] 8°. **14133. f. 18.**

SĀHEBĪ LĪLĀ. সাহেবী-লীলা। [Sāhebī līlā. The story of a penniless Englishman coming to India, and amassing a fortune there. Second edition.] pp. ii. 42. ১২৯৬ *Calcutta*, [1890.] 12°. **14127. d. 40.(1.)**

ṢAILAJĀNANDA OJHĀ. [Begin.] भगवान्-गुणवि-भूषण-राजभक्तिपरायण-भारतजनगण-समीपे सादरमावेदनम्। [A short Sanskrit poem on the Jubilee of Queen Victoria's reign, with English and Bengali translations.] pp. 3. [*Calcutta?* 1887?] 8°. **14076. cc. 2.(1.)**

ṢAILENDRABANDHU RĀYA. বান্ধবং ব্যাকরণম্। [Bāndhavaṃ vyākaraṇam. Rules of Sanskrit grammar, explained in Bengali.] pp. v. 345, iv. কলিকাতা ১২৯৭ [*Calcutta*, 1891.] 8°. **14131. g. 28**

ṢAILEṢACHANDRA MAJUMDĀR. *See* PERIODICAL PUBLICATIONS.—*Calcutta.* সমালোচনী। [Samālochanī. Edited by Ṣaileṣachandra Majumdār.] [1902-05.] 12°. **14133. ee. 1.**

—— *See* RAVĪNDRANĀTHA ṬHĀKURA. কাব্য-গ্রন্থ। [Kāvyagrantha. Edited by Saileṣachandra Majumdār.] [1904.] 12°. **14129. bb. 23.**

—— চিত্র-বিচিত্র। [Chitravichitra. Sketches of Bengali life and character.] pp. iv. 204. কলিকাতা ১৩০৯ [*Calcutta*, 1902.] 12°. **14127. cc. 32.**

ṢAIVALINĪ DEVĪ. *See* MAHĀBHĀRATA.—*Bhagavadgītā.* গীতাকাব্য। [Gītākāvya. A metrical translation of the Bhagavadgītā by Ṣaivalinī Devī.] [1901.] 12°. **14129. bb. 11.**

SAIYID MURTAZĀ. *See* MURTAZĀ, *Saiyid, of Murshidabad.*

SAKHĀRĀMA GAṆEŚA DEUSKAR. দেশের কথা। [Deśer kathā. A collection of articles on India under British rule, the condition of its inhabitants, agriculture, trade, *etc.* Fourth edition.] কলিকাতা ১৩১৪ [*Calcutta*, 1907, *etc.*] 12°.
In progress. **14125. e. 48.**

—— ঝাঁশীর রাজকুমার। [Jhānsīr rājakumāra. A short sketch of the history of Jhansi, dealing chiefly with an account of Rāṇī Lakshmī Bāī, and the events which led to the occupation of the District by the British in 1858. Third edition.] pp. ii. 52. কলিকাতা ১৩১৫ [*Calcutta*, 1908.] 12°. **14127. aaa. 3.**

SAMBHOGA-RATNĀKARA. সুখ সম্ভোগ রত্নাকর। [Sambhoga-ratnākara. A treatise on marriage and sexual pathology.] Pt. i. pp. xv. 266. *Calcutta*, 1889. 12°. **14125. b. 11.**

ŚAMBHUCHANDRA VIDYĀRATNA. ভ্রমনিরাস। [Bhramanirāsa. A criticism on Vidyāsāgara, or Chaṇḍīcharaṇa Vandyopādhyāya's life of Īśvarachandra Vidyāsāgara, pointing out certain inaccurate statements made in that biography.] pp. ii. 89. কলিকাতা ১৩০২ [*Calcutta*, 1895.] 8°. **14131. d. 31.**

—— পণ্ডিতকুলতিলক মহাত্মা তারানাথ তর্কবাচস্পতির জীবনচরিত। [Tārānātha Tarkavāchaspatir jīvanacharita. A biography of Pandit Tārānātha Tarkavāchaspati.] pp. 76. কলিকাতা ১৩০০ [*Calcutta*, 1893.] 8°. **14127. bb. 7.**

—— বিদ্যাসাগর-জীবনচরিত। [Vidyāsāgara-jīvanacharita. The life of Īśvarachandra Vidyāsāgara.] pp. 250. কলিকাতা ১২৯৮ [*Calcutta*, 1891.] 8°. **14127. b. 49.(1.)**

SAMĪR al-DĪN AḤMAD. ছহি জিন্নাতোল কুঞ্জী। [Jannat al-kunjī. A treatise on prayer and religious obligations, in Muhammadan Bengali verse.] pp. 291. ঢাকা ১৩০৮ [*Dacca*, 1901.] 8°. **14123. h. 29.(1.)**

—— معراج الاسلام মোহাম্মদীয় ধর্ম্ম-সোপান। [Mi'rāj al-Islām. An exposition of the principles of Muhammadan faith, extracted from various Arabic sources, with Bengali translations and notes.] কলিকাতা ১৩০৯ [*Calcutta*, 1903, *etc.*] 8°.
In progress. **14123. h. 31.**

SĀMUDRIKA. সানুবাদ বৃহৎ সামুদ্রিক। [Sāmudrika, or Bṛihat sāmudrika. A Sanskrit work on palmistry. Enlarged from several sources, and edited, with a Bengali translation, by Kālīprasanna Vidyāratna Bhaṭṭāchārya.] pp. ii. 160. কলিকাতা ১২৯৯ [*Calcutta*, 1892.] 8°. **14053. cc. 66.**

—— সানুবাদ বৃহৎ সামুদ্রিক। [Bṛihat sāmudrika. Another edition of the Sanskrit text, with Bengali introduction and translation. Edited by Harinārāyaṇa Jyotīratna.] pp. ii. 152. *Calcutta*, [1902.] 8°. **14053. ccc. 4.(4.)**

SAṂVARTA. সংবর্ত্তসংহিতা। [Saṃvarta-saṃhitā. A code of *dharma*, in 227 Sanskrit stanzas. With Bengali translation.] *See* PAÑCHĀNANA TARKARATNA BHAṬṬĀCHĀRYA. ঊনবিংশতি সংহিতা। [Ūnaviṃśati saṃhitā.] pp. 289-302. [1903.] 8°. **14039. c. 20.**

SANĀTANA DHARMOTSĀHINĪ SABHĀ. *See* RANAGHAT.—*Sanātana Dharmotsāhinī Sabhā.*

SANĀTANA GOSVĀMĪ. [*Life.*] *See* AGHORANĀTHA CHAṬṬOPĀDHYĀYA. ভক্ত-চরিতামৃত। [Bhakta-charitāmṛita.] [1894.] 12°. **14127. aa. 2.(2.)**

—— [*Life.*] *See* DHANAKRISHṆA ADHIKĀRĪ. শ্রীল শ্রীযুক্ত সনাতন ... গোস্বামীর জীবন চরিত্র। [Sanātana Gosvāmīr jīvana-charitra.] [1892.] 8°. **14127. b. 47.(2.)**

—— [*Life.*] *See* JĀNAKĪNĀTHA PĀLA, *B.L.* শ্রীরূপ-সনাতন। [Śrīrūpa-Sanātana.] [1904.] 12°. **14127. a. 45.(4.)**

ŚĀṆḌILYA. শাণ্ডিল্যকৃত ভক্তিসূত্র। [Bhaktisūtra. A collection of aphorisms on Vaishṇava devotion; Sanskrit text, with a Bengali translation and commentary.] *See* KRISHṆAPRASANNA SENA. ভক্তি ও ভক্ত [Bhakti o bhakta.] pp. 42-76. [1887.] 8°. **14028. c. 56.**

—— শাণ্ডিল্যসূত্রম্। [Śāṇḍilya-sūtra. Sanskrit text and commentary by Bhavadeva Miśra. Edited, with a Bengali translation, by Hṛishīkeśa Śāstrī.] pp. iii. 299. কলিকাতা ১৮২৭ [*Calcutta*, 1906.] 8°. **14049. b. 41.**

SĀNDRĀNANDA ĀCHĀRYA. *See* UPANISHADS. কৃষ্ণ-যজুর্ব্বেদীয়-উপনিষদঃ। [Taittirīya upanishad. Sanskrit text, edited, with a Bengali translation and notes, by Sāndrānanda Āchārya.] [1896.] 8°. **14010. cc. 3.(2.)**

SAṄGĪTAHĀRA. সঙ্গীতহার। [Saṅgītahāra. A collection of love-songs.] *See* AGHORACHANDRA GHOSHA. সঙ্গীত সাগর। [Saṅgītasāgara.] Vol. i. [1889.] 12°. **14129. b. 33.**

SAṄGĪTAKALPADRUMA. সঙ্গীতকল্পদ্রুম। [Saṅgītakalpadruma. A collection of miscellaneous songs and poems by various authors, with short notices of their lives.] *See* AGHORACHANDRA GHOSHA. সঙ্গীত সাগর। [Saṅgītasāgara.] Vol. ii. [1889.] 12°. **14129. b. 33.**

SAṄGĪTAMĀLĀ. সঙ্গীতমালা। [Saṅgītamālā. A collection of miscellaneous songs.] *See* AGHORACHANDRA GHOSHA. সঙ্গীত সাগর। [Saṅgītasāgara.] Vol. i. [1889.] 12°. **14129. b. 33.**

SAṄGĪTAVILĀSA. অপূর্ব্ব সঙ্গীত বিলাস। [Saṅgītavilāsa. A collection of miscellaneous songs.] pp. 120. কলিকাতা ১৩০২ [*Calcutta*, 1896.] 12°. **14129. b. 44.(5.)**

ṢANIPŪJĀPADDHATI. শ্রীশ্রীশনিপূজাপদ্ধতি ও পাঁচালী। [Ṣanipūjāpaddhati. A Sanskrit poem on the worship of the planet-god Ṣani or Saturn, as prescribed in the Skandapurāṇa. Followed by Ṣanipāṇchālī, a Bengali poem on the legend and cult of Ṣani.] pp. 25. *Calcutta*, [1901.] *obl.* 8°. **14028. dd. 10.(2.)**

SAÑJĪVACHANDRA CHAṬṬOPĀDHYĀYA. কণ্ঠমালা। মাধবীলতার পরভাগ। [Kaṇṭhamālā. A tale of modern life and manners, being a sequel to the author's Mādhavīlatā. Second edition.] pp. 155. কলিকাতা ১৮৮৬ [*Calcutta*, 1886.] 8°. **14127. f. 38.**

—— [Third edition.] pp. 155. কলিকাতা ১৩০৮ [*Calcutta*, 1901.] 8°. **14127. ee. 12.**

—— সঞ্জীবনী সুধা। [Sañjīvanī-sudhā. Extracts from the works of Sañjīvachandra Chaṭṭopādhyāya. With a life of the author by Baṅkimchandra Chaṭṭopādhyāya, and a criticism by Chandranātha Vasu.] pp. 130. *Calcutta*, 1893. 12°. **14127. c. 52.**

—— যাত্রা সমালোচনা। [Yātrā-samālochanā. A review of the native drama.] *See* PYĀRĪCHĀND MITRA. রামারঞ্জিকা *etc.* [Rāmārañjikā.] pp. 103-128. [1907.] 12°. **14125. e. 49.**

ṢAṄKARA ĀCHĀRYA. *See* JAHARLĀL DHARA. শঙ্কর-বিজয় নাটক। [Ṣaṅkara-vijaya nāṭaka. A drama dealing with the life and teachings of Ṣaṅkara Āchārya.] [1897.] 12°. **14131. a. 40.(7.)**

ṢAṄKARA ĀCHĀRYA (*continued*). [*Life.*] *See* ṢARACHCHANDRA ṢĀSTRĪ. শঙ্করাচার্য্য-চরিত। [Ṣaṅkarāchārya-charita.] [1903]. 12°. **14127. aa. 27.**

—— অপরোক্ষানুভূতিঃ। [Aparokshānubhūti. Followed by the Ātmabodha, Sanskrit text, accompanied by a Bengali translation.] *See* MAHEṢACHANDRA PĀLA. বেদান্তরত্নাবলী [Vedānta-ratnāvalī.] Pt. 2. [1883, *etc.*] 8°. **14048. bb. 15.**

—— ଆତ୍ମବୋଧଃ [Ātmabodha. Sanskrit text, with a Bengali translation in Oriya characters.] pp. 24. *Cuttack*, 1885. 12°. **14048. b. 18.(2.)**

—— মোহ-মুদ্গরঃ [Mohamudgara.] Panacea for distraction. [Moral maxims in Sanskrit verse.] By Paramahansa Sankaráchárya. Edited . . . with Bengali, Hindi and English translations, by Durga Das Ray. pp. 16. *Darjeeling*, 1888. 32°. **14048. a. 11.**

—— মোহমুদ্গরঃ (যতিপঞ্চক ও সাধনপঞ্চক।) [Mohamudgara. Also Yatipañchaka and Sādhanapañchaka. Sanskrit text, with Bengali metrical translations.] *See* TĀRĀKUMĀRA KAVIRATNA. পঞ্চামৃত। [Pañchāmṛita.] pp. 11-29. [1892.] 12°. **14028. b. 73.(1.)**

—— শঙ্করাচার্য্যের গ্রন্থমালা। [Ṣaṅkarāchāryer granthamālā. The works of Ṣaṅkara Āchārya, comprising the Ātmabodha, Aparokshānubhūti and Vākyavṛitti, together with 49 of the philosophical and religious poems generally ascribed to him. Edited, with Bengali translations, by Kālīprasanna Vidyāratna. Second edition.] pp. iii. 208. কলিকাতা ১৩০৯ [*Calcutta*, 1903.] 8°. **14033. aa. 30.**

ṢAṄKARĀNANDA, *Disciple of Ānandātmā.* আত্মপুরাণম্। [Ātmapurāṇa. Sanskrit text and commentary of Rāmakṛishṇa, with a Bengali translation successively by Chaṇḍīcharaṇa Smṛitibhūshaṇa, Bhūtanātha Vidyāratna, and Jaganmohana Tarkālaṅkāra.] 6 pts. কলিকাতা ১৯৪২ [*Calcutta*, 1885.] 8°. **14048. e. 13.**

ṢAṄKHA. শঙ্খসংহিতা। [Ṣaṅkha-saṃhitā. A code of *dharma*, in 18 *adhyāyas*. Sanskrit text, with Bengali translation.] *See* PAÑCHĀNANA TARKARATNA BHAṬṬĀCHĀRYA. ঊনবিংশতি সংহিতা। [Ūnaviṃṣati-saṃhitā.] pp. 393-413. [1903.] 8°. **14039. c. 20.**

SAṄKHĀRA-BHĀJANI. বৌদ্ধ-কাহিনী সংগ্রহ। [Bauddhakāhinī-saṅgraha. A collection of Buddhist homilies and stories, translated from the Burmese Saṅkhāra-bhājani by Nagendralāla Baṛuyā Kavirāja.] pp. vi. 61. চট্টগ্রাম ১৩০৯ [*Chittagong*, 1903.] 12°. **14123. k. 4.(2.)**

ṢĀNTIGĪTĀ. শান্তিগীতা। [Ṣāntigītā. A Vedantic poem in 7 chapters, addressed by Krishṇa to Arjuna in consolation for his son's death. Sanskrit text, with Bengali translation.] *See* PAÑCHA GĪTĀ. পঞ্চগীতা। [Pañcha gītā.] pp. 97-286. [1906.] 16°. **14028. a. 33.**

ṢĀNTIMAYA. শান্তিময়। বা দুই ভগ্নি উপন্যাসের উপসংহার ভাগ। [Ṣāntimaya. A sequel to Dāmodara Mukhopādhyāya's Dui bhagnī. By an anonymous authoress.] pp. 47. কলিকাতা ১৩০৬ [*Calcutta*, 1899.] 12°. **14127. c. 30.(5.)**

ṢĀNTIRĀMA DE. কবিরঞ্জন ৺ রামপ্রসাদ সেনের জীবন-বৃত্তান্ত। [Rāmaprasāda Sener jīvana-vṛittānta. An account of the life and writings of the Bengali poet Rāmaprasāda Sena.] pp. 45. কলিকাতা ১৮৯১ [*Calcutta*, 1889.] 12°. **14131. d. 21.(3.)**

ṢARACHCHANDRA BHAṬṬĀCHĀRYA. তান্তিয়া ভীল নাটক। [Tāntiyā Bhīl nāṭaka. A drama describing the exploits of Tāntiyā Bhīl, the notorious dacoit.] pp. 136. *Calcutta*, 1893. 12°. **14131. a. 33.(6.)**

ṢARACHCHANDRA CHAUDHURĪ. *See* PERIODICAL PUBLICATIONS.—*Calcutta.* শিক্ষা-পরিচর। [Ṣikshā-parichara. Edited by Ṣarachchandra Chaudhurī.] [1889-91.] 8°. **14133. f. 12.**

ṢARACHCHANDRA DĀSA. মধু-মালতী। [Madhu-Mālatī. A tale of female domestic life.] pp. 186. কলিকাতা ১৩০২ [*Calcutta*, 1895.] 12°. **14127. c. 57.(1.)**

ṢARACHCHANDRA DATTA. ৺ দয়াময়ী সেনের সংক্ষিপ্ত জীবন চরিত। [Dayāmayī Sener saṃkshipta jīvanacharita. The life of Dayāmayī Sena, an eminent Hindu lady, wife of Navakiṣora Sena.] pp. 36. শ্রীহট্ট ১২৯৭ [*Sylhet*, 1890.] 12°. **14127. a. 37.(1.)**

ṢARACHCHANDRA DATTA and GAṄGĀGATI DĀSA. আসাম প্রদেশের বিশেষ বিবরণ। [Āsām pradeṣer viṣesha vivaraṇa. An account of the province of Assam. Fifth edition.] pp. x. 107. ঢাকা [*Dacca*, 1906.] 12°. **14127. aa. 28.(5.)**

—— [Seventh edition.] pp. ix. 107. ঢাকা ১৩১৩ [*Dacca*, 1906.] 12°. **14131. f. 34.**

ṢARACHCHANDRA DE. শিলাদিত্য। [Ṣilāditya. A drama based on Tod's account of the defeat of Rāṇā Saṅga by the emperor Bābar, through the defection of Ṣilāditya, a feudatory chieftain.] pp. 192. কলিকাতা ১৩০৭ [*Calcutta*, 1900.] 12°. **14131. a. 41.(5.)**

ṢARACHCHANDRA DEVA. নিগূঢ় ধর্ম্ম তত্ত্ব। [Nigudha dharma-tattva. A short sketch in verse of Christianity and the principal religions of India.] pp. 34. *Calcutta*, 1895. 12°. **14123. a. 27.(2.)**

—— পাইকপাড়াতে হুলস্থূল। খেপে গেল যবন কুল। [Pāikpāṛāte hulasthūla. A poem on the disturbances between Hindus and Muhammadans.] Pt. i. pp. 12. [*Calcutta*, 1897.] 12°. **14129. a. 52.(1.)**

ṢARACHCHANDRA GHOSHA. সদ্গোপ জাতি ও সমাজ তত্ত্ব। [Sadgop-jāti. A treatise on the Sadgop caste, their manners and customs, with suggestions for the amelioration of their present condition.] pp. ii. 220. কলিকাতা ১৩১২ [*Calcutta*, 1906.] 12°. **14125. e. 51.**

ṢARACHCHANDRA LĀHIṚĪ, *of Baliyakandi.* বারেন্দ্র কুলীনদিগের বংশাবলী। [Vārendra kulīnadiger vaṃṣāvalī. Genealogical tables of the Vārendra Kulins.] কলিকাতা [*Calcutta*, 1905, *etc.*] *obl.* 4°. **14127. bbb. 7.**
In progress.

ṢARACHCHANDRA MITRA. *See* SCOTT (W.). কেনিলওয়ার্থ। [Kenilworth. Translated by Ṣarachchandra Mitra.] [1898.] 8°. **14127. cc. 13.**

ṢARACHCHANDRA ṢĀSTRĪ. *See* RĀMACHANDRA MUKHOPĀDHYĀYA, *of Harinabhi.* দুর্গামঙ্গল। [Durgāmaṅgala. Edited, with a short account of the author, by Ṣarachchandra Ṣāstrī.] 1898. 12°. **14129. a. 28.(2.)**

—— দক্ষিণাপথ ভ্রমণ। [Dakshiṇāpatha-bhramaṇa. Travels in the Deccan and Central India.] pp. ii. 246. কলিকাতা ১৩০৪ [*Calcutta*, 1898.] 12°. **14127. aa. 10.**

—— দ্বিজ রামচন্দ্রের দুর্গামঙ্গল কাব্য। [Rāmachandrer Durgāmaṅgala. An article on the Durgāmaṅgala, a poem in praise of the goddess Durgā by Rāmachandra, son of Rāmadhana.] ১৩০৬ [1898.] *See* ACADEMIES, *etc.*—Calcutta.—

Bengal Academy of Literature. সাহিত্য-পরিষৎ-পত্রিকা। [Sāhitya-parishat-patrikā.] Vol. v., no. 1. [1894, *etc.*] 8°. **14133. f. 18.**

—— শঙ্করাচার্য্য-চরিত। [Ṣaṅkarāchārya-charita. The life of Ṣaṅkara Āchārya.] pp. xii. 225. কলিকাতা ১৩১০ [*Calcutta*, 1903.] 12°. **14127. aa. 27.**

SĀRADĀCHARAṆA SENA KAVIRATNA. *See* Mādhava, *Son of Indukara.* নিদান। [Nidāna. Translated by Sāradācharaṇa Sena.] [1903.] 8°. **14125. c. 43.(2.)**

SĀRADĀPRASĀDA BHAṬṬĀCHĀRYA. অমরনাথ। . . . Amarnath, or Babu Saroda Prosad Bhattacharje's Travels in Himalaya:—Cashmir and Amarnath. pp. viii. vii. 124. কলিকাতা ১৮৯৫ [*Calcutta*, 1895.] 12°. **14127. a. 51.(2.)**

SĀRADĀPRASĀDA CHAKRAVARTĪ, *Doctor.* ভৈষজ্য-সার-সংগ্রহ। [Bhaishajya-sārasaṅgraha. A concise Materia Medica. Fifth edition.] pp. 588, xiv. কলিকাতা ১৯০৬ [*Calcutta*, 1906.] 12°. **14125. b. 22.**

SĀRADĀPRASĀDA CHAKRAVARTĪ, *Novelist.* সাবিত্রী। সামাজিক উপন্যাস। [Sāvitrī. A story of Hindu domestic life in Bengal.] pp. 332. কলিকাতা ১৩০৪ [*Calcutta*, 1898.] 12°. **14127. cc. 7.**

—— বিমাতা না রাক্ষসী। [Vimātā nā rākshasī. A novel describing the cruel neglect of a step-child by her step-mother.] pp. 144, 10. কলিকাতা ১৩০০ [*Calcutta*, 1894.] 12°. **14127. c. 49.**

SĀRADĀPRASĀDA MITRA. *See* Gopījanavallabha Dāsa. রসিকমঙ্গল। [Rasika-maṅgala. Edited, with an introduction, by Sāradāprasāda Mitra.] [1898.] 8°. **14127. bbb. 5.**

SĀRADĀPRASĀDA MUKHOPĀDHYĀYA. শঙ্কর। [Ṣaṅkara. A tale of the Indian mutiny, and massacre at Cawnpore.] pp. 104. কলিকাতা ১৮৮৮ [*Calcutta*, 1888.] 12°. **14127. d. 32.(1.)**

SARALĀ. সরলা ও চতুরা। [Saralā o chaturā. A picture of modern Hindu society in Calcutta.] pp. 189. কলিকাতা ১২৯৯ [*Calcutta*, 1893.] 12°. **14127. d. 43.(1.)**

SARALĀ DEVĪ. *See* Periodical Publications.—*Calcutta.* ভারতী। [Bhāratī. Vols. 24 to 31, edited by Ṣrīmatī Saralā Devī.] [1877, *etc.*] 8°. **14133. f. 6.**

SARALĀ DEVĪ (*continued*). শত গান। [Ṣata-gāna. A collection of 100 songs by celebrated composers, set to native music.] pp. 216. [*Calcutta*, 1900.] 8°. **14129. c. 53.**

SĀRASVATĀBHIDHĀNA. সারস্বতাভিধান। [Sārasvatābhidhāna. A Sanskrit vocabulary of synonyms in verse, ascribed to the goddess Sarasvatī. With a Bengali translation.] *See* Gopīramaṇa Tarkaratna. কোষচন্দ্রিকা। [Koshachandrikā.] pp. 21-24. [1893.] 12°. **14090. b. 44.(1.)**

ṢARATKUMĀRA GHOSHA. Sarath Kumar Gosh Indische Nächte. [Translated from the Bengali into German by Martin Holle.] pp. 238. *Berlin*, [1906.] 8°. **14128. a. 7.**

ṢARATKUMĀRA SENA. *See* Kālidāsa. কালিদাসের কবিতা। [Kālidāser kavitā. Compiled and edited, with a Bengali translation and biography of the poet, by Ṣaratkumāra Sena.] [1901.] 12°. **14076. b. 26.(2.)**

ṢARATKUMĀRA SENA GUPTA. A short sketch of the life of Ananda Mohan Basu. মহাত্মা আনন্দমোহন বসু। [Mahātmā Ānandamohana Vasu.] ময়মনসিংহ ১৩১৩ [*Mymensingh*, 1907.] 12°. **14127. aa. 18.(3.)**

ṢARAT SUNDARĪ, *Mahārāṇī.* [*Life.*] *See* Girīṣachandra Lāhiṛī. প্রাতঃস্মরণীয়া ৺ মহারাণী শরৎসুন্দরীর জীবন-চরিত। [Mahārāṇī Ṣarat Sundarīr jīvana-charita.] [1894.] 8°. **14127. aa. 3.(2.)**

SARGENT (Henry). *See* Virgilius Maro (Publius). The First Book of Virgil's Æneid, translated ... by H. Sargent. 1810. 8°. **T. 2124.(1.)**

SARKĀR (K. K. G.), *Rev.* মধ্য ভারতে প্রচলিত প্রবাদ মালা। [Pravādamālā. A collection of Bengali and Hindi proverbs in use in Central India: to which are added a few conundrums.] pp. 47. কলিকাতা ১৮৯৪ [*Calcutta*, 1894.] 12°. **14125. f. 35.**

SAROJINĪ DEVĪ. আবেগ। [Āvega. A collection of lyric poems.] pp. iv. 198. কলিকাতা ১৩০৭ [*Calcutta*, 1900.] 8°. **14129. bb. 3.**

SARPĀLAṄKĀRA ṬHĀKURA, *pseud.* দৃশ্য পঞ্চক বা অপ্সরার ভারতভ্রমণ। [Dṛiṣya-pañchaka. A farce on the pernicious effects of Western civilization on Hindu religious life.] pp. 35. কলিকাতা ১৩০৩ [*Calcutta*, 1897.] 12°. **14131. a. 40.(1.)**

SURENDRA DEVA GUPTA MAJUMDĀR. আর্য্য সমাজ-সংস্করণ ... Aryan Samája-sanskarana. A few hints and suggestions regarding the reformation of the Aryan Society of India ... by Surendra Deva Gupta Mazumdára. pp. iv. 192. *Calcutta*, 1885. 8°. **14125. ee. 19.**

SURENDRAMOHANA BHAṬṬĀCHĀRYA. ভবানীর মঠ। উপন্যাস। [Bhavānīr maṭha. An historical tale.] pp. 281. কলিকাতা ১৩১৪ [*Calcutta*, 1907.] 12°. **14128. a. 11.(2.)**

—— ঘুমন্ত ছবি। [Ghumanta chhabi. An hypnotic story.] pp. 112. কলিকাতা ১৩১১ [*Calcutta*, 1904.] 12°. **14127. cc. 20.(2.)**

—— হেমচন্দ্র। [Hemachandra. A novel, written as a sequel to Bankimchandra's Mṛiṇālinī.] pp. 239. *Calcutta*, [1905.] 12°. **14128. a. 4.**

—— জাহানারা। [Jahānārā. A Bengali novel.] pp. 336. *Calcutta*, ১৩১২ [1905.] 12°. **14128. a. 3.**

—— মরা মেম। [Marā mem. The dead lady; a detective story.] pp. 108. কলিকাতা ১৩১২ [*Calcutta*, 1905.] 12°. **14127. d. 19.(4.)**

—— মায়াবিনী উপন্যাস। [Māyāvinī. A tale of life in Bengal.] pp. 218. *Calcutta*, 1901. 12°. **14127. cc. 33.(1.)**

—— কুলীনকুমারী নির্ম্মলা। [Nirmalā. A social novel depicting the evils of Kulin caste-observances.] pp. 142. কলিকাতা ১৩০৩ [*Calcutta*, 1896.] 12°. **14127. d. 43.(3.)**

—— প্রেত-তর্পণ। [Pretatarpaṇa. An historical novel.] pp. 368. কলিকাতা ১৩১৪ [*Calcutta*, 1907.] 12°. **14128. a. 23.**

—— পুরোহিত-দর্পণ। [Purohita-darpaṇa. A handbook of all rites administered by priests. Sanskrit text, with Bengali rubrics, translations, *etc.* Fifth edition.] pp. xvi. 400, 280, 191. *Calcutta*, ১৩১৩ [1906.] 8°. **14033. bbb. 40.**

—— সেনাপতির গুপ্তরহস্য। [Senāpatir gupta-rahasya. The adventures of a general; a novel in 4 parts.] pp. 465. *Calcutta*, 1904. 12°. **14127. cc. 39.**

—— সোণার পারিজাত। [Soṇār pārijāta. A tale of modern Bengali life.] pp. 300. কলিকাতা ১৩১৩ [*Calcutta*, 1906.] 12°. **14128. a. 11.(3.)**

SURENDRAMOHANA BHAṬṬĀCHĀRYA (*continued*). সুর-সুন্দরী। রমন্যাস। [Sura-Sundarī. A tale of life in Bengal during the last century.] pp. 332. *Calcutta*, 1891. 12°. **14127. c. 39.(2.)**

—— সুরেন্দ্র-প্রতিভা। [Surendra-Pratibhā. A Bengali novel.] pp. 88. কলিকাতা ১২৯৪ [*Calcutta*, 1887.] 12°. **14127. c. 37.(4.)**

—— তাপসী-কণ্ঠহার। [Tāpasī kaṇṭhahāra. A tale, aiming at social reforms in Bengali marriage customs. Third edition.] pp. 126. কলিকাতা ১২৯৫ [*Calcutta*, 1888.] 12°. **14127. d. 33.(3.)**

—— যোগরাণী। উপন্যাস। [Yogarāṇī. A novel dealing with the oppressions of Muhammadan rule at the beginning of the 18th century.] pp. 388. *Calcutta*, ১৩১১ [1905.] 12°. **14127. cc. 42.**

SURENDRANĀTHA GHOSHA. সংস্কারক প্রহসন। [Saṃskāraka prahasana. A short tale, in the form of a drama, exposing some of the vices of educated Bengali Babus.] pp. 35. কলিকাতা ১২৯৩ [*Calcutta*, 1886.] 12°. **14131. a. 25.(3.)**

SURENDRANĀTHA GOSVĀMĪ. আর্য্য-ধাত্রীবিদ্যা। [Āryadhātrīvidyā. A treatise on midwifery, with copious quotations from Sanskrit and English authorities.] Pt. i. pp. 72. কুমারখালী ১৩০৬ [*Kumarkhali*, 1900.] 8°. **14043. cc. 11.**

SURENDRANĀTHA RĀYA. উত্তরপশ্চিম-ভ্রমণ। [Uttara-paschima bhramaṇa. Travels in the North-Western Provinces.] pp. iv. 258. কলিকাতা ১৩১৪ [*Calcutta*, 1907.] 12°. **14127. aa. 42.**

SURENDRANĀTHA SMṚITIRATNA. কর্ম্মানুষ্ঠান-সপ্রমাণ ফর্দ্দমালা। [Pharda-mālā. Detailed lists of the articles required in the performance of the various Hindu festivals and religious ceremonies.] pp. iv. 114. কলিকাতা ১৩০৯ [*Calcutta*, 1903.] 12°. **14123. e. 27.(2.)**

SURENDRANĀTHA ṬHĀKURA. মহাভারত। মূল আখ্যান। [Mahābhārata. The incidents of the Sanskrit epic poem, translated in narrative form, in two parts.] pp. ii. 306, 289, xi. কলিকাতা ১৩১৩ [*Calcutta*, 1906.] 8°. **14129. ff. 2.**

—— একটি বসন্ত-প্রাতের প্রস্ফুটিত সকুরা-পুষ্প। [Vasantaprāter sakurāpushpa. A tale of Japan in the 17th century, founded on fact.] pp. 224. কলিকাতা ১৩১১ [*Calcutta*, 1904.] 12°. **14128. a. 8.**

SURENDRANĀTHA VANDYOPĀDHYĀYA. বিজ্ঞান বাবু। [Vijñāna Bābu. A farce, ridiculing the conceited manners of educated Bengali Babus.] pp. 48. কলিকাতা ১২৯৪ [*Calcutta*, 1888.] 12°. **14131. a. 28.(3.)**

SURENDRANĀTHA VASU RĀYA. সমাজ-কলঙ্ক। [Samāja-kalaṅka. A drama illustrative of vices in modern social life in Bengal.] pp. ii. 134. কলিকাতা ১৩১২ [*Calcutta*, 1905.] 12°. **14131. aa. 7.(1.)**

SUREṢACHANDRA CHAṬṬOPĀDHYĀYA, *Deputy Magistrate.* সরল বেদান্ত দর্শন। [Sarala Vedānta-darṣana.] . . . Elementary Vedanta philosophy. By Sures Chandra Chatarji. pp. x. 187. চুঁচুড়া ১৩০৯ [*Chinsurah*, 1903.] 8°. **14123. ff. 12.**

SUREṢACHANDRA SAMĀJAPATI. *See* PERIODICAL PUBLICATIONS.—*Calcutta.* সাহিত্য। [Sāhitya. Edited by Sureṣachandra Samājapati.] [1890-91.] 8°. **14133. f. 10.**

SURES CHANDRA CHATARJI. *See* SUREṢACHANDRA CHAṬṬOPĀDHYĀYA.

SUREṢVARA NĀRĀYAṆA DEVA. *See* BHĀSKARĀNANDA SVĀMĪ. যতীন্দ্র-জীবন-চরিতম্। [Yatīndra-jīvanacharita. With a Bengali translation by Sureṣvara Nārāyaṇa Deva.] 1892. 8°. **14058. b. 26.(2.)**

SŪRYAKUMĀRA CHAṬṬOPĀDHYĀYA. The Antiquities of Kalighat. কালীক্ষেত্র দীপিকা। [Kālīkshetra-dīpikā.] pp. iv. 140. কলিকাতা ১৮৯১ [*Calcutta*, 1891.] 8°. **14127. b. 48.(1.)**

SŪRYAKUMĀRA SARKĀR. মাহিষ্যবিবৃতি। (Mahishyabibriti. A treatise on the origin, status, and history of the Mahishya caste, Bengal. Third edition . . . enlarged.) pp. xvi. 155, v. *Dacca*, 1901. 8°. **14125. e. 44.**

SŪRYANĀRĀYAṆA GHOSHA. A Note book of Surgery in Bengali. অস্ত্র চিকিৎসা। [Astra-chikitsā.] Vol. i. pp. 221. ঢাকা ১৮৯২ [*Dacca*, 1892.] 8°. **14125. c. 38.**

SŪRYASIDDHĀNTA. সূর্য্যসিদ্ধান্ত। মধ্যাধিকার। [Sūryasiddhānta. A Sanskrit work on Hindu astronomy. The Madhyādhikāra, with Raṅganātha's Sanskrit gloss, and a Bengali version of the stanzas.] [1890, *etc.*] *See* PERIODICAL PUBLICATIONS.—*Calcutta.* অরুণোদয়। [Aruṇodaya.] Pt. i., no. 5. [1890, *etc.*] 4°. **14133. g. 16.**

SUṢRUTA. সুশ্রুতসংহিতা। [Suṣruta-saṃhitā. Sanskrit text, and commentary by Ḍallaṇa Miṣra. Edited and translated into Bengali by Avināṣa-chandra Kaviratna.] pp. viii. 1106, 496. *Calcutta*, 1885, *etc.* 8°. **14043. d. 40.**

Incomplete. The text breaks off in the middle of Adhy. 24, and the translation in Adhy. 14 of the Chikitsāsthāna.

—— সুশ্রুত-সংহিতা। [Suṣruta-saṃhitā. With the Sanskrit commentary of Ḍallaṇa. Edited, with a Bengali translation, by Kālīprasanna Kaviṣekhara.] 2 vols. pp. ii. c. 1802. কলিকাতা ১৮৯৮ [*Calcutta*, 1898.] 8°. **14043. dd. 8.**

SUTTAPIṬAKA. ধম্মপদং। [Dhammapada. Pali text in Bengali character, with construing, Sanskrit version, and Bengali translation by Chāruchandra Vasu.] ১৩০৭-১০ [1901-02.] *See* PERIODICAL PUBLICATIONS.—*Calcutta.* সাহিত্য-সংহিতা। [Sāhitya-saṃhitā.] Vol. i., no. 12—iv., no. 11. [1900, *etc.*] 8°. **14133. ff. 1.**

—— ধম্মপদ। [Dhammapada. Another edition, with Chāruchandra Vasu's Bengali translation.] pp. ii. xii. 237. কলিকাতা ১৯০৪ [*Calcutta*, 1904.] 12°. **14098. a. 43.**

—— শ্রীমদ্-ভগবদ্-গৌতমবুদ্ধ-ভাষিতং ধর্ম্মপদম্ . . . The Dharmapada of Bhagavad-Gautama Buddha. Rendered in Sanskrit verse [together with a Bengali translation] by Svámí Hariharánanda Áraṇya. pp. v. 34, 21. *Hugli, Calcutta* [printed], 1905. 8°. **14099. bb. 13.**

SVARṆAKUMĀRĪ. স্বর্ণ-কুমারী। [Svarṇakumārī. A tale of love and adventure.] pp. 83. কলিকাতা ১২৯৭ [*Calcutta*, 1890.] 12°. **14127. c. 39.(1.)**

SVARṆAKUMĀRĪ DEVĪ. *See* PERIODICAL PUBLICATIONS.—*Calcutta.* ভারতী। [Bhāratī. Vol. 32. A new issue under the editorship of Svarṇakumārī Devī.] [1877, *etc.*] 8°. **14133. f. 6.**

—— হুগলীর ইমামবাড়ী। [Huglīr imāmbāṛī. An historical romance.] pp. 256. কলিকাতা ১২৯৪ [*Calcutta*, 1888.] 12°. **14127. d. 32.(2.)**

—— কাহাকে? [Kāhāke? A tale of life in an educated English-speaking Bengali family.] pp. 121. কলিকাতা ১৮৯৮ [*Calcutta*, 1898.] 12°. **14127. cc. 10.(5.)**

SVARṆAKUMĀRĪ DEVĪ (*continued*). মিবার-রাজ। ঐতিহাসিক উপন্যাস। [Miwār Rāja. An historical tale.] pp. 80. কলিকাতা ১২৯৪ [*Calcutta*, 1887.] 12°. **14127. d. 36.(2.)**

—— ফুলের মালা। [Phuler mālā. An historical tale of Hindu rule during the 14th century.] pp. 159. কলিকাতা ১৩০১ [*Calcutta*, 1895.] 12°. **14127. c. 56.(2.)**

—— সখি সমিতি। [Sakhi-samiti. A proposed scheme for the establishment of an association for female education and social progress.] pp. 24. কলিকাতা ১২৯৩ [*Calcutta*, 1886.] 12°. **14125. e. 17.(8.)**

—— স্নেহলতা। [Snehalatā. A novel describing the state of modern Hindu society.] 2 pts. কলিকাতা ১২৯৯ [*Calcutta*, 1892.] 12°. **14127. c. 41.**

—— বিদ্রোহ। [Vidroha. An historical novel, based on Tod's Rajasthan.] pp. 282. কলিকাতা ১২৯৭ [*Calcutta*, 1890.] 12°. **14127. d. 39.(2.)**

SVARṆAMAYĪ, *Rani of Kasimbazar.* [*Life.*] *See* VIHĀRĪLĀLA SARKĀR. মহারাণী স্বর্ণময়ী। [Mahārāṇī Svarṇamayī.] [1907.] 12°. **14127. aa. 35.**

SVARṆAMAYĪ DEVĪ. গীতিমালা। [Gītimālā. Miscellaneous songs.] pp. 135. ঢাকা ১৩১৪ [1907.] 12°. **14129. bb. 28.(5.)**

SVARṆAMAYĪ GUPTĀ. ঊষা-চিন্তা। অর্থাৎ আধুনিক আর্য্য মহিলাগণের অবস্থা সম্বন্ধে কয়েকটি কথা। [Ushā-chintā. A description of the life and position of Bengali women of the present time, with suggestions for their social improvement.] pp. xxiv. 142, ii. কলিকাতা ১২৯৫ [*Calcutta*, 1888.] 12°. **14125. e. 19.(4.)**

SVARŪPACHANDRA RĀYA. An ancient and modern history of Sonargang. By Svarup Chandra Ray. সুবর্ণগ্রামের ইতিহাস। [Suvarṇa grāmer itihāsa.] pp. iv. 146. *Calcutta*, 1891. 12°. **14127. a. 42.(3.)**

SVARŪPA - DĀMODARA. *See* PURUSHOTTAMA ĀCHĀRYA.

SVĀTMĀRĀMA. হঠযোগপ্রদীপিকা। [Haṭhayoga-pradīpikā. A Sanskrit work on Haṭhayoga, with a commentary by Brahmānanda, and a Bengali translation.] pp. 84, ii. [1891, *etc.*] *See* PERIODICAL PUBLICATIONS.—*Calcutta.* অরুণোদয়। [Aruṇodaya.] Pt. i., no. 21. [1890, *etc.*] 4°. **14133. g. 16.**

ṢYĀMACHĀNḌ GUPTA. সারি গান। [Sārigān. Songs sung by boatmen in Eastern Bengal.] pp. 13. কলিকাতা ১৩০৮ [*Calcutta*, 1901.] 12°. **14129. bb. 9.(1.)**

ṢYĀMĀCHARAṆA KAVIRATNA. *See* DHARMADĀSA. বিদগ্ধ-মুখমণ্ডনম্। [Vidagdha-mukhamaṇḍana. Edited with Sanskrit interpretations, and Bengali translations, by Ṣyāmācharaṇa Kaviratna.] [1905.] 8°. **14072. b. 21.(2.)**

—— *See* KṚISHṆA SĀRVABHAUMA. পদাঙ্কদূতম্। [Padāṅka-dūta. Edited with grammatical analyses, translation, and commentary in Bengali by Ṣyāmācharaṇa Kaviratna.] [1904.] 12°. **14060. b. 17.(2.)**

—— *See* NITYAKARMA. আহ্নিককৃত্যম্। বিশুদ্ধ-নিত্যকর্ম্ম। [Āhnikakṛitya. Edited with Bengali introduction, translation and notes, by Ṣyāmācharaṇa Kaviratna.] [1902.] 12°. **14033. a. 49.**

—— সুধাকর ব্যাকরণ। [Sudhākara vyākaraṇa. A grammar of the Sanskrit language. Second edition.] pp. viii. 372. কলিকাতা ১২৯৮ [*Calcutta*, 1892.] 12°. **14131. e. 23.(3.)**

—— সুপরিশুদ্ধ-সটীক ত্রিবেদীয়-ক্রিয়াকাণ্ড-পদ্ধতিঃ। [Trivedīya kriyākāṇḍa-paddhati. A manual of Vedic domestic rites, with Sanskrit commentary, and Bengali notes. Preceded by Bengali introduction by Ṣyāmācharaṇa, a preface and bibliography of his works by Gurudāsa Chaṭṭopādhyāya; and followed by the section on Vedic grammar from the Siddhāntakaumudī, with Bengali notes, and an appendix on Vedic metres.] pp. 67, xvi. 194, 31. *Calcutta*, 1906. *obl.* 8°. **14033. bbb. 44.**

The introductory matter is printed in the ordinary format. The ritual is printed on yellow paper.

ṢYĀMĀCHARAṆA MUKHOPĀDHYĀYA. চূড়ালা উপাখ্যান। [Chuṛālā-upākhyāna. A tale illustrative of Hindu philosophy, adapted from the Nirvāṇa-prakaraṇa of the Yogavāsishṭha.] pp. v. 90. কলিকাতা ১২৮৪ [*Calcutta*, 1877.] 8°. **14127. f. 42.(3.)**

ṢYĀMĀDHAVA RĀYA. *See* KṚISHṆAKĀNTA BHĀDURĪ, called RASASĀGARA. Life of Rasha Sagur and some of his ex-tempore poems. Collected by Syamadhuba Roy. 1898. 12°. **14127. aa. 14.(2.)**

ṢYĀMALĀLA BASĀK. *See* JAYADEVA, *Son of Bhojadeva.* মহাকবি জয়দেবের গীতগোবিন্দের প্রাকৃত পদ্যানুবাদ। [A metrical translation of Jayadeva's Gītagovinda. Edited, with notes and an account of the life and works of Jayadeva, by Ṣyāmalāla Basāk.] [1889.] 12°. **14129. a. 21.(2.)**

ṢYĀMALĀLA GOSVĀMĪ, *Siddhāntavāchaspati.* *See* BĀDARĀYAṆA. বেদান্তদর্শন। [Vedānta-darṣana. With a Bengali translation by Ṣyāmalāla Gosvāmī of the Sanskrit commentary called Govindabhāshya.] [1891, *etc.*] 8°. **14048. dd. 23.**

—— *See* BALADEVA VIDYĀBHŪSHAṆA. সিদ্ধান্তরত্নম্। [Siddhāntaratna. Edited, with a Bengali translation, by Ṣyāmalāla Gosvāmī.] [1897.] 8°. **14048. cc. 24.**

—— *See* NĀRADA. ভক্তিসূত্রম্। [Bhaktisūtra. With a Bengali exposition by Ṣyāmalāla Gosvāmī.] [1904.] 16°. **14028. bb. 15.**

—— *See* PURĀṆAS.—*Bhāgavatapurāṇa.* শ্রীকৃষ্ণলীলা। [Krishṇalīlā. Compiled and edited by Ṣyāmalāla Gosvāmī.] [1904.] 8°. **14016. dd. 10.**

—— *See* PURĀṆAS.—*Bhāgavatapurāṇa.* শ্রীমদ্ভাগবতান্তর্গত নবযোগেন্দ্রোপাখ্যান *etc.* [Navayogendropākhyāna, and Uddhavagītā. Sanskrit text, with analysis, translation, and commentary in Bengali. Edited by Ṣyāmalāla Gosvāmī.] [1900.] 8°. **14018. b. 19.**

—— *See* UPANISHADS. উপনিষদঃ। *etc.* [Īṣā, Kena, and Kaṭha Upanishads, with commentary and Bengali translations. Edited by Ṣyāmalāla Gosvāmī.] [1906.] 16°. **14010. a. 12.(2.)**

—— *See* UPANISHADS. উপনিষদঃ *etc.* [Taittirīya, Aitareya, and Ṣvetāṣvatara Upanishads, with commentary and Bengali translations. Edited by Ṣyāmalāla Gosvāmī.] [1907.] 12°. **14010. b. 28.**

—— *See* UPANISHADS. সামবেদীয়া ছান্দোগ্যোপনিষৎ। [Chhāndogya Upanishad. Edited with Sanskrit notes and a Bengali translation by Ṣyāmalāla Gosvāmī.] [1906.] 12°. **14010. b. 29.**

—— *See* UPANISHADS. Isa-Upanishad ... With a Bengali translation and commentary. Edited by Syamalala Gosvami Siddhanta Vachaspati. 1895. 8°. **14010. cc. 3.**

ṢYĀMALĀLA GOSVĀMĪ, *Siddhāntavāchaspati (continued).* *See* UPANISHADS. ঋগ্বেদান্তর্গতা কৌষীতকিব্রাহ্মণারণ্যকোপনিষৎ। [Kaushītaki. With grammatical analyses and exegetic notes, and a Bengali translation. Edited by Ṣyāmalāla Gosvāmī.] [1903.] 16°. **14010. a. 12.**

—— *See* VIṢVANĀTHA CHAKRAVARTĪ. শ্রীপ্রেমসম্পুটঃ [Premasampuṭa. With interpretations in Sanskrit and Bengali by Ṣyāmalāla Gosvāmī.] [1906.] 12°. **14060. b. 17.(3.)**

—— শ্রীশ্রীগৌরসুন্দর অর্থাৎ শ্রীকৃষ্ণচৈতন্য মহাপ্রভুর চরিত। [Gaura-sundara. The life of Chaitanya.] pp. iv. 544. কলিকাতা ১৩১৩ [*Calcutta*, 1907.] 8°. **14127. bb. 26.**

ṢYĀMALĀLA MAJUMDĀR. বসন্ত। গার্হস্থ্য উপন্যাস। [Vasanta. A story of domestic life.] pp. 247. *Calcutta*, ১৩০৪ [1898.] 12°. **14127. cc. 10.(4.)**

ṢYĀMĀNANDA, *Disciple of Jīva Gosvāmī.* [*Life.*] *See* PRIYANĀTHA RĀYA. শ্যামানন্দ প্রকাশ। [Ṣyāmānanda-prakāṣa.] [1895.] 12°. **14129. b. 44.(1.)**

T., J. M. *See* YATĪNDRAMOHANA ṬHĀKURA.

TAJAMMUL 'ALĪ, *of Kanihati.* তোওয়ারিখ-হেলিমী। [Tawārikh i Ḥalīmī. The family history of Shāh Ḥalīm al-Dīn of Kanihati, in the District of Sylhet.] Pt i. pp. ii. 18. ঢাকা ১৮৯৪ [*Dacca*, 1894.] 12°. **14127. a. 53.**

TĀJ al-DĪN MUḤAMMAD. *See* GHULĀM NABĪ ibn 'INĀYAT ALLĀH. সর্ব্ববৃহৎ কাছাছুল আম্বিয়া চারইয়ারী *etc.* [Ḳiṣaṣ al-anbiyā. Translated by Tāj al-Dīn Muḥammad and others.] [1902.] 4°. **14123. hh. 1.**

TANTRAS. *See* KĀLĪPRASANNA VIDYĀRATNA. নিত্যতন্ত্রম্। [Nityatantra. A work on Tantric practices of religion.] 1908. 8°. **14033. aa. 18.**

—— *See* KRISHṆĀNANDA VĀGĪṢA BHAṬṬĀCHĀRYA. বৃহৎ তন্ত্রসার। [Bṛihat Tantrasāra. A synopsis of the Tantras, with a Bengali translation.] [1896.] 4°. **14033. c. 39.**

—— ভূতডামরঃ। [Bhūtaḍāmaratantra. Sanskrit text, with a Bengali translation.] pp. 40. [1891.] *See* PERIODICAL PUBLICATIONS.—*Calcutta.* অরুণোদয়। [Aruṇodaya.] Pt. i., no. 12. [1890, *etc.*] 4°. **14133. g. 16.**

TANTRAS (*continued*). দত্তাত্রেয়ঃ ষট্‌কর্ম্মদীপিকা। [Dattātreyatantra. Followed by the Shaṭkarma-dīpikā, a work treating of six modes of magic, by Kṛishṇānanda Vāgīṣa Bhaṭṭāchārya. Sanskrit text, edited, with a Bengali translation, by Rasikamohana Chaṭṭopādhyāya.] pp. 93. কলিকাতা ১২৯২ [*Calcutta*, 1885.] 4°. **14033. bb. 24.(1.)**

Reprinted in an expurgated form from the editor's collection Indrajālādi-saṅgraha.

—— দত্তাত্রেয়ঃ। [Dattātreyatantra. Sanskrit text, with a Bengali translation.] pp. 28. [1891, *etc.*] *See* PERIODICAL PUBLICATIONS. — *Calcutta.* অরুণোদয়। [Aruṇodaya.] Pt. i., no. 14. [1890, *etc.*] 4°. **14133. g. 16.**

—— অথ গৌরীকাঞ্জলিকা। [Gaurīkāñjalikā. A Sanskrit tantra containing charms for the cure of diseases and the like. With a Bengali translation, and additional matter.] pp. 66. [1893, *etc.*] *See* PERIODICAL PUBLICATIONS. — *Calcutta.* অরুণোদয়। [Aruṇodaya.] Pt. i., no. 30. [1890, *etc.*] 4°. **14133. g. 16.**

—— গুপ্তসাধনতন্ত্রম্। [Guptasādhanatantra. Sanskrit text, edited with a Bengali translation by Harihara Sādhakendra.] pp. 61. কলিকাতা ১৮০৮ [*Calcutta*, 1886.] 8°. **14028. d. 29.(2.)**

—— জ্ঞানসঙ্কলিনীতন্ত্রম্। [Jñānasaṅkalinītantra. Sanskrit text, with a Bengali translation.] pp. 8. [1891.] *See* PERIODICAL PUBLICATIONS.—*Calcutta.* অরুণোদয়। [Aruṇodaya.] Pt. i., no. 20. [1890, *etc.*] 4°. **14133. g. 16.**

—— জ্ঞান-সঙ্কলিনী-তন্ত্রম্। [Jñānasaṅkalinītantra. Sanskrit text, with a Bengali translation by Vaishṇavacharaṇa Basāk. Third edition.] pp. 31. কলিকাতা [*Calcutta*, 1901.] 12°. **14033. a. 41.(3.)**

—— কালীতন্ত্রম্। [Kālītantra. Sanskrit text, with a Bengali translation by Kālīprasanna Vidyāratna.] pp. 368. *Calcutta*, 1892. 8°. **14033. bb. 44.**

—— মহানির্ব্বাণতন্ত্রম্। [Mahānirvāṇatantra. A Ṣaiva work in Sanskrit verse, with a Bengali prose translation.] 2 pts. কলিকাতা ১২৯৪ [*Calcutta*, 1888.] 8°. **14033. bb. 25.**

—— [Another edition.] pp. 994. কলিকাতা ১৩০৩ [*Calcutta*, 1896.] 32°. **14033. a. 30.**

TANTRAS (*continued*). মহানির্ব্বাণ তন্ত্র। মূল ও অনুবাদ। [Mahānirvāṇatantra. Sanskrit text, with a Bengali translation by Gopāladāsa Mukhopādhyāya.] pp. 223, 232. কলিকাতা ১৩০৭ [*Calcutta*, 1901.] 8°. **14033. aa. 17.**

—— সানুবাদ মহানির্ব্বাণ-তন্ত্র ও সর্ব্ব-দেবদেবীর মন্ত্র-কোষ। [Mahānirvāṇatantra. Sanskrit text, with a Bengali translation by Kālīprasanna Vidyāratna, and an appendix of Sanskrit spells. Edited by Upendranātha Mukhopādhyāya. Eighth edition.] pp. xii. 164. কলিকাতা ১৩১৪ [*Calcutta*, 1907.] 8°. **14028. dd. 18.**

—— সানুবাদ-রাধাতন্ত্রম্। [Rādhātantra. A Sanskrit work in 34 chapters on the Tantric cult of Rādhā. Edited with a Bengali version by Kālīprasanna Vidyāratna.] pp. 188. কলিকাতা ১৩১৩ [*Calcutta*, 1906.] 8°. **14033. bbb. 42.**

—— সিদ্ধিশঙ্করতন্ত্র। [Siddhiṣaṅkaratantra. Sanskrit text, edited with a Bengali translation by Navīnakṛishṇa Lāhā.] pp. 50. কলিকাতা ১২৯৫ [*Calcutta*, 1886.] 12°. **14033. a. 41.(1.)**

—— গুরুগীতা। [Gurugītāstotra, from the Viṣvasāratantra. Sanskrit text, with a Bengali paraphrase and prefatory notes on the practice of Yoga by Prasādadāsa Gosvāmī.] pp. iv. 40. কলিকাতা ১৮০৭ [*Calcutta*, 1885.] 12°. **14033. a. 12.(2.)**

—— গুরুগীতা। শ্রীগুরুগীতাস্তোত্র ও অনুষ্ঠান। [Second edition.] pp. 36. শ্রীরামপুর ১৯০১ [*sic*] [*Serampur*, 1892.] 12°. **14028. b. 72.(1.)**

—— যক্ষডামর ও রসায়ন। [Selections from the Yakshaḍāmaratantra, followed by Rasāyana, a compilation of directions for alchemic rites. With Bengali translations and commentary.] pp. 4. [1893.] *See* PERIODICAL PUBLICATIONS.—*Calcutta.* অরুণোদয়। [Aruṇodaya.] Pt. i., no. 27. [1890, *etc.*] 4°. **14133. g. 16.(vol. 3.)**

TĀRĀCHAND CHAKRAVARTĪ. *See* RĀMACHANDRA VIDYĀVĀGĪṢA. Sixth discourse on the spiritual worship of God ... Translated ... [into English] by Tarachand Chukruvurtee. 1844. 8°. **14123. d. 15.(2.)**

TĀRĀDHANA TARKABHŪSHAṆA. Memoir of Professor Taranath Tarkavachaspati, and progress of Sanskrit learning. By Taradhan Tarkabhushan. (তারানাথ তর্কবাচস্পতির জীবনী এবং সংস্কৃত বিদ্যার উন্নতি.) pp. vi. 102. *Calcutta*, 1893. 8°. **14127. aa. 3.(1.)**

TĀRAKACHANDRA DĀSA GUPTA. চট্টগ্রামের ইতিবৃত্ত। [Chaṭṭagrāmer itivṛitta. A history of Chittagong from the earliest times, compiled chiefly from English works.] pp. iv. 124. চট্টগ্রাম ১৩০৪ [*Chittagong*, 1897.] 8°. **14127. aa. 9.(1.)**

TĀRAKANĀTHA GAṄGOPĀDHYĀYA. Lalita and Saudamini; or The Mother's Device. A tale by Tarak Nath Ganguli. Translated by Mrs. J. B. Knight. (Journal of the National Indian Association, nos. 242 and 243.) *London*, 1891. 8°. **P.P. 1423. ld.**

—— Shornalata: a tale of Hindu life. By Tarak Nath Ganguli. [Translated by M. S. Knight.] (Journal of the National Indian Association, nos. 150-165.) *London*, 1883-84. 8°. **P.P. 1423. ld.**

—— A glimpse into the Indian inner home, being a faithful rendering into English of the late Babu Taraknath Ganguli's popular Bengali novel, Svarnalata. By Bidhubhushan Mukerjee. pp. viii. 301. *Calcutta*, 1903. 8°. **14127. cc. 35.**

—— Svarnalata, or Scenes from Hindu village life in Bengal, by the late Dr. T. N. Ganguli, translated into English by D. C. Roy. With a preface by Charles H. Tawney. Second edition. Revised and improved. pp. ii. iii. 504, 4. *Calcutta*, 1906. 8°. **14128. a. 14.**

TĀRAKANĀTHA VIṢVĀSA. তারকনাথ গ্রন্থাবলী। [Tārakanātha-granthāvalī. The complete works of Tārakanātha Viṣvāsa.] Vol. i. pp. ii. 440. কলিকাতা ১২৯৩ [*Calcutta*, 1886.] 8°. **14127. g. 6.**

—— তারকনাথ-গ্রন্থাবলী। [Tārakanātha-granthāvalī. Another edition.] *Calcutta*, ১৩০৬ [1899, *etc.*] 8°. **14127. ee. 9.**

In progress.

TĀRĀKĀNTA DEVAṢARMĀ. *See* TĀRĀKĀNTA KĀVYATĪRTHA BHAṬṬĀCHĀRYA.

TĀRĀKĀNTA KĀVYATĪRTHA BHAṬṬĀCHĀRYA. *See* PAÑCHATANTRA. পঞ্চতন্ত্র। [Pañchatantra. Translated by Tārākānta Kāvyatīrtha.] [1906.] 12°. **14128. a. 12.**

TĀRĀKĀNTA KĀVYATĪRTHA BHAṬṬĀCHĀRYA (*continued*). *See* PURĀṆAS.—*Agnipurāṇa.* অগ্নিপুরাণম। [Agnipurāṇa. With a Bengali translation by Tārākānta Kāvyatīrtha.] [1907.] 8°. **14016. dd. 29.**

—— *See* PURĀṆAS.—*Brahmāṇḍapurāṇa.* ব্রহ্মাণ্ডপুরাণম। *etc.* [Brahmāṇḍapurāṇa. With a Bengali translation by Tārākānta Kāvyatīrtha.] [1908.] 8°. **14018. b. 22.(1.)**

—— *See* PURĀṆAS.—*Kalkipurāṇa.* কল্কিপুরাণম্। *etc.* [Kalkipurāṇa. With a Bengali translation by Tārākānta Kāvyatīrtha.] [1908.] 8°. **14018. b. 22.(2.)**

—— *See* PURĀṆAS.—*Vāmanapurāṇa.* বামনপুরাণম্। [Vāmanapurāṇa. With a Bengali translation by Tārākānta Kāvyatīrtha.] [1908.] 8°. **14016. dd. 28.(2.)**

—— *See* PURĀṆAS.—*Varāhapurāṇa.* বরাহপুরাণম্। [Varāhapurāṇa. With a Bengali translation by Tārākānta Kāvyatīrtha.] [1906.] 8°. **14016. dd. 23.**

TĀRAKEṢVARA BHAṬṬĀCHĀRYA. *See* JÑĀNADĀSA. নিকুঞ্জ-সাজান। [Nikuñja-sājān. Edited by Tārākeṣvara Bhaṭṭāchārya.] [1902.] 8°. **14133. f. 18.**

—— *See* MAṄGALACHAṆḌĪ. মঙ্গলচণ্ডীর পাঁচালী। [Maṅgalachaṇḍīr pāñchālī. Edited by Tārākeṣvara Bhaṭṭāchārya.] [1902.] 8°. **14133. f. 18.**

—— *See* VṚINDĀVANA DĀSA. গোলোক-সংহিতা। [Goloka-saṃhitā. Edited by Tārākeṣvara Bhaṭṭāchārya.] [1902.] 8°. **14133. f. 18.**

—— কবিবল্লভের রসকদম্ব। [Kavivallabher rasakadamba. An article on the Vaishṇava poet Kavivallabha, and his poem Rasakadamba.] ১৩০৯ [1902.] *See* ACADEMIES, *etc.*—Calcutta.—*Bengal Academy of Literature.* সাহিত্য-পরিষৎ-পত্রিকা। [Sāhitya-parishat-patrikā.] Vol. ix., no. 1. [1894, *etc.*] 8°. **14133. f. 18.**

TĀRĀKUMĀRA KAVIRATNA. *See* DAṆḌĪ. A Complete Key to the Sanskrit Course . . . for F.A. Examination for 1889 . . . Edited by Tárá Kumár Kaviratna. 1888. 12°. **14072. cc. 36.**

—— *See* HITOPADEṢA. হিতোপদেশঃ [Hitopadeṣa. Sanskrit text, with a Bengali translation in prose and verse, notes, and appendices, by Tārākumāra Kaviratna.] [1889.] 8°. **14076. d. 43.**

—— কৃষ্ণভক্তিরসামৃতম্ . . . কৃষ্ণভক্তিরসামৃত। [Kṛishṇa-bhakti-rasāmṛita. A Sanskrit poem on the worship of Kṛishṇa, accompanied by a metrical translation and notes in Bengali.] pp. iii. 154, v. ১৯৪৯ *Calcutta,* [1892.] 8°. **14028. c. 66.**

—— [Second edition.] pp. iv. ii. 152. *Calcutta,* ১৩০৬ [1900.] 8°. **14076. e. 75.(2.)**

—— পঞ্চামৃত। [Pañchāmṛita. A collection of five Hindu religious poems in Sanskrit, compiled with Bengali metrical translations and notes by Tārākumāra Kaviratna. Second edition.] pp. ii. 67. কলিকাতা ১৯৪৯ [*Calcutta,* 1892.] 12°. **14028. b. 73.(1.)**

The Sanskrit is in Devanagari characters.

TĀRĀNĀTHA TARKAVĀCHASPATI BHAṬṬĀ-CHĀRYA. [*Life.*] *See* ŚAMBHUCHANDRA VIDYĀ-RATNA. পণ্ডিতকুলতিলক মহাত্মা তারানাথ তর্কবাচস্পতির জীবনচরিত। [Tārānātha Tarkavāchaspatir jīvana-charita.] [1893.] 8°. **14127. bb. 7.**

—— *See* TĀRĀDHANA TARKABHŪSHAṆA. Memoir of Professor Taranath Tarkavachaspati, *etc.* 1893. 8°. **14127. aa. 3.(1.)**

TARAṄGIṆĪ. তরঙ্গিণী। [Taraṅgiṇī. A tale of love and adventure in the form of a drama. Second edition.] pp. 51. কাশীপুর ১২৯৫ [*Cossipur,* 1888.] 8°. **14131 c. 17.(3.)**

TĀRĀPADA KĀVYATĪRTHA. *See* BHAṬṬI. ভট্টিকাব্যম্। [Bhaṭṭikāvya. Sargas i.-v., with a Bengali translation by Tārāpada Kāvyatīrtha.] [1895-1896.] 8°. **14076. d. 49.**

TĀRĀPADA VIDYĀLAṄKĀRA. *See* PURĀṆAS.—*Padmapurāṇa.* শ্রীশ্রীপদ্ম-পুরাণ। [Padmapurāṇa. An abridged metrical version by Tārāpada Vidyā-laṅkāra.] [1904.] 8°. **14123. gg. 3.**

TĀRĀṢAṄKARA TARKARATNA. *See* JOHNSON (S.), *LL.D.* রাসেলাস। [Rasselas. Translated by Tārāṣaṅkara Tarkaratna.] [1907.] 12°. **14128. a. 16.**

TĀRIṆĪCHARAṆA SENA. *See* PERIODICAL PUBLICATIONS.—*Calcutta.* বঙ্গ-জীবন। [Vaṅga-jīvana. Edited by Tāriṇīcharaṇa Sena.] [1896.] 8°. **14133. f. 14.**

TĀRIṆĪCHARAṆA ṬHĀKURA. ভবানীপুর কাহিনী। [Bhavānīpura-kāhinī. A Pauranic and historical account of Bhawanipur.] pp. ii. 185. কলিকাতা ১৩০৮ [*Calcutta,* 1902.] 8°. **14127. bb. 23.**

TĀRIṆĪPRASĀDA JYOTISHĪ. The Plague-sanhitá. প্লেগ-সংহিতা। বা আর্য্য-স্বাস্থ্যবিধান। The Aryan hygiene. [The plague and its treatment according to Hindu pathology.] By T. P. Jyotishi. pp. iii. x. 151. কলিকাতা [*Calcutta,* 1899.] 12°. **14127. b. 7.(2.)**

TARKARAHASYA. Tarkarahasya. An elementary treatise on logic. (তর্করহস্য।) pp. 24. *Calcutta,* [1892.] 12°. **14125. f. 40.(1.)**

TASLĪM al-DĪN AḤMAD. *See* ḲUR'ĀN. কোর-আন। . . . তবারকল্লজী নামক পারা। [A translation of the 29th Section of the Koran, with notes. By Taslīm al-Dīn Aḥmad.] [1907.] 8°. **14123. h. 38.**

TATTVAVICHĀRA. তত্ত্ব-বিচার। [Tattvavichāra. Thoughts on creation and existence according to the Vedānta system of philosophy.] pp. iv. 72, vi. কলিকাতা ১২৯৩ [*Calcutta,* 1887.] 12°. **14125. f. 31.(2.)**

TAWNEY (CHARLES HENRY). *See* TĀRAKANĀTHA GAṄGOPĀDHYĀYA. Svarnalata . . . Translated into English by D. C. Roy. With a preface by C. H. Tawney. 1906. 8°. **14128. a. 14.**

TEACHER. A Key to Æsop's Fables, containing meanings of difficult words, explanation of difficult passages . . . of eighty fables. By a Teacher. pp. 51. *Calcutta,* [1889.] 12°. **14131. g.**

ṬEKCHĀṆD ṬHĀKUR. *See* PYĀRĪCHĀṆD MITRA.

TEN COMMANDMENTS. দশ আজ্ঞা। [Daṣa ājñā.] The Ten Commandments. [A Christian tract. Second edition.] pp. 18. কলিকাতা [*Calcutta,*] 1881. 16°. **14123. a. 23.**

ṬHĀKURA DĀSA, *Son of Rāmamohana.* *See* VYOMAKEṢA MUSTAFĪ. পাঁচালিকার ঠাকুরদাস। [Pāñ-chālikāra Ṭhākura Dāsa. An account of the poet Ṭhākura Dāsa and his Pāñchālī poems.] [1898.] 8°. **14133. f. 18.**

ṬHĀKURADĀSA CHŪḌĀMAṆI. *See* PURĀṆAS.—*Vāmanapurāṇa.* বামনপুরাণং। [Sanskrit text, with a prose translation by Ṭhākuradāsa Chuḍāmaṇi.] [1886.] 8°. **14016. b. 16.**

ṬHĀKURADĀSA MUKHOPĀDHYĀYA. সাহিত্যমঙ্গল। [Sāhitya-maṅgala. A treatise on literary composition.] pp. 88. কলিকাতা ১২৯৫ [Calcutta, 1888.] 12°. **14131. d. 22.**

ṬHĀKURADĀSA SENA. ভক্তিবিরোধীদিগের আপত্তি খণ্ডন। [Bhakti-virodhīdiger āpatti-khaṇḍana. A treatise in support of the Brahmist religion.] pp. 52. কলিকাতা ১৭৯১ [Calcutta, 1869.] 8°. **14123. d. 19.(2.)**

THOMAS (JOSEPH WILSON). *See* BIBLE.—*Psalms.* গীতসংহিতা। [Gītasaṃhitā.] The Psalms in Bengali. [Translated by J. W. Thomas.] 1881. 16°. **3070. aaa. 30.**

TINKARI GHOSHĀL. Arya Vansavali, or a History of the principal Hindu castes in Bengal, by Tincari Ghoshal, . . . আর্য্যবংশাবলী। pp. ii. 284. কলিকাতা ১২৯২ [Calcutta, 1886.] 8°. **14127. b. 32.**

TINKARI SMṚITIRATNA, *of Sibpur.* জ্ঞানতত্ত্ব নিরূপণম্। [Jñānatattvanirūpaṇa. A Sanskrit anthology treating of the conditions of knowledge, with a Bengali translation. Part i.] pp. 146. কলিকাতা ১৩০৬ [Calcutta, 1899.] 12°. **14048. b. 38.(3.)**

TINKARI VANDYOPĀDHYĀYA. গুরুগোবিন্দ সিং। [Guru Govinda Singh. A life of Govinda Singh, the 10th Guru of the Sikhs, with introductory chapters containing an account of the rise of the Sikh religion, and the lives of the other Gurus.] pp. ii. 238. ১৩০৩ Calcutta, [1896.] 12°. **14127. aa. 6.(6.)**

TINKARI VIṢVĀSA. *See* PURĀṆAS.—*Brahmavaivartapurāṇa.* ব্রহ্মবৈবর্ত্ত পুরাণ। [Translated into verse by Tinkaṛi Viṣvāsa.] [1885.] 8°. **14123. g. 16.**

TITU MĪR, *of Haidarpur.* *See* VIHĀRĪLĀLA SARKĀR. তিতুমীর। [Titu Mīr. An account of Titu Mīr, a Wahhābī of Haidarpur, of his opposition to the local authorities, and defeat and death at Narikelberia, in A.D. 1831.] [1897.] 12°. **14127. aa. 19.**

TOD (JAMES), *Lieutenant Colonel.* সচিত্র রাজস্থান। [Rājasthāna. Tod's 'Annals and Antiquities of Rajast'han,' translated into Bengali by Upendranātha Mukhopādhyāya. Second edition, revised, with the addition of an appendix, by Yajñeṣvara Vandyopādhyāya.] pp. xvi. 608. কলিকাতা ১৩০৬ [Calcutta, 1898.] 8°. **14127. bbb. 4.**

—— [Third edition.] pp. xiv. 618. কলিকাতা ১৩১৩ [Calcutta, 1906.] 8°. **14127. bbb. 8.**

TRAILIṄGA SVĀMĪ. [*Life.*] *See* BHŪDHARA CHAṬṬOPĀDHYĀYA. সাধুদর্শন। [Sādhudarṣana.] Pt. i. [1888.] 12°. **14127. a. 35.**

—— [*Life.*] *See* NIVĀRAṆACHANDRA DĀSA. মহাত্মা ত্রৈলিঙ্গ স্বামির জীবনচরিত। [Trailiṅga Svāmīr jīvanacharita.] [1893.] 12°. **14127. aa. 2.(1.)**

TRAILOKYANĀTHA BHAṬṬĀCHĀRYA. ঐতিহাসিক প্রবন্ধমালা। [Aitihāsika prabandhamālā. Essays on ancient Sanskrit authors.] Pt. i. pp. vi. 144. কলিকাতা ১৮৯৬ [Calcutta, 1896.] 8°. **14131. d. 30.**

—— কবি বিদ্যাপতি ও অন্যান্য বৈষ্ণব কবিবৃন্দের জীবনী। [Kavi Vidyāpati. An account of Vidyāpati and other early Vaishṇava poets, and their writings.] pp. xi. v. 146. কলিকাতা ১৮৯৫ [Calcutta, 1895.] 12°. **14131. d. 33.**

TRAILOKYANĀTHA MUKHOPĀDHYĀYA. *See* RAṄGALĀLA MUKHOPĀDHYĀYA. বিশ্বকোষ। [Viṣvakosha. Edited in part by Trailokyanātha Mukhopādhyāya.] [1885, *etc.*] 4°. **14133. c. 5.**

—— ভূত ও মানুষ। [Bhūta o mānusha. Four short stories.] pp. 157. কলিকাতা ১৩০২ [Calcutta, 1896.] 8°. **14127. c. 50.**

—— মুক্তা-মালা। [Muktāmālā. A collection of short stories.] pp. 4, 320. কলিকাতা ১৯০১ [Calcutta, 1901.] 8°. **14127. cc. 31.**

TRAILOKYANĀTHA PĀLA. Annals of Midnapur, . . . by Trailokya Nath Pal. মেদিনীপুর ইতিহাস। [Medinīpura-itihāsa.] 2 pts. *Calcutta, Midnapur,* 1888-1895. 8°. **14127. b. 40.**

—— Annals of Midnapur. Parts ii. and iii. [A revised edition of Pt. ii., the latter portion of it being amplified and made into a third part] pp. viii. 90, 66. কলিকাতা ১৮৯৬ [Calcutta, 1896.] 8°. **14127. bb. 5.**

TRAILOKYANĀTHA RAKSHITA. Short history of Tamluk. By Trailokya Nath Rakshit . . . তমোলুক-ইতিহাস। [Tamoluk-itihāsa.] pp. vii. 135. *Calcutta,* 1902. 12°. **14127. aa. 22.**

TRIPURĀCHARAṆA RĀYA. মোহ-কানন। [Moha-kānana. An historical romance.] pp. 249. *Calcutta,* ১৮৯৮ [1898.] 12°. **14127. cc. 21.(1.)**

TUKĀRĀMA, *Marathi poet.* [*Life.*] *See* YOGĪNDRANĀTHA VASU. তুকারাম-চরিত। [Tukārāma-charita.] [1901.] 12°. **14127. aa. 20.**

TULASĪCHARAṆA DATTA. সংক্ষিপ্ত ভৈষজ্য-রত্নাবলী। [Saṃkshipta bhaishajya-ratnāvalī.] A sketch of Materia-medica . . . Compiled by Tulshi Charan Dutt. Pt. i. pp. 84. *Calcutta,* 1905. 12°. **14125. b. 23.**

TULASĪ DĀSA. *See* VAISHṆAVACHARAṆA BASĀK. দোহাবলী। [Dohāvalī. A collection of Hindi *dohās,* by Tulasī Dāsa and other poets, with Bengali translations, and a life of the poet.] [1899.] 12°. **14158. c. 44.**

—— গোসাঁই তুলসীদাস কৃত দোহাবলী। [Dohāvalī. A collection of Hindi *dohās* of Tulasī Dāsa with Bengali translations.] *See* KĀLIDĀSA. সঞ্জীবনী কালিদাসের কবিতা। [Kālidāser kavitā.] [1897.] 12°. **14127. aa. 14.(1.)**

—— তুলসীদাস কৃত রামায়ণ। [Rāmāyaṇa. Hindi text, with a transliteration in the Bengali character, and accompanied by a Bengali translation and notes by Jagannātha Ṣukla.] কলিকাতা ১২৯০ [*Calcutta,* 1884.] 8°. **14158. f. 23.**

As far as the beginning of Ayodhyākāṇḍa.

—— তুলসীদাসকৃত রামায়ণ। [Rāmāyaṇa. Hindi text, with a Bengali transliteration and translation by Bhuvanachandra Basāk.] কলিকাতা ১৮৮৭-৮৯ [*Calcutta,* 1887-89.] 8°. **14158. d. 27.**

The Aranya, Kishkindhā, and Sundara kāṇḍas only. Apparently a continuation under a new form of the edition and translation by Jagannātha Ṣukla.

—— রামায়ণ। [Rāmāyaṇa. A metrical translation by Harinārāyaṇa Miṣra.] pp. 318. কলিকাতা ১৩১১ [*Calcutta,* 1905.] 8°. **14129. cc. 14.**

'UBAID ALLĀH ibn MAS'ŪD (ṢADR al-SHARĪ'AH). শরে বেকায়া। বঙ্গানুবাদ। [Sharh i Wikāyah. A digest of Muhammadan Law, being a Bengali translation by Shaikh 'Abd al-Ḳādir of the first two parts of 'Ubaid Allāh's Arabic commentary on Maḥmūd ibn 'Ubaid Allāh's treatise entitled Wikāyat al-riwāyat.] pp. 557, iii. কলিকাতা ১৩০৮ [*Calcutta,* 1902.] 8°. **14125. a. 30.**

UDĀSĪNA PATHIKA, *pseud.* উদাসীন পথিকের মনের কথা। [Udāsīna Pathiker maner kathā. A story of the Indigo riots at Kushtia in 1860.] pp. 197. কলিকাতা ১২৯৭ [*Calcutta,* 1890.] 8°. **14127. e. 38.**

UDAYAKRISHṆA DATTA. আর্য্যালোক। অর্থাৎ আত্মজ্ঞানে তত্ত্ব-জ্ঞান। [Āryāloka. A physico-philosophical treatise on the separate existence of mind and matter, and on different kinds of *yoga.*] pp. iii. 263. কলিকাতা ১২৯৯ [*Calcutta,* 1892.] 8°. **14123. f. 45.**

UDDHAVĀNANDA. রাধিকা-মঙ্গল। [Rādhikā-maṅgala. A poem on the birth of Rādhā. With an account of the author and his writings by Mahendranātha Vidyānidhi.] ১৩০৩ [1896.] *See* ACADEMIES, *etc.*—Calcutta.—*Bengal Academy of Literature.* সাহিত্য-পরিষৎ-পত্রিকা। [Sāhitya-parishat-patrikā.] Vol. iii., no. 3. [1894, *etc.*] 8°. **14133. f. 18.**

UMĀCHARAṆA DATTA. Praśna samádhánam, or Sanskrit questions of Entrance Examinations of the Calcutta University, with the answers, and translations, from English to Bengali, from the year 1872 [to 1880]. প্রশ্ন-সমাধানম্। *Calcutta,* 1880. 8°. **14085. c.**

UMEṢACHANDRA BHAṬṬĀCHĀRYA SMṚITIRATNA. গৌড়াদ্য দ্রাবিড় বৈদিকশ্রেণী ব্রাহ্মণ-কুলপরিচায়ক প্রশ্নোত্তরমালা। [Praṣnottaramālā. An account, in catechetical form, of the origin, functions, and history of the Gauḍa, Drāviḍa, and Vaidika Brahmans. With quotations from Sanskrit texts.] pp. 39. *Calcutta,* 1900. 12°. **14058. a. 8.(2.)**

UMEṢACHANDRA DĀSA GUPTA. জাতিতত্ত্ব-বারিধি। [Jātitattva-vāridhi. A work on Hindu castes, their origin, rites, and ceremonies.] কলিকাতা ১৯০২ [*Calcutta,* 1902, *etc.*] 8°. **14125. ee. 37.**

In progress.

UMEṢACHANDRA GUPTA KAVIRATNA. Vaidyakaśabdasindhu, or A comprehensive lexicon of Hindu medical terms and names of drugs, with their synonyms in Latin, Sanskrit, Hindi, Telugu, Bengali, *etc.* (বৈদ্যকশব্দসিন্ধুঃ) pp. 48, 1112. *Calcutta,* 1894. 8°. **14043. e. 30.**

UMEṢACHANDRA VAITĀLIKA. বৈতালিক বিরচিত সদানন্দ। রঙ্গরস। [Sadānanda, also called Raṅgarasa. Short tales and anecdotes illustrative of

Bengali wit and humour.] pp. 94. কলিকাতা ১২৯৪ [*Calcutta*, 1888.] 12°. 14127. c. 37.(5.)

UMESACHANDRA VIDYĀLAṄKĀRA. সাংখ্য-দর্শন। [Sāṅkhyadarṣana. An exposition of the principles of Sāṅkhya philosophy.] pp. iii. x. 149. কলিকাতা ১৩০৬ [*Calcutta*, 1900.] 12°. **14123. e. 26.**

UṆADISŪTRA. উণাদিসূত্রম্। [Uṇādisūtra. Selections from the Sanskrit text, with a commentary in Sanskrit and Bengali by Mukundadayāla Vasu.] pp. 10. কোচবিহার ১৩০০ [*Cooch Behar*, 1893.] 12°. **14092. a. 17.(2.)**

UPANISHADS. ঋগ্বেদীয়-ঐতরেয়োপনিষৎ (রাজসনেয়-সংহিতোপনিষৎ *etc.*) [A series of Upanishads, compiled and published with ancient Sanskrit commentaries and Bengali translations by Maheṣachandra Pāla.] কলিকাতা ১৯০৩-১১ [*Calcutta*, 1881-89.] 8°. **14007. cc. 8.**

—— উপনিষদ-গ্রন্থাবলী। [Upanishad-granthāvalī. A metrical translation of the Upanishads by Ṣaṣadhara Rāya.] কলিকাতা ১৩১৩- [*Calcutta*, 1906, *etc.*] 12°. **14123. e. 35.**

In progress.

—— উপনিষদঃ। ঈশাকেনকঠৈতিত্রিঃ [Īṣā, Kena, and Kaṭha Upanishads. Sanskrit text, with commentary and Bengali translations. Edited by Ṣyāmalāla Gosvāmī.] pp. i. 160. *Calcutta*, ১৯০৬ [1906.] 16°. **14010. a. 12.(2.)**

—— অথ শান্তিপাঠঃ ॥ [Ṣāntipāṭha. A series of prayers to be said on reading the 10 great Upanishads, compiled chiefly from the Taittirīya, Bṛihadāraṇyaka, Nṛisiṃhatāpani, and Ṣvetāṣvatara Upanishads, and in part from Āraṇyakas. With the commentaries of Ṣaṅkara and Sāyaṇa, and a Bengali translation by Hārāṇachandra Vandyopādhyāya.] pp. 24. 1892. *See* PERIODICAL PUBLICATIONS.—*Calcutta*. ঊষা [Ushā.] Vol. ii., no. 4. [1889-]1893. 8°. **14010. c. 43.(vol. 2.)**

—— হিন্দুশাস্ত্র। . . . ব্রাহ্মণ আরণ্যক ও উপনিষদ্। [Selections from the Upanishads. Edited with Bengali translations, notes, and a preface on the Brāhmaṇa literature by Rameṣachandra Datta and Satyavrata Sāmaṣramī.] pp. i. 117. [1895.] *See* RAMEṢACHANDRA DATTA. হিন্দুশাস্ত্র। [Hinduṣāstra.] Pt. ii. [1895-97.] 8°. **14085. c. 45.(vol. i.)**

UPANISHADS (*continued*). উপনিষদঃ . . . শ্বেতাশ্বতর তৈত্তিরীয় ও ঐতরেয় . . . উপনিষদ্। [Ṣvetāṣvatara, Taittirīya, and Aitareya Upanishads. Sanskrit text, with a Sanskrit gloss styled Ṣaṅkarakṛipā, and a Bengali interpretation, called Prabodhaka, by Sītānātha Tattvabhūshaṇa. Edited by Satyavrata Sāmaṣramī. Second edition.] pp. xii. 132. কলিকাতা ১৯০৮ [*Calcutta*, 1908.] 8°. **14007. b. 32.**

Forms pt. 2 of a general collection of Upanishads.

—— উপনিষদঃ। তৈত্তিরীয়ৈতরেয়শ্বেতাশ্বতরেতিত্রিঃ [Taittirīya, Aitareya, and Ṣvetāṣvatara Upanishads. Sanskrit text, with commentary and Bengali translations. Edited by Ṣyāmalāla Gosvāmī.] pp. 52, 27, 85. কলিকাতা ১৩১৩ [*Calcutta*, 1907.] 12°. **14010. b. 28.**

—— উপনিষদাবলী। [Upanishadāvalī. A collection of 10 Upanishads, viz. Muktikā, Garbha, Brahma, Sarva, Kaivalya, Brahmavindu, Rāma, Nādavindu, Muṇḍaka, and Kaṭha Upanishads, with the Sanskrit commentary of Ṣaṅkara Āchārya, and *dīpikās* of Nārāyaṇa and of Ṣaṅkarānanda. Edited with Bengali translations by Prasannakumāra Ṣāstrī.] pp. 184. কলিকাতা ১৩০২ [*Calcutta*, 1896.] 12°. **14010. b. 12.**

—— সামবেদীয়া ছান্দোগ্যোপনিষৎ। ব্যাখ্যানুবাদ-সমেতা। [Chhāndogya Upanishad. Sanskrit text, edited with Sanskrit notes and a Bengali translation by Ṣyāmalāla Gosvāmī.] pp. ii. 343. কলিকাতা ১৩১৩ [*Calcutta*, 1906.] 12°. **14010. b. 29.**

—— Isa Upanishad . . . text, easy Sanskrit notes, English and Bengali translation . . . ঈশা উপনিষদ্। *See* YADUNĀTHA MAJUMDĀR. The Indian Sage. Pt. i. 1893, *etc.* 12°. **14048. a. 20.**

—— Isa-Upanishad. [Sanskrit text] with the Bhasyas of Baladeva Vidyabhushana, Sri Sankaracharya, and the Tika of Anandagiri . . . With a Bengali translation and commentary. Edited by Sri Syamalala Gosvami Siddhanta Vachaspati. With an English translation and commentary (ঈশোপনিষৎ). pp. 52, 6. *Calcutta*, 1895. 8°. **14010. cc. 3.(1.)**

—— কৈবল্যোপনিষৎ। [Kaivalya Upanishad. Sanskrit text, accompanied by a Bengali prose translation by Pūrṇānanda.] pp. 8. কলিকাতা [*Calcutta*, 1870 ?] 12°. **14010. b. 8.(1.)**

UPANISHADS (*continued*). ঋগ্বেদান্তর্গতা কৌষীতকি ব্রাহ্মণারণ্যকোপনিষৎ। [Kaushītaki. Sanskrit text, with grammatical analyses and exegetic notes, and a Bengali translation. Edited by Śyāmalāla Gosvāmī.] pp. 121. *Calcutta*, ১৯০৩ [1903.] 16°. **14010. a. 12.**

No. 1 of the Kamalamālikā.

—— অথর্ব্ববেদীয়-ক্ষুরিকোপনিষৎ। [Kshurikopanishad. Sanskrit text and commentary, with a Bengali translation.] *See* KĀLĪPRASANNA VIDYĀRATNA BHAṬṬĀCHĀRYA. যোগাঙ্কুর। [Yogāṅkura.] pp. 85-96. [1894.] 12°. **14048. b. 28.(2.)**

—— ମୁକ୍ତିକୋପନିଷଦ [Muktikopanishad. Sanskrit text, with a Bengali translation.] pp. 21. *Cuttack*, 1884. 8°. **14010. c. 30.(3.)**

In Oriya characters.

—— কৃষ্ণ-যজুর্ব্বেদীয়-উপনিষদঃ। [Taittirīya Upanishad. Sanskrit text, edited with a Bengali translation and notes by Sāndrānanda Āchārya.] 4 pts. কলিকাতা ১৩০৩ [*Calcutta*, 1896.] 8°. **14010. cc. 3.(2.)**

—— চৈতন্যোপনিষদ্। [Chaitanyopanishad. A modern work in 19 stanzas of the school of Chaitanya, in the form of an Upanishad. Sanskrit text and commentary, with a Bengali translation, called Amṛitavindu, by Madhusūdana Dāsa.] pp. 8. কলিকাতা, শ্রীচৈতন্যাব্দ ৪০০ [*Calcutta*, 1885.] 12°. **14010. b. 7.(1.)**

—— শিবোপনিষৎ। [Śiva-upanishad. A Sanskrit anonymous poem in 67 cantos in praise of Śiva, professing to give the substance of the Upanishads and other sacred works. With a Bengali prose translation by Rohinīnandana Sarkār.] pp. vi. 256. কলিকাতা ১২৯৬ [*Calcutta*, 1890.] 8°. **14028. c. 59.**

UPENDRACHANDRA MUKHOPĀDHYĀYA. চরিতাভিধান। (Charitabhidhan, or a Dictionary of Biography and Indian Mythology . . . By Upendra Chandra Mukherjee.) pp. vii. 606, 163, 5. *Dacca*, 1908. 8°. **14127. bb. 32.**

UPENDRACHANDRA VASU. *See* RAṄGALĀLA MUKHOPĀDHYĀYA and others. বিশ্বকোষ। [Viśvakosha. Edited in part by Upendrachandra Vasu.] [1885, *etc.*] 4°. **14133. c. 5.**

UPENDRAKṚISHṆA DATTA, *M.D., of Aberdeen.* খৃষ্টানের হিন্দু-সমাজে পুনঃপ্রবেশ সম্বন্ধে ব্যবস্থা। [Khṛishṭāner Hindu samāje punaḥ-praveṣa. Decisions of Hindu Pandits refusing to re-admit Dr. U. K. Dutt, a Christian convert, to membership in the Kāyastha caste.] pp. 37. [*Calcutta*, 1894.] 8°. **14125. ee. 28.(3.)**

UPENDRAKṚISHṆA VANDYOPĀDHYĀYA. A Handbook of Proverbs: English and Bengali. Being a collection of English proverbs in daily use, with necessary explanations, Bengali synonymous proverbs, and equivalent renderings. By Upendro Krishna Bonerjea. New edition. pp. 163. *Calcutta*, 1891. 12°. **14125. f. 38.**

UPENDRAKUMĀRA GHOSHA. আর্য্য-মহিলা। [Ārya-mahilā. Lives of five famous Hindu women, viz. Mīrābāi, Rāṇī Bhavānī, Asāmanyā the daughter of Jagat Śeṭh, Khanā, and Rāṇī Durgāvatī of Garmandal.] pp. 60. *Calcutta*, 1895. 12°. **14127. aa. 2.(5.)**

—— শ্রীচৈতন্য-চরিত। [Chaitanya-charita. A short sketch of the life of Chaitanya.] pp. 66. *Calcutta*, [1895.] 12°. **14127. aa. 3.(4.)**

UPENDRANĀTHA CHAKRAVARTĪ. *See* KRAMADĪŚVARA. সংক্ষিপ্ত সারব্যাকরণ। [Saṃkshipta sāra-vyākaraṇa. An abridgment of the sūtras of Kramadīśvara. Edited with a Bengali translation by Upendranātha Chakravartī.] 1891. 8°. **14090. c. 38.(1.)**

UPENDRANĀTHA MUKHOPĀDHYĀYA. *See* AMṚITALĀLA VASU. অমৃতগ্রন্থাবলী। [Amṛita-granthāvalī. Edited by Upendranātha Mukhopādhyāya.] [1906, *etc.*] 8°. **14127. g. 18.**

—— *See* ATULAKṚISHṆA MITRA. অতুল-গ্রন্থাবলী। [Atula-granthāvalī. Edited by Upendranātha Mukhopādhyāya.] [1904.] 8°. **14127. ee. 24.**

—— *See* BAṄKIMCHANDRA CHAṬṬOPĀDHYĀYA. বঙ্কিমচন্দ্রের গ্রন্থাবলী। [Baṅkimchandrer granthāvālī. Edited by Upendranātha Mukhopādhyāya.] [1904, *etc.*] 8°. **14127. g. 14.**

—— *See* DĪNABANDHU MITRA. রায় দীনবন্ধু মিত্রের গ্রন্থাবলী। [Granthāvalī. Edited by Upendranātha Mukhopādhyāya.] [1901.] 8°. **14127. ee. 16.**

UPENDRANĀTHA MUKHOPĀDHYĀYA (*continued*). *See* GIRIṢACHANDRA GHOSHA. গিরীশ-গ্রন্থাবলী। [Girișa-granthāvalī. Edited by Upendranātha Mukhopādhyāya.] [1905, *etc.*] 8°. **14127. g. 17.**

—— *See* HEMACHANDRA VANDYOPĀDHYĀYA. হেমচন্দ্রের গ্রন্থাবলী। [Hemachandrer granthāvalī. Edited by Upendranātha Mukhopādhyāya.] [1906.] 8°. **14127. g. 16.**

—— *See* TANTRAS. সানুবাদ মহানির্ব্বাণ-তন্ত্র *etc.* [Mahānirvāṇa-tantra. Sanskrit text, with a Bengali translation. Edited by Upendranātha Mukhopādhyāya.] [1907.] 8°. **14028. dd. 18.**

—— *See* TOD (J.), *Lieutenant Colonel.* সচিত্র রাজস্থান। [Rājasthāna. Tod's "Annals and Antiquities of Rajast'han," translated by Upendranātha Mukhopādhyāya.] [1898.] 8°. **14127. bbb. 4.**

—— —— [1906.] 8°. **14127. bbb. 8.**

—— বাসর কৌতুক নাটক। [Bāsar kautuka nāṭaka. A short play describing the songs, jokes, and entertainments that take place amongst the relations of a Hindu married couple on the marriage night.] pp. 35. কলিকাতা ১২৯৬ [*Calcutta*, 1889.] 12°. **14131. a. 28.(6.)**

—— ভারত উপন্যাস। [Bhārata-upanyāsa. A collection of short stories and fairy tales.] pp. 245. কলিকাতা ১৩০৮ [*Calcutta*, 1901.] 8°. **14127. ee. 13.(1.)**

—— [Another edition.] pp. 245. কলিকাতা ১৩১৩ [*Calcutta*, 1907.] 8°. **14127. ee. 28.**

—— দোঁহাবলী। [Dohāvalī. Hindi religious verses by Tulasī Dāsa, Kabīr, Mīrā Bāi, Gharīb Dās, and others. Compiled and edited with Bengali translations by Upendranātha Mukhopādhyāya.] pp. 182. কলিকাতা [*Calcutta*, 1901.] 12°. **14158. c. 51.**

—— Raj-bhasha. A guide to the art of writing and speaking English correctly . . . রাজ-ভাষা। 3 pts. pp. vii. 252. *Calcutta*, 1891. 12°. **14131. e. 21.(2.)**

—— বৈষ্ণব-গ্রন্থাবলী। [Vaishṇava-granthāvalī. A collection of poems by Vaishṇava writers.] Pt. i. pp. 148. কলিকাতা ১৩০৪ [*Calcutta*, 1899.] 8°. **14129. e. 22.**

UPENDRANĀTHA SARKĀR. কোচবিহার রাজবংশী জাতির বিবরণ। [Rājavaṃṣī jātir vivaraṇa. An account of the Rājavaṃṣī caste.] pp. viii. 52. *Cooch Behar*, 1894. 12°. **14125. e. 30.(2.)**

UPENDRANĀTHA SENA and YATĪNDRANĀTHA SENA. The Indian Student's Letter-writer. By Upendra Nath Sen . . . and Jatindra Nath Sen. Anglo-Bengali edition. pp. vi. 284. *Allahabad*, 1902. 12°. **14131. f. 33.**

UPENDRANĀTHA SENA GUPTA. *See* DEVENDRANĀTHA SENA GUPTA and UPENDRANĀTHA SENA GUPTA. আয়ুর্ব্বেদ-সংগ্রহ। [Āyurveda-saṅgraha.] [1908.] 4°. **14043. ddd. 4.**

UPENDRANĀTHA VIDYĀBHŪSHAṆA. *See* BHAṬṬI. Bhatti-kavyam. Cantos i. and ii. . . . With . . . introduction in English, easy Sanskrit commentary . . . notes . . . English and Bengali translations . . . by Pandit Upendra Nath Vidyabhushana. [1904.] 12°. **14085. b. 47.**

UṢANAS. উশনঃ সংহিতা। [Uṣanaḥ-saṃhitā, or Auṣanasa-smṛiti. A code of *dharma* in 9 *adhyāyas*. Sanskrit text with Bengali translation.] *See* PAÑCHĀNANA TARKARATNA BHAṬṬĀCHĀRYA. ঊনবিংশতি সংহিতা। [Ūnaviṃṣati saṃhitā.] pp. 219-263. [1903.] 8°. **14039. c. 20.**

UTTARAGĪTĀ. উত্তরগীতা। [Uttaragītā. Three chapters on Yoga philosophy, forming a sequel to the Bhagavadgītā. Sanskrit text, with Bengali translation.] *See* PAÑCHA GĪTĀ. পঞ্চগীতা। [Pañcha gītā.] pp. 35-96. [1906.] 16°. **14028. a. 33.**

VAIKUṆṬHACHANDRA DĀSA GUPTA. ফটিকচন্দ্র-দাস গুপ্তের সংক্ষিপ্ত জীবন চরিত। [Phaṭikachandra Dāsa Gupter jīvanacharita. A short sketch of the life of Phaṭikachandra Dāsa Gupta, and other members of the Gaila family in the district of Bakarganj.] pp. 8, 79. বরিশাল ১৩০৩ [*Barisal*, 1896.] 12°. **14127. aa. 6.(2.)**

VAISHṆAVACHARAṆA BASĀK. *See* KĀLIDĀSA. সঞ্জীবনী কালিদাসের কবিতা। [Kālidāser kavitā. Compiled and edited by Vaishṇavacharaṇa Basāk.] [1897.] 12°. **14127. aa. 14.(1.)**

—— *See* TANTRAS. জ্ঞান-সঙ্কলিনী তন্ত্রম্। [Jñāna-saṅkalinītantra. With a Bengali translation by Vaishṇavacharaṇa Basāk.] [1901.] 12°. **14033. a. 41.(3.)**

VAISHṆAVACHARAṆA BASĀK (*continued*). দোহাবলী। [Dohāvalī. A collection of Hindi *dohās*, in Bengali characters, by Tulasī Dāsa, Kabīr, and other poets. Compiled with Bengali translations, and lives of Tulasī Dāsa and Kabīr, by Vaishṇavacharaṇa Basāk.] pp. x. 192. কলিকাতা ১৩০৪ [*Calcutta*, 1899.] 12°. **14158. c. 44.**

—— ইন্দ্রচন্দ্র বা আলালের ঘরের নন্দদুলাল। [Indrachandra, also called Ālāler gharer Nandadulāl. A tale of domestic life in Bengal. Second edition.] pp. 142. কলিকাতা [*Calcutta*, 1903.] 12°. **14127. cc. 33.(2.)**

—— সাধনা ও সিদ্ধি *etc.* [Sādhanā o siddhi. A manual of instruction on Yoga and other matters relating to Hindu religion and philosophy.] pp. ii. 248. *Calcutta*, [1908.] 12°. **14123. e. 40.**

VAISHṆAVACHARAṆA MALLIKA. সুবর্ণবণিক্ বৈশ্য। [Suvarṇa-baṇik Vaiṣya. A treatise on the Suvarṇa-baṇik caste, proving that they are Vaiṣyas.] pp. 48. হুগলি ১৩০২ [*Hooghly*, 1895.] 8°. **14125. ee. 28.(4.)**

VAISHṆAVA GRANTHĀVALĪ. বৈষ্ণব গ্রন্থাবলী। [Vaishṇava granthāvalī. A collection of 5 Vaishṇava poems, viz.: (1) Kṛishṇakarṇāmṛita by Yadunandana Ṭhākura. (2) Dinamaṇichandrodaya by Manohara Dāsa. (3) Tattvavilāsa by Vṛindāvana Dāsa. (4) Bālyavilāsa by Krishṇadāsa Kavirāja. (5) Vīraratnāvalī by Ṣrīnivāsasuta.] pp. 88, 135. কলিকাতা ১৩০৬ [*Calcutta*, 1900.] 12°. **14123. e. 20.(3.)**

VĀLMĪKI. *See* JAGADRĀMA RĀYA. অষ্ট কাণ্ডে সম্পূর্ণ জগদ্রামী-রামায়ণ। [Rāmāyaṇa. A metrical version of the Sanskrit epic.] [1906.] 8°. **14129. e. 32.**

—— *See* KṚITTIVĀSA. সরল কৃত্তিবাস। [Sarala Kṛittivāsa. A simplified metrical version of the Rāmāyaṇa of Kṛittivāsa.] [1907.] 4°. **14129. f. 8.**

—— *See* RAGHUNANDANA GOSVĀMĪ. শ্রীশ্রীরামরসায়ন। [Rāmarasāyana. A metrical version of the Rāmāyaṇa.] [1889.] 8°. **14129. e. 17.**

—— *See* VIṢVANĀTHA TARKABHŪSHAṆA. বিশ্বনাথ রামায়ণ। [Viṣvanātha-Rāmāyaṇa. A philosophical interpretation of the Ādi-kāṇḍa of the Rāmāyaṇa.] [1890.] 8°. **14123. f. 41.**

VĀLMĪKI (*continued*). অদ্ভুত রামায়ণ। [Adbhuta Rāmāyaṇa. A prose version of the Rāmāyaṇa, by Chandranātha Vasu.] pp. iii. 183. কলিকাতা ১৩০৮ [*Calcutta*, 1902.] 8°. **14129. cc. 9.**

—— রামায়ণম্। [Rāmāyaṇa. Sanskrit text, with a Bengali prose translation. Edited by Pañchānana Tarkaratna. Third edition.] pp. i. ix. 1469. কলিকাতা ১৩১১ [*Calcutta*, 1904.] 8°. **14068. c. 18.**

—— হিন্দুশাস্ত্র। . . . রামায়ণ। [Rāmāyaṇa. A Bengali prose version by Hemachandra Vidyāratna.] pp. i. 178. [1896.] *See* RAMEṢACHANDRA DATTA. হিন্দুশাস্ত্র। [Hindu-ṣāstra.] Pt. vi. [1895-1897.] 8°. **14085. c. 45.(vol. ii.)**

—— কৃত্তিবাসী রামায়ণ। [Rāmāyaṇa. A metrical translation by Kṛittivāsa. Collated from ancient manuscripts, and edited, with a glossary and index of obsolete words, by Hīrendranātha Datta.] কলিকাতা ১৩১০ [*Calcutta*, 1904, *etc.*] 8°. **14129. cc. 15.**
In progress. No. 1 *of the* Parishad-granthāvali.

—— রামায়ণ। [Rāmāyaṇa. Another edition of Kṛittivāsa's metrical translation. With an extensive introduction and life of Kṛittivāsa.] pp. vi. 15, 499. কলিকাতা ১৩১৩ [*Calcutta*, 1906.] 8°. **14129. cc. 18.**

—— কৃত্তিবাসী রামায়ণ *etc.* [Rāmāyaṇa of Kṛittivāsa. Edited, with a life of the poet, by Subalachandra Mitra.] pp. xvi. 560. কলিকাতা [*Calcutta*, 1908.] 8°. **14129. e. 35.**

—— রামায়ণ-তত্ত্ব। [Rāmāyaṇa-tattva. A classified Bengali encyclopaedia to the Rāmāyaṇa. Published by the Vangīya Sāhitya Parishad under the editorship of Rāmendrasundara Trivedī.] ১৩০৯ [1902, *etc.*] 8°. *See* ACADEMIES, *etc.*—Calcutta.—*Bengal Academy of Literature.* সাহিত্য-পরিষৎ-পত্রিকা। [Sāhitya-parishat-patrikā.] Vol. ix. [1894, *etc.*] 8°. **14133. f. 18.**
In progress.

VĀMĀCHARAṆA VASU. সুরো যে সন্ন্যাসী! বা অষ্টাহে কাব্য। [Sūro je sannyāsī. The story of an unfortunate woman, in verse.] pp. ii. 348. কলিকাতা ১৩১১ [*Calcutta*, 1904.] 12°. **14129. bb. 27.**

—— বিবিধ বস্ত্রবয়ন শিক্ষা। [Vastravayana-ṣikshā. A treatise on the art of weaving cloth.] pp. viii. 93. কলিকাতা ১৩১৩ [*Calcutta*, 1906.] 12°. **14125. ddd. 2.**

VĀMĀ SUNDARĪ. [*Life.*] *See* CHANDRAKĀNTA SENA. বামাস্থন্দরী বা আদর্শনারী। [Ādarṣa-nārī.] [1896.] 12°. **14127. aa. 6.(5.)**

VAMṢĪDĀSA. *See* PURĀṆAS.—*Padmapurāṇa.* শ্রীশ্রী-পদ্মপুরাণ। [Padmapurāṇa. Translated into verse by Vamṣīdāsa.] [1904.] *obl.* 12°. **14123. gg. 2.**

VAMṢĪVADANA CHAṬṬOPĀDHYĀYA. আসল নূতন বিদ্যাস্থন্দর টপ্পা। [Vidyā-Sundara ṭappā. The romance of Vidyā and Sundara, in verse, based on the poem of Bhāratachandra Rāya.] pp. 60. কলিকাতা ১২৯৩ [*Calcutta,* 1886.] 12°. **14129. b.**

VAMṢĪVADANA ṢARMĀ. পুণ্ডরীককুলকীর্ত্তিপঞ্জিকা ফতেসিংহ জমিদারীর ইতিবৃত্ত [Puṇḍarīkakulakīrtti-pañjikā. A Sanskrit poem in five chapters, narrating the history of the Puṇḍarīka family, or zamindars of Fatehsingh, from its settlement to about 200 years ago. Edited, with a Bengali translation and appendices on the subsequent history of the family, by Rāmendrasundara Trivedī.] pp. 2, 88. *Calcutta,* ১৩০৭ [1901.] 8°. **14058. b. 47.**

VANAMĀLĪ DĀSA. জয়দেব-চরিত। [Jayadeva-charita. An old Bengali poem on the life of Jayadeva.] pp. 34. ১৩০৭ [1900-1901.] *See* PERIODICAL PUBLICATIONS.—*Calcutta.* প্রাচীন বাঙ্গালা গ্রন্থাবলী। [Prāchīna Bāṅgālā granthāvalī.] nos. 1 and 2. [1900, *etc.*] 8°. **14133. ff. 2.**

VANAVIHĀRĪ CHAKRAVARTĪ. বঙ্গ-বিজয়। [Vaṅga-vijaya. The conquest of Bengal: an historical drama.] pp. iv. 141. কলিকাতা ১৩১৩ [*Calcutta,* 1906.] 12°. **14131. aa. 5.(3.)**

VAṄGAKOSHA. বঙ্গকোষ অভিধান। [Vaṅgakosha. A small dictionary of Sanskrit synonyms for ordinary Bengali words.] pp. 33. কলিকাতা ১২৯৬ [*Calcutta,* 1899.] 12°. **14133. a. 11.**

VAṄGĪYA SĀHITYA PARISHAD. *See* ACADEMIES, *etc.*—Calcutta.—*Bengal Academy of Literature.*

VARADĀCHARAṆA DEVA. নিত্য তন্ত্র। [Nitya tantra. A compilation of Tantric forms of worship, with notes and quotations from Sanskrit authorities.] Vol. ii., pt. i. কলিকাতা ১২৯৯ [*Calcutta,* 1892.] 8°. **14123. f. 48.**

VARADĀCHARAṆA MITRA. অবসর। [Avasara. Miscellaneous poems.] pp. 122, 17. *Calcutta,* ১৩০২ [1895.] 12°. **14129. b. 42.(1.)**

VARADĀKĀNTA SENA GUPTA. ভারত ভ্রমণ। [Bhārata-bhramaṇa. Travels in India; containing chiefly an account of places of interest on the East Indian Railway.] Pt. i. pp. ii. 234. কলিকাতা ১২৮৪ [*Calcutta,* 1888.] 12°. **14127. a.**

VARADĀPRASĀDA MAJUMDĀR. An enlarged and illustrated Prakritibodha abhidhána, or a comprehensive dictionary of the Bengali language . . . বৃহৎ সচিত্র প্রকৃতিবোধ অভিধান। pp. ii. xxiv. 1232. ১২৯৪ *Calcutta,* [1887.] 8°. **14133. b. 10.**

VARADĀPRASĀDA VASU. তীর্থদর্শন। [Tīrtha-darṣana. An account of the author's visit to Hindu places of pilgrimage, with historical notices of each place.] 5 pts. কলিকাতা ১৮১২-১৫ [*Calcutta,* 1891-94.] 12°. **14127. a. 49.**

VARĀHAMIHIRA. বৃহজ্জাতকম্। [Bṛihaj-jātaka. A Sanskrit work on nativities, with Utpala's Sanskrit commentary, and a Bengali commentary.] pp. 156. ১৩০০ [1893.] *See* PERIODICAL PUBLICATIONS. — *Calcutta.* অরুণোদয়। [Aruṇodaya.] Pt. i., no. 1. [1890, *etc.*] 4°. **14133. g. 16.**

—— বৃহৎসংহিতা। [Bṛihat-saṃhitā. Sanskrit text, with a Bengali translation.] pp. 232. [1890, *etc.*] *See* PERIODICAL PUBLICATIONS.—*Calcutta.* অরুণোদয়। [Aruṇodaya.] [1890, *etc.*] 4°. **14133. g. 16.**

VASANTAKUMĀRA RĀYA. *See* PĀṆINI. সিদ্ধান্ত-সন্দীপনী *etc.* [Siddhāntasandīpanī. A rearrangement of the Aphorisms, with a Bengali commentary by Vasantakumāra Rāya.] [1901.] 12°. **14092. a. 17.(3.)**

VASISHṬHA. বসিষ্ঠসংহিতা। [Vasishṭha-saṃhitā. A code of *dharma,* in 21 *adhyāyas.* Sanskrit text, with Bengali translation.] *See* PAÑCHĀNANA TARKARATNA BHAṬṬĀCHĀRYA. ঊনবিংশতি সংহিতা। [Ūna-viṃṣati saṃhitā.] pp. 479-509. [1903.] 8°. **14039. c. 20.**

VĀSUDEVA GHOSHA. বাস্থদেব ঘোষের পদাবলী। [Padāvalī. Vaishṇava poems.] pp. 24. ১৩০৭ [1900-01.] *See* PERIODICAL PUBLICATIONS. — *Cal-*

cutta. প্রাচীন বাঙ্গালা গ্রন্থাবলী। [Prāchīna Bāṅgālā granthāvalī.] nos. 1 and 2. [1900, *etc.*] 8°. **14133. ff. 2.**

VEDĀNTACHANDRIKĀ. An Apology for the present system of Hindoo worship. Written in the Bengalee language, and accompanied by an English translation. (বেদান্তচন্দ্রিকা) pp. 67, 50. *Calcutta*, 1817. 8°. **14123. g. 19.**

VEDAS. *See* SĀYAṆA ĀCHĀRYA. ঋগ্বেদভাষ্যোপোদ্ঘাত প্রকরণ। [Ṛigvedabhāshyopodghāta. The introduction to Sāyaṇa's commentary on the Ṛigveda, with a Bengali translation.] [1901.] 12°. **14007. b. 16.**

—— *See* ŚYĀMĀCHARAṆA KAVIRATNA. স্বপরিশুদ্ধ-সটীক ত্রিবেদীয়-ক্রিয়াকাণ্ড-পদ্ধতিঃ। [Trivedīya kriyā-kāṇḍa-paddhati. A manual of Vedic domestic rites, with Sanskrit commentary and Bengali notes. Followed by the Vedic grammar from the Siddhāntakaumudī.] 1906. *obl.* 8°. **14033. bbb. 44.**

—— ঋগ্বেদ সংহিতা। [Ṛigveda-saṃhitā. Translated, in accordance with the Sanskrit commentary of Sāyaṇa Āchārya, with notes, by Rameśachandra Datta.] 8 pts. কলিকাতা ১৮৮৫-৮৭ [*Calcutta*, 1885-87.] 8°. **14123. f. 35.**

—— ত্রয়ীভাষা। [Trayī-bhāshā. Translations of selected texts from the 4 Vedas, with explanatory notes. By Satyavrata Sāmaśramī Bhaṭṭāchārya.] pp. xvi. 148, iv. কলিকাতা ১৮৯৭ [*Calcutta*, 1897.] 8°. **14123. f. 54.**

The 4th and last part of a series entitled Trayī-chatushṭaya.

—— হিন্দুশাস্ত্র। . . . বেদ সংহিতা। [Vedasaṃhitā. Selections from the Atharvaveda, Ṛigveda, and Vājasaneyisaṃhitā. Edited with Bengali translations, preface and notes, by Rameśachandra Datta and Satyavrata Sāmaśramī.] pp. i. 107. [1895.] *See* RAMEŚACHANDRA DATTA. হিন্দুশাস্ত্র। [Hindu-śāstra.] Pt. i. [1895-97.] 8°. **14085. c. 45.(vol. 1.)**

VEṆĪMĀDHAVA BHAṬṬĀCHĀRYA. প্রকৃতি ও প্রত্যয় সহিত বৃহৎ সচিত্র বাঙ্গালা অভিধান। [Bāṅgālā abhidhāna. An etymological Bengali dictionary.] pp. 700. কলিকাতা ১৮৮৮ [*Calcutta*, 1888.] 8°. **14133. c. 6.**

VEṆĪMĀDHAVA CHAṬṬOPĀDHYĀYA. পরামুক্তি বা রাধিকার গোলোক-মিলন। [Parāmukti. A mythological drama on the loves of Rādhā and Krishṇa.] pp. 142. কলিকাতা ১৩১১ [*Calcutta*, 1905.] 8°. **14131. b. 25.(2.)**

VEṆĪMĀDHAVA GAṄGOPĀDHYĀYA. Beginners' Dictionary of English Words, Phrases and Idioms done into Bengali by Benimadhav Ganguli. Third edition. pp. iv. 851, 21. *Calcutta*, 1901. 8°. **12906. de. 26.**

—— The Student's Dictionary of Bengali words and phrases, done into English. By Benimadhav Ganguli. pp. viii. 829, xii. *Calcutta*, 1903. 8°. **14133. a. 14.**

VEṆĪMĀDHAVA GAṄGOPĀDHYĀYA and VIŚVEŚVARA CHAKRAVARTĪ. A Junior Text-book of translation from Bengali into English. By Benimadhav Ganguli . . . and Bisvesvar Chakravarti. Second edition. pp. ii. iii. 142. *Calcutta*, 1892. 12°. **14131. e. 22.**

—— Fifth edition. pp. ii. iv. 166. *Calcutta*, 1893. 12°. **14131. e. 28.**

—— A Manual of translation from Bengali into English. By Benimadhav Ganguli and Bisvesvar Chakravarti. Fourth edition. pp. vi. 266. *Calcutta*, 1891. 8°. **14131. g. 26.**

VEṆĪMĀDHAVA NYĀYARATNA. *See* YĀJÑAVALKYA. যোগিযাজ্ঞবল্ক্যম্। [Yogī-yājñavalkya. Edited with a prose translation by Veṇīmādhava Nyāyaratna.] [1893.] 8°. **14048. bb. 50.**

VENSTER (JOSEPH DE). [*Life.*] *See* YOGENDRACHANDRA VASU. অমর কীর্ত্তি। [Amara-kīrti.] [1891.] 12°. **14127. aa. 6.(1.)**

VICTORIA, *Queen of Great Britain and Ireland.* [*Life.*] *See* BHAGAVATĪCHARAṆA MITRA. জুবিলি বা পরার্দ্ধ্য-উৎসব। [Parārddhya-utsava.] 1887. 12°. **14127. a. 31.(2.)**

—— *See* DURGĀDĀSA DE. জুবিলী যজ্ঞ। [Jubilī-yajña. A dramatic composition on the Diamond Jubilee of the reign of Queen Victoria.] [1897.] 12°. **14131. a. 40.(9.)**

—— [*Life.*] *See* KRISHṆAKUMĀRA MITRA. ভিক্টোরিয়া-চরিত সচিত্র। [Bhikṭoriyā-charita.] [1898.] 8°. **14127. bb. 12.**

VICTORIA, *Queen of Great Britain and Ireland* (*continued*). ভিক্‌টোরিয়া-ভারত। [Bhikṭoriyā Bhārata. An anonymous poem addressed to Queen Victoria, extolling her reign, and praying for the redress of wrongs done to her subjects in India.] pp. 29. *Calcutta*, [1885.] 12°. **14129. a. 22.(2.)**

VIDHUBHŪSHAṆA GOSVĀMĪ, *of Dacca College.* *See* BHAṬṬI. Bhatti Kavyam. Canto xii. [With Sanskrit commentary, notes in Sanskrit and English, and English and Bengali translations. Edited by] Bidhubhushan Goswami. 1907. 12°. **14072. b. 26.(4.)**

VIDHUBHŪSHAṆA MUKHOPĀDHYĀYA. *See* TĀRAKANĀTHA GAṄGOPĀDHYĀYA. A Glimpse into the Indian inner home, being a faithful rendering into English of the . . . Bengali novel Svarnalata. By Bidhubhushan Mukerjee. 1903. 8°. **14127. cc. 85.**

VIDHUBHŪSHAṆA RĀYA. আজগুবি হিন্দুয়ানী। [Ājgubi Hinduyānī. A poem condemning the hypocritical Hinduism now in vogue.] pp. 11. মুর্শিদাবাদ ১৩০১ [*Murshidabad*, 1895.] 12°. **14129. b. 44.(2.)**

VIDHUBHŪSHAṆA VASU. লক্ষ্মীমেয়ে। [Lakshmī meye. A story of Bengali domestic life.] pp. 82. কলিকাতা ১৩০৪ [*Calcutta*, 1897.] 12°. **14127. cc. 10.(2.)**

VIDYĀPATI. [*Life.*] *See* TRAILOKYANĀTHA BHAṬṬĀCHĀRYA. কবি বিদ্যাপতি *etc.* [Kavi Vidyāpati.] [1895.] 12°. **14131. d. 33.**

—— বিদ্যাপতি। [The poems of Vidyāpati, with notes and a biography of the poet.] *See* AKSHAYAKUMĀRA DE. মহাজন পদাবলী। চণ্ডীদাস ও বিদ্যাপতি। [Mahājana-padāvalī.] [1903.] 8°. **14129. e. 26.**

—— [Fourth edition.] [1905.] 8°. **14129. e. 30.**

—— [Fifth edition.] [1907.] 8°. **14129. e. 33.**

—— বিদ্যাপতি কৃত পদাবলি। [Padāvalī. The poetical works of Vidyāpati.] *See* AKSHAYACHANDRA SARKĀR. প্রাচীন কাব্য সংগ্রহ। [Prāchīna kāvya-saṅgraha.] Pt. i. [1884-85.] 8°. **14129. g. 8.**

—— বিদ্যাপতি . . . পদাবলী। [Padāvalī. Edited, with critical and explanatory notes, and a short life of the poet, by Pañchānana Tarkaratna.] pp. 187, 29. কলিকাতা ১৩০১ [*Calcutta*, 1895.] 12°. **14129. b. 44.(3.)**

—— নব আবিষ্কৃত বিদ্যাপতির পদাবলী। [Padāvalī. A collection of songs by Vidyāpati, hitherto unpublished, discovered by Haraprasāda Ṣastrī in a manuscript at Khatmandu.] ১৩০৭ [1900.] *See* PERIODICAL PUBLICATIONS.—*Calcutta.* প্রাচীন বাঙ্গালা গ্রন্থাবলী। [Prāchīna Bāṅgālā granthāvalī.] no. i. pp. 1-8. [1900, *etc.*] 8°. **14133. ff. 2.**

—— The Poets of Bengal. Bidyapati. A comprehensive collection of his Bengali songs, compiled from various ancient manuscripts . . . with copious notes and an introduction by Kaliprasanna Kavyabisharad. (বিদ্যাপতি।) pp. xxxii. 215, ii. *Calcutta*, ১৩০১ [1894.] 8°. **14129. cc. 10.**

—— শৈবসর্ব্বস্ব-সার। [Ṣaivasarvasvasāra. A collection of extracts from the Purāṇas and other religious works, on the worship of Ṣiva. Edited, with Bengali translations, by Bhāgyavān Vidyālaṅkāra.] pp. 162, 5. দ্বারভাঙ্গা ১৩০৪ [*Darbhangah*, 1897.] 12°. **14028. d. 57.(2.)**

—— বিদ্যাপতি। [Vidyāpati. An essay on the life and writings of Vidyāpati.] *See* RĀJAKṚISHṆA MUKHOPĀDHYĀYA. নানা প্রবন্ধ। [Nānā prabandha.] p. 11. 1885. 8°. **14133. h. 11.**

—— বিদ্যাপতি। শব্দের তালিকা। [Vidyāpati. Ṣabder tālikā. An alphabetical list of difficult words in the poems of Vidyāpati, with equivalents in modern Bengali, and references to the passages where they occur.] ১৩০২-০৩ [1896.] *See* ACADEMIES, *etc.*—Calcutta.—*Bengal Academy of Literature.* সাহিত্য পরিষৎ-পত্রিকা। [Sāhitya-parishat-patrikā.] Vols. ii., no. 4, and iii., nos. 1 and 2. [1894, *etc.*] 8°. **14133. f. 18.**

VIHĀRĪLĀLA CHAKRAVARTĪ. গ্রন্থাবলী। [Granthāvalī. The complete works of Vihārīlāla Chakravartī, edited, with an introduction, by Avināṣachandra Chakravartī.] pp. ii. 288. কলিকাতা ১৩০৭ [*Calcutta*, 1900.] 12°. **14129. bb. 5.**

—— সারদামঙ্গল। [Sāradāmaṅgala. A mythological poem of the neo-Hindu school of religious thought.] pp. 67. কলিকাতা ১২৮৬ [*Calcutta*, 1880.] 8°. **14129. c. 41.(2.)**

VIHĀRĪLĀLA CHAṬṬOPĀDHYĀYA. গ্রন্থাবলী। [Granthāvalī. The complete works of Vihārīlāla Chaṭṭopādhyāya.] Pt. i. pp. 259. কলিকাতা ১২৯৯ [*Calcutta*, 1893.] 8°. **14129. e. 19.**

—— মুই হ্যাঁন্ডু! [Mui Hyāndu, or "I am a Hindu." A farce directed against female education amongst Hindus.] pp. 55. কলিকাতা ১৩০০ [*Calcutta*, 1894.] 12°. **14131. a. 38.(2.)**

VIHĀRĪLĀLA HĀLDĀR. চিত্ত সংস্কার। [Chittasaṃskāra. Poems inculcating a higher standard of purity in Hindu religion.] pp. 49. কলিকাতা ১৩০২ [*Calcutta*, 1895.] 8°. **14129. f. 6.(2.)**

VIHĀRĪLĀLA MITRA. কথোপকথন-রহস্য। [Kathopakathana-rahasya. Suggestions for the religious and social improvement of India, in the form of a dialogue between a Guru and his disciple.] pp. 94. কলিকাতা ১৮২০ [*Calcutta*, 1898.] 8°. **14125. e. 32.(2.)**

VIHĀRĪLĀLA PĀIN. ভবসিন্ধু-তরণী। [Bhavasindhutaraṇī. A Sanskrit and Bengali anthology, chiefly of poems, for the edification of Vaishṇavas.] pp. xiii. 342; 2 *plates*. [*Calcutta*, 1902.] 8°. **14033. bbb. 17.**

VIHĀRĪLĀLA SARKĀR. মহারাণী স্বর্ণময়ী। [Mahārāṇī Svarṇamayī. A short account of the life of Svarṇamayī, Rani of Kasimbazar, in the District of Murshidabad.] pp. 70. কলিকাতা ১৩১৪ [*Calcutta*, 1907.] 12°. **14127. aa. 35.**

—— শকুন্তলা-রহস্য। [Ṣakuntalā-rahasya. A criticism on the Ṣakuntalā nāṭaka of Kālidāsa.] pp. xxiv. 144. কলিকাতা ১৩০৩ [*Calcutta*, 1896.] 12°. **14131. d. 28.**

—— তিতুমীর। [Titu Mīr. An account of Titu Mīr, a Wahhābī of Haidarpur, of his opposition to the local authorities, and defeat and death at Narikelberia in A.D. 1831.] pp. 101. কলিকাতা ১৩০৪ [*Calcutta*, 1897.] 12°. **14127. aa. 19.**

—— বঙ্গে বর্গী। [Vaṅge Bargī. An historical account of Bengal during the rule of the Nawab 'Alī Vardī Khān, and of the depredations of the Maratha freebooters called Bargīs.] pp. ii. 143. কলিকাতা ১৩১৪ [*Calcutta*, 1907.] 12°. **14127. aa. 41.**

—— বিদ্যাসাগর। [Vidyāsāgara. The life of Īṣvarachandra Vidyāsāgara, with notices of several illustrious contemporaries.] pp. xii. viii. 660. কলিকাতা ১৩০২ [*Calcutta*, 1895.] 12°. **14127. a. 50.**

VIJAYACHAND MAHTĀB, *Maharaja of Burdwan.* বিজয় গীতিকা। [Vijayagītikā. Miscellaneous poems.] 2 pts. *Calcutta*, ১৩০৬-০৮ [1900-01.] 8°. **14129. e. 21.**

VIJAYACHANDRA MAJUMDĀR. কথা ও বীথি। [Kathā o vīthi. Five stories in verse.] pp. 112, iv. কলিকাতা ১৯৫১ [*Calcutta*, 1895.] 12°. **14127. c. 54.(3.)**

—— যুগপূজা বা ধর্ম্মভাব বিকাশ। [Yugapūjā. Poems describing the gradual development of religious ideas in the human mind.] pp. viii. 52. কলিকাতা ১৯৪৯ [*Calcutta*, 1893.] 12°. **14129. b. 35.(7.)**

VIJAYA GUPTA, *the Poet, of Gailā-phullaṣrī.* মনসা-মঙ্গল বা পদ্মাপুরাণ। [Manasā-maṅgala, also called Padmāpurāṇa. An old Bengali poem, written in Ṣaka 1406, relating to the myth of the snake-goddess Manasā. Edited with an introduction by Rāmacharaṇa Ṣiroratna.] pp. xii. 232. বরিশাল ১৩০৩ [*Barisal*, 1896.] 8°. **14129. f. 6.(3.)**

—— শ্রীশ্রীপদ্মপুরাণ বা মনসা-মঙ্গল গীত। [Manasā-maṅgala. Revised and edited by Kālīmohana Vidyāratna.] pp. iii. 112. কলিকাতা ১৩০৭ [*Calcutta*, 1900.] *obl.* 8°. **14123. i. 14.**

VIJAYAKEṢAVA MITRA. ফোজদারী আইন সংগ্রহ। [Phojdārī āin-saṅgraha. A collection of Criminal enactments from A.D. 1882.] Pt. i. কলিকাতা ১৮৯৫ [*Calcutta*, 1895.] 8°. **14125. a. 25.**

VIJAYAKṚISHṆA GHAṬAKA CHŪḌĀMAṆI. *See* DĪNABANDHU GHAṬAKA KULABHŪSHAṆA. কায়স্থ-কারিকা ও বংশাবলি। [Kāyastha-kārikā. Compiled with the assistance of Vijayakṛishṇa Ghaṭaka.] [1886, *etc.*] 4°. **14123. i. 11.**

VIJAYAKṚISHṆA GOSVĀMĪ. ব্রাহ্মসমাজের বর্ত্তমান অবস্থা *etc.* [Brāhma Samājer vartamāna avasthā. An account of the various changes which have taken place in the doctrines and institutions of the Brāhma Samāj. Second edition.] pp. ii. 55. কলিকাতা [*Calcutta*, 1885.] 12°. **14123. c. 8.(6.)**

—— বক্তৃতা ও উপদেশ। [Vaktṛitā o upadeṣa. Brahmist lectures and sermons.] Pt. i. pp. ii. 128. ঢাকা [*Dacca*, 1891.] 8°. **14123. d. 18.(1.)**

VIJAYA PAṆḌITA. *See* MAHĀBHĀRATA. মহাভারত। [Mahābhārata. A metrical version by Vijaya Paṇḍita.] [1899, *etc.*] 8°. **14129. ff. 1.**

—— *See* NAGENDRANĀTHA VASU. বিজয় পণ্ডিতের মহাভারত। [Vijaya Paṇḍiter Mahābhārata. A paper on the Mahābhārata of Vijaya Paṇḍita, with extracts from the poem.] [1896.] 8°. **14133. f. 18.**

VIKRAMĀDITYA, *King of Ujjayinī.* শ্রী বিক্রমাদিত্যের বত্রিশ পুত্তলিকা সিংহাসন সংগ্রহ *etc.* [Siṃhāsana battiṣī. The Thirty-two tales of king Vikramāditya, translated from the Hindi by Mṛityuñjaya Vidyālaṅkāra.] pp. 124. *London,* ১৮১৬ [1816.] 8°. **14127. e. 42.**

—— Contes Indiens. Les Trente-deux Récits du Trône, Batris-sinhasan, ou les merveilleux exploits de Vikramaditya, traduits du Bengali (de Mrityunjaya) et augmentés d'une étude et d'un index par Léon Feer. pp. iv. lxxiv. 258. *Paris,* 1883. 12°. **2348. aa. 34.**

Vol. vi. of a series entitled "Collection de contes et chansons populaires."

—— দ্বাত্রিংশৎ পুত্তলিকা। [Dvātriṃṣat puttalikā, or Vikramārkacharita. Thirty-two tales of the images of Vikramāditya's throne; Sanskrit text, with Bengali translation.] *See* KĀLIDĀSA. মহাকবি কালিদাসের গ্রন্থাবলী। [Granthāvalī.] Vol. ii., pp. 965-1225. [1895.] 8°. **14070. d. 34.(vol. ii.)**

VILVAMAṄGALA GOSVĀMĪ. কৃষ্ণকর্ণামৃত। [Kṛishṇakarṇāmṛita. A Vaishṇava poem on the sports of Kṛishṇa at Vṛindāvana. Sanskrit text, with a Sanskrit commentary by Kṛishṇadāsa Kavirāja, entitled Rasika-raṅgadā, and two Bengali translations, one in verse by Yadunandana Dāsa, the other in prose by the editor Rāmanārāyaṇa Vidyāratna.] মুর্শিদাবাদ ১২৯৭ [*Murshidabad,* 1890, *etc.*] 8°. **14076. d. 44.**

In progress.

VIMALACHANDRA DEVA VARMĀ. গোপ-বালা। [Gopabālā. Kṛishṇa and the Gopīs; a poem in 5 cantos.] pp. iv. 147. *Agartala, Tippera,* ১৩১১ [1904.] 12°. **14129. bb. 21.**

VIMALĀCHARAṆA CHAṬṬOPĀDHYĀYA. *See* BRAHMĀNANDA BHĀRATĪ. সন্ধ্যা-যোগরহস্য। [Sandhyāyogarahasya. Edited with an introduction by Vimalācharaṇa Chaṭṭopādhyāya.] [1901.] 12°. **14123. e. 27.**

VINAYAKṚISHṆA DEVA. কলিকাতার ইতিহাস। [Kalikātār itihāsa.] . . . The Early History and Growth of Calcutta. [Translated from the English by Subalachandra Mitra.] pp. ii. 348. কলিকাতা ১৩১৪ [*Calcutta,* 1907.] 12°. **14127. aa. 33.**

VINAYAKṚISHṆA MUKHOPĀDHYĀYA. গুপ্তবন্ধু। [Guptabandhu. A treatise on the manufacture of gold and silver ornaments.] pp. 32. কলিকাতা [*Calcutta,* 1899.] 16°. **14125. bb. 27.**

VINAYAKUMĀRĪ VASU. নিঝর। [Nijhara. Short poems.] pp. vii. 102. *Calcutta,* 1891. 12°. **14129. b. 35.(4.)**

VINDUVĀSINĪ DĀSĪ. রুক্মিণী কাব্য। [Rukmiṇī. A mythological poem.] pp. 101. ১৩১৩ [*Calcutta,* 1906.] 16°. **14129. bb. 32.**

VINODALĀLA CHAṬṬOPĀDHYĀYA. মতিয়া। [Matiyā. A story of love and adventure.] pp. iv. 84. কলিকাতা ১৩০৩ [*Calcutta,* 1897.] 12°. **14127. cc. 4.(1.)**

VINODALĀLA SĀHĀ. শ্রীকৃষ্ণ চরিত। [Kṛishṇa charita. An account of the life and exploits of Kṛishṇa.] pp. 190. কলিকাতা ১৩০৪ [*Calcutta,* 1897.] 12°. **14127. aa. 18.**

VINODALĀLA SENA GUPTA. *See* PĀṆINI. সিদ্ধান্ত-কৌমুদী। . . . Siddhanta Kaumudi . . . With a Bengali translation. Edited . . . by Kaviraj Binod Lal Sen. [1890-92.] 8°. **14090. d. 29.**

VINODAVIHĀRĪ GOSVĀMĪ. *See* RĀJAVALLABHA GOSVĀMĪ. শ্রীমুরলী-বিলাস। [Muralī-vilāsa. Edited with notes by Vinodavihārī Gosvāmī.] [1894.] 12°. **14129. b. 41.**

VIPINACHANDRA KĀVYARATNA. আর্য্যাহ্নিকাচার কৌমুদী। [Āryāhnikāchāra-kaumudī. An anthological treatise upon the daily religious observances of the Hindus. With numerous Sanskrit quotations.] pp. xii. ii. iv. 131. কলিকাতা [*Calcutta,* 1901.] 8°. **14123. f. 49.(3.)**

VIPINAMOHANA SENA GUPTA. চাঁদরাণী। [Chāṇd Rāṇī. A tale of Hindu society during the time of Raja Kṛishṇachandra in the middle of the 18th century.] 2 pts. কলিকাতা ১৩০১-০২ [*Calcutta,* 1894-95.] 12°. **14127. c. 56.(3.)**

VIPINAVIHĀRĪ DE. সচিত্র বাসর ঘরে রসের গান বা রমণীগণের ঠাট্টা তামাসা। [Bāsar-ghare raser gāna, also called Ramaṇīgaṇer ṭhāṭṭā. A dramatised description in prose and verse of the songs and entertainments at the *bāsar-ghar*, or bridal chamber.] pp. 116. কলিকাতা ১৩০৯ [*Calcutta*, 1902.] 12°. **14131. aa. 1.(1.)**

VIPINAVIHĀRĪ GHOSHA. বিধবা দর্শনে ও পুনর্ভূ। [Vidhavā-darṣane. A poem advocating the marriage of widows, followed by an appendix, entitled Punarbhū, proving its legality according to the Hindu Ṣāstras.] pp. 120. *Calcutta*, 1896. 8°. **14125. e. 32.**

VIPINAVIHĀRĪ GHOSHĀL. মুক্তি এবং তাহার সাধন সম্বন্ধে হিন্দুশাস্ত্রের উপদেশ। [Mukti evaṃ tāhār sādhana. A treatise on salvation and the means to its attainment, copiously illustrated from Sanskrit texts. Third edition.] pp. vi. 224. কলিকাতা ১৯০১ [*Calcutta*, 1901.] 8°. **14123. f. 57.**

VIPINAVIHĀRĪ GOSVĀMĪ. মধুর-মিলন। [Madhura-milana. Poems on the amours of Krishṇa with Rādhā and the milkmaids.] pp. iii. ii. 264. কলিকাতা ১৮২৮ [*Calcutta*, 1906.] 12°. **14129. bb. 28.(6.)**

VIPINAVIHĀRĪ GUPTA. মুষ্টিযোগ সার সংগ্রহ। [Mushṭiyoga-sārasaṅgraha. A collection of *mushṭiyoga* remedies for the cure of diseases, and various ailments.] pp. 107. কলিকাতা ১৩০৮ [*Calcutta*, 1902.] 8°. **14125. b. 18.(2.)**

VIPINAVIHĀRĪ VANDYOPĀDHYĀYA and KULACHANDRA DE DĀSA. হুঁকাপুরাণ মাহাত্ম্যং। [Huṇkā-purāṇa-māhātmya. A Sanskrit burlesque poem on the merits of *hukā*-smoking, accompanied by a Bengali prose translation.] pp. 11. কলিকাতা ১২৯৮ [*Calcutta*, 1892.] 8°. **14072. b. 21.**

VIPINAVIHĀRĪ VAṬAVYĀLA. বৃহৎ সূক্ষ্ম-আয়ুর্ব্বেদ বা প্রাকৃতিক স্বাস্থ্যবিজ্ঞান। [Sūkshma āyurveda. A treatise on medicine, on a peculiar system of treatment, based on European and native medical works.] pp. xi. xxi. 604, vi. কলিকাতা ১৩০৮ [*Calcutta*, 1901.] 8°. **14125. b. 17.**

VIPRADĀSA MUKHOPĀDHYĀYA. যুবতী-জীবন। [Yuvatijīvana. A practical treatise on marriage, midwifery, and the rearing of children, written in the form of a dialogue between a husband and his wife.] pp. vi. 222. কলিকাতা ১৩০৮ [*Calcutta*, 1902.] 12°. **14125. e. 46.**

VĪRACHARITA. বীর-চরিত। [Vīracharita. Short sketches of the lives of notable Bengalis.] pp. 42. যশোহর ১৩০৩ [*Jessore*, 1896.] 12°. **14127. aa. 6.(3.)**

VĪREṢANĀTHA KĀVYATĪRTHA. *See* PURĀṆAS.—*Padmapurāṇa.* পদ্মপুরাণম্। পাতালখণ্ডম্। [Pātāla-khaṇḍa. With a Bengali translation by Vīreṣanātha and others.] [1903.] 8°. **14018. b. 20.**

—— ব্রতমালা-বিধান। [Vratamālāvidhāna. A treatise on the observance of Hindu festivals. Compiled from Sanskrit texts, with Bengali explanations.] pp. iii. v. 532. কলিকাতা ১৩১০ [*Calcutta*, 1903.] 12°. **14033. a. 55.**

VĪREṢVARA KĀVYATĪRTHA. *See* VĪREṢANĀTHA KĀVYATĪRTHA.

VĪREṢVARA PĀṆḌE. ঊনবিংশ শতাব্দীর মহাভারত। [Ūnaviṃṣa ṣatābdīr Mahābhārata. An adverse criticism on Navīnachandra Sena's poems Raivataka, Kurukshetra and Prabhāsa.] pp. iv. 250. *Calcutta*, 1897. 12°. **14131. d. 6.(2.)**

VĪREṢVARA PRĀMĀṆIKA. শ্রী অদ্বৈত-বিলাস। [Advaita-vilāsa. The life of Advaitāchārya, the disciple and contemporary of Chaitanya.] Pt. i. pp.ii. 593. কলিকাতা ১৮২১ [*Calcutta*, 1899.] 12°. **14127. aa. 13.**

VIRGILIUS MARO (PUBLIUS). The First Book of Virgil's Æneid, translated into the Bengali language by H. Sargent. (বর্জ্জিলীয় মারো কর্ত্তৃক রচিত আইনেয়িদ। প্রথম পর্ব্ব।) pp. 65. *Serampore*, 1810. 8°. **T. 2124.(1.)**

VIṢĀKHADATTA. মুদ্রা-রাক্ষস। [Mudrārākshasa. Translated from the Sanskrit by Jyotirindranātha Ṭhākura.] pp. vi. 157. কলিকাতা ১৩০৭ [*Calcutta*, 1901.] 12°. **14131. a. 43.(3.)**

VISHṆU. বিষ্ণুসংহিতা। [Vishṇu-saṃhitā. A code of *dharma*, in 100 *adhyāyas*. Sanskrit text, with Bengali translation.] *See* PAÑCHĀNANA TARKARATNA BHAṬṬĀCHĀRYA. ঊনবিংশতি সংহিতা। [Ūnaviṃṣati saṃhitā.] pp. 25-121. [1903.] 8°. **14039. c. 20.**

VISHṆUCHANDRA BHAṬṬĀCHĀRYA, *of Bajrapur.* ৺ জয় গোপাল তর্কালঙ্কার মহাশয়ের জীবনচরিত। [Jayagopāla Tarkālaṅkāra-jīvanacharita. Life of Jayagopāla Tarkālaṅkāra.] pp. v. 10. ১৩০৮ [*Calcutta*, 1901.] 12°. **14127. aa. 21.(1.)**

VISHṆU ŚARMAN. [For editions of the Hitopadeśa and of the Pañchatantra ascribed to this sage, *see* HITOPADEŚA and PAÑCHATANTRA respectively.]

VIŚVADEVA ĀCHĀRYA. রাঘব দীপিকা। [Rāghavadīpikā. A Sanskrit poem in 9 cantos on the life of a devotee named Rāghava Rāma, and his wife Jayadurgā, said to have been an incarnation of Ardhakālī. Edited, with a Bengali prose translation, introduction, and additional matter, by Durgāmohana Smṛititīrtha.] 2 pts. বারাণসী [*Benares*, 1892.] 8°. **14028. d. 48.(2.)**

VIŚVAMBHARACHARAṆA DĀSA. পত্রমালা। [Patramālā. A Bengali letter-writer. Second edition.] pp. 57. *Calcutta*, 1882. 12°. **14131. f. 31.(1.)**

VIŚVAMBHARA DĀSA. জগন্নাথ মঙ্গল। আদি ও ক্ষেত্রখণ্ড। [Jagannātha-maṅgala. A poem in glorification of the god Jagannātha and his worship, in two parts, styled Ādikhaṇḍa and Kshetrakhaṇḍa.] pp. 183, 115. কলিকাতা ১২৯৪ [*Calcutta*, 1888.] 8°. **14129. c. 40.**

VIŚVAMBHARA JYOTISHĀRṆAVA. *See* RĀMACHANDRA ŚARMĀ, *Āchārya.* দিনকৌমুদী। [Dinakaumudī. Edited, with a preface and translation, by Viśvambhara Jyotishārṇava.] [1898.] 12°. **14053. b. 31.(3.)**

—— গ্রহবিপ্র-সংহিতা। [Grahavipra-saṃhitā. A treatise on the Grahavipra, or astrologer-caste of Brahmans.] pp. ii. 58. কলিকাতা ১৩০৩ [*Calcutta*, 1897.] 12°. **14125. e. 31.(3.)**

VIŚVAMBHARA PĀṆI. *See* PURĀṆAS.—*Padmapurāṇa.* বৃন্দাবন প্রাপ্ত্যুপায়। [Vṛindāvana-prāptyupāya. The Sanskrit text of *adhyāyas* 99-108 of the Pātālakhaṇḍa, with a Bengali metrical paraphrase by Viśvambhara Pāṇi.] [1900.] 8°. **14076. c. 75.(1.)**

VIŚVAMBHARA RĀYA. ঢাকুর বা বারেন্দ্র-কায়স্থ-তত্ত্ব নাগ বংশ। [Ḍhākura. A genealogical account in verse of the Nāga family of the Vārendra Kāyasthas.] pp. ii. iii. 88. কলিকাতা [*Calcutta*, 1908.] 12°. **14127. aaa. 4.**

VIŚVANĀTHA CHAKRAVARTĪ, *Vaishṇava poet.* শ্রীকৃষ্ণভাবনামৃত মহাকাব্য। [Kṛishṇa-bhāvanāmṛita. A prose translation of a poem by Viśvanātha on the sports of Kṛishṇa and the Gopīs, with a brief account of the poet, and a list of his works. By Rādhikānātha Gosvāmī.] pp. xxii. 348. বৃন্দাবন ১৯৫৯ [*Brindaban*, 1902.] 8°. **14123. ff. 10.(2.)**

—— শ্রীপ্রেমসম্পুটঃ। [Premasampuṭa. A Sanskrit poem in 141 stanzas on the legend of Kṛishṇa and Rādhā. With interpretations in both Sanskrit and Bengali by Śyāmalāla Gosvāmī.] pp. 106. বৃন্দাবন [*Brindaban*, 1906.] 12°. **14060. b. 17.(3.)**

VIŚVANĀTHA TARKABHŪSHAṆA. বিশ্বনাথ রামায়ণ। ... আদি কাণ্ড। [Viśvanātha Rāmāyaṇa. A philosophical interpretation of the Ādi-kāṇḍa of the Rāmāyaṇa of Vālmiki. Edited by Harinātha Smṛitibhūshaṇa.] pp. vii. 85. হুগলী ১২৯৭ [*Hooghly*, 1890.] 8°. **14123. f. 41.**

VIŚVEŚVARA, *Dvija.* সত্যনারায়ণের পাঁচালী। [Satyanārāyaṇer pāṇchālī. A poem in praise of the god Satyanārāyaṇa. Edited, with an introduction, by Vrajasundara Sānnyāla.] ১৩০৮ [1902.] *See* ACADEMIES, *etc.*—Calcutta.—*Bengal Academy of Literature.* সাহিত্য-পরিষৎ-পত্রিকা। [Sāhitya-parishat-patrikā.] Vol. viii., no. 3. [1894, *etc.*] 8°. **14133. f. 18.**

VIŚVEŚVARA CHAKRAVARTĪ. *See* VEṆĪMĀDHAVA GAṄGOPĀDHYĀYA and VIŚVEŚVARA CHAKRAVARTĪ. A Junior Text-book of translation from Bengali into English, *etc.* 1892. 12°. **14131. e. 22.**

—— Fifth edition. 1893. 12°. **14131. e. 28.**

—— *See* VEṆĪMĀDHAVA GAṄGOPĀDHYĀYA and VIŚVEŚVARA CHAKRAVARTĪ. A Manual of translation from Bengali into English. 1891. 8°. **14131. g. 26.**

VIVARTAVILĀSA. বিবর্ত্ত বিলাস। অর্থাৎ বৈষ্ণব সম্প্রদায়দিগের নিগূঢ় তত্ত্বাবলী। [Vivartavilāsa. An exposition of mystic teachings of Vaishṇavas, in verse.] pp. 111. কলিকাতা ১২৯৬ [*Calcutta*, 1889.] *obl.* 12°. **14123. f. 42.**

VIVEKĀNANDA, *Svāmī* [*i.e.* NARENDRANĀTHA DATTA]. চিকাগো বক্তৃতা। [Chikāgo-vaktṛitā. A Bengali translation of Svāmī Vivekānanda's Lecture on Hinduism delivered at the World's Fair of Religions at Chicago.] pp. iii. 33. কলিকাতা ১৩০৮ [*Calcutta,* 1902.] 12°. **14123. e. 32.**

—— জ্ঞানযোগ। [Jñānayoga. Lectures on Jñānayoga, translated from the English original of Svāmī Vivekānanda, by Svāmī Ṣuddhānanda.] pp. ii. 276. কলিকাতা ১৩০৮ [*Calcutta,* 1902.] 8°. **14123. ff. 7.(2.)**

—— স্বামী বিবেকানন্দ প্রণীত রাজযোগ। [Rājayoga. A Bengali translation of Svāmī Vivekānanda's English lectures on Rājayoga. By Svāmī Ṣuddhānanda.] pp. v. 237. কলিকাতা ১৩০৫ [*Calcutta,* 1899.] 8°. **14123. ff. 7.(1.)**

VOPADEVA. সানুবাদ সটীকং মুগ্ধবোধঃ ব্যাকরণং [Mugdhabodha. Sanskrit text with Durgādāsa's commentary as far as the end of the *kṛidantādhyāya,* and Rāma Tarkavāgīṣa's commentary thence to the end, together with a Bengali paraphrase of each *sūtra.*] pp. xxii. 800. কলিকাতা ১৮৯৪ [*Calcutta,* 1894.] 8°. **14090. e. 24.**

VRAJALĀLA CHAKRAVARTĪ. বঙ্গদেশস্থ হিন্দু-সমাজ ও প্রচলিত শিক্ষা প্রণালীর সংস্কার। [Vaṅgadeṣastha Hindu samāja. The Hindu society of Bengal, and hints on the reform of the existing system of education.] pp. 16. [*Calcutta,* 1902.] 8°. **14125. ee. 39.**

VRAJAMOHANA RĀYA. ৺ ব্রজমোহন গ্রন্থাবলী। [Vrajamohana-granthāvalī. The complete works of Vrajamohana Rāya, with a life of the author.] কলিকাতা ১৩১৩ [*Calcutta,* 1906, *etc.*] 8°. **14127. ee. 29.**

In progress.

VRAJANĀTHA CHANDRA. মেদিনীপুরপ্রদেশ-নিবাসী শোলাঙ্কি বা শুক্লিজাতির আদি-বৃত্তান্ত। [Ṣolāṅkijātir ādivṛittānta. A brief account of the Ṣolāṅki or Ṣukli caste of Midnapur.] pp. 43. কলিকাতা ১৩১৪ [*Calcutta,* 1907.] 12°. **14125. e. 50.**

VRAJANĀTHA MITRA. ক্রীড়া-তরঙ্গ। তাস পাসা দশ-পঁচিশ। [Krīḍā-taraṅga. Cards, dice-playing, and other games.] pp. 80. কলিকাতা ১৩০৩ [*Calcutta,* 1896.] 12°. **14133. h. 13.**

VRAJASUNDARA SĀNNYĀLA. *See* VIṢVEṢVARA, *Dvija.* সত্যনারায়ণের পাঁচালী। [Satyanārāyaṇer pāṉchālī. Edited, with an introduction, by Vrajasundara Sānnyāla.] [1902.] 8°. **14133. f. 18.**

—— কবির ইতিহাস। [Kavir itihāsa. A series of articles on Bengali poetry, with short biographies of poets.] ১৩১২ [1905, *etc.*] *See* PERIODICAL PUBLICATIONS.—*Calcutta.* সাহিত্য-সংহিতা। [Sāhitya-saṃhitā.] Vol. vi., no. 3, *etc.* [1900, *etc.*] 8°. **14133. ff. 1.**

In progress.

—— মাণিক গাঙ্গুলী ও ধর্ম্মমঙ্গল। [Māṇik Gāṅgulī o Dharmamaṅgala. An account of the poet Māṇik Gāṅgulī and his Dharmamaṅgala.] ১৩১২ [1906.] *See* ACADEMIES, *etc.*—Calcutta.—*Bengal Academy of Literature.* সাহিত্য-পরিষৎ-পত্রিকা। Sāhitya-parishat-patrikā.] Vol. xii., no. 1. [1894, *etc.*] 8°. **14133. f. 18.**

—— মুসলমান বৈষ্ণব কবি। [Musalmān Vaishṇava kavi. The poems of Muhammadan Vaishṇava poets, compiled and edited with biographical notices by Vrajasundara Sānnyāla.] রাজসাহী ১৩১১ [*Rajshahi,* 1906, *etc.*] 12°. **14129. cc. 17.**

In progress. Wanting pt. 2.

VRAJENDRALĀLA BHAṬṬĀCHĀRYA. Amply illustrated, syllabically divided and pronouncing dictionary of the English language, with various English and Bengali meanings of every word. Compiled . . . by Dr. Brojendra Lall Bhattacharjee. pp. 801. *Calcutta,* 1902. 8°. **14133. b. 18.**

VRAJENDRANĀTHA GHOSHĀL. *See* CAREY (W.), *D.D.* A Dictionary of the Bengalee Language. Vol. I. Bengalee and English . . . Revised and edited by Brojendra Nath Ghosal. 1890. 8°. **12907. cc. 31.**

—— *See* CAREY (W.), *D.D.* A Dictionary of the Bengali Language. Vol. I. Bengali and English . . . Revised and edited by Rasamay Mitra . . . and Brojendra Nath Ghosal. 1902. 8°. **14133. b. 19.**

VṚINDĀVANA DĀSA. শ্রীশ্রীভজননির্ণয় গ্রন্থ। [Bhajananirṇaya. A poem on Vaishṇava devotion and religious obligations. Edited by Rādheṣachandra Dāsa.] pp. iv. 139. কলিকাতা ১৩০৮ [*Calcutta,* 1901.] 12°. **14129. bb. 12.**

VṚINDĀVANA DĀSA (*continued*). শ্রীশ্রীচৈতন্যভাগবত। [Chaitanya-bhāgavata. The life and teachings of Chaitanya in verse.] pp. iv. 376. কলিকাতা ১২৯২ [*Calcutta*, 1886.] 8°. **14123. i. 10.**

—— শ্রীচৈতন্যভাগবত। [Chaitanya-bhāgavata. Edited, with notes, life of the author and glossary, by Atulakṛishṇa Gosvāmī.] 2 pts. কলিকাতা [*Calcutta*, 1899-1900.] 8°. **14123. i. 12.**

—— শ্রীচৈতন্যভাগবত। [Chaitanya-bhāgavata. Edited by Kālīprasanna Vidyāratna.] pp. 418. কলিকাতা ১৩১০ [*Calcutta*, 1903.] 8°. **14123. ff. 11.**

—— গোলোক-সংহিতা। [Goloka-saṃhitā. A Vaishṇava poem. Edited by Tārakeṣvara Bhaṭṭāchārya.] ১৩০৯ [1902.] *See* ACADEMIES, *etc.*—Calcutta.—*Bengal Academy of Literature.* সাহিত্য-পরিষৎ-পত্রিকা। [Sāhitya-parishat-patrikā.] Vol. ix., no 1. [1894, *etc.*] 8°. **14133. f. 18.**

—— শ্রীশ্রীনিত্যানন্দচরিতামৃত। [Nityānanda-charitāmṛita. The life of Nityānanda Dāsa, in verse.] pp. iv. 190, iv. কলিকাতা ১৩০৯ [*Calcutta*, 1902.] 8°. **14127. bb. 24.**

—— তত্ত্ববিলাস। [Tattvavilāsa. A poem on Vaishṇava worship.] *See* VAISHṆAVA GRANTHĀVALĪ. বৈষ্ণব গ্রন্থাবলী। [1900.] 12°. **14123. e. 20.(3.)**

VYĀSA. ব্যাসসংহিতা। [Vyāsa-saṃhitā. A code of *dharma*, in 4 *adhyāyas*. Sanskrit text, with Bengali translation.] *See* PAÑCHĀNANA TARKARATNA BHAṬṬĀCHĀRYA. ঊনবিংশতি সংহিতা। [Ūnaviṃṣati saṃhitā.] pp. 377-392. [1903.] 8°. **14039. c. 20.**

VYOMAKEṢA CHAṬṬOPĀDHYĀYA. বাসন্তী। ইতিবৃত্ত-মূলক উপন্যাস। [Vāsantī. An historical novel.] pp. 326. কলিকাতা ১৩১১ [*Calcutta*, 1904.] 12°. **14128. a. 6.**

VYOMAKEṢA MUSTAFĪ. *See* AYODHYĀRĀMA RĀYA, called KAVICHANDRA. সত্যনারায়ণ কথা। [Satyanārāyaṇa-kathā. Edited with an introduction by Vyomakeṣa Mustafī.] [1901.] 8°. **14133. f. 18.**

—— *See* GANGĀRĀMA, *Kavi.* কবি গঙ্গারাম ও মহারাষ্ট্রপুরাণ। [Mahārāshṭra-purāṇa. Edited by Vyomakeṣa Mustafī.] [1907.] 8°. **14133. f. 18.**

VYOMAKEṢA MUSTAFĪ (*continued*). *See* KṚISHṆARĀMA DĀSA, *Son of Bhagavatīcharaṇa Dāsa.* রায়মঙ্গল। [Rāyamaṅgala. With critical notes by Vyomakeṣa Mustafī.] [1896-97.] 8°. **14133. f. 18.**

—— *See* RĀMABHADRA, *Dvija.* সত্যদেব-সংহিতা। [Satyadeva-saṃhitā. Edited by Vyomakeṣa Mustafī.] [1901.] 8°. **14133. f. 18.**

—— পাঁচালিকার ঠাকুরদাস। [Pāṉchālīkāra Ṭhākura Dāsa. An account of the poet Ṭhākura Dāsa and his pāṉchālī poems.] ১৩০৫ [1898.] *See* ACADEMIES, *etc.*—Calcutta.—*Bengal Academy of Literature.* সাহিত্য-পরিষৎ-পত্রিকা। [Sāhitya-parishat-patrikā.] Vol. v., no. 3. [1894, *etc.*] 8°. **14133. f. 18.**

—— রাজকবি জয়নারায়ণ। [Rājakavi Jayanārāyaṇa. The life and poems of Jayanārāyaṇa.] ১৩০৭ [1900.] *See* ACADEMIES, *etc.*—Calcutta.—*Bengal Academy of Literature.* সাহিত্য-পরিষৎ-পত্রিকা। [Sāhitya-parishat-patrikā.] Vol. vii., no. 1. [1894, *etc.*] 8°. **14133. f. 18.**

—— শীতলা-মঙ্গল। [Ṣītalāmaṅgala. A critical examination of two poems in praise of Ṣītalā, the goddess of small-pox, one by Devakīnandana, the other by Nityānanda, with biographical notices of the authors.] ১৩০৪ [1898.] *See* ACADEMIES, *etc.*—Calcutta.—*Bengal Academy of Literature.* সাহিত্য-পরিষৎ-পত্রিকা। [Sāhitya-parishat-patrikā.] Vol. v., no. 1. [1894, *etc.*] 8°. **14133. f. 18.**

WAJH al-DĪN AḤMAD. গো-বধে আপত্তি কেন। [Govadhe āpatti kena. A defence of the Muhammadan practice of killing cattle.] pp. 63. *Noakhali*, ১৩০৭ [1900.] 12°. **14125. e. 41.**

WĀḲIDĪ. *See* MUḤAMMAD ibn ʻUMAR, *Wāḳidī.*

WALLACE (*Sir* DONALD MACKENZIE). রুষীয়া। . . . Russia . . . Translated by Gopal Chandra Mukhopadhyaya. pp. xxiii. 590, x. লক্ষ্ণৌ ১২৯৫ [*Lucknow, Calcutta* printed, 1888.] 4°. **14127. bb. 2.**

WENGER (JOHN). *See* BIBLE. The Holy Bible . . . Translated . . . by [W. Yates and] the Calcutta Baptist Missionaries. [Revised by J. Wenger.] 1861. 8°. **3068. e. 13.**

—— —— 1892. 8°. **14123. b. 17.**

WENGER (JOHN) (*continued*). *See* BIBLE.—*New Testament.* The New Testament . . . Eighth edition [Revised by J. Wenger.] 1846. 12°. **3070. bb. 27.**

—— *See* BIBLE.—*Matthew.* মথিলিখিত সুসমাচার। Gospel of Matthew. [Revised by J. Wenger.] [1854.] 8°. **3070. bb. 1.**

—— *See* BIBLE.—*Mark.* মার্কলিখিত সুসমাচার। Gospel of Mark. [Revised by J. Wenger.] [1854.] 8°. **3070. bb. 4.**

—— *See* BIBLE.—*Luke.* লুকলিখিত সুসমাচার। Gospel of Luke. [Revised by J. Wenger.] [1854.] 8°. **3070. bb. 6.**

—— *See* BIBLE.—*John, Gospel of.* যোহন লিখিত সুসমাচার। Gospel of John. [Revised by J. Wenger.] [1854.] 8°. **3070. bb. 7.**

—— *See* BIBLE.—*Acts.* প্রভু যীশু খ্রীষ্টের প্রেরিতদের ক্রিয়ার বিবরণ। [Revised by J. Wenger.] [1880.] 12°. **3070. aaa. 29.**

Y. N. M. *See* EMERSON (R. W.). এমার্সন সন্দর্ভ। Emerson sandarva, or Translations from the essays of R. W. Emerson . . . By a Villager [signing himself in the preface য, ন, ম। *i.e.* Y. N. M.]. 1890. 8°. **14125. ee. 24.**

YĀDAVACHANDRA RĀYA. Patal Das Mahaprabhur lila sambaran, or The mysteries of Byraggis and their religion . . . By Jadub Chandra Rai. পোটল দাস মহাপ্রভুর লীলা সম্বরণ। pp. 75. কলিকাতা ১২৯৯ [*Calcutta*, 1892.] 12°. **14123. e. 15.(3.)**

YADUNANDANA, *Kavi.* মূল ঢাকুর ও সমালোচনা অর্থাৎ বারেন্দ্র কায়স্থ সমাজের বিবরণ। [Ḍhākura. An ancient poem on the Vārendra Kāyastha caste, compiled from a larger work by Kāṣīdāsa entitled Ādi Ḍhākura. Edited, with an introduction and notes, by Kṛishṇacharaṇa Majumdār, and followed by a criticism on the treatise of the same name, founded on this poem, by Govindamohana Rāya Vidyāvinoda.] pp. ii. 113. কলিকাতা ১৮১৩ [*Calcutta*, 1891.] 12°. **14127. a. 20.**

—— বারেন্দ্র ঢাকুর *etc.* [Ḍhākura. Another, and slightly different edition, with a supplementary part on Vārendra Kāyasthas of modern times by Prasannakumāra Rāya.] pp. 112. কলিকাতা ১৩১৪ [*Calcutta*, 1908.] 12°. **14127. aa. 40.(2.)**

YADUNANDANA DĀSA. *See* KṚISHṆADĀSA KAVIRĀJA, *Gosvāmī.* কৃষ্ণকর্ণামৃত। [Kṛishṇakarṇāmṛita. A metrical translation by Yadunandana Dāsa of Kṛishṇadāsa's Sanskrit commentary, entitled Sāraṅgaraṅgadā.] [1900.] 12°. **14123. e. 20.(3.)**

—— *See* VILVAMAṄGALA GOSVĀMĪ. কৃষ্ণকর্ণামৃত। [Kṛishṇakarṇāmṛita. Sanskrit text, with a verse translation in Bengali by Yadunandana Dāsa.] [1890, *etc.*] 8°. **14076. d. 44.**

—— কর্ণানন্দ। [Karṇānanda. A Vaishṇava poem, containing an account of Ṣrīnivāsa Āchārya and other celebrated Vaishṇava teachers.] pp. iv. 129, iii. মুর্শিদাবাদ ১২৯৯ [*Murshidabad*, 1892.] 8°. **14129. e. 17.(1.)**

YADUNĀTHA BHAṬṬĀCHĀRYA. কালাপাহাড় ঐতিহাসিক উপন্যাস। [Kālāpāhāṛ. An historical tale.] pp. 341. কলিকাতা ১৩১৪ [*Calcutta*, 1907.] 12°. **14128. a. 24.**

—— রাজা সীতারাম রায়। [Rājā Sītārāma Rāya. An historical account of Raja Sītārāma Rāya, son of Udayanārāyaṇa, and of other notable Rajas of Bengal.] pp. iv. 264. কলিকাতা ১৩১১ [*Calcutta*, 1905.] 12°. **14127. aa. 28.(4.)**

—— [Second edition.] pp. v. 250. কলিকাতা ১৩১৩ [*Calcutta*, 1906.] 8°. **14127. aa. 9.(2.)**

YADUNĀTHA CHAṬṬOPĀDHYĀYA. Riju britti, or A complete Key to the Rijupatha [of Īṣvarachandra Vidyāsāgara]. ঋজুবৃত্তি Pt. i. Fourth edition. pp. 252. *Sansk.*, *Beng.*, and *Eng.* *Calcutta*, 1880. 12°. **14085. b.**

YADUNĀTHA MAJUMDĀR. *See* BĀDARĀYAṆA. বেদান্ত সূত্র। [Vedāntasūtra. With a Bengali commentary by Yadunātha Majumdār.] [1904, *etc.*] 8°. **14049. b. 27.**

—— আমিত্বের প্রসার। [Āmitver prasāra. An exhortation to Hindus to practise self-abnegation, avoidance from pernicious habits, and sympathy with all men.] Pt. i. pp. v. 130. যশোহর ১৮২১ [*Jessore*, 1899.] 8°. **14125. e. 37.**

—— The Indian Sage . . . [Select Sanskrit works on Hindu philosophy. Edited with Sanskrit notes and English and Bengali translations] by Jadunath Mozoomdar. *Jessore*, 1893. 12°. **14048. a. 20.**

The first part only of this series appears to have been published, containing the Īṣā Upanishad.

YADUNĀTHA MUKHOPĀDHYĀYA. পল্লিগ্রাম। [Palligrāma. An essay on the degeneracy of villages in Bengal, and of the Bengali race in general.] pp. iv. 107. গরিবপুর ১২৯৯ [*Garibpur,* 1892.] 12°. **14125. e. 26.(2.)**

YADUNĀTHA VIṢVĀSA. হিন্দু জাতিভেদ তাহার ফল ও বর্ত্তমান অবস্থা। [Hindu jātibheda. A discussion of the Hindu caste system, its effect, and present condition.] pp. 30. *Calcutta,* [1902.] 8°. **14125. ee. 36.**

YĀJÑAVALKYA. যোগিযাজ্ঞবল্ক্যম। [Yogīyājña-valkya, or Yājñavalkya-gītā. A Sanskrit metrical treatise on the Yoga. Edited with a Bengali prose translation by Veṇīmādhava Nyāyaratna.] pp. 89. কলিকাতা ১৩০০ [*Calcutta,* 1893.] 8°. **14048. bb. 50.(1.)**

—— যোগিযাজ্ঞবল্ক্যম্। [Yogīyājñavalkya. Sanskrit text, with a Bengali translation.] pp. 128. *See* PRASANNAKUMĀRA ŚĀSTRĪ BHAṬṬĀCHĀRYA. যোগাম্বুধি। [Yogāmbudhi.] [1896.] 32°. **14048. a. 19.**

—— যাজ্ঞবল্ক্যসংহিতা। [Yājñavalkya-saṃhitā. Another edition of the Sanskrit text, with Bengali translation.] *See* PAÑCHĀNANA TARKARATNA BHAṬṬĀCHĀRYA. ঊনবিংশতি সংহিতা। [Ūnaviṃśati saṃhitā.] pp. 135-218. [1903.] 8°. **14039. c. 20.**

YAJÑEŚVARA VANDYOPĀDHYĀYA. *See* PURĀṆAS.—*Bṛihan-nāradīyapurāṇa.* বৃহন্নারদীয়পুরাণ। [Bṛihan-nāradīyapurāṇa. Translated by Yajñeśvara Vandyopādhyāya.] [1901.] 8°. **14123. e. 25.**

—— *See* TOD (J.), *Lieutenant-Colonel.* সচিত্র রাজস্থান। [Rājasthāna. Second edition, revised, with the addition of an appendix, by Yajñeśvara Vandyopādhyāya.] [1898.] 8°. **14127. bbb. 4.**

YAMA. যমসংহিতা। [Yama-saṃhitā. A code of *dharma,* in 78 Sanskrit stanzas. With Bengali translation.] *See* PAÑCHĀNANA TARKARATNA BHAṬṬĀCHĀRYA. ঊনবিংশতি সংহিতা। [Ūnaviṃśati saṃhitā.] pp. 269-274. [1903.] 8°. **14039. c. 20.**

YAŚODĀNANDA PRĀMĀṆIKA. *See* HARIMOHANA PRĀMĀṆIKA. কমলাকরুণাবিলাসোনাম শুভাঙ্কঃ [Kamalākaruṇāvilāsa. Edited with notes by Yaśodānanda Prāmāṇika.] [1899.] 8°. **14079. c. 42.(2.)**

YAŚODĀNANDANA SARKĀR. অঙ্গুরীয়-বিনিময়। [Aṅgurīya-vinimaya. An historical drama on incidents in the life of Śivājī.] pp. 96. কলিকাতা ১৩০২ [*Calcutta,* 1896.] 12°. **14131. a. 37.(7.)**

YATES (WILLIAM), *D.D.* *See* BIBLE. The Holy Bible . . . Translated . . . by [W. Yates and] the Calcutta Baptist Missionaries, *etc.* 1845. 8°. **3070. dd. 1.**

—— —— 1861. 8°. **3068. e. 13.**

—— —— 1877. 8°. **3068. f. 25.**

—— *See* BIBLE.—*Old Testament.* The Old Testament . . . Translated . . . by [W. Yates and] the Calcutta Baptist Missionaries, *etc.* 1844. 8°. **1108. k. 7.**

—— *See* BIBLE.—*Genesis.* মুসালিখিত আদিপুস্তক ... Genesis and part of Exodus (ch. i.-xx.) Translated . . . by [W. Yates and] the Calcutta Baptist Missionaries. 1847. 12°. **3070. b. 35.**

—— —— 1858. 12°. **3070. aa. 13.**

—— *See* BIBLE.—*New Testament.* The New Testament . . . Translated . . . by [W. Yates and] the Calcutta Baptist Missionaries. 1833. 8°. **3068. aaa. 69.**

—— *See* BIBLE.—*New Testament.* Dharmapustaker Antabhág. The New Testament, *etc.* [Translated by W. Yates.] 1839. 8°. **3068. cc. 17.**

—— *See* BIBLE.—*Matthew.* মথিলিখিত সুসমাচার। Gospel of Matthew. [Translated by W. Yates.] [1854.] 8°. **3070. bb. 1.**

—— *See* BIBLE.—*Mark.* মার্কলিখিত সুসমাচার। Gospel of Mark. [Translated by W. Yates.] [1854.] 8°. **3070. bb. 4.**

—— *See* BIBLE.—*Luke.* লুকলিখিত সুসমাচার। Gospel of Luke. [Translated by W. Yates.] [1854.] 8°. **3070. bb. 6.**

—— *See* BIBLE.—*John, Gospel of.* যোহন লিখিত সুসমাচার। Gospel of John. [Translated by W. Yates.] [1854.] 8°. **3070. bb. 7.**

—— *See* BIBLE.—*Acts.* প্রভু যীশু খ্রীষ্টের প্রেরিতদের ক্রিয়ার বিবরণ। [Translated by W. Yates.] [1880.] 12°. **3070. aaa. 29.**

YATĪNDRAMOHANA GHOSHA. *See* SHAKSPERE (W.). লীয়ার। ... কিং লীয়ার নাটকের বঙ্গানুবাদ। [King Lear, Translated by Yatīndramohana Ghosha.] [1902.] 12°. **14131. aa. 3.(1.)**

YATĪNDRAMOHANA SIṂHA. সাকার ও নিরাকার-তত্ত্ববিচার। [Sākāra o nirākāra tattvavichāra. A vindication of Hinduism and Hindu image-worship, in reply to arguments by Brāhma Samājists.] pp. iii. iv. 278. কলিকাতা ১৩০৫ [*Calcutta*, 1898.] 12°. **14123. e. 23.(2.)**

YATĪNDRAMOHANA ṬHĀKURA. Welcome Song. [A Bengali song, with an English translation, composed on the occasion of the visit of the Prince of Wales to India, and set to Bengali music. By J. M. T. *i.e.* Yatīndramohana Ṭhākura.] [*Calcutta*, 1876?] Fol. **14003. e. 2.(13.)**

YATĪNDRANĀTHA SENA. *See* UPENDRANĀTHA SENA and YATĪNDRANĀTHA SENA. The Indian Student's Letter-writer, *etc.* 1902. 12°. **14131. f. 33.**

YOGAVĀSISHṬHA-RĀMĀYAṆA. *See* ŚYĀMĀCHARAṆA MUKHOPĀDHYĀYA. চুড়ালা-উপাখ্যান। [Chuṛālā-upākhyāna. A tale, adapted from the Nirvāṇa-prakaraṇa of the Yogavāsishṭha.] [1877.] 8°. **14127. f. 42.(3.)**

—— বাশিষ্ঠমহারামায়ণম্। [Yogavāsishṭha-rāmāyaṇa. An epic poem popularly ascribed to Vālmīki, in which are conveyed doctrines of Yoga and Vedānta. Sanskrit text, and commentary by Ānandabodhendra Sarasvatī. Edited with a Bengali translation of the text and notes by Kālīvara Vedāntavāgīśa.] কলিকাতা ১৮১৪ [*Calcutta*, 1893, *etc.*] 8°. **14049. a. 2.**

In progress.

—— যোগবাশিষ্ঠ-রামায়ণ। [Yogavāsishṭha-rāmāyaṇa. Translated into prose by Pandit Pañchānana Tarkaratna Bhaṭṭāchārya. Second edition.] pp. viii. 854. কলিকাতা ১৩১২ [*Calcutta*, 1905.] 4°. **14123. i. 15.**

YOGENDRACHANDRA VASU, *Head Master, Deoghar School.* অমর কীর্ত্তি অথবা ফাদার দামিয়েনের জীবনচরিত। [Amara-kīrti. A life of Father Damien, with an introduction appealing for funds for ameliorating the condition of lepers at Deoghar.] pp. 9, 128, 3. কলিকাতা ১২৯৭ [*Calcutta*, 1891.] 12°. **14127. aa. 6.(1.)**

YOGENDRACHANDRA VASU, *Novelist.* বাঙ্গালী চরিত। [Bāṅgālī charita. Satirical sketches of Bengali life and character, showing the evil effects of an English education. Second edition.] 3 pts. কলিকাতা ১২৯২-৯৩ [*Calcutta*, 1886-87.] 12°. **14125. e. 15.**

—— [Another edition.] 3 pts. কলিকাতা ১২৯২-৯৩ [*Calcutta*, 1886-87.] 12°. **14125. e. 18.**

Pts. i. and ii. are of the second edition.

—— কালাচাঁদ। [Kālāchāṇd. A tale of social life in Bengal. Third edition.] pp. iii. 394, ii. কলিকাতা ১৩১৫ [*Calcutta*, 1908.] 12°. **14128. a. 30.**

—— মডেল ভগিনী। [Maḍel bhaginī. A story of domestic life in Bengal.] 3 pts. কলিকাতা ১২৯৩ [*Calcutta*, 1886.] 12°. **14127. e. 24.**

Wanting the second section of pt. 3.

—— [Twelfth edition.] pp. 503. কলিকাতা ১৩১২ [*Calcutta*, 1905.] 12°. **14128. a. 26.**

YOGENDRAMOHANA DATTA. আদর্শ লিখন ও পত্রদলিলশিক্ষা। [Ādarśa-likhana. A letter-writer, with specimens of revenue, legal, and commercial documents.] pp. 172. ঢাকা [*Dacca*, 1906.] 12°. **14131. e. 37.**

YOGENDRA NĀRĀYAṆA RĀYA, *of Lalgola.* *See* BHUVANAMOHANA BHAṬṬĀCHĀRYA, *of Murshidabad.* যোগেন্দ্র মাহাত্ম্য। [Yogendra-māhātmya. A poetical panegyric on Yogendra Nārāyaṇa Rāya.] [1901.] 12°. **14072. b. 25.(2.)**

YOGENDRANĀTHA CHAṬṬOPĀDHYĀYA. জঙ্গলী মেয়ে। [Jaṅgalī meye. The wild girl; a tale of Bengali life.] pp. 146. *Calcutta*, [1902.] 12°. **14127. d. 19.(2.)**

—— প্রসন্নকুমারের উইল। [Prasannakumārer 'will.' A tale of Bengali domestic life.] pp. 170. *Calcutta*, [1900.] 12°. **14127. cc. 21.(4.)**

YOGENDRANĀTHA DE. *See* ARABIAN NIGHTS. সচিত্র আরব্য-উপন্যাস। [Ārabya upanyāsa. The Arabian Nights, translated by Yogendranātha De.] [1901.] 8°. **14127. ee. 13.(2.)**

—— —— [Ninth edition.] [1908.] 8°. **14128. b. 2.**

YOGENDRANĀTHA GHOSHA. A Dictionary of Medical Terms, in English and Bengali . . . by Jogender Nath Ghose. pp. ii. 304. *Calcutta,* 1887. 12°. **14125. bb. 22.**

—— A Dictionary of Medical Terms . . . Second edition. Thoroughly revised, greatly modified, and enlarged. pp. iv. 380. *Calcutta,* 1904. 12°. **14125. b. 19.**

YOGENDRANĀTHA MITRA. Dissection of human body and essentials of anatomy. Compiled by J. N. Mitra . . . শরীর-ব্যবচ্ছেদ ও শরীর-তত্ত্ব-সার [Śarīra-vyavachchheda.] pp. v. 315. *Calcutta,* 1894. 12°. **14125. b. 12.**

YOGENDRANĀTHA MUKHOPĀDHYĀYA. Rachaná-sopán, or Helps to Bengali composition . . . by Jogendra Nath Mukhopadhyay. রচনা-সোপান। pp. vi. 132. *Calcutta,* 1885. 12°. **14131. f. 31.(3.)**

YOGENDRANĀTHA RĀYA. উৎকলের পঞ্চতীর্থ। [Utkaler pañcha-tīrtha. An account of the five principal Hindu places of pilgrimage in Orissa.] pp. ii. vi. 234. কলিকাতা ১৯০৬ [*Calcutta,* 1906.] 12°. **14127. aa. 37.**

YOGENDRANĀTHA SARKĀR. কবির তাহার সংক্ষিপ্ত জীবনী ও উপদেশাবলী। [Kabīr. A biography of the Hindi poet, with selections from his poems in Bengali characters, accompanied by a Bengali translation.] pp. ii. 60. কলিকাতা, ব্রাহ্মসম্বৎ ৬৩ [*Calcutta,* 1893.] 12°. **14127. a. 37.(6.)**

YOGENDRANĀTHA ŚARMĀ. স্বদেশ-সঙ্গীত। [Svadeśa-saṅgīta. A collection of patriotic songs by modern Bengali poets. Second edition.] pp. iv. 72, xii. iv. ভবানীপুর [*Bhawanipur,* 1907.] 12°. **14129. bb. 82.(7.)**

YOGENDRANĀTHA SENA. ঊষা। [Ūshā. Miscellaneous short poems.] pp. ii. 120. কলিকাতা ১৩০৪ [*Calcutta,* 1898.] 12°. **14129. a. 28.(4.)**

YOGENDRANĀTHA ṬHĀKURA. পুনর্বসন্ত। [Punarvasanta. A mythological comedy.] pp. 32. কলিকাতা ১৩০৫ [*Calcutta,* 1899.] 12°. **14131. a. 41.(3.)**

YOGENDRANĀTHA VANDYOPĀDHYĀYA VIDYĀBHŪSHAṆA. জন্ ষ্টুয়ার্ট মিলের জীবন-বৃত্ত। [Jan Shṭuyārṭ Miler jīvanavṛitta. A life of John Stuart Mill. Third edition.] pp. xxi. 173, iii. *Calcutta,* 1884. 12°. **14127. aa. 5.**

—— যোগেন্দ্র গ্রন্থাবলী। [Yogendra-granthāvalī. The collected works of Yogendranātha Vandyopādhyāya.] কলিকাতা ১৩১৫ [*Calcutta,* 1908.] 8°. **14128. b. 3.**

Each work has a separate pagination.

YOGENDRANĀTHA VASU, called DHŪRJAṬI. একাদশ অবতার বা পঞ্চানন্দ মঙ্গল। [Ekādaśa avatāra, or Pañchānanda-maṅgala. A mock heroic poem, representing Babu Indranātha Vandyopādhyāya, who used to write satirical articles in the "Vaṅgavāsī" newspaper, under the *nom de plume* of Pañchānanda, as the eleventh incarnation of Vishṇu, fighting, in defence of the Hindu religion, against the Brahmists.] pp. 272. কলিকাতা ১২৯৩ [*Calcutta,* 1886.] 12°. **14129. a. 28.(1.)**

YOGEŚACHANDRA RĀYA. খনা। [Khanā. A paper on Khanā and her astrological sayings.] ১৩১০ [1903.] *See* ACADEMIES, *etc.*—Calcutta.—*Bengal Academy of Literature.* সাহিত্য-পরিষৎ-পত্রিকা। [Sāhitya-parishat-patrikā.] Vol. x., no. 1. [1894, *etc.*] 8°. **14133. f. 18.**

—— শংকু-নির্মাণ *etc.* [Śaṃku-nirmāṇa. A treatise on the construction of sun-dials.] pp. iii. 120. কলিকাতা ১৮৩০ [*Calcutta,* 1908.] 12°. **14125. ddd. 4.**

YOGEŚVARA GHOSHA. A short poem in Bengali, with an English translation, on the Coronation of His Most Gracious Majesty Edward VII. . . . By Joggeshur Ghose. (রাজ্যাভিষেক-মহোৎসব।) [Rājyābhisheka-mahotsava.] pp. ii. 23. *Calcutta,* 1902. 12°. **14129. bb. 13.(3.)**

YOGĪNDRANĀTHA BHAṬṬĀCHĀRYA. মহম্মদীয় আইন সার-সংগ্রহ। [Mahammadīya āin sāra-saṅgraha. A compendium of Muhammadan law.] pp. iv. 194. কলিকাতা ১৮৯৫ [*Calcutta,* 1895.] 8°. **14128. h. 28.(2.)**

YOGĪNDRANĀTHA SARKĀR. খুকুমণির ছড়া। [Khukumaṇir chhaṛā. A collection of illustrated nursery rhymes. Edited with an introduction by Rāmendrasundara Trivedī.] pp. 176, xx. কলিকাতা ১৩০৬ [*Calcutta,* 1899.] 12°. **14129. a. 43.**

YOGĪNDRANĀTHA SARKĀR (*continued*). বন্দে মাতরম্। [Vande mātaram. Patriotic songs. Sixth edition.] pp. 200. কলিকাতা ১৯০৮ [*Calcutta*, 1908.] 16°. **14129. bbb. 2.**

YOGĪNDRANĀTHA TARKACHŪḌĀMAṆI. The essay on Meghanada badha of Michael Madhusudana Datta, by Jogindra Natha Tarkachudamani . . . মেঘনাদবধ প্রবন্ধ। [Meghanādavadha-prabandha.] pp. 89, 32. *Calcutta*, 1887. 8°. **14131. d. 19.**

—— The minute essay on Abhijnana Sacuntalam of Calidasa. By Jogindra Natha Tarkachudamani . . . শকুন্তলাসরস্বতীতত্ত্ব। [Ṣakuntalā-sarasvatītattva.] pp. 48. *Calcutta*, 1890. 12°. **14131. d. 27.**

—— মহাপ্রস্থান নাটক। [Mahāprasthāna nāṭaka. A drama on the Mahābhārata story of the ascension of Yudhishṭhira to heaven.] pp. ii. 39. কলিকাতা ১৮৮৭ [*Calcutta*, 1887.] 8°. **14131. c. 18.(1.)**

—— যজ্ঞসংহিতা। . . . Yajna sanhita, or The religion of sacrifices . . . By Jogindra Natha Tarkachudamani. 4 pts. *Calcutta*, 1893. 8°. **14123. f. 47.**

YOGĪNDRANĀTHA VASU. *See* KṚITTIVĀSA. সরল কৃত্তিবাস। [Sarala Kṛittivāsa. A simplified metrical version of the Rāmāyaṇa of Kṛittivāsa, with an account of the author and his poem, by Yogīndranātha Vasu.] [1907.] 4°. **14129. f. 8.**

YOGĪNDRANĀTHA VASU (*continued*) [Ahalyābāi. A life of Ahalyābāi H dore.] pp. vi. 74, 33. কলিকাতা ১৩০২ 1895.] 12°. **1**

—— কবিতা-প্রসঙ্গ। [Kavitāprasaṅga. Ins poems.] pp. 129. কলিকাতা ১৩০৩ [*Calcutta*, 12°. **14129.**

—— মাইকেল মধুসূদন দত্তের জীবন-চরিত। [Māi Madhusūdana Datter jīvana-charita. The life Michael Madhusūdana Datta, with a collection o unpublished poems and letters, and a critical examination of his works. Second edition.] pp. vi. 466, iii. 48. কলিকাতা ১৩০১ [*Calcutta*, 1893.] 8°. **14127. bb. 2.**

—— তুকারাম-চরিত। [Tukārāma-charita. Life of the Marathi poet Tukārāma.] pp. vi. 182. কলিকাতা ১৩০৮ [*Calcutta*, 1901.] 12°. **14127. aa. 20.**

YUDHISHṬHIRA NĀRĀYAṆA DĀSA ADHIKĀRĪ. কুমার পরিণয়। [Kumārapariṇaya. The marriage of a prince; a poem.] pp. ii. 176. কলিকাতা ১৩১২ [*Calcutta*, 1905.] 12°. **14129. bb. 16.(3.)**

YŪTHĪ. যূথী। [Yūthī. Short lyrical pieces by an anonymous author.] pp. ii. 84. কলিকাতা [*Calcutta*, 1900.] 12°. **14129. a. 48.(3.)**

ZUHŪR al-ḤUSAIN. কেতাব নুরনাজাত। দর এস্কে মারেফত। [Nūr i najāt. Sufic religious poems, in Muhammadan Bengali.] pp. 216. শ্রীহট্ট ১৩১৪ [*Sylhet*, 1907.] 8°. **14123. h. 41.**

In Sylhet Nagari characters.

ADDENDA.

ABD al-ḲĀDIR, *Munshī.* হেকমতে জানানা বা রমণীর কৌশল। [Ḥikmat i zanānah. The wiles of unchaste women, in verse. Second edition.] pp. 140. কলিকাতা ১৩১৫ [*Calcutta*, 1908.] 8°. **14129. bbb. 5.**

AMARENDRANĀTHA DATTA. অমর-গ্রন্থাবলী। [Amara-granthāvalī. The complete works of Amarendranātha Datta. Edited by Upendranātha Mukhopādhyāya.] কলিকাতা ১৩১৫ [*Calcutta*, 1908, *etc.*] 8°. **14127. g. 19.**
In progress.

ĀSANNABANDHU BHAṬṬĀCHĀRYA ṬHĀKURA, *of Mehar.* *See* [Addenda] ŚIVANĀTHA BHAṬṬĀCHĀRYA, *Son of Sarvānanda.* সর্ব্বানন্দ-তরঙ্গিণী। [Sarvānanda-taraṅgiṇī. With a Sanskrit commentary and a Bengali translation by Āsannabandhu.] [1909.] 8°. **14028. bbb. 18.(4.)**

BANERJI (SATIS K.). *See* SATĪŚAKUMĀRA VANDYOPĀDHYĀYA.

BIBLE.—GOSPELS. আমাদের প্রভু যেশু খ্রীস্তের পবিত্র সমাচার ও প্রেরিতদের ক্রিয়া সটীক। . . . The Holy Gospel of Jesus Christ according to the four Evangelists, and the Acts of the Apostles. Translated from the Latin Vulgate, compared with the original Greek, and with annotations by the Right Rev. S. Taveggia, Vic.-Gen., *etc.* pp. viii. 784. 1906. 8°. **14123. b. 24.**

—— The gospel according to Mark in Bengali, being "A Teacher's Commentary" by Richard Glover . . . adapted by the Rev. . . . with the help of Bengali . . . মার্কলিখিত সুসমাচার।) pp. iii. vi. 1908. 12°. **14123. a. 48.**

—— Bengali. নিষ্কলঙ্ক অবতার। pp. 88. *Calcutta*, 1908. 12°. **14123. a. 40.(5.)**

BIBLE (*continued*). ACTS. প্রেরিতদের ক্রিয়া। The Acts of the Apostles. Translated from the Latin Vulgate . . . with annotations by the Right Rev. S. Taveggia. *See* above: GOSPELS. আমাদের প্রভু যেশু খ্রীস্তের পবিত্র সুসমাচার . . . The Holy Gospel of Jesus Christ, *etc.* pp. 570-732. 1906. 8°. **14123. b. 24.**

CHAITANYA. [*Life.*] *See* [Addenda] VṚINDĀVANA DĀSA. শ্রীশ্রীচৈতন্য ভাগবত। [Chaitanya-bhāgavata.] [1908.] 4°. **14127. bbb. 10.**

—— নিমাই-সন্ন্যাস। বৈরাগ্য খণ্ড। [Nimāi-sannyāsa. An account in verse of Chaitanya's renunciation of the world by becoming a *sannyāsī.* Second edition.] pp. 56. কাঁথী ১৩১৫ [*Contai*, 1908.] 12°. **14123. e. 34.(3.)**

DEVENDRANĀTHA ṬHĀKURA. মহর্ষি দেবেন্দ্রনাথ। [Maharshi Devendranātha. A life of Devendranātha Ṭhākura.] pp. ii. 77. কলিকাতা ১৩১৫ [*Calcutta*, 1908.] 12°. **14127. aaa. 5.**

GLOVER (RICHARD), *Baptist Minister.* *See* [Addenda] BIBLE.—*Mark.* The Gospel according to Mark in Bengali, being "A Teacher's Commentary" by the Rev. Richard Glover . . . adapted by the Rev. Arthur Jewson, *etc.* 1908. 12°. **14123. a. 48.**

GMELIN (FREDERICK), *Rev.* A Manual of Divinity or an exposition of the Catechism of the Church of England . . . ঐশ্বরিক বিদ্যার সারসংগ্রহ। [Aiśvarika vidyār sārasaṅgraha.] pp. iv. vi. 214. *Calcutta*, 1908. 12°. **14123. a. 46.(4.)**

HARIHARĀNANDA, *Sāṅkhyayogāchārya.* অথ বররত্নমালা। [Three Sanskrit tracts on devotion, viz. Vararatnamālā, in prose; Mumukshāchatushka, in 4 verses; and Samādhishaṭka, in 6 verses. With Bengali paraphrases, and a Pali version of the last.] *See* [Addenda] SACHCHIDĀNANDA ĀRAṆYA. সটীকং পরভক্তিসূত্রম্। [Parabhakti-sūtra, *etc.*] pp. 21-31. [1908.] 8°. **14049. aaa. 14.(3.)**

HARIHARA ṢETH. অভিশাপ। [Abhiṣāpa. A social novel.] pp. ii. 286. কলিকাতা ১৩১৫ [*Calcutta*, 1908.] 12°. **14128. a. 32.**

JEWSON (ARTHUR), *Baptist Missionary.* *See* [Addenda] BIBLE.—*Mark.* The Gospel according to Mark in Bengali, being "A Teacher's Commentary" by the Rev. Richard Glover . . . adapted by the Rev. Arthur Jewson, *etc.* 1908. 12°. **14123. a. 48.**

JĪVA GOSVĀMĪ. সংকল্পকল্পদ্রুমঃ। . . . বিমলানাম্নী-টীকয়া অনুবাদেনচ সহিতঃ। [Saṃkalpakalpadruma. A Sanskrit poem on the legend of Kṛishṇa as narrated in the Bhāgavatapurāṇa. Edited with a Sanskrit commentary styled Vimalā, and a Bengali translation of the text by Ṣachīnandana Gosvāmī Bhaktiratna of Nadia.] pp. iii. 355. বৃন্দাবন ৪২২ [*Brindaban*, 1907.] 8°. **14070. cc. 4.**

KRISHṆADĀSA BĀBĀJĪ. শ্রীশ্রীভক্তমাল গ্রন্থ। [Bhaktamāla. Lives of Vaishṇava saints, in verse, based on the Hindi work of Nābhājī and the commentary of Priyādāsa. Edited by Upendranātha Mukhopādhyāya.] pp. ii. 405. কলিকাতা, চৈতন্যাব্দ ৪২৩ [*Calcutta*, 1908.] 8°. **14123. gg. 5.**

KRITTIVĀSA. সরল কৃত্তিবাস। [Sarala Kṛittivāsa. Second edition.] pp. xviii. 232, viii. কলিকাতা ১৩১৫ [*Calcutta*, 1908.] 4°. **14129. f. 9.**

KSHĪRODAPRASĀDA VIDYĀVINODA. অশোক। [Aṣoka. An historical drama relating to the king Aṣoka.] pp. 164. [*Calcutta*, 1908.] 12°. **14131. aa. 12.(2.)**

KUR'ĀN. قرآن شريف . . . কোরাণ শরীফ। [The Koran. Arabic text, with a Bengali interlineary translation, and a Bengali commentary translated and compiled from the most authoritative sources.] কলিকাতা ১৯০৮ [*Baptist Mission Press: Calcutta*, 1908, *etc.*] 4°. **14509. b. 24.**
In progress.

MĀṆIKCHANDRA GHOSHA. ক্ষুদিরামের ফাঁসির কাণ্ড। [Kshudirāmer phāṇsir kāṇḍa. Extracts from native newspapers containing an account of the execution of Kshudirāma Vasu of Midnapore, the murderer in the Muzaffarpur bomb case. Compiled by Māṇikchandra Ghosha.] pp. 11. কলিকাতা [*Calcutta*, 1908.] 12°. **14125. a. 34.**

MANMATHA MUSTAFĪ. The Speaker, Parts I. & II. for Entrance and Lower Class students, by M. Mustafi. Fourth edition. pp. ii. ii. 321. *Calcutta*, 1894. 12°. **14131. e. 38.**

MANOHARA DĀSA. বৈদগ্ধবিলাসঃ। [Vaidagdhavilāsa. A poem on the loves of Kṛishṇa and Rādhā.] pp. ii. iv. 190. ৪২২ [*Brindaban*, 1907.] 8°. **14129. cc. 1.(5.)**

MUSTAFI (M.). *See* MANMATHA MUSTAFĪ.

NĀBHĀJĪ. *See* [Addenda] KRISHṆADĀSA BĀBĀJĪ. শ্রীশ্রীভক্তমাল গ্রন্থ। [Bhaktamāla. Based on the Hindi work of Nābhājī.] [1908.] 8°. **14123. gg. 5.**

NĀRADA. নারদসূত্র বা ভক্তিজিজ্ঞাসা। [Nārada-sūtra, or Bhakti-jijñāsā. Sanskrit aphorisms of the Vaishṇava doctrine of devotion. With a Bengali translation and commentary by Sureṣachandra Datta.] pp. 40. কলিকাতা ১৩১৫ [*Calcutta*, 1908.] 12°. **14049. aa. 5.(3.)**

NAVAKUMĀRA DATTA. *See* [Addenda] PERIODICAL PUBLICATIONS.—*Calcutta.* অনুশীলন। [Anuṣīlana. Edited by Navakumāra Datta.] [1908, *etc.*] 8°. **14133. ff. 5.**

NIDHIRĀMA MUKHOPĀDHYĀYA. মৎস্যের চাষ। [Matsyer chāsh. Another edition, with a different arrangement of the chapters.] pp. 103, ii. কলিকাতা ১৩১৫ [*Calcutta*, 1908.] 12°. **14125. bb. 30.**

PARABHAKTI. সটীকং পরভক্তিসূত্রম্। [Parabhakti-sūtra. Sanskrit aphorisms on the Vedantic theory of devotion, in 4 *āhnikas*, with Sanskrit and Bengali commentaries.] *See* [Addenda] SACHCHIDĀNANDA ĀRAṆYA. সটীকং পরভক্তিসূত্রম্। [Parabhakti-sūtra, *etc.*] pp. 1-20. [1908.] 8°. **14049. aaa. 14.(3.)**

PERIODICAL PUBLICATIONS.—CALCUTTA. অনুশীলন। মাসিক পত্র ও সমালোচন। [Anuṣīlana. A monthly magazine and review. Edited by Navakumāra Datta.] কলিকাতা [*Calcutta*, 1908, *etc.*] 8°. **14133. ff. 5.**
In progress.

PREMCHĀṆD DĀSA. বিরহিনী ভাদু সঙ্গীত। [Virahinī bhādu saṅgīta. Songs on the lament of a woman separated from her lover.] pp. 12. বাঁকুড়া ১৩১২ [*Bankura*, 1905.] 12°. **14129. bbb. 6.**

PRIYĀDĀSA. *See* [Addenda] KṚISHṆADĀSA BĀBĀJĪ. শ্রীশ্রীভক্তমাল গ্রন্থ। [Bhaktamāla. Based on the Hindi work of Nābhājī and the commentary of Priyādāsa.] [1908.] 8°. **14123. gg. 5.**

RAGHUNĀTHADĀSA GOSVĀMĪ. মুক্তাচরিত্রম্। [Muktācharitra. A Sanskrit legend of Kṛishṇa and his loves, in prose, relating to the origin of pearls. Edited with a Bengali translation by Ṣachīnandana Gosvāmī Bhaktiratna of Nadia, with a Bengali preface by Nityasvarūpa Brahmachārī.] pp. iii. 242. বৃন্দাবন ৪২২ [*Brindaban*, 1907.] 8°. **14070. cc. 5.**

RĀMANĀRĀYAṆA VIDYĀRATNA. *See* [Addenda] RŪPA GOSVĀMĪ. ললিতমাধব নাটকং। [Lalita-Mādhava nāṭaka. Edited with a Bengali translation by Rāmanārāyaṇa Vidyāratna.] [1902, *etc.*] 8°. **14079. d. 47.**

RAVĪNDRANĀTHA ṬHĀKURA. গল্পগুচ্ছ। [Galpaguchchha. Second edition.] 2 pts. কলিকাতা [*Calcutta*, 1908.] 12°. **14128. a. 31.**

—— গান। [Gāna. Songs, divided into 5 parts, including the author's Vālmīki-pratibhā.] pp. xvi. 400. কলিকাতা [*Calcutta*, 1908.] 12°. **14129. bbb. 4.**

RŪPA GOSVĀMĪ. ললিতমাধব নাটকং। [Lalita-Mādhava nāṭaka. A Sanskrit drama on the legend of Kṛishṇa, with the author's Sanskrit commentary. Edited with a Bengali translation by Rāmanārāyaṇa Vidyāratna. Second edition.] মুর্শিদাবাদ ১৩০৯ [*Murshidabad*, 1902, *etc.*] 8°. **14079. d. 47.**

In progress. No. 2 did not appear till 1314 *B.S. or* 1908 *A.D.*

SACHCHIDĀNANDA ARAṆYA. সটীকং পরভক্তিসূত্রম্ বররত্নমালা-সমাধিষট্ক-মুমুক্ষাচতুষ্ক-সমেতম্। . . . সটীক ও সানুবাদ পরভক্তিসূত্র *etc.* [Parabhakti-sūtra. Anonymous aphorisms on the Vedantic theory of devotion in Sanskrit, with Sanskrit and Bengali commentaries. Followed by 3 similar Sanskrit works by Hariharānanda Āraṇya, viz. Vararatnamālā, a prose tract, and Mumukshāchatushka and Samādhishaṭka, short poems, with Bengali paraphrases. Edited by Sachchidānanda.] pp. 31. কলিকাতা ১৯০৮ [*Calcutta*, 1908.] 8°. **14049. aaa. 14.(3.)**

ṢACHĪNANDANA GOSVĀMĪ, *Bhaktiratna, of Nadia. See* [Addenda] JĪVA GOSVĀMĪ. সংকল্পকল্পদ্রুমঃ। *etc.* [Saṃkalpakalpadruma. Edited with a Sanskrit commentary, and a Bengali translation of the text, by Ṣachīnandana Gosvāmī.] [1907.] 8°. **14070. cc. 4.**

—— *See* [Addenda] RAGHUNĀTHADĀSA GOSVĀMĪ. মুক্তাচরিত্রম্। [Muktācharitra. Edited with a Bengali translation by Ṣachīnandana Gosvāmī.] [1907.] 8°. **14070. cc. 5.**

SATĪṢAKUMĀRA VANDYOPĀDHYĀYA. An Up-to-date Bengali-to-Bengali-and English Dictionary with Phrases, Idioms and Proverbs. By Satis K. Banerji. Second edition. pp. vii. 614. *Calcutta*, [1908.] 8°. **14133. a. 18.**

ṢIVANĀTHA BHAṬṬĀCHĀRYA, *Son of Sarvānanda.* সর্ব্বানন্দ-তরঙ্গিণী। [Sarvānanda-taraṅgiṇī. An account of Ṣaiva Tantric doctrines and rites, in dialogue form. Sanskrit text, with a Sanskrit commentary and a Bengali translation by Āsannabandhu Bhaṭṭāchārya Ṭhākura. Edited by Atulachandra Bhaṭṭāchārya.] pp. 86. কুমিল্লা [*Comillah*, 1909.] 8°. **14028. bbb. 18.(4.)**

SUREṢACHANDRA DATTA. *See* [Addenda] NĀRADA. নারদসূত্র বা ভক্তিজিজ্ঞাসা। [Nārada-sūtra. With a Bengali translation and commentary by Sureṣachandra Datta.] [1908.] 12°. **14049. aa. 5.(3.)**

TAVEGGIA (S.). *See* [Addenda] BIBLE.—*Gospels.* আমাদের প্রভু যেশু খ্রীস্তের পবিত্র সুসমাচার ও প্রেরিতদের ক্রিয়া সটীক। . . . The Holy Gospel of Jesus Christ according to the four Evangelists, and the Acts of the Apostles. Translated from the Latin Vulgate . . . with annotations by the Right Rev. S. Taveggia, *etc.* 1906. 8°. **14123. b. 24.**

UPENDRANĀTHA MUKHOPĀDHYĀYA. *See* [Addenda] AMARENDRANĀTHA DATTA. অমর-গ্রন্থাবলী। [Amara-granthāvalī. Edited by Upendranātha Mukhopādhyāya.] [1908, *etc.*] 8°. **14127. g. 19.**

VṚINDĀVANA DĀSA. শ্রীশ্রীচৈতন্যভাগবত। [Chaitanya-bhāgavata. Another edition.] pp. iii. 393. কলিকাতা ১৩১৫ [*Calcutta*, 1908.] 4°. **14127. bbb. 10.**

YOGĪNDRANĀTHA VASU. *See* [Addenda] KṚITTIVĀSA. সরল কৃত্তিবাস। [Sarala Kṛittivāsa. Second edition.] [1908.] 4°. **14129. f. 9.**

CORRIGENDA.

Col.	Line
67	7 from bottom. For "vaṇik" read "baṇik"
86	17 from top. For **VANDHYOPĀDHYĀYA** read **VANDYOPĀDHYĀYA.**
124	21 from top. Alter **14048. dd. 16.** to **14049. a. 2.**
161	18 from top. Alter **2348. a.** to **2348. aa. 34.**
164	2 from bottom. For **MU'IZ** read **MU'IZZ**
222	2 from top. For "Rāmachandra" read "Rāmakṛishṇa"
229	7 from bottom. After **VIDYĀRṆAVA** add *See* PURĀṆAS.—*Bṛihad-dharmapurāṇa.*
237	last line. Alter **14129. a. 23.** to **14129. aa. 3.**
239	5 from top. For "nibandha" read "nirbandha."

INDEXES.

The references are to the names of authors or other headings under which the works are catalogued. Anonymous works catalogued under their titles are designated by the phrase in loco.

I. GENERAL INDEX OF TITLES.

Haripura-Majumdār-vaṃṣāvalī. KĀLĪKUMĀRA MAJUMDĀR.
Hariṣchandra-charita. LOKANĀTHA DATTA.
Hariṣchandra Mukhopādhyāyer jīvanī. RĀMAGOPĀLA SĀNNYĀLA.
Hārita-saṃhitā. HĀRĪTA.
Harivaṃṣa. MAHĀBHĀRATA.
Hārmoniyam-ṣikshā. KṚISHṆADHANA VANDYOPĀDHYĀYA.
Hastāmalaka. HASTĀMALAKA ĀCHĀRYA.
Hastasāra. DHARMARĀJA BAṚUYĀ.
Hastatantra-vayana. GHOSH (H. H.).
Hastī-chikitsā. KEṢAVACHANDRA ĀCHĀRYA.
Hāsya-kautuka. RAVĪNDRANĀTHA ṬHĀKURA.
Hāṭapattana. NAROTTAMA DĀSA.
Haṭhayogapradīpikā. SVĀTMĀRĀMA.
Hekṭar-vadha. HOMER.
Hemachandra. HARIDĀSA VANDYOPĀDHYĀYA.
——— SURENDRAMOHANA BHAṬṬĀCHĀRYA.
Hemachandrer granthāvalī. HEMACHANDRA VANDYOPĀDHYĀYA.
Hemahāra. HĀRĀṆACHANDRA RAKSHITA.
Ḥikāyāt al-ṣālihīn. MUḤAMMAD 'ABD al-RAḤMĀN KHĀN.
Ḥikmat i zanānah. [Addenda] 'ABD al-ḲĀDIR, *Munshī*.
Hindudarṣana. CHANDRAKĀNTA TARKĀLAṄKĀRA.
Hindudharma sambandhīya chitrāvalī. HINDU SACRED PICTURES.
Hindudharmer āndolana. DĪNANĀTHA GAṄGOPĀDHYĀYA.
Hindudharmer punarutthāna. GAURAGOVINDA RĀYA.
Hindu jātibheda. YADUNĀTHA VIṢVĀSA.
Hindu melār uddeṣya. MANOMOHANA VASU.
Hindu Mosalmān. 'ABD al-SUBḤĀN.
Hindu Practice of Medicine. RASIKALĀLA GUPTA.
Hindu ṣāstra. RAMEṢACHANDRA DATTA.
Hindu tīrthataraṅgiṇī. KĀLĪPRASANNA VIDYĀRATNA BHAṬṬĀCHĀRYA.
Hindutva. CHANDRANĀTHA VASU, *M.A.*
Hindu vivāha o kanyā-vikraya. KĀLĪṢAṄKARA DĀSA.
Hints on composition and translation. DVĀRAKĀNĀTHA VASU.
Hīre mālinī. RĀJAKṚISHṆA RĀYA, *Dramatist.*
Hitopadeṣa [*in loco*].
Hitopadeṣa-saṅgraha. BIBLE.—*Proverbs.*
Homaṣikhā. SATYENDRANĀTHA DATTA.
How to translate from Bengali into English. DHANAVALLABHA ṢEṬ.
Hugli̇r imāmbāṛī. SVARṆAKUMĀRĪ DEVĪ.
Ḥujjat al-Mūminīn. MUḤAMMAD NI'MAT ALLĀH.
Huṇkā-purāṇa-māhātmya. VIPINAVIHĀRĪ VANDYOPĀDHYĀYA and KULACHANDRA DE DĀSA.

Idiomat… MUKHOPĀDHYĀYA.
Iḥsān al… -RAḤMĀN, *Saiyid.*
I'jāz i G… ḲĀSIM, *Maulavī.*
Ilchhobā… NA.
Imlaṇḍe … LADY.
Imrejī var… LLING-BOOK.
Indian Sa… MDĀR.
Indian Stu… UPENDRANĀTHA SENA… NA.
Indirā. … OPĀDHYĀYA.
Indische N… GHOSHA.
Indrachandr… ṆA BASĀK.
Indrajāla [*in*…
Indra-kumārī. … RĀYA.
Intellectual O… NDRA, *of Benares.*
Īṣā Upanishad. …
Islām. 'ABD …
Islāmīya mantra. … VA'Z al-DĪN.
Īṣopanishad. U…
Iurop-bhramaṇa. … A VASU.
Iyurope tin batsar. … NDRA DATTA.
Jaḍabharata. DĪN… ENA.
Jagadānanda-padāvalī. … NDA, *Vaishṇava poet.*
Jagadrāma Rāyer Rāmā… NCHKAṚI GHOSHA.
Jagannātha-līlā [Vol. iv … rāvali]. RĀDHĀMĀDHAVA GHOSH…
Jagannātha-maṅgala. … ARA DĀSA.
Jagannātha-vijaya o Kav… da. RASIKACHANDRA VASU.
Jāgaraṇa. MĀDHAVĀCHĀ…
Jahānārā. SURENDRAMOH… AṬṬĀCHĀRYA.
Jāmālpureṣvara-buṛārājastotra… RIPADA MUKHOPĀDHYĀYA.
Jamidārī darpaṇa. ṢAṢIṢEKHA… GHOSHA.
Jamidārī kāryaṣikshā. ṢAṢIBHŪSHAṆA GHOSHA.
Jamīdār o rāyater galpa. JAMĪDĀR.
Jānakīvallabha-charita. RAJANĪKĀNTA BHAṬṬĀCHĀRYA.
Jaṅgalī meye. YOGENDRANĀTHA CHAṬṬOPĀDHYĀYA.
Janmāntara-rahasya. BHAVENDRANĀTHA DE.
Jannat al-kunjī. SAMĪR al-DĪN AḤMAD.
Jan Shṭuyārṭ Miler jīvanavṛitta. YOGENDRANĀTHA VANDYOPĀDHYĀYA VIDYĀBHŪSHAṆA.
Japjī. NĀNAK, *Bābā.*
Jarāvairāgya. HARIṢCHANDRA BHAṬṬĀCHĀRYA KAVIRATNA.
Jātitattva. GIRIṢACHANDRA VASU.
Jātitattva-vāridhi. UMEṢACHANDRA DĀSA GUPTA.
Jātīyanigraha [Pt. ii. of Āryasaṅgīta]. NAVĪNACHANDRA MUKHOPĀDHYĀYA.
Jātīya sāhityer āvaṣyakatā o unnati. DEVENDRANĀTHA MUKHOPĀDHYĀYA.
Jawāhir al-Islām. ḲUDRAT ALLĀH.

II. SUBJECT-INDEX.

Works the titles of which are marked by an asterisk will be found in the Catalogue of 1886 *only; those marked by a dagger are in that and also in the present Catalogue.*

The classification is as follows:—

ARTS AND SCIENCES.

1. Agriculture, Horticulture, and Botany.
2. Astronomy and Astrology.
3. Calligraphy.
4. Chemistry.
5. Letter-writing, Book-keeping, Documents, etc.
6. Medicine, Surgery, and Hygiene.
7. Music.
8. Occult Arts, Divination, and Magic.
9. Physical Science and Natural History.
10. Sports and Games.
11. Other Arts and Sciences.

BIBLIOGRAPHY.

BIOGRAPHY AND GENEALOGY.

CASTE AND ETHNOGRAPHY.

DICTIONARIES AND VOCABULARIES.

DRAMA.

EDUCATION.

1. Dialogues and Phrase-books.
2. Pedagogy.
3. Readers.
4. General.

ETHICS AND POLITY.

FICTION AND LEGEND.

1. Epic and Mythical.
2. Fables, Fairy-tales, and Folklore.
3. Miscellaneous Narratives.

GEOGRAPHY AND TOPOGRAPHY.

GRAMMAR.

1. Arabic.
2. Bengali.
3. Burmese.
4. English.
5. Hindi.
6. Hindustani.
7. Oriya.
8. Persian.
9. Sanskrit.
10. Tipperah.
11. Miscellaneous.

HISTORY.

1. Chronology.
2. General Histories.
3. History of Literature.

LAW AND ADMINISTRATION.

1. British.
2. Hindu.
3. Muhammadan.
4. Native States.

LITERATURE.

1. Anthologies.
2. Collected Works of Individual Authors.
3. Erotic and Genre Literature.
4. Essays, Lectures, and Speeches.
5. Literary Criticism.
6. Periodical Publications, and Proceedings of Societies.
7. Miscellaneous Literature.

MATHEMATICS.

1. Algebra.
2. Arithmetic.
3. Geometry and Mensuration.
4. Trigonometry.

PHILOSOPHY.

POETRY.

1. Epic and Mythical.
2. Historical.
3. Narrative.
4. Religious.
   (i.) *Hindu.*
   (ii.) *Muhammadan.*
5. Miscellaneous.

POLITICAL ECONOMY.

PROSODY AND METRE.

PROVERBS AND ADAGES.

RELIGION.

1. Buddhism.
2. Christianity.
3. Hinduism.
4. Islam.
5. Sikh Church.
6. Theistic Churches. (Ārya and Brāhma Samāj.)

RHETORIC (*Alaṅkāra*).

SOCIOLOGY.

TRAVEL AND GUIDE-BOOKS.

ARTS AND SCIENCES.

1. AGRICULTURE, HORTICULTURE, AND BOTANY.

2. ASTRONOMY AND ASTROLOGY.

3. CALLIGRAPHY.

4. CHEMISTRY.

5. LETTER-WRITING, BOOK-KEEPING, DOCUMENTS, ETC.

6. MEDICINE, SURGERY, AND HYGIENE.

7. MUSIC.

8. OCCULT ARTS, DIVINATION, AND MAGIC.

9. PHYSICAL SCIENCE, AND NATURAL HISTORY.

10. SPORTS AND GAMES.

11. OTHER ARTS AND SCIENCES.

BIBLIOGRAPHY.

BIOGRAPHY AND GENEALOGY.

CASTE AND ETHNOGRAPHY.

DICTIONARIES AND VOCABULARIES.

DRAMA.

EDUCATION.

1. DIALOGUES AND PHRASE-BOOKS.

2. PEDAGOGY.

3. READERS.

4. GENERAL.

ETHICS AND POLITY.

FICTION AND LEGEND.

(*See also* Poetry.)

1. EPIC AND MYTHICAL.

2. FABLES, FAIRY-TALES, AND FOLKLORE.

3. MISCELLANEOUS NARRATIVES.

GEOGRAPHY AND TOPOGRAPHY.

5. LITERARY CRITICISM.

6. PERIODICAL PUBLICATIONS, AND PROCEEDINGS OF SOCIETIES.

7. MISCELLANEOUS LITERATURE.

MATHEMATICS.

1. ALGEBRA.

2. ARITHMETIC.

3. GEOMETRY AND MENSURATION.

4. TRIGONOMETRY.

PHILOSOPHY.

POETRY.

(*See also* Literature: 1. *Anthologies* and 2. *Collected Works.*)

1. EPIC AND MYTHICAL.

2. HISTORICAL.

3. NARRATIVE.

4. RELIGIOUS.

(i.) *Hindu.*

(*See also* Religion.—*Hinduism.*)

3. HINDUISM.

(*See also* Poetry.—*Religious.*)

4. ISLAM.

5. SIKH CHURCH.

6. THEISTIC CHURCHES. (ĀRYA AND BRĀHMA SAMĀJ.)

RHETORIC.

SOCIOLOGY.

TRAVEL AND GUIDE-BOOKS.